EIGHTH EDITION

The Aims of Argument
A Text and Reader

MLA Updated Edition

Timothy W. Crusius
Southern Methodist University

Carolyn E. Channell
Southern Methodist University

THE AIMS OF ARGUMENT: TEXT AND READER, EIGHTH EDITION, MLA UPDATED EDITION
Published by McGraw-Hill Education, 2 Penn Plaza, New York, NY 10121. Copyright © 2015 by McGraw-Hill Education. All rights reserved. Printed in the United States of America. Previous editions © 2011, 2009, and 2006. No part of this publication may be reproduced or distributed in any form or by any means, or stored in a database or retrieval system, without the prior written consent of McGraw-Hill Education, including, but not limited to, in any network or other electronic storage or transmission, or broadcast for distance learning.

Some ancillaries, including electronic and print components, may not be available to customers outside the United States.

This book is printed on acid-free paper.

2 3 4 5 6 7 8 9 0 LCR 21 20 19

ISBN 978-1-260-09465-7
MHID 1-260-09465-0

Senior Vice President, Products & Markets: *Kurt L. Strand*
Vice President, General Manager, Products & Markets: *Michael Ryan*
Vice President, Content Production & Technology Services: *Kimberly Meriwether David*
Managing Director: *David Patterson*
Director: *Susan Gouijnstook*
Senior Brand Manager: *Nancy Huebner*
Director of Development: *Lisa Pinto*
Digital Product Analyst: *Janet Smith*
Director, Content Production: *Terri Schiesl*
Content Project Manager: *Laura L. Bies*
Senior Buyer: *Laura Fuller*
Designer: *Jana Singer*
Cover Image: *Don Smith/Photodisc/Getty Images*
Content Licensing Specialist: *Shawntel Schmitt*
Compositor: *Laserwords Private Limited*
Typeface: *9.5/12 Sabon Garamond*
Printer: *LSC Communications*

All credits appearing on page or at the end of the book are considered to be an extension of the copyright page.

Library of Congress Cataloging-in-Publication Data

Crusius, Timothy W., 1950-
  The aims of argument: a text and reader/Timothy W. Crusius, Southern Methodist University; Carolyn E. Channell, Southern Methodist University.—Eighth Edition.
      pages cm
  Includes index.
  ISBN 978–0–07–759220–2—ISBN 0–07–759220–4 (hard copy)   1. English language—Rhetoric—Problems, exercises, etc.   2. Persuasion (Rhetoric)—Problems, exercises, etc.   3. Report writing—Problems, exercises, etc.   4. College readers.   I. Channell, Carolyn E.   II. Title.
  PE1431.C78 2014
  808'.0427—dc23   2013021209

The Internet addresses listed in the text were accurate at the time of publication. The inclusion of a website does not indicate an endorsement by the authors or McGraw-Hill Education, and McGraw-Hill Education does not guarantee the accuracy of the information presented at these sites.

www.mhhe.com

For W. Ross Winterowd

NEW TO THIS EDITION

Now in its eighth successful edition, *The Aims of Argument: A Text and Reader* presents a unique approach to studying and teaching argument. Focusing on the aims (or purposes) of argument—to inquire, to convince, to persuade, and to mediate—the book emphasizes rhetorical contexts, helping students become experts in reading, analyzing, and writing arguments.

In addition to retaining the essential elements that make *The Aims of Argument* a comprehensive argument textbook, the eighth edition now includes:

- *Twenty-five new readings* on such topics as consumerism, immigration, civility, and global warming

- *Expansion of readings chapters to include more options for assignments*

- Significant revisions of the first five chapters to strengthen content on *reading arguments, analyzing arguments, and using visual appeals in convincing and persuading*

- *Additional Activities and Collaborative Activities throughout all chapters* to provide more options for assignments and provide self-reflection points for students

- *Connect Composition Essentials Plus 3.0* provides instructors and program administrators with the tools to assess students, sections, courses, or entire writing programs based on learning outcomes. McGraw-Hill offers simple LMS integration with one-click access and grade sync to Connect Composition from any campus learning management system.

LET CONNECT COMPOSITION ESSENTIALS 3.0 HELP YOUR STUDENTS SET THEIR GOALS

With Connect Composition Essentials Plus 3.0, students and instructors have access to the following resources:

- **LearnSmart Achieve™** assesses an individual student's proficiency in critical areas of composition with a continuously adaptive learning plan (see below for a list of topics). LearnSmart Achieve provides an individualized path to improvement and eventual mastery at the student's own pace. Instructors and administrators have access to valuable reports about student and class performance.

- **Customizable writing assignments** allow instructors to easily grade and annotate student writing. **The Outcomes Based Assessment tool** allows instructors to tie specific learning outcomes to each writing assignment; this provides students with a clear view of what they are being graded on for that task. Instructors and administrators have access to customizable reports that demonstrate achievement levels for learning outcomes at the student, class, and program level. The reports can be exported in a format suitable for accreditation documents.

- A **digital handbook** offers students **four years of access** to McGraw-Hill's trusted content—including up-to-date documentation standards, genre models, and guidance on the writing and research processes. Instructors and students have the ability to highlight, bookmark, and add notes to the handbook.

- A **three-week free trial period** gives students access to their course materials right away so they can be ready to go on the first day of class.

- The **Digital Success Team**, a group of Connect specialists, is dedicated to working one-on-one with instructors to demonstrate how Connect Composition works and to help integrate the available resources into their course based on an instructor's specific needs.

- **McGraw-Hill's Digital Success Academy** offers a wealth of online training resources and course creation tips to help get you started. Go to connect-successacademy.com

UNIT	TOPIC	
THE WRITING PROCESS	The Writing Process Generating Ideas Planning and Organizing	Writing a Rough Draft Revising Proofreading, Formatting, and Producing Texts
CRITICAL READING	Reading to Understand Literal Meaning Evaluating Truth and Accuracy in a Text	Evaluating the Effectiveness and Appropriateness of a Text
THE RESEARCH PROCESS	Developing and Implementing a Research Plan Evaluating Information and Sources	Integrating Source Material into a Text Using Information Ethically and Legally
REASONING AND ARGUMENT	Developing an Effective Thesis or Claim Using Evidence and Reasoning to Support a Thesis or Claim	Using Ethos (Ethics) to Persuade Readers Using Pathos (Emotion) to Persuade Readers Using Logos (Logic) to Persuade Readers
MULTILINGUAL WRITERS	Helping Verbs, Gerunds and Infinitives, and Phrasal Verbs Nouns, Verbs, and Objects Articles	Count and Noncount Nouns Sentence Structure and Word Order Subject-Verb Agreement Participles and Adverb Placement
GRAMMAR AND COMMON SENTENCE PROBLEMS	Parts of Speech Phrases and Clauses Sentence Types Fused (Run-on) Sentence Comma Splices Sentence Fragments Pronouns	Pronoun-Antecedent Agreement Pronoun Reference Subject-Verb Agreement Verbs and Verbals Adjectives and Adverbs Dangling and Misplaced Modifiers Mixed Constructions Verb Tense and Voice Shifts
PUNCTUATION AND MECHANICS	Commas Semicolons Colons End Punctuation Apostrophes Quotation Marks Dashes	Parentheses Hyphens Abbreviations Capitalization Italics Numbers Spelling
STYLE AND WORD CHOICE	Wordiness Eliminating Redundancies Sentence Variety Coordination and Subordination	Faulty Comparisons Word Choice Clichés, Slang, and Jargon Parallelism

LearnSmart Achieve can be assigned by units and/or topics.

ABOUT *THE AIMS OF ARGUMENT* APPROACH

This book is different from other argument texts because it focuses on four aims, or purposes, of argument:

- Arguing to inquire
- Arguing to convince
- Arguing to persuade
- Arguing to mediate

Central Tenets of the Approach

- *Argumentation is a mode or means of discourse, not an aim or purpose for writing.* Consequently, we need to teach the aims of argument.
- *The aims of argument are linked in a learning sequence so that convincing builds on inquiry, persuasion on convincing, and all three contribute to mediation.* Consequently, we offer a learning sequence for conceiving a course or courses in argument.

FAQs about the Approach

Here are the questions we are most frequently asked about this approach:

- *What is the relative value of the four aims? Because mediation comes last, is it the best or most valued?* No aim is "better" than any other aim. Given needs for writing and certain audiences, one aim is more appropriate than another for the task at hand. Mediation comes last because it integrates inquiry, convincing, and persuading.
- *Must inquiry be taught as a separate aim?* No. It *may* be taught as a separate aim, but we do not intend this "may" as a "must." Teaching inquiry as a distinct aim has certain advantages. Students need to learn how to engage in constructive dialogue, which is more disciplined and more focused than most class discussion. Once they see how it is done, students enjoy dialogue with one another and with texts. Dialogue helps students think through their arguments and imagine reader reaction to what they say, both of which are crucial to convincing and persuading. Finally, as with mediation, inquiry offers avenues for assignments other than the standard argumentative essay.
- *Should inquiry come first?* For a number of reasons, inquiry has priority over the other aims. Most teachers are likely to approach inquiry as prewriting, preparatory to convincing or persuading. And commonly, we return to inquiry when we find something wrong with a case we are trying to construct, so the relationship between inquiry and the other aims is also recursive.

Moreover, inquiry has psychological, moral, and practical claims to priority. When we are unfamiliar with an issue, inquiry comes first psychologically, as a felt need to explore existing opinion. Regardless of what happens in the "real world," convincing or persuading without an open, honest, and earnest search for the truth is, in our view, immoral. Finally, inquiry goes hand in hand with research, which requires questioning the opinions encountered.

- *Isn't the difference between convincing and persuading more a matter of degree than kind?* Convincing and persuading do shade into one another so that the difference is clearest at the extremes. Furthermore, the "purest" appeal to reason—a legal brief, a philosophical or scientific argument—appeals in ways beyond the sheer cogency of the case. Persuasive techniques are submerged but not absent in arguing to convince.

  Our motivation for separating convincing from persuading is not theoretical but pedagogical. Case-making is complex enough that attention to logical appeal by itself is justified. Making students conscious of the appeals to character, emotion, and style while they are learning to cope with case-making can overburden them to the point of paralysis.

  Regardless, then, of how sound the traditional distinction between convincing and persuading may be, we think it best to take up convincing first and then persuasion, especially because what students learn in the former can be carried over intact into the latter. And because one cannot make a case without unconscious appeal to character, emotional commitments (such as values), and style, teaching persuasion is a matter of exposing and developing what is already there in arguing to convince.

About the Readings

- We have avoided the "great authors, classic essays" approach. We try instead to find bright, contemporary people arguing well from diverse viewpoints—articles and chapters similar to those that can be found in better journals and trade books, the sort of publications students should read most in doing research.

- We have not presented any issue in simple pro-and-con fashion, as if there were only two sides.

- Included in the range of perspectives are arguments made with both words and images. We include a full chapter examining visual arguments, such as editorial cartoons, advertisements, public sculpture, and photographs.

LET CUSTOMIZABLE RESOURCES HELP YOU TO ACHIEVE YOUR COURSE'S GOALS

A CREATE edition of *The Aims of Argument: A Brief Guide* is available. With McGraw-Hill CREATE, you can easily arrange and customize material from a variety of sources, including your own. You can choose your format (print or electronic) and what you want from

- *The Aims of Argument*'s print text chapters—choose only those chapters that you cover
- Any of the reading selections currently in the text
- A range of additional selections from other McGraw-Hill collections such as *The Ideal Reader* (800 readings by author, genre, mode, theme, and discipline), *Sustainability* (readings with an environmental focus), and many more
- Your own resources, such as syllabi, institutional information, study guides, assignments, diagrams, artwork, student writing, art, photos, and more

You can benefit from all of the customization listed above with a ready-made version that contains Parts One and Two plus the Appendixes.

TABLE OF CONTENTS FOR THE BRIEF GUIDE IN CREATE

PART ONE
RESOURCES FOR READING AND WRITING ARGUMENTS 1

1 **Understanding Argument 3**
2 **Reading Arguments 17**
3 **Analyzing Arguments: The Toulmin Method 39**
4 **Critiquing an Argument 51**
5 **Analyzing and Using Visual Arguments 73**
6 **Writing Research-Based Arguments 91**
7 **Ethical Writing and Plagiarism 163**

PART TWO
THE AIMS OF ARGUMENT 173

8 **Joining the Conversation: Arguing to Inquire 175**
9 **Making Your Case: Arguing to Convince 201**
10 **Motivating Action: Arguing to Persuade 235**
11 **Resolving Conflict: Arguing to Mediate 265**

Go to www.mcgrawhillcreate.com and register today.

Our goal in this book is not just to show you how to construct an argument but also to make you more aware of why people argue and what purposes argument serves. Consequently, Part Two of this book introduces four specific aims that people have in mind when they argue: to inquire, to convince, to persuade, and to mediate. Part One precedes the aims of argument and focuses on understanding argumentation in general, reading and analyzing arguments, writing a critique, doing research, and working with such forms of visual persuasion as advertising.

The selections in Parts One and Two offer something to emulate. All writers learn from studying the strategies of other writers. The object is not to imitate what a more experienced writer does but to understand the range of strategies you can use in your own way for your own purposes.

Included are arguments made with words and images. We have examples of editorial cartoons, advertisements, and photographs.

The additional readings in Part Three serve another function. To learn argument, we have to argue; to argue, we must have something to argue about. So we have grouped essays and images around central issues of current public discussion.

People argue with one another because they do not see the world the same way, and they do not see the world the same way because of different backgrounds. Therefore, in dealing with how people differ, a book about argument must deal with what makes people different, with the sources of disagreement itself—including gender, race/ethnicity, class, sexual orientation, and religion. Rather than ignoring or glossing over difference, the readings in this book will help you better understand it.

This book concludes with two appendixes. The first is on editing, the art of polishing and refining prose, and finding common errors. The second deals with fallacies and critical thinking. Consult these resources often as you work through the text's assignments.

Arguing well is difficult for anyone. We have tried to write a text no more complicated than it has to be. We welcome your comments to improve future editions. Write us at

The English Department
Dallas Hall
Southern Methodist University
Dallas, Texas 75275

or e-mail your comments to

cchannel@mail.smu.edu
tcrusius@mail.smu.edu

Timothy W. Crusius is professor of English at Southern Methodist University, where he teaches beginning and advanced composition. He's the author of books on discourse theory, philosophical hermeneutics, and Kenneth Burke.

Carolyn E. Channell taught high school and community college students before coming to Southern Methodist University, where she is now a senior lecturer and specialist in first-year writing courses.

Acknowledgments

The authors are grateful for the comments of professors and students who have used this book over the years. Reviewers of the current edition include the following: Joanna Brooks, San Diego State University; Xiongya Gao, Southern University at New Orleans; Jennifer G. Herbert, University of Akron; Matthew Hollrah, University of Central Oklahoma; Anne Marie Reid, Colorado State University, Fort Collins; Eileen B. Seifert, DePaul University; Catherine Vieira, University of Wisconsin, Madison; and Lawrence White, Tacoma Community College.

BRIEF CONTENTS

PART ONE

RESOURCES FOR READING AND WRITING ARGUMENTS 1

1 **Understanding Argument** 3
2 **Reading Arguments** 17
3 **Analyzing Arguments: The Toulmin Method** 39
4 **Critiquing an Argument** 51
5 **Analyzing and Using Visual Arguments** 73
6 **Writing Research-Based Arguments** 91
7 **Ethical Writing and Plagiarism** 163

PART TWO

THE AIMS OF ARGUMENT 173

8 **Joining the Conversation: Arguing to Inquire** 175
9 **Making Your Case: Arguing to Convince** 201
10 **Motivating Action: Arguing to Persuade** 235
11 **Resolving Conflict: Arguing to Mediate** 265

PART THREE

READINGS: ISSUES AND ARGUMENTS 301

12 **Consumer Society: Achieving Balance** 303
13 **Global Warming: What Should Be Done?** 343
14 **The Millennials: Issues Facing Young Adults** 381
15 **Immigration Revisited: A New Look at a Permanent Issue** 415
16 **Declining Civility: Is Rudeness on the Rise?** 453
17 **Enhancing Humans: How Far Is Too Far?** 485

APPENDIXES

A **A Brief Guide to Editing and Proofreading** 523
B **Fallacies—and Critical Thinking** 541

 appears at top right, decorative

CONTENTS

PART ONE

RESOURCES FOR READING AND WRITING ARGUMENTS   1

CHAPTER 1
Understanding Argument   3

What Is Argument?   3
What Is Rhetoric?   4
An Example of Argument   6
    Steven Johnson, From *Everything Bad Is Good for You*   6
Arguing Responsibly   7
Four Criteria of Responsible Reasoning   8
    Responsible Reasoning Is Well Informed   9
    Responsible Reasoning Is Open to Constructive Criticism from Others   9
    Responsible Reasoning Considers the Audience   9
    Responsible Reasoning Understands an Argument's Contexts   10
Reading   10
    Kelby Carlson, "Fighting Words: Why Our Public Discourse Must Change"   10
What Are the Aims of Argument?   13
    Arguing to Inquire   13
    Arguing to Convince   13
    Arguing to Persuade   14
    Arguing to Mediate   14

CHAPTER 2
Reading Arguments   17

Strategies for Critical Reading: Once Through Is Not Enough   18
    First Encounters: Skimming for Context, Reading for Content   18
        Strategy: Before Reading, Skim (and Surf) for Context   18
        Strategy: Skim to Preview the Whole Argument   19
        Strategy: Annotate as You Read   19
    Sally Jenkins, "A Major Gain for College Sports"   21
    Second Encounters: Reading to Detect the Case   23
        Strategy: Outlining the Case   24
    Third Encounters: Responding to an Argument   25
        Strategy: Paraphrasing   26
        Strategy: Summarizing   27
        Strategy: Joining the Conversation   29
    Mariah Burton Nelson, Response to "A Major Gain for College Sports"   33

Reading Alternative Forms of Argument   33

Keith A. Williams, "A Technological Cloud Hangs over
Higher Education"   35

CHAPTER 3

Analyzing Arguments: The Toulmin Method   39

An Overview of the Toulmin Method   39

Art Carden, "Let's Be Blunt: It's Time to End the Drug War"   42

A Step-by-Step Demonstration of the Toulmin Method   44

Analyzing the Claim   44

Identify the Claim   44

Look for Qualifiers and Exceptions   44

Analyzing the Reasons and Evidence   45

State the Reasons   45

Find the Evidence   45

Examine the Evidence   46

Examining the Warrants   46

Noting Rebuttals   47

Summarizing Your Analysis   47

A Final Note about Logical Analysis   48

CHAPTER 4

Critiquing an Argument   51

What Is a Critique?   51

Why Critique an Argument?   52

How a Critique Differs from a Reaction   52

Strategies for Critiquing Arguments   53

Tom Stafford, "Why Sherry Turkle Is So Wrong"   54

The Assignment   58

Topic and Focus   58

Audience   58

Voice and Ethos   58

Writing Assignment Suggestions   58

Choosing an Argument   59

Exploring Your Topic   59

David Fryman, "Open Your Ears to Biased Professors"   59

Forming a First Impression   61

Stepping Back: Analyzing the Argument   61

Doing Research   64

The Reality Test for Arguments   64

Preparing to Write   65

Formulating Your Stance   65
Consider Your Reader, Purpose, and Tone   66
Drafting Your Paper   66
Organization   67
 Introduction   67
 Body   67
 Conclusion   67
Development   67
 Introduction   67
 Body   67
 Conclusion   68
Revising Your Draft   68
Excerpts from a Sample Discovery Draft   68
 Excerpt 1: Introduction   68
 Excerpt 2: A Counterargument   68
Example Assessment: Sizing Up D. D. Solomon's First Draft   70
Develop a Revision Strategy   70
Revised Draft: D. D. Solomon's Evaluation of Fryman's Argument   70
D. D. Solomon, "How Professors Should Deal with Their Biases"   70
Responding to the Revised Student Draft   71
Edit Your Paper   72
Chapter Summary   72

CHAPTER 5
Analyzing and Using Visual Arguments   73

Understanding Visual Arguments   74
"Reading" Images   74
Analysis: Five Common Types of Visual Argument   75
Advertisements   75
Editorial Cartoons   76
Public Sculpture   77
News Photographs   81
Graphics   83
Writing Assignment: Analyzing an Advertisement or Editorial Cartoon   85
STUDENT SAMPLE—Analysis of Visual Rhetoric: **Ryan Herrscher,** "The Image of Happiness: An Analysis of Coca-Cola's 'Open Happiness' Campaign"   86
Alternative Assignment 1   88
Alternative Assignment 2   89
Alternative Assignment 3   89

CHAPTER 6
Writing Research-Based Arguments   91

Finding an Issue   92
  Understand the Difference between a Topic and an Issue   92
  Find Issues in the News   93
  The Internet   93
  Library Online Databases and Resources   93
  Magazines and Newspapers   93
  Lectures, Panel Discussions, Class Discussions, Conversations   94
  Personal Observations   94
  Finding an Issue on the Topic of Global Warming: A Student Example   94
Finding Sources   95
Field Research   96
  Observations   96
  Questionnaires and Surveys   96
  Interviews   97
Library and Internet Research   98
  Kinds of Sources   98
  Books   98
  Periodicals   99
  Audiovisual Materials   100
  Websites   100
  Blogs, Listservs, Usenet Groups, Message Boards   101
  Choosing Precise Search Terms   101
  Use Keyword Searching   102
  Use Phrase Searching   102
  Use Boolean Searching   102
  Use Subject Words   102
Searching Your Library   103
  Your Library's Online Catalog   104
  Your Library's Online Resources   106
Internet Research   108
  Domains   108
  Commercial (.com)   109
  Nonprofit Organizations (.org)   109
  Educational Institutions (.edu)   109
  Government Agencies (.gov)   109
  Advanced Features for Searching the Web   109
  Advanced Searches   109
  Google Specialized Searches   110
  Google Scholar   110

Subject Directories to the Web   110

Blogs, Listservs, Message Boards, and Chat Groups   111

Evaluating Sources   111

Eliminate Inappropriate Sources   111

Carefully Record Complete Bibliographic Information   111

Read the Source Critically   111

Who Is the Writer, and What Is His or Her Bias?   112

How Reliable Is the Source?   112

When Was This Source Written?   113

Where Did This Source Appear?   113

What Is the Author's Aim?   114

How Is the Source Organized?   114

Special Help with Evaluating Websites   114

Using Sources   117

Richard Moe, "Battling Teardowns, Saving Neighborhoods"   117

Writing Informally to Gain Mastery over Your Sources   121

1. Annotate the Source   121

2. Respond to the Source in Your Notebook   121

3. Paraphrase Important Ideas from the Source   122

Examples of Adequate and Inadequate Paraphrasing   123

4. Write Summaries of Portions of a Source   124

5. Write Capsule Summaries of Entire Sources   126

6. Dialogue about Sources   127

Incorporating and Documenting Source Material   128

Different Styles of Documentation   128

MLA Style   128

APA Style   129

Direct Quotations   129

MLA Style   129

APA Style   129

Altering Direct Quotations with Ellipses and Square Brackets   130

Using Block Quotations   131

Indirect Quotations   131

MLA Style   131

APA Style   132

In-Text References to Electronic Sources   133

Creating Works Cited and Reference Lists   133

MLA Style for Entries in the Works Cited List   133

Books   134

Articles in Periodicals   138

Other Genres as Sources   139

Sources on the Internet   139

Student Sample of a Research Paper in MLA Style   143

Using APA Documentation Style   143

In-text Citations   143

Reference List Examples   146

Books   146

Articles in Periodicals   148

Sources on the Internet   150

Other Genres as Sources   151

Sample of a Research Paper in APA Style   151

STUDENT SAMPLE—A Research Paper (MLA Style): **Julie Ross,** "Why Residential Construction Needs to Get a Conscience"   152

CHAPTER 7

Ethical Writing and Plagiarism   163

Why Ethics Matter   163

What Plagiarism Is   164

The Ethics of Using Sources   164

Purchasing a Paper   164

Using a Paper Found Online   165

Using Passages from Online Sources without Citing the Source   165

Inadequate Paraphrasing   167

Paraphrasing Ideas or Information without Naming the Source   168

When Opinions Coincide   170

The Ethics of Giving and Receiving Help with Writing   170

Ethical Writing and Good Study Habits   172

PART TWO

THE AIMS OF ARGUMENT   173

CHAPTER 8

Joining the Conversation: Arguing to Inquire   175

What Is Comparing Perspectives?   176

Why Write to Compare Perspectives?   176

How Does Comparing Perspectives Work?   177

What to Ask When Comparing Perspectives   177

The Writer as Inquirer   177

Andy Rudd, "Which Character Should Sports Develop?"   177

Readings   180

John F. Schumaker, "The Paradox of Narcissism"   181

Jean M. Twenge, "Changes in Narcissism"   185

Duncan Greenberg, "Generation Y and the New Myth of Narcissus"   187

The Assignment   189
  Topic and Focus   189
  Audience   189
  Voice and Style   189
  Writing Assignment Suggestions   189
Choosing a Topic   190
Exploring Your Topic   190
  Paraphrase or Summarize the Main Points   191
  Turn Main Points into Questions   192
  Paraphrase and Comment   192
  Keep Track of Connections across Perspectives   193
  Maintain an Exploratory Stance   194
Drafting Your Paper   194
  Planning the Draft   194
  The Art of Questioning: Planning the Body   194
  Development and Organization   195
Revising Your Draft   195
  REVISED STUDENT EXAMPLE—Ian Fagerstrom, "Comparison of Perspectives on Narcissism"   197
Chapter Summary   200

CHAPTER 9

Making Your Case: Arguing to Convince   201

What Is a Case?   202
Why Make a Case?   202
How Do You Make a Case?   203
  Examining Your Audience's Beliefs   205
Readings   205
  Olivia Judson, "Optimism in Evolution"   205
  Strategies Used in Case-Making: Structure and Readership   207
Putting Your Voice into Your Argument   208
  Wilbert Rideau, "Why Prisons Don't Work"   209
  Strategies Used in Case-Making: Problem-Solution, Cause-and-Effect Reasoning   211
  T. Boone Pickens, "A Plan for Reducing American Dependence on Foreign Oil"   212
  Strategies Used in Case-Making: Lines of Reasoning   216
The Assignment   218
  Topic and Focus   218
  Audience   218
  Voice and Style   219
  Writing Assignment Suggestions   219

Choosing a Topic   219

Exploring Your Topic   220

Find the Issues   220

Order the Issues (Stasis)   220

Do More Research   222

Analyze Your Sources: Information versus Interpretation   222

Start Your Working Bibliography   223

A Key Question before Drafting: Is My Opinion Defensible?   223

Assessing Your Opinion from Research Results   224

Preparing to Write   224

State Your Opinion as a Thesis   224

Writing Defensible Claims   225

Unpack Your Thesis   226

Examine Possible Reasons   226

Arrange Your Evidence under Each Reason   227

Examine Possible Evidence   227

STUDENT EXAMPLE: Noelle Alberto's Draft Case Outline   227

Drafting Your Paper   229

Development and Organization   229

STUDENT EXAMPLE: Excerpts from Alberto's Draft   230

Revising Your Draft   231

Formulate a Plan to Guide Your Revision   231

REVISED STUDENT EXAMPLE: **Noelle Alberto,** "Multitasking: A Poor Study Habit"   231

Chapter Summary   233

CHAPTER 10

Motivating Action: Arguing to Persuade   235

What Is Persuasion?   235

Why Write to Persuade?   236

How Does Persuasion Work?   236

The Art of Questioning: What Really Persuades Us?   237

Readings   238

Subaru Advertisement   238

Tom Beaudoin, "Consuming Faith"   239

Strategies for Appealing for Action   242

Katharine Weber, "The Factories of Lost Children"   243

Strategies for Appealing for Action   245

Using Your Voice in Appealing for Action   246

The Assignment   247

Topic and Focus   247

Audience   247

Voice and Ethos   247
Writing Assignment Suggestions   247

Choosing a Topic   248

Exploring Your Topic   248

Focus, Audience, and Need   248
Establishing Need   249
Doing Research   250

Preparing to Write: Thinking about Persuasive Appeals   250

The Appeal through Logos: Deciding on a Claim and Reasons   251
Developing Reasons for Your Claim   252
Making a Brief of Your Case   252
STUDENT EXAMPLE: Natsumi Hazama's Brief   252
The Appeal through Ethos: Presenting Good Character   254
Establishing Ethos with Your Readers   254
The Appeal through Pathos: Using Emotional Appeals   254

Drafting Your Paper   255

Development and Organization   255

Revising Your Draft   256

Getting Feedback from Others   256
Practicing Revision   257
Revising to Bring Out the Structure of the Argument   258
Revising to Improve Incorporation of Quoted Material   259
REVISED STUDENT EXAMPLE: **Natsumi Hazama**, "Is Too Much Pressure Healthy?"   260

Chapter Summary   263

CHAPTER 11

Resolving Conflict: Arguing to Mediate   265

Mediation and the Other Aims of Argument   266

The Process of Mediation   267

Mediation and Rogerian Argument   267

A Conflict to Mediate   268
Understanding the Positions   268
Roger Kimball, "Institutionalizing Our Demise: America vs. Multiculturalism"   268
Elizabeth Martínez, "Reinventing 'America': Call for a New National Identity"   275
Analysis of the Writers' Positions   280
Kimball's Position   280
Martínez's Position   281
Locating the Areas of Agreement and Disagreement   282
Differences over Facts   282
Differences over Interests, Values, and Interpretations   282

Finding Creative Solutions: Exploring Common Ground   285

Exploring Common Ground in the Debate over National Identity   286

The Mediatory Essay   287

Bharati Mukherjee, "Beyond Multiculturalism: A Two-Way Transformation"   287

Analyzing Mukherjee's Essay   293

Ethos: Earning the Respect of Both Sides   293

Pathos: Using Emotion to Appeal to Both Sides   293

Logos: Integrating Values of Both Sides   294

The Assignment   295

Prewriting   295

Drafting   296

Revising   296

STUDENT EXAMPLE—Arguing to Mediate: Angi Grellhesl, "Mediating the Speech Code Controversy"   297

Chapter Summary   299

PART THREE
READINGS: ISSUES AND ARGUMENTS   301

CHAPTER 12
Consumer Society: Achieving Balance   303

Consumerism: Ten Quotations   305

Virginia Postrel, "The Aesthetic Imperative"   306

Erik Kain, "In Defense of Consumerism"   310

David Brooks, "The Grill-Buying Guy"   312

Alex Kotlowitz, "False Connections"   315

Three Cartoons about the Consumer Society   320

Caroline Heldman, "Out-of-Body Image"   322

Alissa Quart, "X-Large Boys"   327

Don Peck and Ross Douthat, "Does Money Buy Happiness?"   331

John F. Schumaker, "The Happiness Conspiracy: What Does It Mean to Be Happy in a Modern Consumer Society?"   336

For Further Reading   340

CHAPTER 13
Global Warming: What Should Be Done?   343

Text of the American College and University Presidents' Climate Commitment   344

National Geographic, "Global Warming: An Overview"   347

Scientific American, "15 Ways to Make a Wedge"   352

Bill Blakemore, "Who's 'Most to Blame' for Global Warming?"   353

Gregg Easterbrook, "Some Convenient Truths"   358

Tim Appenzeller, "The Coal Paradox"   362

Al Gore, "Existing Technologies for Reducing CO_2 Emissions"   367

Michelle Nijhuis, "Selling the Wind"   368

Union of Concerned Scientists, "Ten Personal Solutions"   372

William F. Ruddiman, "Consuming Earth's Gifts"   375

For Further Reading   378

CHAPTER 14

The Millennials: Issues Facing Young Adults   381

Pew Research Center, "Millennials: Confident. Connected. Open to Change"   383

Kit Yarrow and Jayne O'Donnell, "Gen Y Is from Mercury"   391

Kim Brooks, "Is It Time to Kill the Liberal Arts Degree?"   395

Stuart Rabinowitz, "A Liberal Arts Education Is Still Relevant"   399

Dale Archer, "College Debt: Necessary Evil or Ponzi Scheme?"   402

Richard Vedder, "Forgive Student Loans?"   405

Anya Kamenetz, "Waking Up and Taking Charge"   408

For Further Reading   413

CHAPTER 15

Immigration Revisited: A New Look at a Permanent Issue   415

Historical Images: Our Contradictory Attitudes toward Immigration   417

Tamar Jacoby, "The New Immigrants and the Issue of Assimilation"   418

Samuel Huntington, "One Nation, Out of Many: Why 'Americanization' of Newcomers Is Still Important"   425

Jeff Koterba, Cartoon: "Playing POLITICS with the Border"   429

Ross Douthat and Jenny Woodson, "The Border"   430

Linda Chavez, "The Realities of Immigration"   434

Chris Farrell, "Obama's Next Act: Immigration Reform"   441

Dava Castillo, "Comprehensive Immigration Reform—Past, Present, and Future"   444

Leslie Marmon Silko, "The Border Patrol State"   447

For Further Reading   451

CHAPTER 16

Declining Civility: Is Rudeness on the Rise?   453

P. M. Forni, "What Is Civility?"   455

Sara Rimer, "Play with Your Food, Just Don't Text"   459

Elizabeth Bernstein, "Why We Are So Rude Online"   462

Leonard Pitts, Jr., "Going beyond Edgy—and Falling off the Cliff"   465

Tufts Now, "Left Is Mean But Right Is Meaner, Says New Study of Political Discourse"   467

Brian McGee, "Can Political Rhetoric Be Too Civil?"   470

Frank D. Adams and Gloria J. Lawrence, "Bullying Victims: The Effects Last into College"   472

Emily Bazelon, "Don't Be a Bystander"   479

For Further Reading   482

CHAPTER 17

Enhancing Humans: How Far Is Too Far?   485

Carl Elliott, "The Tyranny of Happiness"   487

Benedict Carey, "Brain Enhancement Is Wrong, Right?"   492

Barbara Sahakian and Nora Volkow, "Professor's Little Helper?"   495

Gregory Stock, "Choosing Our Genes"   501

John Naish, "Genetically Modified Athletes"   506

Arthur L. Caplan, "A Shot in the Rear: Why Are We Really against Steroids?"   509

Ed Smith, "Lance Armstrong and the Cult of Positive Thinking"   514

Larry Gonick and Mark Wheelis, Cartoon: "Gene-Splicing as Big Business"   517

C. Ben Mitchell, "On Human Bioenhancements"   519

For Further Reading   521

APPENDIXES

A   A Brief Guide to Editing and Proofreading   523

B   Fallacies—and Critical Thinking   541

Glossary   557

Credits   562

Index   565

BOXES BY TYPE

CONCEPT CLOSE-UP BOXES

Defining Rhetoric   5

Defining Responsible Reasoning   6

Four Criteria of Responsible Reasoning   8

Comparing the Aims of Argument   15

Defining Critical Reading   18

Understanding Case Structure   25

Model Toulmin Diagram for Analyzing Arguments   48

Context and Critique   52

Sample Entry in an Annotated Bibliography   127

Plagiarism: The Presentation or Submission of Another's Work as Your Own   165

Understanding the Ethics of Plagiarism   166

What Is Synthesis?   176

From Inquiry to Convincing   202

Understanding the Functions of Case Structure   203

Key Questions for Case-Making   204

When Should You Persuade?   236

The Four Forms of Appeal   237

Audience Analysis   249

Characteristics of Mediation   266

BEST PRACTICES BOXES

Questions for Determining Rhetorical Context   19

Annotating as You Read   20

Guidelines for Paraphrasing   27

Questions for Responding to an Argument   31

Toulmin Analysis   49

Concepts and Questions for Analyzing an Argument   62

Critique Revision Checklist   69

Guidelines for Using Visuals   90

Additional Guidelines for Evaluating Internet Sources   114

Guidelines for Summarizing   125

Guidelines for Writing with Sources   126

Leading into Direct Quotations   132

Strategies for Comparing Perspectives   190

Organizing around Questions   195

Revision Checklist for Comparing Perspectives   196

Doing Team Research   221

Drafting a Case Outline   228

Drafting Your Case   229

Revision Checklist for Arguing a Case   230

Key Questions for Preparing to Write   251

Places to Find Audience-Based Reasons   253

Revision Checklist for Appealing to Action   257

Questions for Understanding Difference   283

Resources for Reading and Writing Arguments

1 Understanding Argument *3*

2 Reading Arguments *17*

3 Analyzing Arguments: The Toulmin Method *39*

4 Critiquing an Argument *51*

5 Analyzing and Using Visual Arguments *73*

6 Writing Research-Based Arguments *91*

7 Ethical Writing and Plagiarism *163*

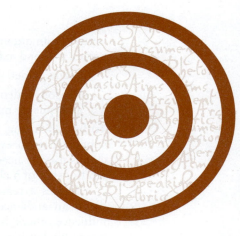

CHAPTER 1

Understanding Argument

For some people, the word *argument* suggests conflict and heated debate; however, it has a much broader and more positive meaning, as the following pages will explain. College writing classes include argument as a key feature of critical thinking because most academic writing, by professors and students, takes the form of argument.

The perception of argument as verbal combat should not overshadow the positive role of reasoned argument in conducting human affairs. Through arguments based on good reasons and evidence, scientists advance our understanding of the world, citizens improve their communities, business leaders make decisions, and families work out compromises when interests conflict.

WHAT IS ARGUMENT?

The Aims of Argument is based on two related concepts: *argument* and *rhetoric*. We will define **argument** very simply, as *reasoned thinking*. The essence of an argument is a **claim**, which is also called a *thesis* because it is what an argument attempts to prove, and a *reason* that supports the claim. A **reason** is a *sentence telling why the claim should be accepted as true*. An example of the minimal kernel of an argument would be Steven Johnson's case in favor of playing video games, as found in his book *Everything Bad Is Good for You:*

Claim: Video games are intellectually stimulating.

Reason: Video games force players to weigh evidence, analyze situations, and quickly make correct decisions.

To be convincing, however, arguments need much more: Reasons need to be supported with evidence, facts, examples, expert testimony, and so on. And claims usually need the support of more than one reason. However, the basic relationship of a claim and a reason underlies all self-aware rational thinking.

Besides a reasoned case, real-life arguments need another crucial ingredient: an audience. No one argues into the air; arguments are intended to influence others' beliefs, opinions, and behavior. For example, Steven Johnson wrote his book to convince critics of video games and TV shows that these forms of popular entertainment are not some kind of wasteland where brains go to rot. The need to win over a skeptical audience brings us to the other important concept of this book, rhetoric.

WHAT IS RHETORIC?

Like the word *argument, rhetoric* has a common negative meaning today, as it is often used to describe the empty promises and demagoguery common in political speeches. You hear people dismiss a candidate's words as "mere rhetoric." This meaning of *rhetoric* confers a judgment, and not a positive one. In this book, we define **rhetoric** in a positive way, as *the art of effective persuasion.*

In ancient Greece, where rhetoric was invented about 2,500 years ago, *rhetoric* referred to persuasive public speaking, as theirs was an oral culture. The Greeks had a goddess of persuasion (see Figure 1.1), and they respected the power of the spoken word to move people. Oral argument dominated their law courts, their governments and their public ceremonies and events.

Since the time of Aristotle, teachers of rhetoric have taught ways of reasoning well and arguing persuasively. The study of rhetoric, therefore, includes both what we have defined as reasoned thinking, the appeal through logic, and other ways of appealing to an audience. What are some other ways?

In addition to reasoning, which the Greeks called the appeal through logos, a speaker could persuade by presenting himself as a person of good, or ethical, character (ethos). The ancients put a high value on good character. Not just sounding ethical but being ethical contributed to a speaker's persuasive power. They also studied how to use emotional appeals (pathos) to move the audience. Obviously, emotional appeals can be abused, but they are, and have always been, a legitimate part of the art of rhetoric. Because the ancient Greeks made their arguments orally, the presentation or delivery of the speech was also part of the art of rhetoric for them. In written arguments today, we might see the style and written voice of the writer as an equivalent kind of appeal.

Defining Rhetoric

Rhetoric is the art of argument as responsible reasoning. The study of rhetoric develops self-conscious awareness of the principles and practices of responsible reasoning and effective arguing.

This old, highly valued meaning of rhetoric as oratory survived well into the nineteenth century. In Abraham Lincoln's day, Americans assembled by the thousands to hear speeches that went on for hours. For them, a good speech held the same level of interest as a big sporting event does for people today. In this book, we are interested primarily in various ways of using *written* argument, but the rhetorical tradition informs our understanding of all kinds of arguments.

Today, rhetoric has become so broadly defined as to include almost any kind of communication or symbol that has the potential to influence people.

Figure 1.1

Peitho, the goddess of persuasion, was often involved in seductions and love affairs. On this piece (a detail from a terra-cotta kylix, c. 410 BCE), Peitho, the figure on the left, gives advice to a dejected-looking woman, identified as Demonassa. To the right, Eros, the god of love, stands with his hand on Demonassa's shoulder, suggesting the nature of this advice.

Defining Responsible Reasoning

Argument as responsible reasoning means

- Defending *not the first position* you might take on an issue *but the best position,* determined through open-minded inquiry
- Providing reasons for holding that position that can earn the respect of an audience

---

A classic textbook, *The Rhetoric of Popular Culture,* by Barry Brummett of the University of Texas, argues that almost anything in popular culture, from blue jeans to hairstyles to shopping malls, can be rhetorical. He means that anything we find meaningful has the potential to influence us. This is an interesting view of the power of rhetoric; however, in this book we will focus on rhetoric and reasoned thinking in purposefully crafted arguments, whether written, spoken, or visual.

AN EXAMPLE OF ARGUMENT

Most books are long arguments, containing many smaller arguments, such as the passage below, which is excerpted from Steven Johnson's book on popular culture, *Everything Bad Is Good for You.* In this excerpt Johnson anticipates that his audience might associate video games with stupid and socially unacceptable content. He claims that the content is not relevant to the educational value of the game. As you read, consider how he uses reasoning and other rhetorical appeals to persuade readers to see the value of video games.

From *Everything Bad Is Good for You*

STEVEN JOHNSON

1   De-emphasizing the content of game culture shouldn't be seen as a cop-out. We ignore the content of many activities that are widely considered to be good for the brain or the body. No one complains about the simplistic, militaristic plot of chess games. ("It always ends the same way!") We teach algebra to children knowing full well that the day they leave the classroom, ninety-nine percent of those kids will never again directly employ their algebraic skills. Learning algebra isn't about acquiring a specific tool; it's about building up a mental muscle that will come in handy elsewhere. You don't go to the gym because you're interested in learning how to operate a Stairmaster; you go to the gym because operating a Stairmaster does something laudable to your body, the benefits of which you enjoy the many hours of the week you're not on a Stairmaster.

2 | So it is with games. It's not *what* you're thinking about when you're playing a game, it's the *way* you're thinking that matters. The distinction is not exclusive to games, of course. Here's John Dewey, in his book *Experience and Education:* "Perhaps the greatest of all pedagogical fallacies is the notion that a person learns only that particular thing he is studying at the time. Collateral learning in the way of formation of enduring attitudes, of likes and dislikes, may be and often is more important than the spelling lesson or lesson in geography or history that is learned. For these attitudes are fundamentally what count in the future."

QUESTIONS FOR DISCUSSION

1. What is the point, or claim, Johnson is attempting to get his readers to accept?
2. What reason does he give to support this claim? What evidence supports the reason?
3. Besides the reason and evidence, do you see any other kind of rhetorical appeals operating in this passage?
4. Do you find this argument convincing? Why or why not?

ARGUING RESPONSIBLY

By now it has probably occurred to you that argument is something that everyone does all the time. After all, we are usually expected to offer reasons for our opinions, such as why we think Lady Gaga is a great performing artist or a shallow publicity stunt, or whether the Red candidate or the Blue one would make a better governor. In addition to making our own arguments, we hear them all the time, from the candidates who want our vote, from businesses who want our dollar, from friends who want us to think the way they do on an issue. The point to remember is that the intelligent person is one who can distinguish good arguments from bad ones—whether he or she agrees with the argument or not.

In fact, responsible argument is not a one-way street, as Walter Lippmann said in his classic 1939 essay "The Indispensable Opposition." He wanted to correct the common notion that freedom of speech simply means that all opinions can be expressed. Lippmann calls the opposition "indispensable" because a free society depends not only on the right of free speech but also on the responsibility to actually listen to (and not just tolerate), those with opposing views. In Lippmann's words, "If we truly wish to understand why freedom is necessary in a civilized society, we must begin by realizing that, because freedom of discussion improves our own opinions, the liberties of other men are our own vital necessity."

Too often people do not think about whether an argument shows good reasoning. People tend to approve of arguments that align with their opinions and dismiss those that do not. They also tend to be convinced by arguments that appeal to their fears, their egos, their family's political views, and so on. In this book, we will use the term **responsible argument** to distinguish those that show responsible reasoning from those that show poor, or careless, reasoning.

Four Criteria of Responsible Reasoning

RESPONSIBLE REASONERS ARE WELL-INFORMED

Their opinions develop out of knowledge and are supported by reliable and current evidence.

RESPONSIBLE REASONERS ARE SELF-CRITICAL AND OPEN TO CONSTRUCTIVE CRITICISM FROM OTHERS

They balance their passionate attachment to their opinions with willingness to evaluate and test them against differing opinions, acknowledge when good points are made against their opinions, and even, when presented with good reasons for doing so, change their minds.

RESPONSIBLE REASONERS ARGUE WITH THEIR AUDIENCES OR READERS IN MIND

They make a sincere effort to understand and connect with other people and other points of view because they do not see differences of opinion as obstacles to their own point of view.

RESPONSIBLE REASONERS KNOW THEIR ARGUMENTS' CONTEXTS

They recognize that what we argue about now was argued about in the past and will be argued about in the future, that our contributions to these ongoing conversations are influenced by who we are, what made us who we are, where we are, what is going on around us.

Responsible arguments can be forceful but never are rude or insult the opposition. More than half of Americans today disapprove of Congress because the members on both sides of the aisle would rather demonize the opposition than listen to each other's arguments and reason together to pass legislation. The media, especially talk radio, is full of irresponsible arguments aimed at stirring up the speakers' followers. These are fake arguments, not even intended to change opponents' thinking.

FOUR CRITERIA OF RESPONSIBLE REASONING

If you read the letters to the editor in almost any daily newspaper, you will see many short arguments by citizens. You might notice that some of them sound more intelligent than others. Whether you agree or disagree with the author's point, you may find yourself respecting some of the letters and dismissing others as laughable or at least not deserving any serious consideration. In this book, we will stress qualities of arguments that deserve respect. Such arguments display what we call responsible reasoning. Some criteria, or standards, for responsible reasoning are listed below.

Responsible Reasoning Is Well Informed

To argue responsibly, a person must support his or her opinions with reliable and current evidence. If the author has not made any effort to dig up and include some specific knowledge on the topic, the reader will dismiss the argument as having no weight or force.

You may have noticed that people have opinions about all sorts of things, including subjects they know little or nothing about. The general human tendency is to have the strongest opinions on matters about which we know the least. Ignorance and inflexibility go together because it is easy to form an opinion when few or none of the facts get in the way and people can just assert their prejudices. Conversely, the more we know about most topics, the harder it is to be dogmatic. We find ourselves changing or at least refining our opinions more or less continuously as we gain more knowledge and learn from well-argued opposing views.

Responsible Reasoning Is Open to Constructive Criticism from Others

We have opinions about all sorts of things that do not matter much to us, but we also have opinions in which we are heavily invested, sometimes to the point that our whole sense of reality, right and wrong, good and bad—our very sense of ourselves—is tied up in them. These opinions we defend passionately.

On this count, popular argumentation and responsible reasoning are alike. It is not a fault to be passionate about our convictions. A crucial difference, however, separates the fanatic's argument from that of the responsible person. The fanatic is all passion; the responsible person is willing to step back and ask himself or herself, "I may have believed this for as long as I can remember, but is this conviction really justified? Do the facts support it? When I think it through, does it really make sense? Can I make a coherent and consistent argument for it?" These are questions that do not concern the fanatic and are seldom posed in the popular argumentation we hear on talk radio or TV.

In practical terms, being open to well-intended criticism boils down to this: the ability to change our minds when good reasons to do so are presented. In popular argumentation, changing one's mind can be taken as a weakness, as being wishy-washy, and so people tend to go on advocating what they believe, regardless of what anyone else says. But there is nothing wishywashy about confronting the facts and realizing that our point of view is not supported by available evidence. In such a case, changing one's mind is a sign of intelligence and responsible reasoning.

Responsible Reasoning Considers the Audience

Nothing drains energy from an argument more than the feeling that it will accomplish nothing. As one student put it, "Why bother? People just go on thinking what they want to." This attitude is understandable. Popular, undisciplined argument often does seem futile: Minds are not changed; no progress is made; it is doubtful that anyone learned anything. Sometimes the opposing positions only harden, and the people involved are more at odds than before.

Why does this happen so often? One reason is that nobody is listening to anyone else. We tend to hear only our own voice and see only from our own point of view. But there is another reason: The people making the arguments have made no effort to reach their audience. This is the other side of the coin of not listening: When we do not take other points of view seriously, we cannot make our points of view appealing to those who do not already share them.

To argue persuasively, we have to respect the opposition, see them—rather than others on our own side—as the audience for our arguments. We have to write in ways that will not turn off the very people whose minds we want to change. Because we have to imagine this audience as our readers, *adapting to the audience* is the biggest challenge of argument.

Responsible Reasoning Understands an Argument's Contexts

All arguments are part of an ongoing conversation, not the isolated events they seem to be in the news. Part of being well-informed means knowing something about the history of an argument. An argument's history tells us how and why people's viewpoints formed and gives us a context for our own views. Knowing context means knowing the current range of opinion on an issue. We have to know what other people are saying to make our own reasoning relevant. To some extent, we need to see into the future of an argument, recognizing the cutting-edge issues that people might argue about in the future. In sum, knowing the past, present, and future of arguments on an issue helps ensure that we are making arguments on issues that matter and will continue to matter.

READING

As citizens, we all have a stake in the quality of arguments in the public arena, whether in newspapers, talk shows, political speeches, or, on a more personal level, class discussions, lunch-table debates, and campus forums. As a college student, you may be concerned about how debates on public policy are shaping the world you are inheriting. In this opinion column from a student newspaper, Vanderbilt University student Kelby Carlson worries that responsible reasoning is in decline.

Fighting Words: Why Our Public Discourse Must Change

KELBY CARLSON

1   Americans have always loved to argue. From our country's founding, debates over political principles, the nature of government, and the relation between liberty and equality have been vigorously and vociferously argued. The most famous debates of

our country's history were perhaps the Lincoln-Douglas debates in 1860. In some (though only some) respects, it was a time quite like our own: Americans were polarized (over, obviously, the nature of slavery) and the rapidly deteriorating relations between Northern and Southern states (with some secession and more yet to come) caused no end of consternation. A quick study of those debates, however, reveals that both candidates for the presidency in 1860 had rhetorical skills that few today can match: their debate points sound like they've been ripped straight from a political treatise.

2   Today's landscape of argument is quite different. Technology has radically re-shaped the ways in which discourse is connected in public life. Television transformed a word-oriented culture into one more focused on images; the recent advent of social media, by contrast, brought words back—and made the process of argument more public than ever before. In the wake of these changes lies a landscape of sound bite polemic and rhetorical politics desperately in need of re-appraisal. I'd like to offer a case in point (with which readers will likely be quite familiar) and a couple of suggestions on where things went wrong and how to chart a new course.

3   In early February [2012], a new amendment to health care legislation began the process of working its way through Congress. This amendment modified employer requirements and would mandate that private institutions include medical contraceptives in their health care plans. Almost immediately, an outcry arose among private religious institutions, spearheaded by the United States Conference of Catholic Bishops. Furthered by Rick Santorum's opposition to the amendment, an increasing groundswell of public opinion developed on both sides of the debate. Later that month, Sandra Fluke, a first-year law student at Georgetown University, testified before the Senate regarding the legislation and made a case for compliance (particularly at schools).

4   This may not have been national news if it were not for a number of incendiary comments by well-known talk-radio kingpin Rush Limbaugh. In his comments, Limbaugh called Fluke a "slut" and a "prostitute" and insinuated that Fluke should be required to video-tape herself having sex for Limbaugh (and those like him) to watch. This led to almost immediate outrage, with many of Limbaugh's sponsors quickly pulling their advertisements and public opinion supporting the sponsors' decisions.

5   This is a case-in-point of the kind of public discourse we see regarding both important and unimportant issues, and showcases the good and the bad in American public life. First, the bad: Limbaugh's comments were inappropriate and offensive on every level imaginable. From publicly shaming Ms. Fluke to more generally placing sexual objectification on women, his acidic remarks reveal deep problems with the way many in America see sex, gender, and their intersections with politics, regardless of what anyone believes about this specific legislation. But, there is a glimmer of hope in this situation: Social media allowed the public instantly and massively to pressure sponsors to respond. Even ten years ago, a mass reaction this visible and immediate would not have been possible.

6   If I were more cynical, I could list dozens of examples from both left and right, from inappropriately sexualized attacks to caricatures that would make most cartoonists blush. But a more important question is: How did we get here?

7   In his trenchant and prophetic book *Amusing Ourselves to Death,* Neal Postman dissects the last century of cultural changes, backed by technology. Postman's basic thesis is that Western culture became strongly word-oriented after the invention of the printing press. Along with an orientation around words came a love for rationality, tempered argument and civility.

8   Television completely changed the way discourse was conducted. It moved culture in a visual direction, focusing on a successive series of rapid images. This appealed to different centers of the human mind, concentrating more on instinct and emotions and leading to what Postman calls a culture of the sound bite. This new need for fast, punchy delivery—style over substance—leaked into the culture of speech and print. Now, the ability to fire a sarcastic barb—no matter how hurtful or unnecessary—is seemingly more prized than the ability to construct a rational argument.

9   As explored above, social media has had both negative and positive effects on this trend. While it has allowed more participation in political action and protest, sites like Facebook—with its constant updates, pictures, and incomplete life snapshots—do as much to encourage the current sound bite culture as suppress it. If a cultural dominance of style and image over substance and dialogue has combined with political uncertainty and unrest, is it any wonder our public discourse appears to be in such a shambles?

10   What is the solution? Quite frankly, there is no simple answer to that question. The technology we have is affecting our culture in ways that are still difficult to predict. The only advice I can offer that I think has any semblance of hope is not political, and not cultural. It is personal. Those who communicate in public forums must seek to reaffirm kindness and respect. This means more than just putting on a nice face. It means making a genuine attempt at dialogue with those with whom we disagree. It means assuming benevolent, rather than malicious, motivations of those with whom we differ. It means not resorting to insults, objectification, and personal attacks, but instead focusing on concrete issues and ways to solve them.

11   No one person can single-handedly solve the problem of a dominantly polemical and aggressive public discourse. Instead, each one of us—in our writing, in our speech and in our actions—must do what we can to set an example of how real debate must happen.

QUESTIONS FOR DISCUSSION

1. Carlson gives evidence of the decline in public discourse by summarizing an incident in which a talk radio host crossed the line of decency by failing to respect a person whose ideas differed from his and his listeners'. Why is it important to maintain civility toward those with whom you disagree?

2. What influences does Carlson see as contributing to a decline in public discourse, especially the decline in the quality of arguments? Do you agree? Can you think of other influences?

3. What can you as a college student, a citizen, and a member of various communities do to contribute to a solution to the problem of "fighting words" dominating Americans' idea of argument?

WHAT ARE THE AIMS OF ARGUMENT?

The heart of this book is Part Two, the section titled "The Aims of Argument." In conceiving this book, we worked from one basic premise: Responsible reasoners do not argue just to argue; rather, they use argument to accomplish something: *to inquire* into a question, problem, or issue (commonly part of the research process); *to convince* their readers to assent to an opinion, or claim; *to persuade* readers to take action, such as buying a product or voting for a candidate; and *to mediate* conflict, as in labor disputes, divorce proceedings, and so on.

Below, we explain each of these aims in more detail.

Arguing to Inquire

Arguing to **inquire** is using reasoning to determine the best position on an issue. We open the "Aims" section with **inquiry** because responsible reasoning is not a matter of defending what we already believe but of questioning it. Arguing to inquire helps us form opinions, question opinions we already have, and reason our way through conflicts or contradictions in other people's arguments on a topic. Inquiry is open-minded, and it requires that we make an effort to find out what people who disagree think and why.

The ancient Greeks called argument as inquiry *dialectic;* today we might think of it as **dialogue** or serious conversation. There is nothing confrontational about such conversations. We have them with friends, family, and colleagues, even with ourselves. We have these conversations in writing too, as we make notations in the margins of the arguments we read.

Inquiry centers on questions and involves some legwork to answer them—finding the facts, doing research. This is true whether you are inquiring into what car to buy, what major to choose in college, what candidate to vote for, or what policy our government should pursue on any given issue.

Arguing to Convince

The goal of inquiry is to reach some kind of conclusion on an issue. Let's call this conclusion a **conviction** and define it as "an earned opinion, achieved through careful thought, research, and discussion." Once we arrive at a conviction, we usually want others to share it. The aim of further argument is to secure the assent of people who do not share our conviction (or who do not share it fully).

Argument to **convince** centers on making a case, which means offering reasons and evidence in support of our opinion. Arguments to convince are all around us. In college, we find them in scholarly and professional writing.

In everyday life, we find arguments to convince in editorials, courtrooms, and political speeches. Whenever we encounter an opinion supported by reasons and asking us to agree, we are dealing with arguing to convince.

Arguing to Persuade

Like convincing, persuasion attempts to earn agreement, but it wants more. **Persuasion** attempts to influence not just thinking but also behavior. An advertisement for Mercedes-Benz aims to convince us not only that the company makes a high-quality car but also that we should go out and buy one. A Sunday sermon asks for more than agreement with some interpretation of a biblical passage; the minister wants the congregation to live according to its message. Persuasion asks us to do something—spend money, give money, join a demonstration, recycle, vote, enlist, acquit. Because we do not always act on our convictions, persuasion cannot rely on reasoning alone. It must appeal in broader, deeper ways.

Persuasion appeals to readers' emotions. It tells stories about individual cases of hardship that move us to pity. It often uses photographs, as when charities confront us with pictures of poverty or suffering. Persuasion uses many of the devices of poetry, such as patterns of sound, repetitions, metaphors, and similes to arouse a desired emotion in the audience.

Persuasion also relies on the personality of the writer to an even greater degree than does convincing. The persuasive writer attempts to represent something higher or larger than him- or herself—some ideal with which the reader would like to be associated. For example, a war veteran and hero like Senator John McCain naturally brings patriotism to the table when he makes a speech.

Arguing to Mediate

By the time we find ourselves in a situation where our aim is **mediation**, we will have already attempted to convince an opponent to settle a conflict or dispute our way. Our opponent will have done the same. Yet neither side has secured the assent of the other, and "agreeing to disagree" is not a practical solution because the participants must decide what to do.

In most instances of mediation, the parties involved try to work out the conflict themselves because they have some relationship they wish to preserve—as employer and employee, business partners, family members, neighbors, even coauthors of an argument textbook. Common differences requiring mediation include the amount of a raise and the terms of a contract. In private life, mediation helps roommates live together and families decide on everything from budgets to vacation destinations.

Just like other aims of argument, arguing to mediate requires sound logic and the clear presentation of positions and reasons. However, mediation challenges our interpersonal skills more than do the other aims. Each side must listen closely to understand not just the other's case but also the emotional commitments and underlying values. When mediation works, the opposing

Comparing the Aims of Argument

The aims of argument have much in common. For example, besides sharing argument, they all tend to draw on sources of knowledge (research) and to deal with controversial issues. But the aims also differ from one another, mainly in terms of purpose, audience, situation, and method, as summarized here and on the inside back cover.

	Purpose	Audience	Situation	Method
Inquiry	Seeks truth	Oneself, friends, and colleagues	Informal; a dialogue	Questions
Convincing	Seeks assent to a thesis	Less intimate; wants careful reasoning	More formal; a monologue	Case-making
Persuading	Seeks action	More broadly public, less academic	Pressing need for a decision	Appeals to reason and emotions
Mediating	Seeks consensus	Polarized by differences	Need to cooperate, preserve relations	"Give-and-take"

We offer this chart as a general guide to the aims of argument. Think of it as the big picture you can always return to as you work your way through Part Two, which deals with each of the aims in detail.

sides begin to converge. Exchanging viewpoints and information and building empathy enable all parties to make concessions, to loosen their hold on their original positions, and finally to reach consensus—or at least a resolution that all participants find satisfactory.

Reading Arguments

Reading arguments takes a different kind of concentration than reading to retain information; you have to assess the soundness of the author's reasoning. As we explain in Chapter 1, the essence of an argument is reasoning—asserting a claim, also called a thesis, and supporting it with a reason or reasons. Because arguments lay out a case in support of a claim, to judge them, you must use many **critical reading** skills.

For example, critical readers must detect the relationship between the claim and its supporting material. They must also evaluate the relevance and validity of the support. Often they must "read between the lines," meaning they must infer meanings that are not obvious, such as when a writer is being ironic. Critical reading is at least equal parts reading and thinking.

Many students think that good reading is fast reading, but that is not always the case. Depending on your purpose for reading, you should shift speeds and use different tactics, such as writing comments or paraphrasing ideas so that you can think carefully about them. This is especially important when reading an argument.

Like anything involving mental effort, the more you do critical reading, the easier it becomes and the sooner you will start to see benefits. From careful and attentive reading of well-made arguments, you will learn how to craft your own arguments, how to choose reasons to suit particular audiences, and how to use style to best effect. You can learn from reading flawed arguments, too, by detecting weaknesses in the reasoning and other mistakes such as tone-deaf writing that would turn readers away.

Defining Critical Reading

Critical reading goes beyond finding out what a text says. Critical reading means engaging through questioning the text. When reading an argument, critical reading requires that you ask who wrote the text and why, and to whom the argument is being made. Critically reading an argument also means detecting the case, that is, the claim and the reasons and the evidence in support of each reason, and asking how well the reasons and evidence support the claim. Finally, critical reading requires you to think about how you would respond to what the author has said.

Finally, critical reading works best if your mind is fresh and dedicated to the task, not tired, hurried, or distracted. Find a place free from noise and force yourself to turn off social media. To read critically, you need to stay focused.

STRATEGIES FOR CRITICAL READING: ONCE THROUGH IS NOT ENOUGH

Critical reading takes you through an argument more than once. It is recursive: You move through, loop back, move on. You reread. In this chapter, we will demonstrate some strategies that will help you master critical reading of arguments. We break the process down into three encounters with the text, each with its own strategies, to take you deeper into thinking about any argument.

First Encounters: Skimming for Context, Reading for Content

You have probably heard the expression "Study smarter, not harder." This slogan definitely applies to reading. For example, it is not efficient to start with the opening sentence and zip (or slog) your way to the end. Although this kind of linear approach might be best for reading a mystery novel, it is not a smart way to read arguments, especially long and difficult ones.

Strategy: Before Reading, Skim (and Surf) for Context

Become informed about the **rhetorical context** of an argument before reading it. By rhetorical context, we mean the background for the text, such as who wrote it, when, why, and to whom. Read headnotes or endnotes about the author or surf the Internet for biographical information. Just as a traveler gets more out of a trip by gathering information before embarking, a reader gets more out of a text by finding information about its creation before starting to read.

Questions for Determining Rhetorical Context

To determine an argument's rhetorical context, answer the following questions:

Who wrote this argument? What are the writer's occupation, personal background, and political leanings?

To whom is the author writing? Arguments are usually aimed at a specific audience, such as entertainment industry moguls, undecided voters, or parents of teenagers.

Where does the argument appear? If it is reprinted or inserted into a website, where did it originally appear? Is the source reliable?

When was the argument written? If not recently, what do you know about the circumstances in which it was written?

Why was the argument written? What is the author's purpose?

For example, if you picked up Jonathan Swift's famous essay "A Modest Proposal" without considering the context, you might be bewildered by the following statement:

> I have been assured by a very knowing American of my acquaintance in London, that a young healthy child well nursed is at a year old a most delicious, nourishing, and wholesome food, whether stewed, roasted, baked, or boiled; and I make no doubt that it will equally serve in a fricassee or a ragout.

To appreciate Swift's satire, a reader has to know when and why this famous essay was written and the historical facts about poverty in Ireland and the inhumane "solutions" proposed by the English absentee landowners. Reading without knowing the context can be a waste of time.

Strategy: Skim to Preview the Whole Argument

Skimming the text is another way to become informed before reading. Do a quick overview of the whole argument. How long is it? What is the writer going to talk about? Skim the introduction; read some topic sentences and subheadings if the text has them. Read the conclusion. It is good to know where the argument will end up, and the main point can often be found at the end.

Strategy: Annotate as You Read

Most students are highlighters, not annotators. But highlighting is a very superficial way of marking a text. It can tell you what seemed important, but not why it seemed important, what it connects to in the rest of the text, or what you thought about it. In other words, highlighting does not help you hold on to the thoughts you had while reading.

Marginal annotations can improve reading comprehension and retention in ways that highlighting cannot. Use **annotations** (literally "notes added on")

Annotating as You Read

1. An argument consists of a claim and a reason or reasons. As you detect these elements, label them. If you are not sure about the label, add a question mark and come back later.

2. If a word seems important, especially if it seems to be a key term, circle it. If you think the author should have explained the meaning of any key word, note that omission in the margin. Look up unfamiliar words and jot definitions in the margin. Take advantage of ways to build up your vocabulary.

3. Use annotations to monitor your comprehension. If a passage is confusing, make a note such as: "What does this mean?" or "I don't get it." These are places to revisit and to ask about in class.

4. If you question the author's ideas or facts, mark the passage, and later, after reading, do a fact check.

5. It is just as important to note what is not there as what is. If you think of something that the author has ignored or omitted, make a note.

6. React to the text. Even simple annotations like "Right" or "Who says?" or "But what about . . ." will help you be an active reader.

7. Mark any opposing views. Not everything in the argument will necessarily be the view of the author; sometimes the author will present an opposing view, with or without a formal introduction of the person who holds it. Opposing views can even slip in as irony. Read for tone, and mark changes in tone and point of view.

8. Write down anything you want to remember after you are done reading. Good insights do not wait around; catch them while you can.

to track the author's line of thought: the main points, the turning points, the points you might challenge. If you have not developed the annotation habit, the box on this page will give you some ideas about what to write.

Do not skip annotations. Students who mark up their readings comprehend them better and write about them with more confidence. If you are reading a print copy, you should make marginal notes as you read. And if you are reading online or do not want to mark your textbook, it is worth making a copy that you can mark up.

◎ ACTIVITY: Practicing the Strategies

The first argument to read critically in this chapter is an opinion column by Sally Jenkins, a sports commentator for *The Washington Post*. The column appeared in the fall of 2011 when the illegal paying and recruiting of athletes in NCAA sports was a major issue in the news.

1. Before reading the argument, apply the rhetorical context questions on page 19. Skim, surf for context information, and be ready to say more in class discussion about Jenkins and her topic, audience, and possible bias.

2. Skim to preview the whole text. After reading the first and last paragraphs, what do you think Jenkins's main point will be?

3. Now read more slowly through the argument, making annotations. To help you get started, we have made a few annotations to the first several paragraphs.

A Major Gain for College Sports

SALLY JENKINS

1   If we would quit being half-ashamed of college sports and assign them some real value, we might just cure some of their corruptions. The NCAA should stop treating athletic departments as ticket offices attached to universities like tumors and instead treat them as legitimate academic branches. In fact, why shouldn't we let kids major in sports? Aspiring athletes should be able to pursue their real interest, as a business and an art.

2   High-performance athletes study a craft, with a science, theory, history and literature, just like music or dance or film majors do. Varsity athletes deserve significant academic credits for their incredibly long hours of training and practice, and if they fulfill a core curriculum they deserve degrees, too. A school could design a rigorous Performance of Sport major by requiring the following:

3   Introduction to Sports Law: a broad overview of antitrust law, labor law and contract law, via memorable sports legal battles such as *Tarkanian v. NCAA,* and *Flood v. Kuhn.* Textbook: "Sports Law: Cases and Materials" by Michael J. Cozzillio and Mark Levenstein.

4   The Origins of Sport: a survey of the history of ritual athletics from the Bronze Age to the modern Olympics. Textbooks: "Combat Sports in the Ancient World," by Michael Poliakoff and "Reading Football" by Michael Oriard.

5   Making Up the Rules: an ethical-studies examination of moral and philosophical issues from amateurism to performance enhancement. Textbook: "Ethics in Sport," edited by William Morgan.

6   Sports and Public Policy: how our sports-entertainment industries intersect with economics, urban planning, public health, and political science. Textbook: "Sport and Public Policy: Social, Political, and Economic Perspectives," by Charles Santo and Gerard Mildner.

7   Think about it. Why is an Alabama football player or Tennessee women's basketball player less worthy than a Yale drama student? According to Yale's Theater Studies course guide, drama students learn a "complex cultural practice," and "combine practical training with theory and history, while stressing creative critical thinking." Now substitute the word sport for theater. Isn't sport a complex cultural practice with a body of knowledge, history, and theory? Just to be sure I haven't jumped the shark, I e-mailed the director of the Yale Theater Studies program, Toni Dorfman, to ask whether this is nonsense. "What a wonderful idea," she replied. "The theory and practice of sport are certainly as ancient as those of theater."

Annotations (right margin):

Who is we? Who does she think is ashamed?

Corruptions like illegal recruiting and paying athletes. Example: University of Miami scandal.

What actually is the meaning of academic? Can a sport be academic? Is it anything connected with a school?

The crux of the argument—her claim.

A reason.

This curriculum is academic. And it might help athletes find a job in sports if they can't go pro.

Less worthy of what? Respect? Academic credit? She needs to pin down some definitions.

Annotations (bottom):

It would be hard to argue with this expert's opinion. But she means studying the sport, not just playing it.

Voice here—she's funny.

8   With a fundamental shift in the way we think about college sports, by designating them intellectually worthwhile exercises instead of mere obsessions, we might gain some clarity. For one thing, the worth of an athletic scholarship would suddenly be clearer. We could stop worrying about "exploiting" athletes and whether to pay them. Yale drama undergraduates don't get a cut of the box office—their recompense is first-rate training for the stage. They aren't exploited. They're privileged.

9   Too many college presidents harbor the secret conviction that athletics are trivial, if not evil, entertainments that exist merely to please donors. Back in 2004, former NCAA president Myles Brand was scandalized to learn that some schools gave athletes limited academic credits for varsity participation. "We can't have that," he said.

10   That attitude has to change. Sports aren't trivial. Among the things college athletes strive to learn: how to bring their best every day, how to deal with the fact that their minds and bodies will betray them under pressure, how to accept the consequences of public performance, and how to withstand violence or pain and create something beautiful and excellent despite it—or even from it. The vast majority of them, even the so-called cheats and chokers, are highly focused, dedicated, self-appraising, self-motivated and highly aspirational.

11   The NCAA's stated mission is "to integrate intercollegiate athletics so that the educational experience of the student athlete is paramount." So do it. Stitch college sports into the rest of the university by recognizing their value as an academic major. Once college presidents make that fundamental shift in their thinking, they might be inclined to make other changes too. They might mandate that athletics be answerable to an academic dean, like any other discipline. They might decide that coaches should be faculty members who teach.

12   "Athletics needs to be acknowledged as something legitimate and serious," says Oriard, a former Notre Dame and NFL football player who is now an associate dean and literature professor at Oregon State. Given that college sports have become multibillion dollar industries and national institutions, he says, students should "understand the ethical, cultural, social and historical dimensions of their activity."

13   Oriard observes that athletes devote as much time to their craft as a student violinist, and "there is an intelligence that is required of athletes that is similar to music, too." We congratulate music majors for their passion, and tell them that even if they don't make it in the symphony, they are acquiring an art and a method of thought that will be theirs forever. But for some reason we tell athletes who aspire to the highest levels that they are academically illegitimate, and look down on them as vocational students (forgetting that without vocational students, our cars wouldn't start).

14   But what if we taught and talked to them differently? What if we pulled available college courses together into a more coherent, meaningful way for them, instead of herding them into General Studies. What if we taught that athleticism, like musicality, is a "lifelong discovery," Oriard says. Above all, surely we should teach that their performance "is valuable in itself," quite apart from commercial value.

15   Such thinking would not only benefit athletes, it would sharpen the decision-making of administrators. Because frankly, any resistance to this idea begs the question, "Then why have sports on campus at all?" Why do universities build sports stadiums? Well, why does a university build a hospital? Not to gouge and rip off the infirm for profit. They do it because the research and teaching in a hospital is vital and enhances a university's standing.

16   There's no reason the NCAA can't reconcile commerce with education in a more honorable way. If presidents see athletes as worthy students, instead of unpaid labor, then they themselves might act more like educators, instead of carnival barkers grabbing for easy cash. What a concept. College sports are salvageable. But first, we have to correct an underlying fallacy—that despite all that money, they are worthless.

QUESTIONS FOR DISCUSSION

1. This is an example of a proposal argument. Jenkins sees that there are problems with NCAA sports on campus and proposes a means of correcting the problems. How controversial is her proposed solution? Who might agree with her? Who do you think would disagree most strongly, and why?

2. Defining key terms in any argument is important. In this argument, a key term is *academic*. What is your understanding of the word? Look it up in a good dictionary to see how it is defined. Look over Jenkins's argument to see how she describes sports and athletes to convince readers that they belong in the category of *academic study* rather than "trivial entertainment."

3. In paragraph 15, Jenkins says "any resistance to [her argument] begs the question, 'Then why have sports on campus at all?' Why do universities have sports stadiums?" What does *begging the question* mean? (See page 554 in Appendix B, "Fallacies—and Critical Thinking.") What does Jenkins see as a logical flaw in the opposition's argument? How would you explain the connection between sports and higher education?

COLLABORATIVE ACTIVITY: Discussing Your Annotations

As a class or in small groups, compare the annotations you made to this text. Which of the suggestions on page 19 did you use when finding places to make annotations? What other questions or reactions caused members of your class or group to make an annotation?

Second Encounters: Reading to Detect the Case

Readers are more likely to stay engaged when they are not just reading, but reading to find answers to questions. With an argument, an important question is, What is the author's case? By **case,** we mean a combination of three levels of reasoning:

(1) **the claim,** or main point,

(2) **the reasons** given to support the claim, and

(3) **the evidence** given to make each reason credible.

Strategy: Outlining the Case

When you scrutinize someone's argument, it helps to pull out these three levels of reasoning and put them into an outline or tree diagram. In Jenkins's column, her claim is stated many times in slightly different wording. No one sentence stands out as the thesis sentence, but the second sentence in the first paragraph contains the main point: "The NCAA [and college presidents] should . . . treat [athletic departments] as legitimate academic branches." (Using square brackets, we modified this sentence to include college presidents, since the argument includes them as well as the NCAA as a source of the problem.) You see this main idea again in paragraphs 8 and 16, and also in the words of one of Jenkins's sources, Michael Oriard, in paragraph 12.

Using the outline form, we can begin to analyze Jenkins's case, starting with the claim.

> **Claim:** "The NCAA [and college presidents] should . . . treat [athletic departments] as legitimate academic branches."

Once you are certain of the claim, look for how the author tries to get the readers to see the claim as valid, or at least reasonable. You are looking for the reasons, and this may take some rereading. Reasons answer the question: Why is the claim true? You should be able to put an imaginary *because* between the claim and a reason. In paragraph 2, we find one of Jenkins's reasons:

> **Reason:** [Because] Sports are a craft similar to other performance majors, with long hours of practice, a history, science, theories, and body of literature for study.

Jenkins is using a common type of reasoning, the **analogy.** In an analogy, two things are compared in the hope that if the audience accepts something as true for one half of the comparison, then they will accept it as true for the other half. For example, a familiar argument states that because consuming sugar is known to cause disease, sugar should be taxed like other disease-causing substances, such as tobacco.

Returning to Jenkins's analogy, if the audience accepts performance in music or art or theater as a legitimate academic major, they should also accept performance in a sport as a legitimate academic major. Because this reason would not sit well with many people who see sports as "less worthy," to use Jenkins's phrase, she has to shore up the reason with evidence—specifics that make the reason credible.

> **Evidence:** Course titles and reading materials for a major in Performance of Sport (paragraphs 3–6)
> **Evidence:** E-mail testimony from Yale theater professor (paragraph 7)

⊚ ACTIVITY: Schematic Layout of an Argument

Using either a tree diagram or an outline, continue the schematic layout of the logical case structure of Jenkins's argument. Use direct quotations or paraphrases for additional reasons; indicate the paragraph numbers where you find these.

Understanding Case Structure

All arguments include a claim, at least one reason, and evidence to support that reason. Most arguments have more than one reason, and most reasons are supported by multiple offerings of evidence. The template below can be expanded to show the structure of a case of any size.

Claim _____

    Reason _____

        Evidence _____

        Evidence (if present) _____

        Additional evidence _____

    Reason (if present) _____

        Evidence _____

        Evidence (if present) _____

    Additional reasons _____

Do not try to list the reasons in the order they appear; just read and reread until you see the case emerge clearly. For each reason, indicate briefly, as we have above, what Jenkins uses as evidence to make the reason convincing to an opposing audience.

◎ COLLABORATIVE ACTIVITY: Filling Out Jenkins's Case

In pairs or groups of three, use the template above to complete an analysis of the case Jenkins makes for making college sports part of the academic curriculum.

Third Encounters: Responding to an Argument

Arguments are voices in a conversation. We hope that when you read an argument on an interesting topic, you will want to respond to what the writer says. Your third encounter with an argument, your response, contributes to the conversation with constructive criticism or a new perspective on what has already been said. In other words, you will refer specifically to points in the argument you read.

The deepest thinking about an argument comes when you try to answer the following questions: "Is this a good argument or not? Does it show good thinking? Is it based on good facts? Does the argument depend on unstated assumptions that may or may not be true? What would be the implications of accepting this argument?"

Begin your response by giving an argument a fair reading, regardless of your initial position on the issue. When you read with an open mind, you may find that you respect an argument you had initially opposed.

Strategy: Paraphrasing

A fair reading begins with a careful reading. If you are going to critique what somebody else has said, your first responsibility is to get it right. Paraphrasing and summarizing are both ways to give an accurate account of someone else's argument.

Paraphrase requires very close reading and the ability to translate an entire idea into your own words. A paraphrase is as specific as the original and about the same length or even longer. Think of paraphrasing as explaining an idea. A paraphrase puts the author's ideas into your own words, your own sentences, and your own voice.

What do we mean by **voice**? Notice that Jenkins uses a satiric tone; she is angry at the big-money folks in college sports who do not value the effort and intelligence of the players. She uses figurative language, the simile of the ticket office as tumor, to characterize the NCAA's idea of how athletic departments are not really legitimate parts of a university. Looking again at Jenkins's opening paragraph, you can hear the disgust in her voice:

> If we would quit being half-ashamed of college sports and assign them some real value, we might just cure some of their corruptions. The NCAA should stop treating athletic departments as ticket offices attached to universities like tumors and instead treat them as legitimate academic branches. In fact, why shouldn't we let kids major in sports?

When paraphrasing, you want to restate and explain the author's point in your own voice. Remember, you are just reporting on what she says, so your voice is likely to be calmer and cooler and you may state ideas more directly. Notice that the following paraphrase drops the "tumor" simile:

> Sally Jenkins argues that colleges could solve the problem of corruption in athletic departments by redefining sports as part of the academic life of the university instead of just profit-making entertainment. When sports get the academic respect they deserve, colleges could even allow athletes to major in sports.

Paraphrase is not easy, but it helps you absorb the ideas and makes you think harder about them. In the box on page 27, you will find some tips about how to write good paraphrases.

⊚ ACTIVITY: Practicing Paraphrase

The concluding paragraph in Jenkins's argument is highly charged and sarcastic. Write a paraphrase that explains Jenkins's position, using a tone more appropriate for explaining an idea that is not your own.

Guidelines for Paraphrasing

1. Read the whole argument before trying to paraphrase any part of it. Look carefully at the context, that is, at the sentences surrounding the passage you plan to paraphrase. You may want to include some of that information to clarify the passage.

2. Look up any unfamiliar words or allusions.

3. Read through the passage slowly, thinking of how you would explain it to someone who had not read it.

4. Set the original passage aside. Looking at the original wording while paraphrasing will tempt you to copy it.

5. Write your own version as if you were telling someone what the passage said. Do not merely replace the author's words with synonyms. Write your own sentences. You may make your sentences longer or shorter than those in the original.

6. Use your own words, but do not strain to find a different word for every single one in the original. Using some of the author's plain words, like *college sports* or *athletes,* is fine.

7. If you take a phrase or loaded word from the original, enclose it in quotation marks.

Original Passage to Paraphrase:

There's no reason the NCAA can't reconcile commerce with education in a more honorable way. If presidents see athletes as worthy students, instead of unpaid labor, then they themselves might act more like educators, instead of carnival barkers grabbing for easy cash. What a concept. College sports are salvageable. But first, we have to correct an underlying fallacy—that despite all that money, they are worthless.

◎ COLLABORATIVE ACTIVITY:
Comparing Paraphrases

After drafting your paraphrase, exchange drafts with another student. Did you both cover all the same points? Did you both use your own words and sentences? Did you both use your own voices? Make suggestions for improvement, and revise.

Strategy: Summarizing

Summarizing also requires that you put someone else's ideas into your own words, sentences, and voice, but it uses slightly different thinking skills than paraphrasing. A **summary** includes just the main points of the original argument. When you summarize, you must see the big picture and boil it down to less than one-third of the original's length. In a summary, you find the main ideas, paraphrase them, and then combine your paraphrases into a smooth-flowing abbreviated version of the original text.

Writing a summary is usually not an end in itself. In your own writing, you will use summaries to serve many real purposes: in book reviews, in critiques of an argument, in responses to an argument, and in your own arguments as evidence to support your opinions or as opposing views that you want to refute.

The following sections give more advice on methods for writing a good summary.

Chunking the Argument   A useful strategy for summarizing a text is to find its component parts. In any text, paragraphs work singly or in tandem to play different roles. Spotting the paragraph groupings and determining the function of each helps you recognize the author's overall plan and how the argument is developed. Typical moves in argument are listed below. Note that some of these moves may require multiple paragraphs.

Set up the topic or issue in a way that gets the readers' attention.

State the claim.

Qualify the claim, explaining any exceptions.

Define a key term or terms.

Give background information on the topic.

Give a reason and support it with evidence.

Give an opposing view and refute it.

Make a concession by agreeing with an opposing point.

Conclude by driving home the point.

◎ ACTIVITY: Finding the Moves in Jenkins's Argument

We will discuss the components of Jenkins's argument on college sports, but before reading on, look at Jenkins's argument on pages 21–23 to determine on your own which paragraphs work together to accomplish any of the functions listed above. Annotate your text so that you can compare the chunks you find with our analysis in the pages that follow.   •

Writing a Descriptive Outline   One writing teacher, Kenneth Bruffee, suggests that students make an outline of the component parts of any text, noting the function and the content of each paragraph or group of paragraphs. The descriptive outline consists of a series of entries, each including two parts:

1.   What each component does. This sentence describes the author's move.
2.   What each component says. This sentence summarizes the author's point.

Here is an example of a descriptive outline of Jenkins's argument. Note that the summary statements are shorter than paraphrases, because the goal of a summary is to strip the passage of details and leave only the bare bones of the argument.

First Part: Paragraph 1

Does: Introduces the argument by stating the problem and the solution.

Says: Colleges could clean up the corruption in varsity sports by recognizing that sports have academic value and even allowing athletes to major in sports.

Second Part: Paragraphs 2–7

Does: Gives a reason for recognizing sports as academic.

Says: Sports performance is comparable to other performance majors like theater because sports have a similar intensity of effort and a body of serious scholarship that could form the basis for a rigorous academic major.

Third Part: Paragraph 8

Does: Gives a second reason for recognizing the academic value of sports.

Says: If sports were seen as a legitimate part of higher education, an athletic scholarship would have academic value, undercutting the argument that athletes should be paid for playing.

Fourth Part: Paragraphs 9–10

Does: Gives a third reason for recognizing the academic value of sports.

Says: Athletics are not "evil" or "trivial"; athletes work hard and suffer pain to create beautiful performances.

Fifth Part: Paragraphs 11–15

Does: Gives a fourth reason for recognizing the academic value of sports.

Says: Intercollegiate athletics either have a place in higher education, as the NCAA claims, or they do not. If they do, they should be administered and taught like other academic departments.

Sixth Part: Paragraph 16

Does: Concludes by restating the problem and the solution.

Says: If administrators would recognize that sports have more than just commercial value to the school, they could save varsity sports from the current embarrassing corruptions.

You can create a good summary of the entire argument by combining the "says" statements from your outline and adding a few transitions and references to the author of the argument. Following is a summary written in this way.

Strategy: Joining the Conversation

Once you are confident about an argument's claim and reasoning, you are ready to say what you think about it. What do think about the argument we have been working with? What do you have to say back to Jenkins?

EXAMPLE SUMMARY OF "A MAJOR GAIN FOR COLLEGE SPORTS"

According to *The Washington Post* sports columnist Sally Jenkins, colleges could solve the problem of sports scandals by giving athletics academic credit and even allowing athletes to major in sports. Jenkins makes a case for sports as academic. First, sports are comparable to other performance majors like theater; athletes have to put forth the same intense effort, and sports performance has a body of serious scholarship like other performance arts. She also points out that making sports a legitimate academic major would eliminate the argument that athletes should be paid for their work, and it would disprove the idea that sports are trivial or immoral. In fact, it would help end corruption by bringing academic oversight, such as faculty and deans, to the athletic department. The bottom line is athletics either have a place in higher education, as the NCAA claims, or they don't. If they do, then they should be integrated into the school's educational programs. If administrators would treat athletics like any other academic department, they could avoid the embarrassing scandals and corruption.

The first time you are asked to respond to someone else's argument, especially a professional one, you may be a bit intimidated. How do you challenge someone's thinking? The questions in the Best Practices box will give you ideas of what to say when talking back to an argument.

You have several options for writing your responses to an argument. If space in a text allows, you can just write your responses in the margin, as annotations. However, other strategies allow for a more in-depth response and public response.

The Double-Entry Notebook   A useful tool for responding to any kind of reading is a notebook with two columns. The left-hand column is the "observations" column, because that is where you note things you observe, things that caught your attention in the text. Put quotations and paraphrases in the observations column. Observations include passages that made you think, question, react, and talk back. The column on the right is the "responses" column, where you write what you think about each passage you observed.

Questions for Responding to an Argument

1. Are key terms defined or left ambiguous? It is important that writer and reader know the meaning of words that are central to the case. A writer might purposely leave a key term vague instead of spelling out just what he or she means by it. In Jenkins's argument, what does she mean by "less worthy" in paragraph 7? How does she define *academic,* because the argument hinges on that concept?

2. Are reasons supported with evidence? Is the evidence specific, credible, and relevant? If readers might doubt facts, has the author named the source? To accept a reason, would you need to know more facts?

3. The relationship between a claim and a reason depends on assumptions, which are usually not stated. To accept the argument as valid, the reader would have to share the author's underlying assumptions. Consider the following argument. Is the assumption a safe one?

    Claim: Colleges need to shut down Wi-Fi connections in large lecture halls.

    Reason: The distractions offered by laptops prevent students from paying attention to the lecture.

    Assumption: Students would pay attention if they did not have Internet distractions.

    Looking over Jenkins's argument, do you find any unstated assumptions that you would have to accept in order to accept the logic of the argument? Would you challenge any of her assumptions?

4. Do you see any contradictions in the author's argument? Does the argument contradict itself? Does it contradict any facts you know from other reading and experiences?

5. What do you think about the author's priorities, ethics, and values? For example, Jenkins gives athletes' educations a higher priority than their ability to generate revenue for their schools.

6. Consider the implications of the argument. If people believe or do what the author argues, what is likely to happen?

7. Even if you agree with the argument, think of someone who would disagree with the claim or any of the reasoning. Why would they not accept the argument? What might account for their holding different values, beliefs, or assumptions from the author?

8. If you see any opposing views in the argument, has the author presented them accurately? One fallacy in argument is the straw man, a metaphor for a falsely overstated description of the opposing view that makes it easy to knock down, like a scarecrow. See pages 541–556 in Appendix B on Fallacies for more on the straw man fallacy.

9. Can you think of anything the author is overlooking or leaving out that would either weaken or strengthen the case?

10. Does the argument exemplify responsible reasoning, as explained in Chapter 1, "Understanding Argument"?

11. What kind of person does the author sound like? Mark places where you hear the author's voice. Describe the tone. How does the author establish credibility—or fail to?

12. Do you see emotional as well as logical appeals in the argument? If you see emotional appeals, would you evaluate them as ethical or manipulative? Do you think the author is pandering to audience fears, prejudices, stereotypes, desire for power, or other emotional appeals? See pages 541–556 in Appendix B on Fallacies for more about misuse of emotional appeals.

The "responses" column is for your inferences, judgments, questions, challenges, and any other thoughts in response.

Observations of the text	Responses to the text
. . . drama students "combine practical training with theory and history, while stressing creative critical thinking." Now substitute the word sport for theater. Isn't sport a complex cultural practice with a body of knowledge, history, and theory? (Par. 7)	But drama students are preparing for a life-time career. Would athletes be likely to want to learn that much about sports since the life of their sports career is likely to be less than five years? Her own example of Michael Oriard works against her since he probably majored in English.
. . . by designating [sports] intellectually worthwhile exercises instead of mere obsessions, we might gain some clarity. For one thing, the worth of an athletic scholarship would suddenly be clearer. We could stop worrying about "exploiting" athletes and whether to pay them. (Par. 8)	She's assuming that all scholarship athletes would be able to study sports in that way. Many athletes are exploited because they are special admits who will never graduate and are only in college because they must be in order to get to the pros.

◎ ACTIVITY: Making a Double-Entry Notebook

Use the example above as a template for making more observations and responses to the argument on college sports. If you use direct quotations in the left-hand column, be sure to enclose them in quotation marks as we have done. Depending on your instructor's preference, you may handwrite your responses in a lined notebook, making two columns, or you may create columns in a Word document and post your notebook online.

Writing a Comment   If you have ever had a blog, you know that writers like to know they have readers. They welcome comments, even constructive and polite criticism, because it at least shows that someone has paid attention.

Good comments add value to an argument by pointing out flaws in the reasoning or helping make the case with new reasons and evidence. Comments can also offer a fresh perspective on the issue.

Most online newspaper editorials have a comment thread for readers to write their opinions and interact with the author and each other. Below is one of many comments readers sent to Sally Jenkins after her *Washington Post* column. (By going online, you should be able to find others.)

Response to "A Major Gain for College Sports"

MARIAH BURTON NELSON

I sometimes joke that at Stanford University, I "majored in basketball." Truth is, I spent hours each day immersed in a highly educational experience involving leadership and team-building lessons that were far more hands-on than anything I might have picked up at the Biz School. I also took those lessons and used them as a foundation for a career as a sportswriter.

Sally Jenkins' proposal is a game-changer because it would legitimize sports participation for the educational experience that it is—and encourage universities to create integrated curricula including existing courses such as sport science, sport psychology, sport sociology, sport management, physical education, kinesiology—and the currently-missing piece, the connection between theory and practice: varsity participation.

Most athletes are not football players, and most sports do not generate revenue (nor do most football teams, but that's another story). Her main point has nothing to do with money, and everything to do with challenging the way we think about sports as an educational experience. Congrats, Sally, for raising a fascinating new subject. Wish I'd thought of it myself!

QUESTIONS FOR DISCUSSION

1. How does Nelson establish her own ethos, or credibility, to comment on this topic?

2. How does she show that she read Jenkins's column carefully?

3. Does her comment strengthen Jenkins's case, in your opinion? Why or why not?

READING ALTERNATIVE FORMS OF ARGUMENT

There are many ways to make an argument. Laying out a case with a claim, reasons, and evidence is the most common form that argument takes in academic writing, business, law, and politics. However, less structured forms of argument can sometimes work more effectively, especially when the goal is to move the audience to take some action. An argument does not have to be structured tightly to express an opinion and give reasons in support. Readers may have to work a little harder to uncover and examine the reasoning in alternative arguments, but it is important to do so because this kind of persuasion is a powerful aspect of popular culture. Movies and music can influence people's thinking on a topic more effectively than many outright arguments made in a speech.

Advertisements are arguments that often rely more on visual appeals than on verbal appeals. These images tell us why we will be happier, handsomer, and more popular if we choose one cologne, cellphone, or pair of sneakers over another. Chapter 5, "Analyzing and Using Visual Arguments," covers this common alternative to the case format. Another alternative to case-making is Rogerian argument, named after psychologist Carl R. Rogers, in which opposing sides work at understanding each other's positions. Chapter 11, "Resolving Conflict: Arguing to Mediate," covers this alternative form.

Another alternative to making a case is to tell a story. By narrating an experience, whether your own or someone else's, you can indirectly make a case for your viewpoint on a subject. An example is Katharine Weber's "In the Factories of Lost Children" (see pages 249–251), which narrates a historical event, a famous New York sweatshop fire, to argue against overseas sweatshops today. She uses the tragedy as evidence of the danger posed to sweatshop workers.

Vivid description of a scene can also make an argument and is often combined with narrative; the writer chooses words and images that make the reader see the scene according to his or her point of view. Many alternative arguments combine various modes of development, such as narrative, description, dialogue, reflection, and exploration.

Voice and style play a role in any argument; in alternative forms, they often play a large role. Some writers use humor to make their points. One example is the use of satire, which exposes the wrongheadedness or evil of some human activity by mocking and exaggerating it, as Jonathan Swift did in "A Modest Proposal." Another stylistic device is irony, in which the writer says the opposite of what he or she really thinks. Readers must infer irony from context clues, such as how a passage either conforms to or contradicts the thinking of the argument as a whole.

◎ ACTIVITY: Preparing to Read an Alternative Argument

The argument that follows, "A Technological Cloud Hangs over Higher Education," differs from the style of Sally Jenkins's argument. However, you should use the same process to read it critically. Begin by surfing and skimming for rhetorical context before digging in to read all the way through with pen in hand. The author of this piece, Keith A. Williams, is a physics professor at University of

Virginia, and the essay was originally published in *The Chronicle of Higher Education.* What can you find out about Williams and this publication?

Skim the reading. To whom do you think Williams is addressing his argument? What are the two meanings of the word *cloud* in the title? What does the title lead you to expect Williams's claim will be?   •

◎ ACTIVITY: Making Annotations while Reading

This argument is on a topic most students have had some experience with—the use of technology in classrooms. As you read, write your questions and responses as marginal annotations (explained on page 20) or in a double-entry notebook (explained on pages 30–32).   •

A Technological Cloud Hangs over Higher Education

KEITH A. WILLIAMS

1   I was there when it happened. And for the record: I did object. I was but a teaching assistant; the decision was not mine. The decision was to replace the pendulums and other demonstration gizmos in the undergraduate physics teaching laboratory with computers and software.

2   To be sure, the change would be convenient: no more time-consuming preparation of experiments, no more lectures on how to make demonstrations work, no more disinclined planes or springs sprung too far. This was cutting-edge. The students would love it. Students like computers. And aren't computers the future? Don't we need to get with the times and prepare students for the information age?

3   With great reluctance, I packed up the pendulums one last time, helped install the computers, and then stood witness as another three-dimensional classroom was replaced with a computer lab. The students would now be greeted by glowing screens and a printer for their data.

4   I didn't return to the demonstration lab the following semester; probably a good thing, as I was busy with my own experiments. To be fair, the students probably did enjoy the computers. They could press a button and make a pendulum swing across their screen. With a few keystrokes, they could change the hanging mass and the length of the string supporting it. They could even change the strength of the gravitational field. The software did everything, and there would be no more experimental complications, such as higher-order friction and drag. If students wanted to observe what Foucault observed, I suppose they could rotate their screens. Best of all, the students now recorded all quantities with perfect accuracy, so they wouldn't need to learn how to account for errors. There were no more experimental errors.

5   Countless other exciting innovations have ensued since that day in 1993 when one teaching laboratory shed one of its dimensions. Long gone are the overhead projectors—the noisy appliances with which we showcased our patiently handwritten

transparencies. I confess that I miss those; we physicists tend to have innovative symbols. It seems unlikely we would have if PowerPoint had been around in the 18th century.

6   To its credit, PowerPoint did relieve us of hot projectors, smelly pens, and staticky transparencies spread out to dry, and students have certainly benefited from more-legible typefaces. Many students don't even need to labor on their own handwritten notes; they can simply download a scanned lecture or PowerPoint file and view it at their leisure on a laptop, iPad, or iPhone. It is all so irresistibly convenient and . . . cool.

7   The tasks of asking and answering questions in the classroom, and the taking of the attendance, were solved by placing a clever new technology in the hands of each student: This "clicker" sends signals to a computer, somewhat like a television remote control. Colleagues informed me that clickers would solve the problems of low attendance and lack of student engagement. The added benefit is that instructors can take attendance without learning any names, and they can administer a quiz without subjecting students to the embarrassment of direct inquiry. (Predictably, the improvement in attendance was short-lived: It seems that some mischievous students are capable of wielding more than one clicker at a time and might even find financial incentive for doing so, particularly in the case of early-morning lectures.) I do wonder whether the clicker is designed to confirm the attendance of the student or the absence of a teacher.

8   Textbooks are rapidly becoming a thing of the past. We'll spare many trees that way. Old knowledge can be scanned. Instructors and students can annotate their PDF's. Unfortunately, the few textbooks that are still written tend to be horribly expensive by the time they reach the bookstore. With fewer instructors requiring books, and fewer students buying them, publishers say they need to set a higher price.

9   It has been a long while since I have beheld an innovative new textbook. With the incentive to write them virtually gone, what does appear is usually rehashed and cluttered with "Web resources." On an accompanying disc, one typically finds lectures and exercises that can be done on a computer. The instructor needn't invent questions—there is a bank full of them.

10   Busy professors certainly appreciate the time that these innovations have saved them. One can now summon a lecture from the bank, project it on a screen, and simply narrate it, if he or she wishes. There is far less risk of actually interacting with the students, who can ask troublesome questions if given the opportunity. And for homework crises, Cramster is only a few clicks away.

11   The Internet certainly channels a great deal of wonderful, fresh information into the classroom. During one recent lecture, I couldn't recall the year that Tycho Brahe observed the supernova, but I was saved by a student with a smartphone, who then narrated the whole tale from Wikipedia. I am actually rather fond of the Internet's capabilities; I use Twitter to disseminate hints and links. Some instructors don't permit laptops—too much distraction from the compelling PowerPoint lectures—but members of a generation that had keyboards beside their cradles are far more comfortable with the technology than we ever will be, we who remember fingers blistered from

typing out a manuscript on a manual typewriter, long before floppy disks or even the Selectric [an early electric typewriter].

12   Students of today are adept at taking notes on laptops and tablets and phones, should they choose to do so. Unfortunately for those students whose instructors haven't found a way to format test questions compatible with bubble sheets, test-taking remains arduous. Students must write with an analog pencil or pen, relying on the trained dexterity of the whole hand, not merely the opposable thumbs so adept at texting.

13   It is virtually miraculous how much information the laptops, tablets, and phones can bring into the classroom, almost free of cost. A steady torrent of fresh information has transformed the classroom. Gone or concealed in dust are most periodic tables, encyclopedias, and globes. All of that can now be called up on a screen.

14   The whole apparatus of instruction has moved into the cloud. (And at my institution, the cloud is present most of the time; only foul weather or an occasional IT glitch decouples us from it.) Whether we need the YouTube video of the astronaut dropping a hammer and feather on the moon or Newton's *Principia* translated, narrated, or lectured, we delight in using Google to retrieve it quickly from the cloud.

15   And so the instructor is the multimedia rainmaker who summons from the cloud everything that the modern American scholar must learn. The student is spared the necessity of a library; the library is in the cloud. Lecture demonstrations are also in the cloud, in the form of flashlets and applets sanitized of any complicating realities, non-idealities, and inefficiencies. And if a student should miss a lecture, the cloud will oblige: The student need no longer request notes from an instructor or colleague. Everything is in the cloud—even some of the most popular instructors. And that cloud hangs over all of America's institutions of higher education.

QUESTIONS FOR DISCUSSION

1. The first three paragraphs use a story to introduce the topic and Williams's position on computers in the physics lab. Besides announcing that he voiced his objection to the change, what stylistic choices reveal and reinforce Williams's angle on the subject?

2. How would you put Williams's claim into a specific assertion, in your own words? Is he just talking about physics labs, or do you think he includes other labs and classrooms? If you do, be ready to point out passages that apply to other teaching situations.

3. Williams is ironic and humorous in places. Where does he seem to be praising some aspect of technology while at the same time showing that the praise is not sincere or deserved? Where is he obviously kidding? How would you describe the personality of the speaker?

◎ COLLABORATIVE ACTIVITY: Using the Chunking Strategy

In pairs or groups of three, use the "chunking" strategy (see page 28) to break this argument into constituent parts. Look more closely into each part to find its function. Which paragraph units seem to offer reasons in support of Williams's objection to the rise of technology in the classroom and higher education in general? How many reasons do you find? Does he provide evidence for each reason? After the groups have made their lists of reasons, form a whole-class discussion to compare the results.   •

◎ ACTIVITY: Responding to the Argument

Look over the list of questions for responding to an argument on pages 31–32. What would you question about this argument and Williams's portrayal of educational technology? How does his description of technology for teaching compare with your own experiences in computer labs and lecture classes? Compose a short response that first summarizes the claim and reasons and then goes on to assess the merits of the argument. Be ready to read your commentary to the class or post it on a class blog or bulletin board.   •

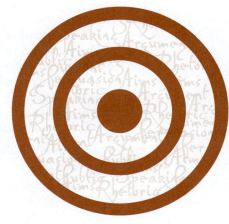

CHAPTER 3

Analyzing Arguments: The Toulmin Method

In Chapter 2, we discussed the importance of reading arguments critically: breaking them down into their parts to see how they are put together, noting in the margins key terms that are not defined, and raising questions about the writer's claims or evidence. Although these general techniques are sufficient for analyzing many arguments, sometimes—especially with intricate arguments and with arguments we sense are faulty but whose weaknesses we are unable to specify—we need a more systematic technique.

In this chapter, we explain and illustrate such a technique based on the work of Stephen Toulmin, a contemporary philosopher who contributed a great deal to our understanding of argumentation. This method will allow you to analyze the logic of any argument; you will also find it useful in examining the logic of your own arguments as you draft and revise them.

AN OVERVIEW OF THE TOULMIN METHOD

In his 1958 book, *The Uses of Argument,* Stephen Toulmin describes several key elements of an argument. In Chapter 2 of this text, you were introduced to three of these: the *claim* and the *reasons* and *evidence* (also called *data*) offered to support the claim.

The example argument outlined below depicts these three main elements. The examples of reasoning here are taken from a longer argument by Alfie Kohn, who has written many books on education. Kohn is an outspoken critic of the practice of grading students at any level, from kindergarten through college. Below is one of the many reasons he offers for abolishing grading. You can find the text of the full argument on Kohn's website at <http://www.alfiekohn.org/teaching/tcag.htm>.

Claim: Grading should be abolished in schools from elementary through college.

> *Reason:* Focusing on a grade reduces students' quality of thinking while studying.

>> *Evidence:* An experiment showed that students who were told they would be graded on their understanding of a social studies text were less able to grasp the main point of the text than students who were told they would not be graded.

As this example shows, specific evidence makes a reason convincing to skeptical readers.

However, all the reasons and evidence in the world will not make an argument convincing if readers do not accept certain underlying beliefs or assumptions that connect the reasons and evidence to the claim. A great strength of the Toulmin method of analysis is that it asks readers to look for these unstated assumptions, an element of argument that Toulmin calls *warrants*.

For example, if you accept the argument that grades should be abolished because "Focusing on a grade reduces students' quality of thinking while studying," you probably accept the **warrant,** or belief, that critical thinking, and not just grabbing facts, is important to education. As in this example argument, warrants usually go unstated. The writer assumes that readers already share the belief and do not need to be convinced of its truth. Below, we show the argument again, this time with the unstated warrant included in parentheses.

Claim: Grading should be abolished in schools from elementary through college.

> *Reason:* Focusing on a grade reduces students' quality of thinking while studying.

>> *Evidence:* An experiment showed that students who were told they would be graded on their understanding of a social studies text were less able to grasp the main point of the text than students who were told they would not be graded.

> (*Warrant:* Critical thinking, and not just learning information, is an important part of education.)

Writers usually leave warrants unstated because they assume their readers share their core beliefs. In this example, the warrant is a pretty safe assumption: Most people would agree that education should improve one's thinking. But it is good for readers of all arguments to think about the missing statements and decide for themselves whether or not an argument's warrant is sound and true. In fact, a writer may intentionally keep warrants unstated to discourage readers from thinking too hard about an argument's underlying principles.

◎ COLLABORATIVE ACTIVITY: Finding Warrants

Uncover the assumptions underlying the following arguments about grading; then, in each case, discuss whether you accept the truth of the warrant or not.

1. *Claim:* In an ideal world, grading would not be necessary, but in schools today, grading is a necessary practice if students are to learn.

    Reason: Without grades to motivate them, most students today would not work hard enough to learn what they have to learn.

    Warrant: _____

2. *Claim:* Students will learn better if we eliminate the practice of grading.

    Reason: Grading encourages competition rather than cooperation in the classroom.

    Warrant: _____

3. *Claim:* Grades in high school are necessary preparation for college.

    Reason: Students will be graded in college, so they have to learn how to work for grades and be competitive.

    Warrant: _____   •

In addition to looking for warrants, the Toulmin method of analysis helps critical readers detect other weaknesses in an argument. A common flaw in arguing is stating the claim as absolute, or universally true, when in fact there may be exceptions or situations where it is not true. The Toulmin method therefore asks readers to consider a fifth element, known as *qualifiers*.

A **qualifier** limits or clarifies the claim. By limiting the claim to reasonable circumstances or specifying the meaning of key terms, a qualifier deprives opponents of opportunities to point out exceptions to the claim or other objections that would shoot down the argument. Continuing with our example argument for abolishing grading, imagine that an opponent says, "Wait a minute—teachers have to set some standards. They have to distinguish between success and failure." To defuse this objection, the writer might qualify the claim by making the wording more specific:

Claim with a *qualifier: Although instructors should distinguish between passing and failing work,* letter or numerical grades should be abolished.

Even simple qualifiers such as "in most cases" or "on the whole" can diffuse objections to a claim. When analyzing an argument, find the claim and ask yourself what possible exceptions might exist. When writing your own claims, think about possible exceptions. You can make your argument stronger by acknowledging exceptions before your readers think of them.

Finally, the Toulmin method includes an element known as rebuttals. A **rebuttal** is a statement that shows that the writer has anticipated counterarguments and diffused them by showing their flaws. Entire arguments can take the form of rebuttals, especially if the counterargument is a commonly held opinion. For example, an entire argument could be a rebuttal of arguments for or against the death penalty.

It is not difficult to think of counterarguments to the case against grading, because grading is so entrenched in education all over the world. Most teachers, administrators, and students assume it serves a purpose. For example, hard-working students might want grades as a reassurance that they are making progress in learning. They might offer the following counterargument to Kohn's case against grades:

Claim: Grades are an important part of education.

> *Reason:* Grades help students know where they stand in the learning process and encourage them to progress.

In his argument, Kohn anticipated this counterargument and nullified it by showing that teachers' written and oral comments were more effective than grades in helping students learn.

We have now covered the six most basic elements in the Toulmin method: claims, reasons, evidence, warrants, qualifiers, and rebuttals. The diagram on page 48 gives you an overview of these elements and their relationships. The reading below gives you an opportunity to apply the terms to another argument on a controversial issue, the legalization of drugs.

Let's Be Blunt: It's Time to End the Drug War

ART CARDEN

This argument was originally published in *Forbes* magazine. The author is a regular columnist for *Forbes* and a professor of economics at Samford University in Birmingham, Alabama.

1   April 20 is the counter-culture "holiday" on which lots and lots of people come together to advocate marijuana legalization (or just get high). Should drugs—especially marijuana—be legal? The answer is "yes." Immediately. Without hesitation. Do not pass Go. Do not collect $200 seized in a civil asset forfeiture. The war on drugs has been a dismal failure. It's high time to end prohibition. Even if you aren't willing to go whole-hog and legalize all drugs, at the very least we should legalize marijuana.

2   For the sake of the argument, let's go ahead and assume that everything you've heard about the dangers of drugs is completely true. That probably means that using drugs is a terrible idea. It doesn't mean, however, that the drug war is a good idea.

3   Prohibition is a textbook example of a policy with negative unintended consequences. Literally: it's an example in the textbook I use in my introductory economics classes (Cowen and Tabarrok, *Modern Principles of Economics* if you're curious) and in the most popular introductory economics textbook in the world (by N. Gregory Mankiw). The demand curve for drugs is extremely inelastic, meaning that people don't change their drug consumption very much in response to changes in prices. Therefore, vigorous enforcement means higher prices and higher revenues for drug dealers. In fact, I'll defer to Cowen and Tabarrok—page 60 of the first edition, if you're still curious—for a discussion of the basic economic logic:

> The more effective prohibition is at raising costs, the greater are drug industry revenues. So, more effective prohibition means that drug sellers have more money to buy guns, pay bribes, fund the dealers, and even research and develop new technologies in drug delivery (like crack cocaine). It's hard to beat an enemy that gets stronger the more you strike against him or her.

4   People associate the drug trade with crime and violence; indeed, the newspapers occasionally feature stories about drug kingpins doing horrifying things to underlings and competitors. These aren't caused by the drugs themselves but from the fact that they are illegal (which means the market is underground) and addictive (which means demanders aren't very price sensitive).

5   Those same newspapers will also occasionally feature articles about how this or that major dealer has been taken down or about how this or that quantity of drugs was taken off the streets. Apparently we're to take from this the idea that we're going to "win" the war on drugs. Apparently. It's alleged that this is only a step toward getting "Mister Big," but even if the government gets "Mister Big," it's not going to matter. Apple didn't disappear after Steve Jobs died. Getting "Mr. Big" won't win the drug war. As I pointed out almost a year ago, economist and drug policy expert Jeffrey Miron estimates that we would have a lot less violence without a war on drugs.

6   At the recent Association of Private Enterprise Education conference, David Henderson from the Naval Postgraduate School pointed out the myriad ways in which government promises to make us safer in fact imperil our safety and security. The drug war is an obvious example: in the name of making us safer and protecting us from drugs, we are actually put in greater danger. Without meaning to, the drug warriors have turned American cities into war zones and eroded the very freedoms we hold dear.

7   Freedom of contract has been abridged in the name of keeping us "safe" from drugs. Private property is less secure because it can be seized if it is implicated in a drug crime (this also flushes the doctrine of "innocent until proven guilty" out the window). The drug war has been used as a pretext for clamping down on immigration. Not surprisingly, the drug war has turned some of our neighborhoods into war zones. We are warehousing productive young people in prisons at an alarming rate all in the name of a war that cannot be won.

8   Albert Einstein is reported to have said that the definition of insanity is doing the same thing over and over again and expecting different results. By this definition, the drug war is insane. We are no safer, and we are certainly less free because of concerted efforts to wage war on drugs. It's time to stop the insanity and end prohibition.

QUESTIONS FOR DISCUSSION

1. As pointed out in Chapter 2, "Reading Arguments," you should begin reading with some knowledge of rhetorical context. The author is a professor of economics, and the article was published in *Forbes*, a business magazine. How does the rhetorical context help to explain the focus of Carden's argument?

2. Carden's claim is obvious: It appears in the title. What do you know about the range of opinions on this issue? What are some of the most common arguments made for continuing to keep marijuana and other street drugs illegal? Do you see places in the argument where Carden acknowledges any of the opposing views? If so, where?

A STEP-BY-STEP DEMONSTRATION OF THE TOULMIN METHOD

When evaluating the logic of an argument, follow the steps outlined below to ensure that you have considered the most important elements. The Toulmin method requires you to analyze the claim, the reasons offered to support the claim, and the evidence offered to support the reasons, along with the warrants that make the reasons and evidence relevant to the claim. Finally, you will look to see if the argument attempts to rebut any counterarguments.

Analyzing the Claim

Logical analysis begins with identifying the *claim*, the thesis or central contention, along with any specific qualifications or exceptions.

Identify the Claim

First, ask yourself, "What statement is the author defending?" In Carden's argument for legalizing drugs, he makes his claim clear in the first paragraph. He asks, "Should drugs—especially marijuana—be legal? The answer is yes." Note that although he says "especially marijuana," he is not arguing for the legalization of marijuana only.

Look for Qualifiers and Exceptions

Next, ask, "How is the claim qualified?" Is it absolute, or does it include words or phrases such as "on the whole," "usually," or "in most cases" to indicate that it may not hold true in every situation or set of circumstances? Does the writer acknowledge any exceptions to what he or she is arguing for? Careful arguers are wary of making absolute claims. Qualifying words or phrases are used to restrict a claim and improve its defensibility. For example, a qualifier for an argument legalizing drugs might stipulate that it pertains only to certain drugs, such as marijuana. Another way of qualifying this argument might be to stipulate a minimum age for legal purchase and use of drugs. An exception might stipulate a drug or drugs that should not be legalized under any circumstances.

◎ ACTIVITY: Freewriting or Notebook Entry

Prepare for class discussion by writing a response to the following questions:

1. Is Carden claiming that all drugs, including heroin and methamphet-amines, should be legal? Does the argument imply that these drugs should be legal?
2. Do you think the words "especially marijuana" qualify the claim?

Analyzing the Reasons and Evidence

Once you have analyzed the claim, you should next identify and evaluate the reasons offered for the claim.

State the Reasons

Begin by asking yourself, "According to the author, why should I accept this claim as true?" Look for any statements that are used to justify the thesis.

When you state the reasons, you need not preserve the exact words of the arguer; often, you cannot do so, because reasons are not always spelled out. Be very careful, however, to adhere as closely as possible to the writer's language. Otherwise, your analysis can easily go astray, imposing a reason of your own that the writer did not have in mind.

Carden's reason for ending the war on drugs is found in the opening sentence of paragraph 3:

> Prohibition is a textbook example of a policy with negative unintended consequences.

He builds his argument around some of these unintended consequences, all of which are reasons for ending the prohibition of drugs.

> Enforcement of prohibition "means higher prices and higher revenues for drug dealers" (para. 3).
>
> "In the name of making us safer and protecting us from drugs, we are actually put in greater danger" (para. 6).
>
> The war on drugs has "eroded the very freedoms we hold dear" (para. 6).

Find the Evidence

As you identify each reason, ask, "What kinds of evidence (data, anecdotes, case studies, citations from authority, and so forth) are offered as support for this reason?" Some arguments advance little in the way of evidence. Therefore, lack of evidence is not always a fault.

For example, Carden supports his argument that "the stronger the enforcement of prohibition, the higher the profits for drug dealers" with specific references to an economics textbook. However, his argument that enforcement increases violence goes unsupported with statistics or examples. Carden assumes that his readers already know about the violence in the drug trade and in neighborhoods where drugs are dealt.

Examine the Evidence

Two questions apply. First, Is the evidence good? That is, is it sufficient, accurate, and credible? Second, Is it relevant to the reason it supports? For example, evidence and quotations from Cowen and Tabarrok's textbook are relevant to Carden's argument about the enrichment of drug sellers—provided that Cowen and Tabarrok themselves have proof of the relationship among enforcement, higher prices, and greater profit. Raising the question of relevance brings us to the question of warrants, which readers must examine in every argument.

Examining the Warrants

Recall that warrants are unstated beliefs or principles that connect a reason to the claim. Even if the argument looks logical, you need to question whether the underlying principles are sound. There are two questions to ask as you examine the warrants. First, ask, "Is the reason relevant to the thesis?" In other words, does the warrant connecting the claim and the reason hold up to examination? For example, the argument "You should buy a new car from Fred Freed" because "Fred is a family man with three cute kids" falls apart when you examine the warrant: Family men will give you a good deal on a car. Having children, no matter how cute, does not make a man or woman a better car dealer—or a better politician, although many ads attempt to influence voters with this argument.

Second, when you have uncovered the warrants, ask, "Are they really good values and beliefs? How might they be questioned?" A reason is only as good as the values it invokes or implies. A value is something we think is good—that is, something that is worth pursuing for its own sake or because it helps us attain other goods. Let's look again at Carden's argument:

Claim: We should end the war on drugs.

> *Reason:* This policy has "negative unintended consequences" such as increased profit for drug dealers, increased violence, and decreased personal freedoms.

> *Warrant:* Any policy with negative unintended consequences is a bad policy that should be ended.

◎ COLLABORATIVE ACTIVITY: Small-Group Discussion

In pairs or groups of three, consider the validity of the warrant in Carden's argument. Do you agree that any policy that results in unintended but harmful consequences is a bad policy that should be ended? Can you think of examples of other policies that have unintended negative consequences? Do you agree that it would be right to end such policies? How might someone rebut the warrant for Carden's argument? Would legalization also have negative unintended consequences?   •

Noting Rebuttals

A final step is to note if a writer anticipates counterarguments and successfully rebuts or refutes them. In a good argument, the writer anticipates potential objections to his or her position and tries to show why they do not undermine the basic argument. A skilled arguer uses rebuttals to deal with any obvious objections a reader is likely to have.

First ask, "What counterarguments does the writer offer?" Then ask, "How does the writer answer or refute each objection?" In paragraph 6, Carden rebuts the counterargument that the war on drugs is worth fighting because it has been successful in wiping out some powerful drug dealers. In rebutting this argument, he uses an analogy, or comparison, between the deaths of powerful drug dealers and the deaths of powerful corporate executives. In both cases, the businesses find new leaders and continue to thrive.

◎ ACTIVITY: Freewriting or Notebook Entry

Write informally to prepare to discuss your assessment of this argument's rebuttal of counterarguments.

1. How would you evaluate Carden's handling of opposing views? What else might he have done to rebut these counterarguments?
2. Can you think of other counterarguments that he has not anticipated?   •

Summarizing Your Analysis

Once you have used the Toulmin method to examine the logic of this argument or any other argument, write up a brief assessment. Restrict your focus to the logic of the argument, showing its strengths and weaknesses. Refer to the elements of argument discussed in this chapter. You may also note what you noticed about the argument as a result of using the Toulmin method that you might not otherwise have noted.

Model Toulmin Diagram for Analyzing Arguments

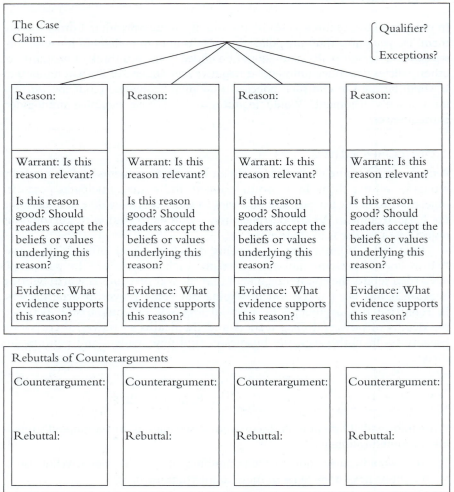

A FINAL NOTE ABOUT LOGICAL ANALYSIS

No method for analyzing arguments is perfect, and no method can guarantee that everyone using it will assess an argument the same way. Uniform results are not especially desirable anyway. What would be left to talk about? The point of argumentative analysis is to step back and examine an argument carefully, to detect how it is structured, to assess the cogency and power of its logic. The Toulmin method helps us move beyond a hit-or-miss approach to logical analysis, but it cannot yield a conclusion as compelling as mathematical proof.

Toulmin Analysis

A. ANALYZE THE CLAIM

1. **Find the claim.** In many arguments, the claim is never explicitly stated. When it is not, make the implied claim explicit by stating it in your own words. (Note: If, after careful analysis, you are not sure *exactly* what the writer is claiming, you've found a serious fault in the argument.)

2. **Look for qualifiers.** Is the claim absolute? Or is it qualified by some word or phrase like *usually* or *all things being equal?* If the claim is absolute, can you think of circumstances in which it might not apply?

3. **Look for explicit exceptions to the claim.** If the writer has pointed out conditions in which he or she would not assert the claim, note them carefully.

B. ANALYZE THE REASONS AND EVIDENCE

1. **Find the reason or reasons offered to justify the claim.** All statements of reason will answer the question, Why are you claiming what you've claimed? They can be linked to the claim with *because.* As with claims, reasons may be implied. Dig them out and state them in your own words. (Note: If, after careful analysis, you discover that the reasons are not clear or relevant to the claim, you should conclude that the argument is either defective and in need of revision or invalid and therefore unacceptable.)

2. **For each reason, locate all evidence offered to back it up.** Evidence is not limited to hard data. Anecdotes, case studies, and citations from authorities also count as evidence. (Note: Not all reasons require extensive evidence, but we should be suspicious of reasons without evidence, especially when it seems that evidence ought to be available. Unsupported reasons are often a sign of bad reasoning.)

3. **Consider each piece of evidence.** Is it good? That is, is it accurate and believable? Is it relevant to the reason it supports? Note any problems.

C. CONSIDER THE WARRANT OR WARRANTS FOR EACH REASON

1. **What unstated beliefs or principles connect each reason to the claim?**

2. **Do you share these assumptions or would you challenge any of them? Explain.**

D. LOOK FOR COUNTERARGUMENTS AND REBUTTALS

If there are rebuttals—efforts to refute objections to the case—examine them. If you do not see rebuttals, consider what objections you think the writer should have addressed.

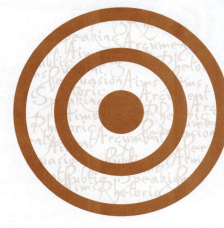

CHAPTER 4

Critiquing an Argument

Chapter 2 presented methods for reading an argument critically, and Chapter 3 presented a method for analyzing one. This chapter shows how you can apply critical reading and analysis to write a critique of an argument.

WHAT IS A CRITIQUE?

A **critique** is a written evaluation of some kind of performance. Examples of this genre, or kind of writing, are reviews, such as book or concert reviews, and evaluations, such as the terminal comments a teacher might write at the end of a paper when assigning a grade. We encounter critiques in "Letters to the Editor" in newspapers, in magazines that include reader responses to articles in previous issues, and in blogs devoted to some controversial issue or cause. Some, but not all, comments on blog posts are critiques.

A critique is not just a response but a close look at the quality of an argument someone else has made. In a critique, the writer explains what deserves respect in the argument and what does not—and why. It is not an attack on someone's argument, but rather a rational assessment, part of a search for truth.

Context and Critique

Most written arguments are "stand-alone" texts—such as an opinion column in a newspaper or online or an article in a magazine or on a website. However, they are not as isolated as they seem. Authors create **context**, a background against which they want you to see their argument—current events, an ongoing debate about the topic, and so on.

Context *always* matters for the following reasons:

- *Context is the key to understanding an argument.* For example, increasing the availability of loans for college students makes sense within the context of the rapid increase of higher education costs.

- *Context is the key to understanding why people disagree.* Those who favor increasing loans often see the issue in the context of opportunity, making college possible for modest-income students. Those who oppose it often see loans in the context of too much personal debt.

- *Context is the key to understanding your response.* If you or your family cannot afford college and you have taken full advantage of other forms of aid, loans may be very appealing.

WHY CRITIQUE AN ARGUMENT?

Every day, you will hear or read the arguments of other people, in conversation, in books and magazines, on television, radio, and the Net, in business meetings and community gatherings. Short of becoming a hermit, there is no way to avoid arguments designed to influence what you think and do. In college, you should sharpen your abilities to judge good from bad reasoning, even when you agree with the writer's position.

HOW A CRITIQUE DIFFERS FROM A REACTION

You may have noticed that most people merely react to arguments. They just agree or disagree, usually with anger and closed minds rather than any serious consideration of other views. A good example is what you hear on talk radio: Listeners call in to voice opinions on topics from political issues to the performance of their local sports team. Many people tune out such exchanges because they feel nothing is accomplished.

Why does public discussion often seem pointless? The problem is not in exchanging opinions. Saying what we think gets things off our chest. Finding out what other people think is stimulating. The problem is that public discussion tends to *stop* at exchanging opinions and reacting to them. People seldom get to the next level: real critique of each other's arguments.

Critical thinking is the difference between reacting and critiquing. To think critically, you need to step back and judge the quality of the argument, whether you agree with it or not. Keep in mind that a critique can point out strengths as well as weaknesses in an argument, but the key to writing a good critique is to take an analytical stance or position.

People use the term *critical distance* to describe the space between a first reaction, which may be hot, and a cooler, more studied analysis. You can use some of the analytical strategies discussed below to open up critical distance and find good points to make in a critique of an argument.

Strategies for Critiquing Arguments

A critique requires analysis, so you will want to apply the strategies discussed in Chapter 2, on reading arguments critically, and Chapter 3, on analyzing arguments using the Toulmin method.

Begin by reading analytically and marking up the text of the argument with annotations that note where the author has stated his or her claim, or thesis. That statement may be explicit, or you may have to read between the lines to extract it for close examination. Consider whether you can think of exceptions to the claim and whether it applies in some circumstances but not all.

Consider key terms in the claim, in the reasons, and in background material that sets up the issue. How has the author defined important words? Or have some words been left vague, perhaps deliberately?

Next, ask what reasons and evidence the writer gives to convince readers that they should accept the claim as true. An argument may have just one reason or several, and for each reason, some further support should be offered in the form of specific facts or expert opinion. Do you see much specific evidence? Is it anecdotal, just a few examples from the writer's experiences, or has the writer found or done serious research to make a solid argument?

Most arguments are based on some kind of underlying beliefs or assumptions that can be questioned. In the Toulmin scheme, we called these assumptions *warrants*. To find warrants or assumptions, ask yourself, "In order to accept this reason as true, what prior belief would I have to hold?" For example, an argument showing that a seawall can protect homes along the shore of a barrier island is based on the assumption that barrier islands should be developed for commercial and residential use. Consider what the author has assumed that may or may not be true.

Another important question to consider in a critique of an argument is this: What will happen if everyone agrees with the author's position and what he or she is arguing for prevails? In other words, what are the implications of the argument? Sometimes even a policy that will bring about some positive results will have collateral or unplanned consequences. Project the situation into the future and imagine what will happen if the author has failed to anticipate some problems down the road.

Consider the context of the argument as you read. How have the author's background, profession, personal biographical experiences, or other formative forces influenced his or her perspective on the topic? Consider also the context of the topic itself: What might have brought this topic to the author's attention? Has it been in the news? Consider what other people are saying on the issue, and why. Arguments do not exist in a vacuum; they are part of ongoing conversations situated in time and place.

Finally, if you disagree with the argument or find the reasoning weak, ask yourself what counterarguments you might offer that would be more valid and convincing to readers. Be sure that you can support any counterarguments with evidence.

The reading that follows shows how one writer critiqued the argument of a major figure in debates about the social and psychological effects of digital media. We have annotated it to show how the critic, Tom Stafford, asked some of the questions described above in his critique.

Stafford's article is a book review, a common genre for critiques of nonfiction books that argue a position on a debatable topic. The book being reviewed is by Sherry Turkle, a professor at the Massachusetts Institute of Technology, who argues that even though technology is connecting us on one level, it is actually getting in the way of our ability to form close human relationships. Stafford, the author of the review, is a lecturer in psychology and cognitive science at the University of Sheffield, in England. The review appeared on his blog *idiolect* (http://idiolect.org.uk/notes/).

Why Sherry Turkle Is So Wrong

TOM STAFFORD

1 *(Attention conservation notice: a rambling 1800 word book review in which I am rude about Sherry Turkle and psychoanalysis, and I tell you how to think properly about the psychology of technology)*

2 This book annoyed me so much I wasn't sure at page 12 if I could manage the other 293. In the end I read the introduction and the conclusion, skimming the rest. Turkle's argument is interesting and important[;] I just couldn't face the supposed evidence she announced she was going to bring out in the body of the book.

3 Psychoanalysts are conspiracy theorists of the soul, and nowhere is that clearer than in Turkle's reasoning about technology. Page after page of anecdotes are used to introduce the idea that communications technologies such as email, [F]acebook and Twitter offer an illusion of intimacy, but in fact drive us into a new solitude. This might be true, it's an important idea to entertain, but pause for a moment to think how you would establish if it really was the case or not.

Stafford writes his critique in first person and in a humorous and informal style, beginning with this cautionary note to his readers. This style is appropriate for the medium in which the review appeared, a personal blog.

Stafford is reacting here rather than critiquing; however, he quickly moves into thinking critically about Turkle's evidence.

This is the claim, or main point of the critique. Stafford qualifies his claim by saying that the argument could be worth making but is flawed because of weak evidence.

Stafford considers context for Turkle's argument here; psychoanalysis is one of Turkle's research interests.

Anecdotes, which are often hearsay or personal observations, may not be truly representative. Anecdotal evidence is less convincing than scientific studies.

Stafford summarizes Turkle's claim.

Stafford shows the need to think critically about Turkle's argument.

4   For Turkle, the evidence is all around, discerned by her keen psychoanalytically-trained psychologist's eye. A young woman chats to her grandmother on [S]kype for an hour a week—[a] touching example of a relationship deepened and sustained? No! Unbeknownst to the grandmother the young woman uses that hour to catch up on her emails, leaving her unsatisfied with the [S]kype conversation, with vague feelings of guilt and a failure to connect. Turkle combines stories like these of people she's met with sweeping generalisations about how "we" feel—increasingly disconnected, overwhelmed and unable to tell where the boundary between work and home life is. Text messages, originally a substitute of the phone call you couldn't make, "very quickly . . . became the connection of choice" she announces. Really? For everyone?

Stafford gives examples of Turkle's evidence to show why he does not accept it as convincing.

5   Throughout Turkle seems to assume that this new age of communications technology has accelerated us into an age of dislocation and disconnection. This may be so, but a few anecdotes about people's unsatisfactory relationships and yearning for deeper intimacy and authenticity don't establish this. Here is the news: it was ever so. Now people wonder if their [F]acebook friends are true friends[;] previously we wondered if our friends on the team, or in the pub, were our true friends. Now we wish for romantic relationships without betrayal and inconvenience[;] previously this is what we wished for too. Ambiguity, failure and fear of disconnection are not a novel part of online relationships[.T]hey are part of the human condition and it is mighty irksome that Turkle assumes the novelty of these things. She is seeing what she wants to see in the world around her. There is also an inherent conservatism in her assumption that things were better before this anarchy of technology was loosed upon the world, the assumption that not only were things better before, but that this was the way they were "supposed to be[.]" The comic thing is that her historical benchmark is just as arbitrary—as if phone calls were a good and proper means of communication, a ceremony of innocence drowned by the destructive forces of text messaging and [S]kype. When the phone was invented there was a moral panic about what this technology would do for relationships, the same as there was a moral panic when printed books became widespread. There's no reason why we shouldn't invent a new form of communication, such as the text message, and it come to fill a niche in the ecology of how we relate to each other. People haven't stopped making phone calls[;] they have augmented the way they communicate with text messages, not substituted texting for phoning.

Critiques look at the assumptions behind an argument. Stafford says that Turkle is assuming effects of technology rather than proving them.

6   Reading the book, it is hard to shake the impression that everything Turkle says is in a slightly dismayed and hysterical tones[:] "Oh no! The kids are using text messaging" "Oh no! People underestimate the distracting effect of checking their email!" "Oh no! The kids find face to face conversations threatening, the little dears can't live in the real world[."]

A critique can include observations of ethical or emotional appeals, not logical appeals only.

7   Again: it was ever so. And of course, with anything new, you can always find some genuinely [misled] and bewildered people. Turkle has some striking examples of people who wish for relationships—both romantic and sexual—with robots. This shows, she says, that we are in the "robotic moment[."] It is not that robots are ready for our desires, but that our desires are now ready for the idea for intimacy with robots. A young woman yearns for a robot lover, wanting to trade her human boyfriend for a "no risk relationship"; an elderly woman saying that her robot dog "won't die suddenly and abandon you and make you very sad"; the genuinely astounding

argument of David Levy's "Love and Sex with Robots" which proposes that soon we'll be fighting for the right to marry robots in the same way we fought for the right to marry people of the same sex. Are we only discussing these possibilities, asks Turkle, because we are failing each other in human relationships?

8 The impression I get is of a very earnest anthropologist, speaking to the young people of a alien tribe, ready to be shocked and titillated by their revelations. Do the people speaking to Turkle really believe what they say, or are they egged on by her credulity, just as the tribespeople compete to tell the anthropologist ever more outrageous things? Yes, yes I would prefer a robot lover. Yes, yes, real men are a disappointment—irritating, changeable—and the simulation of intimacy would be better than a risk on authentic intimacy.

9 My problem is not that people are seeking to escape human frailty and ambiguity with robots, but that Turkle seems to assume that there was ever a time when some people didn't try to escape human frailty and ambiguity. It isn't that we are newly dissatisfied with our relationships, that we are newly struggling for authenticity. Rather it is that the old struggle has found a new form, that the eternal uncertainties we have of ourselves and each other are given a new light by technology.

10 Turkle has an important point disguised by a boring pessimism. "Relationships with robots are ramping up; relationships with people are ramping down"; she says, "of every technology, we must ask, Does it serve our human purposes?" This later point is vitally important. The idea that Turkle has proven that human relationships are "ramping down" due to the current communications technology is the distraction. This is just a generational cry of despair, common to every age, when one age group realise they don't understand or don't like how their children behave.

11 True, we must ask how technology can be built to enhance our relationships, and [whether] true intimacy and authenticity are endangered, but it was always so and Turkle's speculations of doom help only to muddy the waters.

12 I find myself wondering why Turkle has this pervasive pessimism about our ability to sensibly navigate these new technologies. Perhaps, it is related to the stance she seems to adopt to the characters that populate her anecdotes, which is of subjects under her microscope, an amorphous mass of "them" rather than as unique individuals with stories and weaknesses just like all of us. This may just be my knee-jerk dislike of psychoanalysts but her stance towards these characters in her argument always felt condescending and arrogant, as if she alone possessed the objective stance, as if only she, with her psychoanalytic training, was expert enough to discern the loneliness and feel what they themselves didn't know they felt. Again, the tone reminded me of the naive anthropologist—aren't they strange?! Isn't their confusion fascinating?!

13 I would have had more faith in Turkle's reasoning if she talked more about her experience, rather than relating [these] anecdotes from people she met at conferences and at Parisian dinner parties.

14 Turkle's underlying assumption is that technology is a thing separate from, or gets in between, authentic relationships. (There's a comparison to those who diagnose an addiction to the internet, as if the internet were a substance, when it is just a medium). In fact, technology is part of relationships because it is part of our minds (see Andy Clark's book *Natural Born Cyborgs* for an exploration of this idea). Technology cannot get in the way of some kind of natural detection of reality because we never have direct

A critique acknowledges what is both good and bad in an argument. He points out that a concern over human relationships "ramping down" is a valid point, but placing the blame on technology is a faulty assumption.

This paragraph returns to the question of the author's context; what does she bring to the topic that causes her to interpret the evidence in such a negative way?

This paragraph offers a counterargument to Turkle's assumption that humans related more directly before the new technology.

contact with reality—it is always mediated by culture, history, language, expectations, and the whole architecture of our minds for understanding the world. As every psychologist should know, the idea of "virtual reality" is a misnomer because reality has always been virtual. A concrete example of this confusion is when Turkle assumes that she (alone) can tell the real (flesh and blood) encounters from the fake (technologically mediated) encounters. "The ties we form through the internet are not, in the end, the ties that bind[,]" she says solemnly. This is a ridiculous generalisation, and must be confusing to all those who met over the internet, or have had relationships deepened because of the internet. Can you imagine how ridiculous Turkle would sound if she'd made such a generalisation about another medium. "The ties formed through writing are not the ties that bind[.]" "The ties formed by those speaking French are not the ties that bind[.]" Nonsense! Again Turkle has been distracted by her pessimism and her conservatism. The problem of human bonds is not a new one[;] we've always struggled to find rapprochement with each other[;] the internet doesn't change that. It does give the problem interesting new dimensions, and I've no doubt that we'll struggle collectively with these new dimensions for decades, but I don't see Turkle doing anything to make clear the outlines of the problem or advance any solutions.

15   New technology is easy to think about, partly because the novel always stands out against the background of the old, and partly because it is easier to think about the material aspects of things, and the material aspects of technology can be ubiquitous (like text messages and email) or particularly entrancing (like robots). But let me give an alternative vision to Turkle's Cassandra wail. Rather than technology, a far more real threat to intimacy and authenticity in the modern world is the continuous parade of advertising which tries to hock material goods with the promise that they can give access to transcendent values. Cars which give freedom, cameras which give friendship, diamonds that give love and clothes that give confidence. Here is a cultural force, with a massive budget and the active intention to make us dissatisfied with our possessions, our lifestyles, our bodies and our relationships. How about we worry a bit more about that, and less about the essentially democratic technologies of communication.

Cassandra was a figure in Greek mythology who had powers to predict the future.

Stafford offers a counterargument to show a better cause of "ramping down" of human relationships today

QUESTIONS FOR DISCUSSION

1. Any reader of this critique who has not read Turkle's book will have to depend on Stafford's summary of Turkle's argument to judge the fairness of the critique. Do you think Stafford gives enough examples to show that Turkle's evidence is not representative of people's experiences with technology? Have you observed evidence to support Turkle's point that technology is causing a breakdown in real human interaction?

2. Do you share the assumption that human relationships were more genuine at some earlier point in time, such as in the generation before yours? Why or why not?

3. What do you think of Stafford's argument about advertising's effects on human relationships, in the final paragraph? What is his point? What messages does advertising send us that could explain a "ramping down" of human relationships?

◎ ACTIVITY: Finding Arguments to Critique

Choose some short arguments from the op-ed pages or letters to the editor of your local newspaper or from an online news and opinion source. Examine the opinions and cases made to convince readers of the author's position. Using our list of strategies on pp. 53–54 and the Best Practices Box on page 62, be ready to share one of the arguments with the class. Find at least two points that you would make if you were to write a critique of that argument.

THE ASSIGNMENT

If your instructor does not assign one, locate any short (750–1,000 words) argument on a controversial topic and write a paper of about the same length critiquing it.

Topic and Focus

Obviously, you need to respond to what the article says. However, you can relate the argument's topic to matters the author does not mention. For example, an article advocating laws prohibiting handheld cell phone use by drivers may focus entirely on this particular device. You might respond by pointing to other driver distractions that also contribute to accidents, such as putting CDs in audio equipment. Perhaps the real problem is driver distraction in general, not cell phone use in particular?

Audience

Usually you will write to the same readership your argument addresses. However, when an argument you are responding to targets only one of several readerships with a stake in the topic, it is legitimate to respond by addressing your critique to one of the other audiences. For example, an argument addressed only to parents about a public school issue, such as classes that are too large, might well address the students affected by too large classes instead.

Voice and Ethos

Be sincere, project confidence, have command of the facts and what they mean, and show respect for the argument you are evaluating.

Writing Assignment Suggestions

This assignment could be written in many genres, the most common being a letter to the editor of a newspaper or magazine. Others include an op-ed piece; a response to a blog; a short article for a newspaper, magazine, or newsletter; or an assessment of a classroom discussion, debate, chat room exchange, public speech, or some other oral argument.

We suggest that you pick an argument you disagree with or an argument you partly agree with and partly disagree with in almost equal measure. It makes little sense to critique an argument you find wholly convincing.

CHOOSING AN ARGUMENT

When you have a choice, opt for the provocative or extreme argument. They almost beg for critique, and evaluating them is more fruitful than the predictable position defended in predictable ways.

You can locate suitable arguments by recalling something you read in a newspaper, magazine, or on a website, by doing subject searches on LexisNexis (see page 107 for how to use this resource), and by Googling a topic in the news. Consider also the following possibilities:

- *Class readings*. Class readings can provide arguments for critique, especially if the readings themselves are arguments.

- *Local news or observation*. Read your local and campus newspapers for arguments relating to your community. Sometimes these can be more interesting than overworked topics like abortion or gun control.

- *Internet discussions*. Blogs are often good sources for arguments. Visit blogs on issues of public concern, such as one of National Public Radio's blogs at www.npr.org/blogs/.

EXPLORING YOUR TOPIC

So that you can see how to explore the argument you have selected or been assigned, we need to work with an example argument. Here's one on an issue of some concern on most college campuses. Read it once or twice, just to understand what it says and to form a first reaction to it.

Open Your Ears to Biased Professors

DAVID FRYMAN

> David Fryman was a senior at Brandeis University when he wrote this opinion column for the school's newspaper, *The Justice*. He's offering advice to younger college students who often encounter professors with political opinions different from those endorsed at home or in their local communities. Fryman's question is, How should they respond?

1   One of the most important lessons I've learned in three years of higher education is the value of creativity and critical thinking, particularly when confronted with a professor whose ideology, political leanings or religious viewpoint fly in the face of what I believe. In fact, with a good professor, this should happen often. It is part of a professor's job to challenge you, force you to reconsider, encourage you to entertain new ideas and the like.

2   My first year here, it bothered me. Some professors subtly endorsed certain ways of thinking over others without always justifying their biases. They offered opinions on issues beyond their academic expertise. Many showed partiality to the political left or right.

3   How should we react when a professor with a captive audience advances a perspective we find offensive, insulting or just ridiculous? Perhaps we would

benefit from treating our professors, who often double as mentors and advisers, the same way that we're taught to approach great works of literature: With critical respect.

4   The truth is many faculty members are at the top of their fields. They read, write and teach for a living. We're generally talking about the most well-educated and well-read members of society. So when a professor has something to say about politics, religion, war or which movie should win the Academy Award, I think it's a good idea to take him seriously.

5   It certainly doesn't follow, though, that there's a direct relationship between what a professor says and what's true. In fact, there may be no relationship at all. While our professors generally are leading scholars, some are also biased and fallible. I don't mean this as an insult. Professors are human beings and, as such, carry with them a wide array of hang-ups and prejudices.

6   Interestingly enough—if not ironically—our professors often teach us how to deal with biased and opinionated scholars like themselves. When we read novels, journal articles, essays and textbooks for class, we're taught—or at least this has been my experience—to be critical. We're expected to sift through material and distinguish between what holds water and what doesn't, what is based on reasoned analysis and what is mere speculation.

7   If we treat our professors similarly it should no longer bother us when they use the classroom as their soapbox. They have important things to say and we're here to learn from them. I've come to appreciate professors' opinions on a variety of issues not directly related to the subject at hand, and I think it helps us build relationships with them. While it's unfair for a professor to assign high grades only to students who echo their view or to make others feel uncomfortable to disagree, I prefer that professors be honest about what they think.

8   While it's a disservice to our own education to be intimidated or too easily persuaded by academic clout, it's just as problematic, and frankly silly, to categorically reject what a professor has to say because we take issue with his ideology, political leanings, religious views or cultural biases.

9   It's become popular, particularly among conservatives responding to what they perceive as a liberal bias in academia, to criticize professors for espousing personal views in the classroom. The ideal, they argue, is to leave students ignorant to their instructors' beliefs.

10   First of all, I think there's a practical problem with this strategy. It's more difficult to be critical if we're unsure where our professors stand. For the same reason that it's often helpful to have background information about an author before analyzing his work, it's useful to see our professors' ideological cards on the table. For instance, if I know my professor loves hunting and believes everybody should have firearms in his basement then when I hear his interpretation of the Second Amendment, I'm better equipped to evaluate his thoughts.

11   Secondly, if we proscribe what views may or may not be expressed in the classroom, we limit our own access to potentially useful information. Even if most of the extraneous digressions aren't worthy, every once in a while we might hear something

12 | that goes to the heart of an important issue. To limit this because we don't trust our own critical abilities is cowardly.

To return to the question I posed above: How should we respond to politically charged, opinionated, biased professors? I think we should listen.

Forming a First Impression

It is impossible to read an argument without having some kind of response to it. Objectivity or neutrality is either possible or desirable. Start by being honest with yourself about what your first impression is.

◎ ACTIVITY: First Response

After reading your argument, state your reaction simply and directly. Write it down in your notebook or a computer file reserved for this assignment. Read the selection again. Is your reaction changing? How? Why?

The first response of most of our students to Fryman was favorable. He offered practical advice, and more appealing yet, *safe* advice. You may have had an entirely different reaction. First reactions cannot be right or wrong, good or bad. They just are what they are. The important thing is that *you* know what your reaction is.

Stepping Back: Analyzing the Argument

Critiques require **critical distance** from first responses. "Critical distance" does not mean "forget your first response." On the contrary, first impressions often turn out to be sound. Critical distance does mean setting your first response aside for a while so that you can think the argument through carefully.

Use the questions in the Best Practices box to guide your analysis. It deals with parts of an argument that can be challenged. In contrast, there is nothing to be gained by challenging the following items:

- *Values everyone in our culture accepts.* For example, Fryman appeals to "creativity and critical thinking" (paragraph 1). Who can argue against these two values?

- *Statements of personal feelings.* For example, Fryman states that he was bothered at first by opinionated professors (paragraph 2). We can't say, "No you weren't."—or "You shouldn't have been." What would be the point?

- *Information only the author would know.* For example, if Fryman had mentioned something he read or heard that caused him to be more tolerant of bias in the classroom, we would just have to accept what he says.

- *Incidental facts whose accuracy is not important for the argument.* For example, if Fryman had referred to a particular class and professor, we would have to accept the information as factual. Even if his memory was faulty, it does not matter so far as assessing the argument is concerned.

Concepts and Questions for Analyzing an Argument

1. *The claim or thesis.* Find the main point the writer wants you to believe and/or be persuaded to do. Sometimes the claim will be stated, sometimes implied. Ask, Is the claim clear and consistent? Is it absolute, no exceptions allowed? Assess the claim: Is it reasonable, desirable, practical?

2. *The reasons.* Find answers to the question, Why? That is, given the claim, what explains or justifies it? Like the claim, reasons will be stated or implied. Ask, Does each reason actually explain or justify the thesis? How convincing is the reason?

3. *The evidence.* Reasons will be supported or developed with something: more reasoning, examples, data, or expert opinion. Look at the evidence offered for each reason and ask, Does the evidence actually support the reason? How convincing is each piece of evidence, and how convincing is the evidence for each reason taken together?

4. *Key terms.* Often without defining them, writers use words that should be carefully pondered. When a claim is justified, for instance, as the right or moral thing to do, we need to ask what "right" or "moral" means in this case.

5. *Assumptions.* It is impossible to argue without assuming many things—and "assume" means "often not stated." Ask, What must I believe to accept that claim, or reason, or piece of evidence? Is the assumption "safe," something that any reasonable person would also assume?

6. *Implications.* Like assumptions, implications are usually not stated. To uncover them, ask, If I accept this statement, what follows from it? Are its implications acceptable or not?

7. *Analogies.* Many arguments use comparisons and some depend on them—on reasoning based on something being like something else. Look for analogies. Ask, Are the items compared close enough to permit reasoning by similarity? How important are the differences between the items compared?

Here are some illustrations of how the analytical concepts and questions apply to Fryman's argument:

1. *Thesis*

   Fryman: College students should listen to biased and opinionated professors with critical respect.

   Comment: Note that you have to piece together the thesis from several statements he makes. We can respond by saying, "What sort of opinions *merit* critical respect?"

2. *Reasons*

   Fryman: "Many faculty members are at the top of their fields."

   Comment: Clearly, this statement is a reason—it explains why the author thinks students should accord professors respect. We can respond by saying, "Yes, some professors are quite accomplished *in their fields*. But when they venture outside them, do their opinions count for more than any other relatively well-informed person's?"

3. *Evidence*

   Fryman: "Many [professors] showed partiality to the political left or right."

   Comment: In backing up one of his statements—that it bothered him at first when professors offered their opinions—he points to political bias as one of the irritating factors. We can respond by saying, "*Under what circumstances* would expression of political opinions be appropriate?"

4. *Key terms*

   Fryman: "hang-ups and prejudices"

   Comment: Fryman admits that professors have such things when he talks about the relationship between opinions and truth (paragraph 5). We can respond by saying, "What exactly is a 'hang-up,' and how do we distinguish it from a legitimate concern with something?" Or "We *all* have 'prejudices.' When are they justified and therefore worth taking seriously?"

5. *Assumptions*

   Fryman: He assumes that there are no ethical constraints on what professors should talk about in class.

   Comment: We can respond by asking, "Shouldn't there be professional ethics at work here? What moral or ethical principles should govern what's discussed and under what conditions?"

6. *Implications*

   Fryman: He implies that students should tolerate whatever the professor dishes out.

   Comment: We can respond by saying, "How much student toleration is too much toleration? Suppose that a professor is openly sexist, for instance? Shouldn't we not only reject the opinions but also report the behavior to university authorities?"

7. *Analogies*

   Fryman: He compares the approach students should take to opinionated professors with the critical respect accorded great works of literature (paragraph 3).

   Comment: We can respond by saying, "Great works of literature have typically survived for years. We call them classics. Does it make sense to meet the casual opinions of professors the same way that we approach Shakespeare?"

⦿ ACTIVITY: Analyzing the Argument

If you are working alone on an argument, use the seven questions in the Best Practices box. Record the results in your notebook, your computer file for this assignment, or online as a blog that presents the argument and your analysis of it.

If your class is working on the same argument, divide into small groups of about three or four people and do an analysis. Share what your group found with the class as a whole in discussion.   •

Doing Research

Logical analysis focuses on *what an argument says*. The challenge of analysis is to discover what you can say back.

As important as analysis is, there is another way to explore an argument. Test what it says *against reality*, your experience with life and the world, what you know about the topic, and what you can find out from research.

The Reality Test for Arguments

The following questions should help you test the argument against reality:

1. What is my own experience with the topic or issue or problem the argument takes up?

    In the case of Fryman's argument, when have the comments of "biased teachers" been illuminating or helpful to you? When have they been boring, irritating, or useless? What is the difference between the two?

2. What relevant information do I have from reading or from some other source?

    Perhaps you have heard other students complain about professors pushing their political convictions on their students. What did they say? Did their complaints seem justified? Why or why not?

3. What could I find out from research that might be relevant to assessing the argument?

    Most arguments suggest opportunities for at least checking up on information relevant to the argument. For instance, you might investigate the idea of academic freedom. How does it apply to professors? How does it apply to students? (For detailed guidance on ways to research any topic, see Chapter 6, pages 95–111.)

4. If the argument reasons from data, in what other ways might the data be interpreted?

    Research will often lead you to other arguments that interpret the same or similar data differently or that supply additional data the argument you are critiquing did not know or ignored. For example, arguments for stronger border patrol enforcement sometimes fail to mention that about 40% of illegal immigrants got here legally and simply stayed. Enhanced border control obviously will have no effect on that group.

5. In what other contexts might the argument be placed?

All arguments state or assume a context within which what they say is valid or true. What other contexts might be relevant? For instance, using the Constitution as context, the Supreme Court has ruled that public flag-burning qualifies as free speech. You could reason based on some other context, such as the wisdom of burning a flag as a gesture of protest. Does it make a point or just make people mad?

◎ ACTIVITY: Summing Up

In your notebook or computer file, sum up the results of applying the above questions. Highlight the best insight you gained. It could be a major point in your critique, perhaps even the central point around which you structure it.   •

Preparing to Write

Thoughtful exploration of an argument—responding to what it says and pondering its fit with reality—results in much you *could* say. However, a critique is not a collection of comments or a list of criticisms. Rather it is *a coherent evaluation from a particular point of view,* your view. Consequently, in preparing to write, formulating your stance matters most.

Formulating Your Stance

Stances toward an argument range from total acceptance to total rejection, with many possibilities in between. You can reject an argument in general, but see value in a part of it. You can accept an argument in general, but with major reservations. The key question is, *What do you really think?*

Here are a few of the stances our students took on "Open Your Ears to Biased Professors."

1. He focuses entirely on what *students* should do. He's one-sided. The key question is, What should professors do to deserve the critical respect Fryman says students should have?

2. He says students should listen with critical respect. Fine, but shouldn't we do more than that? If professors are free to give their opinions on just about anything in class, shouldn't students have at least the freedom to question the opinions offered?

3. Professors should limit their opinions to the subject matter of the course and topics they have special knowledge about. They shouldn't offer opinions on "politics, religion, war, or which movie should win the Academy Award" if these topics do not arise from the course's subject matter.

◎ ACTIVITY: Determining Your Stance

Using the examples above as models, write down your stance. If you are having difficulty, consider the following possibilities:

- *Return to your first impression.* Perhaps a revised version can be your stance.
- *Review the statements in the argument that you found open to question.* Is there a pattern in your criticisms? Or perhaps one statement stands out from the rest and seems central? Your stance may be implied in your most important criticism.
- *Do you detect one place where the reasoning breaks down?* Try fashioning your stance around the reasoning you think the author should have used to reach conclusions you favor.
- *Look for places where the author's view of reality or what is needed or desirable parts company with yours.* Your stance may be implied in it.
- *Talk through possible stances with another student or your instructor.* Just talking helps, and sometimes a comment from someone else can help your stance emerge.

Sometimes you will discover your best stance only through writing a first draft. For now, try out the stance that appeals to you most. You can always revise and rewrite. •

Consider Your Reader, Purpose, and Tone

As you approach the first draft, review the key variables discussed earlier (page 58). In sum,

Reader. Most critiques address the same audience as the argument.

Purpose. A critique contributes to a conversation seeking the truth about a controversial issue or question. Connect your criticisms with the truth as you see it.

Tone. You want to sound engaged, fair, balanced, and respectful. Assert your criticisms firmly and forcefully.

◎ ACTIVITY: Refining Your Stance

Add notes about the key variables to your stance statement. Answer these questions: Do you intend to address the same readers that the argument does? Why or why not? How *exactly* does your version of the truth differ from the author's and how great is the difference? How friendly to the author do you want to sound? •

DRAFTING YOUR PAPER

As you write your paper, focus on organization and development. The following advice should help.

Organization

Whether you write first drafts in chunks and then fit them together or write from a plan more or less in sequence, beginning to end, have the following organizational principles in mind:

Introduction

Begin by identifying the argument you are critiquing: who wrote it and for what group of readers, when and where it appeared, what it is about, and the position the author takes. Make your main point about your overall evaluation of the argument clear and give it an emphatic position, near the end of your introduction.

Body

From everything you found questionable in the argument, select *only* what is relevant to your main point. No one expects a critique to deal with everything an argument says or everything that can be said about it.

   Do not let the order of the argument determine the order of your critique. Order in relation to your stance and for maximum impact on your readers.

   If you can say positive things, deal with these points first. Readers listen to the negative more willingly after hearing the positive.

Conclusion

Short critiques of short arguments do not need summarizing conclusions. Strive instead for a clincher, the memorable "parting shot" expressing the gist or main thrust of your response.

Development

For each part of your critique, you have many options for development. Here are some of them.

Introduction

Besides identifying the argument and taking your stance, you can also include material about context, background information, and a preview of your critique. A critique of Fryman, for instance, might deal with his argument in the context of efforts to restrict academic freedom; research about the author might reveal relevant background information, such as what was happening at Brandeis University when he wrote the article. Previews summarize the points you are going to make in the order in which you are going to discuss them.

Body

Take up one point at a time. Each point will challenge either the reasoning of the argument or its fit with reality. If the former, be sure to explain inconsistencies or contradictions fully, so that your reader understands exactly where and why the reasoning went wrong. If the latter, provide counter-evidence from personal experience, general knowledge, or research.

Conclusion

To clinch your critique, consider the following possibilities: a memorable quotation with a comment on it from you; a return to a key statement or piece of information in your introduction that you can now develop more fully; remind the reader of your strongest point with additional support or commentary.

REVISING YOUR DRAFT

Whenever time permits, it is best to get away from your draft for a day or two, come back to it fresh, assess it first yourself, and then seek input from others. The Best Practices checklist should help both you and the persons you consult in assessing the first draft.

Excerpts from a Sample Discovery Draft

The following excerpts come from student D. D. Solomon's draft in response to the Fryman argument.

Excerpt 1: Introduction

"Open Your Ears to Biased Professors," by David Fryman, deals with a common complaint among students: teachers who express their political or religious views in class. The article was published in *The Justice,* Brandeis University's student newspaper. In the article Fryman discusses how students should deal with a professor's opinion that differs from a student's own. By examining the situation from a student perspective, Fryman illuminates the implications and ramifications of professor bias. The author concludes that bias should be avoided, but if it isn't, students should deal with the situation by following several basic guidelines.

Excerpt 2: A Counterargument

Although Fryman is right about how students should respond, he left out the obligations professors have. Fryman dealt with how teachers sometimes deviate from the topic at hand, and begin to speak of their own personal opinions on a topic. In my ethics class last year, my teacher told us she was a lesbian. In one of our discussions we spoke about gay rights, and whether or not marriage should be legal for homosexuals. She believed strongly in the right of homosexuals to marry. Some of the students, including myself, did not agree with her. Yet, when we tried to discuss our side of the issue, she cut us off. Fryman neglected to discuss such instances when a teacher's opinions infringe on the students' right to open debate.

Critique Revision Checklist

1. Look at all places where you have summarized or paraphrased the argument. Compare them against the text. Are they accurate? Do they capture the author's apparent intent as well as what she or he says?

2. Locate the argument's context—the existing view or views the author addressed. If the critique does not mention context, would it improve if it did? If so, where might a discussion of context work best?

3. Critiques are written either to the same readers the author attempted to reach or for readers with a stake in the argument the author left out. Where in the critique can you detect the writer appealing to readers? Compare the opening paragraphs with the ending ones. Is the reader conception consistent?

4. Critiques seek the truth about some controversial issue or question. What is the issue or question the argument addresses? Is it stated in the critique? Does the difference between the author's view of the truth and the view in the critique emerge clearly? If not, what could be done to make the difference sharper?

5. Underline the critique's stance. Is it stated explicitly and early in the essay? Examine each critical point. How does it develop, explain, or defend the stance? Consider cutting anything not related to the stance.

6. Check the flow of the critical points. Does each connect to the one before it and the one after? If not, consider rearranging the sequence. How might one point set up or lead to another better?

7. How does the critique sound? The tone should be thoughtfully engaged, fair, balanced, and respectful, but also confident and forceful. Look for places where the tone might make the wrong impression. Consider ways to improve it.

Fryman believed that professors should express their stands on controversial issues. When expressing his or her opinion, professors should not neglect to introduce all aspects of the issue at hand. Sometimes professors get caught up in their own view too much and fall into preaching, rather than sharing what they know with the class. Students should hear about other viewpoints so they can view many sides of the issue. The professor should offer his own position as an opinion, not as fact, and should encourage students to form their own opinions.

Fryman fails to deal with the negative impact when teachers stray from the subject matter of the course. His point that teachers should express their opinions is relevant only when related to the topic at hand. In my ethics class, the teacher was always returning to the issue of gay rights, even when the topic of discussion didn't relate to it. She wanted to convert students to her point of view more than teach us ethics.

Example Assessment: Sizing Up D. D. Solomon's First Draft

Solomon felt that his first draft lacked punch and that the body of his critique did not unfold the way he wanted it to. Questions 4 and 5 in the revision checklist helped him see why he felt his paper lacked punch. Fryman sees biased professors as a fact that students must cope with as constructively as they can. For Solomon the professor–student relationship should be a two-way street. He did not bring out this fundamental difference well.

A student collaborator helped him see why his critical points did not flow as well as he wished. "What should come first," Solomon's partner asked, "staying on topic or not ignoring student opinions?"

Finally, Solomon's instructor helped him detect another problem, a place where he did not represent Fryman's position accurately. "The author concludes that bias should be avoided," Solomon claimed. "Does he?" his teacher asked, adding, "Where?" Solomon could not find it in the argument because Fryman does not say it.

Solomon had much to consider and a number of decisions to make. The revised draft appears below and on page 71.

Develop a Revision Strategy

Make a list of both your assessments of the draft and those of anyone who responded helpfully to it. Which criticisms seem valid or sound? Take these and plan your second draft. It can be a sentence or two, "I'll cut this, rearrange that, and add a point here," a full-blown outline, or something in between. *The important thing is to have a clear idea of what you plan to do and in what order.*

Before attempting your revision, read Solomon's revised draft. It is a good example of what cutting, adding, and rearranging can do.

REVISED DRAFT: D. D. SOLOMON'S EVALUATION OF FRYMAN'S ARGUMENT

How Professors Should Deal with Their Biases

D. D. SOLOMON

1   "Open Your Ears to Biased Professors," by David Fryman, deals with a common complaint among students: teachers who express their political or religious views in class. Fryman believes that students should treat the personal opinions of professors with critical respect. I agree, but think that his view is one-sided and therefore not fully persuasive.

2   Because he is writing only to students, he has very little to say about how professors should conduct themselves. Fryman deals with the problem of bias as if only what students should do matters. Actually, professors have more responsibility.

They're older, more knowledgeable, and more experienced. I think if professors are going to express their political and religious views in class, they should do so in certain ways or not do it at all.

3   Fryman fails to consider professors who try to convert students to their own ideology. Because professors know so much, they can appear very appealing to students who have not encountered an issue before. By leaving out other interpretations, the professor assures that students hear only the teacher's side, which does not allow students to form their own conclusions. I saw this happen in a government class which discussed the 2008 Presidential election. Most of the class did not know much about politics, and therefore accepted the professor's view completely. They didn't have the critical capacity Fryman assumes all college students have. Certainly professors should challenge students, but what my government professor did was convert.

4   Sometimes professors get caught up in their own view too much and fall into preaching, rather than sharing all they know with the class. Students should hear about other viewpoints so they can view all sides of the issue. Furthermore, the professor should offer his own opinion as an opinion, not as a fact, and encourage students to form their own opinions.

5   Unfortunately, professors who want to convert students don't want students to form their own opinions but rather believe what the professor thinks. In my ethics class last year, my teacher told us she was a lesbian. In one of our discussions we spoke about gay rights, and whether or not marriage should be legal for homosexuals. She believed strongly in the right of homosexuals to marry. Some of the students, including me, did not agree with her. Yet, when we tried to discuss our side of the issue, she cut us off. Fryman neglects to discuss such instances when a teacher's opinions infringe on the students' right to open debate. I believe that if teachers can express their opinions openly in class, the students should be able to express theirs.

6   Finally, Fryman fails to deal with the negative impact when teachers stray from the subject matter of the course. In my ethics class, the teacher was always returning to the issue of gay rights, even when the topic of discussion didn't relate to it. She wanted to convert students to her point of view more than teach us ethics. Because she lacked restraint, the class spent too much class time on one issue.

7   I agree that professors should share their opinions with the class and students should listen and learn from them. But opinions must be distinguished from facts. Students should hear about other opinions besides the professor's. There should be open discussion, and students who have opinions different from the professor's should feel free to express them. Professors should stay on topic and not allow themselves to talk about just whatever happens to be on their mind. Most of all, education shouldn't be conversion. A professor is not a preacher and shouldn't take that role.

Responding to the Revised Student Draft

It is remarkable how much a paper can improve if genuine effort goes into revising. Note especially in Solomon's revised draft that

- He stated clearly in the introduction his main point about the weakness of Fryman's reasoning.

- He brought out his key critical point, that education should not be a process of conversion.
- He pulled his whole view together well at the end.

Edit Your Paper

Edit your own draft to eliminate errors.

It is easy to overlook small-scale editing problems. Someone else's eyes and ears can be a big help. Exchange your edited paper with another student. Help each other find and correct any remaining errors.

Make a list of the editing problems. List words you misspelled. If you did not punctuate a sentence correctly, write the sentence down and circle or underline the correct mark of punctuation. Add to this list when you get the marked paper back from your instructor.

Always check your next paper for the problems listed first. In this way you can gradually reduce error. Continue this practice with everything you write. It will improve your grades and make you a better writer.

CHAPTER SUMMARY

For nearly everything people do, there is a natural way to go about it and an educated way. The natural way to approach disagreement is to "have at it" in a free-for-all kind of way. People want to be heard, but too often they do not want to listen; hardly anything receives careful thought or discussion. The natural way is open, democratic, often exciting, and even therapeutic. But too often the point of it all—finding the truth insofar as we can hope to discover it—gets lost.

The educated way of critique works by listening, taking in what other people say, and probing it through questions, testing it thoughtfully for both logical cogency and for its adequacy in coping with reality. It enables thought and discussion rather than merely an exchange of opinion.

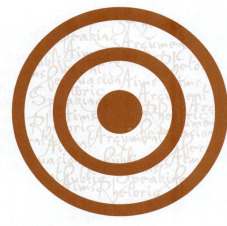

CHAPTER 5

Analyzing and Using Visual Arguments

We live in a world awash in pictures. We turn on the TV and see not just performers, advertisers, and talking heads but also dramatic footage of events from around the world, commercials as visually creative as works of art, and video images to accompany popular music. We boot up our computers and surf the Net; many of the waves we ride are visual swells, enticing images created or enhanced by the very machines that take us out to sea. We drive our cars through a gallery of street art—on billboards and buildings and on the sides of buses and trucks. We go to malls and window-shop, entertained by the images of fantasy fulfillment each retailer offers. Print media are full of images; in our newspapers, for instance, photos, drawings, and computer graphics vie with print for space. Even college textbooks, once mostly blocks of uninterrupted prose with an occasional black-and-white drawing or photo, now often have colorful graphics and elaborate transparency overlays.

Like language, visual images are rhetorical. They persuade us in obvious and not-so-obvious ways. As both readers and writers of arguments, we need to understand the power of visual rhetoric and learn to use it effectively and responsibly.

UNDERSTANDING VISUAL ARGUMENTS

Visual rhetoric is *the use of images, sometimes coupled with sound or appeals to the other senses, to make an argument or persuade us to act as the image-maker would have us act.* Probably the clearest examples are advertisements and political cartoons, a few of which we will examine shortly. But visual rhetoric is everywhere. We do not ordinarily think, say, of a car's body style as "rhetoric," but clearly it is, because people are persuaded to pay tens of thousands of dollars for the sleekest new body style when they could spend a few thousand for an older car that would get them from home to work or school just as well.

"READING" IMAGES

Rhetorical analysis of visual rhetoric involves examining images to see how they attempt to convince or persuade an audience. Pictures are symbols that must be read, just as language is read. To read an argument made through images, a critic must be able to recognize allusions to popular culture. For example, Americans know that the white mustaches on the celebrities in the "Got milk?" commercials refer to the way children drink milk; more recently, the milk mustache symbolizes the ad campaign itself, now part of our culture.

As with inquiry into any argument, we ought to begin with questions about rhetorical context: When was the visual argument created and by whom? To what audience was it originally aimed and with what purpose? Then we can ask what claim a visual argument makes and what reasons it offers in support of that claim. Finally, as with verbal texts that make a case, we can examine visual arguments for evidence, assumptions, and bias, and we can ask what values they favor and what the implications of accepting their argument are.

However, many visuals do not even attempt reasoning; they rely instead on emotional appeals. Such appeals are most obvious in advertising, where the aim is to move a target audience to buy a service or product. In many advertisements, especially for products like beer, cigarettes, and perfume, where the differences between brands are subjective, emotional appeal is all there is. Most emotional appeals work by promising to reward our desires for love, status, peace of mind, or escape from everyday responsibilities.

Advertisements also use ethical appeals, associating their claim with values the audience approves of and wants to identify with—such as images that show nature being preserved, races living in harmony, families staying in touch, and people attaining the American dream of upward mobility.

In evaluating the ethics of visual rhetoric, we need to consider whether the argument is at least reasonable: Does the image demonstrate reasoning, or does it oversimplify and mislead? We will want to look at the emotional and ethical appeals to decide if they pander to audience weaknesses and prejudices or manipulate fantasies and fears.

ANALYSIS: FIVE COMMON TYPES OF VISUAL ARGUMENT

In this section, we analyze some visual arguments in various genres: advertisements, editorial cartoons, public sculpture, news photographs, and graphics. We show how "reading" visual texts requires interpretive skills and how interpretive skills, in turn, depend on cultural knowledge.

Advertisements

Advertisements are a good starting place for analysis of visual arguments because they are aimed at a specific target audience and their purpose is clear: to get the audience to buy a product, service, or idea. A classic ad for Charlie perfume created quite a stir when it first appeared in 1988 (see Figure C-1 in the color section). Although *The New York Times* refused to print it, saying it was in "poor taste," the ad proved irresistibly appealing to women because it showed sexism in reverse. Why did it work so well?

In his book *Twenty Ads That Shook the World,* James B. Twitchell argues that "Charlie is not just in charge, she is clearly enjoying dominance."

> She is taller than her partner. . . . Not only does he have part of his anatomy removed from the picture so that the Charlie bottle can be foregrounded, and not only does she have the jaunty scarf and the cascading hair of a free spirit, but she is delivering that most masculine of signifiers, the booty pat. . . . In football especially, the pat signifies comradeship . . . and is applied dominant to submissive. . . . The coach delivers it to a hulking [player] returning to the field of battle. . . . When Charlie bestows it on her gentleman friend . . . , she is harvesting a rich crop of meaning. The tide has turned, and now men are getting their butts slapped, by of all people, women. (170)

Women found the ad amusing because the fanny pat was the kind of thing a dominant man might do to a subordinate woman at the office, inappropriate behavior now widely understood as sexual harassment. But no matter how you read it, there is no doubt that the ad tapped into the woman's movement at a time when women routinely endured sexism at work.

QUESTIONS FOR DISCUSSION

1. Figure C-2 may look like a poster but it is actually a "semi-postal" stamp, so called because a percentage of its cost goes to the cause it advocates. Depicting a goddess of the hunt, it was issued in 1998. By 2012, this stamp had raised over $76.3 million for breast cancer research. Why do you think this visual argument has had such lasting appeal?

2. Figure C-3, from the Southampton Anti-Bias Task Force, depends for full impact on remembering a crayon labeled *flesh* that was the color of the center crayon in the photo. People in their forties and fifties or older remember that crayon. What, then, is the ad's appeal for them? What does it say about skin color to younger people who do not remember the crayon?

3. Figure C-4 is an example of digital photography's magical and often deceptive power. Photographs of models and celebrities, both female and male, are often digitally enhanced, stretched, or altered in other ways. This kind of manipulation is so common that researchers estimate the average person sees six hundred altered images per day. On the Internet, you can find many other examples of real and enhanced photographs. Discuss the effects on the average viewer's self-image.

4. Figure C-5, an Adidas ad, ingeniously exploits how the eye can be fooled by what it expects to see rather than what is actually there. Did you see the shadow at first simply as the runner's shadow? What made you reevaluate what you were seeing? What is the impact of playing with perception in this case?

◎ ACTIVITY: Comparing Rhetorical Appeals in Visual Arguments

Find two or more advertisements for similar products (although the brands may differ), and consider how the visual presentations differ. For each ad, describe the target audience, and then consider the elements of the visual argument such as photographs, drawings, print text, graphics, special effects, colors, and so on. How do the ads make different rhetorical appeals to persuade different audiences?

Editorial Cartoons

Editorial cartoons comment on events and issues in the news. They are funny but offer concise arguments too. Most political cartoons rely on captions and dialogue to make their argument, combining the visual and verbal. Consider the one by Mike Keefe (Figure 5.1) that comments on the impact of computers.

The cartoon illustrates well how "reading" a visual argument depends on shared cultural knowledge. The image of a thirsty man crawling on hands and knees through a desert stands for anything important that humans lack. The cartoon depicts our common metaphor for the Internet, the "information superhighway," literally. The man has too much information and not enough wisdom. To read the argument of the cartoon and appreciate its humor, the viewer has to know about the overwhelming glut of information on the Internet, suggested by the size of the letters on the road. The cartoon "argues" that relying on the Internet will deprive a civilization of the wisdom to sustain a good life.

QUESTIONS FOR DISCUSSION

1. Cartoons probably are most persuasive when they satirize common behavior and attitudes, as in the cartoon satirizing people's dependence on the Internet in Figure 5.1. You can see a similar approach in Tom Toles's cartoon about

Figure 5.1

Mike Keefe, InToon.com

people's attitudes toward global warming in Figure 5.3 (page 79). What is the point of the tiny caption in the bottom right-hand corner of the cartoon? How common is the attitude being satirized here?

2. Some cartoons are "factional," created by one side in a controversy to ridicule the position of the other side. Contrasting positions on the issue of immigration appear in Figure 5.2 (page 78). Do you think that either faction might reconsider its position because of the points made in these cartoons? If not, what is the purpose of such cartoons?

⊚ ACTIVITY: Explaining the Persuasive Power of an Editorial Cartoon

Find an editorial cartoon that you think is amusing and effective, something that makes a point you think is important. Reproduce the cartoon to present to the class and be ready to explain the following: What is the issue addressed by the cartoon and what is the cartoonist's main point? How do the verbal and visual elements make the point and support it? How does humor add to the argument's appeal? Would the cartoon appeal to someone with an opposing view? Why or why not?   •

Public Sculpture

Public sculptures, such as war memorials, aim to teach an audience about a nation's past and to honor its values. An example that can be read as an argument is the Marine Corps Memorial, erected in 1954 on the Mall in Washington, D.C. (see Figure 5.4). It honors all Marines who have given their lives by

Figure 5.2

By permission of Mike Luckovich and Creators Syndicate, Inc.

By permission of Michael Ramirez and Creators Syndicate, Inc.

Figure 5.3

Figure 5.4

Figure 5.5

Figure 5.6

depicting one specific act of bravery, the planting of the American flag on Iwo Jima, a Pacific island captured from the Japanese in 1945. The claim the sculpture makes is clear: Honor your country. The image of the soldiers straining every muscle gives the reason: These men made extreme sacrifices to preserve the values symbolized by this flag. The sculpture also communicates through details like the wind-whipped flag.

The Iwo Jima sculpture is traditional, glorifying victory on enemy soil. Compare it with the Vietnam War Memorial, dedicated in Washington, D.C., in November 1982. Maya Lin designed what we now call "the Wall" while an undergraduate student at Yale. Her design was controversial because it was so unconventional (see Figures 5.5 and 5.6, page 80) and antiwar. Its black granite slates are etched with the names of war dead; it honors individuals who died in a war that tore the nation apart.

QUESTIONS FOR DISCUSSION

1. Because it does not portray a realistic scene as the Iwo Jima Memorial does, the Wall invites interpretation and analysis. If you have visited it, try to recall your reaction. What details led to your interpretation? Could you characterize the Wall as having logical, ethical, and emotional appeals?

2. Find public sculpture or monuments to visit and analyze. Alone or with some classmates, take notes and photographs. Then develop your interpretation of the sculpture's argument, specifying how visual details contribute to the case, and present your analysis to the class. Compare your interpretation with those of your classmates.

News Photographs

While some news photographs may seem merely to record an event, the camera is not objective. The photographer makes many decisions—whether to snap a picture, when to snap it, what to include and exclude from the image—and decisions about light, depth of field, and so on. Figure 5.7 (page 82), a photograph that appeared in the *Washington Post*, shows a scene photographer Astrid Riecken encountered while covering the issue of homelessness in Washington, D.C., in February of 2015. The city endured several rounds of snow that year, and the homeless were particularly affected. Without the caption supplied by the *Washington Post*, readers might not recognize the object in the foreground as a man in a wheelchair near a bench, covered by undisturbed snow.

The picture depicts homelessness in America as a national disgrace. The image is from Lafayette Square, surrounded by grand and lavishly decorated buildings, symbols of our national wealth. In the foreground, the homeless man looks like a bag of garbage, marring the picture of the snow-covered landscape. No blame attaches to the homeless man for his condition; he is too pathetic under his blanket of snow. The picture shows the homeless as a fact of life in our cities, challenging the idealized image of our nation.

Figure 5.7

© Astrid Riecken/The Washington Post/Getty Images

QUESTIONS FOR DISCUSSION

1. Figure C-6 in the color section depicts the family of Sergeant Jose M. Velez standing over his casket. Sgt. Velez was killed in Iraq. Any thoughtful response to such a photo has to be complex. How would you describe your response? To what extent is your view of the war in Iraq relevant?

2. Figure C-7 is a shot of the Tour de France, the annual bicycling race. What impression does the photo convey? What details in the photo convey the impression?

3. The news photos in Figure 5.8 show damage Hurricane Sandy inflicted on an amusement park pier at Seaside Heights, New Jersey, and on the beach community of Rockaway in the borough of Queens in New York City. In both images, the photographer showed an individual walking on the beach. What do you think the inclusion of these people adds to the meaning of the images?

⊚ ACTIVITY: Analyzing the Persuasiveness of News Photographs

In a recent newspaper or newsmagazine, look for photos you think are effective when combined with a story about a controversial issue. What perspective or point of view do the pictures represent? How do you read their composition, including camera angle, light conditions, foreground, background, and so on? •

Figure 5.8A
*Remains of pier
at Fun Town*

Figure 5.8B
*Houses on
the beach at
Rockaway, New
York City*

Graphics

Visual supplements to a longer text such as an essay, article, or manual are
known as **graphics.** Most graphics fall into one of the following categories:

Tables and charts (typically an arrangement of data in columns and rows
that summarizes the results of research)

Graphs (including bar, line, and pie graphs)

Photographs

Drawings (including maps and cartoons)

Although charts and tables are not images, they, like graphs, present data in visual form. They display information economically in one place so that readers can assess it as they read and find it easily afterward if they want to refer to it again. Graphs are usually no more than tables transformed into visuals we can interpret more easily. Bar graphs are best at showing comparisons at some single point in time. In contrast, line graphs reveal trends—for example, the performance of the stock market. Pie graphs highlight relative proportions well. When newspapers want to show us how the federal budget is spent, for example, they typically use pie graphs with the pieces labeled in some way to represent categories such as national defense, welfare, and entitlement programs. What gets the biggest pieces of the pie becomes *instantly clear* and *easy to remember*—the two major purposes of all graphs. Graphs do not make arguments, but they deliver evidence powerfully.

An article in *BBC News Magazine* reported on self-esteem among first-year college students as measured by an annual survey conducted by University of California at Los Angeles. The line graph in Figure C-8 shows changes in how first-year students rate themselves on various traits associated with self-esteem. Try presenting the same information in words alone, and then consider the advantages, in addition to brevity, of using a graphic to present it visually. (If you are curious or skeptical about the survey's findings, you might want to do more research into the work of the lead author of the original source for this information, psychologist Jean Twenge of San Diego State University. Also, see Chapter 8 in this textbook, pp. 185–187, for an excerpt from Twenge's book *Generation Me.*)

As graphics, photographs represent people, objects, and scenes realistically. For instance, owner's manuals for cars often have a shot of the engine compartment that shows where fluid reservoirs are located. Clearly, such photos serve highly practical purposes, such as helping us locate the dipstick. Photographs are also used, for example, in biographies; we get a better sense of, say, Abraham Lincoln's life and times when pictures of him, his family, his home, and so on are included. But photographs can do much more than inform. They can be highly dramatic and powerfully emotional in ways that only the best writers can manage with prose. Photos are often potent persuaders.

Photographs, however, are not analytical—by their nature, they give us the surface, only what the camera can "see." A different type of graphic, the drawing, is preferable when we want to depict how something is put together or structured. For instance, instructions for assembling and installing a ceiling fan or a light fixture usually have many diagrams—a large one showing how all the parts fit together and smaller ones that depict steps in

Figure C-1

Figure C-2

SOUTHAMPTON ANTI-BIAS TASK FORCE • 516-287-5734

Figure C-3

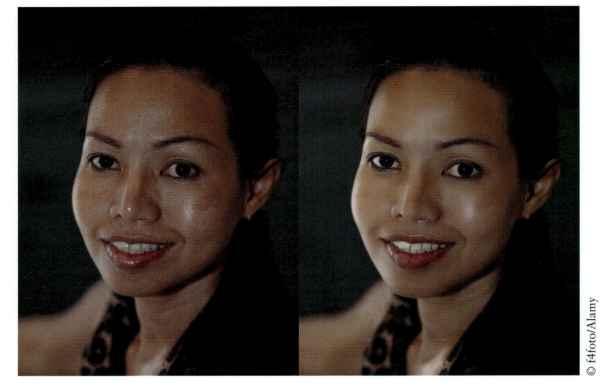

Figure C-4

The World's Fastest Man, Donovan Bailey, wears the adStar Sprint. See our complete new line of track & field spikes at www.adidas.com.

Figure C-5

Figure C-6

Figure C-7

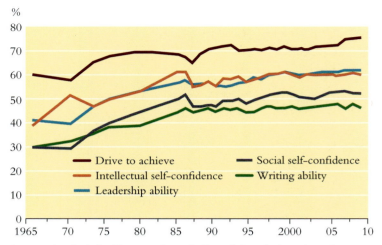

Source: Analysis by Twenge, Campbell, and Gentile based on the American Freshman Survey from William Kramer, "Does Confidence Really Breed Success?" *BBC News Magazine,* 3 Jan. 2013; Web.

Figure C-8

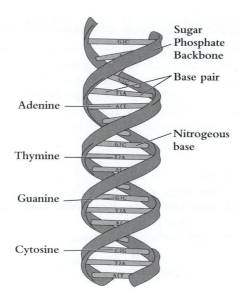

Figure 5.9

the process in more detail. Corporate publications often include diagrams of the company's organizational hierarchy. Scientific articles and text-books are full of drawings or illustrations created with computer graph-ics; science writers want us to understand structures, particularly internal structures, impossible to capture on film. For example, our sense of DNA's double-helical structure comes entirely from diagrams, such as the one in Figure 5.9.

WRITING ASSIGNMENT: ANALYZING AN ADVERTISEMENT OR EDITORIAL CARTOON

Choose an ad or cartoon from a current magazine or newspaper. First, inquire into its rhetorical context: What situation prompted its creation? What pur-pose does it aim to achieve? Where did it originally appear? Who is its intended audience? What would they know or believe about the product or issue? Then inquire into the argument being made. Consider the following points: What visual metaphors or allusions appear? What prior cultural knowledge and experiences would the audience need to "read" the image? Consider how the visual argument might limit the scope of the issue or how it might play to the audience's biases, stereotypes, or fears. After thorough inquiry, reach some conclusion about the effectiveness and ethics of your ad or cartoon. Write your conclusion as a thesis or claim. Use your analysis to convince, supporting it with evidence gathered during inquiry.

The following student essay is an example of the writing assignment for this chapter. Note that this student used secondary sources and cited them according to APA (American Psychological Association) style, commonly used in the social sciences. We were not able to receive permission from Coca-Cola to reprint the advertisements discussed in this paper.

THE IMAGE OF HAPPINESS   1

The Image of Happiness:
An Analysis of Coca-Cola's "Open Happiness" Campaign
Ryan Herrscher
Southern Methodist University

- - - - - - - - - - - - - [separate page] - - - - - - - - - - - - - -

The Image of Happiness:
An Analysis of Coca-Cola's "Open Happiness" Campaign

1   The goal of advertising is to persuade consumers to buy not just a product but an idea. To this end, advertisers employ a variety of methods to associate a product with an idea that will appeal to possible consumers. From colorful graphics and eye-catching designs to clever jingles and celebrity endorsements, advertisements make a product stand out from its competitors. To make Coca-Cola one of the best-selling brands in the world, advertisers have conjured up mental associations of a feel-good, upbeat attitude as seen in the 2009 "Open Happiness" campaign. Because of their simplicity and lack of information, these ads target an audience already familiar with these themes in previous ads for the Coca-Cola brand.

2   All the ads in this series appear plain and devoid of much content at first glance. There are no people pictured, and the ads tell no stories. The simplest contains nothing more than a monotone red Coke Classic bottle and the words "open happiness." Indeed, the product could be any kind of soda, but viewers recognize the silhouette of the iconic bottle shape, the cursive script of the Coca-Cola logo, and the red and white color scheme. To people familiar with Coca-Cola, these visuals are symbols loaded with meaning beyond what is visually obvious. According to University of Texas professor Barry Brummett (2011) in his book *Rhetoric in Popular Culture*, "Rhetorical critics

THE IMAGE OF HAPPINESS 2

should not assume that an image just 'is' or that it conveys clear and obvious meanings to an audience. Images may be thought of as placeholders for a meaning that the audience must assemble" (p. 168). These simple visuals stand for a brand identity over 100 years in the making that has brought in and captivated people around the world.

At the heart of this culture is an idea that this ad campaign expresses with the phrase "open happiness." The concept is that the soda provides a burst of joy and satisfaction that can brighten anyone's day. By popping the top off of a bottle of Coke, one enjoys a refreshing moment of happiness. Some versions on this theme feature complex digitalized pictures that attempt to show the experience of happiness in formations of suspended soda around the bottle. One depicts the word "Aaahhh" with a smiling mouth forming the shape of that sound to remind people of the sensations that accompany drinking the beverage.

In some of the other advertisements from the series, the idea of opening happiness is not ever explicitly stated. The idea is conveyed only through the image of magnified carbonated soda bubbles exploding out of and around the bottle in a playful, artistic way. For viewers already familiar with other ads associating the effervescence of a freshly opened Coke with the effervesance of feeling happy, this image is easy to interpret. The bubbles stand for happiness. In his book *Ads, Fads, and Consumer Culture,* Arthur Asa Berger (2011) says that signs are "anything that can be used to stand for something else, to deliver some kind of a message, to generate some kind of meaning" (p. 155). In this ad, the soda bubbles around the bottle are a metaphor for the explosion of happiness that opening a Coke can bring.

The simplicity of the symbolism in these Coca-Cola ads is a relatively new development for the company. While they have always utilized icons like their bottle shape, in the past Coke advertisements frequently depicted a happy person, such as Santa Claus in his red and white suit, drinking a Coke, along with a verbal text such as "The pause that refreshes." As the culture of the brand has developed over time, it has gotten to the point where the ideas of refreshment can be conveyed to an audience through nothing more than a red silhouette of a Coke bottle or a few letters of its name in cursive script. As Barry Brummett explains, images "appear in contexts," and we use our knowledge of the past ads as a context to interpret what the new ones mean (p. 167). Berger tells us that "[T]exts store a tremendous amount of information in themselves and are a great deal more complicated than we might imagine" (p. 152). The amount of information stored in the shape of a Coca-Cola bottle or the image of some soda bubbles is a testament to the power of their brand and what it has stood for over the years.

6

At one point in time Coke had trouble differentiating itself from copycats; for many years it used the slogan "It's the real thing" to try and show people that it was different. As the brand has become stronger, the company has moved towards relying on nothing more than their name, the shape of their bottle, and a simple image to convey the entirety of their culture and message. When Coca-Cola advertises, their aim is not to inform their audience about what Coke is, but rather to harness the power of their brand, the identity built through years of slogans and images that associate Coca-Cola with happiness and refreshment.

References

Berger, A. (2011). *Ads, fads, and consumer culture: Advertising's impact on American character and society* (4th ed.). Lanham, MD: Rowman & Littlefield.

Brummett, B. (2011). *Rhetoric in popular culture* (3rd ed.). Los Angeles, CA: SAGE.

Coca-Cola. (2009). Aaahhh. Open happiness [Advertisement]. Retrieved from http://www.discoverdigitalphotography.com/2012/ensuring-your-photos-have-a-clearconcept/

Coca-Cola. (2009). Bubbles [Advertisement]. Retrieved from http://www.anch.com/coca-cola-ads-from-campaign-open-happiness/coca-cola_bubbles_2009/

Coca-Cola. (2009). Open happiness [Advertisement]. Retrieved from http://creativestudiosng.com/blog/2011/03/16/coke-moves-further-with-open-happiness/

Alternative Assignment 1

As a class project, collect copies of posters or flyers you find around your campus. It is true that information in our culture is plentiful and cheap, but attention is at a premium. Creators of posters and flyers must compete not only with each other but with all other visual sources of information to catch and keep our attention. How well do the posters and flyers your class found work? Why do some catch and hold attention better than others?

Create a poster or flyer to publicize an event, an organization, a student government election, or anything else relevant to your campus life. Use the best posters and flyers you found as a model, but do not be reluctant to use color, type sizes, images, and so on in your own way.

Alternative Assignment 2

Colleges and universities compete fiercely for students and are therefore as concerned about their image as any corporation or politician. As a class project, collect images your school uses to promote itself, including brochures for prospective students, catalogs, class lists, and Web home pages. Choose three or four of the best ones, and in class discussions analyze them. Then, working in groups of three or four students or individually, do one or all of the following:

1. Find an aspect of your college or university overlooked in the publications that you believe is a strong selling point. Employing photographs, drawings, paintings, or some other visual medium, create an image appropriate for one of the school publications. Compose an appealing text to go with it. Then, in a page or two, explain why you think your promotional image would work well.

2. If someone in the class has the computer knowledge, create an alternative to your school's home page, or make changes that would make it more appealing to prospective students and their parents.

3. Imagine that for purposes of parody or protest you wanted to call attention to aspects of your school that the official images deliberately omit. Proceed as in item 1. In a short statement, explain why you chose the image you did and what purpose(s) you want it to serve.

4. Select a school organization (a fraternity or sorority, a club, etc.) whose image you think could be improved. Create a promotional image for it either for the Web or for some other existing publication.

5. As in item 3, create a visual parody of the official image of a school organization, perhaps as an inside joke intended for other members of the organization.

Alternative Assignment 3

If you are writing an argument to convince or an argument to persuade, which are projects assigned in Chapters 9 and 10 of this textbook, consider how graphics might help make your argument more effective. For help with using graphics effectively in your writing, see the Best Practices box "Guidelines for Using Visuals."

Guidelines for Using Visuals

Graphics come in a variety of useful forms: as tables to display numerical data economically, as graphs to depict data in a way that permits easy comparison of proportions or trends, as photographs to convey realism and drama, and as drawings to depict structures. Whatever graphics you use, be sure to do the following:

- Make sure every graphic has a definite function. Graphics are not decorative and should never be "thrown" into an essay.
- Choose the kind or form of visual best suited to convey the point you are trying to make.
- Design graphics so that they are easy to interpret. That is, keep them simple, make them large enough to be read without strain, and use clear labeling.
- Place graphics as close as possible to the text they explain or illustrate. Remember, graphics should be easier to understand than the text they supplement.
- Refer to all your graphics in the text. Readers usually need both the graphic and a text discussion for full understanding.
- Acknowledge the creator or source of each graphic next to the graphic itself. As long as you acknowledge the source or creator, you can borrow freely, just as you can with quotations from texts. Of course, if you wish to publish an essay that includes borrowed graphics, you must obtain written permission.

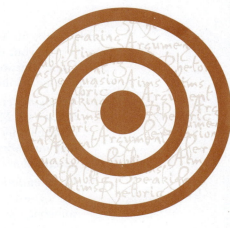

CHAPTER 6

Writing Research-Based Arguments

Most arguments are researched writing. You read sources to inform your-self about your topic, and then you cite sources to convince your readers that you have a good case. An argument with no research behind it is gener-ally weak. Many published arguments do not appear to have research behind them. In journalism, sources may not be documented, but the authors have had to dig to learn the facts, and when they use someone else's views, they introduce that person as an authority because naming authorities' credentials strengthens a case.

Nevertheless, a researched argument must be your own case, with your own angle on the topic, not a case borrowed from your sources. The trick to writing well with sources is to keep them from taking over. You must be in charge, using your sources as supporting characters in what must remain your own show. This chapter will cover finding sources, evaluating them, using them in your own writing, and citing them correctly. To help you stay in charge through this whole process, we will emphasize the role of writing "behind the scenes" *before* you begin drafting your paper. The more you use writing to interact with your sources, to know them well, and to see what supporting parts they might play, the more you will be ready to write as the author—the authority—of an argument of your own: an argument with your own claim, your own voice, your own design.

Using your sources with this kind of confidence helps reduce the possibility of misusing a source. Misuse of a source includes

- *Taking material out of context and misrepresenting the viewpoint of the author.* Most texts include "multiple voices"—that is, writers may describe opposing views, or they may speak ironically, so a casual reader may misunderstand their viewpoint. Applying the critical reading skills described in Chapter 2 will keep you from misusing a source.

- *Using material without giving credit to the source.* If you use someone else's words, you must put quotation marks around them. If you use someone else's ideas, even in your own words, you must give that other person credit. Failure to do so is plagiarism.

Because plagiarism is a growing problem, partly owing to the ease with which material can be cut and pasted from online sources, we have devoted Chapter 7 to ethical writing and plagiarism. Because some plagiarism is not intentional—students may not understand what constitutes fair use of a source or may not realize how to paraphrase adequately and accurately—we recommend that you read that brief chapter before you start working with the sources you find.

Research takes time and patience; it takes initiative; it takes genuine curiosity. You have to recognize what you do not know and be willing to accept good evidence even if it contradicts what you previously believed. The first step in research is finding an issue that is appropriate to write about.

FINDING AN ISSUE

Let's say you have been assigned to write an argument on an issue of current public concern. How should you choose a topic?

Understand the Difference between a Topic and an Issue

People argue about issues, not about topics. For example, global warming is a topic. It is the warming of the earth's atmosphere, a scientific observation. However, people argue about many issues related to the topic of global warming, such as whether human activity has contributed to the temperature increase. The conversation on that issue is subsiding because most people now accept the evidence about the effects of manmade greenhouse gases. But other issues remain, such as what sources of energy are the best alternatives to the fuels that produce greenhouse gases and how individuals might change their lifestyles to make less of an impact on global climate. The point here: To write a good argument, you must explore genuine questions at issue, not just topics.

Find Issues in the News

Pay attention to the news and to the opinions of newsmakers, political leaders, and commentators. College students are busy, but there are some easy ways to keep abreast of issues in the news.

The Internet

Set one of the major news organizations, such as NBC, ABC, CBS, or CNN, as your home page so that when you turn on your computer, the news will be first thing you see. Other options are online news sites and aggregators such as Google News or any of the following sites:

The Daily Beast	www.thedailybeast.com
The Huffington Post	www.huffingtonpost.com
National Public Radio News	www.npr.org/
The New York Times	www.nytimes.com
The Wall Street Journal	www.wsj.com

If you moved away to go to college, choose the online version of your hometown paper as a way of keeping in touch with events back home as well as around the world.

Library Online Databases and Resources

Your college library likely subscribes to many online databases and resources that you can search to find issues of current interest. See pages 106–108 for more about online library resources. A good place to look for issues is CQ Researcher. Do a title search in your school library's catalog to see if you have free access to this resource. This publication of CQ Press allows you to search for issues and browse reports and pro–con statements from professional researchers. Although the reports offer only a general overview, they are a good starting point for further research, as each report concludes with a bibliography listing books, articles, and websites about the issue. Another useful tool created by librarians is ipl2: Information You Can Trust. See Figure 6.1 for a look at this website.

Magazines and Newspapers

Browse your campus bookstore, library, and the Internet for magazines devoted to news and current affairs. In the library, ask for directions to the "recent periodicals" area. To find news magazines and newspapers on the Internet, go to Magazine Directory <http://magazine-directory.com/index-s.htm> and Internet Public Library <http://www.ipl.org/div/subject>. In addition to the obvious choices such as *Time* and *U.S. News & World Report,* look for the more opinionated magazines such as *Utne Reader, The New Republic,* and *National Review.* For more coverage of issues, look for *The Atlantic Monthly, Harper's, Science,* and *National Geographic.*

Figure 6.1

The Internet Public Library and the Librarians' Internet Index maintain the ipl2 website, an Internet tool for researching according to areas of academic interest.

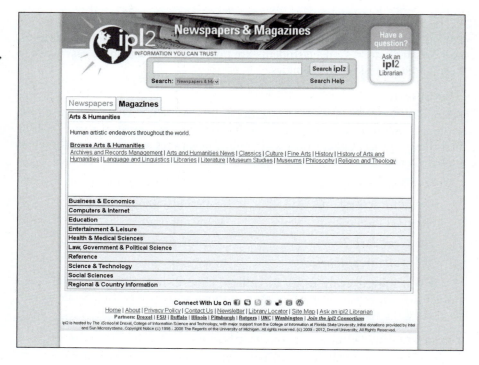

Lectures, Panel Discussions, Class Discussions, Conversations

Hearing in person what others have to say on an issue will help expose the important points and raise questions for research. Seek out discussion of issues you are considering for research.

Personal Observations

The best way to find an engaging issue is to look around you. Your instructor may not give you total freedom to choose an issue, but many current events and social concerns touch our daily lives. For example, the student whose paper we use as an example of researched writing found her issue when she realized the connection between something close to home that had been bothering her and the general topic area her instructor had specified for the class: global warming.

Finding an Issue on the Topic of Global Warming: A Student Example

Student Julie Ross was in a class that had been assigned the topic of global warming. To find an issue, Ross attended an on-campus screening of *An Inconvenient Truth*, followed by a panel discussion featuring representatives of government agencies, environmentalists, and professors of earth science. Ross asked the panelists what individual citizens could do to reduce their contributions to greenhouse gases. One panelist suggested that consuming "less stuff" would make a difference because the production of consumer goods contributes to carbon dioxide and other greenhouse gases. Because Ross was already fuming about old houses on her street being torn down and replaced with supersized McMansions, she decided to research the question of how destructive this kind of development is, not just to the immediate neighborhood, but also to the planet. She began wondering about its contribution to global warming and how much more energy it demands, because the new houses use much more energy than the ones they replace. She decided to write her paper to an audience of home buyers. If she could discourage them from buying these huge new houses, the developers would have to stop building them. To make a convincing case, Ross needed to find good arguments for preserving the older homes and evidence about how much more energy the large new homes use than the older, smaller ones. Ross's paper appears on pages 152–161.

FINDING SOURCES

The prospect of doing research can be overwhelming, given the many possible avenues to explore: the Internet, newspapers, magazines and journals, and all kinds of books. You need a strategy to guide you most efficiently to the best sources on your topic. The quality of your paper depends on its ingredients; you want to find not just *any* sources but the most credible, appropriate, and—if you are writing about current events—the most recent.

As you begin your research, two tips will make the journey much more efficient and orderly—and less stressful.

1. **Keep a research log.** Keep a record of your research by writing informally about what you do in each session of searching. Some things to record are

   - search terms you used, noting which ones were good and which were less productive
   - ideas and questions that occur to you while browsing and reading
   - notes about catalogs and indexes you searched on any particular day
   - complete bibliographical information about each source you plan to use and notes about what the source contains and how you might use it
   - personal responses to sources you read and notes about how different sources compare or contrast on the same topic or issue

   Your research log could be handwritten in a notebook or typed into a computer file or an electronic source management tool like Zotero or EndNote, available through many schools' library websites. You may have folders for different kinds of notes (such as search terms or responses to sources). You may organize all or part of your log like a diary with daily notes on the progress of your research. In whatever form or forms you choose, a research log helps you keep track of sources so you do not have to retrace steps, and it positions you to have your own views and voice when writing your argument.

2. **Make and store complete copies of sources that you may use.** Depending on the source, you may make photocopies or printouts or download documents (such as PDFs) of sources you think you will use. You will want to annotate all your sources and mark them up, and your instructor might require that you submit them with your paper. When copying, be sure to get all the information; avoid cutting off page numbers. With a book, capture the title page and the copyright page on the flip side; you will need this information when citing the source. With online sources, when given the option, choose to print out PDF files because these have page numbers, which makes citing much easier. Also copy any information about the author. Clip, clamp, and label these copies. Keep them in a file folder or binder.

FIELD RESEARCH

Consider beginning your research with what you can observe. That means going out into the "field," as researchers call it, and recording what you see, either in written notes or with photographs or drawings. Field research also can include recording what you hear, in audiotapes and in notes of interviews and conversations. An interview can take place online, through e-mails or a chat, if you can preserve it. Following are some suggestions for field research.

Observations

Do not discount the value of your own personal experiences as evidence in making a case. You will notice that many writers of arguments offer as evidence what they themselves have seen, heard, and done.

Alternatively, you may seek out a specific personal experience as you inquire into your topic. For example, one student writing about homelessness in Dallas decided to visit a shelter. She called ahead to get permission and schedule the visit. Her paper was memorable because she was able to include the stories and physical descriptions of several homeless women, with details of their conversations.

Julie Ross began her research by walking the streets of her neighborhood, photographing the stark contrasts of size and style between the older homes and the new ones built on the sites of torn-down houses. Her photographs provided evidence for her case against supersized homes in historic communities.

Questionnaires and Surveys

You may be able to get information on some topics, especially if they are campus related, by doing surveys or questionnaires. This can be done very efficiently in electronic versions (web-based or e-mail). Be forewarned, however, that it is very difficult to conduct a reliable survey.

First, there is the problem of designing a clear and unbiased survey instrument. If you have ever filled out an evaluation form for an instructor or a course, you will know what we mean about the problem of clarity. For example, one evaluation might ask whether an instructor returns papers "in a reasonable length of time"; what is "reasonable" to some students may be too long for others. As for bias, consider the question "Have you ever had trouble getting assistance from the library's reference desk?" To get a fair response, this questionnaire had better also ask how many requests for help were handled promptly and well. If you do decide to draft a questionnaire, we suggest you do it as a class project so that students on all sides of the issue can contribute and troubleshoot for ambiguity.

Second, there is the problem of getting a representative response. For the same reasons we doubt the results of certain magazine-sponsored surveys of people's sex lives, we should be skeptical about the statistical accuracy of surveys targeting a group that may not be representative of the whole. For example, it would be impossible to generalize about all first-year college students in the United States based on a survey of only your English class—or even the entire first-year class at your college.

Surveys can be useful, but design, administer, and interpret them carefully.

Interviews

You can get a great deal of current information by talking to experts. As with any kind of research, the first step in conducting an interview is to decide exactly what you want to find out. Write down your questions.

The next step is to find the right person to interview. As you read about an issue, note the names (and possible biases) of any organizations mentioned; these may have local offices, the telephone numbers of which you could easily find. In addition, institutions such as hospitals, universities, and large corporations have public relations offices whose staffs provide information. Also, do not overlook the expertise available from faculty members at your own school.

Once you have determined possible sources for interviews, you must begin a patient and courteous round of telephone calls, continuing until you connect with the right person; this can take many calls. If you have a subject's e-mail address, you might write to introduce yourself and request an appointment for a telephone interview.

Whether your interview is face to face or over the telephone, begin by acknowledging that the interviewee's time is valuable. Tell the person something about the project you are working on, but withhold your own position on any controversial matters. Sound neutral and be specific about what you want to know. Take notes, and include the title and background of the person being interviewed and the date of the interview, which you will need to cite this source. If you want to record the interview, ask permission first. Finally, if you have the individual's mailing or e-mail address, send a thank-you note after the interview.

If everyone in your class is researching the same topic and more than one person wants to contact the same expert, avoid flooding that person with requests. One or two students could do the interview and report to the class, or the expert could visit the class.

LIBRARY AND INTERNET RESEARCH

Since much of what is now published in print is also available online, the distinction between library and Internet research has blurred. You will be able to find many magazines, scholarly journals, and newspapers through the Internet, and many Internet sites through your library's online directories. Because so many documents are now electronic—even if they appeared first in print—librarians have coined the term "born digital" to distinguish purely cyberspace documents from documents that were born in print but have been made available online.

With the daily additions to information, articles, images, and even books available online, the resources for searching it are constantly being upgraded. The advice in this chapter should get you started, but it is always a good idea to consult your library's reference librarians for help with finding sources on your topic. They know what is in your school's library, what is online, and what the latest tools are for finding any kind of source. You will find these librarians at the reference desk; every library has one.

Kinds of Sources

The various kinds of sources available in print and online include books and periodicals as well as electronic media.

Books

Nonfiction books generally fall into three categories:

Monographs: Monographs are sustained arguments on a single topic. To use them responsibly, you should know the complete argument; that means reading the entire book, which time may not allow. Possibly, reading the introduction to a book will acquaint you with the author's argument well enough that you can selectively read sections of the book. Decide if you have time to use a book responsibly. Sometimes you can find a magazine or journal article by the author that covers some of the same ground as the book but in a condensed way.

Anthologies: These are collections of essays and articles, usually by many different writers, selected by an editor, who writes an introductory essay. Anthologies are good sources for short papers because they offer multiple voices, and each argument can be read in one sitting. Pay attention to whether a book is an anthology because you will cite these anthology selections differently from a regular book. Look near the back of the book for information about the author of any selection you choose to use.

Reference books: These are good for gathering background information and specific facts on your topic. You can find these online and on the library shelves; they cannot be checked out. Reference books include specialized encyclopedias on almost any subject, such as *The Encyclopedia of Politics and Religion* (CQ Press, 2007). We will tell you below how to search for encyclopedias and other reference books. Many reference books are now available electronically.

A note of caution about Wikipedia: *Wikipedia* is not a scholarly publication. It is a general encyclopedia, meaning it contains commonly available information, not the kind of specialized knowledge professors would cite in their research. (See the note about general encyclopedias below.) In addition, on many topics, *Wikipedia* is not considered a reputable source because it encourages a democratic notion of knowledge in which anyone can contribute, add to, alter, or delete material that has been posted on a topic. Although the editors scan it regularly for misinformation, errors, and deliberate lies, there is no guarantee that what you find there is credible. We suggest you use it for background information and for links to other, more authoritative sources whose authors' credentials you can confirm. Check any facts you plan to use in your papers against other, more scholarly sources.

A note of caution about general encyclopedias: Multivolume online and print encyclopedias such as *Britannica* are good for background knowledge as you begin research on a topic or for fact-checking while you are writing. However, college students should not use general encyclopedias as primary sources. The entries do not cover topics in depth and are not usually products of original research. It is better to use specialized encyclopedias and reference works or books and articles by specialists in your topic.

Periodicals

Periodicals are published periodically—daily, weekly, monthly, quarterly. They include the following types:

Articles in scholarly journals: These journals are usually published by university presses and aimed at readers in a particular scholarly discipline: Both the authors and intended readers are professors and graduate students. Scholarly articles are contributions to ongoing debates within a discipline. Therefore, they are credible sources, but scan them for accessibility. If you are not familiar with the debate they are joining, you may not find them accessible enough to use responsibly. Seek your instructor's help if you find a source hard to comprehend. Scholarly journals are usually born in print and put online, but some are born digital.

Articles in magazines: Magazines—print, online, and the born digital "e-zines"—are good sources for short papers. Magazine articles vary greatly, depending on their intended readership. Some magazines, such as *The Atlantic Monthly, Harper's, National Review, The New Republic, The New Yorker,* and even *Rolling Stone,* offer articles by scholars and serious journalists. They give arguments on current public issues by the same people who write for scholarly journals, but the articles are aimed at an educated public readership, not other scholars. These are perfect for familiarizing yourself with viewpoints on an issue. You can find even more accessible articles and arguments in weekly newsmagazines, including columns by nationally syndicated writers. Trade magazines are good for business-related topics; Julie Ross found several online magazines published for the building industry. Many advocacy groups also publish magazines in print and online. Ross found ecological advocacy groups' magazines, such as *E: The Environmental Magazine,* helpful in her research.

Newspapers: Newspapers are ideal sources for arguments and information on current as well as historical issues. Feature articles, which are long and in-depth, usually present the reporter's angle on the topic; opinion columns are arguments and therefore good for getting perspectives on your topic. Major national newspapers such as *The Washington Post, The Wall Street Journal,* and *The New York Times* are available online, although you may have to use your school's library databases to find archived articles if you do not want to pay to access them. Below, we tell more about how to search library databases for newspaper articles.

Audiovisual Materials

You should be aware of the many resources for finding visuals to use in your paper and also to view as sources of information. You can find images by searching the Internet. Also, your library's online resources page may have a link to digital resources, as does the Library of Congress's Digital Collections and Services, which is a free resource available online. See Figure 6.2 for a look at this website.

Websites

Websites include nearly every kind of source described above and more. You have to evaluate everything you find in the wild and open world of cyberspace, but nearly all research institutes and centers associated with universities, advocacy groups, government bureaus, and political organizations are excellent sources for your arguments. Also, most writers these days have their own page on the web, where you can go to find more about their lives, views, and other writing, so the web is a great resource for learning more about your sources. The only problem is searching the web efficiently, and we offer advice later in this chapter on how to zero in on the best sites for your topic.

Figure 6.2
This page from the Library of Congress website gives you an idea of the range of audiovisual material available to you.

Blogs, Listservs, Usenet Groups, Message Boards

The web has become an exciting place for dialogue, where scholars within an area of interest can argue with each other and ask each other for help with their research. Although a first-year student may not feel ready to enter these discussions, "lurking"—reading a discussion without contributing to it—is a great way to learn about the debates firsthand. And an intelligent question will find people ready to share their knowledge and opinions. We'll tell you later in this chapter about directories that will take you to the most relevant resources for your topic.

Choosing Precise Search Terms

The success of your search depends on what terms you use. Before beginning, write down, in your notebook or research log, possible terms that you might use in searching for sources on your topic. Do this by examining your research question to find its key terms. As you begin doing your research, you will discover which of these terms are most productive and which you can cross out. Adapt your search terms as you discover which ones are most productive.

We'll use Ross's search to illustrate how to find the best search terms. Ross's research question was, What are the negative effects of tearing down older homes and replacing them with bigger new ones? Ross wanted to know more about the environmental effects of large homes, both on climate change globally and on the local neighborhoods.

Use Keyword Searching

Keyword searches use as search terms the words that most often are used to refer to your topic. Ross's topic, the construction of large new houses replacing old ones, is often referred to as the teardown trend, so Ross used "teardowns" in a keyword search.

Use Phrase Searching

You can combine words to create a search term. When you do this, your search engine may want you to put quotation marks or parentheses around the combined terms so it recognizes them as one idea. For example, Ross also used the phrase "neighborhood preservation" to find sources on her topic.

Use Boolean Searching

Boolean searching (named after nineteenth-century English logician George Boole) allows you to narrow or broaden your search by joining words with AND OR NOT

AND: "home size" AND "energy consumption"

Using AND narrowed Ross's search. However, she found nothing by combining "home size" AND "global warming." She needed to think more specifically about the connection between home size and global warming: Energy consumption is the link. (Note: Google and most other search engines automatically put AND in when you type words in succession.)

OR: "green houses" OR "sustainable homes"

Using OR broadened the search, yielding more hits. Using OR is helpful if you know your subject has many synonyms, such as *youth, teenagers, students*.

NOT: "green house" NOT agriculture

Using NOT limited the search by eliminating references to hothouses in agriculture.

Use Subject Words

Keyword searches may not work well in some indexes and databases that have been compiled under strict subject headings. Different search engines and databases will have different official subject headings. For example, the Library of Congress uses "electric automobiles" as a subject heading, whereas the online library subscription database Academic OneFile uses the subject heading "electric cars."

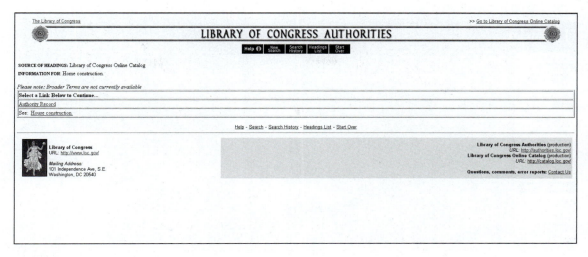

Figure 6.3

The Library of Congress Authorities website will tell you the correct search term for finding books on your topic.

Most university libraries use the Library of Congress subject words for books in their online catalogs. You can go to the Library of Congress Subject Authorities website at <http://authorities.loc.gov/> to find the correct subject headings. When Ross went to the Library of Congress Subject Authorities site, she found that "house construction" was the correct search term, not "home construction."

Figure 6.3 shows the results of a search for correct subject headings. Or you can go directly to your library's catalog and type what you think might be a good search term. The catalog should then direct you to the correct subject heading for that topic. For example, if you type in "electric cars" in your library catalog, you will be told to "See 'electric automobiles'."

SEARCHING YOUR LIBRARY

Because much of the research material on the Internet is available for free through your school's library, it makes sense to start with your library's resources. Why pay for something that you already have free access to through your college or university? Also, unlike much of what you find on the Internet, the materials available through your library have been selected by scholars, editors, and librarians, so you can be more confident about the credibility of what you find.

Do not assume that searching the library means using bound books and periodicals only, or even going there in person. Libraries are going electronic, giving you online access to more high-quality, full-text sources than you will find on the web. Libraries subscribe to online indexes and journals that cannot

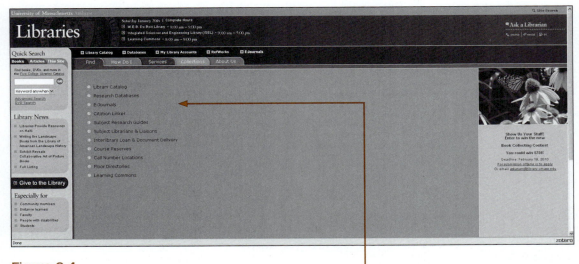

Figure 6.4
A library home page

Use the link to research databases (often called online resources) to find articles in magazines, newspapers, and scholarly journals.

be found through search engines like Google and Yahoo!. Your enrollment at school gives you access to these resources, which are described later in this chapter. Your library's online home page is the gateway to all the library's resources. Figure 6.4 is an example of a library home page. Many librarians create research guides to the resources their library offers in various subject areas, including first-year writing, as shown in Figure 6.5.

Your Library's Online Catalog

Your library's online catalog is the gateway to a wealth of sources: books, both printed and online in the form of e-books that you can "check out" and download; full-text online newspapers, including the complete archives of these papers; indexes to individual articles in magazines, newspapers, and scholarly journals, including links to the full text of most of them online; audiovisual materials; maps; and reference books of all kinds. Visit the home page of your library's online catalog and explore the places it will take you. In the library catalog, you can search for books by title, author, subject, and keyword, as well as their Library of Congress call numbers. Here are some tips:

In a title search: If you know a title you are looking for, do a title search with as much of the title needed to distinguish it from other titles. Omit initial articles (*a, the, an*).

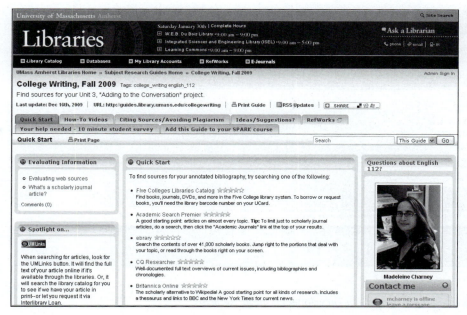

Figure 6.5

A research guide to college writing

In a subject search: You will need to know what "subject heading" the Library of Congress has given your topic. Julie Ross, for example, found no books in her library catalog when she typed in "home construction" but found twenty-five books when she typed in "house construction." See pages 102–103 for more about subject headings. Or just try a keyword search, described below.

In a keyword search: This kind of search is more forgiving than a subject search and can be helpful if you do not know the exact right word. Put quotation marks around phrases: "global warming." You can use AND or OR to combine terms: "teardowns" AND "neighborhood preservation."

The library's online catalog will also tell you if your library subscribes to a particular newspaper or magazine. The catalog will not tell you about individual articles or stories in these periodicals, but you can find them by searching the publication's own online index or the online databases in your library, described on the next page. Most university libraries now subscribe to major U.S. newspapers and have full-text archives online. Do a title search to find out if your library has a particular newspaper.

To locate reference books, combine your keyword search with words like *encyclopedia, dictionary,* or *almanac,* and you will find both online and

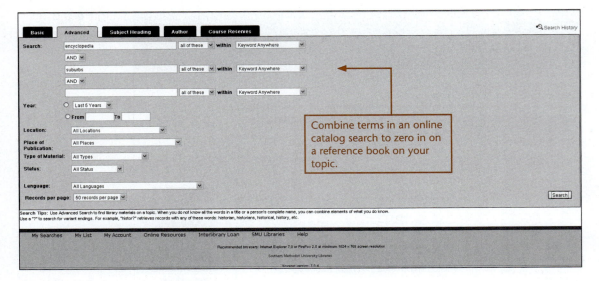

Figure 6.6

A search in an online catalog for specialized encyclopedias about suburbs

on-the-shelf reference books. For an example of such a search and an example of a result, see Figures 6.6 and 6.7.

Your Library's Online Resources

Your school library's purchased online resources are available only to students, faculty, and staff. Students can access them on campus or off campus by using a password. The main web page of most university libraries offers a link to a page listing the online resources available to you. These usually include reference resources: dictionaries such as *The Oxford English Dictionary*; electronic encyclopedias, journals, and magazines; and most important, licensed databases to help you search for a wide variety of sources on any topic, both on and off the web.

These databases are indexes to articles in periodicals: magazines, scholarly journals, and newspapers. You search them by typing in a subject, keyword, author, or title. In most cases the search will produce a list of articles, an abstract of the article, and often, a link to full text of the article, which you can then save or print out.

If the full text is not available online, the database will tell you if the periodical is in your library's holdings. You may be able to access it electronically through the online catalog. This is why it is good to know which magazines, journals, and newspapers are cataloged along with the books in your library's online catalog.

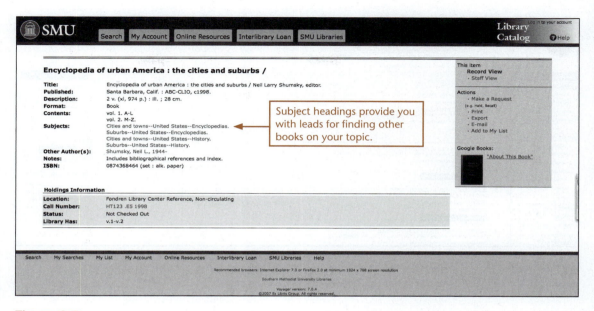

Figure 6.7

The result of an online search for encyclopedias about suburbs

Never use the abstract of an article as a source. Abstracts may not be written by the source's author; they may not be accurate. Most important, you cannot get the in-depth understanding of a source that would allow you to use it accurately.

The following are some common databases subscribed to by college libraries:

Academic Search Complete

Academic OneFile

LEXIS-NEXIS Academic

Business Source Complete

Communication and Mass Media Complete

Film and Television Literature Index

TOPICsearch (good for social, political, and other topics popular in classroom discussions)

Using the "advanced search" in databases like Academic OneFile and Academic Search Complete (illustrated in Figure 6.8) allows you to combine terms to narrow your search. Ross eliminated all hits not related to housing by including "houses" as a second term in her search. Note that both databases

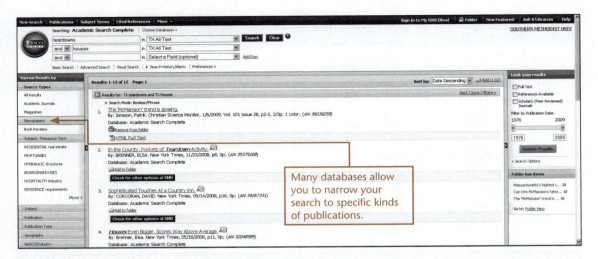

Figure 6.8

Results of an advanced search for newspaper articles in a database

allow you to select from academic journals, popular magazines, newspapers, or all three. The search in Figure 6.8 targeted newspapers only.

INTERNET RESEARCH

Because the Internet is so large—estimated to contain over 11.5 billion web pages—we want to caution you about the potential for wasting time if you start browsing with one of the common search engines such as Yahoo! or Google. However, there are some ways to use search engine features to narrow your search. One of those ways is to limit your search to certain domains.

Domains

Every Internet address or URL (Uniform Resource Locator) has certain components; it helps to know a little about them. What is known as the "top level domain name" tells you something about who put the site on the web. For websites from the United States, the following are the four most common top level domain names. Websites from other nations typically have instead an abbreviation of the country's name.

Commercial (.com)

"Dot com" sites include businesses and their publications—such as the real estate newsletter at <http://www.teardowns.com>—other commercial publications, such as magazines; and personal web pages and blogs, such as those created on Blogger.com. The example, www.teardowns.com, is a site assisting builders who want to construct on the sites of torn-down houses. Although you will find magazine and newspaper articles through search engines like Yahoo! and Google, a better way to ensure that you get them in full text for free is to find them through your library's licensed databases, as described on page 106. Because so much of the web is commercial sites, you will probably want to use the advanced search options explained in the next section to filter "dot com" sites from your search.

Nonprofit Organizations (.org)

"Dot org" sites include organizations and advocacy groups, such as the National Trust for Historic Preservation at <http://www.nationaltrust.org /teardowns/>. Their purpose is to raise awareness of, participation in, and donations to their causes.

Educational Institutions (.edu)

"Dot edu" sites contain research and course materials of public and private schools, colleges, and universities. The URL <http://sciencepolicy.colo rado.edu/> is a site for a center at University of Colorado at Boulder doing research on science, technology, and public policy. Although mostly what you find at these sites is the work of professors, some of the material may be by graduate and undergraduate students, so as always, check out the author's credentials.

Government Agencies (.gov)

"Dot gov" sites are useful for getting the latest information about any aspect of American government or about government agencies and policies. The URL <http://www.census.gov/> leads to articles published by the U.S. Census Bureau.

Advanced Features for Searching the Web

Search engines provide a variety of ways to focus your search, and Google has some that are especially useful for students.

Advanced Searches

Search engines will let you customize your search, allowing you to limit your search to just one or two of the domains listed above, or to exclude one. Filtering out the "dot com" sites is like turning on a spam blocker, so you will get fewer hits by writers with no academic or professional credentials. Figure 6.9 shows how to filter web searches.

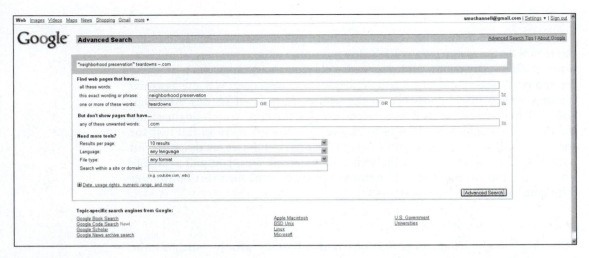

Figure 6.9

Narrow your Google searches by using the advanced search window to combine terms and exclude websites in specific domains, like .com.

Google Specialized Searches

Google offers an ever-increasing number of specific kinds of searches, such as Books, Images, and Earth. Many link you to materials that you will have to pay for. However, you can probably find many of these for free through your school library, which subscribes to the archives of many magazines and newspapers. See the earlier section, "Your Library's Online Resources," on page 106.

Google Scholar

Google Scholar is where your library and the Internet intersect. Google Scholar is an index to scholarly articles and book reviews, many of them available at your university library. If you open Google Scholar from a computer on campus or if your home computer connects to your school's network (or if you have a password that will grant you off-campus access to your school's network), you will be able to access full texts of materials available from your school's library.

Subject Directories to the Web

You can narrow your search for websites by going first to a subject directory that organizes websites by topic. Some examples are

    Yahoo!

    Open Directory

    Exalead

    Infomine (assembled by librarians, not machines)

    About.com

Blogs, Listservs, Message Boards, and Chat Groups

Do not overlook the potential of interactive sites on the Internet. Many authors of your sources have blogs and personal web pages where they try out new ideas and get feedback from others interested in their topics. As a student, you may not feel ready to join these conversations, but you can learn a lot by lurking—that is, just reading them. You can find them by using "blogs," "list-servs," "message board," or "chat room" as a search term in your browser.

EVALUATING SOURCES

Before beginning to read and evaluate your sources, you may need to reevaluate your issue. If you have been unable to find many sources that address the question you are raising, consider changing the focus of your argument.

Once you are sure that sources are available on your topic, use the following method to record and evaluate them.

Eliminate Inappropriate Sources

You may find that some books and articles are intended for audiences with more specialized knowledge than you have. If you have trouble using a source, put it aside, at least temporarily.

Also, carefully review any electronic sources you are using. Although search engines make it easy to find material on the web, online documents often have met no professional standards for scholarship. Material can be "published" electronically without review by experts, scholars, and editors that must occur in traditional publishing. Nevertheless, you will find legitimate scholarship on the Internet—news reports, encyclopedias, government documents, and even scholarly journals appear online. The freedom of electronic publishing creates an exciting and democratic arena, but it also puts a much heavier burden on students and researchers to ensure that the sources they use are worthy of readers' respect.

Carefully Record Complete Bibliographic Information

For every source you consider using, be sure to record full bibliographic information (Figure 6.10). Take this information from the source itself, not from an index, which may be incomplete or inaccurate. If you make a record of this information immediately, you will not have to go back later to fill in omissions.

Read the Source Critically

As discussed in Chapter 2, critical reading depends on having some prior knowledge of the subject and the ability to see a text in context. As you research a topic, your knowledge naturally becomes deeper with each article you read. But your sources are not simply windows, giving you a clear view; whether argumentative or informative, they have bias. Before looking through them, you must look *at* your sources. Know the answers to the following questions.

Figure 6.10

Working bibliography entries

Print Sources	Electronic Sources
Book • Author's full name (or authors' names) • Title of book, including subtitle • City where published (for APA style) • Publisher • Year published	**Document found on the Internet:** • Author's full name (or authors' names) • Title of the work • Original print date, if applicable • Title of the database or website • URL
Article or essay in a collection • Author's full name (or authors' names) • Title of article or essay • Title of book • Editor's name (or editors' names) • City where published (for APA style) • Publisher • Year published • Inclusive page numbers of the article.	**Website, listserv, or blog:** • Author's full name (or authors' names) • Title of post or subject line • Title of website or blog • Date of the posting • URL
Article in a periodical • Author's full name (or authors' names) • Title of the article • Title of the periodical • Date of the issue • Volume number, if given • Library database if retrieved online (example, Academic OneFile) and URL for article • Page numbers on which article appears	

Who Is the Writer, and What Is His or Her Bias?

Is there a note that tells about the writer's professional title or institutional affiliation? If not, search the Internet for the writer's personal home page or university website. Do an author search in your library's catalog and online databases to find other books and articles by the writer.

How Reliable Is the Source?

Again, checking for credibility is particularly important when you are working with electronic sources. For example, one student found two sites on the web, both through a keyword search on "euthanasia." One, entitled "Stop the Epidemic of Assisted Suicide," was posted by a person identified only by name, the letters MD, and the affiliation "Association for Control of Assisted Suicide." There was no biographical information, and the "snail mail" address was a post office box. The other website, "Ethics Update: Euthanasia," was posted by a professor of philosophy at the University of San Diego whose home page included a complete professional biography detailing his education, titles, and the publishers of his many books and articles. The author gave his address at

"I just feel fortunate to live in a world with so much disinformation at my fingertips."

© P. C. Vey/The New Yorker Collection/www.cartoonbank.com

USD in the Department of Philosophy. The student decided that, although the first source had some interesting information—including examples of individual patients who were living with pain rather than choosing suicide—it was not a source that skeptical readers would find credible. Search engines often land you deep within a website, and you have to visit the site's home page to get any background information about the source and its author. Be suspicious of sites that do not contain adequate source information; they probably are not reliable.

When Was This Source Written?

If you are researching a current issue, decide what sources are too old. Arguments on current issues often benefit from earlier perspectives.

Where Did This Source Appear?

If you are using an article from a periodical, be aware of the periodical's readership and editorial bias. For example, *National Review* is conservative, *The Nation* liberal. An article in the *Journal of the American Medical Association* will usually defend the medical profession. Looking at the table of contents and scanning editorial statements will give you a feel for the periodical's

Additional Guidelines for Evaluating Internet Sources

1. Look at the last segment of the domain name, which will tell you who developed the site. The most reliable ones are developed by colleges and universities (.edu) or by the government (.gov). Of course, commercial sites (.com, .biz) are profit-minded.

2. Does the site have a link to information about the person or organization that put it on the Internet? What can you find out about the education and professional credentials of the author or publisher?

3. If the site is run by an organization, how is it funded? On the site or elsewhere, look for information about funding and donations. Look for conflict of interest or bias in, for example, a site that publishes about the environment but whose corporate donors have been charged with violating environmental protection laws.

4. Check whether the source includes a bibliography, a sign of scholarly work.

5. A tilde (~) indicates a personal page; these pages must be evaluated with special care.

politics. Also look at the page that lists the publisher and editorial board. You will find, for example, that *The New American* is published by the ultra-right-wing John Birch Society. If you need help determining bias, ask a librarian. A reference book that lists periodicals by subject matter and explains their bias is *Magazines for Libraries*.

What Is the Author's Aim?

First, determine whether the source informs or argues. Both are useful, and both will have some bias. When your source is an argument, note whether it aims primarily to inquire, to convince, to persuade, or to mediate.

How Is the Source Organized?

If the writer does not use subheadings or chapter titles, break the text into parts yourself and note what function each part plays in the whole.

Special Help with Evaluating Websites

The Internet is a dangerous place for researchers in a hurry. If you are not careful to look closely at what you find on the web, you could embarrass yourself badly. For example, why would a college student want to cite a paper written for a high school class? Many high school teachers put their best student papers on class sites—good papers, but nevertheless, not exactly the kind of authority a college student should be citing. So before choosing to use something from the web, go through the following checklist:

1. **Know the site's domain.** See pages 108–109 for how to read a web address and what the various domain suffixes tell you about the site.

Note if the site is commercial, educational, governmental, or some kind of advocacy group. Advocacy groups are usually indicated by *.org* in the domain name. Commercial sites may be advertising something—they are not disinterested sources.

2. **Find the home page.** A search engine or online directory may take you to a page deep within the site; always look for links back to the home page because that is where you can find out more about the bias of the site and the credentials of the people behind it.

3. **Read about the bias and mission of the site.** At the home page, you should see a link to more information about the site—often the link is called "About Us" or "Mission Statement." Follow it and learn about the ideology of the site and how it compares with your own bias and that of other sources you are using.

4. **Read about the credentials of the site's creators.** The creators' degrees and professional affiliations should be easy to find. Regard any site as bogus if the only link to finding more about the authors is an e-mail address. Also, note whether the credentials of its board of directors or trustees are in the fields of specialization for your topic. For example, many writers for some websites on global warming dispute scientific findings but are not scientists. They may be economists or historians.

5. **Note if the site reports on its funding and donors.** The rule of "follow the money" becomes important when you are using sources outside the academic world. Think tanks and advocacy groups receive money from large corporations. Consider how the funding might influence their research and reported findings. There should be a link to material about funding, corporate sponsors, and the group's annual tax reports.

6. **Note how current the site is.** Near the beginning or the end of any website or part of a website, you should be able to find a note about when the site was last updated. You will need this information in order to cite the site—a site that has not been updated in years is not a good choice.

The website for the National Trust for Historic Preservation (Figure 6.11), where Ross found a speech about the effects of teardowns on neighborhoods, checks out as a credible site. From the home page, Ross was able to link to a page titled "About the National Trust" (Figure 6.12), where she learned that it is a private, nonprofit organization founded in 1949 and dedicated to saving historical places. It advocates for legislation to protect communities and places of cultural heritage. The home page also provides a link titled "Funding," with information about donations, corporate sponsors, and tax returns. A link to the organization's "Management" gave the credentials of its trustees and its executive staff, including Richard Moe, the author of the speech. Ross learned that Moe graduated from Williams College in 1959 and from the University of Minnesota Law School in 1966. He has been president of the National Trust

Figure 6.11

The home page of the website of the National Trust for Historic Preservation

Credible websites have a link that tells you about the organization responsible for the site.

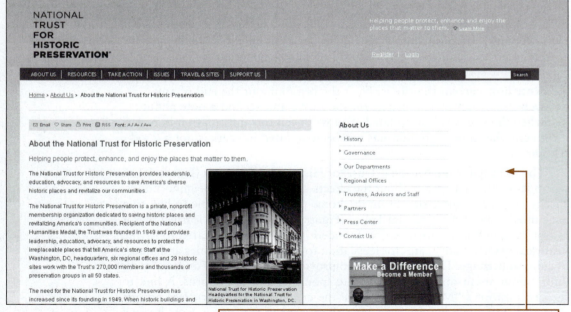

Figure 6.12

"About Us" page on website

The organization should provide information about its purpose, history, governance and annual financial reports, and leaders. Reject websites that do not provide such information.

since 1993. He is an honorary member of The American Institute of Architects and coauthor of a book titled *Changing Places: Rebuilding Community in the Age of Sprawl*, published in 1997. Clearly, this source from a website passed the test.

USING SOURCES

The first way to use your sources is to familiarize yourself with viewpoints on your topic. Your thesis will grow out of your research; you do not do research to find information to support a position you have not investigated. In high school, you may have grabbed quotations or facts from a source; in college you must know the source itself, including something about the author and the author's argument, unless your source is an encyclopedia or almanac or other reference work. For more on getting to know sources, read Chapter 2, "Reading Arguments," and the preceding section in this chapter, "Evaluating Sources," pages 111–117.

When you have gathered and evaluated some sources, you should next spend some time with each one, reading it, marking it up, and writing about it in your notebook or on a notepad. This essential step will help you use your sources confidently and accurately in a paper with your own angle and voice. One teacher calls this step "writing in the middle" because it bridges the gap between the sources you have found and the paper you will turn in. If you skip this step, you risk misrepresenting your source, taking material out of context, plagiarizing (see Chapter 7, "Ethical Writing and Plagiarism"), or, more commonly, letting your sources take over with too much of their voice and wording, resulting in a paper that sounds patched together.

Because you should not use a source that you have not read in its entirety, we reproduce below one of Julie Ross's sources for her argument on neighborhood preservation. We will demonstrate various kinds of informal writing about this source.

Note that we have annotated this reading, an important step you should perform for every source you plan to use.

Battling Teardowns, Saving Neighborhoods

RICHARD MOE, president of the National Trust for Historic Preservation

Note author's credentials

Speech given to the Commonwealth Club, San Francisco, CA; June 28, 2006.

A growing disaster is tearing apart many of America's older neighborhoods. They're being devoured, one house at a time, here in the Bay Area, across California, and in scores of communities from coast to coast.

I'm talking about teardowns—the practice of purchasing and demolishing an existing house to make way for a new, much bigger house on the same site. Teardowns wreck neighborhoods. They spread through a community like a cancer, destroying

Quotable passage here

the character and livability that are a neighborhood's lifeblood. I believe teardowns represent the biggest threat to America's older neighborhoods since the heyday of urban renewal and interstate highway construction during the 1950s and 60s.

Here's how it works: Developers and home-buyers look through desirable neighborhoods for a building lot that can lawfully accommodate a much bigger house than that which currently stands on it. The property is acquired, the existing house is torn down and a bigger house is constructed in its place. There are variations: Sometimes a large estate is leveled and subdivided to accommodate several new houses; in others, several smaller houses are cleared to make way for a single, massive new one.

Extent of the problem

It's a simple process, but it can totally transform the streetscape of a neighborhood and destroy its character. It's especially destructive in older and historic communities.

5   Teardowns are occurring all over America—from fashionable resorts such as Palm Beach and Palm Springs to the inner-ring suburbs around Washington and Chicago and the Richmond District here in San Francisco. The trend has become so alarming that the National Trust included "Teardowns in Historic Neighborhoods" on our list of America's 11 Most Endangered Historic Places in 2002. Back then, we identified 100 communities in 20 states that were having major problems with teardowns. That statistic was troubling in 2002—but four years later, the news is much worse: Today we can document the impact of teardowns in more than 300 communities in 33 states. The National Association of Home Builders says that 75,000 houses are razed and replaced with larger homes each year. . . .

Background information

This disaster goes by many names. In New Jersey, the practice is often called "bash-and-build." In Colorado, teardowns are known as "scrape-offs." In Oregon, the new houses are sometimes called "snout houses" because of the big, protruding garages that dominate their facades. In other places they're known simply—and aptly—as "bigfoots" or "monster homes."

Extent of the problem

Whatever you call it, one teardown usually sparks others. A New Jersey builder says, "It's a trend that keeps on rolling. Builders used to be afraid to be the first person in a neighborhood to tear a house down. Now they're looking around and saying they don't mind taking the risk."

Why is this happening?

Three factors are at work in the spread of teardowns.

10   The first is the rise in real-estate prices. In some areas, home values have doubled or tripled over the past decade, and this leads developers to look for "undervalued" properties—many of which exist in older neighborhoods.

More background

The second factor is the trend toward bigger houses. In 1950, the average American home incorporated less than 1,000 sq. ft. By 2005, the average new home had more than doubled in size, to 2,412 sq. ft. According to the National Association of Home Builders, almost 40% of new homes have four or more bedrooms; that's more than twice as many as in the early 1970s—despite the fact that the average family size decreased during that same period. Subdivisions of luxury homes of 5,000 sq. ft. and more are becoming commonplace. Clearly, burgers and french fries aren't the only things in America being "super-sized."

One reason for teardowns

The final factor is that many people are looking for an alternative to long commutes or are simply fed up with the soulless character of sprawling new subdivisions. For these people, older in-town neighborhoods and inner-ring suburbs are enormously appealing because of their attractive architecture, mature landscaping, pedestrian orientation, easy access to public transportation and amenities such as local shopping districts, libraries and schools.

Other reasons for teardowns

The problem is that too many people try to impose their preference for suburban-style mini-mansions on smaller-scale neighborhoods where they just don't fit. And since most of these older areas offer few vacant lots for new construction, the pressure to demolish existing houses can be intense. A modest cottage gets torn down and hauled off to the landfill, and what goes up in its place is "Tara" on a quarter-acre lot.

Neighborhood livability is diminished as trees are removed, backyards are eliminated, and sunlight is blocked by bulky new structures built right up to the property lines. Economic and social diversity are reduced as costly new "faux chateaux" replace more affordable houses—including the modest "starter homes" that our parents knew and that first-time homebuyers still search for today. . . .

15   While the destruction of historic houses is wasteful, environmentally unsound and unnecessary, it's often just the beginning of the problems caused by teardowns.

Reason against tearing down: effect on neighborhood

It's not uncommon for a demolished older home to be replaced with a new one that is three times as big as any other house on the block. These structures loom over their neighbors and break the established building patterns of the area. Front yards are often given over to driveways, and three- or four-car garages are the dominant elements in the façade. Floor plans are often oriented to private interior spaces, making the new houses look like fortresses that stand totally aloof from their surroundings. . . .

Apart from their visual impact, teardowns can profoundly alter a neighborhood's economic and social environment. A rash of teardowns can cause property taxes to rise—and while this may be a good thing for communities in search of revenue, it can drive out moderate-income or fixed-income residents. Those who remain start to feel they've lost control of their neighborhood to developers and speculators. A house that once might have been praised as "charming and historic" now gets marketed as "older home on expansive lot"—which is realtor language for "teardown." Once that happens—once the value of an older house is perceived to be less than that of the land it's built on—the house's days are probably numbered. And sadly, the neighborhood's days as a viable historic enclave may be numbered too.

Another reason against teardowns

It doesn't have to be this way. There are alternatives to teardowns.

First of all, prospective builders should realize that most older, established neighborhoods simply can't accommodate the kind of sprawling new mini-mansion that is appropriate on a suburban cul-de-sac. People who want to move into the city can often find development opportunities in underused historic buildings and vacant land in older areas. Even in areas where vacant land is scarce, existing older houses can be enlarged in sensitive ways: A new zoning ordinance in Coronado, California, for example, gives homebuilders "bonus" square footage if they incorporate design elements that maintain the historic character of the community.

Alternatives to tearing down

20

Qualification of his argument

No one is saying that homebuyers shouldn't be able to alter or expand their home to meet their needs, just as no one is saying that older neighborhoods should be frozen in time like museum exhibits. A neighborhood is a living thing, and change is both inevitable and desirable. The challenge is to manage change so that it respects the character and distinctiveness that made these neighborhoods so appealing in the first place.

Let me mention a few things that people and communities can do.

Solutions to the problem

First and most important, communities must realize that they aren't helpless in the face of teardowns. They have choices: They can simply take the kind of community they get, or they can go to work to get the kind of community they want. They have to decide what they like about the community and don't want to lose. They must develop a vision for the future of their community, including where and how to accommodate growth and change. Then they must put in place mechanisms to ensure that their vision is not compromised.

Ideally, this consensus-building should take place as part of a comprehensive planning process—but that can take time, and sometimes the pressure of teardowns calls for immediate action. In those situations, some communities have provided a "cooling-off" period by imposing a temporary moratorium on demolition. This moratorium prevents the loss of significant structures while allowing time for residents and city officials to develop effective means of preserving neighborhood character.

More solutions

One of those means is local historic district designation. Notice that I said "local historic district." Many people believe that listing a property in the National Register of Historic Places is enough to protect it, but that isn't true. The only real protection comes through the enactment of a local ordinance that regulates demolition, new construction and alteration in a designated historic area. More than 2,500 communities across the country have enacted these ordinances. Most of them require that an owner get permission before demolishing or altering a historic building; many also offer design guidelines to ensure that new buildings will harmonize with their older neighbors.

25

If historic district designation isn't feasible or appropriate, other forms of regulation may work. Conservation districts or design-review districts can address issues such as demolition and new construction with less administrative burden than historic districts. Floor-area ratios or lot-coverage formulas can remove the economic incentive for teardowns by limiting the size of new buildings. In the same way, setback requirements, height limits and open-space standards can help maintain traditional neighborhood building patterns. At least two communities in San Mateo County have recently adopted regulations of this sort to limit the height and floor area of newly built homes.

Not all approaches require government involvement. Local preservation organizations or neighborhood groups can offer programs to educate realtors and new residents about the history of older neighborhoods and provide guidance in rehabbing or expanding older houses. They can acquire easements to ensure that the architectural character of historic buildings is permanently protected. They can provide low-interest loans to help encourage sensitive rehabilitation. Incentives such as these are particularly effective when combined with technical assistance and some form of tax abatement from state or local government.

Some people go so far as to claim that teardowns actually support smart growth by directing new-home construction to already-developed areas, thereby increasing density and offering an alternative to suburban sprawl. Again, I disagree.

Opposing view and rebuttal

Tearing down a smaller house to build a bigger one simply adds square footage, not population density. In addition, teardowns affect neighborhood livability, reduce affordability, consume energy, and send thousands of tons of demolition debris to landfills. That doesn't sound like smart growth to me.

Equally important, teardowns exact too high a price in the wasteful destruction of our nation's heritage. Of course we need to encourage investment in existing communities as an alternative to sprawl—but not at the expense of the historic character that makes older neighborhoods unique, attractive and livable. Some say that change is simply the price of progress—but this kind of change isn't progress at all; it's chaos.

30 The National Trust is committed to helping local residents put the brakes on teardowns. It will be a huge job—but it's eminently worthy of our best efforts.

America's older neighborhoods are important chapters in the story of who we are as a nation and a people. Working together, we can keep that story alive. Working together, we can keep America's older and historic communities intact so that generations to come can live in them, learn from them, be sheltered and inspired by them—just as we are today.

Writing Informally to Gain Mastery over Your Sources

The more you engage your sources with informal "talk-back" such as annotations, notebook responses to the ideas in the sources, notebook entries that make connections between and among ideas in sources, and paraphrases and summaries that make you really think about the key points and passages, the easier it will be for you to assume the voice of authority when it is time to start drafting your paper. Here are some suggestions for writing in the middle zone between researching and drafting.

1. Annotate the Source

Use the advice in Chapter 2, "Reading Arguments," which suggests things to look for in sources that are arguments. If a source is not an argument, annotate to comment on the author's angle, bias, and main points.

2. Respond to the Source in Your Notebook

After annotating, write more in your notebook about how you might use the source. If you have roughed out a case, note which reason or reasons of your own case this source could help you develop. If you find a new reason for your case, note it and think how you could develop it with your own observations and other sources you have found.

If you think the source will be mainly useful for facts, make a note about what kind of facts it has and the page numbers, so that when you start drafting, you can find them quickly.

If the author is an expert or authority, note the credentials or at least where you can go to find these as you start drafting—perhaps the author's web page or a biographical note at the end of the book or article.

If this will be a major source for your paper, you should be sure you grasp the most important concepts in it. Look for the passages that pose a challenge; to use the source with authority, you need to own, not borrow, these ideas. That means instead of just dropping them in as quotations, you will have to work them in, explaining them in your own words. Try out *paraphrases* (see more on paraphrases in item 3 in this list) to make these points completely clear to you and then respond to the major ideas with what you think about them: If it is a good idea, why do you think so? What in your own experiences (field research) confirms it? What can you add of your own as you discuss this idea in your paper?

Look for memorable passages that are worth *direct quotations* (see more on direct quotations in this chapter's section on incorporating source material). The best quotes are strongly worded opinions and writing that cannot be paraphrased without losing its punch.

Think about how additional research might help you develop an idea given to you by this source.

The box on page 123 shows some notes Ross put in her notebook after deciding to use the National Trust source.

3. Paraphrase Important Ideas from the Source

Although you will use paraphrases as you incorporate material from your sources into your essay, consider paraphrase as a study skill that helps you understand key ideas by putting them into your own words. It helps you to "own" the key ideas rather than simply borrowing the author's words to insert into your paper. Here are some suggestions for paraphrasing:

- Read the entire source or section in which the passage appears. You cannot write a good paraphrase of a passage you have taken out of context. Surrounding sentences will provide information essential for understanding the material you are paraphrasing, and to make the idea clear to yourself, you may need to add some of that information to your paraphrase. Later, if you use the paraphrase in your paper, you will need to provide enough context so that your readers will understand the idea as well.

- Read the passage several times through, including surrounding text, until you think you understand it. Annotate it. Look up any words that are even slightly unfamiliar to you.

- Put the text away so that you will not be tempted to look at it. Then think of the main ideas and try to put each one into your own words and your own wording. A paraphrase must not be an echo of the original's sentence patterns with synonyms plugged in. That is really a form of

---

Notes on Moe, Richard. "Battling Teardowns."

- *Perfect source for my paper. I need to mention the National Trust for Historic Preservation. This source supports my "preserve the neighborhood character" reason. Good description of the garages—"snout houses." Also mention the way these new houses block the sunlight. Good on the economic impact on the older people in my neighborhood. Many can't afford to stay. This source helps explain why.*

- *I also hadn't thought about how these homebuyers are destroying the very thing that makes them want to live here. Old charm won't last if everybody does what they are doing. This could appeal to their interest—restore, not tear down.*

- *I like the part about allowing for change. I'll use this quote: "A neighborhood is a living thing. Change is both inevitable and desirable." What kinds of changes would I consider OK? Could a new house of different architectural style actually add character to the neighborhood? Maybe look for a source that describes some kind of acceptable change.*

- *He mentions the other part of my case, the environment, but not enough to use this source for that part.*

---

plagiarism because it involves "stealing" the author's sentence pattern. You may want to break up complex sentences into shorter, more simple ones that make the idea easier to comprehend.

- Do not feel that you must find a substitute word for every ordinary word in the passage. For example, if a passage has the word *children*, do not feel you have to say *kids*.

- Go back and check your paraphrase against the original to see if you have accurately represented the full content of the original passage. Make adjustments as needed.

Examples of Adequate and Inadequate Paraphrasing

Original Passage:

> Some people go so far as to claim that teardowns actually support smart growth by directing new-home construction to already-developed areas, thereby increasing density and offering an alternative to suburban sprawl. Again, I disagree. Tearing down a smaller house to build a bigger one simply adds square footage, not population density.

Inadequate Paraphrase: This example borrows too much of the wording and sentence patterns (underlined) from the original text by Moe.

> Some people even claim that tearing down old houses supports smart growth by increasing new-home construction and density in already developed areas. Therefore, teardowns are an alternative to suburban sprawl. Moe disagrees because tearing down small houses and building bigger ones only adds more square footage, not more people.

Inadequate Paraphrase: The paraphrase below does not do justice to the idea: It does not include the concept of smart growth; it does not mention the problem of new development in suburban areas versus rebuilding in existing neighborhoods; and it does not give Moe credit for the opinion.

> It's not smart to tear down old houses and replace them with bigger ones because you don't get more population density.

Good Paraphrase: This explains "smart growth," gives Moe credit, and represents all the points in original sentence patterns. It even offers an interpretation at the end.

> Smart growth is an attempt to develop cities while minimizing suburban sprawl. According to Moe, tearing down older, small homes in close-in neighborhoods and replacing them with bigger ones is not really "smart growth" because bigger houses do not necessarily increase population density; they just offer more square footage for the same size household. So they are really a kind of urban sprawl.

4. Write Summaries of Portions of a Source

As a way to help get your own handle on important sections of a source, write a summary of it in your notebook. That means putting just the most important parts of the text into your own words (paraphrase) and joining them into a smooth paragraph. To write a summary, follow these steps.

1. Read and reread the portion of a text you want to summarize, looking up unfamiliar words.
2. Choose the main points.
3. Paraphrase them, using the advice on paraphrasing above.
4. Combine sentences to make the new version as concise as possible.

Here is an example of a portion of Richard Moe's speech that Julie Ross used in her paper by shortening it and presenting it in her own words. The underlined sections are the ones she deemed important enough to go into the summary.

Original Passage:

> Three factors are at work in the spread of teardowns.
>   The first is the rise in real-estate prices. In some areas, home values have doubled or tripled over the past decade, and this leads developers to look for "undervalued" properties—many of which exist in older neighborhoods.
>   The second factor is the trend toward bigger houses. In 1950, the average American home incorporated less than 1,000 sq. ft. By 2005, the average

Guidelines for Summarizing

1. Read and reread the original text until you have identified the claim and the main supporting points. You ought to be able to write an outline of the case, using your own words. Depending on your purpose for summarizing and the amount of space you can devote to the summary, decide how much, if any, of the evidence to include.

2. Make it clear at the start whose ideas you are summarizing.

3. If you are summarizing a long passage, break it down into subsections and work on summarizing one at a time.

4. As with paraphrasing, work from memory. Go back to the text to check your version for accuracy.

5. Maintain the original order of points, with this exception: If the author delayed presenting the thesis, refer to it earlier in your summary.

6. Use your own words.

7. Avoid quoting entire sentences. If you want to quote keywords and phrases, incorporate them into sentences of your own, using quotation marks around the borrowed words.

new home had more than doubled in size, to 2,412 sq. ft. According to the National Association of Home Builders, almost 40% of new homes have four or more bedrooms; that's more than twice as many as in the early 1970s—despite the fact that the average family size decreased during that same period. Subdivisions of luxury homes of 5,000 sq. ft. and more are becoming commonplace. Clearly, burgers and french fries aren't the only things in America being "super-sized."

The final factor is that many people are looking for an alternative to long commutes or are simply fed up with the soulless character of sprawling new subdivisions. For these people, older in-town neighborhoods and inner-ring suburbs are enormously appealing because of their attractive architecture, mature landscaping, pedestrian orientation, easy access to public transportation and amenities such as local shopping districts, libraries and schools.

Ross's Summary:

Moe sees three reasons for the increase in teardowns:

- In the past decade, the value of houses has doubled or tripled, except in some older neighborhoods. Developers look for these "'undervalued' properties" to build on.

- Homebuyers want more space, with the average home size going from 1,000 square feet in 1950 to 2,412 square feet in 2005.

- Some homebuyers desire to move from the "soulless . . . sprawling subdivisions" to close-in neighborhoods that have more character and more amenities, such as public transportation and local shopping.

Guidelines for Writing with Sources

Avoid plagiarism by *distinguishing sharply* between quoting and paraphrasing. Anytime you take exact words from a source, even if it is only a phrase or a significant word, you are quoting. You must use quotation marks and documentation. If you make any change at all in the wording of a quotation, you must indicate the change with square brackets. If you remove any words from a direct quotation, use ellipses (three spaced dots) to indicate the deletion. If you use your own words to summarize or paraphrase portions of a source, name that source in your text and document it. Be careful to use your own words when paraphrasing and summarizing.

1. Use an attributive tag such as "According to . . ." to introduce quotations both direct and indirect. Do not just drop them in.

2. Name the person whose words or idea you are using. Provide the full name on first mention.

3. Identify the author(s) of your source by profession or affiliation so that readers will understand the significance of what he or she has to say. Omit this if the speaker is someone readers are familiar with.

4. Use transitions into quotations to link the ideas they express to whatever point you are making.

5. If your lead-in to a quotation is a phrase, follow it with a comma. But if your lead-in can stand alone as a sentence, follow it with a colon.

6. Place the period at the end of a quotation or paraphrase, after the parenthetical citation, except with block quotations. (See page 131 for treatment of block quotations.)

5. Write Capsule Summaries of Entire Sources

Writers frequently have to summarize the content of an entire source in just a brief paragraph. Such summaries appear in the introduction to a volume of collected essays, in an opening section of scholarly articles in which the author reviews previously published literature on the topic, and at the end of books or articles in annotated bibliographies or works cited lists. The purpose of these is to let other scholars know about sources they might also want to consult.

If your class is working on a common topic, your instructor may ask the class to assemble a working bibliography of sources all of you have found, including a brief summary of each one to let other students know what the source contains. This is called an "annotated bibliography." Following is some advice on creating capsule summaries and annotated bibliographies.

1. As explained in Chapter 2, "Reading Arguments," read and annotate the entire source, noting claims, reasons, the subdivisions into which the text breaks down, and definitions of words you looked up.

2. Working with one subdivision at a time, write paraphrases of the main ideas in each. Decide how much specific evidence would be appropriate

Sample Entry in an Annotated Bibliography

Here is an annotated bibliography entry for Ross's National Trust source.

> Moe, Richard. "Battling Teardowns, Saving Neighborhoods." *The National Trust for Historic Preservation*, 28 June 2006, www.nationaltrust.org/news/news/2006/20060628_speech_sf.html.
>
> In this transcript of a speech given to a San Francisco civic organization, Moe, who is president of the National Trust for Historic Preservation, argues that builders should respect the integrity of older neighborhoods and that local residents should join the Trust's efforts to block the teardown trend, which is fueled by rising real estate values, homebuyers' desire for bigger houses, and fatigue with life in the distant suburbs. Teardowns "wreck neighborhoods" by removing trees and backyards, blocking the sun, ruining historic character, raising taxes so that poorer residents are forced out, and generating environmental waste. Communities can organize to fight teardowns by applying for historical designation or other kinds of government regulations on building as well as offering incentives for realtors and new buyers to respect neighborhood quality.

to include, depending on the purpose of your summary. As with any paraphrase, work from memory and recheck the original later for accuracy.

3. You may include brief direct quotations, but avoid quoting whole sentences. That is not efficient.

4. Join your paraphrases into a coherent and smooth paragraph.

5. Edit your summary to reduce repetitions and to combine points into single sentences where possible.

Note that a good capsule summary restates the main points; it does not just describe them.

Not: Moe gives three reasons for the rise of the teardown trend.

But: Moe argues that the teardown trend is fueled by rising real estate values, homebuyers' desire for bigger houses, and fatigue with life in the distant suburbs.

6. Dialogue about Sources

Inside or outside of class, any conversations you can have about your research with others researching the same topic will help you get an angle and an understanding of your sources. This is the reason many scholars keep blogs—a blog is a place to converse about ideas. Your instructor may set up an electronic bulletin board for students to chat about their research, or you might make your own blog with friends and start chatting.

INCORPORATING AND DOCUMENTING SOURCE MATERIAL

We turn now to the more technical matter of how to incorporate source material in your own writing and how to document it. You incorporate material through direct quotation or through summary or paraphrase; you document material by naming the writer and providing full publication details of the source—a two-step process. In academic writing, documenting sources is essential, with one exception: You do not need to document sources of factual information that can easily be found in common references, such as an encyclopedia or atlas, or of common knowledge. See page 164 in Chapter 7, "Ethical Writing and Plagiarism," for more explanation of the concept of common knowledge.

Different Styles of Documentation

Different disciplines have specific conventions for documentation. In the humanities, the most common style is the Modern Language Association (MLA). In the physical, natural, and social sciences, the American Psychological Association (APA) style is most often used. We will illustrate both in the examples that follow. Both MLA and APA use parenthetical citations in the text and simple, alphabetical bibliographies at the end, making revision and typing much easier. (For a detailed explanation of these two styles, visit the websites for the MLA and the APA.)

In both MLA and APA formats, you provide some information in the body of your paper and the rest of the information under the heading "Works Cited" (MLA) or "References" (APA) at the end of your paper. The following summarizes the essentials of both systems.

MLA Style

In parentheses at the end of both direct and indirect quotations, supply the last name of the author of the source and the exact page number(s) where the quoted or paraphrased words appear. Online sources often have no page numbers. If an online source is a PDF file, it should have page numbers. You need to use them. If the name of the author appears in your sentence that leads into the quotation, omit it in the parentheses.

Direct quotation with source identified in the lead-in:

> According to Jessie Sackett, a member of the U.S. Green Building Council, home ownership is "the cornerstone of the American dream. Recently, however, we've realized that keeping that dream alive for future generations means making some changes to how we live today" (36).

Indirect quotation with source cited in parenthetical citation:

> A spokesperson for the U.S. Green Building Council reminds us that home ownership is fundamental to the American dream; however, in order to preserve that dream for the generations to come, we need to develop more energy efficient houses and lifestyles today (Sackett 36).

APA Style

In parentheses at the end of direct or indirect quotations, place the author's last name, the date published, and the page number(s) where the cited material appears. If the author's name appears in the sentence, the date of publication should follow it in parentheses; the page number still comes at the end of the sentence. Unlike MLA, the APA style uses commas between the parts of the citation and "p." or "pp." before the page numbers. For an example paper using APA documentation, see pages 177–180.

Direct quotation with source cited in the lead-in:

> Jessie Sackett (2006), a member of the U.S. Green Building Council, writes, "Owning a home is the cornerstone of the American dream. Recently, however, we've realized that keeping that dream alive for future generations means making some changes to how we live today" (p. 36).

Indirect quotation with source cited in parenthetical citation:

> A spokesperson for the U.S. Green Building Council reminds us that home ownership is fundamental to the American dream; however, in order to preserve that dream for the generations to come, we need to develop more energy efficient houses and lifestyles today (Sackett, 2006, p. 36).

Direct Quotations

Direct quotations are exact words taken from a source. The simplest direct quotations are whole sentences worked into your text, as illustrated in the following excerpt. Any citations in the text of your paper must match up with an entry on the works cited or reference list.

MLA Style

> Richard Moe of the National Trust for Historic Preservation explains, "The problem is that too many people try to impose their preference for suburban-style mini-mansions on smaller scale neighborhoods where they just don't fit."

This source will be listed in the MLA Works Cited list as follows:

> Moe, Richard. "Battling Teardowns, Saving Neighborhoods." The National Trust for Historic Preservation, 28 June 2006, www.nationaltrust.org/news/news/2006/20060628_speech_sf.html.

APA Style

> Richard Moe (2006) of the National Trust for Historic Preservation explains, "The problem is that too many people try to impose their preference for suburban-style mini-mansions on smaller scale neighborhoods where they just don't fit."

This source will be listed in the APA reference list as follows:

> Moe, R. (2006, June 28). Battling teardowns, saving neighborhoods.
> Retrieved from *The National Trust for Historic Preservation* website:
> http://www.nationaltrust.org/news/2006/20060628_speech_sf.html

Altering Direct Quotations with Ellipses and Square Brackets

Although there is nothing wrong with quoting whole sentences, it is often more economical to quote some words or parts of sentences from the original in your own sentences. When you do this, use *ellipses* (three evenly spaced periods) to signify the omission of words from the original; use square *brackets* to substitute words, to add words for purposes of clarification, and to change the wording of a quotation so that it fits gracefully into your own sentence. (If ellipses already appear in the material you are quoting and you are omitting additional material, place your ellipses in square brackets to distinguish them.)

The following passages illustrate quoted words integrated into the sentence, using ellipses and square brackets. The citation is in MLA style.

Square Brackets   Use square brackets to indicate any substitutions or alterations to a direct quotation.

Original passage:

> Teardowns wreck neighborhoods. They spread through a community like a cancer, destroying the character and livability that are a neighborhood's lifeblood.

Passage worked into the paper: Part of the quotation has been turned into paraphrase.

> Moe compares the teardown trend to a cancer on the community: "Teardowns wreck neighborhoods. They [destroy] the character and livability that are a neighborhood's lifeblood."

Ellipses   Use three spaced periods to indicate where words have been removed from a direct quotation.

Original passage:

> Almost every one of these new, large homes is made out of wood—roughly three-quarters of an acre of forest. Much of the destructive logging around the world is fueled by our demand for housing. But homebuilding doesn't have to translate into forest destruction. By using smart design and forest-friendly products, builders can create new homes that save trees and money.
>
> Many houses today are still built using outdated, inefficient construction methods. About one-sixth of the wood delivered to a construction site is never used, but simply hauled away as waste.

Passage worked into the paper: Two entire sentences have been removed, replaced with ellipses, because they were not relevant to the point Ross was making. There are no quotation marks because this will be a blocked quotation in the paper.

> Almost every one of these new, large homes is made out of wood—roughly three-quarters of an acre of forest. Much of the destructive logging around the world is fueled by our demand for housing. . . . Many houses today are still built using outdated, inefficient construction methods. About one-sixth of the wood delivered to a construction site is never used, but simply hauled away as waste.

Using Block Quotations

In MLA style, if a quoted passage runs to more than four lines of text in your essay, indent it one-half inch (five spaces of type) from the left margin, double-space it as with the rest of your text, and omit quotation marks. In block quotations, a period is placed at the end of the final sentence, followed by one space and the parenthetical citation.

> In a consumer society, when people see their neighbors driving a new car, they think they need to buy a new one too. This is called "keeping up with the Joneses." Gregg Easterbrook has coined a new phrase, "call and raise the Joneses." He explains his new term this way:
>
>> In call-and-raise-the-Joneses, Americans feel compelled not just to match the material possessions of others, but to stay ahead. Bloated houses, for one, arise from a desire to call-and-raise-the-Joneses—surely not from a belief that a seven-thousand-square-foot house that comes right up against the property setback line would be an ideal place in which to dwell. (140)

In APA style, use the block form for quotations of more than forty words. Indent the block five spaces from the left margin. Double-space all blocked quotations.

Indirect Quotations

Indirect quotations are paraphrases or summaries of a source. Here is how this quotation might be incorporated in a paper as an indirect quotation.

MLA Style

> A spokesperson for the U.S. Green Building Council reminds us that home ownership is fundamental to the American dream; however, in order to preserve that dream for the generations to come, we need to develop more energy efficient houses and lifestyles today (Sackett 36).

Leading into Direct Quotations

Direct quotations need to be set up, not dropped into your paper. Setting up a quotation means leading into it with words of your own. A lead-in may be a short introductory tag such as "According to Smith," if you have already introduced Smith, but lead-ins usually need more thought. You need to connect the quotation to the ideas surrounding it in the original source.

Provide enough of the original context to fit the quotation coherently into your paragraph. You may need to paraphrase some of the surrounding sentences from the original source from which the quotation was taken. If you have not done so already, you may need to introduce the speaker of the words, along with his or her credentials if the speaker is an important writer or authority.

Here is an example of a quotation that does not fit coherently into the student's paper.

Quotation dropped in:

> Affluent Americans are buying new super-sized homes in older, urban residential areas. These lots were once occupied by historic and humble homes. "Teardowns wreck neighborhoods. They [destroy] the character and livability that are a neighborhood's lifeblood" (Moe).

Here is how Julie Ross led into the same quotation so that her readers would know more about the speaker and his point.

Quotation worked in:

Introduces the speaker.

Provides context for the quotation.

Parenthetical citation of author's name not needed because author is cited in text.

> Affluent Americans are buying new super-sized homes in older, urban residential areas. These lots were once occupied by historic and humble houses. The older houses are now known as "teardowns." In their place, towering "McMansions" dominate the street. Richard Moe, President of the National Trust for Historic Preservation, reports that teardowns affect over 300 U.S. cities, with a total of 75,000 older houses razed each year. Moe compares the teardown trend to a cancer on the community: "Teardowns wreck neighborhoods. They [destroy] the character and livability that are a neighborhood's lifeblood."

The entry in the Works Cited list would appear as follows:

> Sackett, Jessie. "The Green American Dream: LEED for Homes Is Currently Being Piloted." *The LEED Guide: Environmental Design & Construction,* vol. 9, no. 6, 2006, pp. 36+. *Academic OneFile.* www.academiconefile. com/leedguide/2006/jsackett/the_green_american_dream.htm.

APA Style

A spokesperson for the U.S. Green Building Council reminds us that home ownership is fundamental to the American dream; however, in order to preserve that dream for the generations to come, we need to develop more energy efficient houses and lifestyles today (Sackett, 2006, p. 36).

The entry in the References list would appear as follows:

Sackett, J. (2006). The green American dream: LEED for homes is currently being piloted. *The LEED Guide: Environmental Design & Construction.* 9.6 (2006): 36+. Retrieved from Academic OneFile.

In-Text References to Electronic Sources

The conventions just described apply to print sources. Adapt the examples to Internet and other electronic sources. Because you must include the electronic sources in your works-cited or reference list, your in-text citations should connect the material quoted or paraphrased in your text to the matching work or posting on the list. Therefore, your in-text citation should begin with the author's name or, lacking that, the title of the work or posting. The APA format requires that you also include the posting date.

CREATING WORKS CITED AND REFERENCE LISTS

At the end of your paper, include a bibliography of all sources that you quoted, paraphrased, or summarized. If you are using MLA style, your heading for this list will be *Works Cited;* if you are using APA style, it will be *References.* In either case, the list is in alphabetical order based on either the author's (or editor's) last name or—in the case of unidentified authors—the first word of the title, not counting the articles *a, an, the.* The entire list is double-spaced both within and between entries. See the Works Cited page of the sample student paper at the end of this chapter for the correct indentation and spacing. Note that MLA format requires that the first line of each entry be typed flush with the left margin; subsequent lines of each entry are indented half an inch (five spaces on a keyboard). The APA recommends the same indentation.

The following examples illustrate the correct MLA and APA style for the types of sources you will most commonly use.

MLA Style for Entries in the Works Cited List

The following pages show examples of how to cite the most commonly used kinds of sources in papers for first-year writing assignments. When putting entries into the Works Cited list,

- Put all entries, regardless of their genres and media, in alphabetical order according to the first word in each entry. This will usually be the lead author's or editor's last name or—if no author is named—the first word in the title that is not an article (*a, an, the*). See page 134 for an example.

- Do not number the entries.
- Double-space within and between entries; the list should look like the spacing in the rest of the paper.
- Begin each entry at the left margin and indent all subsequent lines by five spaces (one-half inch).
- Italicize titles of books, periodicals like magazines and journals, films, and other major works like websites and blogs.
- Put quotation marks around titles of articles and essays contained in periodicals or books of collected works, and around pages or posts found on a website.
- Capitalize all words in titles and subtitles except for articles (*a, an, the*), coordinating conjunctions (*and, or, but*) and prepositions. Always capitalize the first and last word of a title, regardless of its part of speech.
- Include subtitles of works; separate them from the title with a colon.

Books

The first word in each entry on the Works Cited list must match the in-text citation. The essential items are the

1. author's or editor's name, followed by a period (unless no author or editor is listed);
2. title of the work, followed by a period;
3. publisher, followed by a comma; and
4. date of publication.

Do not cite page numbers for chapters or portions of entire books. Do cite page numbers for items in an anthology or collected set of works.

Book by a Single Author

> Urrea, Luis Alberto. *The Devil's Highway: A True Story.* Little, Brown, 2004.

Two or More Books by the Same Author Instead of repeating the author's name in your Works Cited list, give the name in the first entry only. For subsequent works, use three hyphens in place of the name, followed by a period. Arrange the works in alphabetical order according to the first word in the title of the work, excluding articles (*a, an, the*).

> Obama, Barack. *The Audacity of Hope: Thoughts on Reclaiming the American Dream.* Crown, 2006.
>
> ———. *Dreams from My Father: A Story of Race and Inheritance.* 1995. Three Rivers, 2004.

Note: For republished works, include the original date of publication immediately after the book's title.

Book by Two Authors Put the name of the principal author (first author) first, beginning with his or her last name. Place a comma after the first author's name. Put the name of second author in the regular order from first name to last name.

> Small, Gary, and Gigi Vorgan. *iBrain: Surviving the Technological Alteration of the Modern Mind.* HarperCollins, 2008.

Book by Three or More Authors Use only the first author's name and the Latin abbreviation et al., meaning "and others."

> Bellah, Robert N., et al. *Habits of the Heart: Individualism and Commitment in American Life.* Harper, 1958.

Book with No Author or Editor Begin the citation with the title. In the Works Cited list, ignore articles *a, an,* and *the* when placing in alphabetical order.

> *The New York Times Guide to Essential Knowledge: A Desk Reference for the Curious Mind.* St. Martin's, 2004.

Book by a Corporate Author or Government Agency Treat the corporation or agency as an author. If the book author is also the publisher, begin with the title of the book.

> *MLA Handbook,* 8th ed., Modern Language Association of America. 2016.

Anthology or Edited Compilation Place a comma after the editor's name and add the word "editor."

> Shreve, Susan Richards, editor. *Dream Me Home Safely: Writers on Growing Up in America.* Houghton Mifflin, 2003.

Work in an Anthology For works in collections of essays, poetry, and short stories, put the author of the individual work first, followed by its title in quotation marks, then the title of the collection in italics. The editor's name follows in normal order. Note that entries for works in anthologies do include the inclusive page numbers of the selection.

> Nguyen, Bich Minh. "Toadstools." *Dream Me Home Safely: Writers on Growing Up in America,* edited by Susan Richards Shreve. Houghton Mifflin, 2003, pp. 129–32.

Two or More Works from the Same Anthology   If you are using more than one selection from an anthology, you will need three entries in your Works Cited list, one for the entire work, opening with the name of its editor, and one for each of the items, opening with the name of its author. Following the title of the work, you simply put the last name of the editor to refer your readers to the entire book, followed by the inclusive page numbers of each selection. Place each entry in its alphabetically determined spot on the Works Cited list, as illustrated below.

> Griffith, Patricia. "The Spiral Staircase." Shreve, pp. 73–81.

> MacDonald, Michael Patrick. "Spitting Image." Shreve, pp. 112–22.

> Shreve, Susan Richards, editor. *Dream Me Home Safely: Writers on Growing Up in America.* Houghton Mifflin, 2003.

Translation

> Eco, Umberto. *The Name of the Rose.* Translated by William Weaver, San Diego: Harcourt, 1983.

Later Edition of a Book   Directly after the title, abbreviate the edition number without italics.

> Williams, Joseph M. *Style: Ten Lessons in Clarity and Grace.* 9th ed., Pearson, 2007.

Preface, Introduction, Foreword or Afterword Not by the Book's Author or Editor   Open the entry with the name of the author of the part of the book; then provide the name of the section, followed by title of the book. If the book is a reprint, follow the title with the original date of publication. Use the word *by* before the author of the book. Indicate the inclusive page numbers for the part of the book you used as your source.

> Brogan, D. W. Introduction. *The Education of Henry Adams: An Autobiography.* 1918, by Henry Adams. Houghton, 1961, pp. v–xviii.

Reprinted Book   Directly after the title, include the original date of publication.

> Adams, Henry. *The Education of Henry Adams: An Autobiography.* 1918. Houghton, 1961.

One Volume of a Multivolume Work   Directly after the title of the work, indicate the volume number you used.

> Churchill, Winston. *A History of the English-speaking Peoples.* Vol. 3, Cassell, 1956–58.

More than One Volume of a Multivolume Work   After the title, indicate the total number of volumes in the work.

> Churchill, Winston. *A History of the English-speaking Peoples.* Cassell, 1956–58. 4 vols.

Book That Is Part of a Series   After the medium (print) put the name of the series and a series number for the work if available. Do not italicize the series title.

> Horning, Alice, and Anne Becker, editors. *Revision: History, Theory, and Practice.* Parlor Press, 2006. Reference Guides to Rhetoric and Composition.

Signed Article in a Reference Book   Cite the name of the author, the title of the entry, the title of the reference work, name of the editor, and publication information. Do not include page numbers if entries appear in alphabetical order.

> Zangwill, O. L. "Hypnotism, History of." *The Oxford Companion to the Mind.* Edited by Richard L. Gregory, Oxford UP, 1987.

Unsigned Article in a Reference Book   Open with the title of the entry. Include page numbers if entries do not appear in alphabetical order.

> "A Technical History of Photography." *The New York Times Guide to Essential Knowledge: A Desk Reference for the Curious Mind.* St. Martin's, 2004, pp. 104–12.

Religious Text   Italicize the title and provide names of editors and/or translators and the publication information.

> *The Holy Bible.* Revised Standard Version. World, 1962.

> *The Bhagavad Gita: According to Paramhansa Yogananda.* Edited by Swami Kriyananda, Crystal Clarity, 2008.

Articles in Periodicals

The essential items in entries for articles in periodicals are the

1. author's name, followed by a period;
2. title of the article, followed by a period, all in quotation marks;

3. title of the publication, italicized;
4. volume number (if given);
5. date (if given);
6. inclusive page numbers followed by a period.

Article in a Weekly Magazine   In the following example, the magazine was dated both July 6 and July 13. In such a case, use a comma between the two dates.

> Levy, Ariel. "Nora Knows What to Do." *The New Yorker*, 6, 13 July 2009, pp. 60–69.

Article in a Monthly Magazine   Abbreviate all months except May, June, and July.

> Mooney, Chris. "Climate Repair Made Simple." *Wired*, July 2008, pp. 128–33.

Article in a Print Newspaper   Give the day, month, year, and edition, if specified; use abbreviations. Give section and page number. If pages are not consecutive, put a plus sign after the first page number.

> Yoon, Carol Kaesuk. "Reviving the Lost Art of Naming the World." *The New York Times*, 11 Aug. 2009, natl. ed, pp. D1+.

Review   Open with name of reviewer and title of review, if there is one. Add "review of," not italicized, followed by the title of the work being reviewed, and its author or performer.

> Hofferth, Sandra. "Buying So Children Belong." Review of *Longing and Belonging: Parents, Children, and Consumer Culture*, by Allison J. Pugh. *Science*, 26 June 2009, p. 1674.

Editorial in a Newspaper—No Named Author

> "Disfigured Democracy: Health Care Extremism Exposes Our Uglier Side." Editorial. *The Dallas Morning News*, 13 Aug. 2009, p. A14.

Letter to the Editor of a Newspaper or Magazine

> Reed, Glenn. "Not Enough Fish in the Sea." Letter. *Harper's*, Aug. 2009, p. 5.

Article in a Journal with Volume Numbers   Put the volume number and the issue number after the title of the article, followed by the month (if given) and the year.

> Bracher, Mark. "How to Teach for Social Justice: Lessons from *Uncle Tom's Cabin* and Cognitive Science." *College English*, vol. 71, no. 4, Mar. 2009, pp. 363–88.

Other Genres as Sources

Advertisement in Print Medium   Open with the name of the item or service being advertised.

> Daedalus Books. Advertisement. *Harper's,* Aug. 2009, p. 6.

Art Reproduction   Treat art found in books in the same way you treat essays found in edited collections. Open the entry with the artist's name, followed by the title of the work and the date it was created, if available. Before the publication information, include where the original work of art may be found.

> O'Keefe, Georgia. *Light/17: Evening Star, No. V.* 1917. The Marion
> Koogler McNay Art Museum, San Antonio. Republished in *O'Keefe*
> *and Texas,* by Sharyn R. Udall. The Marion Koogler McNay Art
> Museum, 1998.

Personal Interview   Give the name of the person interviewed, the kind of interview (personal, telephone), and the date it took place.

> Coman, Carolyn. Telephone interview. 15 Aug. 2009.

Sources on the Internet

The essential items in entries for electronic sources are as follows (as available):

1. Name of author, editor (ed.), performer (perf.), or translator (trans.)
2. Title of work
3. Version or edition
4. Publisher of the site
5. Date last updated

Website or Independent Online Work   It is not necessary to include the URL of a website unless your reader would have difficulty finding the site through a search engine.

Example Entry for Entire Website

> Taylor, Paul, director. *Pew Hispanic Center.* Pew Research Center, 22 July
> 2009, www.pewhispanic.org.

Example Entry for Document Found on a Website

> Fry, Richard. "The Changing Pathways of Hispanic Youths into Adulthood."
> *Pew Hispanic Center.* Pew Research Center, 7 Oct. 2009, http://www.
> pewhispanic.org/2009/10/07/the-changing-pathways-of-hispanic-
> youths-into-adulthood/.

Personal Website   If the site has no title, use "home page" or other descriptive title. If there is no publisher noted, do not list one in your entry.

Langer, Ellen. Home page. 2009, ellenlanger.com.

Find the person responsible for the site by clicking on the links that tell more about the website. Clicking on "About" tells that Michael Dimock is the Director of the Pew Hispanic Center. If there is no author, editor, director, compiler, or corporate author, begin your works cited entry with the title of the website.

Date of most recent update of the site.

Title of the website.

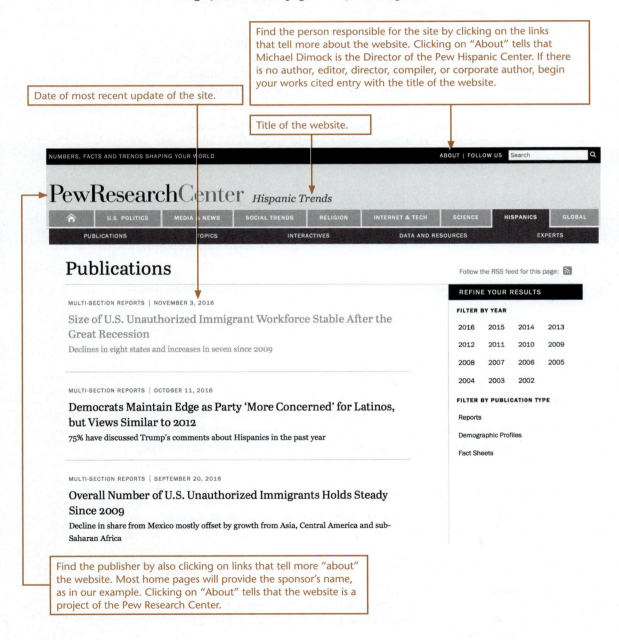

Find the publisher by also clicking on links that tell more "about" the website. Most home pages will provide the sponsor's name, as in our example. Clicking on "About" tells that the website is a project of the Pew Research Center.

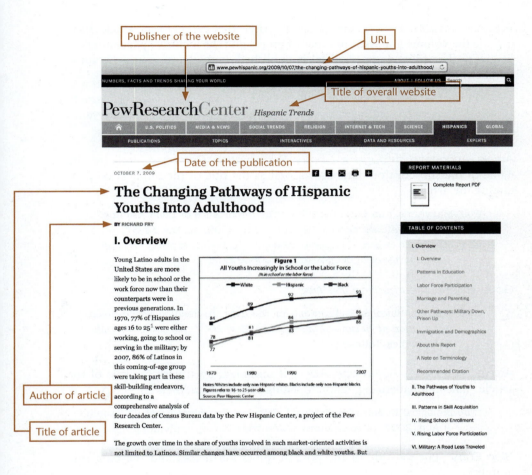

Article in an Online Newspaper   Put the website in italics; follow with the date of the article, followed by the URL.

> Hotz, Robert L. "Some Creative Destruction on a Cosmic Scale: Scientists Say Asteroid Blasts, Once Thought Apocalyptic, Fostered Life on Earth by Carrying Water and Protective Greenhouse Gas." *The Wall Street Journal,* 14 Aug. 2009, www.wsj.com/articles/SB125020578491030557.

Article in an Online Magazine

> MacFarquhar, Larissa. "Who Cares If Johnny Can't Read? The Value of Books Is Overstated." *Slate,* 17 April 1997, www.slate.com/articles/news_and_politics/high_concept/1997/04/who_cares_if_johnny_cant_read.html.

Article in an Online Scholarly Journal After the author and article title, include the volume and issue number (if given) and the inclusive page numbers (if given). The following periodical is published annually, so it has a volume number only.

> O'Dwyer, Kathleen. "Nietzsche's Reflections on Love." *Minerva—An Internet Journal of Philosophy*, vol. 12, Nov. 2008, pp. 37–77, www.minerva.mic.ul.ie/vol12/Nietzsche.pdf.

Article Accessed through a Library Subscription Database Italicize the name of the subscription database as well as the title of the publication containing the article.

> Wolf, Maryanne, and Mirit Barzillai. "The Importance of Deep Reading." *Educational Leadership*, vol. 66, 6 Mar. 2009, pp. 66: 32–37. *Academic Search Complete*, www.ebscohost.com/ezproxy/wolf_m/the-importance-of-deep-reading/030609.htm.

Government Document on the Web

> United States, National Endowment for the Arts. *To Read or Not to Read: A Question of National Consequence,* Nov. 2007, www.arts.gov/sites/default/files/ToRead.pdf.

Article in an Online Reference Work If unsigned, open with the title of the article. When alphabetizing, ignore opening article (*a, an, the*).

> "The Biological Notion of Individual." *Stanford Encyclopedia of Philosophy,* 9 Aug. 2007, plato.stanford.edu/entries/biology-individual/.

Blog Entry Put the title of the post in quotation marks and the blog title in italics.

> Postrel, Virginia. "Naomi Wolf and the Phenomenology of Angelina Jolie." *Dynamist,* 19 June 2009, vpostrel.com/deep-glamour/naomi-wolf-and-the-phenomenology-of-angelina-jolie.

Broadcast or Published Interview Open with the names of the interviewee or interviewees; then provide the title of the interview, followed by the interviewer. Include the date of the interview and the URL.

> Ganguly, Sumit, and Minxin Pei. "Balancing India and China." Interview by Jayshree Bajoria. *Council on Foreign Relations*, 6 Aug. 2009, www.cfr.org/india/balancing-india-china/p19979.

Student Sample of a Research Paper in MLA Style

See pages 152–161 for a student's paper using MLA documentation.

Using APA Documentation Style

The American Psychological Association style of documentation is used not only in the field of psychology but also in education, anthropology, social work, business, and other behavioral and social sciences. The conventions of APA style aim to achieve an objective and impersonal tone. In the text, authors are usually referred to by last name only, and direct quotations are rare.

Like MLA, the APA system requires that a writer acknowledge the source of all direct quotations, paraphrased and summarized ideas from sources, and information that is not common knowledge. Citing is a two-step process: a brief in-text reference to the author and date of publication, and a longer entry with complete bibliographical information in the References list at the end of the article or book. Citing page numbers is required for direct quotations and highly specific data but not for summarizing or paraphrasing ideas found throughout a text.

In-text Citations

For both direct and indirect quotations, including paraphrased information that is not common knowledge, the basic in-text citation provides the last name of the author of the source, directly followed by the year the source was published. The following examples show options for citing in-text.

Paraphrased Reference to Source by One Author Named in the Sentence

> The playground is a space where gender identities are constructed. Paechter (2007) argues that boys who are physically passive on the playground move into the marginal spaces occupied by girls and younger children, and thus become stigmatized by other boys as effeminate.

Paraphrased Reference to Source by One Author Cited Only in Parenthetical Citation

> The playground is a space where gender identities are constructed. Boys who are physically passive on the playground move into the marginal spaces occupied by girls and younger children, and thus become stigmatized by other boys as effeminate (Paechter, 2007).

Direct Quotation with Author Named in the Sentence

> According to Yoon (2009) anthropologists have found that people around the world create remarkably similar categories when labeling plants and animals, a phenomenon known as folk taxonomy. Yoon finds consensus about such categories as trees, vines, and bushes especially interesting

"since there is no way to define a tree versus a bush" (p. D4). In naming the world around them, people appear "unconsciously to follow a set of unwritten rules" (p. D1).

Direct Quotation with Author Named in Parenthetical Citation

Anthropologists have found that people around the world create remarkably similar categories when labeling plants and animals, a phenomenon known as folk taxonomy (Yoon, 2009). Consensus about such categories as trees, vines, and bushes is especially interesting "since there is no way to define a tree versus a bush" (p. D4). In naming the world around them, people appear "unconsciously to follow a set of unwritten rules" (p. D1).

Source with Two Authors   Give both authors' last names each time you refer to the source. If you name them as part of your sentence, use *and* to join them: Wolf and Barzillai (2009). If you name them in parentheses, use an ampersand as shown in the example below.

Reading is far from our other natural human functions of seeing, moving, speaking, and thinking. Reading is an invented cognitive function, and understanding how it works illustrates the amazing plasticity of the brain (Wolf & Barzillai, 2009).

Source with Three or More Authors   In your in-text citation, give all authors' last names in your first reference to the work. Write out *and* when the list is part of your sentence. Subsequent references should give only the first author's name followed by et al. (not in italics).

First reference:

Radeloff, Hammer, and Stewart (2005) studied the impact of housing density on forests in the Midwestern United States.

Later references:

Radeloff et al. (2005) argue that rural sprawl has more impact on forests than urban sprawl because even though rural sprawl is less dense, its effects are spread over larger areas that once were forests.

Two Authors with the Same Last Name   Include identifying initials before each last name.

S. Young (2007) complains that scientists study earth-eating, or geophagia, only from the standpoint of their own disciplinary interests. Thus, there is no "global perspective of all the possible benefits and all the possible negative consequences of geopaghia" (p. 67).

Citations within Quotations   You will often find that your source cites other sources. Do not put these sources on your References list unless you also read them and used them in your paper. When quoting, include the citations as they appear in the passage you are quoting.

> Cantarero (2007) notes that moral, political, and economic factors enter in to what people think is good to eat. He offers the example of advertising:
>> By associating values with products, producers seek to increase their sales. According to the principle of incorporation (Rozin and Nemeroff, 1989; Fischler, 1992) subjects acquire the symbolic qualities of ingested food. Thus, ingestion goes beyond the satisfaction of hunger, deep into the sphere of mentalities and internalizes an ideological language which is "artificially" built. (p. 207)

If you have more than one source for the same point or information, you put both in the parenthetical citation.

With blocked quotations, place final period before the parenthetical citation.

Long Quotations   For direct quotations of forty or more words, omit quotation marks and display the quotation as a block of text set in from the left margin by about one-half inch (in the same place as a new paragraph's opening). Double-space the entire quotation. See the example above on Citations within Quotations.

Work with No Author or Editor   If no author or editor is named, you will use the title of the work in both in-text citations and Reference entries. If the title is long, you should abbreviate it. Use double quotation marks around the title of an article, a chapter, or a web page. Italicize the title of a periodical, book, or report. The example below shows a website.

> The Law School Aptitude Test (LSAT) measures ability to read and comprehend in-depth texts with insight, to draw "reasonable inferences" from readings, and to analyze and evaluate the reasoning of others' arguments ("About the LSAT," 2009).

Personal Communications   Personal communications such as letters and interviews are cited in text only, as in the following example.

> Carolyn Coman described her use of storyboarding to focus on the emotional impact of significant scenes in her fiction (C. Coman, personal communication, August 15, 2009).

Reference List Examples

Below are examples of how to cite the most commonly used kinds of sources in papers using the APA style of documentation. First, some general advice:

- Begin the list on a new page and center the word "References" at the top. (Do not enclose it in quotation marks.)

- Put all entries, regardless of their genres and media, in alphabetical order according to the author's (or editor's) last name, followed by the initials of the author's given name or names.
- If no author is named, use the first word in the title that is not an article (*a, an, the*). See page 179 for an example.
- Put the year, month, and date of publication immediately after the author's (or editor's) name, in parentheses.
- Do not number the entries.
- Double-space within and between entries; the list should look like the spacing in the rest of the paper.
- Begin each entry at the left margin and indent all subsequent lines by five spaces (one-half inch).
- Italicize titles of books and periodicals like magazines and journals.
- Do not enclose titles of articles in quotation marks.
- Capitalize only the first words of titles and subtitles, unless they are proper nouns (names).
- Capitalize the full names of periodicals, journals, and newspapers.

See the following list of examples for more help with citing specific kinds of sources.

Books

Book by a Single Author

> Paechter, C. F. (2007). *Being boys, being girls: Learning masculinities and femininities.* New York: McGraw-Hill.

Two or More Books by the Same Author   List the works in order of publication, with the earliest first.

> Obama, B. (2004). *Dreams from my father: A story of race and inheritance.* New York: Three Rivers. (Original work published 1995)

> Obama, B. (2006). *The audacity of hope: Thoughts on reclaiming the American dream.* New York: Crown.

Book by Two or More Authors   List all authors by last name and initials. Put commas between items in this list. Use an ampersand (&) before the final name.

> Small, G., & Vorgan, G. (2008). *iBrain: Surviving the technological alteration of the modern mind.* New York: HarperCollins.

> Booth, W., Colomb, G., & Williams, J. (2003). *The craft of research* (2nd ed.). Chicago: U of Chicago Press.

Book by a Corporate Author or Government Agency   Treat the corporation or agency as an author. If the author and publisher are the same, put "author" after the place of publication.

> American Psychological Association. (2010). *Publication manual of the American Psychological Association* (6th ed.). Washington DC: Author.

Edited Compilation   Between the editor's name and the date, put the abbreviation for editor(s).

> MacClancy, J., Henry, J., & Macbeth, H. (Eds.). (2007). *Consuming the inedible: Neglected dimensions of food choice.* New York: Berghahn Books.

Selection in an Edited Compilation   For articles in edited works, put the author of the individual work first, followed by the year of publication, and then the title of the article, followed by the word "In" and the editor or editors' names and the title of the collected work. The inclusive pages of the selection follow the title of the book, in parentheses. End the citation with place and name of publisher.

> Young, S. (2007). A vile habit? The potential biological consequences of geophagia, with special attention to iron. In J. MacClancy, J. Henry, & H. Macbeth (Eds.), *Consuming the inedible: Neglected dimensions of food choice* (pp. 67–79). New York: Berghahn Books.

Edition Other than the First   Put the edition number in parentheses after the title.

> Williams, J. M. (2007). *Style: Ten lessons in clarity and grace* (9th ed.). New York: Pearson Longman.

Translation   Put the translator's initials and last name, followed by the abbreviation for translator in parentheses, after the book's title.

> Durkheim, E. (1984). *The division of labor in society.* (W. D. Halls, Trans.). New York: Free Press. (Original work published 1933)

Preface, Introduction, Foreword or Afterword Not by the Book's Author or Editor   Open the entry with the name of the author of the part of the book; then put the date in parentheses and write out the name of the section written by this author. Follow with publication information for the rest of the book. Do not give page numbers in the References list.

> Coser, L. A. (1984). Introduction. In E. Durkheim, *The division of labor in society.* (W. D. Halls, Trans.). New York: Free Press. (Original work published 1933)

Reprinted Book   Indicate original date of publication in parentheses.

> Obama, B. (2004). *Dreams from my father: A story of race and inheritance.* New York: Three Rivers. (Original work published 1995)

Note: The in-text citation should include both dates. (2004/1995).

One Volume of a Multivolume Work   Directly after the author, indicate the inclusive dates of the volumes. After the title of the work, indicate in parentheses the volume number you used.

> Churchill, W. (1956–58). *A history of the English-speaking peoples* (Vol. 3). London: Cassell.

Article in a Reference Book   Include inclusive page numbers for the entry after the title of the book. Put parentheses around page number or numbers.

> Zangwill, O. L. (1987). "Hypnotism, history of." In R. L. Gergory (Ed.), *The Oxford companion to the mind* (pp. 330–334.) New York: Oxford University Press.

Unsigned Article in a Reference Book   Open with the title of the entry. Put parentheses around page numbers.

> A technical history of photography. (2004). *The New York Times guide to essential knowledge: A desk reference for the curious mind* (pp. 104–112). New York: St. Martin's.

Articles in Periodicals

For newspaper articles, use p. and pp. before page number. For magazine and journal articles, do not use p. or pp. Instead, put volume # in italics followed by the page numbers, separated with a comma.

Article in a Newspaper   Give the day, month, year, and edition if specified. List all page numbers if the article appeared on discontinuous pages.

> Yoon, C. K. (2009, August 11). Reviving the lost art of naming the world. *The New York Times,* pp. D1, D4.

Article in a Monthly Magazine

> Mooney, C. (2008, July). Climate repair made simple. *Wired,* 128–133.

Article in a Weekly Magazine   Include the day as well as the month and year.

Gladwell, M. (2009, October 19). "Offensive play: How different are dogfighting and football?" *The New Yorker*, 50–59.

Article in a Journal Paginated by Volume   Put the volume number, a period, and the issue number after the title of the article. Put the month (if given) and the year in parentheses. Include inclusive page numbers for the article.

Bracher, M. (2009, March). How to teach for social justice: Lessons from *Uncle Tom's Cabin* and cognitive science. *College English 71*(4), 363–388.

Article in a Journal Paginated by Issue   Put the issue number in parentheses after the volume. The volume number is italicized. The issue number is not.

Wolf, M., & Barzillai M. (2009, March). The importance of deep reading. *Educational Leadership, 66*(6), 32–37.

Newspaper Article with an Anonymous Author   Open citation with title of the article. When alphabetizing, ignore opening articles (*a, an, the*).

Moon travel uncertain. (2009, August 14). *Dallas Morning News*, p. 12A.

Review   Open with name of reviewer and title of review, if there is one. Put "Review of," followed by the item being reviewed, all in square brackets. Note that the volume number of the magazine is in italics, followed by a comma and the page number, not italicized.

Hofferth, S. (2009, June 26). Buying so children belong. [Review of the book *Longing and belonging: Parents, children, and consumer culture*]. *Science, 324*, 1674.

Editorial in a Newspaper—No Author Given   Put the genre (editorial) in square brackets.

Disfigured democracy: Health care extremism exposes our uglier side. (2009, August 13). [Editorial]. *Dallas Morning News*, p. A14.

Letter to the Editor of a Newspaper or Magazine   Put the genre (letter to the editor) in square brackets.

Meibers, R. (2009, July). Thou shall kill. [Letter to the editor]. *Harper's*, 4.

Advertisement in Print Medium

Daedalus Books. (2009, August). [Advertisement]. *Harper's*, 6.

Sources on the Internet

Article in an Online Newspaper   Put the title of the newspaper in italics, followed by the URL of the paper's website.

> Hotz, R. L. (2009, August 14). Creative destruction on a cosmic scale: Scientists say asteroid blasts, once thought apocalyptic, fostered life on earth by carrying water and protective greenhouse gas. *Wall Street Journal*. Retrieved from http://online.wsj.com/home-page

Article in a Journal Accessed through Library Subscription Database   Include the name of the database only if you think it unlikely that multiple databases would carry the article or that the article would be difficult to find.

Online Journal Article with Digital Object Identifier (DOI)   Because uniform resource locators (URLs) often change, a new method of locating online materials has been developed. Increasingly, you will find that articles have an alphanumeric identification string, usually located near the copyright date in the article. You can also find it in the bibliographic information in the library's full record display. Use the DOI, if available, instead of the URL from which you retrieved the online article. Include the issue number in italics after the journal title. Conclude the entry with inclusive page numbers and the DOI.

> McGrevey, M., & Kehre, D. (2009). Stewards of the public trust: Federal laws that serve servicemembers and student veterans. *New Directions for Student Services, 126*, 89–94. doi:10.1002/ss.320

Article in an Online Magazine without a DOI   If there is no DOI, conclude the entry with "retrieved from" and the URL.

> MacFarquhar, L. (1997, April 17). Who cares if Johnny can't read? The value of books is overstated. *Slate*. Retrieved from http://www.slate.com/id/3128/

Article in an Online Scholarly Journal without DOI   Volume number follows the journal title. If there is an issue number, it goes in parentheses after the volume number. In this case, there is no issue number because the journal is published annually.

> O'Dwyer, K. (2008). Nietzsche's reflections on love. *Minerva—An Internet Journal of Philosophy, 12*, 37–77. Retrieved from http://www.mic .ul. ie/stephen/vol12/Nietzsche.pdf

Article in an Online Encyclopedia or Reference Work   If the entry is unsigned, open with its title, as in the second example below.

> Botstein, L. (2005). Robert Maynard Hutchins and the University of Chicago. In J. Reiff, A. D. Keating, & J. R. Grossman (Eds.),

Encyclopedia of Chicago. Retrieved from http://www.encyclopedia
.chicagohistory.org

The biological notion of individual. (2007, August 9). In E. N. Zalta (Ed.),
Stanford Encyclopedia of Philosophy. Retrieved from http://plato
.stanford.edu/

Blog Post   Give the URL but not the title of the blog.

Postrel, V. (2009, June 19). Naomi Wolf and the phenomenology of Angelina
Jolie. [Web log message]. Retrieved from http://www.dynamist.com/
weblog/

Other Genres as Sources

Published or Broadcast Interview   Include the medium in which the interview was published.

Ganguly, S., & Pei, M. (2009, August 6). Interview by J. Bajoria. Balancing India and China. [Audio podcast]. Council on Foreign Relations.
Retrieved from http://www.cfr.org/

Personal Interviews   Personal communication such as interviews and letters are not included in the list of references in APA style. However, you need to cite them in the text as described on page 146.

Sample of a Research Paper in APA Style

See pages 177–180 for a paper using APA documentation.

STUDENT SAMPLE: A RESEARCH PAPER (MLA STYLE)

Ross 1

Standard heading

Julie Ross

ENGL 1301, Section 009

April 20, 2007

Professor Channell

Title centered

Why Residential Construction Needs to Get a Conscience

Entire essay is double-spaced

Introduction announces topic

Home ownership is a significant part of the American dream. Americans take great pride in putting down roots and raising a family in a good neighborhood. And, if a recent boom in residential construction is any indication, more Americans are realizing that dream. In addition to the number of new homes being built, the average home size has also grown significantly, almost twice as large as in the 1960s ("How to Build"). The question is: what is the impact of super-sized houses on our neighborhoods and our environment?

Poses issue the argument will address

No word breaks at end of lines

Author's last name and page number in MLA style

In big cities like Dallas, huge new houses are springing up in the outer-ring suburbs like Frisco and Flower Mound. The National Association of Homebuilders reports that the average size of a single-family home has grown from 983 square feet in 1950 to 2,434 square feet in 2005, "even as the average household shrunk from 3.4 to 2.6 people" (Brown 23). This desire for more living space keeps cities sprawling outward as developers look for open land. However, urban residential areas are also now impacted by new building. Affluent Americans are buying new super-sized homes in older, urban residential areas. These lots were once occupied by historic and humble houses. The older houses are now known as "teardowns." In their place, towering "McMansions" dominate the street. Richard Moe, President of the National Trust for Historic Preservation, reports

Full name and credentials of authors who have expertise

Ross 2

that teardowns affect over 300 U.S. cities, with a total of 75,000 older houses razed each year.

Moe compares the teardown trend to a cancer on the community: "Teardowns wreck neighborhoods. They [destroy] the character and livability that are a neighborhood's lifeblood." He sees three reasons for the rise in teardowns:

- In the past decade, the value of houses has doubled or tripled, except in some older neighborhoods. Developers look for these "'undervalued' properties" to build on.

- Homebuyers demand more space.

- Some homebuyers want to move from the "soulless . . . sprawling subdivisions" to close-in neighborhoods that have more character and more amenities, such as public transportation and local shopping.

Moe explains, "The problem is that too many people try to impose their preference for suburban-style mini-mansions on smaller scale neighborhoods where they just don't fit."

My neighborhood in Dallas, known as Lakewood Heights, has been plagued by more than its share of tearing down and building up. Once famous for its 1920s Craftsman and Tudor architecture, my quiet residential street is now marred by rows of McMansions, bustling traffic, and noisy, new construction. These colossal residences vary little in outward appearance from one to the next. "Starter mansions" as they are often called, have no particular architectural style and only remotely resemble Tudor or Craftsman styles. No matter where you look, these giants tower over their single-story neighbors, blocking the sunlight and peering into once-private backyards from their tall, garish peaks.

Annotations:

Paraphrases for information from source, quotations for opinions

Colon after full-sentence as introductory tag

Reasons against teardowns begin

Personal observation as support for this reason

Another reason against tearing down

Ross 3

A super-sized new home towers over its older next-door neighbor.

The builders and buyers of these giant homes are callous to community and environmental concerns. Preserving an old Dallas neighborhood's rich architectural history and green landscape is of little importance to them. For example, most McMansions occupy an extremely large footprint, leaving little or no yard space. Original homes in my neighborhood occupied about a third of their rectangular lot. This design permitted a sizable back yard with room for a small one-car garage as well as an inviting front lawn where children could play. By contrast, mega homebuilders show no appreciation for conventional site planning. They employ bulldozers to flatten the lot and uproot native trees. Their goal is to make room for as much house as possible, raking in more profit with each square foot. Furthermore, each tall fortress has a wide cold, concrete driveway leading to the grandiose two-Tahoe garage, equivalent to nearly half the size of my one-story house.

Ross 4

What was once a grassy lawn is now paved with concrete.

Only ten years ago pecan trees, the official state tree of Texas, and flowering magnolias graced every lawn on my block. These beautiful native trees, some over a century old, shaded our homes from the harsh Texas sun and our sidewalks from the triple-digit, summer heat. There is no way the new home owners' landscaping can replace what is lost. The charm of the neighborhood is being destroyed.

Aside from changing the face of my neighborhood, these monster houses, many selling for half a million or more, have skyrocketed property taxes and pushed out many older, lower-income, long-time residents. As a result, several senior citizens and other long-time residents of Lakewood have been forced to sell their homes and move to apartments. Many custom homeowners argue that more expensive, larger homes positively contribute to a neighborhood by increasing the resale value of smaller, older homes. This may be true to a certain extent. However, from a wider perspective, short-term gains in resale

Transition into another reason

Ross 5

prices are no compensation for the irreversible harm done to our neighborhoods.

But the destruction of a neighborhood is only half the story. These over-sized homes, and others like them everywhere, are irresponsible from a larger environmental perspective. According to Peter Davey, editor of the *Architectural Review*, "Buildings [residential and commercial combined] take up rather more than half of all our energy use: they add more to the pollution of the atmosphere than transport and manufacture combined." Not only is pollution a consequence of this surge in residential structure size, but also the building of larger homes drains our natural resources, such as lumber. The National Resource Defense Council notes that forested areas, necessary for absorbing greenhouse gas emissions, are being depleted by the super-sizing trend in residential building:

> Almost every one of these new, large homes is made out of wood—roughly three-quarters of an acre of forest. Much of the destructive logging around the world is fueled by our demand for housing. . . . Many houses today are still built using outdated, inefficient construction methods. About one-sixth of the wood delivered to a construction site is never used, but simply hauled away as waste. And much of the wood that goes into the frame of a house is simply unnecessary. ("How to Build")

Obviously, residential construction must "go green" in an effort to save valuable resources and conserve energy. But what does it mean to "go green"? As Earth Advantage, a green building certification organization, explains: "Green building entails energy efficiency, indoor air quality, durability and minimal site impact" (Kaleda). However, whether a home can be designated as "green" depends on more than just

[margin notes:]

Double-space blocked quotations; use no quotation marks

Period ends sentence. Ellipses of three dots indicates material omitted

With block form, period goes before parenthetical citation

Ross 6

energy-efficient construction methods and materials. According to Martin John Brown, an ecologist and independent consultant, green homebuilding is being used to describe a wide range of residential construction, and not all homes should qualify. Essentially, while some homebuilders are selling "environmentally-friendly" design, the epic scale of these new homes outweighs any ecological benefits provided through materials and construction methods. So, size does matter. A recent article in the *Journal of Industrial Energy*, published by M.I.T. Press, reports that a 1,500 square foot house with "mediocre energy-performance standards" will consume far less energy than a 3,000 square foot house with all the latest energy-saving materials and details (Wilson 284). In Boston, a house rated "poor" in terms of energy standards used 66% less energy than one rated "good" but twice the size (Wilson 282).

For articles by reporters or staff writers, rather than experts and authorities, their names can be cited parenthetically only

Brown argues that practically minded, ecologically conscious homebuilding should be part of our overall effort to decrease our consumption of limited resources and energy. Evidence from the Department of Energy supports his claim: "From 1985 to 2002, total residential energy consumption per capita climbed eight percent, and residential consumption for the nation—the figure most relevant to global effects like carbon dioxide (CO_2) emissions—climbed 32 percent" (Brown 23).

Unfortunately, many Americans who can afford it won't stop buying environmentally irresponsible, un-humble abodes. Their motives may stem from the competitive nature of consumer society. When people see their neighbors driving a new car, they think they need to buy a new one too. This is called "keeping up with the Joneses." Discussing the supersized house, best-selling author Gregg Easterbrook has coined a new phrase, "call and raise the Joneses." As he explains it,

Ross 7

> In call-and-raise-the-Joneses, Americans feel compelled not just
> to match the material possessions of others, but to stay ahead.
> Bloated houses . . . arise from a desire to call-and-raise-the-
> Joneses—surely not from a belief that a seven-thousand-square-
> foot house that comes right up against the property setback line
> would be an ideal place in which to dwell. (140)

Daniel Chiras, the author of *The Natural House: A Complete Guide to Healthy, Energy-Efficient, Environmental Homes,* warns: "People tell themselves that if they can afford a 10,000-square-foot house, then that's what they should have . . . but I wonder if the earth can afford it" (qtd. in Iovine).

Fortunately, other Americans are starting to recognize the folly of buying more space than they need. A survey by Lowe's and Harris Interactive found that "46% of homeowners admit to wasting up to half of their home" ("Are McMansions Giving Way"). Felicia Oliver of *Professional Builder* magazine suggests that the marriage of conservation and construction is the next natural step in the evolution of residential building. One example of a builder taking this step is the Cottage Company in Seattle, which specializes in "finely detailed and certified-green" houses of between 1,000 and 2,000 square feet. Company co-owner Linda Pruitt says Cottage Company houses "'live as big' as McMansions because they're better designed, with features like vaulted ceilings and abundant built-ins. 'It's kind of like the design of a yacht,' she says. The theme is quality of space, not quantity" (qtd. in Brown 24).

Even Richard Moe of the National Trust for Historic Preservation admits that responsible new construction has a place in older neighborhoods:

Margin notes:

Cite author of article, not speaker. Use "qtd." to indicate quotation appeared in the source

If no author, use shortened form of title
Shows possible solution to problem

Ross 8

Trees tower over this stretch of original modest-scale homes in Lakewood Heights, reminding us of what is being lost.

No one is saying that homebuyers shouldn't be able to alter or expand their home to meet their needs, just as no one is saying that older neighborhoods should be frozen in time like museum exhibits. A neighborhood is a living thing, and change is both inevitable and desirable. The challenge is to manage change so that it respects the character and distinctiveness that made these neighborhoods so appealing in the first place.

This is the challenge that must be met in my own neighborhood. If new construction and additions are as architecturally interesting as the older homes and comparable with them in size and footprint, preserving lawns and trees, the neighborhood can retain its unique character.

Jessie Sackett, a member of the U.S. Green Building Council, writes: "Owning a home is the cornerstone of the American dream. Recently, however, we've realized that

Conclusion returns to idea used in introduction

Ross 9

keeping that dream alive for future generations means making some changes to how we live today" (36). We must ensure that the American Dream doesn't translate into a horrific nightmare for our planet or future generations. Therefore, I ask would-be homebuyers to consider only the more conscientious construction in both urban and suburban areas. When we demand more modest and responsible homebuilding, we send a clear message: younger generations will know that we value our planet and our future more than we value excessive personal living space.

- - - - - - - - - - - - - [separate page] - - - - - - - - - - - - - -

Works Cited

Use alphabetical order according to author's last name or if no author, according to first word in title, ignoring articles (a, an, the)

"Are McMansions Giving Way to Smaller, Cozier Homes?"
    Coatings World. Aug. 2004, p. 12. *Academic OneFile*, www.
    academiconefile.com/coatings_world/mcmansions/0804.hml.

Brown, Martin John. "Hummers on the Homefront: At 4,600
    Square Feet, Is It an Eco-House?" *E, The Environmental
    Magazine*, Sept.–Oct. 2006, pp. 23–24. *Academic One-
    File*, www.academiconefile.com/e_environmental_
    magazine/091006/jmbrown/hummers_on_homefront.htm.

Double-space in and between entries

Davey, Peter. "Decency and Forethought: It Is Foolish to Behave
    As If We as a Race Can Go on Treating the Planet As We
    Have Been Doing Since the Industrial Revolution." *The
    Architectural Review*, vol. 213, no. 1281, 2003, pp. 36–37.
    Academic OneFile, www.academiconefile.com/architectural_
    review/213.1281.03/pdavey/decency_and_forethought.htm.

Easterbrook, Gregg. *The Progress Paradox: How Life Gets Better
    While People Feel Worse.* Random House, 2003.

"How to Build a Better Home: A New Approach to Homebuilding
    Saves Trees and Energy—and Makes for Economical,

Ross 10

Comfortable Homes." *National Resources Defense Council*,
22 July 2004, www.nrdc.org/build_better_home.htm.

Iovine, Julie V. "Muscle Houses Trying to Live Lean; Solar
Panels on the Roof, Five Cars in the Garage." *The New York
Times,* 30 Aug. 2001, p. B9. *Academic OneFile,* www.aca-
demiconefile.com/nytimes/083001/jviovine/muscle_houses_
trying_to_live_lean.htm.

Kaleda, Colleen. "Keeping It 'Green' with Panels and More." *The
New York Times,* 15 Oct. 2006, p. 11. *Academic OneFile,*
www.academiconefile.com/nytimes/101506/ckaleda/
keeping_it_green_with_panels.htm.

Moe, Richard. "Battling Teardowns, Saving Neighborhoods."
The National Trust for Historic Preservaion, 28 June 2006,
www.nationaltrust.org/news/news/2006/20060628_
speech_sf.html.

Oliver, Felicia. "The Case for Going Green." *Custom Builder,*
July 1, 2006, www.custombuilderonline.com/case-
going-green.

Sackett, Jessie. "The Green American Dream: LEED for Homes
Is Currently Being Piloted." *The LEED Guide: Environmental
Design & Construction,* vol. 9, no. 6, 2006, pp. 36+. *Academic OneFile,* www.academiconefile.com/leedguide/2006/
jsackett/the_green_american_dream.htm.

Wilson, Alex, and Jessica Boehland. "Small Is Beautiful: U.S.
House Size, Resource Use, and the Environment." *Journal
of Industrial Energy,* vol. 9, no. 1, Winter/Spring 2005, pp.
277–87. *Academic Search Complete,* www.ebscohost.com/
ezproxy/wilson_a/small_is_beautiful/ws2005.htm.

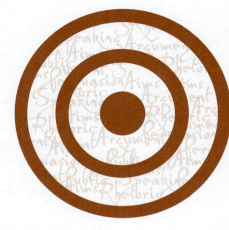

CHAPTER 7

Ethical Writing and Plagiarism

WHY ETHICS MATTER

To write well, you need to be informed about your topic, which means doing research into what others have already said about it. You will want to put some of these ideas into your papers, but it is unethical to do so in a way that does not give credit to the source.

By citing your sources, you also earn your reader's respect. Readers are more likely to accept your views if you project good character, what the ancient rhetoricians called *ethos*. Honesty is part of good character. Part of writing honestly is distinguishing your ideas from the ideas of others.

The news has been filled in recent years with stories about unethical writers, people who have been caught using other writers' words and ideas without citing the source. One university president who borrowed too freely in a convocation speech was forced to resign. Recently, some professors' books were found to contain long passages taken word-for-word from sources, the result—they claimed—of careless note-taking. Whether deliberate or accidental, such mistakes can destroy a person's career.

Plagiarism by students also has become an increasing problem, partly as a result of the Internet. Students may plagiarize by accident, not realizing that material that is so easy to copy and paste from the web must be treated as a quotation and cited as a source. The Internet has also become part of the solution to this problem: Professors using programs like Turnitin.com can check submitted work for originality. At schools using this software, plagiarism dropped by 82%.*

For students, the consequences of plagiarizing are severe, ranging from failure on the writing project to failure in the course and even to suspension or expulsion from the university. Many universities will indicate on a student's transcript if there has been an honor violation, something that potential employers will see.

The purpose of this chapter is to help you avoid plagiarizing.

WHAT PLAGIARISM IS

We like the definition of plagiarism on Fairfield University's online honor tutorial because it includes the various kinds of media that count as sources and must be acknowledged when you draw from them. See Concept Close-Up, on the next page, to read this definition.

As we explain in Chapter 6, "Writing Research-Based Arguments," you must document the sources of all direct quotations, all paraphrased ideas taken from sources, and even information paraphrased from sources, unless it is "common knowledge."

A good definition of *common knowledge* comes from Bruce Ballenger's excellent book *The Curious Researcher:* "Basically, common knowledge means facts that are widely known and about which there is no controversy."† If you already knew something that shows up in your research, that is a good indication that it is common knowledge, but you also have to consider whether your *readers* would already know it. If your readers know less about your topic than you do, it is good to cite the source, especially if the information might surprise them.

THE ETHICS OF USING SOURCES

There are five major kinds of violations of ethics in using sources.

Purchasing a Paper

A simple Internet browser search for most topics will turn up services that offer pre-written essays for sale. These services claim that the essays are merely "examples" of what could be written on the topic, but we all know better. In almost every arena of life, people are ruthlessly trying to make a buck off

---

*"Largest Study of Cheating in the World Reveals 82% Drop in Plagiarism After Using Turnitin.com for Five or More Years." *PR Newswire,* 4 Oct. 2006.
†Bruce Ballenger, *The Curious Researcher: A Guide to Writing Research Papers,* 3rd ed., Allyn and Bacon, 2001, p. 236.

Plagiarism: The Presentation or Submission of Another's Work as Your Own.

Plagiarism includes summarizing, paraphrasing, copying, or translating words, ideas, artworks, audio, video, computer programs, statistical data, or any other creative work, without proper attribution.

Plagiarism can be deliberate or accidental. It can be partial or complete. No matter which, the penalties are often similar. Understanding what constitutes plagiarism is your first step to avoiding it.

SOME ACTS OF PLAGIARISM:

- Copying and pasting from the Internet without attribution
- Buying, stealing, or ghostwriting a paper
- Using ideas or quotations from a source without citation
- Paraphrasing an author too lightly

"What Constitutes Plagiarism?" by Ramona Islam, Senior Reference Librarian and Instruction Coordinator at Fairfield University. Reprinted with permission.

---

the gullible or the desperate. These services are counting on college students to take the bait. It is a bad idea for all these reasons:

- You learn nothing about writing, so you are cheating yourself.
- College professors can find the same essays by searching the Internet and by using more sophisticated search engines designed by textbook publishers to help them find plagiarism.
- The paper will be a poor fit with the prompt your teacher has given you, and the style of the writing will not match previous examples of your own voice and style—red flags professors easily detect.
- Some of these papers are poorly written, often filled with generalizations, bad thinking, and errors of grammar and punctuation.

Using a Paper Found Online

Many college professors and high school teachers have class websites where they post the best work of their students. These papers will often turn up in online searches. Do not be tempted to use these papers or parts of them without citing them, and that includes giving the qualifications of the author.

Using Passages from Online Sources without Citing the Source

It is easy to copy and paste material from the Internet, and much of it is not protected by copyright. Nevertheless, to take passages, sentences, or even

CONCEPT CLOSE-UP

Understanding the Ethics of Plagiarism

A student who plagiarizes faces severe penalties: a failing grade on a paper, perhaps failure in a course, even expulsion from the university and an ethics violation recorded on his or her permanent record. Outside of academe, in the professional world, someone who plagiarizes may face public humiliation, loss of a degree, rank, or job, perhaps even a lawsuit. Why is plagiarism such a serious offense?

Plagiarism is theft. If someone takes our money or our car, we rightly think that person should be punished. Stealing ideas or the words used to express them is no less an act of theft.

Plagiarism is a breach of ethics. In our writing, we are *morally obligated* to distinguish between our ideas, information, and language and somebody else's ideas, information, and language. Human society cannot function without trust and integrity—hence the strong condemnation of plagiarism.

Plagiarism amounts to taking an unearned and unfair advantage. You worked hard to get that "B" on the big paper in your political science class. How would you feel if you knew that another student had simply purchased an "A" paper, thereby avoiding the same effort? At the very least, you would resent it. You should report it. Plagiarism is not just a moral failure with potentially devastating consequences for an individual. *Plagiarism, like any form of dishonesty, damages human society and hurts everyone.*

---

phrases or single significant words from another text is plagiarism. Significant words express strong judgment or original style, such as metaphors.

Compare the source text below with the uses of it. It comes from an interview with Al Gore about his film *An Inconvenient Truth*. The interview appeared in *Sierra* magazine, found on the Sierra Club website.*

> **Sierra:** In your movie, you cite U.S. determination in World War II as an example of the kind of resolve we need to confront global warming. But it took the attack on Pearl Harbor to galvanize the country. Are we going to have a similar moment in this crisis?
>
> **Gore:** Obviously, we all hope it doesn't come to that, but for hundreds of thousands of people in New Orleans, that moment has already been reached. And for millions of people in Africa's Sahel, that moment has already been reached with the disappearance of Lake Chad. For an untold number of species, it has been reached. The challenge for the rest of us is to connect the dots and see the picture clearly. H. G. Wells wrote

*Pat Joseph, "Start by Arming Yourself with Knowledge: Al Gore Breaks Through with His Global-Warming Message." *Sierra*, Sept.–Oct. 2006 vault.sierraclub.org/sierra/200609/interview.asp.

that "history is a race between education and catastrophe." And this is potentially the worst catastrophe in the history of civilization. The challenge now is to seize our potential for solving this crisis without going through a cataclysmic tragedy that would be the climate equivalent of wartime attack. And it's particularly important because, by the nature of this crisis, when the worst consequences begin to manifest themselves, it will already be too late.

Unethical use of source:

> It will take an environmental crisis to galvanize the country into confronting the problem of global warming, and for hundreds of thousands of people in New Orleans, that moment has already been reached. The challenge for the rest of us is to connect the dots and see the picture clearly. H. G. Wells wrote that "history is a race between education and catastrophe." And this is potentially the worst catastrophe in the history of civilization, so we must step up our efforts to learn about global warming and the means to keep it in check.

In this example, the writer has made no reference to the source of the words or ideas. This is wholesale theft of another's words and ideas. This kind of borrowing from sources is every bit as unethical as buying a paper online and turning it in as your own writing.

Ethical use of source:

> There are two routes to discovering the need to confront the problem of global warming, as Al Gore explained to Sierra magazine. We can wait for catastrophes like Hurricane Katrina, or we can learn from other environmental crises that are occurring around the globe and take action now. Quoting H. G. Wells, who said that "history is a race between education and catastrophe," Gore argues that we need to get educated because global warming is "potentially the worst catastrophe in the history of civilization. . . . " (Joseph).

The ethical way to use a source is

- to integrate paraphrase and direct quotation into a paragraph of your own, and
- to cite the source.

Notice that good paraphrasing does not borrow either the language or the sentence pattern of the original text. The source is cited and the style of the sentences is the student's own.

Inadequate Paraphrasing

Paraphrasing is tricky because paraphrases must be *entirely* your own words, not a mixture of your words and the words of the source. Even if you cite the source, it is plagiarism to borrow words and phrases from another author.

Therefore, you must put quotation marks around sentences, parts of sentences, and even significant words taken directly from another text.

Here is a source text and on page 169 is the picture to which the examples of paraphrase that follow refer:

> Subversive masculine modes in the second half of this century began with the tee-shirts and blue jeans of rural laborers, later adopted by rebellious urban youth.
>
> —Anne Hollander, *Sex and Suits* (Alfred A. Knopf, 1994)

Unethical use of source:

> Marlon Brando symbolizes the subversive masculine mode of the second half of the twentieth century with the tee-shirts and blue jeans of rural laborers (Hollander 186).

Even though the student cited his source, this is plagiarism because his sentence contains words from the source without quotation marks. This example illustrates the most common kind of unintentional plagiarism. This passage also fails to identify Hollander as the interpreter of the image.

To avoid this accidental plagiarism:

- When taking notes, highlight in color any wording that you copy directly from a source.
- When paraphrasing, study the original passage but then put it aside when you write your paraphrase, so that you will not be tempted to use the wording of the source. Then go back and check your paraphrase for accuracy and for originality of expression. As the ethical version below shows, any quoted parts must be treated as quotations.

Ethical use of source:

> According to art historian Anne Hollander, Marlon Brando's tee-shirt and blue jeans illustrate a rebellious kind of late-twentieth-century masculinity, a look originally associated with "rural laborers" (186).

This version has reworded the sentence into an adequate paraphrase and used quotation marks around a phrase taken word for word from Hollander. It also identifies Hollander as an art historian, which establishes her credibility. When you tell your readers something about your source, you increase the credibility of your own writing.

Paraphrasing Ideas or Information without Naming the Source

Although it is not necessary to cite sources of commonly available information, such as the percentage of high school graduates who go to college, you must give credit when a source presents someone's idea, interpretation, or opinion, or when the information would be difficult for your readers to verify on their

Marlon Brando in A Streetcar Named Desire, *1951.*

own. If in doubt, it is always better to cite. The source text below comes from a book about the college experience:

> Many [college] seniors single out interdisciplinary classes as the courses that meant the most to them. As a corollary, they cite faculty members who, while expert in their own fields, are able to put the fields in proper perspective. Students find this important. They believe that the real world, and the way people think about the world, does not divide neatly into categories called history, chemistry, literature, psychology, and politics.
> —Richard J. Light, *Making the Most of College: Students Speak Their Minds* (Harvard UP, 2001)

Unethical use of source:

> Studies have shown that college students find interdisciplinary courses the most meaningful. They also prefer professors who can think outside the box of their own areas of academic specialization.

Richard Light's research led him to this information; he deserves credit for his work.

Ethical use of source:

> In interviews with seniors at Harvard, where he teaches, Richard Light found that college students say that interdisciplinary courses are the most meaningful. They also prefer professors who can think outside the box of their own areas of academic specialization (126).

By citing Light as the source of this information, the writer has also added credibility to his or her own essay.

When Opinions Coincide

Students often ask what to do when they have an idea, opinion, or interpretation and then encounter that same idea, opinion, or interpretation as they are doing research. For example, after looking into the problem of global warming, a student could easily come to the conclusion that rising temperatures and ocean levels could become a threat to civilization. Reading the *Sierra* interview with Al Gore, that student sees that she and Gore share the opinion that global warming "is potentially the worst catastrophe in the history of civilization." If the student does not use Gore's exact words, is it plagiarism to use the opinion without citing him? A classic book on the subject of research, *The Craft of Research,* advises the cautious approach: "In the world of research, priority counts not for everything, but for a lot. If you do not cite that prior source, you risk having people think that you plagiarized it, even though you did not."* You do not have to check to see that all of your own ideas are not already out there; however, if you encounter one of your own in a source, you should acknowledge that source.

THE ETHICS OF GIVING AND RECEIVING HELP WITH WRITING

Writing is not a solitary act. Most professional writers seek feedback from colleagues, editors, family, and friends, and they thank those who have contributed in the acknowledgments section of the book. Students benefit from help with their projects—in conferences with their instructors, peer exchanges with other students in class, and visits to their campus's tutorial services. Whether you are giving help or receiving it, you need to realize that inappropriate help is also plagiarism because it involves using someone else's ideas and language. If someone tells you what to write, rewrites your work for you, or even proofreads or "edits" your work, that is plagiarism, because you are using someone else's work as if it were your own. Likewise, it is unethical for you to provide

---

*Wayne C. Booth, et al., *The Craft of Research*. U of Chicago P, 2003, p. 203.

such help to anyone else, a practice known as "facilitating plagiarism" and equally punishable at most schools.

The following list describes three unethical ways of giving and receiving help.

1. **Having someone "ghostwrite" your paper.** College campuses attract unscrupulous people who offer to "help" students with their writing. It is dangerous to use an off-campus tutor because his or her primary interest is income, not education.

2. **Having someone edit your paper for style.** It is plagiarism to have someone else change your wording and word choices for you. Your instructor will teach you about elements of style and illustrate principles of editing. This textbook covers such material in Appendix A.

    After you have used this advice to edit your own paper, it is okay to ask someone else to point out passages that need more attention and even to explain why those passages are wordy or unclear. But it is up to you to improve the expression.

3. **Having someone proofread your paper for grammar and punctuation.** As with editing for style, proofreading is your responsibility. You plagiarize

"My parents didn't write it—they just tweaked it."

© Barbara Smaller/The New Yorker Collection/www.cartoonbank.com

if you hand your paper to someone else to "clean it up," whether as a favor or for money. Many students need help with proofreading, and your instructor or on-campus tutorial service can offer instruction that will help you catch errors in the future.

ETHICAL WRITING AND GOOD STUDY HABITS

Good study habits are central to ethical writing.

- **Do not procrastinate.** Students who procrastinate are more likely to make the kind of careless errors that lead to accidental plagiarism. They are also more likely to use intentional plagiarism as the only way to meet a deadline.

- **Take careful notes.** Use your notebook or notecards to write about your sources, being sure to distinguish your own ideas from the material you copy directly or paraphrase. Use quotation marks around any words you take directly from a source.

- **Ask your instructor about proper sources of help with your writing.** Avoid using untrained family members and friends as tutors. If your school has a writing center, take advantage of the tutors there.

- **Work on improving your reading skills.** Good reading skills will empower you to use sources more confidently. Read Chapter 2, "Reading Arguments," for advice on how to improve your comprehension and analysis of texts.

PART TWO

The Aims of Argument

8 Joining the Conversation: Arguing to Inquire *175*

9 Making Your Case: Arguing to Convince *201*

10 Motivating Action: Arguing to Persuade *235*

11 Resolving Conflict: Arguing to Mediate *265*

CHAPTER 8

Joining the Conversation: Arguing to Inquire

In Chapter 2, "Reading Arguments," and Chapter 3, "Analyzing Arguments," we offered what you need to respond critically to any argument you encounter. Chapter 4 took you through the process of writing a critique, an application of what you learned in Chapters 2 and 3.

What you learned in these chapters applies to arguing to inquire. However, inquiry is different from responding to single arguments. **Inquiry** *is joining a conversation, an ongoing exchange of opinions about some controversial topic,* and therefore involves many arguments advanced by many people.

To join any conversation, you have to know already or become familiar with what is going on. This is the case whether you are talking in a group, posting on a blog, working on a term paper, drafting a business proposal, or composing a letter to your mayor or city council. In short, *having something to say depends on knowing what others have said.* It depends on *comparing perspectives,* analyzing and evaluating existing viewpoints.

CONCEPT CLOSE-UP

NCEPT

What Is Synthesis?

All the genres that use comparisons *synthesize*—a Greek word that means "putting together." Typically the views you encounter in comparing perspectives are at odds with one another enough to make point-by-point reconciliation impossible. In other words, no one could fashion a single, consistent view out of everything they say. Therefore, aim for a *partial synthesis,* selecting what you consider the best insights from each, combining them with your own insights, thereby creating a new perspective. The result is your viewpoint, matured and refined by open and thoughtful engagement with the viewpoints of others.

WHAT IS COMPARING PERSPECTIVES?

Many situations call for written comparisons of people's perspectives on a problem, issue, or question. Money managers compare stock analysts' reports; land developers compare architectural concepts for a new building; government administrators compare reports from advocacy groups; a consumer compares product reviews. Among many others, genres that compare perspectives include

- Book reviews that evaluate two or three recently published books on the same topic
- Market research that analyzes the results of in-depth interviews to find patterns and commonalities in consumers' preferences and attitudes
- Introductions to articles in the sciences that provide overviews of past research
- Exploratory essays that question and evaluate the viewpoints of other people writing on the same topic

WHY WRITE TO COMPARE PERSPECTIVES?

All researched writing begins with reading and comparing other people's perspectives on a topic. Writing out this exploration helps us to

- Sort out the specific points being discussed
- See where opinions intersect and diverge
- Pin down, point by point, the differences and similarities
- Reflect on the points under debate
- Formulate our own view

Put another way, what do you do *after* you find sources for a paper? The answer is, compare their perspectives. Without understanding your sources' perspectives, you cannot make sense out of them or use them to say anything yourself. Comparing perspectives, then, is an essential part of doing research for anything you write.

HOW DOES COMPARING PERSPECTIVES WORK?

Writing that compares perspectives usually proceeds by asking and answering a series of questions about the readings selected for comparison.

What to Ask When Comparing Perspectives

1. What is the central question addressed in all the readings?
2. What are the key terms or concepts used in discussing this question, and how do the writers define these terms? Is there disagreement about the meaning of key terms?
3. What do the authors have to say about the question, and where do their answers agree or disagree? When perspectives disagree, how do you assess the arguments of each author? Whose views have more validity, and why?
4. What conclusions or insights into the central question have you been able to reach as a result of comparing perspectives on it?

Of these four items, the third is especially important. Locate the points of agreement; they will reveal the *current state of informed opinion.* Locate the points where there is disagreement; they will reveal the *live issues,* what is currently in dispute. We must know both to join a conversation—what is accepted as true, and what people are arguing about.

The Writer as Inquirer

In addition to the perspectives you read, you will probably have a perspective of your own on the central question you are investigating. Acknowledge it, but keep an open mind as you read through others' opinions. Read all perspectives with an equally critical stance. You will be reading arguments, but *you will be arguing to inquire, writing an exploration.* Your paper should open with the central question to explore, not with your own thesis on the question.

It is important to keep the central question open and to present all views fairly and accurately. Use your own thinking to evaluate the views. Keeping a question open does not mean accepting everything you read. Give reasons for saying what you accept as the better perspective as you work through the points of agreement and disagreement. Expect your exploration to lead you to a more informed viewpoint than you had before writing.

Which Character Should Sports Develop?

ANDY RUDD

Andy Rudd is a psychologist on the faculty at Florida State University. The following selection is the opening from a much longer article on the relationship of sports and character. It is widely assumed that participation in sports builds character in young people. If it does, Rudd asks, what kind of character does it build? As you read, identify the differing informed opinions Rudd presents. Where do you stand on this issue, and what might you add to the conversation?

ABSTRACT

For years, strong claims have been made that sport builds character. Despite such claims, a "winning at all cost" mentality can frequently be seen within all of sport. The reason for this paradox may relate to confusion around what it means to demonstrate character. The purpose of this article is to show that there are indeed two distinct types of character that are espoused in the sport milieu. One type is related to social values (social character) the other related to moral values (moral character). Following an explication and comparison of these types of character, a recommendation is made for a needed emphasis towards the development of moral character.

INTRODUCTION

In his *A Way Out of Ethical Confusion*, Zeigler (2004) asks the question: "What character do we seek for people?" He refers to Commager's 1966 list of 12 traits—i.e., "common denominators"—that can be attributed to Americans. In this list are many traits, some of which apply directly to the topic of sport's relationship to character. These are "self-confidence; materialism; complacency bordering occasionally on arrogance; cultivation of the competitive spirit; and indifference to, and exasperation with laws, rules, and regulations" (p. 7). Zeigler believes that the situation deteriorated further by the end of the 20th century. In the dedication to this work, he states: "I believe there is an urgent need to challenge the underlying human values and norms that have determined the direction the United States is heading in the 21st century" (p. iii). This comment, if true, has significance in a search for an answer to the topic at hand. Which "character" should sport develop?

Typically when an athlete or team at any level of sport is considered to have displayed character, the word "character" is associated with a host of values such as teamwork, loyalty, self-sacrifice, perseverance, work ethic, and mental toughness. As a specific example, a high school athletic director defined an athlete's character as "a willingness to try no matter what the situation. An attempt to continually improve; a willingness to give all up for the cause; and sacrificing without expectations." In another example, a high school coach asserted: "Character is the belief in self-worth and your own work ethic. . . . " (Rudd, 1999).

In professional sport, character has been defined similarly. For instance, consider a newspaper article that headlined, "The Arizona Diamondbacks Attribute Their Success to Character." Specifically, the article highlighted the Diamondbacks as players who work hard and don't complain about salaries (Heyman, 2000). Consider also an issue of *Sports Illustrated* in which New England Patriots' Troy Brown commented on former teammate Drew Bledsoe's ability to play with a broken finger and lead his team to victory. Brown stated, "It showed a lot of character" (Zimmerman, 2001, p. 162).

Margin notes:

A convention in science articles, abstracts help researchers decide whether an article is relevant to their research without having to read the article itself.

First paragraph "frames" the article by answering key questions: What is character as Americans understand and value it? How does character relate to sports? How does character developed by sports relate to the future of American values?

This article uses APA notational conventions. Use it as a model for papers you write that require APA style.

Specifies what character means in sports, as generally understood by athletic directors and coaches. Author must establish this understanding of character to serve as a contrast with "moral character" in paragraph 4.

4   However, in contrast to the notion that an athlete of character is one who displays values such as teamwork, loyalty, self-sacrifice, perseverance, work ethic, and mental toughness, sport scholars in the area of character development have defined character with a different set of values. Sport scholars, including sport philosophers and sport psychologists, more commonly define an athlete of character as one who is honest, fair, responsible, respectful, and compassionate (Arnold, 1999; Beller & Stoll, 1995; Gough, 1998; Shields & Bredemeier, 1995). For example, Arnold (1999) states, "In terms of moral goodness, or what I refer to as moral character, it involves a life that complies with such virtues as justice, honesty, and compassion" (p. 42).

5   It does indeed seem, therefore, that there are two distinct definitions of character maintained by two camps. The first camp consists of coaches, administrators, and players who may typically define character with social values such as teamwork, loyalty, self-sacrifice, and perseverance. This could be designated as "social character." The second camp consists of sport scholars, and people of earlier generations still alive, who typically define character with moral values such as honesty, fairness, responsibility, compassion, and respect. This is commonly referred to by many of them as "moral character." The existence of these two camps, each with their respective definitions of character, suggests that there is confusion and disagreement concerning the definition of character in sport. (Of course, there may be some "in the middle" who accept an overlapping, possibly conflicting set of values to describe the term "character.")

6   As a result of the above, the differences in the way character is defined may provide strong evidence why many feel there is a lack of sportsmanship in competitive sport today. Similarly, these same people decry the "winning-at-all-cost" mentality that seems to prevail in athletics (see, for example, "A Purpose," 1999; Hawes, 1998; Spencer, 1996). Many coaches, athletic administrators, and parents may indeed place such a premium on social values such as teamwork, loyalty, self-sacrifice, and work ethic that they forget, or at least downplay, any emphasis on time-honored moral values such as honesty, fairness, responsibility, and respect.

7   The purpose of this paper is to define and discuss in detail two types of character (moral and social) that are espoused by two distinct groups in the sport milieu. The ramifications of the "social character view" in sport are explained below. At the same time, what the author feels is the need for greater emphasis on the development of moral character in sport and physical education will also be discussed.

Sidenotes

Specifies what author means by "moral character" and contrasts it with "social character." This is the second perspective the article develops.

Summarizes the social versus moral character contrast. It is weighted to favor moral character.

Anticipates objection: That the contrast between social and moral character is too sharp, as if there is no middle ground. Author concedes that the values can be combined.

Points to a commonly recognized problem in contemporary sports that makes the author's research and conclusions relevant, worth reading and studying.

Prepares the reader for the rest of the article by stating what the author is doing and why.

REFERENCES

Arnold, P. (1994). Sport and moral education. *The Journal of Moral Education, 23*(1), 75–89.
Beller, J. M., & Stoll, S. K. (1995). Moral reasoning of high school student athletes and general students: An empirical study versus personal testimony. *Pediatric Exercise Science, 7*(4), 352–363.
Gough, R. (1998). A practical strategy for emphasizing character development in sport and physical education. *Journal of Physical Education, Recreation, & Dance, 69*(2), 18–23.
Hawes, K. (1998). Sportsmanship: Why should anybody care? *NCAA news*, pp. 1, 18.
Heyman, J. (2000, May 22). They're 'good guys, good players.' *Statesman Journal*, p. 3B.
A purpose pitch. (1999, May 17). *Sports Illustrated, 90*, 24.
Rudd, A. (1999). [High school coaches' definitions of character]. Unpublished raw data.
Shields, D., & Bredemeier, B. (1995). *Character development and physical activity*.
    Champaign, IL: Human Kinetics.

Note APA "References" section, rather than the MLA "Works Cited" list. See Chapter 6, pages 129–133 for more on APA conventions.

Spencer, A. F. (1996). Ethics in physical and sport education. *Journal of Physical Education, Recreation & Dance, 67*(7), 37–39.

Zeigler, E. F. (2004). *A way out of ethical confusion.* Victoria, Canada: Trafford.

Zimmerman, P. (2001, September 3). New England Patriots. *Sports Illustrated, 95*(9), 162–163.

QUESTIONS FOR DISCUSSION

1. Notice that the Rudd reading is organized around questions addressed by various writers rather than around what each writer says, taken up one by one. Why does organizing around questions work so well?

2. One of the keys to responding to anything we read, including exploratory writing, is to evaluate it according to our own experience. What have you learned from participating in sports or from observing sports events? Does your experience mirror what this article says?

READINGS

See Chapter 2, "Reading Arguments," pages 18–21, for more on preparing to read any challenging text.

To demonstrate the process of exploring perspectives, we present three readings with different views on whether narcissism is increasing in Western culture, particularly among young people.

Take time to consider the topic and your first response to it. In this case, what is narcissism? A good place to find in-depth definitions is *The Oxford English Dictionary (OED).* As defined by the *OED, narcissism* is

1. Excessive self-love or vanity; self-admiration, self-centredness.

2. *Psychol.* The condition of gaining emotional or erotic gratification from self-contemplation, sometimes regarded as a stage in the normal

Figure 8.1

Narcissus contemplating his own image

psychological development of children which may be reverted to in adulthood during mental illness.

The term *narcissism* alludes to a character in Greek mythology. (See Figure 8.1.) The *OED* defines Narcissus as:

> *Greek Mythol.* (The name of) a beautiful youth who fell in love with his own reflection in water and pined to death. Hence (allusively): a person characterized by extreme self-admiration or vanity; a narcissist.

◎ COLLABORATIVE ACTIVITY: Finding Examples of Narcissism

In small groups, discuss your collective observations of peers' behavior. What examples of excessive self-love have you observed? What kind of behavior do you consider narcissistic? What conditions might contribute to such behavior? Do members of your group agree or disagree that young people exhibit narcissistic behavior? Be ready to report your group's conclusions to the class. •

The Paradox of Narcissism

JOHN F. SCHUMAKER

This selection comes from *In Search of Happiness: Understanding an Endangered State of Mind.* John F. Schumaker is a clinical psychologist who lives in Australia and has published nine books on issues of culture and mental health. As you read, consider the concepts of self-esteem, happiness, and consumer culture Schumaker introduces and how he uses them to compare perspectives on narcissism.

1   While walking through the local Botanical Gardens recently, a woman wearing a "Love Yourself" T-shirt jogged past me. T-shirts like that were non-existent in the 1960s, when they all read "Love" or "Love One Another." But preachers of self-love are everywhere today. There are even numerous books extolling the virtues of self-love, including Peter McWilliams's *Love 101: To Love Oneself Is the Beginning of a Lifelong Romance.* The subtitle of that book is actually a tongue-in-cheek comment once made by Oscar Wilde. But it seems that many people have come to take that idea literally.

2   Today the self-esteem movement is in full swing. As an arm of feel-good culture, this movement has persuaded us that it is not good enough to feel good within ourselves. We must also feel good *about* ourselves. It has grown in force to the extent that it has reshaped childhood education. Teachers in recent years have been trained that a high level of self-esteem is the child's passport to happiness and success in life, as well as to a good education. Less and less emphasis is being paid to self-discipline, hard work, integrity, and helping students gain realistic appraisals of themselves. Instead, young people are being told automatically that they are infinitely talented, phenomenally creative, and erupting with potential in any area that takes their fancy.

One zealous school in Alabama went so far as placing banners over all bathroom mirrors that read "You are now looking at one of the most special people in the whole world."

3   Young people find themselves in a culture that tells us to feel good about ourselves regardless of what we are as people. It does not matter if we are spoiled, selfish, indifferent, wasteful, or cruel. We have done our best to make self-esteem unconditional. But many education theorists are now conceding that the self-esteem extravaganza is proving to be a dismal failure in terms of education and personality development.

4   For instance, it was once thought that high self-esteem was crucial for effective leadership, social skills, and cooperation. The same was said about the ability to resist risky, anti-social, and self-destructive behaviours such as drug taking, smoking, drinking, and unsafe sex. But in all the cases, high self-esteem offers no advantages. In fact, research shows that high self-esteem increases people's likelihood to experiment and to take chances, which can make them more vulnerable to certain problems.

5   Once considered to be essential for advanced social skills and interpersonal effectiveness, high self-esteem has been shown to give no additional edge in these areas as well. It can even impair social judgement and conscience development. Recent research has found that "self-enhancers" with highly favourable views of themselves were more prone to acts of aggression such as bullying. They were also more inclined toward irritating behaviour patterns such as bragging, being overly opinionated, and interrupting others in conversation.

6   Those with high self-esteem appear to have their trumped-up pride hurt more easily, which can trigger in them hostility and other reactions that turn people off. High self-esteem individuals find themselves even more alienated from others when they are not able to conceal their elevated perception of themselves. While high self-esteem leads people to perceive themselves to be more popular and socially adept than other people, this does not correspond to reality when others are asked to rate them. While it is still promoted as a happiness helper, it has become clear that high self-esteem is not all that it was once cracked up to be.

7   . . . The notion that we are not worthy of being happy unless we are big, and full of ourselves, is a thoroughly Western one. Happiness in modern Western culture unfolds in the context of individualism. So it follows that our perceptions of ourselves would be crucial in judging our own degree of happiness. If we are self-satisfied, we are likely to say that we are satisfied with life. This contrasts with collectivist cultures where happiness is tied to cooperation and social harmony, and to being a worthwhile and valued member of the group. In such settings, less effort would be put into self-enhancement, and more into group-enhancement, as a pathway to happiness.

8   The worst problem comes when self-esteem becomes completely blown out of proportion to the extent that it gives way to narcissism. Unwarranted self-esteem may in many respects be a forerunner of the modern type of "unwarranted happiness" that has been criticised because it is not founded on anything substantial. In this regard, the type of narcissism and unjustified self-esteem that prevails today is

quite interesting in light of the history of the self-esteem movement, which many say was begun by Los Angeles psychotherapist and corporate consultant Dr Nathaniel Branden. While he tried to soften our negative connotations about self-centredness, he was careful to distinguish between healthy and unhealthy types of self-attention. He professed self-esteem that was built on the recognition of the need for love, healthy relationships, and spiritual awareness that he called "soulfulness." Since its origins, the self-esteem movement has given way to unbridled me-ism that lacks much scope for a meaningful shared happiness.

9   The ego has become so artificially inflated in today's cultural climate that the idea of being famous is seen as a requirement for happiness. Local fame is no longer enough. Fame seekers want the whole world as their audience, which may in part be a reaction to the absence of true carers in their local environments. If nobody around me cares, maybe I can get the whole world to care. As our need for affection has been relocated to the public sphere, wooing the mass media has become a popular form of courtship. Ignored people of every description are coming out of the woodwork to set world records or be the first to unicycle blindfolded across the Utah salt flats or leapfrog a thousand beer barrels in less than fifteen minutes.

10   The familiar cry "Look at me!" of the neglected child begging for parental attention has spread across the entire Western world as people have become increasingly invisible. For many, fame is imagined to be the only touch that can soothe their gnawing separation anxiety. The problem from a happiness standpoint is that there are very few winners in the fame game. As desperate as we are to be seen and recognised, getting anonymous fans is no easy task. Yet the quest for fame has become inseparable from the quest for happiness.

11   This trend is eating away at people's prospects for happiness by way of condemning them to almost certain disappointment. They become slaves to a public that is largely a fiction propagated by Hollywood-style hype. The lucky few who make it into the limelight often fall prey to their anxieties about the fickleness of their unknown worshippers, not to mention the loss of privacy and the relationship breakdowns that are part of the package. Despite this, the desire for public fame grows more powerful as our local worlds continue to weaken as a source of recognition. Mixed in with our own ambitions for fame is a trend to bow down further and further to those who have already become famous.

12   Consumer culture has a large investment in narcissism, just as it does with fame. A lot has been said about today's culture of narcissism, but almost always from a negative point of view. The upside of narcissism is that it is always associated with a high degree of entitlement that sways people to think that they deserve to have things— lots of things. The advertising industry is geared toward selling on the back of rising narcissism. Some of it is blatant, such as commercials that blurt out various messages to the effect ". . . because you deserve it." Others are subtler at selling things as part of people's growing desire to romance themselves. As narcissism becomes a dominant personality trait, the person gradually becomes shallower and loses the ability

to feel deeply for other people. This too increases consumption potential by making people more accepting of the fictionalised world of objects.

13   The perfect psychological incubator for narcissism is a combination of overindulgence and neglect, which is the story for so many people growing up under modern cultural conditions. It is also the classic condition for the emergence of sociopaths whose main attribute is an absence of social conscience. Narcissists, like sociopaths, experience little guilt, or sense of sin. But sin is not good for the economy. As the cult of the individual has gradually made narcissism acceptable, the sense of sin has been overtaken by the feeling that one has the right to do whatever it takes to satisfy oneself and to feel good.

14   The sins that remain in our culture of narcissism are largely sins against oneself. We feel that we have done something wrong if we have not gotten the most for ourselves, done the most, or made the most of our opportunities. Other than that, the old-fashioned sins that stemmed from offending others or God are virtually obsolete. The worst sin today is to deprive oneself, which once again is music to the ears of a consumer economy. While feelings of being a sinful person can tarnish happiness, the wholesale erasure of social responsibility can be even more destructive to one's prospects for happiness.

15   An unceasing preoccupation with personal happiness is in many ways an expression of narcissism. Or at least this is the case with a large percentage of happiness seekers who are looking for happiness by way of what they can draw toward themselves, rather than what they can share with others. Jean-Jacques Rousseau once alluded to narcissism in saying that "man's nature is not fully mature until it becomes social." One could say the same thing about happiness; that is, happiness is not fully mature until it becomes social.

16   The myth of Narcissus is a tragic one. Because he will not surrender himself, Narcissus blows his chances with the beautiful nymph Echo, only to be cursed by an unrelenting self-devotion that robs him of his vigour and beauty. His beloved self never returns his affections, and finally he pines to death, leaving in his place only a lonely flower to preserve his memory. Fittingly, the tale lacks a happy ending. Yet it could be argued that narcissism is not a bad plan of attack. Put yourself first at all times and devote your full energies to feeling good. But narcissism has little to offer by way of happiness, or even self-love. Societies that generate narcissism among their members are dysfunctional ones that have lost sight of the reciprocal nature of human happiness.

17   The unofficial labels "middle-class narcissism" and "normal narcissism" have been used to describe the garden variety of narcissism that is generated by modern consumer culture, which has removed all taboos on selfishness in order to stimulate consumption. As a personality structure, collective narcissism has some advantages since it allows people in a hyper-competitive environment to exploit others without guilt. At the same time, it promotes a low tolerance for frustration that destroys relationships. People often end up fluctuating between expressions of hostility and ungainly attempts to get the approval of others.

Changes in Narcissism

JEAN M. TWENGE

Jean M. Twenge is Associate Professor of Psychology at San Diego State University. This selection is from *Generation Me: Why Today's Young Americans Are More Confident, Assertive, Entitled—and More Miserable Than Ever Before*. Notice the number and variety of sources Twenge cites. What do the number and variety of sources Twenge cites reveal about her position on the prevalence of narcissism in today's society?

1   Narcissism is one of the few personality traits that psychologists agree is almost completely negative. Narcissists are overly focused on themselves and lack empathy for others, which means they cannot see another person's perspective. (Sound like the last clerk who served you?) They also feel entitled to special privileges and believe that they are superior to other people. As a result, narcissists are bad relationship partners and can be difficult to work with. Narcissists are also more likely to be hostile, feel anxious, compromise their health, and fight with friends and family. Unlike those merely high in self-esteem, narcissists admit that they don't feel close to other people.

2   All evidence suggests that narcissism is much more common in recent generations. In the early 1950s, only 12% of teens aged 14 to 16 agreed with the statement "I am an important person." By the late 1980s, an incredible 80%—almost seven times as many—claimed they were important. Psychologist Harrison Gough found consistent increases on narcissism items among college students quizzed between the 1960s and the 1990s. GenMe students were more likely to agree that "I would be willing to describe myself as a pretty 'strong' personality" and "I have often met people who were supposed to be experts who were no better than I." In other words, those other people don't know what they're talking about, so everyone should listen to me.

3   In a 2002 survey of 3,445 people conducted by Joshua Foster, Keith Campbell, and me, younger people scored considerably higher on the Narcissistic Personality Inventory, agreeing with items such as "If I ruled the world it would be a better place," "I am a special person," and "I can live my life anyway I want to." (These statements evoke the image of a young man speeding down the highway in the world's biggest SUV, honking his horn, and screaming, "Get out of my way! I'm important!") This study was cross-sectional, though, meaning that it was a one-time sample of people of different ages. For that reason, we cannot be sure if any differences are due to age or to generation; however, the other studies of narcissism mentioned previously suggest that generation plays a role. It is also interesting that narcissism scores were fairly high until around age 35, after which they decreased markedly. This is right around the cutoff between GenMe and previous generations.

4   Narcissism is the darker side of the focus on the self, and is often confused with self-esteem. Self-esteem is often based on solid relationships with others, whereas narcissism comes from believing that you are special and more important than

other people. Many of the school programs designed to raise self-esteem probably raise narcissism instead. Lillian Katz, a professor of early childhood education at the University of Illinois, wrote an article titled "All About Me: Are We Developing Our Children's Self-Esteem or Their Narcissism?" She writes, "Many of the practices advocated in pursuit of [high self-esteem] may instead inadvertently develop narcissism in the form of excessive preoccupation with oneself." Because the school programs emphasize being "special" rather than encouraging friendships, we may be training an army of little narcissists instead of raising kids' self-esteem.

5   Many young people also display entitlement, a facet of narcissism that involves believing that you deserve and are entitled to more than others. A scale that measures entitlement has items like "Things should go my way," "I demand the best because I'm worth it," and (my favorite) "If I were on the *Titanic,* I would deserve to be on the *first* lifeboat!" A 2005 Associated Press article printed in hundreds of news outlets labeled today's young people "The Entitlement Generation." In the article, employers complained that young employees expected too much too soon and had very high expectations for salary and promotions.

Teachers have seen this attitude for years now. One of my colleagues said his students acted as if grades were something they simply deserved to get no matter what. He joked that their attitude could be summed up by "Where's my A? I distinctly remember ordering an A from the catalog." Stout, the education professor, lists the student statements familiar to teachers everywhere: "I need a better grade," "I deserve an A on this paper," "I *never* get B's." Stout points out that the self-esteem movement places the student's feelings at the center, so "students learn that they do not need to respect their teachers or even earn their grades, so they begin to believe that they are entitled to grades, respect, or anything else . . . just for asking."

6   Unfortunately, narcissism can lead to outcomes far worse than grade grubbing. Several studies have found that narcissists lash out aggressively when they are insulted or rejected. Eric Harris and Dylan Klebold, the teenage gunmen at Columbine High School, made statements remarkably similar to items on the most popular narcissism questionnaire. On a videotape made before the shootings, Harris picked up a gun, made a shooting noise, and said "Isn't it fun to get the respect we're going to deserve?" (Chillingly similar to the narcissism item, "I insist upon getting the respect that is due me.") Later, Harris said, "I could convince them that I'm going to climb Mount Everest, or I have a twin brother growing out of my back. I can make you believe anything" (virtually identical to the item "I can make anyone believe anything I want them to"). Harris and Klebold then debate which famous movie director will film their story. A few weeks after making the videotapes, Harris and Klebold killed thirteen people and then themselves.

7   Other examples abound. In a set of lab studies, narcissistic men felt less empathy for rape victims, reported more enjoyment when watching a rape scene in a movie, and were more punitive toward a woman who refused to read a sexually arousing passage out loud to them. Abusive husbands who threaten to kill their wives—and tragically sometimes do—are the ultimate narcissists. They see everyone and everything in terms of fulfilling their needs, and become very angry and aggressive when

things don't go exactly their way. Many workplace shootings occur after an employee is fired and decides he'll "show" everyone how powerful he is.

8   The rise in narcissism has very deep roots. It's not just that we feel better about ourselves, but that we even think to ask the question. We fixate on self-esteem, and unthinkingly build narcissism, because we believe that the needs of the individual are paramount. This will stay with us even if self-esteem programs end up in the dustbin of history.

QUESTIONS FOR DISCUSSION

1. How would you summarize Twenge's perspective on the topic of narcissism? How does it compare with Schumaker's?

2. Twenge is a psychology professor—a teacher and researcher. How might her profession affect her purpose and audience?

Generation Y and the New Myth of Narcissus

DUNCAN GREENBERG

At the time he wrote this column for his campus newspaper, *The Yale Herald*, Duncan Greenberg was a senior.

1   In our 10 or 20 years of existence as an age group, we've been called a lot of things, but "narcissistic" is the slur du jour. A controversial study at San Diego State University, which trickled down to papers this week, found that "30 percent more college students showed 'elevated narcissism' in 2006 compared with 1982." The study was authored by Jean Twenge, the cynic behind the book *Generation Me: Why Today's Young Americans Are More Confident, Assertive, Entitled—and More Miserable Than Ever Before*. Twenge consolidated data from 25 years of surveys and found—or claimed to find—that the Millennials had reached unhealthy heights of self-esteem.

2   To you and me, narcissism remains an elusive term. But words have different meanings in common parlance than in academic jargon, and there is a general consensus in the psychology community as to the symptoms of "narcissism." Some of the more familiar characteristics, as defined by the Mayo Clinic, include a "need for constant praise," a "grandiose sense of one's own abilities or achievements," a "lack of empathy for other people," and an "expectation of special treatment."

3   Twenge's study hasn't been published yet, but newspaper articles give us glimpses of her methodology: In an annual poll conducted for 25 years, students were asked if they agreed with statements like, "If I ruled the world, it would be a better place," "I think I am a special person," and "I can live my life any way I want to." Each student's answers were ranked on a scale from egocentric to empathetic.

4   Having circumscribed the malady, though, we are left with the problem of diagnosis. You can't just flat-out ask people if they're narcissistic (a true narcissist will never admit it); your only hope is to trick your subject into signing off on statements

that indirectly expose his inflated ego. That's why psychologists use oblique and ambiguous statements like, "I think I am a special person." The downside of obliquity, however, is questionable results.

5   Take the second question for example: if someone thinks he's special, does that make him a narcissist? Isn't everyone "special," in the etymologically related sense of "species," implying a unique combination of color, shape, and size? And where exactly is the line between narcissism and self-confidence? Given our high achievement and low rates of violence, maybe we Millennials are entitled to some self-esteem. Remember, surveys are like a house of mirrors: You can appear fat or thin, tall or short, depending on which study you happen to be looking at. UCLA's annual report, "The American Freshman National Norms for 2006," for example, paints a radically different picture. Its finding? "A record number [of college freshmen]— 83 percent—say they volunteered at least occasionally during their senior year of high school."

6   Either we're narcissistic, or we're compassionate—we can't be both. But rather than reconcile the two studies, Twenge dismisses the redeeming evidence, arguing that more and more high schools require students to meet a not-for-profit quota— the drive to do community service, she suggests, is coming from without, not from within. Admittedly, as university acceptance rates have fallen, students have turned increasingly to volunteer work to gild their applications. But if you eliminate competitive pressure from the equation, two-thirds of college freshman still believe it is "essential or very important to help others who are in difficulty, the highest percentage in a quarter century." I'm not calling Twenge a quack, but for every study that supports her point, there's another that contradicts it. And the fact of the matter is that when it comes to giving back, we've more than done our part.

7   "Okay," the critics say, "maybe you're not selfish, but you're self-absorbed." True, Millennials have been known to flaunt their lives on YouTube and MySpace. But it's not as if our predecessors didn't get attention other ways—you're telling me the hippie and grunge movements weren't attempts to attract eyeballs by raising eyebrows. Besides, while there's no denying that YouTube and MySpace are perfect outlets for the world's narcissists, vanity is not the only trait those websites cater to. Would YouTube be worth $1.65 billion to Google if users only posted videos of themselves without so much as a glance at others' postings? Critics get hung up on the egotism of the prefixes "my" and "you," but these sites are only successful because they're about other people—about meeting other people, about seeing what hidden talents other people have. Social networking, whether virtual or in person, is always going to entail a little window-dressing; the quasi-narcissistic practice of putting one's best foot forward in social settings is hardly confined to cyberspace.

8   In a recent *Los Angeles Times* editorial, William Strauss and Neil Howe ["Will the Real Gen Y Please Stand Up?" 2 March 2007] hit upon a baffling phenomenon: "Whenever youth behavior seems clearly positive, critics cynically find a way to dismiss it." Maybe these critics begrudge us our youth, maybe they mistake young-looking bodies for immature minds—your guess is as good as mine. For not only do we care about what other people think, seeking the approval of our peers through YouTube ratings and FaceBook friend requests, but we care about how other people

feel, volunteering for heroic causes on unprecedented scale. Yes, we feel entitled—to a world without terrorism and global warming and to politicians who will take these scourges seriously. And, no, we don't need constant praise—but a little positive feedback, when we deserve it, would be nice.

QUESTIONS FOR DISCUSSION

1. Greenberg was prompted to write this column by a news story about research by Jean Twenge into the topic of narcissism. How does his description of the research compare to Twenge's perspective?

2. What arguments and evidence does Greenberg give to refute Twenge's conclusions? Which author do you find more credible?

THE ASSIGNMENT

Read at least two perspectives addressing a topic you care about. In an essay explore the perspectives by noting where different authors address the same or similar questions, and compare their answers. Decide which views seem most valid and which have deepened your own understanding of the topic and its relevance to your life.

Topic and Focus

Pick a topic of current interest on which many people are expressing their views. The point is to explore the views, examine and question them carefully. Keep your mind open until you have explored the viewpoints, then draw your conclusions.

Audience

Think of your audience as people interested in your topic but who have not read what you have read. Consequently, you will need to tell your readers enough about each view for them to know who says what, using quotations and paraphrases as needed.

Voice and Style

Imagine that you are participating in a conversation with your readers about the perspectives and your opinions of them. You should sound fair, thoughtful, and receptive, willing to ponder points of view you do not find persuasive but which may contain valuable points or insights. Be willing also to look for problems in perspectives you do find persuasive.

Writing Assignment Suggestions

Comparing perspectives is a common occurrence in our everyday lives. For a film you have seen or a performance you have attended, find two or more reviews of substantial length, and compare the reviewers' interpretations and

Strategies for Comparing Perspectives

With each reading

1. Paraphrase or summarize the main points
2. Find the questions each point answers
3. Write down your response to each point
4. Keep track of connections across perspectives
5. Maintain an exploratory stance

We take you through these five steps, showing why they are worth doing and how they work with the narcissism topic.

evaluations. Conclude by explaining how reading the perspectives added to your ideas about the film. If your library has a collection of history textbooks, find ones from different time periods and compare their treatments of events or people. Have "the facts" changed? How has interpretation of the facts changed?

CHOOSING A TOPIC

Your instructor may assign a topic and readings arguing from different perspectives about it. If not, here are some possibilities for finding topics.

- *Reading and research.* Most authors will mention the names of people who agree and disagree with their point of view. For example, a news article about Jean Twenge also mentioned a psychologist whose work disputed Twenge's conclusions. To bring that perspective into your comparison, do an Internet or library database search of that person's name.

- *Library databases.* Research the topic in an index to periodicals, such as Academic OneFile (see Chapter 6, pages 107–108). The advantage is that you will find readings grouped according to topic and time, some of which will likely refer to each other.

- *Internet discussions.* If you find a reading on the Internet, it will often link you to what other writers have said. Online journals and magazines often contain lengthy comments in which readers exchange opinions with the original author and with each other.

EXPLORING YOUR TOPIC

See Chapter 6, pages 122–125, for guidance on paraphrasing and summarizing.

Before reading, begin by clarifying key definitions as we did with narcissism, using a good dictionary. Write to record your own viewpoints on the topic. Then, move on to explore the perspectives through your selection of readings.

Paraphrase or Summarize the Main Points

Paraphrasing or summarizing will help you digest the ideas and talk about them in your own voice. Mark the major subdivisions (paragraphs that discuss the same point) as you read. For each subdivision, put the main point in your own words. Reread the first two paragraphs of the Schumaker reading, "The Paradox of Narcissism," reproduced below and compare them with our student, Ian Fagerstrom's, paraphrase.

I. Schumaker, Paragraphs 1–2

> While walking through the local Botanical Gardens recently, a woman wearing a "Love Yourself" T-shirt jogged past me. T-shirts like that were nonexistent in the 1960s, when they all read "Love" or "Love One Another." But preachers of self-love are everywhere today. There are even numerous books extolling the virtues of self-love, including Peter McWilliams's *Love 101: To Love Oneself Is the Beginning of a Lifelong Romance.* The subtitle of that book is actually a tongue-in-cheek comment once made by Oscar Wilde. But it seems that many people have come to take that idea literally.
>
> Today the self-esteem movement is in full swing. As an arm of feel-good culture, this movement has persuaded us that it is not good enough to feel good within ourselves. We must also feel good about ourselves. It has grown in force to the extent that it has reshaped childhood education. Teachers in recent years have been trained that a high level of self-esteem is the child's passport to happiness and success in life, as well as to a good education. Less and less emphasis is being paid to self-discipline, hard work, integrity, and helping students gain realistic appraisals of themselves. Instead, young people are being told automatically that they are infinitely talented, phenomenally creative, and erupting with potential in any area that takes their fancy. One zealous school in Alabama went so far as placing banners over all the bathroom mirrors that read "You are now looking at one of the most special people in the whole world."

Fagerstrom's Paraphrase of Schumaker's Paragraphs 1–2

> Schumaker compares self-love now to the 1960's to show a change in focus. He also makes the point that the schools have worked too hard to bring up kids' self esteem at the expense of old-fashioned values like hard work.

◎ COLLABORATIVE ACTIVITY: Finding Subdivisions

Mark up the text of one of the readings to indicate its subdivisions. For each subdivision, write a paraphrase of its main point or points. As a class, discuss what students selected as main points and compare your paraphrases. •

Turn Main Points into Questions

Turn the main points into questions by asking, What question is this an answer to? Turning the main points into questions will help you in two ways: (1) *to connect the readings,* because writers will address the same questions; and (2) *to organize your paper,* because exploratory writing is structured around questions. These are the questions the main points in Fagerstrom's paraphrase of Paragraphs 1–2 answer:

- Has there been an increase in narcissism? Schumaker says yes.
- What has caused this increase? Schumaker says a cause is the self-esteem movement in the schools.

◎ COLLABORATIVE ACTIVITY: Rephrasing in Your Own Words

In groups of two or three, take paraphrases or quotations that the group agrees represent key points in the reading. As we have illustrated, rephrase the point to show what question the author is addressing.

Paraphrase and Comment

Write informally, such as in your notebook or on a class discussion board, to respond to the main points in each reading. Draw on your own experiences to test the merit of the author's ideas.

Here is an example of a notebook entry in response to Schumaker's reading. Notice how Fagerstrom moves back and forth between quoted and paraphrased passages in the text and his own response to the passages. To show the texture of moving from what the text says to what Fagerstrom says back, we have bolded the references to Schumaker's text.

> Shumaker seems to be very cynical about self-esteem, without pointing out that self-esteem in moderation is actually not a bad thing. **He says that "high self-esteem is not all that it was once cracked up to be" (169) and shows a correlation between people with high self-esteem and negative traits like risky sexual behavior, bragging, and hostility when they think they have been slighted.** Yes, I agree that too-high self-esteem is detrimental to happiness, but he could at least say that moderate self-esteem isn't bad. Without some self-esteem, I would not push myself to take on new challenges. Sure, **Western culture says that we always need to feel good about ourselves (169),** but he could at least admit that positive self-worth doesn't automatically lead to narcissism. He says, **"Societies that generate narcissism among their members are dysfunctional ones that have lost sight of the reciprocal nature of human happiness" (173).** This is a good point because individualism won't ever result in true happiness, but why can't he talk about people who balance self-worth with respect and love for others?

Question	Schumaker	Twenge
What is narcissism? How does it compare with self-esteem?	Paragraph 8	Paragraphs 1, 4
Is narcissism greater today than in the past?	Paragraphs 1, 3, 9	Paragraphs 2–3, 5–6
Is high self-esteem a good thing or a bad thing?	Paragraphs 3–6	Paragraph 4
If narcissism is increasing, what is contributing to this change?	Paragraphs 2, 9–13	Paragraphs 4, 9
What effects does narcissism have on personality and behavior?	Paragraphs 5–6, 9, 11, 15, 17	Paragraphs 1, 7–8

Figure 8.2

Comparative grid used to map differences and similarities among perspectives

As you read other perspectives, write more comparative notebook entries. In a notebook entry responding to more than one reading, show how both provide answers to a single question, either agreeing or disagreeing. If you organize these informal comparisons around questions in common, you will be creating material to use in the rough draft.

◎ ACTIVITY: Creating a Comparative Grid

As you read and reread each of the perspectives, record key points in a reading and interact with them by stating your own evaluations of the text, connections with the topic, and comparisons to other readings.

Create a comparative grid to map your comparisons (see Figure 8.2). When reading to compare what different authors have to say on similar topics, focus on where they agree and disagree on the same points. If you look at the list of questions raised in the first reading, you will see whether the second reading addresses any of the same questions. A comparative grid makes these connections easier to see. Review the following comparative grid to get a sense of how the points made about narcissism in the Schumaker and Twenge essays compare. •

Keep Track of Connections across Perspectives

As you read a second or third person's perspective, try one or more of these suggestions to help keep control over your sources:

- Annotate each reading with references to page numbers in other sources that address the same questions.
- Use color-coded highlighters to mark passages addressing the same questions in different readings.

- Consult previous informal writings often to recall ideas already responded to. Add quotes and paraphrases from new sources as they relate to points already explored.
- Add to your idea grid if you prefer this way of tracking ideas across sources.

Maintain an Exploratory Stance

It is important not to limit your observations to personal experience; doing this will limit your ability to compare effectively. For example, on the question of what causes narcissism, Twenge says that elementary schools praise kids who have done nothing to deserve praise. Some students said, "She's wrong; that didn't happen at my school. We had to work for our A's." A more exploratory stance would be to say, "While some schools may give kids false praise, in my experience I haven't seen it." And then you could go on to say more about how your schools did not have grade inflation, allowed students to fail, and so on. But you might also ask other students what their experiences have been at their schools. Inquiry, comparing perspectives, is all about opening your mind to the way others see the world. Doing so will enhance your own point of view.

DRAFTING YOUR PAPER

Drafting the essay for this project should not be difficult if you have been doing informal writing as you explored the sources. Read through your material again, and then consider the following advice.

Planning the Draft

Before you start drafting you need a plan to give your paper focus, purpose, and organization. For your introduction, you could

- open with your own view before reading. In the body and conclusion, indicate how your thinking changed.
- open with the question that is the focus of your exploration. State it clearly and explain its importance.
- open with one of the main questions that cut across the readings, such as "Some people think narcissism is a growing problem. Is it?" You could move directly into your paper this way.

You also need to mention the writers whose viewpoints you are exploring. You could devote one paragraph to background for all of them, citing full names, credentials, titles of the works you read, and main points. Or you could save this information for the body of your paper, introducing the authors as you bring them into your discussion.

The Art of Questioning: Planning the Body

Do not try to cover every point that comes up in the readings. *Be selective;* explore a few questions in depth. Choose ones you wrote most about in the informal writing you did.

Organizing around Questions

A paper that synthesizes ideas from multiple authors needs to be organized around the questions that cut across the readings, *not around the readings themselves.* If you devote the first part of your paper to just one author's views, the second to the second author's views, and so on, your paper will read like a summary rather than an exploration. Here are some suggestions for organizing around questions:

- Check the lists of questions you have made for each perspective. Put these lists together now and identify questions that appear in multiple readings.

- Consider whether narrowing the focus of your exploration might help. An exploration of narcissism, for instance, might deal only with the difference between healthy self-esteem and genuine narcissism.

- Based on length requirements for the paper and how much you have to say about the questions, select the ones you intend to address.

- Order the questions logically. For example, a definition question makes more sense at the paper's beginning. Discuss causes, then effects.

- Plan on multiple paragraphs for each question. You could, for instance, devote one paragraph to one source's answer, and another to what the others say on the same question.

- Create transitions so that your reader will know when discussion of one question is over and another is beginning.

Take up the general questions first and then more specific ones. It would not make sense to look at the role of schools in creating narcissists before taking up the questions "What is narcissism?" and "Is it increasing?"

Bear in mind that you need not agree with a viewpoint to explore interesting questions it raises. You could say, "While I see Greenberg's position on my generation as more realistic than Twenge's, is there anything valid in her idea that American culture encourages self-absorption?" Once you have worked out your answers to these questions, start drafting your paper.

Development and Organization

The Best Practices box above summarizes a key point about structure in comparing perspectives.

REVISING YOUR DRAFT

Revising this kind of paper usually involves improving the organization, looking more closely at the perspectives to make your exploration more specific, and including more of your own reactions to the authors' views. The Best Practices box on page 196 provides a checklist to help you revise your paper.

Revision Checklist for Comparing Perspectives

The checklist moves in descending order, from the major challenges of the project to concerns in every piece of formal writing.

1. *How much did you explore?* Exploring means entertaining a question. To entertain a question is to hold it open and consider it thoughtfully. If you disputed a point before considering its merits, revise and give it a chance.

2. *How well did you represent the ideas of all the authors?* Did you draw on the sources enough to represent their views accurately and fully?

3. *How well did you work quotations into your paper?* Set them up rather than drop them in, and follow up with explanation and commentary about context as needed.

4. *How well did you organize the paper?* Check to see that you are focusing on one question at a time.

5. *How well did you respond to the sources?* Use specifics to show exactly what you agreed or disagreed with and why.

6. *How smoothly did the sentences flow?* Each sentence sets up the reader's expectations for the one coming next. Read your draft aloud, listening for places where flow could be improved.

7. *Did you introduce the authors adequately?* Provide full name on first mention and something about their credentials.

The paragraph answers two questions: about effects of narcissism and whether there has been an increase in narcissism. This causes loss of focus and makes the paragraph too long.

When you have limited time to revise a paper, you have to prioritize. Take care of the bigger problems first, the ones that alter your essay substantially. If smaller problems remain, solve as many as you can in the time you have.

The following excerpts from Ian Fagerstrom's draft focus on three problems his peer reviewers found, common problems your draft also may have.

1. One large paragraph addressed two questions rather than one.

    Does narcissism create unhappiness, and more important, is narcissism a growing problem? Schumaker, concerned that happiness is an "endangered state of mind," does well to show that narcissism will lead to a false sense of happiness. Coming from the belief that you must surround yourself with good people to be happy, I completely agree with his point that "happiness is almost impossible if one is unable to escape the prison of self-interest" (175). Considering that happiness is typically the goal of one's life, Schumaker has effectively proved that narcissism ends any chances of that. He does not make any convincing points about it being a significant problem, though—just illustrating with an example of a woman wearing a "love yourself" T-shirt. What does that prove? Twenge says in an interview with National Public Radio that if you are narcissistic, "you may be happy—probably very happy—with how you feel about yourself, but you're going to end up in the long run alienating other people"

Addresses first question.

Addresses second question.

Addresses first question.

("Study"). So they would agree that narcissism really leads to a false kind of happiness that would not be satisfying. In fact, Twenge shows the even darker side of narcissism. Much more than just unhappiness, she believes that in extreme cases narcissism can lead to hostility and aggression of the worst kind, including murder (70–71).

> The paragraph was too long and not unified. In the revised version, Fagerstrom uses three focused paragraphs: 4, 5, and 6.

2. Fagerstrom did not mention Twenge's use of the NPI (Narcissistic Personality Inventory). In this excerpt, Fagerstrom refers to data misinterpretation, but he does not say what the data are.

   Jean M. Twenge, an Associate Professor of Psychology at San Diego State University and author of *Generation Me*, also tends to put the young generation in a negative light, accusing us of being obsessed with ourselves and putting the blame for it on the schools, media, and parents. She believes narcissism is on the rise, almost an epidemic. To put things back in perspective, Duncan Greenberg, an undergraduate student at Yale, wrote an editorial in his campus newspaper, "Generation Y and the New Myth of Narcissus." He would confront both Schumaker and Twenge and say that narcissism is actually not a problem at all, instead a misinterpretation of data. He takes the opposition and points out that our generation is actually more empathetic than most. So, on most issues, the two psychologists would agree, and Greenberg would disagree.

> Fagerstrom has not mentioned what data he is referring to. In the revised version, he added what he needed. See paragraph 2 in the revised version.

3. In many places, Fagerstrom needed to refer to the texts more specifically. There are many perspectives on the topic, some more critical than others. John F. Schumaker, a clinical psychologist and author of *In Search of Happiness*, has a very negative view on it all, arguing that American society is basically going down the drain because of narcissism, saying that it "is an unfulfilling experience that sets the stage for rage and eventual despair" (175).

> The cliché about "going down the drain" does not get at Schumaker's real concern. See paragraph 2 for a better paraphrase.

REVISED STUDENT EXAMPLE
Comparison of Perspectives on Narcissism

IAN FAGERSTROM

You will notice that Fagerstrom added a fourth reading, a National Public Radio interview with Twenge. Multiple readings can represent the same perspective so long as a participant in the conversation does not change his or her position. Twenge was interviewed about new research supporting her views on narcissism.

Living in a bustling city like Dallas, going to a college with many affluent students, and watching the TV every once in a while, I see self-absorbed people everywhere I turn. Many students get caught up in the appealing idea of being special. It's a good feeling to be at the top of the class, or the one with the newest iPod. So strong is the desire to be special that self-absorption or narcissism has become a much-discussed topic.

> Fagerstrom leads into his exploration with a natural voice and shows his connection to the topic.

This wording is more specific than the cliché "going down the drain."

There are many perspectives on it, some more critical than others. John Schumaker, a clinical psychologist and author of *In Search of Happiness*, has a very negative view, arguing that Americans are much less happy than they could be because of their focus on themselves. He says that narcissism "is an unfulfilling experience that sets the stage for rage and eventual despair" (175). While he may acknowledge the positives of healthy self-esteem based in relationships, he is more interested in the downside of high self-esteem.

3

Fagerstrom realized that he had to refer to the survey here to make his later references to it clear.

The second paragraph introduces all three perspectives, one option for introducing them.

Jean M. Twenge, an Associate Professor of Psychology at San Diego State University and author of *Generation Me*, also tends to put the young generation in a negative light, accusing us of being obsessed with ourselves and putting the blame for it on the self-esteem movement in the schools, media, and parents. She believes narcissism is on the rise, almost an epidemic, as indicated by college students' responses over the years to a psychological survey known as the Narcissistic Personality Inventory (NPI). To put things back in perspective, though, Duncan Greenberg, an undergraduate student at Yale, wrote an editorial in his campus newspaper, "Generation Y and the New Myth of Narcissus." He would confront both Schumaker and Twenge and say that narcissism is actually not a problem at all, instead a misinterpretation of the NPI data. He points out that our generation is actually more empathetic than most. So, on most issues, the two psychologists would agree, and Greenberg would disagree.

4

Fagerstrom leads into his first point of comparison: How do the authors define narcissism?

To fully understand what these authors are saying, we must first know how they are defining narcissism. For Schumaker, narcissism consists of "self-esteem . . . completely blown out of proportion" as well as "unwarranted self-esteem" (170). Although he does not necessarily equate high self-esteem with narcissism, he mentions that certain types of high self-esteem are potentially dangerous. His definition leaves room for misinterpretation and could be used to label many people as narcissists.

5

This paragraph synthesizes definitions and compares similarities.

This section of the paper will address the question: Is narcissism really becoming more prevalent?

Twenge describes narcissists as "overly focused on themselves"; they are people who "feel entitled to special privileges and believe that they are superior . . ." (*Generation*, 68). She carefully makes the distinction between high self-esteem and narcissism. She notes that people with high self-esteem feel close to others; narcissists, on the other hand, do not (69). Greenberg wisely uses the Mayo Clinic's definition to define it; traits such as "a need for constant praise" in addition to an "expectation of special treatment" succinctly embody narcissistic tendencies. Instead of trying to make his own definition, he goes with a well-known and respected authority. Still, the Mayo Clinic definitions in Greenberg are similar to the traits Twenge describes; their definitions are the same but they reach different conclusions about the existence of narcissism as a problem.

6

So with these definitions in mind, is narcissism becoming increasingly problematic? Schumaker does not really give evidence to show that rising narcissism is a serious problem. He doesn't have any evidence; he just makes good points that it is a negative trait. While Twenge may have some hard evidence with her survey, saying that 30 percent more college students score above average on the NPI than in 1982 ("Study"), Greenberg makes some compelling points to challenge her findings. He argues that the survey tricks people with "oblique and ambiguous" statements most people would agree with. What's wrong with feeling that you are special? As Greenberg asks, "if someone thinks he's special, does that make him a narcissist? Isn't everyone 'special,' in the etymologically related sense of 'species,' implying a unique combination of color, shape, and size?" He actually goes to the other end of the spectrum by saying that our generation may be "entitled to some self-esteem." Greenberg is savvy enough about surveys to realize that for every Twenge argument, there is probably another survey to refute it with. He does this by citing the UCLA survey of first-year students, which shows that they are volunteering "in record numbers" for community service. I agree with Greenberg: young people cannot be both empathetic and narcissistic.

7   Whether narcissism is increasing or not, these authors do show that it will lead to a false sense of happiness or worse. Coming from the belief that you must surround yourself with good people to be happy, I completely agree with Schumaker's point that "happiness is almost impossible if one is unable to escape the prison of self-interest" (175). Considering that happiness is typically the goal of one's life, Schumaker has effectively proved that narcissism ends any chances of that. Twenge says in an interview with National Public Radio that if you are narcissistic, "you may be happy—probably very happy—with how you feel about yourself, but you're going to end up in the long run alienating other people" ("Study"). So they would agree that narcissism really leads to a false kind of happiness that would not be satisfying.

8   In fact, Twenge shows the even darker side of narcissism. Much more than just unhappiness, she believes that in extreme cases narcissism can lead to hostility and aggression of the worst kind, including murder (*Generation,* 70–71). She uses the example of the Columbine shooters and their video where they make comments about getting the respect they deserve. While this is certainly scary to think about, I would disagree with her here and say that these boys actually had very little self-esteem to begin with. It was their lack of an ego rather than an inflated one that led them to kill thirteen people and commit suicide. Twenge bases her conclusion on the similarities between what the boys said on their video and what some of the items on the NPI say. But that is not enough evidence to make a diagnosis. It simply shows their desire for power after being bullied by other students. Twenge may scare people away from narcissism here, which is not a bad intention, but I believe that her reasoning is flawed.

9   Whatever definition of narcissism is used, everyone will agree that it is in no way a healthy behavior and will lead to unhappiness, just as in the myth of Narcissus. The main question still remains: Is narcissism on the rise? With many interpretations of data, people refute each other using the same evidence, and given the persistent bickering, the question may never be answered. Personally, at first I was inclined to accept Twenge's argument that schools, media, and parents are going too far in telling children they are the best, most special kids ever ("Study"). And Schumaker is right that some societies encourage narcissistic tendencies, very true in the consumer-society of the United States. But I am not so pessimistic as Twenge and Schumaker about the future, based on my generation's values.

10   I tend to agree with Greenberg that Generation Y is not as narcissistic as generations before us. He makes a valid point when he says that older generations often

Fagerstrom revised paragraph 2 to include information about Twenge's research, so he can refer to it again here without confusing his readers.

The focus of this section of the exploration is: What are the consequences or effects of narcissism on a person?

This paragraph is further development of Twenge's answer to the question about the effects of narcissism.

Fagerstrom clearly explains Twenge's point but shows why he reaches a different conclusion.

dismiss positive youth behavior. Whenever a younger generation is praised for something, the older generations put us down, call us spoiled and scoff at us. I have met my fair share of narcissists, but it is hard to prove that it is such a big problem that we need to name my generation "Generation Me."

WORKS CITED

Greenberg, Duncan. "Generation Y and the New Myth of Narcissus." Editorial. *The Yale Herald*, 8 Mar. 2007.

Schumaker, John F. *In Search of Happiness: Understanding an Endangered State of Mind*. Praeger, 2007.

Twenge, Jean M. *Generation Me: Why Today's Young Americans Are More Confident, Assertive, Entitled—and More Miserable Than Ever Before*. Free Press, 2006.

"Study Sees Rise of Narcissism among College Students." Interview by Alex Chadwick and Luke Burbank. *Day to Day*, 27 Feb. 2007, www.npr.org/templates/story/story.php?storyId=7618722.

CHAPTER SUMMARY

This chapter has given you practice in essential skills for other writing assignments in this course and others. You learned that people's perspectives are answers to questions, and that careful reading uncovers the questions that serve as threads, weaving the conversation together, even if authors do not refer to each other directly. Finding the questions at issue is essential to any research project and to making your own arguments.

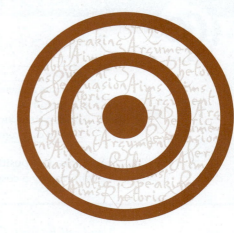

CHAPTER 9

Making Your Case: Arguing to Convince

The last chapter ended where inquiry ends—with the attempt to formulate a position, an opinion that you can assert with some confidence. When your aim shifts from inquiring to convincing, everything changes.

The most significant change is in audience. In inquiry, your audience consists of our fellow inquirers—friends, classmates, and teachers you can talk with face to face. You seek assurance that your position is at least plausible and defensible. In convincing, however, your audience consists of readers whose positions differ from your own or who have no position at all. The audience changes from a small, inside group that helps you develop your argument to a larger, public audience who will either accept or reject it.

As the audience changes, so does the situation or need for argument. Inquiry is a cooperative use of argument; convincing is more competitive. You pit your case against the cases of others to win the assent of readers who will compare the various arguments and ask, Who makes the best case?

Because of the change in audience and situation, your thinking becomes more strategic, calculated to influence readers. In inquiry, you find out what you can believe in; in convincing, you make a case readers can believe in. What you find compelling in inquiry will sometimes also convince readers, but *in convincing you must adapt your reasoning to appeal to their beliefs, values,*

From Inquiry to Convincing

Inquiry	Convincing
Intimate audience	Public readership
Cooperative	Competitive
Earns a conviction	Argues a thesis
Seeks a case convincing *to you*	Makes a case convincing *to them,* the readers

You take the position you discovered through inquiry and turn it into a thesis supported by a case designed to gain the assent of a specific group of readers.

---

and self-interest. Convincing, however, does not mean abandoning the work of inquiry. Your version of the truth, your conviction, gained through inquiry, is what you argue for.

WHAT IS A CASE?

A *case* develops your opinion about a controversial issue or question. The result is an argument with three levels of assertion:

1. A central contention or **claim,** also called a thesis.

    Example: College costs are unjustifiably high.

2. One or more reasons that explain or justify the claim.

    Example: They have increased much more than inflation over the last thirty years.

3. Appropriate evidence to back up each reason.

    Example: Data comparing the cost of living in general with increases in tuition and fees over the last thirty years.

WHY MAKE A CASE?

We make cases to do the following:

1. *Influence the thinking of others.* CEOs make cases for decisions they have made to their board of directors and stockholders; lawyers make cases to convince judges or a jury; special interest groups make cases to bring their causes to the attention of communities and civic leaders.

2. *Avoid violence.* Reason together or fight: These are the alternatives—hence, the Chinese proverb, "He who strikes the first blow has lost the argument." Nothing less than peaceful resolution of differences is at stake in arguing well.

3. *Learn what we really think.* In college, making cases is part of the learning process. We all have casual opinions we have never thought through.

Understanding the Functions of Case Structure

The **thesis** answers the question, *What are you asserting or claiming?*

Reasons explain or justify the thesis; they answer the question, *Why do you hold this thesis?*

Evidence backs up each reason; it answers the question, *What information confirms your reasoning?*

How good are they? Do they stand up to what is known about a subject in dispute? If not, we need to modify our opinion or alter what we think entirely. Reasoning is a way of learning that can change us profoundly.

HOW DO YOU MAKE A CASE?

Cases combine structure with strategy. The structure is the three-part division of reasoning: thesis, reasons, and evidence. The strategy is what you do to *connect with your readers,* to make what you have to say convincing to other people. See the Concept Close-Up, "Key Questions for Case-Making" to understand the concerns of strategic thinking in general. The following example should also help.

Many people, including some college presidents, are in favor of lowering the drinking age from twenty-one to eighteen. The concern is binge drinking, which they partly blame on the current drinking age. Breaking the law is part of the appeal of underaged drinking. Universities cannot advocate responsible drinking when many undergraduates are not supposed to drink at all.

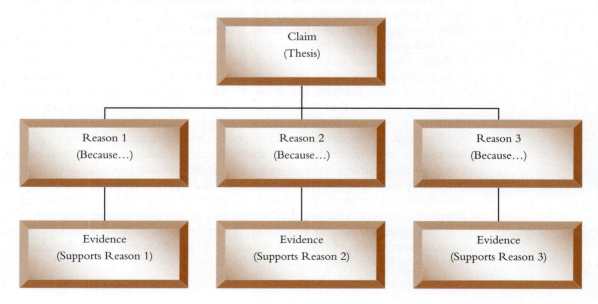

Key Questions for Case-Making

1. Who is your target audience?
2. What preconceptions and biases might they hold about your topic?
3. What claim do you want your readers to accept?
4. What reasons are likely to appeal to this audience?
5. How should you arrange these reasons for maximum impact on your target audience?
6. How might you introduce your case?
7. How might you conclude it?
8. How can you gain the trust and respect of your audience?

Convincing is audience centered. Every choice we make must be made with the target audience in mind.

Organizations such as MADD (Mothers against Drunk Driving) support the twenty-one legal age. They point to thousands of people who die each year in traffic accidents caused by drunk drivers. Lower the drinking age, they say, and you will only make a serious problem worse.

Given the range of opinion, what good case could you make favoring legal access to alcohol at eighteen? The most common reason offered is consistency. If young adults are old enough to fight in Afghanistan or Iraq, shouldn't they be old enough to drink legally?

In making your case, you can offer reasons like this one. However, they will not have much impact on people who support the current law. Reaching them requires strategy, *thinking as the other side thinks*.

Here is one way to cross the divide. All agree that abusing alcohol is a big problem. They differ on how to reduce the problem. Legalize and educate is one way; prohibit by law and strictly enforce the law is the other. In making a case in favor of the lower drinking age, stress the shared goal—reducing alcohol abuse.

You could argue that age is not the issue but rather moderation and responsibility whenever people drink. After all, most drunk drivers are not under legal drinking age. But moderation and responsibility are exactly what the current law cannot promote. Prohibition hardly encourages moderation and responsibility; on the contrary, it drives underaged drinking underground, out of sight but hardly out of common practice. You could go on to support MADD's well-developed measures for preventing drunk driving, such as encouraging designated drivers. You could advocate that universities devote more effort and time to educating college students about drinking. Without a strategy for winning over the opposition, all your argument can do is strengthen the adherence of people who already share your position.

Examining Your Audience's Beliefs

You cannot reach everyone. But you can reach many people, at least enough to get them to reconsider what they think. The problem is not that reasoning lacks power but that its power depends on coming up with ways to appeal to people who do not already agree with you.

Begin by asking these two questions:

- What are the opinions of people who differ from me?
- Why do they hold these opinions?

Based on this understanding, then ask,

- Can I think of goals, values, attitudes, or beliefs that I share with those who differ from me?
- Can I agree with at least some of what they say?
- What exactly do I need to change in their viewpoint to move them toward my position?

In short, *you need to find the common ground you share with those you want to convince.* In this way you can reduce the "us versus them" mentality that makes reasoning seem so frustrating and pointless.

READINGS

We begin with a recent contribution to a long-standing dispute—teaching evolution in public schools—that remains controversial enough in the United States to result in court cases.

Optimism in Evolution

OLIVIA JUDSON

Educated at Stanford and Oxford, Olivia Judson is a biologist at Imperial College, in London. She's best known for her book, *Dr. Tatiana's Sex Advice to All Creation*, an international best-seller that deals in an engaging way with the role of sex in evolution. She writes a weekly blog on evolutionary biology called "The Wild Side," accessible on *The New York Times* website.

The following column appeared in *The New York Times*. As you read, note how well Judson structures her case for teaching evolution in all beginning biology classes.

When the dog days of summer come to an end, one thing we can be sure of is that the school year that follows will see <u>more fights over the teaching of evolution and whether intelligent design, or even Biblical accounts of creation, have a place in America's science classrooms.</u>

In these arguments, evolution is treated as an abstract subject that deals with the age of the earth or how fish first flopped onto land. It's discussed as though it

Reminds readers of the conflict of opinion.

were an optional, quaint and largely irrelevant part of biology. <u>And a common consequence of the arguments is that evolution gets dropped from the curriculum entirely.</u>

3   This is a travesty.

4   It is also dangerous.

5   <u>Evolution should be taught—indeed, it should be central to beginning biology classes—for at least three reasons.</u>

6   <u>First,</u> it provides a powerful framework for investigating the world we live in. Without evolution, biology is merely a collection of disconnected facts, a set of descriptions. <u>The astonishing variety of nature, from the tree shrew that guzzles vast quantities of alcohol every night to the lichens that grow in the Antarctic wastes, cannot be probed and understood.</u> Add evolution—and it becomes possible to make inferences and predictions and (sometimes) to do experiments to test those predictions. All of a sudden patterns emerge everywhere, and apparently trivial details become interesting.

7   The second reason for teaching evolution is that the subject is immediately relevant here and now. The impact we are having on the planet is causing other organisms to evolve—and fast. And I'm not talking just about the obvious examples: <u>widespread resistance to pesticides among insects; the evolution of drug resistance in the agents of disease, from malaria to tuberculosis; the possibility that, say, the virus that causes bird flu will evolve into a form that spreads easily from person to person.</u> The impact we are having is much broader.

8   <u>For instance,</u> we are causing animals to evolve just by hunting them. The North Atlantic cod fishery has caused the evolution of cod that mature smaller and younger than they did 40 years ago. Fishing for grayling in Norwegian lakes has caused a similar pattern in these fish. Human trophy hunting for bighorn rams has caused the population to evolve into one of smaller-horn rams. (All of which, incidentally, is in line with evolutionary predictions.)

9   Conversely, hunting animals to extinction may cause evolution in their former prey species. Experiments on guppies have shown that, without predators, these fish evolve more brightly colored scales, mature later, bunch together in shoals less and lose their ability to suddenly swim away from something. Such changes can happen in fewer than five generations. If you then reintroduce some predators, the population typically goes extinct.

10   <u>Thus,</u> a failure to consider the evolution of other species may result in a failure of our efforts to preserve them. And, perhaps, to preserve ourselves from diseases, pests and food shortages. In short, evolution is far from being a remote and abstract subject. A failure to teach it may leave us unprepared for the challenges ahead.

11   The third reason to teach evolution is more philosophical. It concerns the development of an attitude toward evidence. <u>In his book, "The Republican War on Science," the journalist Chris Mooney argues persuasively that a contempt for scientific evidence—or indeed, evidence of any kind—has permeated the Bush administration's policies, from climate change to sex education, from drilling for oil to the war in Iraq.</u> A dismissal of evolution is an integral part of this general attitude.

12   Moreover, since the science classroom is where a contempt for evidence is often first encountered, it is also arguably where it first begins to be cultivated. A society where

---

Indicates what's at stake, why this topic matters.

States thesis or central claim, signals reader to expect three-part defense of the thesis.

Numbers reasons to help readers identify them.

Note use of specific examples of "astonishing variety."

Makes first point forcefully: that nature cannot be understood without evolution.

Reminds readers of well-known examples of evolution caused by human activity.

Use of transitional phrase.

Another use of a transitional word or phrase.

Cites authority to back up her reason.

ideology is a substitute for evidence can go badly awry. <u>(This is not to suggest that science is never distorted by the ideological left; it sometimes is, and the results are no better.)</u>

13   But for me, the most important thing about studying evolution is something less tangible. It's that the endeavor contains a profound optimism. It means that when we encounter something in nature that is complicated or mysterious, such as the flagellum of a bacteria or the light made by a firefly, we don't have to shrug our shoulders in bewilderment.

14   Instead, we can ask how it got to be that way. And if at first it seems so complicated that the evolutionary steps are hard to work out, we have an invitation to imagine, to play, to experiment and explore. To my mind, this only enhances the wonder.

Acknowledges that distortion of science is not limited to the political right.

Good conclusion that stresses the author's personal view and refutes the notion that evolution takes away from the wonder and beauty of nature.

QUESTIONS FOR DISCUSSION

1. When you took your first biology class, was evolution taught as the foundation of the discipline, or as "an optional, quaint, and largely irrelevant part of biology" (paragraph 2)? How did you feel about evolution then? What is your view now?

2. Judson calls the failure to teach evolution a "travesty"—that is, a gross misrepresentation of something. Does she establish that leaving evolution out of biological instruction distorts the discipline? How?

3. She also calls the failure to teach evolution "dangerous." What in her article confirms that statement?

Strategies Used in Case-Making: Structure and Readership

There could not be a clearer example of how to structure an effective case, one easy for a reader to follow:

Thesis: Evolution should be central to beginning biology classes.

> *Reason 1:* It provides a powerful framework for investigation.
>
>> *Evidence:* moving beyond "disconnected facts" to "inferences and predictions"
>
> *Reason 2:* Evolution is relevant to the here and now.
>
>> *Evidence:* drug resistance in microbes, the impact of hunting, evolution in species whose prey goes extinct, and so on
>
> *Reason 3:* Teaching evolution encourages a respect for evidence.
>
>> *Evidence:* reference to *The Republican War on Science*, the ignoring or suppression of scientific evidence

You can learn much about how to structure a case from Judson's article, including how to develop individual reasons in support of a thesis. Note that the second reason takes four paragraphs (7–10) to explain and support and that she devotes two paragraphs (11–12) to her third reason. *Follow her example, and do not think of each reason as corresponding to a single paragraph.* Reasons often require more than one paragraph to explain and support.

Another feature of the article worth your attention is how to *frame* (provide a context for) a case and how to *close* or conclude a case. Note that Judson has a four-paragraph introduction that precedes her thesis, stated in paragraph 5. The opening paragraphs explain why she is making her case for teaching evolution— because too often it either is not taught or not taught well. Readers need to know *why* you are making a case, the context that makes a case worth making.

Her two-paragraph conclusion (13–14) is a good example of something much better than a summarizing "in conclusion" close. She says that evolution "contains a profound optimism" and "enhances the wonder" of studying nature. It is these positive attitudes that opponents of evolution say teaching evolution destroys. Her conclusion, therefore, addresses an objection the other side has raised.

In addition to its structure, the Judson article offers an important insight into *selecting an appropriate readership* for any case you make. On one hand, Judson is not writing for her fellow biologists. With very few exceptions, they agree with her already. On the other hand, she also makes no effort to convince those unalterably opposed to teaching evolution. Instead, she is making her case for those who may think teaching evolution does not matter much or for those who support equal time for evolution and creationism.

You should do likewise in conceiving readers for the cases you make. Depending on the topic and your position on it, there will always be a segment of readers unalterably opposed to what you have to say. Ignore them and address an audience capable of responding to your reasoning.

PUTTING YOUR VOICE INTO YOUR ARGUMENT

Voice refers to the personality of the writer as it is made apparent in the writing. While making an argument, you want to show genuine conviction. The voice you choose, which may demonstrate moderation, or passion, or sarcasm, or any other quality, helps you do this. However, too much passion, heavy sarcasm, or insults to the other side are not effective in changing minds. Here is a passage from a case for prison reform. The full reading appears later in this chapter.

> Prison has a role in public safety, but it is not a cure-all. Its value is limited, and its use should be limited to what it does best: isolating young criminals long enough to give them a chance to grow up and get a grip on their impulses.

Read these sentences aloud and you can hear a voice appropriate for case-making: It states its position clearly, directly, and forcefully. It is more formal than relaxed chatting with a friend, but not as formal as a speech from President Obama or an emotional sermon from the pulpit on Sunday.

You can miss appropriate voice in two ways. On one hand, you may have been taught to keep your opinions out of your writing. Clearly, the advice does not apply to arguing a case, because the thesis you are defending *is* your opinion. On the other hand, resist being influenced by the phony, overheated sensationalism of much talk radio and TV. Argument is not name-calling, insults, outrageous claims, or partisan bickering—all designed to increase ratings. Argument is the calm voice of reason, of opinions stated precisely and defended well. It is one of the voices most admired and respected at universities, in business meetings, in community gatherings, and wherever productive interaction among people occurs.

Why Prisons Don't Work

WILBERT RIDEAU

Wilbert Rideau was convicted of murder at age nineteen and spent over forty years of his life in Louisiana State Penitentiary at Angola. He edited the prison newspaper and became an award-winning journalist and one of the best-known convicts ever in the United States.

As you read his article, pay special attention to how Rideau depicts the problem of how we deal with criminals in the United States and to the solution he proposes. Note also his use of cause-and-effect reasoning, common in case-making.

1 I was among thirty-one murderers sent to the Louisiana State Penitentiary in 1962 to be executed or imprisoned for life. We weren't much different from those we found here, or those who had preceded us. We were unskilled, impulsive, and uneducated misfits, mostly black, who had done dumb, impulsive things—failures, rejects from the larger society. Now a generation has come of age and gone since I've been here, and everything is much the same as I found it. The faces of the prisoners are different, but behind them are the same impulsive, uneducated, unskilled minds that made dumb, impulsive choices that got them into more trouble than they ever thought existed. The vast majority of us are consigned to suffer and die here so politicians can sell the illusion that permanently exiling people to prison will make society safe.

2 Getting tough has always been a "silver bullet," a quick fix for the crime and violence that society fears. Each year in Louisiana—where excess is a way of life—lawmakers have tried to outdo each other in legislating harsher mandatory penalties and in reducing avenues of release. The only thing to do with criminals, they say, is get tougher. They have. In the process, the purpose of prison began to change. The state boasts one of the highest lockup rates in the country, imposes the most severe penalties in the nation, and vies to execute more criminals per capita than anywhere else. This state is so tough that last year, when prison authorities here wanted to punish an inmate in solitary confinement for an infraction, the most they could inflict on him was to deprive him of his underwear. It was all he had left.

3 If getting tough resulted in public safety, Louisiana citizens would be the safest in the nation. They're not. Louisiana has the highest murder rate among states. Prison, like the police and the courts, has a minimal impact on crime because it is a response after the fact, a mop-up operation. It doesn't work. The idea of punishing the few

to deter the many is counterfeit because potential criminals either think they're not going to get caught or they're so emotionally desperate or psychologically distressed that they don't care about the consequences of their actions. The threatened punishment, regardless of its severity, is never a factor in the equation. But society, like the "incorrigible" criminal it abhors, is unable to learn from its mistakes.

4   Prison has a role in public safety, but it is not a cure-all. Its value is limited, and its use should also be limited to what it does best: isolating young criminals long enough to give them a chance to grow up and get a grip on their impulses. It is a traumatic experience, certainly, but it should be only a temporary one, not a way of life. Prisoners kept too long tend to embrace the criminal culture, its distorted values and beliefs; they have little choice—prison is their life. There are some prisoners who cannot be returned to society—serial killers, serial rapists, professional hit men, and the like—but the monsters who need to die in prison are rare exceptions in the criminal landscape.

5   Crime is a young man's game. Most of the nation's random violence is committed by young urban terrorists. But because of long, mandatory sentences, most prisoners here are much older, having spent fifteen, twenty, thirty, or more years behind bars, long past necessity. Rather than pay for new prisons, society would be well served by releasing some of its older prisoners who pose no threat and using the money to catch young street thugs. Warden John Whitley agrees that many older prisoners here could be freed tomorrow with little or no danger to society. Release, however, is governed by law or by politicians, not by penal professionals. Even murderers, those most feared by society, pose little risk. Historically, for example, the domestic staff at Louisiana's Governor's mansion has been made up of murderers, hand-picked to work among the chief-of-state and his family. Penologists have long known that murder is almost always a once-in-a-lifetime act. The most dangerous criminal is the one who has not yet killed but has a history of escalating offenses. He's the one to watch.

6   Rehabilitation can work. Everyone changes in time. The trick is to influence the direction that change takes. The problem with prisons is that they don't do more to rehabilitate those confined in them. The convict who enters prison illiterate will probably leave the same way. Most convicts want to be better than they are, but education is not a priority. This prison houses 4,600 men and offers academic training to 240, vocational training to a like number. Perhaps it doesn't matter. About 90 percent of the men here may never leave this prison alive.

7   The only effective way to curb crime is for society to work to prevent the criminal act in the first place, to come between the perpetrator and crime. Our youngsters must be taught to respect the humanity of others and to handle disputes without violence. It is essential to educate and equip them with the skills to pursue their life ambitions in a meaningful way. As a community, we must address the adverse life circumstances that spawn criminality. These things are not quick, and they're not easy, but they're effective. Politicians think that's too hard a sell. They want to be on record for doing something now, something they can point to at reelection time. So the drumbeat goes on for more police, more prisons, more of the same failed policies.

8   Ever see a dog chase its tail?

QUESTIONS FOR DISCUSSION

1. According to Rideau, why doesn't the possibility of prison deter criminal acts?

2. What does he say prisons do best? What roles should they play in our society's effort to cope with criminals? Do his proposals make sense, given his analysis of cause and effect? Why or why not?

3. What does Rideau contend would truly be effective in reducing crime, especially the violent crime we fear most? What would have to change to pursue the course of action he favors?

◎ COLLABORATIVE ACTIVITY: Analyzing Case Structure

In groups of two or three, look over Rideau's argument with an eye to **case structure.** Write up an outline of its claim and reasons. Beneath each reason, jot down something about the evidence that he uses to support it. Compare your group's decisions about Rideau's case structure with the outline of at least one other group. Where did you find consensus about the argument's structure? If you found disagreement about structure, how might that be explained or reconciled? •

Strategies Used in Case-Making: Problem-Solution, Cause-and-Effect Reasoning

The difficulty in solving any problem resides in understanding it, which is why cause-and-effect reasoning dominates problem-solution cases. Fail to grasp the causes of a problem, and you will also fail to solve it. It sounds simple, but of course it is not.

Rideau shows us clearly why understanding a problem can be so difficult. First, there is prejudice, often rooted in common sense. Get tough with crime?—certainly, we say. It seems so reasonable that our politicians outdo each other trying to be the toughest. But as Rideau explains, getting tough is only a "mop-up operation" (paragraph 3) after the criminal has been caught and convicted. Do we feel safer when violent criminals receive long prison terms and, in some cases, life without parole? We do, yet murder and other violent crimes are daily news items, and the cost of locking up so many people for so long imposes a huge burden on taxpayers.

With most problems, understanding depends on getting beyond gut reactions and common sense. Ask, *What is really going on?* Answering it requires cool, dispassionate analysis of the information we have. Drawing on his own long experience, Rideau sees a pattern: "Crime is a young man's game," especially the violent crime we fear most (paragraph 5). If this is so, prisons should "[isolate] young criminals long enough to give them a chance to grow up and get a grip on their impulses" (paragraph 4). If this is so, rehabilitation requires more effort; otherwise, paroled prisoners will not be equipped to rejoin society as productive, law-abiding citizens. If this is so, it makes no sense to keep older prisoners in jail for so long, well past their impulsive youth. If this is so, "coming between the perpetrator and the crime"—that is, working with young people in the neighborhoods where so much of the violent crime occurs—is about the only effective way to *prevent* crime, as opposed to reacting to it after it occurs.

The Rideau article shows how problem-solution, cause-and-effect case-making works: Analyze what you know to identify the cause or causes of a problem. The solution, then, follows from understanding the cause: If crime is a young man's game, everything Rideau proposes makes sense.

A Plan for Reducing American Dependence on Foreign Oil

T. BOONE PICKENS

T. Boone Pickens is an internationally prominent Texas oil man, investor, and philanthropist, who used his money and influence to bring the following proposal to the attention of all Americans through newspaper spreads and Internet postings.

We took the following argument from his website. The selection preserves the formatting of the website. As you read, pay special attention to the use of graphics as an efficient way of presenting evidence and to the use of bold print as a way of calling attention to key points.

THE PLAN

1   America is addicted to foreign oil.

2   It's an addiction that threatens our economy, our environment and our national security.

3   It touches every part of our daily lives and ties our hands as a nation and a people.

4   The addiction has worsened for decades and now it's reached a point of crisis.

5   **In 1970, we imported 24% of our oil. Today it's nearly 70% and growing.**

6   Oil prices have come down from the staggering highs of last summer, but lower prices have not reduced our dependence on foreign oil or lessened the risks to either our economy or our security.

7   If we are depending on foreign sources for nearly 70% of our oil, we are in a precarious position in an unpredictable world.

8   In addition to putting our security in the hands of potentially unfriendly and unstable foreign nations, we spent $475 billion on foreign oil in 2008 alone. That's money taken out of our economy and sent to foreign nations, and it will continue to drain the life from our economy for as long as we fail to stop the bleeding.

9   Projected over the next 10 years the cost will be $10 trillion—it will be the greatest transfer of wealth in the history of mankind.

10 Can't we just produce more oil?

11 | America uses a lot of oil. Every day 85 million barrels of oil are produced around the world.

12 | And 21 million of those are used here in the United States.

13 | That's 25% of the world's oil demand. Used by just 4% of the world's population.

14 | Consider this: America imports 12 million barrels a day, and Saudi Arabia only produces 9 million a day. Is there really more undiscovered oil here than in all of Saudi Arabia?

15 | World oil production peaked in 2005. Despite growing demand and an unprecedented increase in prices, oil production has fallen over the last three years. Oil is getting more expensive to produce, harder to find and there just isn't enough of it to keep up with demand.

16 | The simple truth is that cheap and easy oil is gone.

17 | **But America is focused on another crisis: The economy.**

18 | All Americans are feeling the effects of our recent downturn. And addressing this problem is the top priority of our nation. This is more than bailing out a bank, an insurance firm or a car company. The American economy is huge and has many facets.

19 | To make a real and lasting impact we must seek to do more than create new jobs and opportunities today, we must build the platform on which our economy can continue to grow for decades to come.

20 | There is nothing more important to the present and future of our economy than energy. Any effort to address our economic problems will require a thorough understanding of this issue and willingness to confront our dependence on foreign oil and what domestic resources we can use.

21 | It is a crisis too large to be addressed by piecemeal steps. We need a plan of action on scale with the problems we face. That is the spirit in which the Pickens Plan was conceived. The Pickens Plan is a collection of steps that together form a comprehensive approach to America's energy needs.

The Pickens Plan

22 | There are several pillars to the Pickens Plan:

- Create millions of new jobs by building out the capacity to generate up to 22 percent of our electricity from wind. And adding to that with additional solar capacity.

- Building a 21st century backbone electrical grid.

- Providing incentives for homeowners and the owners of commercial buildings to upgrade their insulation and other energy saving options.

- Using America's natural gas to replace imported oil as a transportation fuel.

23 | While dependence on foreign oil is a critical concern, it is not a problem that can be solved in isolation. We have to think about energy as a whole, and that begins by considering our energy alternatives and thinking about how we will fuel our world in the next 10 to 20 years and beyond.

New Jobs from Renewable Energy and Conservation

24   Any discussion of alternatives should begin with the 2007 Department of Energy study showing that building out our wind capacity in the Great Plains—from northern Texas to the Canadian border—would produce 138,000 new jobs in the first year, and more than 3.4 million new jobs over a ten-year period, while also producing as much as 20 percent of our needed electricity.

25   Building out solar energy in the Southwest from western Texas to California would add to the boom of new jobs and provide more of our growing electrical needs—doing so through economically viable, clean, renewable sources.

26   To move that electricity from where it is being produced to where it is needed will require an upgrade to our national electric grid. A 21st century grid which will, as technology continues to develop, deliver power where it is needed, when it is needed, in the direction it is needed, will be the modern equivalent of building the Interstate Highway System in the 1950's.

27   Beyond that, tremendous improvements in electricity use can be made by creating incentives for owners of homes and commercial buildings to retrofit their spaces with proper insulation.

28   Studies show that a significant upgrading of insulation would save the equivalent of one million barrels of oil per day in energy by cutting down on both air conditioning costs in warm weather and heating costs in winter.

A Domestic Fuel to Free Us from Foreign Oil

29   Conserving and harnessing renewable forms of electricity not only has incredible economic benefits, but is also a crucial piece of the oil dependence puzzle. We should

2010 Civic GX Sedan

The Honda Civic GX Natural Gas Vehicle is the cleanest internal-combustion vehicle in the world according to the EPA.

continue to pursue the promise of electric or hydrogen powered vehicles, but America needs to address transportation fuel today. Fortunately, we are blessed with an abundance of clean, cheap, domestic natural gas.

30 Currently, domestic natural gas is primarily used to generate electricity. It has the advantage of being cheap and significantly cleaner than coal, but this is not the best use of our natural gas resources.

31 By generating electricity from wind and solar and conserving the electricity we have, we will be free to shift our use of natural gas to where it can lower our need for foreign oil—helping President Obama reach his goal of zero oil imports from the Middle East within ten years—by replacing diesel as the principal transportation fuel for heavy trucks and fleet vehicles.

32 Nearly 20% of every barrel of oil we import is used by 18-wheelers moving goods burning imported diesel. An over-the-road truck cannot be moved using current battery technology. Fleet vehicles like buses, taxis, express delivery trucks, and municipal and utility vehicles (any vehicle which returns to the "barn" each night where refueling is a simple matter) should be replaced by vehicles running on clean, cheap, domestic natural gas rather than imported gasoline or diesel fuel.

A Plan That Brings It All Together

33 Natural gas is not a permanent or complete solution to imported oil. It is a bridge fuel to slash our oil dependence while buying us time to develop new technologies that will ultimately replace fossil transportation fuels. Natural gas is the critical puzzle piece that will help us keep more of the $350 to $450 billion every year at home, where it can power our economy and pay for our investments in wind energy, a smart grid and energy efficiency.

34 It is this connection that makes The Pickens Plan not just a collection of good ideas, but a plan. By investing in renewable energy and conservation, we can create millions of new jobs. New alternative energies allow us to shift natural gas to transportation; securing our economy by reducing our dependence on foreign oil, and keeping more money at home to pay for the whole thing.

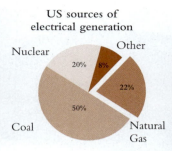

US sources of
electrical generation

How Do We Get It Done?

35   The Pickens Plan is a bridge to the future—a blueprint to reduce foreign oil dependence by harnessing domestic energy alternatives, and to buy us time to develop even greater new technologies.

36   Building new wind generation facilities, conserving energy and better utilizing our natural gas resources can replace more than one-third of our foreign oil imports in 10 years. But it will take leadership.

37   We're organizing behind the Pickens Plan now to ensure our voices will be heard.

38   Together with President Obama and the new Congress, we can take down the old barriers and provide energy security for generations to come, while helping dig out of the recession we are in today.

39   As our new President has said, "Yes, we can." And together, as never before, we will.

QUESTIONS FOR DISCUSSION

1. Cases made online or in other popular, mass media like television and newspapers usually observe special conventions. Describe the conventions in this website posting. In your view, do they work well to communicate the message? Why or why not?

2. This short article uses five graphics, including several types—photographs, a map, and a pie graph. In case-making, graphics present evidence efficiently and memorably. What evidence do the graphics in this piece provide? What statements in the article do they support?

3. The T. Boone Pickens website makes no effort to conceal his personal stake in the plan. He is heavily invested in natural gas and wind power. In your view, does being up front strengthen or weaken his case?

Strategies Used in Case-Making: Lines of Reasoning

Compare the structure of this case with Olivia Judson's in "Optimism in Evolution" (pages 205–207). Judson's is the typical case: State a thesis; defend it with three or four reasons; support each reason with evidence. It works well when your thesis is a single claim, such as "Evolution should be central to beginning biology classes."

In contrast, the Pickens Plan is an example of a case composed of two or more claims or theses, each requiring explanation and evidence. The Pickens Plan makes three claims:

- We must reduce our dependence on foreign oil. (claim 1)
- We can do this by exploiting domestic wind power for generating electricity. (claim 2)
- We can also substitute domestic supplies of natural gas for the gasoline and diesel we are currently using in vehicles. (claim 3)

The three claims are linked together by the contrast between *foreign* crude oil and *domestic* wind energy and natural gas.

Each part of the Pickens Plan also develops differently from Judson's single-thesis case. Think of it as answers to your questions as you read, and the logic is easy to follow. Here is the logic for claim 1, which establishes the problem:

What is the problem your plan would solve?

Answer: America's addiction to foreign oil.

Is that really such a big problem?

Answer: Yes. We import 70% of our oil. It threatens our economy, environment, and national security.

Why not just produce more oil domestically?

Answer: There is not enough to satisfy the current demand. The era of cheap and easy oil is gone.

This way of arguing a point works by anticipating your readers' questions and answering them one by one. The secret to arguing this way is *to imagine what your readers will think based on what you have just said.* If you say that America is addicted to foreign oil, your readers will think, So what? Where's the harm? Then, when you answer that question, your reader will think, Why not produce more domestic oil? When you indicate that doing so will not solve the problem, that brings one line of reasoning to a close, and you are ready to move on to the solutions you advocate.

◎ COLLABORATIVE ACTIVITY: Analyzing the Rest of Pickens's Case

Working with one or two classmates, analyze the reasoning of the remaining parts of the Pickens case. What sequence of questions is being answered in the solution parts of the case?

Then address this question: Is the reasoning as a whole convincing? Why or why not?

⊚ ACTIVITY: Informal Writing in Response to an Argument

Each of the topics addressed in the readings in this chapter—teaching evolution, prison reform, and the energy crisis—is debated vigorously online, especially in blogs and in e-mail responses to web postings and print publications. Why not weigh in on the subject that interests you the most? If you have a blog, post a response to one of the readings, or make your own short case on the subject. If you do not maintain a blog, compose an e-mail response to one of the authors, or get a conversation going online with other members of your class via e-mail or Blackboard or any other online means for exchanging viewpoints and ideas.

The best way to learn to make cases is to get involved in real arguments on genuine issues. You also may find your topic for this chapter's assignment this way.

THE ASSIGNMENT

Make a case that seeks to convince readers to accept your central claim or thesis about any controversial topic, problem, issue, or question. *Controversial* means that various positions or stances are possible—not necessarily that the subject has received media attention. It can address anything from something as personal and local as a family dilemma or a campus concern to something as impersonal and global as U.S. relations with China.

Topic and Focus

Whatever your topic is, avoid thinking in pro–con, us versus them ways. Despite how they are depicted in the media, even highly polarized issues like abortion are not simply "pro-life" versus "pro-choice." Strongly antiabortion cases, for instance, usually allow abortion in instances of rape, incest, or when the woman's life is in danger, and many people labeled "pro-choice" do not oppose reasonable restrictions on abortion after the first trimester. *Think in terms of many possible stances.*

Most topics also consist of many controversial issues. Consider limiting your case to one of them. For instance, standardized testing in public schools raises many issues, including what subject areas should be tested, how standardized testing affects coverage of a subject, what to do about schools that do not meet standards, and how to control cheating. You can easily locate many other areas for debate in newspapers and web searches.

Audience

Cases aim at two audiences: people weakly inclined to agree and those tending toward another stance but open to reason. Your case should strengthen the adherence of those favorably disposed to your thesis by giving them good reasons and strong evidence they may have lacked before. Those good reasons and strong evidence also may appeal to readers entertaining other positions, but reaching them requires strategy (see pages 207–208).

Voice and Style

Cases aim for assent to a thesis. They want to secure agreement by advancing good reasons based on current, accurate information about the topic.

Your voice should be dispassionate, calm, and fair. Treat other positions and arguments with respect, even as you show that your evidence and reasons are more compelling.

Writing Assignment Suggestions

The paper could be written in many possible genres: an editorial, a posting on a website, a magazine article, a text for a speech, an open letter to some group of people, a personal letter, and so on. You might consider writing in one of these genres if your topic and readership seem appropriate and your instructor approves.

A wide range of topics are of interest to college students: college costs, living conditions on campus, and avoiding excessive debt in personal finances; cultural and social issues, such as the impact of electronic communication on how people live and relate to other people, computer gaming, rap music, the behavior of people at sporting events, controversial films, TV shows, and advertisements; political issues, such as counterterrorism policy, the use of torture in interrogating persons suspected of terrorist activity, health care, energy policy, global warming, and immigration. Perhaps your topic can be one of these or related to one of them.

CHOOSING A TOPIC

Often the best topics come from problems and issues you have experienced directly as a student, voter, friend, parent, resident in a foreign country, participant in a sport or other activity—in short, something you have lived. Maybe you are involved in a club, volunteer organization, or student activity that deserves more recognition or support. Maybe you attended a campus event and heard a controversial speaker with a viewpoint you responded to strongly. Civic activities, internships, and jobs can also be rich sources of topics for case-making. Here are some possibilities for finding topics.

- *Class readings.* Class readings can suggest topics for case-making, especially if the readings themselves are cases, like the examples in this chapter. For instance, after reading the Pickens Plan, you may have your own ideas about how to reduce American dependence on foreign oil.

- *Local news or observation.* Read your local and campus newspapers for issues and problems of concern to your community. Take a walk around your neighborhood or campus with an eye for problems that need solutions, such as wasted energy in offices, dorms, and classrooms.

- *Internet discussions.* If you keep a blog, you probably have a store of observations about issues that concern you, things you would like to convince others to see as you do. Also try visiting blogs concerned with public issues.

EXPLORING YOUR TOPIC

The best approach to exploring a topic depends on many variables: how much you know about the topic already, whether you have participated in debates or discussions about it previously, how much time you have to produce the paper, and so on. Let's assume the situation many students face in their classes: an assigned topic about which you know little or nothing.

Find the Issues

An **issue** is a point of controversy always or frequently discussed when a particular topic arises. For any topic, begin by asking, What are the questions that people disagree about when discussing this topic? For instance, the primary purpose of prisons is always an issue when prison reform is discussed. Some see prisons primarily as punishment for crime; others see them primarily as institutions that should rehabilitate criminals.

◎ COLLABORATIVE ACTIVITY: Exploring Questions at Issue on a Topic

Relying on general knowledge, list the issues connected with the topic. The key question is, *What do people argue about whenever this topic is discussed?*

Assign each issue to a group of between two and four students for research and further exploration. Each group should report its results to the class. Here are some key questions class discussion might address:

Did you encounter issues in your group that you were not aware of before research?

What knowledge about the issues struck you as most important?

Given what you know now, what would you like to know more about?

After the discussion is over, consider your view of the topic now. If you had no opinion before discussing the issues, are you beginning to form one now? If you had a strong opinion, is it changing significantly?   •

Order the Issues (Stasis)

Discussing the issues is an important step in exploring a controversial topic. Ordering them can help as well, beginning with the most elementary of questions and moving through to subsequent issues. As an example, here is one way of ordering the issues involved in committing American troops to a foreign country:

Doing Team Research

Sometimes instructors want you to do research on your own. When that is part of the assignment, do not use the team approach suggested here. Otherwise a team approach is best because there is so much information on nearly all topics.

Here are the steps in a team approach to research:

1. Form small groups based on sharing the same opinion.

2. Share all information you have already, so that everyone in the group has the same knowledge base.

3. Make a list of the information you lack.

4. Divide the items on the needed information list among group members and set a deadline for getting the research done.

5. Get together to share and discuss the implications of the new research materials.

The team approach to research is the norm in business settings, community organizations, government, and often in advanced academic work. The advantages are obvious: sharing the work burden and having people with whom to discuss the results.

- Are vital American interests at stake?

  If you say no, make a case against committing the troops. If you say yes, move on to the next question.

- Have nonmilitary alternatives been exploited fully?

  If you say no, make a case for increased diplomatic effort or some other measure not requiring American troops on the ground. If you say yes, move on to the next question.

- Do the announced objectives make sense?

  If you say no, make a case for changing the objectives. If you say yes, move on to the next question.

- Can we realize our objectives in a reasonable amount of time with minimal loss of lives?

  If you say yes, make a case for military intervention. If you say no, make a case against it based on impracticality.

Ordering the issues in this way is sometimes called **stasis,** a word that means "stop" or "stay." That is, if you think a proposed military intervention would not secure vital national interests, you stop with the first question and make a case against it. If you think nonmilitary options have not been pursued far enough, you argue for more diplomacy, economic sanctions, or some other alternative. You stay with the second question—and so on, through the whole list.

You can order the issues connected with any controversial topic this way. Doing so can help you see how the issues relate to one another and on what key questions opinion divides. It can clarify your own thinking as you work toward an opinion or assess the one you have.

⊚ ACTIVITY: Informal Writing

Cases require a *considered opinion*—that is, an opinion *thought through carefully.* Consequently, after finding and ordering the issues, you need to decide what your opinion is on the issue you chose to address. Your opinion may change as you write and assess your first draft, but you cannot write a draft at all without committing to an opinion.

In a blog post or notebook entry, state your opinion and the reasons you have for holding it.   •

Do More Research

The amount of research needed to argue a case depends on such variables as the nature of the topic, how much you know about it already, and what the assignment requires.

Even thought-through opinions need to confront "the facts," current, reliable knowledge about a topic. For controversial topics, the problem is rarely lack of sources. If you use the resources for finding information discussed in Chapter 6, "Writing Research-Based Arguments," you can count on finding much more than you will have time to read.

Therefore, let the opinion you formed after considering the issues dictate the direction for further research. You can then look only for sources relevant to it and take notes (see pages 121–122 for how to do this) only on those sources that provide the best information. You can pass over many articles and book chapters because the titles alone indicate they will not be relevant. Others you can eliminate with a quick, partial reading; the title turns out to be more promising than the content. You can concentrate on what is left, the articles that are most relevant, and among these, the few that are outstanding, most authoritative, recent, and detailed in offering reliable information. (See pages 111–117 for estimating how reliable a source is.)

The Best Practices box offers an approach to research that can make it more efficient yet.

Analyze Your Sources: Information versus Interpretation

Research materials on controversial topics typically are arguments backed by information used as evidence. Consequently, you need to distinguish information from the "spin" or interpretation the writer and his or her sources supply. For example, it is a fact that in a recent year about 6,200 people died in Mexico as a result of the traffic in narcotics. Citing this figure, some writers argue that American tourists should avoid Mexico. There is no reason to doubt the 6,200 figure, but the interpretation is far from certain—drug-related violence seldom involves American tourists, and many destinations in Mexico are no more risky than some of our own cities.

It is also important to distinguish information from speculation. Facts are uncontested, established pieces of data. How the stock market performed over the last month is a matter of fact, as measured, for example, by the Dow Jones average. Speculations are at most probabilities and possibilities. How the stock market will perform over the next year is anyone's guess. When relevant to your opinion, you *must* engage the facts; speculation you can ignore or use if it supports your opinion.

In general, despite what people sometimes say, the facts cannot speak for themselves. *Facts have to be interpreted, put into a context where they have meaning.* For example, newspapers are in significant financial trouble in the United States. Does this mean, as some people claim, that Americans are less well informed about current events than they were thirty years ago, when papers were in much better shape? Or does it mean that people are getting the news from other sources—online, for instance? It is hard to say, but in any case the decline of newspapers, a fact beyond dispute, must be interpreted to have meaning and significance.

Finally, above all, *strive to maintain independence from your sources' views and voices.* Avoid distorting or misrepresenting the information in a source to fit what you want to believe, but feel free to interpret the information your own way, as you see the subject. For instance, you may support screening passengers before boarding commercial airliners as a necessary counterterrorism measure. If so, you cannot ignore considerable evidence that screening often fails to detect prohibited items that could be used for a terrorist act. Instead of ignoring or denying the evidence, argue instead that screening technology must improve.

Start Your Working Bibliography

As you do research, maintain a complete list of your sources, including all information you will need for the concluding bibliography or works cited page. (See examples of the various types of entries for these pages on pages 133–143.) Doing this as you work can save having to relocate the sources later.

Keep the bibliographical information with your drafts, bearing in mind that revision and rewriting usually result in dropping and adding source material.

A Key Question before Drafting: Is My Opinion Defensible?

You are about to make your case, so address the following question coolly and apart from how strongly you are committed to the opinion you had before research: Given what I know now, can I make a good case for my opinion?

One outcome is that current knowledge makes your opinion impossible or very difficult to defend. Change your opinion to accord with the evidence.

More commonly, research yields another result. Your opinion is still defensible, but you need to modify it some to allow for information you lacked prior to research. Perhaps you did not know that the flu vaccine developed each year is never 100% effective. You could still make a case in favor of a more aggressive vaccination campaign. You need only admit that the inoculation is not uniformly reliable. There is still overwhelming evidence of its benefit to public health—of the approximately 36,000 Americans who die from the flu each year, a high percentage did not receive the vaccine.

Assessing Your Opinion from Research Results

Cases are public arguments and therefore must respect what is known about a topic. Ask these questions as you adjust your opinion to the evidence you have gathered:

1. What facts and expert opinion best support my position?
2. What did I learn from research that challenges my position? Do I need to rethink or modify it?
3. What further information should I seek?

Some people believe that arguments require that they take a stand and hold it regardless of what the available evidence says. They elevate saying what they think over responding to the evidence, and often they appeal to honesty to justify their behavior.

We urge a sharply different attitude. Case-making is a rational process, and part of being rational is changing your mind or modifying your opinion as you learn more about a subject. This process is not dishonest. On the contrary, admitting that "I used to believe this, but now that I know more I believe that instead" requires not only being honest with yourself and other people but also being open to experience, which is necessary for intellectual growth and maturity.

PREPARING TO WRITE

Some writers prefer to go straight to drafting, working out their cases in several drafts. We recommend going through the following steps first, which most writers find helpful:

1. State your opinion as a claim or thesis.
2. "Unpack" (analyze) the thesis to determine what you must argue to defend it adequately.
3. State the reasons you will use to explain or justify your thesis.
4. Select and order the evidence you will use to back up each reason.

These steps, described in more detail below, yield a **brief,** an outline of your case. Add ideas for an introduction and a conclusion and you have all you need to guide your first draft.

State Your Opinion as a Thesis

You are still exploring your opinion when your write a first draft of your case because the ultimate test of any opinion is how strong a case you can make for it. However, your first draft will be stronger if you attempt to state your opinion as a thesis before you begin drafting. An opinion is a general stance or point of view. For instance, in the second reading in this chapter (pages 209–210), Wilbert Rideau believes that our prison system is not working because politics rather than reason and an adequate understanding of crime and criminals controls it. That is his opinion. In contrast, his thesis is much more specific: "Society would be well served by releasing some of its older prisoners who pose no threat and using the money to catch young street thugs" (paragraph 5).

In preparing to write a case, the advantage of a thesis over an opinion is a *sharper focus, with carefully selected key terms.* It is worth your time and effort to work toward a thesis before you draft.

Writing Defensible Claims

- Your claim is a statement you'll defend, not just a description of something that is factual.

  Not a claim: Student debt for government loans has grown to over $20,000 for the average graduate, a heavy burden for young people just entering the workplace.

  Claim: The economy as a whole would benefit if the federal government would forgive student debts for higher education, which now average over $20,000 per graduate.

  The first in this pair describes a problem. The second proposes a solution for doing something about the problem.

- The claim should be focused and specific, and directed at a readership.

  Too general: Many professors do not know how to make effective use of technology in teaching.

  Better: Professors who use presentation technology such as PowerPoint too often stifle creativity and student involvement in the class.

  The second example in this pair is more refined, indicating specific directions that the argument will take. The more specific your claim, the easier it will be to decide what your paper will include.

- Some claims may need to be qualified.

  Too absolute: Professors should openly state their opinions on political issues in classes where such opinions are relevant to course content.

  Qualified: Provided that students are encouraged to discuss their own opinions freely, professors should be able to openly state their opinions on political issues so long as the issue is relevant to course content.

  Think of objections your readers might have to your claim and revise it to eliminate the possible objection.

◎ ACTIVITY: Informal Writing

Any opinion can be expressed in many thesis statements. If you are having difficulty formulating yours or hesitating between or among two or more possibilities,
post a blog entry or send an e-mail to your instructor or to some other appropriate person that lays out your thought process and asks for feedback. Just writing
the blog or e-mail can help you think things through and make a good decision.
Any feedback you receive can help you even more.   •

Unpack Your Thesis

To unpack a thesis means to detect the key terms that make the assertion. Judson's thesis, "Evolution should be central to beginning biology classes," contains
terms that demand that the argument show why evolution is *central*, rather
than a theory one can explain and discuss at one meeting and then ignore. It
will also show why biology classes must start with evolution as a foundation.

As another example, consider the thesis: "*Huckleberry Finn* should be
required reading in all American high schools." To defend the thesis adequately
requires addressing all the key terms: why this *particular book* should be a
required title on American literature lists and why *high school* is the best place
to teach it.

Examine Possible Reasons

The reasoning that led you to your claim will supply the reasons you will
offer to explain and justify it to your reader. In listing your reasons, however,
you can avoid potential problems by thinking carefully about the following
questions:

- Does the statement of each reason say exactly what I mean to say? The
  wording of your reason or reasons matters as much as the wording of
  your thesis.

- Do I need all the reasons I am thinking of using? As a general rule, two or
  three reasons are better than four or five because they are easier for the
  reader to remember. *Concentrate on developing your best reasons well
  rather than offering all the reasons you can think of.*

- Does each reason clearly connect to the thesis by either explaining or justifying it? Imagine your reader asking this question, "Why do you believe
  your thesis?" Each reason should answer this question.

- Are there advantages in developing my reasons in a particular order?
  In general, begin and end your argument with your strongest reasons.
  But also consider the possibility that one reason will lead naturally to
  another, and therefore should come first.

- If you have more than one reason, are they consistent with each other?
  Make sure, for instance, that your first reason does not contradict your
  third reason.

ARRANGE YOUR EVIDENCE UNDER EACH REASON

Just as the reasons that led you to your thesis are the reasons you will develop to convince your readers, so the information you found in research that led you to your reasons or confirmed them will supply the evidence. Arrange the evidence you have under each reason.

Examine Possible Evidence

Select and order your evidence in response to the following questions:

- What kind of evidence does each reason require? For example, if you are arguing for making cell phone use by drivers illegal, one of your main reasons will be the link of cell phone use with accidents. You will need data, facts and figures, to back it up. If you also argue that such a law would not restrict personal freedom unduly, you will need other kinds of evidence, such as pointing out that banning cell phones is no more restrictive than laws against driving while intoxicated.

- How much evidence do I need? The answer is, *Enough to overcome the degree of resistance your reader is likely to have.* Many Americans, for instance, assume that the federal government is already too big, too intrusive, and too expensive. Defending any proposal that would increase its role requires significant evidence for both need and positive results.

- Have I mixed evidence types when I can? For example, when a reason requires hard data, you must supply it. But if you also have a statement from a respected expert confirming your reason, consider using it as well. Some readers are convinced more by authoritative statements than by hard data. You could also offer anecdotes, stories from people involved in an event, to confirm a reason. Stories from wounded soldiers who have served in Afghanistan or Iraq, for example, can be used to argue for improvements in Veteran Administration hospitals. Many people find testimony more convincing than any other kind of evidence.

- Have I selected the best pieces of evidence from all that I could use? Just as it is better to develop two or three reasons well than four or five poorly, so it is better to offer two or three strong pieces of evidence than four or five that vary in quality. More is not necessarily better, and too much evidence can confuse and overburden your reader.

Student Example: Noelle Alberto's Draft Case Outline

See Best Practices, "Drafting a Case Outline" for a checklist of the thinking that needs to go into preparing a brief.

Here is an example of a brief from a student urging her fellow students to stop multitasking when they study. Note its three-level structure: the claim is the thesis or statement your paper defends; each reason is subordinate to the

Drafting a Case Outline

1. A position or general outlook on a topic is not a thesis. A **thesis** is a carefully worded claim that your entire essay backs up with reasons and evidence. Experiment with various ways of stating your thesis until it says *exactly* what you want it to say and creates the least resistance in your readers.

2. Be willing to give up or modify significantly a thesis you find you cannot support with good reasons and strong evidence that appeal *to your readers*. We must argue a thesis that fits the available **evidence.**

3. Create a specific audience profile. We are always trying to convince some definite group of possible readers. What are the age, gender, and economic status of your target audience? What interests, beliefs, and values might they bring to your topic and thesis?

4. Unpack your thesis to discover what you must argue. If you say, for instance, that *Huckleberry Finn* should be *required* reading in high school, you must show why *this particular novel* should be an experience shared by all American high school students. It will not be enough to argue that it is a good book.

5. Select your reasons based on what you must argue to defend your thesis combined with what you should say given your audience's prior knowledge, preconceptions, prejudices, and interests.

6. Be prepared to try out different ways of ordering your reasons. The order that seemed best in your brief might not work best as you draft and redraft your essay.

thesis because it explains why you hold your thesis; each piece of evidence is subordinate to the reason it supports.

Claim: **Multitasking between recreational technology and studying impairs students' learning and does not prepare them for the real world of work.**

> *Reason: Multitasking increases the amount of time spent studying.*
>
>> *Evidence:* Homework takes twice as long to complete with multitasking. (Source: Tugend)
>>
>> *Evidence:* Switching tasks makes you have to relearn information to get back on track. (Source: Hamilton)
>
> *Reason: Multitasking impairs the brain's abilities to learn and store information.*
>
>> *Evidence:* It prevents students from being able to store information learned through studying. (Sources: Rosen, Jarmon)
>
> *Reason: Multitasking is poor preparation for the workplace.*
>
>> *Evidence:* Businesses don't want people who multitask; they want people who prioritize. (Source: LPA)
>>
>> *Evidence:* Multitasking decreases production ability of workers. (Source: Rosen)

Drafting Your Case

1. Openers are important. Start your essay by putting your case in context. For example, Judson (page 205) opens hers by referring to the beginning of a school year, when how to teach biology is immediately relevant.

2. Your reader may need background information to understand your case. Part of this will come from establishing the context in the opening, but sometimes additional information your reader lacks or may not remember will be necessary. Pickens (page 212) provides a good example of needed background information in developing his first claim: "America is addicted to foreign oil." Most of his readers are aware of our dependence on foreign crude, but probably not of its full consequences: $700 billion going out of the country to feed our habit every year, $10 trillion over the next ten years, "the greatest transfer of wealth in the history of mankind." Information like this not only provides needed background but also catches reader attention.

3. Cases do not have to deal with opposing points of view. However, if there is an obvious objection to your case you think most readers will think of, better mention it and show why the objection does not hold. Pickens provides good examples of anticipating and responding to objections. For instance, he explains why we cannot overcome our addiction to foreign oil by pumping more domestically (page 213).

4. Consider using visuals as an efficient way to convey evidence. Again, Pickens provides a good example of how effective photos, maps, and graphs can be.

5. Avoid summary, "in conclusion," conclusions. Strive instead for a memorable "parting shot," something with impact. Rideau's "Ever see a dog chase its tail?" is a good example, but you can use, for instance, a well-worded quotation followed by commentary of your own.

6. Strive to maintain throughout your essay the voice described in the assignment—dispassionate, calm, and fair—and the middle style case-making favors: simple, forceful statements that allow the thesis and its supporting reasons and evidence to stand out for your reader.

Reason: Multitasking promotes shallow rather than deep thinking.

> *Evidence:* Ability to pay attention to one thing at a time is a mark of mature thinking. (Source: Rosen)

DRAFTING YOUR PAPER

Using your brief as a guide, write your first draft.

Development and Organization

Start by orienting your reader, providing what she or he needs to know to understand your topic and why it is significant. Establish the point of view toward the topic you have and want your reader to share. Make your own position clear. The Best Practices box offers suggestions to help you as you write.

Revision Checklist for Arguing a Case

1. Who is the target audience? How is the case framed—introduced—to reach that audience? Does the writer keep this audience in mind throughout the essay?

2. Locate the claim as stated or implied. Is it held consistently throughout the essay?

3. Locate the reasons that explain and justify the claim. Does the writer focus on one reason at a time, staying with it until it is completely developed? How effectively does each reason appeal to the audience? Is each reason clearly connected to the thesis it defends?

4. Do you detect a logical progression in the ordering of the reasons, so that the first reason leads to the second, the second to the third, and so on? Is there a better way to order the reasons? Can you find weak reasons that should be cut? Can you suggest reasons not included that would make the case stronger?

5. How much will the audience resist each reason? Is there sufficient evidence to overcome the resistance? Is the evidence for each reason clear and relevant to the reason it supports?

6. Do you see a better way to order the evidence for any of the reasons?

7. Look at the conclusion. How does it clinch the case, leaving the reader with something memorable? Can you see a way to make the conclusion more forceful?

Student Example: Excerpts from Alberto's Draft

The introduction from Alberto's first draft illustrates a common problem with arguments. It opens with generalizations that do not grab the reader's attention and show how the topic of the paper will matter to them.

> Long before the computer, people have always needed to multitask. Mothers dressed their children while getting ready for work and making breakfast. Men drank their morning coffee and ate breakfast on their drive to work. Multitasking has long been a part of our society, and now, technology has granted us new means of multitasking. This multitasking is now crucial to the younger generation's way of life, but it may be hurting them academically.

Alberto did a good job of creating a context for her case against multitasking, and her thesis is clearly stated in the last sentence. However, she could have used a specific example to connect with her intended audience, college and high school students. By using a source, she was able to revise her introduction (see page 231) to engage her readers better immediately.

Another common problem in arguments is using sources to support and develop points, but not using enough from the source to make the evidence clear and convincing. Here is an example that is not easy to follow.

> David Meyer, a professor at University of Michigan, found that when you switch to a new task, the parts of the brain that are no longer being used "start shutting things down—like neural connections to important information" (Hamilton). The work you were focusing on isn't as understandable, and when you finally get back to it you "will have to repeat much of the process that created [the information] in the first place" (Hamilton).

The source actually gave a much more detailed description of the problem Alberto describes above. See the revised version of this passage (paragraph 3 on page 232).

To catch this kind of revision problem, ask a friend to read your draft and to be completely honest about where you may not have been clear enough in explaining evidence from a source.

REVISING YOUR DRAFT

Write a brief assessment of your first draft. Exchange your draft and assessment with at least one other student and help each other decide what needs improvement.

The revision questions in the Best Practices box should help you assess your own and your partner's draft.

Formulate a Plan to Guide Your Revision

The plan can be a single sentence or two: "I'll cut this, rearrange that, and add a section here." The important thing is to have a definite, clear idea of what you want to do and what moves you will make to get the results you want.

REVISED STUDENT EXAMPLE
Multitasking: A Poor Study Habit

NOELLE ALBERTO

1   A recent National Public Radio program described the study habits of a modern teenager, Zach Weinberg of Chevy Chase, Maryland. On a typical evening, he worked on French homework while visiting his e-mail and Facebook, listening to iTunes, messaging a friend, and playing an online word puzzle (Hamilton). According to the story, Zach is a successful student, but many studies of multitasking suggest that he could be better if he focused on one thing at a time. While human beings are capable of doing two things at once if one of those things does not require much attention, like driving and drinking your morning coffee, there are some things that require a single focus, like school work. Multitasking between studies and recreational technology is not an effective way to study.

2   One misconception that students may have about their multitasking is that they are saving time. Some say that they feel they get more done in a shorter amount of time, but they are actually not doing two things at once. They are switching from one task to another, and constant task switching takes more time. Gloria Mark of the University of California, Irvine conducted a study in which business workers were interrupted while working on a project. Each time, it took them about 25 minutes to return their attention to the original project (Tugend). In study terms, if you interrupt yourself to check your e-mail, a chapter that would take thirty minutes to read straight through could take much longer.

3   What happens when people shift from one demanding task to another? David Meyer, a professor at University of Michigan, found that when you switch to a new task, the parts of the brain that are no longer being used "start shutting things down—like neural connections to important information." If a student is studying French and stops to shop online, the neural connections to the French homework start to shut down. To restore full understanding, Meyer says the student "will have to repeat much of the process that created [the connections] in the first place" (qtd. in Hamilton).

Paragraph gives more evidence for the first reason.

4   This frequent reconnecting to prior levels of focus and understanding is a waste of time. It is time lost that could be used more efficiently. If students eliminated technological distractions during study time, they would be able to complete more work in a shorter amount of time with greater understanding. There is always time to socialize after homework and studying has been completed.

A transitional paragraph wrapping up the first reason.

           Another misconception is that multitasking prepares you for the business world. "Able to multitask" used to be considered a positive on employee résumés. However, the researchers found that "extreme multitasking—information overload—costs the U.S. economy $650 billion a year in lost productivity" (Rosen 106). A study conducted at the University of London found that "workers distracted by e-mail and phone calls suffer a fall in IQ more than twice that found in marijuana smokers" (qtd. in Rosen 106). Employers, therefore, do not value multitasking. Now, according to the U.S. Departments of Labor and Education, businesses want an employee who "selects goal-relevant activities, ranks them, allocates time, and prepares and follows schedules" ("Skills and Competencies"). If multitasking is difficult and harmful in the business world, it has no place in university work either.

Second reason.

6   Besides wasted time and money, another unfortunate effect of multitasking is serious damage to students' ability to learn. Studies by psychology professor Russell Poldrack show that multitasking makes "learning . . . less flexible and more specialized, so you cannot retrieve the information as easily" (qtd. in Rosen 107). Studies of blood flow in the brain show why. When people are task-switching, they use the "striatum, a region of the brain involved in learning new skills" (Rosen 107). In contrast, people who are not multitasking "show activity in the hippocampus, a region involved in storing and recalling information" (Rosen 108). Amy Jarmon, Dean at Texas Tech's School of Law, recalls a study comparing two groups of students in a large lecture class. One group of students was allowed to use laptops in class; they performed much more poorly on a memory quiz of lecture content than students not permitted to use laptops. Students who checked their e-mail and updated their Web pages during class did not recall information as well because they were not using the hippocampus.

Third reason.

7   Finally, if students get into the habit of multitasking, they could miss out on developing a personality trait prized by highly successful people. Christine Rosen calls the trait "a finely honed skill for paying attention" (109). The great British scientist Sir Isaac Newton said his discoveries owed "more to patient attention than to any other talent." The American psychologist William James wrote that the ability to pay attention marked the difference between a mature and an immature person: "The faculty of voluntarily bringing back a wandering attention, over and over again . . . is the very root of judgment, character, and will" (qtd. in Rosen 109). Maturity means recognizing that there is "a time and place for everything." When I go to the library to study, I leave my computer behind so that I will not be tempted to multitask. After an hour of focused school work, I have accomplished a great deal.

Fourth reason. This is the last reason because it has weight in showing how multitasking undermines intellectual potential.

Brings personal experience into the paper.

8   Multitasking is now part of every student's life. The facts indicate that we need to resist it more. It is not as helpful as many people think, and its very appeal is part of the problem. It is inefficient, reduces intelligence, and impairs recall. To think deeply rather than shallowly, we need to concentrate. Therefore, the best approach is to divide study time from social time. Focusing on one thing at a time will produce better outcomes now and in the future.

WORKS CITED

Hamilton, Jon. "Multitasking Teens May Be Muddling Their Brains." *NPR,* 9 Oct. 2008, www.npr.org/templates/story/story.php?storyId=95524385.

Jarmon, Amy L. "Multitasking: Helpful or Harmful? Multitasking Has Been Shown to Slow Learning and Reduce Efficiency." *Student Lawyer,* vol. 36, no. 8, Apr. 2008, pp. 30+. *Academic OneFile,* www.academiconefile.com/student_lawyer/0408/aljarmon/multitasking.htm.

Rosen, Christine. "The Myth of Multitasking," *The New Atlantis,* vol. 20, Spring 2008, pp. 105–10.

"Skills and Competencies Needed to Succeed in Today's Workplace." *What Work Requires of Schools: A SCANS Report for America 2000,* docushare3.dcc.edu/docushare/dsweb/Get/Version-3015/.

Tugend, Alina. "Multitasking Can Make You Lose . . . Um . . . Focus." *The New York Times,* 25 Oct. 2008, www.nytimes.com/2008/10/25/business/yourmoney/25shortcuts.html.

CHAPTER SUMMARY

Go back and review the steps you went through in writing this paper, concentrating on what happened when you were preparing to write. Pay special attention to testing your opinion. No matter what the subject or whether you are writing an argument or not, the method and attitude always apply. Internalize it. Make it a part of how you encounter new information and new experience. It boils down to this: Take time to form an opinion on controversial issues you hear and read about. But be constantly open to revising your opinion when you encounter anything new and relevant. Only in this way can your understanding of life and the world deepen and mature.

You know people who seem to gain almost instant respect from others, people who are listened to—part of this special quality is knowing what you think while remaining open to changing what you think. The impact of such people is not surprising at all: When people offer considered and well-informed opinions, they influence others who lack them. That is not only how it is but how it should be.

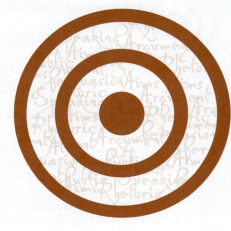

CHAPTER 10

Motivating Action: Arguing to Persuade

We can define persuasion as "convincing plus" because, in addition to reason, three other forms of appeal receive conscious attention: appeals to the writer's character, to the emotions of the audience, and to style, the artful use of language. These three forms of appeal usually are present in case-making but in need of development for full persuasive impact, which means everything you learned in Chapter 9 remains relevant. We are building on Chapter 9 to help you understand and control persuasion's wider range of appeals.

WHAT IS PERSUASION?

Have you ever advocated change in an existing policy or way of doing something at school, in your dormitory or apartment complex, on your job, or at a community meeting? If so, you know about the potential power of persuasion. *Persuasion asks us to do something*—spend money, give money, join a demonstration, recycle, vote, enlist, convict, or acquit. For this reason, we call persuasion "appealing for action."

Persuasion joins a case to other ways of moving people to act, especially by gaining their trust and confidence and by arousing emotions favorable to the action advocated. In a moment, we will look at the means of persuasion,

When Should You Persuade?

Pay close attention to what your course assignments call for because the full range of persuasive appeal is not always appropriate. The more purely intellectual your topic and the more academic your audience, the more you should emphasize logical appeal, or making a good case. A clear thesis, supported by good reasons and backed by solid evidence, is usually what professors want.

When the issue is public, matters of policy or right and wrong, persuasion's fuller range of appeal is appropriate. Making an argument for the creation of a homeless shelter in your community requires establishing your good character and personal involvement with the project as well as appealing to the emotions of your readers. *Persuasion appeals to the whole person:* mind, emotion, the capacity for trust and cooperation, even the virtue of saying things well.

College assignments calling for persuasion will often ask you to take knowledge gained from a course and use it to persuade others who lack it. For example, using what you learned from a course in environmental science, you might write an article urging Americans to buy smaller, fuel-efficient automobiles to reduce carbon dioxide emissions and consumption of oil.

---

often called forms of appeal. First, consider the issue of appropriateness, when to convince and when to persuade, especially in college writing.

WHY WRITE TO PERSUADE?

Persuasion brings about change in the world, whether in national or local politics, in neighborhoods, on campus, in the workplace, or in personal relationships. For example, persuasion can:

- Sway elected officials to favor one policy over another
- Induce people and nations to resolve conflicts peacefully rather than by violent means
- Affect business decisions of all kinds, including how to promote a product or service
- Influence college officials who set tuition rates and housing costs on campus

No other kind of writing has more practical impact. If you want to make a difference in a world that needs to change in many ways, learning how to persuade other people is the key.

HOW DOES PERSUASION WORK?

Getting people to take action requires more than a good case. That's why the ancient Greek philosopher Aristotle identified three kinds of appeal: to reason (*logos*); to the character of the speaker (*ethos*); and to the emotions of the listeners (*pathos*). In all three, you adapt what you are advocating to the interests, beliefs, and values of a target audience.

The Four Forms of Appeal

Form	Function	Presence in Text
Reason	Logical cogency	Your case; any supported contention
Character	Personal appeal	Indications of author's status and values
Emotion	Appeals to feelings	Concrete descriptions, moving images
Style	Appeals through language	Word choice, sentence structure, metaphor

Essentially, persuasion differs from convincing in seeking action, not just agreement; it integrates rational appeal with other ways to influence people.

In the readings that follow this section, you will see the appeals at work in an ad and two articles, all finished texts. Let us consider them at the other end of the writing process, as a *heuristic* (learning device) for coming up with something to say.

To save money and for other reasons, Americans are looking for alternatives to cars. One of these alternatives is the motorcycle or scooter. Suppose you were writing an essay with the title, "Getting Around on Two Wheels." What might you say?

Starting with logos, or the appeal to reason, you could argue that

- Motorcycles cost far less than cars to buy and maintain.

- They use on average about one-third as much gas.

- They take up only about half as much parking space.

- With proper training and equipment, they are not as dangerous to operate as many people think.

Motorcycles could help solve many problems, including reduction in traffic, greenhouse gas emissions, and American dependence on foreign crude oil.

How could you use pathos, or emotional appeal? The main value here is the fun of motorcycling. Motorcycles are the mechanical horse—you do not drive them, you ride them—and it should be fairly easy to appeal to the American love for freedom and adventure.

Finally, how could you appeal to ethos, or character? If you are a motorcyclist yourself, you could draw on your own experience. If not, interview friends who ride and cite what they say: You can borrow ethos from others.

The Art of Questioning: What Really Persuades Us?

Many people say they are persuaded by reasons and evidence. That is, logos matters most. Aristotle thought that ethos might be more powerful: If we think that a writer is intelligent, well informed, trustworthy, and has genuine concern for our needs, we will tend to believe most of what that person says. Look at advertising and you will probably conclude that pathos is the prime persuader. Nearly all ads appeal to emotions and attitudes most of all.

What do you think? Consider the last important decision you made. How did you persuade yourself to do one thing rather than another? If someone tried to persuade you, what kinds of appeal did they use? Which of these appeals had the most impact on the decision you made?

READINGS

The following readings will help you see in more detail how persuasion works and what you can do when you encounter a situation that calls for persuasion.

Advertising is one of the most common examples of moving people to action. We can learn a great deal about persuasion by studying advertisers' creative use of rhetorical appeals, both verbal and visual, to targeted audiences. This advertisement from Subaru's Web site illustrates all of the appeals Aristotle identified as contributing to effective persuasion.

Subaru Advertisement

Although Subaru also advertises in print magazines, appealing to specific readerships like mountain-bike riders, this advertisement is well designed for people who use the Internet to investigate possible automobile choices. The links in the menu across the top enable readers to see the range of vehicles, specifics about Subaru cars, pricing, and dealerships—all good basic information. However, this particular page moves beyond informing to persuading because of its emotional and ethical appeals aimed at people accustomed to the social networking and collaboration made possible by Web 2.0.

The ad invites owners and potential buyers to interact personally with the company and with each other by posting pictures of themselves with their cars and brief testimonials about why they love their Subaru. It is an emotional appeal to be part of a group of happy and fun-loving people swapping their stories. Sharing is emphasized in the text: "Share your love. . . ." "Share your story."

The ad also appeals logically to Internet shoppers who routinely check out other consumers' reviews and opinions about a product. Buyers' testimonials about good mileage, safety, and performance are good reasons and evidence that would also move the reader to choose this line of cars.

Subaru also displays its corporate ethos, or character, in this promotion by showing that it cares about its customers and the pleasure they get from driving their cars. The corporate image is friendly and unpretentious, a company for sporty, adventurous, outdoor lovers. "Share the love" is a theme in Subaru advertisements, referring to Subaru's philanthropic efforts on behalf of five major national charities. Market research told Subaru that its customers are likely to be committed to charitable causes.

Finally, the visuals and layout of the advertisement contribute to the message of personal connection, fun, and adventure. The featured visual looks like a letter with its salutation, "Dear Subaru." The letter's message is the car itself with its balloons, flowing streamers, and "Just Married" sign. These details visually depict the words in the caption at the lower right. The compilation of pictures and stories is a slightly less cluttered version of a Facebook page, completing the appeal to a targeted audience of connected, fun-loving people.

◎ ACTIVITY: Informal Writing

Find an advertisement that you think is effective for its target audience. Who is the audience? Analyze how the ad appeals to ethos, pathos, and logos. Describe the visual and verbal appeals to style.

Consuming Faith

TOM BEAUDOIN

"Consuming Faith" was published in *Tikkun,* the journal of a socially progressive organization that publishes interfaith perspectives on issues of justice, preservation of the environment, and political freedom.

Tom Beaudoin is professor of theology at Santa Clara University in California. The essay comes from his book, *Consuming Faith: Integrating Who We Are with What We Buy*. As you read this essay, think about your own consumer behavior and your relationship to the people who produce the items you purchase.

1   In December, several Honduran women came to Boston College. They were on a speaking tour of New England universities, talking about their work back home sewing shirts for a major brand that many of my students wore.

2   These women told stories that anyone familiar with the global sweatshop workforce will find painfully predictable: verbal abuse, beastly wages, forbidden unions, forced overtime, no holidays, no health insurance or other benefits, the inability to save money so their children can break out of this life, and transportation and food costs that ate up four hours' wages every day. And the workforce consisted entirely of young women, aged 15 to 30.

3   I was outraged, because these women worked for a company that I knew had turned enormous profits. It was not as if the company was going to go broke if it had even minimally met the meager requests of these women. I was outraged because many of my students wore this clothing brand and I hated that they were paying this corporation to brand themselves at these women's expense [. . .] . And I was outraged because I was reminded that this corporation got away with it because I myself spent so many years not doing my part to stop such practices. I had paid lots of money to be a foot soldier for my favorite brands of shoes, jeans, and shirts—even coffee.

4   For me, the turning point came when I started seeing the faces of the women making my favorite brands. I had read a story several years ago about impoverished coffee farmers who harvest coffee beans for wealthy American coffee companies, and saw a picture of one of their faces on the Web or in the paper. I ended up pulling my favorite brands out of my closet and tracking down who made "my" brands, where they were produced, and the conditions under which they were put together. With the exception of my branded sport coat produced in Toronto under Canadian labor laws, the rest of my favorite brands were assembled by non-American faces that were forbidden to join unions, had to submit to pregnancy tests, and were kept in poverty by American companies that had almost eliminated the cost of labor, while avoiding paying any taxes at all due to breaks from the host countries where the factories were placed. Not that any of them volunteered this information. Most of the companies gave me public relations blowback and legal-speak and some outright lied to me. I had to turn to independent reportage to find out exactly what I was supporting, and whose faces I was affecting, by my purchase of my favorite brands. When I called the corporate headquarters of my local outpost of a coffee chain to see if I could travel— at my own expense—to South America to take pictures of the farmers who harvested my coffee and post them in the store, I got a firm and unequivocal "no." Why did so many of my favorite coffee and clothing brands want to hide the faces of those who made my stuff?

5   I was beginning to see that there were relationships in which I was an involved but irresponsible partner—economic relationships. Just as any other common relationship we have has both pleasures and responsibilities (whether as spouse, friend,

or co-worker), so do my economic relationships, I was beginning to see. By enjoying my branded jeans, I was necessarily in relationship with the women who made them. They had done their part by making clothes that protected me and brought me pleasure. What was my obligation to them? What was my part of the relationship?

6   This raised the question for me: how central are economic relationships to faith? Are my economic relationships secondary to who I am before God, or central? The popular picture of Christianity today, unfortunately, does not show the best face of my faith on this issue. As a Catholic Christian, I notice the way Christianity is portrayed in the media, and how it portrays itself in its own advertising, and what I see lately is a religion too often indifferent to war, over interested in individual morality, and defensive about its own institutional abuses. One would almost think that this public image of religiosity was mandated by the Christian scriptures. However, when I turned back to scripture to see how Jesus of Nazareth dealt with economics, I was shocked at what I found. Jesus very seldom talks about God's final judgment, about "heaven" and "hell," but when he does, as his way of talking about what is most important in a life of spiritual maturity before God, he does something interesting. He almost always talks about intimacy with God in the next life as bound up with one's economic relationships in this life. He speaks of a wealthy man who ignores a poor man at his gate finding himself later in hell, crying out to the poor man for help. He talks about those who use their resources of time and money to visit prisoners and clothe the naked as going on to a final happiness with God, and those who do not as having failed to love God and live a truly human life. Jesus was not focused on whom one is sleeping with, whether one has properly obeyed religious authorities, or how religious institutions can preserve themselves. He saw economic relationships as ultimate expressions of one's true faith. Responsibility for the other is where and how one ought to live in relationship to that gracious and mysterious power that sustains us, which he intimately called his "Father."

7   For me, the Jewishness of Jesus' concern for the other is present in a more recent idiom in the philosophy of Emmanuel Levinas. For Levinas, we are everywhere and in each moment dependent on and responsible to others. To be human is to be responsible for the other, whose well-being my very existence may be threatening. This obligation to others is encountered and symbolized in the face-to-face relationship. The faces of others represent persons genuinely different from us, exposed to us. The vulnerability of the human face presents us with the claim: do not kill me. In a sense, Levinas says, the face says to us "do not deface me"; allow me, it says, my otherness and exposure without violation, shame, or indifference.

8   But what if we are systematically excluded, in a brand economy, from seeing the faces of the others who inhabit our lives? What if your local branded coffee shop does not want you to even see the faces of those who harvest your coffee? Would we not think of our brands differently if we had in view the faces of those who make our stuff?

9   A more human brand economy would be a more holy one, one in which we take responsibility for our economic relationships, for the well-being of the faces who make our stuff. In a better world, the brands themselves will better manage the economic

relationships between producers and consumers that they steward. In a better world, we will each think and even pray about our obligations to our economic relationships. In a better world, brands will try to talk us into purchasing them because they give their workers in China, Indonesia, or El Salvador a living wage, holidays, overtime pay, child care, and health insurance. Whether you are more with Jesus of Nazareth or Levinas of Lithuania, this better world is possible. If only we made economics a part of the discourse of spiritual maturity today, it would begin to happen.

QUESTIONS FOR DISCUSSION

1. Beaudoin uses word-pattern repetition to appeal to the readers' emotions. Reread the selection and locate some examples. Why does he employ this strategy in those places rather than others? How effective is it for his intended audience?

2. The article attempts to overcome a common dissociation: Probably most people see religion and economics as separate and at most weakly related. Does it succeed? Are you persuaded to pull them together? Why or why not?

Strategies for Appealing for Action

Beaudoin wants to persuade his readers to see their consumer choices as part of their religious practice. He tailors his argument to his audience (1) by giving them religious reasons for knowing more about the conditions in which goods are produced and (2) by refusing to buy from companies that exploit and abuse their workers.

We can learn something about strategy in appealing for action by examining how Beaudoin arranged the parts of his essay. Like many persuasive writers, he does not present his claim and reasons at the start of the essay but leads the readers gradually to the argument, which does not begin until about the midpoint. Beaudoin's essay falls into three parts:

1. The introductory narrative about the Honduran women. (paragraphs 1–3)

> Stories based on personal experience are often good openings. Beaudoin connects with his readers by assuming that they already know and disapprove of sweatshop conditions. But they are still buying the products, not "doing [their] part."

2. The story of his attempts to find out more about his brand-name goods. (paragraph 4)

> This section, also a narrative, builds up Beaudoin's ethos because it shows his long-term concern for and dedication to finding out about the workers.

3. The argument that responsible economic relationships are central to living a spiritual life. (paragraphs 5–9)

> This section is a case based on reasons and evidence. Paragraph 5 gives his first reason: Economic relationships entail responsibility

just like other relationships. Then, in paragraphs 6–9, he argues that this relationship is religious. He asks, "[H]ow central are economic relationships to faith?" He answers this question by showing that economic relationships are central to religious identity (the *claim*). He justifies the claim with this reason: Both Christianity and Judaism see economic responsibility for others as integral to faith. He supports the reason with evidence from two sources, the Bible and the writings of the Jewish philosopher Emmanuel Levinas.

The Factories of Lost Children

KATHARINE WEBER

Weber's subject matter and claim are similar to Beaudoin's in the previous essay, but she bases her argument on tragic incidents involving child labor. It was originally published in *The New York Times* on the anniversary of a tragic factory fire in New York City.

How does Weber's use of persuasion differ from what you noticed in Beaudoin's essay? As you read, consider which argument is more appealing to you and why.

1   Ninety-five years ago, March 25 also fell on a Saturday. At 4:40 p.m. on that sunny afternoon in 1911, only minutes before the end of the workday, a fire broke out on the eighth floor of the Asch Building, a block east of Washington Square in Manhattan.

2   The Triangle Waist Company occupied the top three floors of the 10-story building. There, some 600 workers were employed in the manufacture of ladies' shirtwaists, most of them teenage girls who spoke little English and were fresh off the boat from Russia, the Austro-Hungarian Empire and Italy. The fire, probably caused by a carelessly tossed match or cigarette butt (there were perhaps 100 men working at the Triangle), engulfed the premises in minutes.

3   The factory owners and the office staff on the 10th floor, all but one, escaped onto the roof and climbed to an adjacent building on Waverly Place. But on the eighth and ninth floors, the workers were trapped by a deadly combination of highly combustible materials, workrooms crowded by dense rows of table-mounted sewing machines, doors that were locked or opened inward, inadequate fire escapes, and the lack of any plan or instruction.

4   Before the first horse-drawn fire engines arrived at the scene, girls—some holding hands, in twos and threes—had already begun to jump from the windows. The hundred-foot drop to the cobbled street was not survivable. The firemen deployed their nets, but the force of gravity drove the bodies of the girls straight through to the pavement, and they died on impact.

5   The ladders on the fire trucks were raised quickly, but the New York City Fire Department of 1911 was not equipped to combat fires above six stories—the limit of those ladders. The top floors of the Asch Building, a neo-Renaissance "fireproof" warehouse completed in 1901 in full compliance with building codes, burned relentlessly.

6   The workers trapped near the windows on the eighth and ninth floors made the fast and probably instinctive choice to jump instead of burning or suffocating in the smoke. The corpses of the jumpers, by some estimates as many as 70, could at least be identified. But the bodies of most of those who died inside the Triangle Waist Company—trapped by the machinery, piled up on the wrong side of doors, heaped in the stairwells and elevator shafts—were hideously charred, many beyond recognition.

7   Before 15 minutes had elapsed, some 140 workers had burned, fallen from the collapsing fire escapes, or jumped to their deaths. Several more, critically injured, died in the days that followed, putting the official death toll at 146.

8   But what happened to the children who were working at the Triangle Waist Company that afternoon?

9   By most contemporary accounts, it was common knowledge that children were usually on the premises. They were hidden from the occasional inspectors, but underage girls, as young as 9 or 10, worked in most New York garment factories, sewing buttons and trimming threads. Where were they on this particular Saturday afternoon?

10   There are no descriptions of children surviving the fire. Various lists of those who died 95 years ago today—140 named victims plus six who were never identified (were some of those charred remains children?)—include one 11-year-old, two 14-year-olds, three 15-year-olds, 16 16-year-olds, and 14 17-year-olds. Were the ages of workers, living and dead, modified to finesse the habitual violation of child labor laws in 1911? How many children actually died that day? We will never know. And now 1911 is almost beyond living memory.

11   But we will also never know how many children were among the dead on May 10, 1993, in Thailand when the factory of the Kader Industrial Toy Company (a supplier to Hasbro and Fisher-Price) went up in flames. Most of the 188 workers who died were described as teenage girls.

12   We will never know with any certainty how many children died on Nov. 25, 2000, in a fire at the Chowdhury Knitwear and Garment factory near Dhaka, Bangladesh (most of the garments made in Bangladesh are contracted by American retailers, including Wal-Mart and the Gap), where at least 10 of the 52 trapped in the flames by locked doors and windows were 10 to 14 years old.

13   And we will never know how many children died just last month, on Feb. 23, in the KTS Composite Textile factory fire in Chittagong, Bangladesh. The official death toll has climbed into the 50's, but other sources report that at least 84 workers lost their lives. It's a familiar story: crowded and unsafe conditions, locked exits, hundreds of undocumented female workers as young as 12, a deadly fire. There may never be another tragic factory fire in America that takes the lives of children. We don't lock them into sweatshops any more. There are child labor laws, fire codes.

14   But as long as we don't question the source of the inexpensive clothing we wear, as long as we don't wonder about the children in those third world factories who make the inexpensive toys we buy for our own children, those fires will occur and young girls and boys will continue to die. They won't die because of natural

catastrophes like monsoons and earthquakes; they will die because it has become our national habit to outsource, and these days we outsource our tragedies, too.

Strategies for Appealing for Action

Detailed arguments are not the only way of being persuasive. Weber shows us how effective narrative can be. It serves the following persuasive purposes:

- It establishes her credibility and ethos with a wealth of detailed information. Readers feel she knows what she is talking about and has the welfare of other people foremost in her concerns.

- In paragraphs 4, 6, and 7, she appeals to pathos well, drawing her readers into this tragic incident with powerful images of brutal, unnecessary deaths.

- In these same paragraphs, she also appeals to the readers' ethics, knowing they would not tolerate such conditions in New York today.

Effective narratives depend on *telling detail,* on statements of fact that imply the writer's judgments without stating them. For instance,

- Many of the workers "were fresh off the boat from Russia, the Austro-Hungarian Empire and Italy."

  Implication: They were expendable. There was a ready supply of labor on the next boat.

- "The factory owners and the office staff on the 10th floor, all but one, escaped."

  Implication: The people that mattered survived. The bosses would not lock themselves or valued employees inside, where they could not escape.

- "The New York City Fire Department of 1911 was not equipped to combat fires above six stories. . . . The top floors of the Asch Building [were] completed in 1901 in full compliance with building codes."

  Implication: You cannot depend on authorities to prevent tragedies or respond to unfolding disasters adequately.

Tell your readers what they need to know and they will draw the conclusions you want them to make.

In the concluding paragraph, Weber makes a summarizing case, stating her claim and her reason in one sentence: "As long as we don't question the source of the inexpensive clothing we wear, as long as we don't wonder about the children in those third world factories who make the inexpensive toys we buy for our own children, those fires will occur and young girls and boys will continue to die." The case brings her general point home, linking her narrative of a past event to present concerns.

◎ COLLABORATIVE ACTIVITY: Analyzing Weber's Strategies

Using the analysis of Beaudoin as a model (pages 242–243), break up into small groups, assign the roles of recorder and reporter, and investigate the following questions:

- Why do you think the author organized her material the way she did?
- In paragraphs 11–13 Weber shifts attention from the past to the present. Does the shift work; that is, do you find the connections to the present persuasive? If so, why? If not, why not?

Share the results of your work with the class and discuss how each group's answers differed. Address this question at some point in your class dialogue: What strategies does Weber use that we can use in our own way? •

USING YOUR VOICE IN APPEALING FOR ACTION

Appealing for action or persuasion is in part the calm voice of reason described in Chapter 9: your opinion stated clearly, directly, forcefully, with confidence. To this persuasion adds the *controlled passion* of emotional appeal, designed to arouse appropriate feelings in your readers.

Look at paragraphs 10–14 in Katharine Weber's "The Factories of Lost Children." Here is the voice of controlled passion:

> We will never know with any certainty how many children died on Nov. 25, 2000, in a fire at the Chowdhury Knitwear and Garment factory near Dhaka, Bangladesh (most of the garments made in Bangladesh are contracted by American retailers, including Wal-Mart and the Gap), where at least 10 of the 52 trapped in the flames by locked doors and windows were 10 to 14 years old. (paragraph 12)

She gives the reader the terrible facts, including the role of American companies in allowing the conditions that result in tragic loss of children's lives. She does not have to say, "This is outrageous, intolerable"; the facts say it for her.

Furthermore, she cites several tragic instances in paragraphs 10–14, all linked together by the repeated statement, "We will never know how many children died." This is how you arouse appropriate emotions in readers and how the voice of controlled passion should sound. Moving people to act requires using this voice as well as the calm voice of reasoning.

◎ COLLABORATIVE ACTIVITY: Comparing Two Authors' Voices

In small groups of two or three people, explore these questions:

1. How is Weber's voice like Beaudoin's? How are they different?
2. Beaudoin wrote in first person (uses "I"), whereas Weber favors third person. Is your sense of the author's presence different in Beaudoin? If so, how would you describe the difference? •

THE ASSIGNMENT

Write an essay on any controversial topic that asks your readers to take action. "Controversial" for this assignment means that various courses of action are possible, genuine choice exists. In some cases, you might advocate doing nothing when other people want to take action or stop doing something that causes more harm than benefit.

Topic and Focus

Your topic may grow out of readings or discussion of current events in your class, or your instructor may have you choose your own topic. Whatever happens, distinguish topics from possible focuses within them. For instance, "illegal immigration" is a highly controversial topic, ideal for persuasion because so many courses of action are possible. However, illegal immigration covers too much ground for anything less than a book. You might focus, for example, on the fences being constructed along the U.S.–Mexico border. Or, because many people here illegally overstay their visas, you might focus on the visa process itself. *Find some part of the topic you can handle in the space you have.*

Audience

Think of your audience as people weakly inclined toward your position, weakly opposed, or uncommitted. Within these possibilities, consider two questions: Who can take action? Which audience can I relate to best? Choose your audience based on how you answer these questions.

Voice and Ethos

Persuasion favors middle style, neither ultra-formal (as in a legal brief) nor informal and off-hand (like an e-mail to a friend). You should sound like someone talking about a serious topic to people you do not know well. The readings provide good examples of middle style and the voice that goes with it.

Good character, or ethos, always matters in writing, but especially in persuasion because you are asking your readers to trust you enough to take action. Be sincere. Project confidence. Show respect for your audience.

Writing Assignment Suggestions

This paper could be written in many possible genres: an editorial, a personal letter, a magazine article, a text for a speech, and so on. You might consider one of these genres, especially if your topic and audience seem appropriate and your instructor approves.

Our students have written on the following topics: U.S. policy in Iraq and Afghanistan; immigration issues, especially border control; all issues connected with "going green"; and many issues connected with consumer society. Be sure to consider local issues as well, including what is going on where you work, where you live, and in organizations to which you belong.

CHOOSING A TOPIC

Persuasive topics arise from *exigency;* that is, *the need for action.* If you are choosing your own topic, pick one you care about and are personally invested in enough to take action yourself. You can then draw on what moves you to motivate your readers to act as you do. Here are some possible places to find topics.

- *Class readings.* Class readings can suggest topics for persuasion, especially if the readings themselves are persuasive, like the examples in this chapter. For instance, if the sweatshop problem interests you, begin by finding out about the labor practices of the companies that make the clothing you and your friends wear.

- *Reading in other classes.* In a political science class, for example, you might study how presidential candidates are selected by the Democratic and Republican parties. The process is highly controversial and many proposals for reform have been advanced. Perhaps one of the reforms struck you as especially desirable. Do some more reading about it; perhaps you have found your topic.

- *Local news or observation.* Read your local and campus newspapers for issues and problems of concern to your community. Take a walk around your neighborhood or campus, looking for problems that need solutions, such as wasted energy in offices, dorms, and classrooms.

- *Internet discussions.* If you keep a blog, you probably have a store of observations about issues that concern you, things you would like to see changed. Or visit blogs on issues of public concern, such as "The Opinionator" at *The New York Times.*

EXPLORING YOUR TOPIC

Whether your topic is assigned or you chose your own, all or some of the following activities can help you gain a better initial sense of your paper.

Focus, Audience, and Need

Consider these questions:

- Can you handle the topic in the space you have? If not, how might you limit the topic?

- What audience do you wish to reach? Usually there are several appropriate choices. Consult the Concept Close-Up, "Audience Analysis," when you have identified your audience.

- How can you establish a need for taking action? See the next section to grasp the importance of need in persuasive writing.

Your answers to these questions may change as you work on your paper. Asking them now, however, can help you gain a sense of focus, audience, and purpose, always important in writing well.

Audience Analysis

To understand any audience we hope to persuade, we must know *both* what separates us from them *and* what common ground we share.

We may differ from our audience in the following ways:

Kind of Difference	Example
Assumptions	Western writers assume that separation of church and state is normal; some Muslim audiences do not make the distinction.
Principles	Most conservative writers believe in the principle of the open market; labor audiences often believe in protecting American jobs from foreign competition.
Value rankings	Some writers value personal freedom over duty and obligation; some audiences place duty and obligation above personal freedom.
Ends and means	Writer and audience may agree about purpose (for example, making America safe from terrorism) but disagree about what policies will best accomplish this end.
Interpretation	Some writers understood the September 11, 2001, attacks as acts of war; some audiences saw them as criminal acts that demanded legal rather than military measures.
Consequences	Some writers think making divorce harder would keep more couples together; some audiences think it would only promote individual unhappiness.

We may **share** the following characteristics with our audience:

Kind of Identification	Example
Local identity	Students and teachers at the same university
Collective identity	Citizens of the same state or the same nation
Common cause	Improving the environment
Common experience	Pride in the success of American Olympic athletes
Common history	Respect for soldiers who have died defending the United States

Essentially, we must understand differences to discover how we need to argue; we must use the resources of identification to overcome differences separating us from our readers.

Establishing Need

Sometimes the need for action is so widely and well understood that it is hardly necessary to mention it. We need a cure for cancer, for instance. Usually, however, need cannot be taken for granted. Consider global warming: Attitudes toward it range from casual dismissal to taking it as the biggest long-term problem we face. If you are trying to persuade an audience to take action to reduce global warming, you must devote a significant portion of your paper to establishing the damage global warming has done already and will do in the next decade or so.

In contrast, sometimes people think that a need to act exists when you think the best course is to do nothing or postpone taking action. When you face such a situation, your entire paper will be devoted to showing that no compelling need to act exists or that no immediate action is required.

In any case, thinking about need—the motivation for action—matters. The temptation is to imagine that everyone sees the need as you do, which is rarely the case.

◎ ACTIVITY: Prewriting

Jot down your first ideas about topic, focus, audience, and need. If you have the beginnings of a case in mind—your claim, reasons, and evidence—write them down as well. Include whatever insights you have gained from personal experience. These entries will help shape your first ideas.

Doing Research

If the assignment calls for research, use the techniques for finding and evaluating sources (pages 98–117) to find articles, books, and online materials about or related to your topic. Arguments require evidence, and research will help with this as well as with refining and developing your thinking.

◎ COLLABORATIVE ACTIVITY: Exchanging Ideas and Suggestions

Break out into pairs or groups of three to discuss your ideas for the persuasive paper. Assess each other's choice of topics, focus within the topics, choice of audience, and your ideas for moving the audience to take action. At the end of your discussion, evaluate the comments made about your ideas and use them to refine your topic.

PREPARING TO WRITE: THINKING ABOUT PERSUASIVE APPEALS

Exploring your topic is a good first step in preparing to write. Some writers go straight to drafting, preferring to work out what they have to say in chunks that they eventually piece together to form a complete first draft. Most, however, need more preparation before drafting. We suggest beginning with the key questions listed in the Best Practices box "Key Questions for Preparing to Write."

Answering these questions will prepare you to dig deeper into the appeals to logic, character, and emotion. Thinking them through now helps many writers build up confidence, energy for drafting, and a more detailed plan to guide the first draft.

Key Questions for Preparing to Write

1. What do you want your readers to do?

2. Who are your readers? Describe them as specifically as you can. What about them will be relevant to your argument? Consider age, religion, income bracket, occupation, political orientation, education, and gender.

3. Reader awareness is important: How much will they know about the problem, question, or issue you intend to address? What is their likely attitude?

4. Why do you care about this topic? What makes you a credible writer on behalf of your position?

5. What is the best reason you can give your readers for doing what you want them to do? State it as a sentence. Do you have a second reason in mind?

6. What additional ideas do you have for appealing to your readers? What values and beliefs can you appeal to?

7. If your topic requires more than general knowledge and personal experience, what sources have you found to support your argument? What additional material might you need?

The Appeal through Logos: Deciding on a Claim and Reasons

You know what you want your readers to do; try formulating it as a claim. These suggestions will help.

1. Your claim is a statement you will defend, not just a description of something factual.

    Not a claim: Students are choosing majors based on future income instead of interests and abilities.

    Claim: Students should find a major that excites their desire to learn rather than one that promises only financial rewards.

2. The claim should be focused and specific, and directed at a readership.

    Too general: Parents need to be stricter.

    Better: Parents need to teach children to be sensitive to other people when they are in restaurants, stores, and other public places.

3. The claim uses concrete nouns and verbs, rather than vague and indirect wording, to make its point.

    Vague: One's natural abilities cannot grow into an established intelligence unless a person learns how to control his or her attention and concentration.

    Better: Even highly talented people need to learn to control attention and concentration to develop their full potential.

4. Some claims may need to be qualified.

   Too absolute: High schools need a vocational track.

   Qualified: Except for high schools where all students go on to college, a high-quality vocational track should exist.

◎ COLLABORATIVE ACTIVITY: Refining Claims

Share several versions of the claim you have in mind by an e-mail exchange with one or several other students. Use the list of suggestions directly above to help each other improve these draft claims. Modify the claim as you draft and revise using this feedback. •

Developing Reasons for Your Claim

Once you have a working version of the claim, begin to formulate reasons for it—why your readers should take the action you are arguing for. Focus on the fit between reasons and the values and beliefs of your readers.

The Best Practices box, "Places to Find Audience-Based Reasons" (page 253), provides some places to look for reader-oriented reasons.

Making a Brief of Your Case

The brief is a concise version of a logical argument. It has three levels:

1. The claim, what you want your readers to do.
2. A reason or reasons explaining why.
3. Evidence to support each reason.

Briefs can help in preparing to write, but keep in mind that new ideas will come to you as you draft. Also bear in mind that a brief is not a plan for the whole paper, only its logical appeal. Beaudoin postponed his argument until the midpoint of his essay (pp. 241–242, paragraphs 6–9); Weber presented her evidence first (pp. 244–245, paragraph 14), then the claim and reasons.

Student Example: Natsumi Hazama's Brief

A student, Natsumi Hazama, wrote a persuasive paper urging Asian parents not to push their children so hard in school. Here is the brief she developed for her argument:

Claim: Asian-American parents need to moderate their demands for high career goals and obedience to parents, allowing their children to find goals and challenges that are right for them.

Reason: Too much pressure can lead to depression and even suicide.

Evidence: CNN.com article on college student suicides; *The Chronicle of Higher Education* online article about depression and suicide at Cornell

Places to Find Audience-Based Reasons

- In the audience's *beliefs and values.* Think about their politics and the values of their culture or subculture.

- In *traditions* and traditional texts. What books, ceremonies, ideas, places, and people do they revere?

- In *expert opinion and data.* Draw on the reasoning of qualified experts your audience will respect—mention them by name and cite their credentials. Construct reasons from information and statistics taken from sources your readers will know and trust.

- In comparisons or *analogies* your audience would accept. Analogies work because they liken the less familiar to the more familiar and known. Those who oppose genetic engineering, for example, often reason that altering human genes is like altering nature—it has bad side effects.

- In establishing *cause and effect.* If you can show that the action you would like the audience to take will lead to positive consequences, you have a good reason. Of course, you will need evidence to show that the cause-and-effect relationship exists.

Reason: Over-protective parenting does not prepare children for the independence of college life.

    Evidence: Asian Outlook website quotes

Reason: Students will be more successful at careers they prefer, not the limited choices of engineering and medicine preferred by their parents.

    Evidence: My personal experience

Reason: Constant pressure to do better rather than praise for what has been accomplished leads to low self-esteem.

    Evidence: Class reading by Csikszentmihalyi.

Note that Hazama's brief "blocks out" (separates into clear, distinct points) what she intends to say. No matter how closely related they are, *do not allow your reasons to run together.* Note also that she uses both statements from experts and personal experience as evidence. The experts lend authoritative support for her argument, whereas personal experience makes it more concrete and demonstrates firsthand knowledge.

◎ ACTIVITY: Informal Writing

In your notebook, electronic bulletin board, or journal, outline the logical case you will make. If possible, include supporting evidence for each reason.

The Appeal through Ethos: Presenting Good Character

Ethos is self-presentation. In general, you should

- Sound informed and engaged with your topic
- Show awareness of your readers' views
- Treat competing courses of action with respect, but show that yours is better
- Refer to your values and beliefs, your own ethical choices
- When appropriate, reinforce your ethos by citing information and expert testimony from sources your readers respect and trust

A more specific list of ideas for establishing good ethos follows.

Establishing Ethos with Your Readers

1. Do you have a shared local identity—as members of the same organization, the same institution, the same town or community, the same set of beliefs?
2. Can you get your audience to see that you and they have a common cause or perspective?
3. Are there experiences you might share? These might include dealing with siblings, helping friends in distress, caring for ailing family members, struggling to pay debts, or working hard for something.
4. Can you connect through a well-known event or cultural happening, perhaps a movie, book, a political rally, something in the news?

◎ ACTIVITY: Informal Writing

In your notebook or other site for informal writing, explain what attitudes you could convey in your paper that will show your good character and values. What can you talk about that will get these appeals across to your readers?   •

The Appeal through Pathos: Using Emotional Appeals

Sharing your own emotions is the most honest way to appeal to your audience's feelings. However, simply saying what your feelings are will not arouse emotion in others. How can you arouse emotions?

Show the audience the *concrete images and facts* that aroused the feelings in you. Beaudoin listed the indignities suffered by the Honduran women he interviewed. Likewise, Weber described the bodies of the burned workers in the Triangle fire, "trapped by the machinery, piled up on the wrong side of doors, heaped in the stairwells and elevator shafts . . . hideously charred, many beyond recognition."

In short, give your readers a verbal picture. You can often give them visual images as well, such as photographs.

◎ ACTIVITY: Informal Writing

Do a freewriting of ideas for specific details and images that moved you. Make lists of what you recall. Visit or revisit places relevant to your topic and take notes or pictures.

DRAFTING YOUR PAPER

By now you have generated many ideas for appealing to your readers. As you move toward drafting, focus attention on two main concerns:

- Voice, how you want to sound to your reader
- A plan to guide the draft

Development and Organization

Here are answers to some common questions that will help you with both development and organization of your paper.

1. *How might I open the paper?*

   Here are some possibilities:

- An anecdote (short narrative) based on your own experience or something you found in a source
- A surprising fact or opinion relevant to your topic
- A question that will stimulate reader interest
- A description of a person or place relevant to your claim
- A memorable quotation, with commentary from you

Introductions are often more than one paragraph, and your claim can appear anywhere in the paper.

2. *What background material should I provide?*

   Here are two principles:

- Offer *only* what your readers need
- Place it just before the section or sections of your essay where the background is relevant

3. *Where will I show my connection to the topic?*

   The introduction is often a good place. Beaudoin's first four paragraphs (p. 240) describe his awakening to a sense of economic responsibility. He wanted his readers to see his personal commitment to the topic.

4. *Will I present opposing views, and, if so, where?*

   How you handle opposing views depends on your reader's relationship to them. If you think your readers will believe them, the best strategy is to engage the opposing views first in several paragraphs. Otherwise handle them after your case and with less space devoted to them.

5. *How will I order my reasons?*

If your case has three or more reasons, starting and ending with your stronger ones is good strategy. In developing your reasons, remember that multiple paragraphs are often necessary to develop a reason.

6. *What visuals might I use, and where should they go?*

For example, a student who wrote against wearing fur added much to the pathos of her argument by including photographs of animals injured by trappers.

7. *How will I conclude my paper?*

Try one of these ending strategies:

- Look back at your introduction. Perhaps some idea you used there to attract your reader's attention could come into play again—a question you posed has an answer, or a problem you raised has a solution.
- Think about the larger context of your argument. For example, Beaudoin puts his argument about responsible consuming into the larger context of a more humane world.
- End with a well-worded quotation, and follow it up with comments of your own.
- Repeat an idea you used earlier in the essay, but with a twist. Weber took the word "outsource" and used it in a new way: People "will die because it has become our national habit to outsource, and these days we outsource our tragedies, too."

REVISING YOUR DRAFT

Writing is revising. Most first drafts need big changes on the way to completion. They need parts taken out, new parts added, and parts rearranged.

The strongest revisions begin with assessing the draft yourself. Put it aside for a day or two. Then go back and give it a critical reading.

Getting Feedback from Others

It always helps to have someone else look at your draft. Be sure that the person understands the assignment and the target audience before they read. Share the Revision Checklist in the Best Practices box with your reader.

◎ ACTIVITY: Informal Writing

After getting a second opinion, formulate a revision strategy:

1. Decide what you think the useful criticisms and comments are. Reassess your self-criticisms—do you still see the same problems?

2. Make a list of specific items you intend to work on. "The first point on page 3 needs more development" is an example of a specific item.

Revision Checklist for Appealing for Action

Take the point of view of someone reading your paper. Ask these questions to assess it.

1. Is it clear what the author wants the readers to do? Where is it stated most clearly? Is this the best place to state it?

2. Does the paper have a shape and sense of direction? Does it have parts that clearly play their individual roles in making the argument? Could you make any suggestions for arranging the parts to make it easier to follow?

3. Do the reasons for taking this action stand out as reasons? Are they good reasons for the intended audience? Is there a better way to order the reasons?

4. Has the author given enough evidence to support each reason?

5. Has the author shown awareness of and sympathy for the audience's perspective?

6. Are the individual paragraphs unified, and is their contribution to the section in which they appear clear?

7. Can you hear the author's voice in this paper? Do you think the readers would find it appealing? Does the author show personal connection with the topic?

8. Where do you see the author using emotional appeals? Are they appropriate? Do they move you?

9. Do you have suggestions to improve the introduction and the conclusion?

10. Has the author smoothly integrated the sources used or just dropped them in?

---

3. Divide your list into two categories: big revisions that will change all or much of the paper and smaller revisions requiring only adding, deleting, or rewriting a paragraph or two.

4. Ponder the best order for doing big revisions. For example, suppose that you need to rearrange the order of your reasons and improve your tone throughout. Rearrange first because attending to tone will require changing many sentences, and each sentence revision can have an impact on the flow of ideas from sentence to sentence.

5. Finalize your plan with a step-by-step list. Usually the spot revisions can be done in any order, but tackle the ones requiring most work first, leaving the easier ones for last.

Practicing Revision

A revised draft of Natsumi Hazama's paper appears on pages 260–263. To see how revision improved it, read the following excerpts from her first draft.

Paragraph 1

> One night in 1990, Eliza Noh got off the phone with her sister in college. Eliza knew her sister was depressed and something bad might happen. She sat down to write a letter to support and encourage her. But it was too late. By the time the letter arrived, her sister was dead. She had taken her own life. Eliza believed that too much pressure to succeed contributed to her sister's death. This tragedy led Noh to pursue a career in studying the effects of pressure on Asian-American students.

Paragraph 7

> Low self-esteem can be a result of too much pressure to be at the top. According to Mihaly Csikszentmihalyi, goals can determine a person's level of self-esteem. Because Asian-Americans' goals are set so high by parents, these students tend to have lower self-esteem (Csikszentmihalyi, 23). A 24-year-old Korean rock star named Jeong-Hyun Lim has turned into a global phenomenon from his rock rendition of Pachelbel's Canon (Lam). Some call him a second Jimi Hendrix and his YouTube video has been viewed more than 24 million times (Lam). But when interviewers ask him to rate himself he said 50 or 60 out of 100 and is always thinking that he needs to improve (Lam). This is an example of a stereotypical Asian.

Compare the first draft's introduction with the introduction to the final version of the paper (page 260). Do you agree that opening with Natsumi's own story is more effective? The original opening was moved to paragraphs 12–13; do you think this arrangement is better?

◎ ACTIVITY: Informal Writing

Look at the opening of your own draft. Why did you choose to open the paper as you did? If you are not happy with the opening, do you see material elsewhere in the draft that might work better? If not, review the opening strategies discussed on page 255 and try one of those instead.   •

Revising to Bring Out the Structure of the Argument

Here is a body paragraph from Hazama's first draft, offering a reason and evidence in support of her claim:

> Dr. Henry Chung, assistant vice president for student health at New York University and executive director of the NYU student Health Center, says "Asian-American/Asian students, especially males, are under unique pressures to meet high expectations of parents by succeeding in such traditional predetermined careers as medicine and engineering" (qtd. in Ramanujan). Asian students feel that even though they aren't interested in these fields they must major in them and they end up stressing themselves out. Because students major in fields that they aren't interested in

they end up not doing as well in school as they could. If you don't have a passion for your job you feel like you are working twice as hard with loads of work on your shoulders.

This paragraph was revised to become paragraph 12 in the final version (page 262). Compare them. In the revised version, how has the argument emerged better in the opening sentence? How has it been better supported?

◎ ACTIVITY: Revising Your Draft

Look over the body paragraphs of your draft. Open with a point of your own; use your sources to support and develop it. Look over your entire draft. How could revising make your reasons stand out more?

Revising to Improve Incorporation of Quoted Material

Using sources responsibly means not only citing the source but also identifying the source by name. Hazama noticed that she was not always clear about whose words were in quotation marks. Here is an example of the problem:

See Chapter 6, "Writing Research-Based Arguments," for more on this important research skill.

Draft Version

> Also when kids come to college they receive conflicting messages. "The message at home is that their priority should be to look after their parents and take care of their families" ("Mental"). But the message you get at college and from your friends is that you need to learn to think for yourself and be who you are and do what is best for you. This is a different value than the Asian culture so Asian students feel guilty for not doing what they are supposed to be doing ("Mental").

Revised Version

> According to Diem Nguyen, a UC Davis student affairs officer, when Asian-American students come to college, they sometimes end up partying too much because they are not used to this freedom (qtd. in "Mental"). Also, when kids come to college they receive conflicting messages. Nadine Tang, a psychotherapist who has counseled students at UC Berkeley, says they get the message at home that family is their top priority, but the message at college is "to be who you are, learn to be yourself and do what is best for you. . . . You feel guilty for not doing what you're supposed to and not fulfilling your obligations" (qtd. in "Mental").

As the underlined phrases show, identifying your sources by name and qualifications not only helps your reader understand who is saying what but also increases the authority of the quoted statements.

◎ ACTIVITY: Editing for Clarity with Direct Quotations

If you are using the words of someone quoted in your source, are you *identifying the actual speaker of the words* as well as citing the source? If not, identify them as Hazama did in the revised version above.

REVISED STUDENT EXAMPLE

Is Too Much Pressure Healthy?

NATSUMI HAZAMA

1   Growing up in an Asian-American family, I was raised to stay close to my family and always to strive to be number one in my class. My parents were both born in Japan and came to America for my father's work. My father was a very intelligent man who wanted me to go into either medicine or engineering. My parents also made me go to Japanese School every Saturday to learn to read and write my native tongue. Going to school six days a week left no time for a social life. The girls at my English school would always have sleepover parties on Friday nights, but I was studying for my next Japanese test. I excelled in school, but that wasn't good enough. Even if I scored a 98 on my math test, my parents would say, "Why didn't you get a 100?"

2   When I was in 8th grade, my father was diagnosed with colon cancer. He grew very ill, and my parents actually knew that he was dying but didn't tell my sister and me. One week, all my relatives from Japan flew in; at the end of that week he passed away. It was a horrible experience, but my mother, sister, and I helped each other, and with the support of all of our family and friends we got through it.

3   Starting high school was completely different. Because my mother knew growing up without a father was hard enough, she just wanted me to be happy. Coming home with a few B's on my report card was okay now. My mother didn't pressure me to get good grades; she basically let me do whatever I wanted. I wasn't in the top 10% of my class, didn't get straight A's, or take all AP courses. However, I was completely satisfied with my high school experience. I was part of the nationally ranked cheerleading team. I had higher self-esteem. I would give anything to have my father still alive, but I have learned to think for myself and to set my own goals.

4   My situation before the death of my father is common among Asian-American families. I understand it is part of my culture, which I value. However, Asian-American parents need to moderate their demands and allow their children to find goals and challenges that are right for them.

5   Wenju Shen and Weimin Mo, experts on educating Asian-Americans, describe our ways as rooted in Confucianism: "The

Confucian ethical code . . . holds that the first loyalty is to the family, even above their allegiance to their country and religion."

6   This closeness to family can bring pressures. In an Asian family the most important thing is to always keep your "face." "Face" means family pride. "Family" means not only immediate relatives, extended relatives, dead ancestors, but also anyone with my last name. To fail in any obligation to the family is to "lose face" and bring shame to myself, my parents, my relatives, and all my ancestors.

7   While family should be important, this cultural pressure to succeed helps to create harmful stereotypes. As Shen and Mo point out, the "whiz kid" stereotype of Asian-American students encourages their parents to maintain practices "not compatible with the values and beliefs of American society." Asian-American parents need to learn how to balance obligations to the family with the more individual values of Americans.

8   A more balanced approach to parenting will lead children to more fulfilling lives. Mihaly Csikszentmihalyi, a psychologist at the University of Chicago, is noted for his work on happiness, creativity, and subjective well-being. His book, Finding Flow, describes the kind of family that leads children to develop their full potential: "they combine discipline with spontaneity, rules with freedom, high expectations with unstinting love. An optimal family system is complex in that it encourages the unique individual development of its members while uniting them in a web of affective ties" (88). Asian-American parents should raise their children more like this. Too much parental pressure hinders what Csikszentmihalyi calls "flow," a state of mind where the person is fully engaged in what he or she is doing for its own sake (29–32).

9   For most Asian students, college is their first significant time away from home. Because they aren't used to the freedom of college life, they sometimes end up partying too much.

10   They also receive conflicting messages. Nadine Tang, a psychotherapist who has counseled students at UC Berkeley, says the message at home is that family matters most, but the message at college is "be who you are, learn to be yourself and do what is best for you. . . . You feel guilty for not doing what you're supposed to and not fulfilling your obligations" (qtd. in "Mental").

11   That is what life is all about, fulfilling your own potential, as Csikszentmihalyi says. Unfortunately, even if Asian-American students receive excellent grades in school, they tend to have lower self-esteem than other students (Csikszentmihalyi 24). I think this is so because their parents never praise them. Asian-American parents see success

as a duty, so children should not receive praise; instead they are told to do even better and aim still higher (Shen).

12   Along with bringing home straight "A's," parents also urge their children to major in a subject that they see as respectable. Dr. Henry Chung, assistant vice president for student health at New York University and executive director of the Health Center, points out that "Asian-American/Asian students, especially males, are under unique pressures to meet high expectations of parents by succeeding in such traditional predetermined careers as medicine and engineering" (qtd. in Ramanujan). Even if these fields are not areas of strength or interest, Asian-American students feel that they must major in them. Their grades may start to slip, but as Nguyen at Berkeley says, "Some stay in these majors because they think that they need to. They're reluctant to leave because their parents don't understand: 'If you're not a doctor or engineer, then what are you?'" (qtd. in "Mental").

13   The result can be destructive to a student's mental health, often leading to anxiety and depression. These problems are more common in Asian-American students than in the general population ("Mental"). When Asian-American students are unhappy, they usually don't seek help, even though the best way to recover is to get counseling. Chung at NYU explains that in Asian culture "suffering and working hard are accepted as part of life, a cultural paradigm" (Ramanujan). Asian-American students don't get counseling because discussing emotional problems is a sign of weakness ("Mental"). They also do not tell their parents about their problems. A psychologist at Baylor University, Dr. Dung Ngo, says, "The line of communication in an Asian culture goes one way. It's communicated from the parents downward" (qtd. in Cohen). If students can't express their anger and frustration, it turns into helplessness; they feel like there is no way out.

14   Suicide is therefore common among Asian-American students. According to CNN, Asian American women age 15–24 have the highest suicide rate of any ethnic group. Suicide is the second-leading cause of death (Cohen). At Cornell University between 1996 and 2006 there were 21 suicides; 13 of these were Asian or Asian-American students (Ramanujan).

15   CNN tells the story of how Eliza Noh, a professor of Asian-American studies at California State University at Fullerton, decided to devote her studies to depression and suicide among Asian-American women. One night in 1990, she had been talking to her sister, a college student, on the telephone. She knew her sister was depressed. She sat down to write a letter to encourage her. It was too late. By the time the

16　　letter arrived, she had taken her life. Noh believes that the pressure to
succeed contributed to her sister's death (Cohen).

I have lived both sides, with pressure and without. Living
without pressure has enabled me think for myself and be happier.
Asian-American parents need to give their children support and
encouragement, allow them to make their own decisions about goals,
and most of all, stop pressuring them so much.

WORKS CITED

Cohen, Elizabeth. "Push to Achieve Tied to Suicide in Asian-American
Women." *CNN.com Health,* 16 May 2007, www.cnn.com/2007/
HEALTH/05/16/asian.suicides/.

Csikszentmihalyi, Mihaly. *Finding Flow: The Psychology of Engagement
with Everyday Life.* Basic Books, 1997.

"Mental Health of Asian Youth a Growing Concern." *Asian Outlook—
Challenges for Today's Asian American Students,* Fall/Winter 2007.

Ramanujan, Krishna. "Health Expert Explains Asian and Asian-American
Students' Unique Pressures to Succeed." *Cornell Chronicle,*
19 Apr. 2006, www.news.cornell.edu/stories/2006/04/
health-expert-explains-asian-students-unique-pressures-succeed.

Shen, Wenju, and Weimin Mo. "Reaching Out to Their Cultures: Building
Communication with Asian American Families." *ERIC,* files.eric.ed.gov/
fulltext/ED351435.pdf.

CHAPTER SUMMARY

In this assignment, you learned to combine logical appeal (logos) with ethos,
pathos, and style to move an audience to action. You will use what you have
learned over and over, in college, at work, and in the community.

What you learn from persuasion applies to other kinds of writing. For
instance, how you present yourself—your ethos—makes a difference. We are
always writing to reach others even when moving readers to act is not on
our mind.

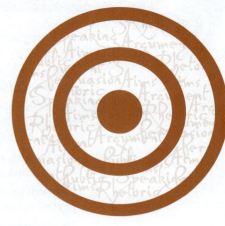

CHAPTER 11

Resolving Conflict: Arguing to Mediate

Private citizens can avoid the big conflicts that concern politicians and activist groups: debates over gay marriage, abortion, taxes, foreign policy, and so on. However, we cannot hide from all conflict. Family members have different preferences about budgeting, major purchases, where to go on vacation, and much else. Furthermore, if you care about what goes on beyond your front door, you will find conflict close to home. The school down the street, for example, wants to expand its athletic stadium. Some parents support the decision because their children play sports at the school. Others oppose it because they think the expansion will bring more traffic, noise, and bright lights to the neighborhood.

One way to resolve conflict is through reasoned arguments. The chapters on convincing and persuading show how appeals to logic and emotion can change minds. But what if we cannot change someone's mind or impose our will in other ways?

Some conflicts do not have to be resolved. The Republican husband can live happily with the Democratic wife. Other conflicts are resolved by compromise. We can go to the mountains this year, the seashore the next. Compromise is better than shouting matches, but it does not result in a common understanding.

CONCEPT CLOSE-UP

Characteristics of Mediation

1. Mediation aims to resolve conflict between opposing and usually hardened positions, often because action of some kind must be taken.
2. Mediation aims to reduce hostility and promote understanding between or among conflicting parties; preserving human relationships and promoting communication are paramount.
3. Like inquiry, mediation involves dialogue and requires that one understand all positions and strive for an open mind.
4. Like convincing, mediation involves making a case that appeals to all parties in the controversy.
5. Like persuasion, mediation depends on the good character of the negotiator and on sharing values and feelings.
6. Mediation depends on conflicting parties' desire to find solutions to overcome counterproductive stalemates.

Essentially, mediation comes into play when convincing and persuading have resulted in sharply differing viewpoints. The task is first to understand the positions of all parties involved and second to uncover a mediating position capable of producing consensus and a reduction in hostility.

This chapter presents **mediation** as argument whose aim is to resolve conflict by thinking more critically about it. People too often see disputes uncritically by simplifying them to their extreme positions, pro and con. *Mediation aims to move disputants beyond the polarized thinking that makes conflicts impossible to resolve.*

MEDIATION AND THE OTHER AIMS OF ARGUMENT

Mediation uses the other three aims of argument: inquiry, convincing, and persuading. Like inquiry, it examines the range of positions on an issue. Mediation requires knowledge of case structure. The mediator scrutinizes the arguments offered by all sides. A mediatory essay must also present a well-reasoned case of its own. Finally, like persuasion, mediation considers the values, beliefs, and assumptions of the people who hold the conflicting positions. Mediators must appeal to all sides and project a character all sides will trust and find attractive.

In short, mediation requires the mediator to rise above a dispute, including his or her own preferences, to see what is reasonable and right in conflicting positions. The mediator's best asset is wisdom.

THE PROCESS OF MEDIATION

Mediation takes place more often in conversation, through dialogue with the opposing sides, than in writing. But essays can mediate by attempting to argue for middle ground in a conflict. Mediation begins where all arguments should—with inquiry.

MEDIATION AND ROGERIAN ARGUMENT

Arguing to mediate resembles an approach to communication developed by a psychologist, Carl Rogers (1902–1987). In "Communication: Its Blocking and Its Facilitation," he urged people in conflict to listen to each other carefully and with empathy as a first step toward resolving differences. The second step is to go beyond listening in an effort to understand one another's background. Finally, a third step is for each person involved in a dispute to state the position of his or her opponents in a way the opponents agree is accurate and fair. The total approach reduces misunderstanding and helps to clarify what the genuine points of difference are, thus opening up the potential to resolve conflict.

In their textbook *Rhetoric: Discovery and Change* (1970), Richard Young, Alton Becker, and Kenneth Pike outlined four stages for Rogerian argument:

1. An introduction to the problem and a demonstration that the opponent's position is understood

2. A statement of the contexts in which the opponent's position may be valid

3. A statement of the writer's position, including the contexts in which it is valid

4. A statement of how the opponent's position would benefit if he were to adopt elements of the writer's position. If the writer can show that the positions complement each other, that each supplies what the other lacks, so much the better.[1]

Our approach to mediation draws on Rogerian argument. As a mediator, rather than a participant in a dispute, you need to consider the validity of opposing positions, including the personal backgrounds of the people involved. In light of these backgrounds, you look for what is good and right in each position.

Rather than face-to-face oral arguments, in this chapter you will be reading written arguments on a controversial issue and exploring them to uncover

---

[1]This summary of the four stages comes from Douglas Brent, "Rogerian Rhetoric: An Alternative to Traditional Rhetoric," *Argument Revisited, Argument Redefined: Negotiating Meaning in the Composition Classroom*, edited by Barbara Emmel, et al., Sage, 1996, www.acs.ucalgary.ca/~dabrent/art/rogchap.html.

exactly how and why their authors disagree. Instead of sitting around a table with parties in conflict as mediators do, you will write a mediatory essay proposing a point of view designed to appeal to both sides.

A Conflict to Mediate

The United States is a nation of immigrants, but recently the immigrant population includes a wider array of races, ethnicities, religions, and cultures than in the past. The result is a population less white and less Protestant. Should we become a multicultural nation or maintain a single culture based on the original northern European settlers?

Some people argue that the influx of diverse people should have no impact on the traditional Eurocentric identity of America. According to this position, America has a distinctive and superior culture, traceable to the Puritan settlers and based more broadly on Western civilization. This culture is the source of our nation's strength. To keep it strong, newcomers need to assimilate, adopting its values and beliefs. In other words, people holding this position advocate the melting-pot metaphor. Because they believe cultural differences should dissolve as new immigrants become "true Americans," they oppose multiculturalism. We have chosen a recent essay by Roger Kimball, an art critic and editor at the conservative journal *The New Criterion,* to represent the assimilationist position.

Opponents argue that newcomers should preserve their distinctive cultures, taking pride in being Mexican, Chinese, African, and so on. Their metaphor is the mosaic, with each culture remaining distinct but contributing to the whole. We have chosen an essay by Elizabeth Martínez to represent the multiculturalist perspective. Martínez is a Chicana writer and an activist on issues of social justice, including racism and women's rights.

Understanding the Positions

Any attempt to mediate positions requires an understanding of opposing cases. Printed below are the two arguments, followed by our analyses.

Institutionalizing Our Demise: America vs. Multiculturalism

ROGER KIMBALL

The following abridged article appeared in *The New Criterion*. Roger Kimball's books include *The Long March: How the Cultural Revolution of the 1960s Changed America* and *Tenured Radicals: How Politics Has Corrupted Our Higher Education.*

There is no room in this country for hyphenated Americanism. When I refer to hyphenated Americans, I do not refer to naturalized Americans. Some of the very best Americans I have ever known were naturalized Americans, Americans born abroad.

But a hyphenated American is not an American at all. This is just as true of the man who puts "native" before the hyphen as of the man who puts German or Irish or English or French before the hyphen.

—Theodore Roosevelt, 1915

1　It is often said that the terrorist attacks of September 11 precipitated a new resolve throughout the nation. There is some truth to that. Certainly, the extraordinary bravery of the firefighters and other rescue personnel in New York and Washington, D.C., provided an invigorating spectacle—as did Todd "Let's roll" Beamer and his fellow passengers on United Airlines Flight 93. Having learned from their cell phones what had happened at the World Trade Center and the Pentagon, Beamer and his fellows rushed and overpowered the terrorists who had hijacked their plane. As a result, the plane crashed on a remote Pennsylvania farm instead of on Pennsylvania Avenue. Who knows how many lives their sacrifice saved?

2　The widespread sense of condign outrage—of horror leavened by anger and elevated by resolve—testified to a renewed sense of national purpose and identity after 9/11. Attacked, many Americans suddenly (if temporarily) rediscovered the virtue of patriotism. At the beginning of his remarkable book *Who Are We? The Challenges to America's National Identity* (2004), the Harvard political scientist Samuel Huntington recalls a certain block on Charles Street in Boston. At one time, American flags flew in front of a U.S. Post Office and a liquor store. Then the Post Office stopped displaying the flag, so on September 11, 2001, the flag was flying only in front of the liquor store. Within two weeks, seventeen American flags decorated that block of Charles Street, in addition to a huge flag suspended over the street close by. "With their country under attack," Huntington notes, "Charles Street denizens rediscovered their nation and identified themselves with it."

3　Was that rediscovery anything more than a momentary passion? Huntington reports that within a few months, the flags on Charles Street began to disappear. By the time the first anniversary rolled around in September 2002, only four were left flying. True, that is four times more than were there on September 10, 2001, but it is less than a quarter of the number that populated Charles Street at the end of September 2001.

4　There are similar anecdotes from around the country—an access of flag-waving followed by a relapse into indifference. Does it mean that the sudden upsurge of patriotism in the weeks following 9/11 was only, as it were, skin deep? Or perhaps it merely testifies to the fact that a sense of permanent emergency is difficult to maintain, especially in the absence of fresh attacks. Is our sense of ourselves as Americans patent only when challenged? "Does it," Huntington asks, "take an Osama bin Laden . . . to make us realize that we are Americans? If we do not experience recurring destructive attacks, will we return to the fragmentation and eroded Americanism before September 11?"

5　One hopes that the answer is No. . . . But I fear that for every schoolchild standing at attention for the National Anthem, there is a teacher or lawyer or judge or politician or ACLU employee militating against the hegemony of the dominant culture, the insupportable intrusion of white, Christian, "Eurocentric" values into the curriculum, the school pageant, the town green, etc., etc. . . .

6   The threat shows itself in many ways, from culpable complacency to the corrosive imperatives of "multiculturalism" and political correctness. . . . In essence, as Huntington notes, multiculturalism is "anti-European civilization. . . . It is basically an anti-Western ideology.". . . [W]herever the imperatives of multiculturalism have touched the curriculum, they have left broad swaths of anti-Western attitudinizing competing for attention with quite astonishing historical blindness. Courses on minorities, women's issues, the Third World proliferate; the teaching of mainstream history slides into oblivion. "The mood," Arthur Schlesinger wrote in *The Disuniting of America* (1992), his excellent book on the depredations of multiculturalism, "is one of divesting Americans of the sinful European inheritance and seeking redemptive infusions from non-Western cultures."

7   A profound ignorance of the milestones of American culture is one predictable result of this mood. The statistics have become proverbial. Huntington quotes one poll from the 1990s showing that while 90 percent of Ivy League students could identify Rosa Parks, only 25 percent could identify the author of the words "government of the people, by the people, for the people." (Yes, it's the Gettysburg Address.) In a 1999 survey, 40 percent of seniors at fifty-five top colleges could not say within half a century when the Civil War was fought. Another study found that more high school students knew who Harriet Tubman was than knew that Washington commanded the American army in the revolution or that Abraham Lincoln wrote the Emancipation Proclamation. Doubtless you have your own favorite horror story.

8   But multiculturalism is not only an academic phenomenon. The attitudes it fosters have profound social as well as intellectual consequences. One consequence has been a sharp rise in the phenomenon of immigration without—or with only partial—assimilation: a dangerous demographic trend that threatens American identity in the most basic way. These various agents of dissolution are also elements in a wider culture war: the contest to define how we live and what counts as the good in the good life. Anti-Americanism occupies such a prominent place on the agenda of the culture wars precisely because the traditional values of American identity—articulated by the Founders and grounded in a commitment to individual liberty and public virtue—are deeply at odds with the radical, de-civilizing tenets of the "multiculturalist" enterprise.

9   To get a sense of what has happened to the institution of American identity, compare Robert Frost's performance at John F. Kennedy's inauguration in 1961 with Maya Angelou's performance thirty-two years later. As Huntington reminds us, Frost spoke of the "heroic deeds" of America's founding, an event, he said, that with "God's approval" ushered in "a new order of the ages." By contrast, Maya Angelou never mentioned the words "America" or "American." Instead, she identified twenty-seven ethnic or religious groups that had suffered repression because of America's "armed struggles for profit," "cynicism," and "brutishness.". . .

10   A favorite weapon in the armory of multiculturalism is the lowly hyphen. When we speak of an African-American or Mexican-American or Asian-American these days,

the aim is not descriptive but deconstructive. There is a polemical edge to it, a provocation. The hyphen does not mean "American, but hailing at some point in the past from someplace else." It means "only provisionally American: my allegiance is divided at best.". . . The multicultural passion for hyphenation is not simply a fondness for syntactical novelty. It also bespeaks a commitment to the centrifugal force of anti-American tribalism. The division marked by the hyphen in African-American (say) denotes a political stand. It goes hand-in-hand with other items on the index of liberal desiderata—the redistributive impulse behind efforts at "affirmative action," for example. . . .

11   Multiculturalism and "affirmative action" are allies in the assault on the institution of American identity. As such, they oppose the traditional understanding of what it means to be an American—an understanding hinted at in 1782 by the French-born American farmer J. Hector St. John de Crèvecoeur in his famous image of America as a country in which "individuals of all nations are melted into a new race of men." This crucible of American identity, this "melting pot," has two aspects. The negative aspect involves disassociating oneself from the cultural imperatives of one's country of origin. One sheds a previous identity before assuming a new one. One might preserve certain local habits and tastes, but they are essentially window-dressing. In essence one has left the past behind in order to become an American citizen.

12   The positive aspect of advancing the melting pot involves embracing the substance of American culture. The 1795 code for citizenship lays out some of the formal requirements.

> I do solemnly swear (1) to support the Constitution of the United States; (2) to renounce and abjure absolutely and entirely all allegiance and fidelity to any foreign prince, potentate, state, or sovereignty of whom or which the applicant was before a subject or citizen; (3) to support and defend the Constitution and the laws of the United States against all enemies, foreign and domestic; (4) to bear true faith and allegiance to the same; and (5) (A) to bear arms on behalf of the United States when required by law, or (B) to perform noncombatant service in the Armed Forces of the United States when required by law. . . .

For over two hundred years, this oath had been required of those wishing to become citizens. In 2003, Huntington tells us, federal bureaucrats launched a campaign to rewrite and weaken it.

13   I shall say more about what constitutes the substance of American identity in a moment. For now, I want to underscore the fact that this project of Americanization has been an abiding concern since the time of the Founders. "We must see our people more Americanized," John Jay declared in the 1780s. Jefferson concurred. Teddy Roosevelt repeatedly championed the idea that American culture, the "crucible in which all the new types are melted into one," was "shaped from 1776 to 1789, and our nationality was definitely fixed in all its essentials by the men of Washington's day."

14   It is often said that America is a nation of immigrants. In fact, as Huntington points out, America is a country that was initially a country of *settlers*. Settlers

precede immigrants and make their immigration possible. The culture of those mostly English-speaking, predominantly Anglo-Protestant settlers defined American culture. Their efforts came to fruition with the generation of Franklin, Washington, Jefferson, Hamilton, and Madison. The Founders are so denominated because they founded, they inaugurated a state. Immigrants were those who came later, who came from elsewhere, and who became American by embracing the Anglophone culture of the original settlers. The English language, the rule of law, respect for individual rights, the industriousness and piety that flowed from the Protestant work ethic—these were central elements in the culture disseminated by the Founders. And these were among the qualities embraced by immigrants when they became Americans. "Throughout American history," Huntington notes, "people who were not white Anglo-Saxon Protestants have become Americans by adopting America's Anglo-Protestant culture and political values. This benefited them and the country."

15   Justice Louis Brandeis outlined the pattern in 1919. Americanization, he said, means that the immigrant "adopts the clothes, the manners, and the customs generally prevailing here . . . substitutes for his mother tongue the English language" and comes "into complete harmony with our ideals and aspirations and cooperate[s] with us for their attainment." Until the 1960s, the Brandeis model mostly prevailed. Protestant, Catholic, and Jewish groups, understanding that assimilation was the best ticket to stability and social and economic success, eagerly aided in the task of integrating their charges into American society.

16   The story is very different today. In America, there is a dangerous new tide of immigration from Asia, a variety of Muslim countries, and Latin America, especially from Mexico. The tide is new not only chronologically but also in substance. First, there is the sheer matter of numbers. More than 2,200,000 legal immigrants came to the U.S. from Mexico in the 1990s alone. The number of illegal Mexican immigrants is staggering. So is their birth rate. Altogether there are more than 8 million Mexicans in the U.S. Some parts of the Southwest are well on their way to becoming what Victor Davis Hanson calls "Mexifornia," "the strange society that is emerging as the result of a demographic and cultural revolution like no other in our times." A professor of Chicano Studies at the University of New Mexico gleefully predicts that by 2080 parts of the Southwest United States and Northern Mexico will join to form a new country, "La Republica del Norte."

17   The problem is not only one of numbers, though. Earlier immigrants made— and were helped and goaded by the ambient culture to make—concerted efforts to assimilate. Important pockets of these new immigrants are not assimilating, not learning English, not becoming or thinking of themselves primarily as Americans. The effect of these developments on American identity is disastrous and potentially irreversible.

18   Such developments are abetted by the left-wing political and educational elites of this country, whose dominant theme is the perfidy of traditional American values. Hence the passion for multiculturalism and the ideal of ethnic hyphenation that goes with it. This has done immense damage in schools and colleges as

well as in the population at large. By removing the obligation to master English, multiculturalism condemns whole subpopulations to the status of permanent second-class citizens. . . .

19   As if in revenge for this injustice, however, multiculturalism also weakens the social bonds of the community at large. The price of imperfect assimilation is imperfect loyalty. Take the movement for bilingualism. Whatever it intended in theory, in practice it means *not* mastering English. It has notoriously left its supposed beneficiaries essentially monolingual, often semi-lingual. The only *bi* involved is a passion for bifurcation, which is fed by the accumulated resentments instilled by the anti-American multicultural orthodoxy. Every time you call directory assistance or some large corporation and are told "Press One for English" and "Para español oprime el numero dos" it is another small setback for American identity. . . .

20   We stand at a crossroads. The future of America hangs in the balance. Huntington outlines several possible courses that the country might take, from the loss of our core culture to an attempt to revive the "discarded and discredited racial and ethnic concepts" that, in part, defined pre-mid-twentieth century America. Huntington argues for another alternative. If we are to preserve our identity as a nation we need to preserve the core values that defined that identity. This is a point that the political philosopher Patrick, Lord Devlin made in his book *The Enforcement of Morals* (1965):

> [S]ociety means a community of ideas; without shared ideas on politics, morals, and ethics no society can exist. Each one of us has ideas about what is good and what is evil; they cannot be kept private from the society in which we live. If men and women try to create a society in which there is no fundamental agreement about good and evil they will fail; if having based it upon a common set of core values, they surrender those values, it will disintegrate. For society is not something that can be kept together physically; it is held by the invisible but fragile bonds of common beliefs and values. . . . A common morality is part of the bondage of a good society, and that bondage is part of the price of society which mankind must pay.

What are those beliefs and values? They embrace several things, including religion. You wouldn't know it from watching CNN or reading *The New York Times,* but there is a huge religious revival taking place now, affecting just about every part of the globe except Western Europe, which slouches towards godlessness almost as fast as it slouches towards bankruptcy and demographic collapse. (Neither Spain nor Italy are producing enough children to replace their existing populations, while the Muslim birthrate in France continues to soar.)

21   Things look different in America. For if America is a vigorously secular country—which it certainly is—it is also a deeply religious one. It always has been. Tocqueville was simply minuting the reality he saw around him when he noted that "[o]n my arrival in the United States the religious aspect of the country was the first thing that struck my attention." As G. K. Chesterton put it a century after Tocqueville, America is "a nation with the soul of a church." Even today, America is a country where an astonishing 92 percent of the population says it believes in God and 80 to 85 percent of the population identifies itself as Christian. Hence Huntington's call for a return to

America's core values is also a call to embrace the religious principles upon which the country was founded, "a recommitment to America as a deeply religious and primarily Christian country, encompassing several religious minorities adhering to Anglo-Protestant values, speaking English, maintaining its cultural heritage, and committed to the principles" of political liberty as articulated by the Founders. . . . Huntington is careful to stress that what he offers is an "argument for the importance of Anglo-Protestant culture, not for the importance of Anglo-Protestant people." That is, he argues not on behalf of a particular ethnic group but on behalf of a culture and set of values that "for three and a half centuries have been embraced by Americans of all races, ethnicities, and religions and that have been the source of their liberty, unity, power, prosperity, and moral leadership."

22   American identity was originally founded on four things: ethnicity, race, ideology, and culture. By the mid-twentieth century, ethnicity and race had sharply receded in importance. Indeed, one of America's greatest achievements is having eliminated the racial and ethnic components that historically were central to its identity. Ideology—the package of Enlightened liberal values championed by the Founders—[is] crucial but too thin for the task of forging or preserving national identity by themselves. ("A nation defined only by political ideology," Huntington notes, "is a fragile nation.") Which is why Huntington, like virtually all of the Founders, explicitly grounded American identity in religion. . . .

23   Opponents of religion in the public square never tire of reminding us that there is no mention of God in the Constitution. This is true. Neither is the word "virtue" mentioned. But both are presupposed. For the American Founders, as the historian Gertrude Himmelfarb points out, virtue, grounded in religion, was presumed "to be rooted in the very nature of man and as such . . . reflected in the *moeurs* of the people and in the traditions and informal institutions of society." It is also worth mentioning that if the Constitution is silent on religion, the Declaration of Independence is voluble, speaking of "nature's God," the "Creator," "the supreme judge of the world," and "divine Providence.". . . Benjamin Rush, one of the signers of the Declaration of Independence, summed up the common attitude of the Founders toward religion when he insisted that "[t]he only foundation for a useful education in a republic is to be laid in religion. Without it there can be no virtue, and without virtue there can be no liberty, and liberty is the object of all republican governments." George Washington concurred: "Reason and experience both forbid us to expect that national morality can prevail in exclusion of religious principles."

24   No nation lasts forever. An external enemy may eventually overrun and subdue it; internal forces of dissolution and decadence may someday undermine it, leaving it prey to more vigorous competitors. Sooner or later it succumbs. The United States is the most powerful nation the world has ever seen. Its astonishing military might, economic productivity, and political vigor are unprecedented. But someday, as Huntington reminds us, it too will fade or perish as Athens, Rome, and other great civilizations have faded or perished. Is the end, or the beginning of the end, at hand?

25   So far, the West—or at least the United States—has disappointed its self-appointed undertakers. How do we stand now, at the dawn of the twenty-first

century? It is worth remembering that besieged nations do not always succumb to the forces, external or internal, that threaten them. Sometimes, they muster the resolve to fight back successfully, to renew themselves. Today, America faces a new external enemy in the form of militant Islam and global terrorism. That minatory force, though murderous, will fail in proportion to our resolve to defeat it. Do we still possess that resolve? Inseparable from resolve is self-confidence, faith in the essential nobility of one's regime and one's way of life. To what extent do we still possess, still practice that faith?

Reinventing "America": Call for a New National Identity

ELIZABETH MARTÍNEZ

> Elizabeth Martínez has written six books, including one on Chicano history. This essay comes from her book, *De Colores Means All of Us: Latina Views for a Multi-Colored Century*.

1   For some 15 years, starting in 1940, 85 percent of all U.S. elementary schools used the Dick and Jane series to teach children how to read. The series starred Dick, Jane, their white middle-class parents, their dog Spot and their life together in a home with a white picket fence.

2   "Look, Jane, look! See Spot run!" chirped the two kids. It was a house full of glorious family values, where Mom cooked while Daddy went to work in a suit and mowed the lawn on weekends. The Dick and Jane books also taught that you should do your job and help others. All this affirmed an equation of middle-class with whiteness with virtue.

3   In the mid-1990s, museums, libraries and 80 Public Broadcasting Service (PBS) stations across the country had exhibits and programs commemorating the series. At one museum, an attendant commented, "When you hear someone crying, you know they are looking at the Dick and Jane books." It seems nostalgia runs rampant among many Euro-Americans: a nostalgia for the days of unchallenged White Supremacy—both moral and material—when life was "simple."

4   We've seen that nostalgia before in the nation's history. But today it signifies a problem reaching a new intensity. It suggests a national identity crisis that promises to bring in its wake an unprecedented nervous breakdown for the dominant society's psyche.

5   Nowhere is this more apparent than in California, which has long been on the cutting edge of the nation's present and future reality. Warning sirens have sounded repeatedly in the 1990s, such as the fierce battle over new history textbooks for public schools, Proposition 187's ugly denial of human rights to immigrants, the 1996 assault on affirmative action that culminated in Proposition 209, and the 1997 move to abolish bilingual education. Attempts to copycat these reactionary measures have been seen in other states.

6   The attack on affirmative action isn't really about affirmative action. Essentially it is another tactic in today's war on the gains of the 1960s, a tactic rooted in Anglo

resentment and fear. A major source of that fear: the fact that California will almost surely have a majority of people of color in 20 to 30 years at most, with the nation as a whole not far behind.

7   Check out the February 3, 1992, issue of *Sports Illustrated* with its double-spread ad for *Time* magazine. The ad showed hundreds of newborn babies in their hospital cribs, all of them Black or brown except for a rare white face here and there. The headline says, "Hey, whitey! It's your turn at the back of the bus!" The ad then tells you, read *Time* magazine to keep up with today's hot issues. That manipulative image could have been published today; its implication of shifting power appears to be the recurrent nightmare of too many potential Anglo allies.

8   Euro-American anxiety often focuses on the sense of a vanishing national identity. Behind the attacks on immigrants, affirmative action and multiculturalism, behind the demand for "English Only" laws and the rejection of bilingual education, lies the question: with all these new people, languages and cultures, what will it mean to be an American? If that question once seemed, to many people, to have an obvious, universally applicable answer, today new definitions must be found. But too often Americans, with supposed scholars in the lead, refuse to face that need and instead nurse a nostalgia for some bygone clarity. They remain trapped in denial.

9   An array of such ostriches, heads in the sand, began flapping their feathers noisily with the publication of Allan Bloom's 1987 best-selling book, *The Closing of the American Mind*. Bloom bemoaned the decline of our "common values" as a society, meaning the decline of Euro-American cultural centricity (shall we just call it cultural imperialism?). Since then we have seen constant sniping at "diversity" goals across the land. The assault has often focused on how U.S. history is taught. And with reason, for this country's identity rests on a particular narrative about the historical origins of the United States as a nation.

THE GREAT WHITE ORIGIN MYTH

10   Every society has an origin narrative that explains that society to itself and the world with a set of stories and symbols. The origin myth, as scholar-activist Roxanne Dunbar Ortiz has termed it, defines how a society understands its place in the world and its history. The myth provides the basis for a nation's self-defined identity. Most origin narratives can be called myths because they usually present only the most flattering view of a nation's history; they are not distinguished by honesty.

11   Ours begins with Columbus "discovering" a hemisphere where some 80 million people already lived but didn't really count (in what became the United States, they were just buffalo-chasing "savages" with no grasp of real estate values and therefore doomed to perish). It continues with the brave Pilgrims, a revolution by independence-loving colonists against a decadent English aristocracy and the birth of an energetic young republic that promised democracy and equality (that is, to white male landowners). In the 1840s, the new nation expanded its size by almost one-third, thanks to a victory over that backward land of little brown people called Mexico. Such has been the basic account of how the nation called the United States of America came into being as presently configured.

12   The myth's omissions are grotesque. It ignores three major pillars of our nationhood: genocide, enslavement and imperialist expansion (such nasty words, who wants to hear them?—but that's the problem). The massive extermination of indigenous peoples provided our land base; the enslavement of African labor made our economic growth possible; and the seizure of half of Mexico by war (or threat of renewed war) extended this nation's boundaries north to the Pacific and south to the Rio Grande. Such are the foundation stones of the United States, within an economic system that made this country the first in world history to be born capitalist.

13   Those three pillars were, of course, supplemented by great numbers of dirt-cheap workers from Mexico, China, the Philippines, Puerto Rico and other countries, all of them kept in their place by White Supremacy. In history they stand alongside millions of less-than-supreme white workers and sharecroppers.

14   Any attempt to modify the present origin myth provokes angry efforts to repel such sacrilege. In the case of Native Americans, scholars will insist that they died from disease or wars among themselves, or that "not so many really did die." At worst it was a "tragedy," but never deliberate genocide, never a pillar of our nationhood. As for slavery, it was an embarrassment, of course, but do remember that Africa also had slavery and anyway enlightened white folk finally did end the practice here.

15   In the case of Mexico, reputable U.S. scholars still insist on blaming that country for the 1846–48 war. Yet even former U.S. President Ulysses Grant wrote in his memoirs that "[w]e were sent to provoke a fight [by moving troops into a disputed border area] but it was essential that Mexico should commence it [by fighting back]" (*Mr. Lincoln's General: Ulysses S. Grant, an illustrated autobiography*). President James Polk's 1846 diary records that he told his cabinet his purpose in declaring war as "acquiring California, New Mexico, and perhaps other Mexican lands" (*Diary of James K. Polk 1845–49*). To justify what could be called a territorial drive-by, the Mexican people were declared inferior; the U.S. had a "Manifest Destiny" to bring them progress and democracy.

16   Even when revisionist voices expose particular evils of Indian policy, slavery or the war on Mexico, they remain little more than unpleasant footnotes; the core of the dominant myth stands intact. PBS's eight-part documentary series of 1996 titled "The West" is a case in point. It devoted more than the usual attention to the devastation of Native Americans, but still centered on Anglos and gave little attention to why their domination evolved as it did. The West thus remained the physically gorgeous backdrop for an ugly, unaltered origin myth.

17   In fact, "The West" series strengthens that myth. White Supremacy needs the brave but inevitably doomed Indians to silhouette its own inevitable conquest. It needs the Indian-as-devil to sustain its own holy mission. Remember Timothy Wight, who served as pastor to Congress in the late 1700s and wrote that, under the Indians, "Satan ruled unchallenged in America" until "our chosen race eternal justice sent." With that self-declared moral authority, the "winning of the West" metamorphosed from a brutal, bloody invasion into a crusade of brave Christians marching across a lonely, dangerous landscape.

RACISM AS LINCHPIN OF THE U.S. NATIONAL IDENTITY

18   A crucial embellishment of the origin myth and key element of the national identity has been the myth of the frontier, analyzed in Richard Slotkin's *Gunfighter Nation,* the last volume of a fascinating trilogy. He describes Theodore Roosevelt's belief that the West was won thanks to American arms, "the means by which progress and nationality will be achieved." That success, Roosevelt continued, "depends on the heroism of men who impose on the course of events the latent virtues of their 'race.'" Roosevelt saw conflict on the frontier producing a species of virile "fighters and breeders" who would eventually generate a new leadership class. Militarism thus went hand in hand with the racialization of history's protagonists.

19   No slouch as an imperialist, Roosevelt soon took the frontier myth abroad, seeing Asians as Apaches and the Philippines as Sam Houston's Texas in the process of being seized from Mexico. For Roosevelt, Slotkin writes, "racial violence [was] the principle around which both individual character and social organization develop." Such ideas have not remained totally unchallenged by U.S. historians, nor was the frontier myth always applied in totally simplistic ways by Hollywood and other media. (The outlaw, for example, is a complicated figure, both good and bad.) Still, the frontier myth traditionally spins together virtue and violence, morality and war, in a convoluted, Calvinist web. That tortured embrace defines an essence of the so-called American character—the national identity—to this day.

20   The frontier myth embodied the nineteenth-century concept of Manifest Destiny, a doctrine that served to justify expansionist violence by means of intrinsic racial superiority. Manifest Destiny saw Yankee conquest as the inevitable result of a confrontation between enterprise and progress (white) versus passivity and backwardness (Indian, Mexican). "Manifest" meant "God-given," and the whole doctrine is profoundly rooted in religious conviction going back to the earliest colonial times. In his short, powerful book *Manifest Destiny: American Expansion and the Empire of Right,* Professor Anders Stephanson tells how the Puritans reinvented the Jewish notion of chosenness and applied it to this hemisphere so that territorial expansion became God's will. . . .

MANIFEST DESTINY DIES HARD

21   The concept of Manifest Destiny, with its assertion of racial superiority sustained by military power, has defined U.S. identity for 150 years. Only the Vietnam War brought a serious challenge to that concept of almightiness. Bitter debate, moral anguish, images of My Lai and the prospect of military defeat for the first time in U.S. history all suggested that the long-standing marriage of virtue and violence might soon be on the rocks. In the final years of the war the words leaped to mind one day: this country is having a national nervous breakdown.

22   Perhaps this is why the Vietnam War continues to arouse passions today. Some who are willing to call the war "a mistake" still shy away from recognizing its immorality or even accepting it as a defeat. A few Americans have the courage to conclude from the Vietnam War that we should abandon the idea that our identity rests on being the world's richest, most powerful and indeed *best* nation. Is it possible

that the so-called Vietnam syndrome might signal liberation from a crippling self-definition? Is it possible the long-standing belief that "American exceptionalism" had made freedom possible might be rejected someday?

23   The Vietnam syndrome is partly rooted in the fact that, although other societies have also been based on colonialism and slavery, ours seems to have an insatiable need to be the "good guys" on the world stage. That need must lie at least partially in a Protestant dualism that defines existence in terms of opposites, so that if you are not "good" you are bad, if not "white" then Black, and so on. Whatever the cause, the need to be seen as virtuous, compared to someone else's evil, haunts U.S. domestic and foreign policy. Where on earth would we be without Saddam Hussein, Qaddafi, and that all-time favorite of gringo demonizers, Fidel Castro? Gee whiz, how would we know what an American really is?

24   Today's origin myth and the resulting concept of national identity make for an intellectual prison where it is dangerous to ask big questions about this society's superiority. When otherwise decent people are trapped in such a powerful desire not to feel guilty, self-deception becomes unavoidable. To cease our present falsification of collective memory should, and could, open the doors of that prison. When together we cease equating whiteness with Americanness, a new day can dawn. As David Roediger, the social historian, has said, "[Whiteness] is the empty and therefore terrifying attempt to build an identity on what one isn't, and on whom one can hold back."

25   Redefining the U.S. origin narrative, and with it this country's national identity, could prove liberating for our collective psyche. It does not mean Euro-Americans should wallow individually in guilt. It does mean accepting collective responsibility to deal with the implications of our real origin. A few apologies, for example, might be a step in the right direction. In 1997, the idea was floated in Congress to apologize for slavery; it encountered opposition from all sides. But to reject the notion because corrective action, not an apology, is needed misses the point. Having defined itself as the all-time best country in the world, the United States fiercely denies the need to make a serious, official apology for anything. . . . To press for any serious, official apology does imply a new origin narrative, a new self-image, an ideological sea change.

26   Accepting the implications of a different narrative could also shed light on today's struggles. In the affirmative-action struggle, for example, opponents have said that that policy is no longer needed because racism ended with the Civil Rights Movement. But if we look at slavery as a fundamental pillar of this nation, going back centuries, it becomes obvious that racism could not have been ended by 30 years of mild reforms. If we see how the myth of the frontier idealized the white male adventurer as the central hero of national history, with the woman as sunbonneted helpmate, then we might better understand the dehumanized ways in which women have continued to be treated. A more truthful origin narrative could also help break down divisions among peoples of color by revealing common experiences and histories of cooperation.

27   A new origin narrative and national identity could help pave the way to a more livable society for us all. A society based on cooperation rather than competition, on the idea that all living creatures are interdependent and that humanity's goal should

28   be balance. Such were the values of many original Americans, deemed "savages." Similar gifts are waiting from other despised peoples and traditions. We might well start by recognizing that "America" is the name of an entire hemisphere, rich in a stunning variety of histories, cultures and peoples—not just one country.

28   The choice seems clear, if not easy. We can go on living in a state of massive denial, affirming this nation's superiority and virtue simply because we need to believe in it. We can choose to believe the destiny of the United States is still manifest: global domination. Or we can seek a transformative vision that carries us forward, not backward. We can seek an origin narrative that lays the groundwork for a multi-cultural, multinational identity centered on the goals of social equity and democracy. We do have choices.

29   There is little time for nostalgia. Dick and Jane never were "America," they were only one part of one community in one part of one country in one part of one continent. Yet we have let their image define our entire society and its values. Will the future be marked by ongoing denial or by steps toward a new vision in which White Supremacy no longer determines reality? When on earth will we transcend the assumptions that imprison our minds?

30   At times you can hear the clock ticking.

Analysis of the Writers' Positions

The first step in resolving conflict is to understand what the parties are claiming and why. Below is our paraphrase of Kimball's and Martínez's arguments.

Kimball's Position

He opposes multiculturalism and wants to preserve an American identity based in Anglo-Protestant culture.

Thesis: Multiculturalism weakens America by keeping people of different cultures from assimilating to the core values of America's Anglo-Protestant identity.

Reason: Educational multiculturalism degrades traditional American values and ignores mainstream history and culture.

Evidence: Opinions of Samuel Huntington and Arthur Schlesinger Jr. Examples of college students' ignorance about history. Maya Angelou's speech at Clinton's inauguration.

Reason: Multiculturalism "weakens the social bond" by denying that immigrants need to assimilate to the language and values of the dominant culture.

Evidence: Rise of hyphenization. Rise of non-English-speaking communities. Calls for affirmative action, which violates the idea of success based on merit.

Reason: America should be defined by one culture and nationality, not many.

Evidence: Quotations from de Crèvecoeur on the "new race of men." Quotations from Theodore Roosevelt, John Jay, Thomas

Jefferson, Benjamin Franklin. The 1795 oath of allegiance for citizenship.

Reason: The single, unifying identity of America should be based in Anglo-Saxon Protestant Christianity.

Evidence: Religious beliefs of original settlers. Historian Himmelfarb on American virtue as deeply rooted in religion. Quotes from Founding Fathers on relation of virtue to religion. Huntington on the need for national identity based in religion.

Martínez's Position

She wants to replace traditional Anglo-American identity with a multicultural one.

Thesis: The United States needs to discard its "white supremacist" identity.

Reason: It's based on racism, genocide, and imperialist expansion.

Evidence: The "origin myth" in common accounts of U.S. history. The historical record of slavery, takeover of Native American land, wars of expansion. Primary sources such as Presidents Grant and Polk. Theodore Roosevelt's statements about racial superiority. Historian Richard Slotkin's analysis of frontier myth.

Reason: It's based on a false sense of moral superiority and favor in the eyes of God.

Evidence: Professor Anders Stephanson on the concept of Manifest Destiny. Protestant moral dualism—seeing the world in terms of good and evil. Social historian David Roediger on the Anglo sense of superiority.

Reason: America will be a more fair and democratic country if we revise our identity to acknowledge Anglo faults and adopt the values of non-Anglo cultures.

Evidence: Racism and sexism not eliminated. The valuable gifts of other cultures, such as cooperation over competition.

◎ ACTIVITY: Analyzing Opposing Views

If you and some of your classmates have written arguments taking opposing views on the same issue, prepare case outlines, as we have done above for the arguments by Kimball and Martínez, of your respective positions to share with one another. (You might also create an outline of your opponents' positions to see how well you have understood one another's written arguments.)

Alternatively, write briefs summarizing the opposing positions offered in several published arguments as a first step toward mediating these viewpoints. •

Locating the Areas of Agreement and Disagreement

Differences over Facts

Most conflicts result from interpreting facts differently rather than disagreement about the facts themselves. For example, in the arguments of Kimball and Martínez, we see agreement on many factual points:

- Whites are becoming the minority in some parts of the United States.
- Assimilation has meant conformity to a culture defined by Anglo-Protestant values.
- Christianity has played a large role in America's sense of identity.

If a mediator finds disagreement over facts, he or she needs to look into them and provide evidence from credible sources that would resolve the disagreement.

◎ ACTIVITY: Informal Writing

For the arguments you are mediating, make a list of facts that the authors both accept. Note facts offered by one side but denied or not considered by the other. Where your authors do not agree on the facts, do research to decide how valid the facts cited on both sides are. Explain the discrepancies. If your class is mediating the same conflict, compare your findings.   •

Differences over Interests, Values, and Interpretations

Facts alone cannot resolve entrenched disputes such as the debate over multiculturalism. For example, a history lesson about white settlers' treatment of Native Americans would not change Kimball's mind. Nor would a lesson in Enlightenment philosophy alter what Martínez thinks. When we attempt to mediate, *we have to look into why people hold the positions they do.* Like persuasion, mediation looks at the contexts of a dispute.

To identify these differences, we can ask questions similar to those that are useful in persuasion for identifying what divides us from our audience (see the Best Practices box, "Questions for Understanding Difference," page 283). We apply below the questions about difference to Kimball's and Martínez's positions.

Is the Difference a Matter of Assumptions?   Every argument has assumptions—unstated assertions that the audience must share to find the reasoning valid and persuasive. Kimball assumes that Anglo-Protestant culture is moral; therefore, he does not show how Christianity has made America a moral nation. Martínez disputes the very assumption that America is moral. But she also makes assumptions. She assumes that the "origin narrative" of the white man's conquest and exploitation is the sole basis for the nation's past and present identity. This assumption allows her to argue that the culture of the United States is simply white supremacist.

Questions for Understanding Difference

1. Is the difference a matter of *assumptions?*

2. Is the difference a matter of *principle?*

3. Is the difference a matter of *values* or a matter of having the same values but giving them different *priorities?*

4. Is the difference a matter of *ends* or *means?*

5. Is the difference a matter of *implications* or *consequences?*

6. Is the difference a matter of *interpretation?*

7. Is the difference a result of *personal background, basic human needs,* or *emotions?*

To our list of questions about difference in persuasive writing, we add this last question because mediators must look not just at the arguments but also at the disputants as people with histories and feelings. Mediators must take into account such basic human needs as personal security, economic well-being, and a sense of belonging, recognition, and control over their lives.

These two assumptions show polarized thinking—one assumes that Anglo-Protestant values are all good, the other that Anglo-Protestant values are all evil. Such polarized assumptions are common in disputes because, as philosopher of ethics Anthony Weston explains, we polarize not just to simplify but to justify: "We polarize . . . to be able to picture ourselves as totally justified, totally right, and the 'other side' as totally unjustified and wrong."[2] It is precisely this tactic that mediation must resist and overcome.

Is the Difference a Matter of Principle?   By principles, we mean informal rules that guide our actions, like the "rule" in sales: "The customer is always right." Kimball's principle is patriotism: Americans should be undivided in loyalty and allegiance to the United States. Martínez's principle is fairness and justice for all, which means rewriting the origin narrative, admitting past mistakes, and recognizing the richness and morality of all the cultures that make up America. A mediator might ask, Can we be patriotic *and* self-critical? Must we repudiate the past entirely to fashion a new national identity?

Is the Difference a Matter of Values or Priorities?   The principles just discussed reflect differing priorities. In the post–9/11 world, Kimball is concerned with America's strength on the world stage, whereas Martínez concentrates more on America's compassion in its domestic policies. This is a significant difference because Martínez supports programs like affirmative action and

---

[2]Anthony Weston, *A Practical Companion to Ethics.* Oxford UP, 2005, p. 50.

multicultural education, the very policies Kimball claims weaken our social bonds. Once we see this difference, we can see the dispute in the context of liberal and conservative opinion in general. Kimball is arguing for a national identity acceptable to conservatives, Martínez for one acceptable to liberals. But what we need, obviously, is something that can cross this divide and appeal to most Americans.

Is the Difference a Matter of Ends or Means?   Martínez and Kimball have different ends in mind, so they also have different means to achieve the ends. For Martínez, a multicultural identity is the means to a more fair and livable society for all. For Kimball, a common identity in Anglo-Protestant culture is the means to remaining "the most powerful nation the world has ever seen." A mediator could reasonably ask: Couldn't we have both? Couldn't the United States be a powerful nation that is also fair and livable for all its citizens?

Is the Difference a Matter of Implications or Consequences?   The mediator has to consider what each side fears will happen if the other side prevails. Kimball fears that multiculturalism will lead Americans to self-doubt, loss of confidence. He also forecasts a large population of "permanent second-class citizens" if subgroups of the population do not assimilate. Martínez fears continuing oppression of minorities if our national self-conception does not change to fit our country's actual diversity. The mediator must acknowledge the fears of both sides while not permitting either to go unquestioned. Fear is a powerful motivator that must be confronted squarely.

Is the Difference a Matter of Interpretation?   A major disagreement here is over how to interpret the values of Anglo-Protestant culture. To Kimball, these values are "individual liberty and public virtue" (paragraph 8), "the rule of law" (paragraph 14), "respect for individual rights" (paragraph 14), devotion to God and a strong work ethic (paragraph 14). In contrast, Martínez interprets Anglo-Protestant values as a belief in whites' moral superiority and favor in the eyes of God (paragraph 20) that enabled them to see their own acts of "genocide, enslavement, and imperialist expansion" (paragraph 12) as morally acceptable and even heroic (paragraph 19). These interpretations stem from the different backgrounds of the writers, which we consider next.

Is the Difference a Matter of Personal Background, Basic Human Needs, or Emotions?   When mediating between positions, it is a good idea to go to the library or an online source for biographical information about the authors. It will pay off with insight into why they disagree.

Kimball and Martínez obviously come from very different backgrounds that are representative of others who hold the same positions they do. For example, as a white male with the financial means to have attended Yale, Kimball represents the group that has benefited most from the traditional national identity. His conservative views have pitted him against liberal academics and social activists.

Martínez identifies herself as a Chicana, an American woman of Mexican descent (her father was an immigrant). She is an activist for social justice and heads the Institute for MultiRacial Justice in San Francisco and has taught women's studies and ethnic studies in the California State University system. She knows the burden of discrimination from personal experience and from her work and research. As a proponent of bilingual and multicultural education, she sees people like Kimball as the opposition.

◎ ACTIVITY: Informal Writing

If you are mediating among printed arguments, write an analysis based on applying the questions in the Best Practices box on page 283 to two or more arguments. Write out your analysis in list form, as we did in analyzing the differences between Kimball and Martínez.   •

Finding Creative Solutions: Exploring Common Ground

Using critical thinking to mediate means looking closely at what people want and why they want it. It also means seeing the dispute in larger contexts. For example, the dispute over national identity is part of a larger debate between liberals and conservatives over social policy and education.

Mediation cannot reach everyone. Some people hold extreme views that reason cannot touch. An example would be the professor Kimball cites who predicts that the southwestern United States and northern Mexico will eventually become a new and separate country. Mediation between this person and Kimball is about as likely as President Obama and Osama bin Laden having dinner together. But mediators can bring reasonable people closer together by trying to arrive at creative solutions that appeal to some of the interests and values of all parties.

The ethicist Anthony Weston suggests trying to see conflict in terms of what each side is right about.[3] He points to the debate over saving owls in old-growth forests versus logging interests that employ people. Preserving the environment and endangered species is good, but so is saving jobs. If jobs could be created that use wood in craft-based ways, people could make a living without destroying massive amounts of timber. This solution is possible if the parties cooperate—but not if corporations are deadlocked with radical environmentalists, neither willing to concede anything or give an inch.

Mediators should aim for "win-win" solutions, which resolve conflict by dissolving it. The challenge for the mediator is keeping the high ground and looking for the good and reasonable in what each side wants.

---

[3] Weston, *Practical Companion* 56.

Exploring Common Ground
in the Debate over National Identity

To find solutions for the national identity–multiculturalism dispute, we used our list of questions for understanding difference to find interests and values Kimball and Martínez might share or be persuaded to share. Here, in sum, is what we found.

Both want Americans to know their history. Kimball is right. It is a disgrace that college students cannot recognize a famous phrase from the Gettysburg Address. But they need to know that *and* the relevance of Harriet Tubman to those words. Martínez is right also that history should not be propaganda for one view of events. The history of all nations is a mix of good and bad.

Neither Kimball nor Martínez wants a large population of second-class citizens, living in isolated poverty, not speaking English, not seeing themselves as Americans, and not having a say in the democratic process. Martínez's multiculturalism would "break down divisions among peoples of color by revealing common experiences and histories of cooperation" with the goal of "social equity and democracy." She would be more likely, however, to achieve her goal if she considered white men and women *as participants* in this multicultural discussion. To exclude whites keeps people of color where they too often are—on the margins, left out. Kimball needs to be reminded that failure to assimilate is not typically a choice. As in the past, assimilation works only when educational and economic opportunities exist. Kimball needs to look into solutions to the problem of poverty among immigrants.

There is agreement too on the need for a national identity. Martínez calls for "a new identity." But asking what culture should provide it is the wrong question. Concentrating on the values themselves will help everyone see that most values are shared across races and cultures. For example, Martínez takes Anglo-Protestant culture as competitive, not cooperative. We need to recall that early Protestant settlers also valued community. The Puritans tried to establish utopian communities devoted to charity. Kimball's "Protestant" work ethic can be found in every ethnic group—for example, in the predominantly Catholic Mexican laborers who do backbreaking work in agriculture and construction.

Finally, what agreement could be reached about assimilation? Kimball suggests that immigrants follow Justice Louis Brandeis's advice—adopting "the clothes, the manners, and the customs generally prevailing here." But would such advice mean that what "prevails" here is based in Protestantism and Anglo-Saxon culture? A more realistic idea of "Americanization" comes from our third writer, Bharati Mukherjee, who suggests in her mediatory essay that "assimilation" is a two-way transformation, with immigrants and mainstream culture interacting, influencing each other. Such a conception *requires* both the preservation of tradition Kimball wants and the respect for diversity Martínez wants.

◎ ACTIVITY: Informal Writing

Either in list form or as an informal exploratory essay, find areas of agreement between the various positions you have been analyzing. End your list or essay with a summary of a position that all sides might accept.   •

THE MEDIATORY ESSAY

The common human tendency in argument is to polarize—to see conflict as "us" versus "them." That is why mediation is necessary: to move beyond polarized thinking. An example of mediation in the multiculturalism debate appears below. The essay's author is the novelist Bharati Mukherjee. She was born into a wealthy family in Calcutta but became an American citizen. She is now Distinguished Professor of English at the University of California at Berkeley.

There is no single model for a mediatory essay. In this case, Mukherjee's essay mediates by making a case against both radical extremes, one way of seeking to bring people together on the remaining middle ground.

Beyond Multiculturalism: A Two-Way Transformation

BHARATI MUKHERJEE

1   The United States exists as a sovereign nation with its officially stated Constitution, its economic and foreign policies, its demarcated, patrolled boundaries. "America," however, exists as image or idea, as dream or nightmare, as romance or plague, constructed by discrete individual fantasies, and shaded by collective paranoias and mythologies.

2   I am a naturalized U.S. citizen with a certificate of citizenship; more importantly, I am an American for whom "America" is the stage for the drama of self-transformation. I see American culture as a culture of dreamers, who believe material shape (which is not the same as materialism) can be given to dreams. They believe that one's station in life—poverty, education, family background—does not determine one's fate. They believe in the reversal of omens; early failures do not spell inevitable disaster. Outsiders can triumph on merit. All of this happens against the backdrop of the familiar vicissitudes of American life.

3   I first came to the United States—to the state of Iowa, to be precise—on a late summer evening nearly thirty-three years ago. I flew into a placid, verdant airport in Iowa City on a commercial airliner, ready to fulfill the goals written out in a large, lined notebook for me by my guiltlessly patriarchal father. Those goals were unambiguous: I was to spend two years studying Creative Writing at Paul Engle's unique Writers Workshop; then I was to marry the perfect Bengali bridegroom selected by my father and live out the rest of a contented, predictable life in the city of my birth, Calcutta. In 1961, I was a shy, pliant, well-mannered, dutiful young daughter from a very privileged, traditional, mainstream Hindu family that believed women should

be protected and provided for by their fathers, husbands, sons, and it did not once occur to me that I might have goals of my own, quite distinct from those specified for me by my father. I certainly did not anticipate then that, over the next three decades, Iowans—who seemed to me so racially and culturally homogeneous—would be forced to shudder through the violent paroxysms of a collective identity in crisis.

4   When I was growing up in Calcutta in the fifties, I heard no talk of "identity crisis"—communal or individual. The concept itself—of a person not knowing who she or he was—was unimaginable in a hierarchical, classification-obsessed society. One's identity was absolutely fixed, derived from religion, caste, patrimony, and mother tongue. A Hindu Indian's last name was designed to announce his or her forefathers' caste and place of origin. A Mukherjee could *only* be a Brahmin from Bengal. Indian tradition forbade inter-caste, inter-language, inter-ethnic marriages. Bengali tradition discouraged even emigration; to remove oneself from Bengal was to "pollute" true culture.

5   Until the age of eight, I lived in a house crowded with forty or fifty relatives. We lived together because we were "family," bonded by kinship, though kinship was interpreted in flexible enough terms to include, when necessary, men, women, children who came from the same *desh*—which is the Bengali word for "home-land"—as had my father and grandfather. I was who I was because I was Dr. Sudhir Lal Mukherjee's daughter, because I was a Hindu Brahmin, because I was Bengali-speaking, and because my *desh* was an East Bengal village called Faridpur. I was encouraged to think of myself as indistinguishable from my dozen girl cousins. Identity was viscerally connected with ancestral soil and family origins. I was first a Mukherjee, then a Bengali Brahmin, and only then an Indian.

6   Deep down I knew, of course, that I was not quite like my girl cousins. Deeper down, I was sure that pride in the purity of one's culture has a sinister underside. As a child I had witnessed bloody religious riots between Muslims and Hindus, and violent language riots between Bengalis and Biharis. People kill for culture, and die of hunger. Language, race, religion, blood, myth, history, national codes, and manners have all been used, in India, in the United States, are being used in Bosnia and Rwanda even today, to enforce terror, to "otherize," to murder.

7   I do not know what compelled my strong-willed and overprotective father to risk sending us, his three daughters, to school in the United States, a country he had not visited. In Calcutta, he had insisted on sheltering us from danger and temptation by sending us to girls-only schools, and by providing us with chaperones, chauffeurs, and bodyguards.

8   The Writers Workshop in a quonset hut in Iowa City was my first experience of coeducation. And after not too long, I fell in love with a fellow student named Clark Blaise, an American of Canadian origin, and impulsively married him during a lunch break in a lawyer's office above a coffeeshop.

9   That impulsive act cut me off forever from the rules and ways of upper-middle-class life in Bengal, and hurled me precipitously into a New World life of scary impro-visations and heady explorations. Until my lunchtime wedding, I had seen myself as an Indian foreign student, a transient in the United States. The five-minute ceremony in the lawyer's office had changed me into a permanent transient.

10   Over the last three decades the important lesson that I have learned is that in this era of massive diasporic movements, honorable survival requires resilience, curiosity, and compassion, a letting go of rigid ideals about the purity of inherited culture.

11   The first ten years into marriage, years spent mostly in my husband's desh of Canada, I thought myself an expatriate Bengali permanently stranded in North America because of a power surge of destiny or of desire. My first novel, *The Tiger's Daughter,* embodies the loneliness I felt but could not acknowledge, even to myself, as I negotiated the no-man's-land between the country of my past and the continent of my present. Shaped by memory, textured with nostalgia for a class and culture I had abandoned, this novel quite naturally became my expression of the *expatriate consciousness.*

12   It took me a decade of painful introspection to put the smothering tyranny of nostalgia into perspective, and to make the transition from expatriate to immigrant. I have found my way back to the United States after a fourteen-year stay in Canada. The transition from foreign student to U.S. citizen, from detached onlooker to committed immigrant, has not been easy.

13   The years in Canada were particularly harsh. Canada is a country that officially— and proudly—resists the policy and process of cultural fusion. For all its smug rhetoric about "cultural mosaic," Canada refuses to renovate its national self-image to include its changing complexion. It is a New World country with Old World concepts of a fixed, exclusivist national identity. And all through the seventies when I lived there, it was a country without a Bill of Rights or its own Constitution. Canadian official rhetoric designated me, as a citizen of non-European origin, one of the "visible minority" who, even though I spoke the Canadian national languages of English and French, was straining "the absorptive capacity" of Canada. Canadians of color were routinely treated as "not real" Canadians. In fact, when a terrorist bomb, planted in an Air India jet on Canadian soil, blew up after leaving Montreal, killing 329 passengers, 90 percent of whom were Canadians of Indian origin, the prime minister of Canada at the time, Brian Mulroney, cabled the Indian prime minister to offer Canada's condolences for India's loss, exposing the Eurocentricity of the "mosaic" policy of immigration.

14   In private conversations, some Canadian ambassadors and External Affairs officials have admitted to me that the creation of the Ministry of Multiculturalism in the seventies was less an instrument for cultural tolerance, and more a vote-getting strategy to pacify ethnic European constituents who were alienated by the rise of Quebec separatism and the simultaneous increase of non-white immigrants.

15   The years of race-related harassments in a Canada without a Constitution have politicized me, and deepened my love of the ideals embedded in the American Bill of Rights.

16   I take my American citizenship very seriously. I am a voluntary immigrant. I am not an economic refugee, and not a seeker of political asylum. I am an American by choice, and not by the simple accident of birth. I have made emotional, social, and political commitments to this country. I have earned the right to think of myself as an American.

17   But in this blood-splattered decade, questions such as who is an American and what is American culture are being posed with belligerence and being answered with violence. We are witnessing an increase in physical, too often fatal, assaults on Asian Americans. An increase in systematic "dot-busting" of Indo-Americans in New Jersey, xenophobic immigrant-baiting in California, minority-on-minority violence during the south-central Los Angeles revolution.

18   America's complexion is browning daily. Journalists' surveys have established that whites are losing their clear majority status in some states, and have already lost it in New York and California. A recent *Time* magazine poll indicated that 60 percent of Americans favor limiting *legal* immigration. Eighty percent of Americans polled favor curbing the entry of undocumented aliens. U.S. borders are too extensive and too porous to be adequately policed. Immigration, by documented and undocumented aliens, is less affected by the U.S. Immigration and Naturalization Service, and more by wars, ethnic genocides, famines in the emigrant's own country.

19   Every sovereign nation has a right to formulate its immigration policy. In this decade of continual, large-scale diasporic movements, it is imperative that we come to some agreement about who "we" are now that the community includes oldtimers, newcomers, many races, languages, and religions; about what our expectations of happiness and strategies for its pursuit are; and what our goals are for the nation.

20   Scapegoating of immigrants has been the politicians' easy instant remedy. Hate speeches fill auditoria, and bring in megabucks for those demagogues willing to profit from stirring up racial animosity.

21   The hysteria against newcomers is only minimally generated by the downturn in our economy. The panic, I suspect, is unleashed by a fear of the "other," the fear of what Daniel Stein, executive director of the Federation for American Immigration Reform, and a champion of closed borders, is quoted as having termed "cultural transmogrification."

22   The debate about American culture has to date been monopolized by rabid Eurocentrists and ethnocentrists; the rhetoric has been flamboyantly divisive, pitting a phantom "us" against a demonized "them." I am here to launch a new discourse, to reconstitute the hostile, biology-derived "us" versus "them" communities into a new *consensual* community of "we."

23   All countries view themselves by their ideals. Indians idealize, as well they should, the cultural continuum, the inherent value system of India, and are properly incensed when foreigners see nothing but poverty, intolerance, ignorance, strife, and injustice. Americans see themselves as the embodiments of liberty, openness, and individualism, even when the world judges them for drugs, crime, violence, bigotry, militarism, and homelessness. I was in Singapore when the media was very vocal about the case of an American teenager sentenced to caning for having allegedly vandalized cars. The overwhelming local sentiment was that caning Michael Fay would deter local youths from being tempted into "Americanization," meaning into gleefully breaking the law.

24   Conversely, in Tavares, Florida, an ardently patriotic school board has legislated that middle school teachers be required to instruct their students that American

culture—meaning European-American culture—is inherently "superior to other foreign or historic cultures." The sinister, or at least misguided, implication is that American culture has not been affected by the American Indian, African American, Latin American, and Asian American segments of its population.

25   The idea of "America" as a nation has been set up in opposition to the tenet that a nation is a collection of like-looking, like-speaking, like-worshiping people. Our nation is unique in human history. We have seen very recently, in a Germany plagued by anti-foreigner frenzy, how violently destabilizing the traditional concept of nation can be. In Europe, each country is, in a sense, a tribal homeland. Therefore, the primary criterion for nationhood in Europe is homogeneity of culture, and race, and religion. And that has contributed to blood-soaked balkanization in the former Yugoslavia and the former Soviet Union.

26   All European Americans, or their pioneering ancestors, gave up an easy homogeneity in their original countries for a new idea of Utopia. What we have going for us in the 1990s is the exciting chance to share in the making of a new American culture, rather than the coerced acceptance of either the failed nineteenth-century model of "melting pot" or the Canadian model of the "multicultural mosaic."

27   The "mosaic" implies a contiguity of self-sufficient, utterly distinct culture. "Multiculturalism" has come to imply the existence of a central culture, ringed by peripheral cultures. The sinister fallout of official multiculturalism and of professional multiculturalists is the establishment of one culture as the norm and the rest as aberrations. Multiculturalism emphasizes the differences between racial heritages. This emphasis on the differences has too often led to the dehumanization of the different. Dehumanization leads to discrimination. And discrimination can ultimately lead to genocide.

28   We need to alert ourselves to the limitations and the dangers of those discourses that reinforce an "us" versus "them" mentality. We need to protest any official rhetoric or demagoguery that marginalizes on a race-related and/or religion-related basis any segment of our society. I want to discourage the retention of cultural memory if the aim of that retention is cultural balkanization. I want to sensitize you to think of culture and nationhood *not* as an uneasy aggregate of antagonistic "them" and "us," but as a constantly re-forming, transmogrifying "we."

29   In this diasporic age, one's biological identity may not be the only one. Erosions and accretions come with the act of emigration. The experiences of violent unhousing from a biological "homeland" and rehousing in an adopted "homeland" that is not always welcoming to its dark-complected citizens have tested me as a person, and made me the writer I am today.

30   I choose to describe myself on my own terms, that is, as an American without hyphens. It is to sabotage the politics of hate and the campaigns of revenge spawned by Eurocentric patriots on the one hand and the professional multiculturalists on the other, that I describe myself as an "American" rather than as an "Asian-American." Why is it that hyphenization is imposed only on non-white Americans? And why is it that only non-white citizens are "problematized" if they choose to describe themselves on their own terms? My outspoken rejection of hyphenization is my lonely

campaign to obliterate categorizing the cultural landscape into a "center" and its "peripheries." To reject hyphenization is to demand that the nation deliver the promises of the American Dream and the American Constitution to *all* its citizens. I want nothing less than to invent a new vocabulary that demands, and obtains, an equitable power-sharing for all members of the American community.

31   But my self-empowering refusal to be "otherized" and "objectified" has come at tremendous cost. My rejection of hyphenization has been deliberately misrepresented as "race treachery" by some India-born, urban, upper-middle-class Marxist "green card holders" with lucrative chairs on U.S. campuses. These academics strategically position themselves as self-appointed spokespersons for their ethnic communities, and as guardians of the "purity" of ethnic cultures. At the same time, though they reside permanently in the United States and participate in the capitalist economy of this nation, they publicly denounce American ideals and institutions.

32   They direct their rage at me because, as a U.S. citizen, I have invested in the present and the future rather than in the expatriate's imagined homeland. They condemn me because I acknowledge erosion of memory as a natural result of emigration; because I count that erosion as net gain rather than as loss; and because I celebrate racial and cultural "mongrelization." I have no respect for these expatriate fence-straddlers who, even while competing fiercely for tenure and promotion within the U.S. academic system, glibly equate all evil in the world with the United States, capitalism, colonialism, and corporate and military expansionism. I regard the artificial retentions of "pure race" and "pure culture" as dangerous, reactionary illusions fostered by the Eurocentric and the ethnocentric empire builders within the academy. I fear still more the politics of revenge preached from pulpits by some minority demagogues. . . .

33   As a writer, my literary agenda begins by acknowledging that America has transformed *me*. It does not end until I show that I (and the hundreds of thousands of recent immigrants like me) am minute by minute transforming America. The transformation is a two-way process; it affects both the individual and the national cultural identity. The end result of immigration, then, is this two-way transformation: that's my heartfelt message.

34   Others often talk of diaspora, of arrival as the end of the process. They talk of arrival in the context of loss, the loss of communal memory and the erosion of an intact ethnic culture. They use words like "erosion" and "loss" in alarmist ways. I want to talk of arrival as gain. . . .

35   What excites me is that we have the chance to retain those values we treasure from our original cultures, but we also acknowledge that the outer forms of those values are likely to change. In the Indian American community, I see a great deal of guilt about the inability to hang on to "pure culture." Parents express rage or despair at their U.S.-born children's forgetting of, or indifference to, some aspects of Indian culture. Of those parents, I would ask: What is it we have lost if our children are acculturating into the culture in which we are living? Is it so terrible that our children are discovering or inventing homelands for themselves? Some first-generation Indo-Americans, embittered by overt anti-Asian racism and by unofficial

"glass ceilings," construct a phantom more-Indian-than-Indians-in-India identity as defense against marginalization. Of them I would ask: Why not get actively involved in fighting discrimination through protests and lawsuits?

36   I prefer that we forge a national identity that is born of our acknowledgment of the steady de-Europeanization of the U.S. population; that constantly synthesizes—fuses—the disparate cultures of our country's residents; and that provides a new, sustaining, and unifying national creed.

Analyzing Mukherjee's Essay

Let's see what we can learn about how to appeal to audiences in mediatory essays. We'll look at ethos (how Mukherjee projects good character), pathos (how she arouses emotions favorable to her case), and logos (how she wins assent through good reasoning).

Ethos: Earning the Respect of Both Sides

Mediatory essays are not typically as personal as this one. But the author is in an unusual position, which makes the personal relevant. By speaking in the first person and telling her story, Mukherjee seeks the goodwill of people on both sides. She presents herself as patriotic, a foreigner who has assimilated to American ways, clearly appealing to those on Kimball's side. But she is also a "person of color," who's been "tested" by racial prejudices in the United States, clearly appealing to Martínez's side. She creates negative ethos for the radical extremists in the identity debate, depicting them as lacking morality and/or honesty. That is why she cites the violence committed by both whites and minorities, the scapegoating by politicians pandering to voter fears, the hypocrisy of professors who live well in America while denouncing its values. She associates her own position with words like *commitment, compassion, consensus, equality,* and *unity.*

By including her own experiences in India and Canada and her references to Bosnia, Rwanda, Germany, and the former Soviet Union, Mukherjee is able to place this American debate in a larger context—parts of the world in which national identity incites war and human rights violations.

Pathos: Using Emotion to Appeal to Both Sides

Appealing to the right emotions can help to move parties in conflict to the higher ground of consensus. Mukherjee displays a range of emotions, including pride, anger, and compassion. In condemning the extremes on both sides, her tone becomes heated. She uses highly charged words like *rabid, demagogues, scapegoaters, fence-straddlers,* and *reactionaries* to describe them. Her goal is to distance the members of her audience who are reasonable from those who are not, so her word choice is appropriate and effective.

Patriotism is obviously emotional. Mukherjee's repeated declaration of devotion to her adopted country stirs audience pride. So does the contrast with India and Canada and the celebrating of individual freedom in the United States.

Her own story of arrival, nostalgia, and transformation arouses compassion and respect because it shows that assimilation is not easy. She understands the reluctance of Indian parents to let their children change. This shows her ability to empathize.

Finally, she appeals through hope and optimism. Twice she describes the consensus she proposes as *exciting*—and also fresh, new, vital, alive—in contrast to the rigid and inflexible ethnic purists.

Logos: Integrating Values of Both Sides

Mukherjee's thesis is that the opposing sides in the national identity debate are two sides of the wrong coin: the mistaken regard for ethnic purity. Making an issue of one's ethnicity, whether it be Anglo, Chicano, Indian-American, or whatever, is not a means to harmony and equality. Instead, America needs a unifying national identity that blends the ever-changing mix of races and cultures that make up our population.

Mukherjee offers reasons to oppose ethnic "purity":

Violence and wars result when people divide according to ethnic and religious differences. It creates an "us" versus "them" mentality.

The multicultural Canadian program created second-class, marginal populations.

Hyphenization in America makes a problem out of non-whites in the population.

We said that mediation looks for the good in each side and tries to show what they have in common. Mukherjee shows that her solution offers gains for both sides, a "win-win" situation. She concedes that her solution would mean some loss of "cultural memory" for immigrants, but these losses are offset by the following gains:

The United States would be closer to the strong and unified nation that Kimball wants because *everyone's* contributions would be appreciated.

The cultural barriers between minorities would break down, as Martínez wants. This would entail speaking to each other in English, but being free to maintain diverse cultures at home.

The barriers between "Americans" and hyphenated Americans would break down, as both Kimball and Martínez want. In other words, there would be assimilation, as Kimball wants, but not assimilation to one culture, which Martínez strongly resists.

By removing the need to prove one's own culture superior, we could all recognize the faults in our past as well as the good things. We would have no schools teaching either the superiority or the inferiority of any culture.

> Emphasizing citizenship instead of ethnicity is a way of standing up for and demanding equal rights and equal opportunity, helping to bring about the social justice and equality Martínez seeks.

> The new identity would be "sustaining," avoiding future conflicts because it would adapt to change.

Mukherjee's essay mediates by showing that a definition of America based on either one ethnic culture or many ethnic cultures is not satisfactory. By dropping ethnicity as a prime concern, both sides can be better off and freer in pursuit of happiness and success.

QUESTIONS FOR DISCUSSION

Look over the essays by Elizabeth Martínez and Roger Kimball. Do you think either of them would find Bharati Mukherjee's essay persuasive? What does Mukherjee say that might cause either of them to relax their positions about American identity? Do you think any further information might help to bring either side to Mukherjee's consensus position? For example, Kimball mentions the "Letter from an American Farmer" by de Crèvecoeur, who describes Americans as a new "race" of blended nationalities, leaving behind their ties and allegiances to former lands. How is Crèvecouer's idea of the "new race" similar to Mukherjee's?

THE ASSIGNMENT

Write an essay that might help readers on opposing sides of an issue come to a better understanding of each other's position or at least find some middle ground to ease the polarization between them. Begin by finding well-written arguments for opposing positions. Then use the advice below to work through the writing process.

Prewriting

In preparing to write a mediatory essay, you should work through the steps described on pages 267–287. Prepare briefs of the various conflicting positions, and note areas of disagreement; think hard about the differing interests of the conflicting parties, and respond to the questions about difference on page 283.

Give some thought to each party's background—age, race, gender, and so forth—and how it might contribute to his or her viewpoint on the issue.

Describe the conflict in its full complexity, not just its polar opposites. Try to find the good values in each position: You may be able to see that people's real interests are not as far apart as they might seem. You may be able to find common ground.

At this point in the prewriting process, think of some solutions that would satisfy at least some of the interests on all sides. It might be necessary for you to do some additional research. What do you think any of the opposing parties might want to know more about in order to accept your solution?

Finally, write up a clear statement of your solution. Can you explain how your solution appeals to the interests of all sides?

Drafting

There is no set form for the mediatory essay. As with any argument, the important thing is to have a plan for arranging your points and to provide clear signals to your readers. One logical way to organize a mediatory essay is in three parts:

Overview of the conflict. Describe the conflict and the opposing positions in the introductory paragraphs.

Discussion of differences underlying the conflict. Here your goal is to make all sides more sympathetic to one another and to sort out the important real interests that must be addressed by the solution.

Proposed solution. Here you make a case for your compromise position, giving reasons why it should be acceptable to all—that is, showing that it does serve at least some of their interests.

Revising

When revising a mediatory essay, you should look for the usual problems of organization and development that you would be looking for in any essay to convince or persuade. Be sure that you have inquired carefully and fairly into the conflict and that you have clearly presented the cases for all sides, including your proposed solution. At this point, you also need to consider how well you have used the persuasive appeals:

The appeal to character. Think about what kind of character you have projected as a mediator. Have you maintained neutrality? Do you model open-mindedness and genuine concern for the sensitivities of all sides?

The appeal to emotions. To arouse sympathy and empathy, which are needed in mediation, you should take into account the emotional appeals discussed on pages 293–294. Your mediatory essay should be a moving argument for understanding and overcoming difference.

The appeal through style. As in persuasion, you should put the power of language to work. Pay attention to concrete word choice, striking metaphors, and phrases that stand out because of repeated sounds and rhythms.

For suggestions about editing and proofreading, see Appendix A.

STUDENT EXAMPLE: ARGUING TO MEDIATE

The following mediatory essay was written by Angi Grellhesl, a first-year student at Southern Methodist University. Her essay examines opposing views on the institution of speech codes at various U.S. colleges and the effect of speech codes on freedom of speech.

Mediating the Speech Code Controversy
Angi Grellhesl

1   The right to free speech has raised many controversies over the years. Explicit lyrics in rap music and marches by the Ku Klux Klan are just some examples that test the power of the First Amendment. Now, students and administrators are questioning if, in fact, free speech ought to be limited on university campuses. Many schools have instituted speech codes to protect specified groups from harassing speech.

2   Both sides in the debate, the speech code advocates and the free speech advocates, have presented their cases in recent books and articles. Columnist Nat Hentoff argues strongly against the speech codes, his main reason being that the codes violate students' First Amendment rights. Hentoff links the right to free speech with the values of higher education. In support, he quotes Yale president Benno Schmidt, who says, "Freedom of thought must be Yale's central commitment. . . . [U]niversities cannot censor or suppress speech, no matter how obnoxious in content, without violating their justification for existence . . . " (qtd. in Hentoff 223). Another reason Hentoff offers against speech codes is that universities must teach students to defend themselves in preparation for the real world, where such codes cannot shield them. Finally, he suggests that most codes are too vaguely worded; students may not even know they are violating the codes (216).

3   Two writers in favor of speech codes are Richard Perry and Patricia Williams. They see speech codes as a necessary and fair limitation on free speech. Perry and Williams argue that speech codes promote multicultural awareness, making students more sensitive to the differences that are out there in the real world. These authors do not think that the codes violate First Amendment rights, and they are suspicious of the motives of those who say they do. As Perry and Williams put it, those who feel free speech rights are being threatened

"are apparently unable to distinguish between a liberty interest on the one hand and, on the other, a quite specific interest in being able to spout racist, sexist, and homophobic epithets completely unchallenged—without, in other words, the terrible inconvenience of feeling bad about it" (228).

4   Perhaps if both sides trusted each other a little more, they could see that their goals are not contradictory. Everyone agrees that students' rights should be protected. Hentoff wishes to ensure that students have the right to speak their minds. He and others on his side are concerned about freedom. Defenders of the codes argue that students have the right not to be harassed, especially while they are getting an education. They are concerned about opportunity. Would either side really deny that the other's goal had value?

5   Also, both sides want to create the best possible educational environment. Here the difference rests on the interpretation of what benefits the students. Is the best environment one most like the real world, where prejudice and harassment occur? Or does the university have an obligation to provide an atmosphere where potential victims can thrive and participate freely without intimidation?

6   I think it is possible to reach a solution that everyone can agree on. Most citizens want to protect constitutional rights; but they also agree that those rights have limitations, the ultimate limit being when one person infringes on the rights of others to live in peace. All sides should agree that a person ought to be able to speak out about his or her convictions, values, and beliefs. Most people can see a difference between that protected speech and the kind that is intended to harass and intimidate. For example, there is a clear difference between expressing one's view that Jews are mistaken in not accepting Christ as the son of God, on the one hand, and yelling anti-Jewish threats at a particular person on the other. Could a code not be worded in such a way as to distinguish between these two kinds of speech?

7   Also, I don't believe either side would want the university to be an artificial world. Codes should not attempt to ensure that no one is criticized or even offended. Students should not be afraid to say controversial things. But universities do help to shape the future of the real world, so shouldn't they at least take a stand against harassment? Can a code be worded that would protect free speech and prevent harassment?

8   The current speech code at Southern Methodist University is a compromise that ought to satisfy free speech advocates and speech code advocates. It prohibits hate speech at the same time that it protects an individual's First Amendment rights.

9   First, it upholds the First Amendment by including a section that reads, "[D]ue to the University's commitment to freedom of speech and

expression, harassment is more than mere insensitivity or offensive conduct which creates an uncomfortable situation for certain members of the community" (*Peruna* 92). The code therefore should satisfy those, like Hentoff, who place a high value on the basic rights our nation was built upon. Secondly, whether or not there is a need for protection, the current code protects potential victims from hate speech or "any words or acts deliberately designed to disregard the safety or rights of another, and which intimidate, degrade, demean, threaten, haze, or otherwise interfere with another person's rightful action" (*Peruna* 92). This part of the code should satisfy those who recognize that some hurts cannot be permitted. Finally, the current code outlines specific acts that constitute harassment: "Physical, psychological, verbal and/or written acts directed toward an individual or group of individuals which rise to the level of 'fighting words' are prohibited" (*Peruna* 92).

10   The SMU code protects our citizens from hurt and from unconstitutional censorship. Those merely taking a position can express it, even if it hurts. On the other hand, those who are spreading hatred will not be protected. Therefore, all sides should respect the code as a safeguard for those who use free speech but a limitation on those who abuse it.

WORKS CITED

Hentoff, Nat. "Speech Codes on the Campus and Problems of Free Speech." *Debating P.C,* edited by Paul Berman. Bantam, 1992, pp. 215–24.

Perry, Richard, and Patricia Williams. "Freedom of Speech." *Debating P.C,* edited by Paul Berman. Bantam, 1992, pp. 225–30.

Peruna Express 1993–1994. Southern Methodist U, 1993.

CHAPTER SUMMARY

We often must deal as constructively as we can with sharp differences of opinion, where people taking opposing positions seem unable or unwilling to explore ways to reduce or eliminate conflict. Sometimes efforts at mediation fail, no matter how skillful the mediator is. However, as you have seen in this chapter, mediation is possible and can result in agreement on a course of action satisfactory to all parties. Mediating involves understanding the positions of all sides, finding common ground, defusing hostilities among the contending sides, and making a good case for the course of action the mediator advocates. It involves, that is, everything you have learned in this book about using argument to inquire, convince, and persuade.

PART THREE

Readings: Issues
and Arguments

12 Consumer Society: Achieving Balance *303*

13 Global Warming: What Should Be Done? *343*

14 The Millennials: Issues Facing Young Adults *381*

15 Immigration Revisited: A New Look at a Permanent
Issue *415*

16 Declining Civility: Is Rudeness on the Rise? *453*

17 Enhancing Humans: How Far Is Too Far? *485*

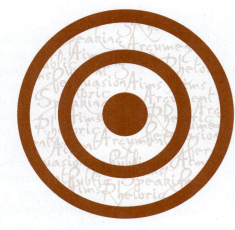

Consumer Society: Achieving Balance

Consumerism: Ten Quotations *305*

Virginia Postrel, The Aesthetic Imperative *306*

Erik Kain, In Defense of Consumerism *310*

David Brooks, The Grill-Buying Guy *312*

Alex Kotlowitz, False Connections *315*

Three Cartoons about the Consumer Society *320*

Caroline Heldman, Out-of-Body Image *322*

Alissa Quart, X-Large Boys *327*

Don Peck and Ross Douthat, Does Money Buy Happiness? *331*

John F. Schumaker, The Happiness Conspiracy: What Does It Mean
  to Be Happy in a Modern Consumer Society? *336*

For Further Reading *340*

When we say we live in a consumer society, we commonly mean that we live with more products and services than our parents and grandparents did; more choices within a product category, including premium labels at the high-priced end; and more information about it all in the form of advertising, media images, and product placement in music, movies, and TV. Even people who would never buy a pair of Manolo Blahnik shoes have heard of them because of the show *Sex and the City*. This casebook takes a close and critical look at how consumerism affects our sense of identity and quality of life.

Scholars who observe consumer societies describe not just the amount of goods available but the importance people place on them. Says Paul Elkins: "A consumer society is one in which the possession and use of an increasing number and variety of goods and services is the principal cultural aspiration and the surest perceived route to personal happiness, social status, and national success."[1]

The readings in this chapter focus on the United States, but the consumer society is really a global village, including the middle- and upper-class populations of developing nations whose workers supply most of the products we buy. In China, for example, parts of Shanghai and other booming cities epitomize the consumer society. A serious problem for China, however, is the disparity of income between rich and poor. The United States also has a vast disparity between rich and poor. Although not as great as Brazil's, the income gap in the United States is larger than that of any other advanced industrialized country.

As the world-renowned Columbia University economist Jeffrey D. Sachs pointed out in *The Price of Civilization,*

> The wealthiest 1 percent of American households today enjoys a higher net worth than the bottom 90 percent, and the top 1 percent of income earners receives more pretax income than the bottom 50 percent. The last time America had such massive inequality of wealth and income was on the eve of the Great Depression . . . . Economic growth was widely shared from the end of [World War II] until the 1980s. Then all the economic benefits tilted toward the rich.[2]

These facts are worth remembering as you read the arguments in this chapter. Some of the authors address the problem of those excluded from the consumer society; others do not. Even those who can afford to participate at some level feel inadequate because they constantly compare themselves to the biggest spenders at the top. Thanks to the media, the "lifestyles of the rich and famous" are highly visible while the lives of the poor can easily be ignored by those who choose not to look.

---

[1]Paul Elkins, qtd. in Neva R. Goodwin, "Overview Essay," *The Consumer Society,* edited by Neva R. Goodwin et al., Island Press, 1997, p. 2.
[2]Jeffrey D. Sachs, *The Price of Civilization.* Random House, 2011, pp. 22–23.

Consumerism: Ten Quotations

As you read these statements about consumerism, consider which views are similar to your own and which make you aware of insights or new ideas. As context for these quotes, we repeat the definition of consumerism quoted on page 304: "A consumer society is one in which the possession and use of an increasing number and variety of goods and services is the principal cultural aspiration and the surest perceived route to personal happiness, social status, and national success."

All over the place, from the popular culture to the propaganda system, there is constant pressure to make people feel that they are helpless, that the only role they can have is to ratify decisions and to consume.

—Noam Chomsky

A person buying ordinary products in a supermarket is in touch with his deepest emotions.

—John Kenneth Galbraith

What's great about this country is America started the tradition where the richest consumers buy essentially the same things as the poorest. You can be watching TV and see Coca-Cola, and you can know that the President drinks Coke, Liz Taylor drinks Coke, and just think, you can drink Coke, too. A Coke is a Coke and no amount of money can get you a better Coke than the one the bum on the corner is drinking. All the Cokes are the same and all the Cokes are good.

—Andy Warhol

Armaments, universal debt, and planned obsolescence—those are the three pillars of Western prosperity. If war, waste, and moneylenders were abolished, you'd collapse. And while you people are overconsuming the rest of the world sinks more and more deeply into chronic disaster.

—Aldous Huxley

If you live for having it all, what you have is never enough.

—Vicki Robin

I was part of that strange race of people aptly described as spending their lives doing things they detest, to make money they don't want, to buy things they don't need, to impress people they don't like.

—Emile Gauvreau

The paramount doctrine of the economic and technological euphoria of recent decades has been that everything depends on innovation. It was understood as desirable, and even necessary, that we should go on and on from one technological innovation to the next, which would cause the economy to "grow" and make everything better and better. This of course implied at every point a hatred of the past, of all things inherited and free. All things superseded in our progress of innovations, whatever their value might have been, were discounted as of no value at all.

—Wendell Berry

We know—it has been measured in many experiments—that children with strong impulse control grow to be better adjusted, more dependable, achieve higher grades in school and college and have more success in their careers than others. Success depends on the ability to delay gratification, which is precisely what a consumerist culture under-mines. At every stage, the emphasis is on the instant gratification of instinct. In the words of the pop group Queen, "I want it all and I want it now." A whole culture is being infantilized.

—Jonathan Sacks

Nothing short of the end of the world would get our eco-conscious techies to toss their latest gadgets onto the street.

—Susan Ee

The system of consumerism may seem like an immovable fact of modern life. But it is not. That the system was manufactured suggests that we can reshape those forces to create a healthier, more sustainable system with a more fulfilling goal than "more stuff."

—Rachel Botsman

QUESTIONS FOR DISCUSSION

1. Some of these quotations point to positive aspects of our consumer society, but most are to varying degrees critical of it. Yet our economy is, by most estimates, 70–80% dependent on consumption. Why do you think so many Americans are critical of the economic system on which they depend?

2. What do you find most attractive about our consumer society? What do you find least attractive? Why?

FOR REFLECTION AND A SHORT ESSAY

Select from the above list one or two quotes and write a blog entry or a short essay of about two paragraphs in response to the quote or quotes. Be sure that what you say is relevant to the quote or quotes, but go beyond what is said to share your own insights, experiences, or thoughts.

The Aesthetic Imperative

VIRGINIA POSTREL

Virginia Postrel, whose degree from Princeton is in English literature, has made a career writing on the subjects of economics, progress, and design. She writes regular columns for *The Atlantic* and *Forbes* magazines and has published two books, *The Future and Its Enemies* and *The Substance of Style: How the Rise of Aesthetic Value Is Remaking Commerce, Culture, and Consciousness*, from which this selection is excerpted.

1   The twenty-first century isn't what the old movies imagined. We citizens of the future don't wear conformist jumpsuits, live in utilitarian high-rises, or get our food in pills.

To the contrary, we are demanding and creating an enticing, stimulating, diverse, and beautiful world. We want our vacuum cleaners and mobile phones to sparkle, our bathroom faucets and desk accessories to express our personalities. We expect every strip mall and city block to offer designer coffee, several different cuisines, a copy shop with do-it-yourself graphics workstations, and a nail salon for manicures on demand. We demand trees in our parking lots, peaked roofs and decorative façades on our supermarkets, auto dealerships as swoopy and stylish as the cars they sell.

2   Aesthetics has become too important to be left to the aesthetes. To succeed, hard-nosed engineers, real estate developers, and MBAs must take aesthetic communication, and aesthetic pleasure, seriously. We, their customers, demand it.

3   "We are by nature—by deep, biological nature—visual, tactile creatures," says David Brown, the former president of the Art Center College of Design in Pasadena, California, and a longtime observer of the design world. That is a quintessential turn-of-our-century statement, a simultaneous affirmation of biological humanity and aesthetic power. Our sensory side is as valid a part of our nature as the capacity to speak or reason, and it is essential to both. Artifacts do not need some other justification for pleasing our visual, tactile, emotional natures. Design, says Brown, is moving from the abstract and ideological—"this is good design"—to the personal and emotional—"I *like* that." In this new age of aesthetics, we are acknowledging, accepting, and even celebrating what a design-museum curator calls our "quirky underside."

4   This trend doesn't mean that a particular style has triumphed or that we're necessarily living in a period of unprecedented creativity. It doesn't mean everyone or everything is now beautiful, or that people agree on some absolute standard of taste. The issue is not *what* style is used but rather *that* style is used, consciously and conscientiously, even in areas where function used to stand alone. Aesthetics is more pervasive than it used to be—not restricted to a social, economic, or artistic elite, limited to only a few settings or industries, or designed to communicate only power, influence, or wealth. Sensory appeals are everywhere, they are increasingly personalized, and they are intensifying.

5   Of course, saying that aesthetics is pervasive does not imply that look and feel trump everything else. Other values have not gone away. We may want mobile phones to sparkle, but first we expect them to work. We expect shops to look good, but we also want service and selection. We still care about cost, comfort, and convenience. But on the margin, aesthetics matters more and more. When we decide how next to spend our time, money, or creative effort, aesthetics is increasingly likely to top our priorities.

6   In this context, "aesthetics" obviously does not refer to the philosophy of art. Aesthetics is the way we communicate through the senses. It is the art of creating reactions without words, through the look and feel of people, places, and things. Hence, aesthetics differs from entertainment that requires cognitive engagement with narrative, word play, or complex, intellectual allusion. While the sound of poetry is arguably aesthetic, the meaning is not. Spectacular special effects and beautiful movie stars enhance box-office success in foreign markets because they offer universal aesthetic pleasure; clever dialogue, which is cognitive and culture-bound, doesn't travel as well. Aesthetics may complement storytelling, but it is not itself narrative.

7   Aesthetics shows rather than tells, delights rather than instructs. The effects are immediate, perceptual, and emotional. They are not cognitive, although we may analyze them after the fact. As a mid-century industrial designer said of his field, aesthetics is "fundamentally the art of using line, form, tone, color, and texture to arouse an emotional reaction in the beholder."

8   Whatever information aesthetics conveys is prearticulate—the connotation of the color and shapes of letters, not the meanings of the words they form. Aesthetics conjures meaning in a subliminal, associational way, as our direct sensory experience reminds us of something that is absent, a memory or an idea. Those associations may be universal, the way Disney's big-eyed animals play on the innate human attraction to babies. Or they may change from person to person, place to place, moment to moment.

9   Although we often equate aesthetics with beauty, that definition is too limited. Depending on what reaction the creator wants, effective presentation may be strikingly ugly, disturbing, even horrifying. The title sequence to *Seven*—whose rough, backlit type, seemingly stuttering film, and unsettling sepia images established a new style for horror films—comes to mind. Or aesthetics may employ novelty, allusion, or humor, rather than beauty, to arouse a positive response. Philippe Starck's fly swatter with a face on it doesn't represent timeless beauty. It's just whimsical fun.

10   Aesthetic effects begin with universal reactions, but these effects always operate in a personal and cultural context. We may like weather-beaten paint because it seems rustic, black leather because it makes us feel sexy, or fluffy pop music because it reminds us of our youth. Something novel may be interesting, or something familiar comforting, without regard to ideal beauty. The explosion of tropical colors that hit women's fashion in 2000 was a relief from the black, gray, and beige of the late 1990s, while those neutrals looked calm and sophisticated after the riot of jewel tones that preceded them. Psychologists tell us that human beings perceive changes in sensory inputs—movement, new visual elements, louder or softer sounds, novel smells—more than sustained levels.

11   Because aesthetics operates at a prerational level, it can be disquieting. We have a love-hate relationship with the whole idea. As consumers, we enjoy sensory appeals but fear manipulation. As producers, we'd rather not work so hard to keep up with the aesthetic competition. As heirs to Plato and the Puritans, we suspect sensory impressions as deceptive, inherently false. Aesthetics is "the power of provocative surfaces," says a critic. It "speaks to the eye's mind, overshadowing matters of quality or substance."

12   But the eye's mind is identifying something genuinely valuable. Aesthetic pleasure itself has quality and substance. The look and feel of things tap deep human instincts. We are, as Brown says, "visual, tactile creatures." We enjoy enhancing our sensory surroundings. That enjoyment is real. The trick is to appreciate aesthetic pleasure without confusing it with other values.

13   Theorist Ellen Dissanayake defines art as "making special," a behavior designed to be "sensorily and emotionally gratifying and more than strictly necessary." She argues that the instinct for "making special" is universal and innate, a part of human beings' evolved biological nature. Hers may or may not be an adequate definition of art, but it does offer a useful insight into our aesthetic age. Having spent a century or more focused primarily on other goals—solving manufacturing problems, lowering costs, making goods and services widely available, increasing convenience, saving

energy—we are increasingly engaged in making our world special. More people in more aspects of life are drawing pleasure and meaning from the way their persons, places, and things look and feel. Whenever we have the chance, we're adding sensory, emotional appeal to ordinary function.

14   "Aesthetics, whether people admit it or not, is why you buy something," says a shopper purchasing a high-style iMac, its flat screen pivoting like a desk lamp on a half-spherical base. He likes the computer's features, but he particularly likes its looks. A computer doesn't have to be a nondescript box. It can express its owner's taste and personality.

15   "Deciding to buy an IBM instead of a Compaq simply because you prefer black to gray is absolutely fine as long as both machines meet your other significant criteria," a writer advises computer shoppers on the female-oriented iVillage Web site. "Not that color can't or shouldn't be a significant criterion; in truth, the market is filled with enough solid, affordable machines that you finally have the kind of freedom of choice previously reserved only for the likes of footwear." Computers all used to look pretty much the same. Now they, too, can be special.

16   A Salt Lake City grocery shopper praises her supermarket's makeover. Gone are the gray stucco exterior, harsh fluorescent lighting, and tall, narrow aisles. In their place are warm red brick, spot and track lighting, and low-rise departments of related items. The "crowning glory" is the Starbucks in the front, which provides both a welcoming aroma and a distinctive look and feel. "The experience is a lot more calm, a lot more pleasant," she says, "an extraordinary change, and a welcome one." Grocery shopping is still a chore, but at least now the environment offers something special.

17   A political writer in Washington, D.C., a city noted for its studied ignorance of style, says he pays much more attention to his clothes than he did ten or fifteen years ago, and enjoys it a lot more. "One thing I try to do is not to wear the same combination of suit, shirt, and tie in a season," he says. "It's another way of saying every day is special." Once seen as an unnecessary luxury, even a suspect indulgence, "making special" has become a personal, social, and business imperative.

NOTES

307 "*We are by nature*" David Brown. Interview with the author. 9 Nov. 2000.

307 "*quirky underside*" Martin Eidelberg, quoted in Linda Hales, "When Designs Delight," *The Washington Post,* 12 Nov. 1998, p. T12.

308 "*As a midcentury industrial designer*" Harold Van Doren, *Industrial Design: A Practical Guide to Product Design and Development,* 2nd ed. McGraw-Hill, 1954, p. 166.

308 "*The power of provocative surfaces*" Stuart Ewen, *All Consuming Images: The Politics of Style in Contemporary Culture.* Basic Books, 1988, p. 2.

308 "*making special*" Ellen Dissanayake, *Homo Aestheticus: Where Art Comes From and Why.* U of Washington P, 1992, 1995, p. 56.

309 "*Aesthetics, whether people admit it . . .* " Dave Caldwell, quoted in Vikas Bajaj, "Electronic Manufacturers Emphasize Form with Function," *The Dallas Morning News,* 4 Apr. 2002, p. 5D.

309 "*Deciding to buy an IBM*" Heidi Pollock, "How to Buy a Computer, Part I." *iVillage,* www.iVillage.com/click/experts/goodbuygirl/articles/0,5639,38862,00.html.

309 "*A Salt Lake City grocery shopper*" Deborah Moeller. E-mail to the author. 27 Dec. 2001. Interview with the author. 8 Apr. 2002.

309 "*A political writer*" Michael Barone. Interview with the author. 8 Apr. 2002.

QUESTIONS FOR DISCUSSION

1. Postrel argues in paragraph 4 that the aesthetic imperative is not limited to the "social, economic, or artistic elite . . ." but pervades our consumer society at all levels. What examples of style does she give in this selection, and how well do they support her argument? How would you describe the relationship between "the aesthetic imperative" and a society's standard of living?

2. Discuss Postrel's definition of aesthetics as presented in paragraphs 6–12. What possible criticisms might people have about the increased importance of aesthetics in "people, places, and things" these days? What criticisms can you think of that are not mentioned here? How does Virginia Postrel answer the critics of aesthetics?

FOR INQUIRY AND PERSUASION

Postrel does not mention the impact of consumer spending on the environment. Look into some particular aspect of the consumer society to determine its impact on the Earth's environment. Do you see a need for people to reduce their consumption in some area that is not often discussed in the media? Write a persuasive essay to raise people's awareness and move them to change their spending.

In Defense of Consumerism

ERIK KAIN

It is easy to find attacks on consumerism, and only slightly harder to find uncritical defenses of it. This wise and intelligent defense may not address some of the bigger issues, such as whether the Earth can sustain our now-global consumerism, but it does point to the perspective that most of us have about the worth of buying things. By implication it asks, "What are your values?" A "value" here means more than a price tag.

1   Values are tricky, especially when they come into conflict with one another. Take consumerism. It's widely unpopular as a concept, and yet we all participate in some form of it or another, especially this time of year as Christmas approaches and stores unveil their holiday deals in spread after spread of glossy ads and energetic commercial segments. Shopping is a national pastime this season. The other national pastime is griping about it and wishing that Americans could be a little less materialistic and a little more in the spirit of the season (once it's stripped of its religiosity, of course). No Jesus and no presents—a holiday of bells and whistles and little colorful lights.

2   Well let me be a defender of consumerism for a moment.

3   Obviously, placing too much value on simply having things is unhealthy. Someone else will always have more of whatever it is you have or want, and so you will always be envious and greedy and unhappy. But placing some value on things isn't necessarily harmful.

4   A new car might actually make you happier. It might be safer, more reliable, handle better, waste less gas. All these things might make you happier. The new

computer might let you surf the web faster or play a game or chat online with family. The new couch might not smell funny. The new clothes might fit better and not have stains in them. All this stuff might actually make you a bit happier—maybe not as much as your friends and family, though some of it might actually bring you closer to them.

5   There's more to it, though. Buying stuff or paying for services creates wealth, and not just for the wealthy. It creates wealth for the poor also, and for the working class. It creates jobs for retail workers and delivery people and many others besides. All that horrible stuff we buy translates somewhere down the line into paychecks for very real people who can use that money to buy other things like food and shelter and maybe even stuff of their own to keep them entertained or comfortable.

6   A lot of jobs in this economy rest on people buying things. That's not a bad thing since overall we have more money to buy things with, and these jobs are uniformly better than the sort of jobs Americans used to have. And yet, we dislike the abstract concept of consumerism so much that we've erected "Buy Nothing Day" events in protest. We even advertise these events online, probably via our shiny new Apple Macbook.

7   Having something to be against, to blame, is very important to many of us. It helps piece our complicated world together into something simple.

8   Of course, the chaos of Black Friday is absurd. I certainly don't understand how anyone could prefer getting up at the crack of dawn to go stand in a freezing cold line at Best Buy to sleeping off the Thanksgiving hangover, but that's just me. It's perhaps just a tiny bit arrogant to begrudge others their own shopping habits. To some, the event itself is good fun. Something to do with loved ones maybe. A way to make that paycheck go a tiny bit further.

9   You see, the problem isn't that we buy things, or that we take pleasure in giving and receiving gifts. The problem comes when too many people distance themselves from deeper meaning in their lives and replace that value with simply possessing things. This has always been a problem. Only now, with capitalism more and more people can afford the luxury, and so more and more of us now suffer from this materialistic impulse—though in fairness, it is a better affliction than those we used to suffer from like starvation and plague.

10   Possessions will possess us if we let them, but having too little is much, much worse.

11   I just wonder if this problem is as bad or as widespread as so many believe it to be. It is a sacred cow of popular culture now that we've entered into some hedonistic age of rampant consumerism and a cultural nihilism devoted to the almighty gods of shopping. This is one point of agreement that many social conservatives and liberals can agree.

12   But I suspect that in many ways this is just what we choose to see. I suspect that beneath the news stories and beyond the popular opinion on the subject, most people still find the greatest joy in spending time with their families and friends. Holidays are still more about getting together than giving gifts. Having things is still secondary to having them for a reason. And meaning is still mostly found in deeper places than the swipe of a credit card or the top shelf of a department store.

QUESTIONS FOR DISCUSSION

1. "The problem comes," Kain says, "when too many people distance them-selves from deeper meaning in their lives and replace that value with simply possessing things." What does "deeper meaning" mean to you? Where did you acquire your sense of it?

2. Kain speaks of the common sentiment that we live in a "hedonistic age" of "cultural nihilism." What does *hedonism* mean? What does *nihilism* mean? Would you say you or anyone you know fits the definition?

3. Kain also claims that, for most of us, "having things is still secondary to hav-ing them for a reason." That is, except for compulsive shoppers, we don't buy just to buy. Think of the last two or three items you bought that were not strictly necessities, such as food. What reasons did you have for buying them?

FOR RESEARCH AND CONVINCING

There is such a thing as being addicted to shopping—or what is sometimes called compulsive buying. Do some research on the topic, paying special attention to why some people become addicted and how the compulsion can be reduced or eliminated. Write a paper assessing our present understanding of shopping addic-tion. Do you think we understand it fully? Do you think ways of coping with it are adequate? Recommend and defend your ideas for handling this problem better.

The Grill-Buying Guy

DAVID BROOKS

David Brooks, a graduate of University of Chicago, is a regular columnist for *The New York Times,* writing with what he describes as a "Hamiltonian or Giuliani" conservative viewpoint. His books of social commentary are *Bobos in Paradise: The New Upper Class and How They Got There, On Paradise Drive: How We Live Now (And Always Have) in the Future Tense,* and *The Social Animal: The Hidden Sources of Love, Character, and Achieve-ment.* Although he pokes fun at consumers' behavior, Brooks reveals a deep appreciation for Americans' work ethic, ingenuity, and tireless pursuit of their dreams. This selection is from *On Paradise Drive.*

1   I don't know if you've ever seen the expression of a man who is about to buy a first-class barbecue grill. He walks into Home Depot or Lowe's or one of the other mega-hardware complexes, and his eyes are glistening with a faraway visionary zeal, like one of those old prophets gazing into the promised land. His lips are parted and twitching slightly.

2   Inside the megastore, the man adopts the stride American men fall into when in the presence of large amounts of lumber. He heads over to the barbecue grills, just

past the racks of affordable house-plan books, in the yard-machinery section. They are arrayed magnificently next to the vehicles that used to be known as riding mowers but are now known as lawn tractors, because to call them riding mowers doesn't fully convey the steroidized M1 tank power of the things. The man approaches the barbecue grills with a trancelike expression suggesting that he has cast aside all the pains and imperfections of this world and is approaching the gateway to a higher dimension. In front of him is a scattering of massive steel-coated reactors with names like Broilmaster P3, Thermidor, and the Weber Genesis, because in America it seems perfectly normal to name a backyard barbecue grill after a book of the Bible.

3   The items in this cooking arsenal flaunt enough metal to survive a direct nuclear assault. Patio Man goes from machine to machine comparing their various features— the cast-iron/porcelain-coated cooking surfaces, the 328,000-BTU heat-generating capacities, the 2,000-degree tolerance linings, multiple warming racks, lava-rock containment dishes, or built-in electrical meat thermometers. Certain profound questions flow through his mind. Is a 542-cubic-inch grilling surface enough, considering he might someday get the urge to roast a bison? Can he handle the TEC Sterling II grill, which can hit temperatures of 1,600 degrees, thereby causing his dinner to spontaneously combust? Though the matte-steel overcoat resists scratching, doesn't he want a polished steel surface so he can glance down and admire his reflection while performing the suburban manliness rituals such as brushing tangy teriyaki sauce on meat slabs with his right hand while clutching a beer can in an NFL foam insulator in his left?

4   Pretty soon a large salesperson in an orange vest—looking like an SUV in human form—comes up to him and says, "Howyadoin'," which is "May I help you?" in Home Depot talk. Patio Man, who has so much lust in his heart, it is all he can do to keep from climbing up on one of these machines and whooping rodeo-style with joy, still manages to respond appropriately. He grunts inarticulately and nods toward the machines. Careful not to make eye contact at any point, the two manly suburban men have a brief exchange of pseudo-scientific grill argot that neither of them understands, and pretty soon Patio Man comes to the reasoned conclusion that it would make sense to pay a little extra for a grill with V-shaped metal baffles, ceramic rods, and a side-mounted smoker box.

5   But none of this talk matters. The guy will end up buying the grill with the best cup holders. All major purchases of consumer durable goods these days ultimately come down to which model has the most impressive cup holders.

6   Having selected his joy machine, Patio Man heads for the cash register, Visa card trembling in his hand. All up and down the line are tough ex-football-playing guys who are used to working outdoors. They hang pagers and cell phones from their belts (in case a power line goes down somewhere) and wear NASCAR sunglasses, mullet haircuts, and faded T-shirts that they have ripped the sleeves off of to keep their arm muscles exposed and their armpit hair fully ventilated. Here and there are a few innately Office Depot guys who are trying to blend in with their more manly Home Depot brethren, and not ask Home Depot inappropriate questions, such as "Does this tool belt make my butt look fat?"

7   At the checkout, Patio Man is told that some minion will forklift the grill over to the loading dock around back. He is once again glad that he's driving that Yukon XL so he can approach the loading-dock guys as a co-equal in the manly fraternity of Those Who Haul Things.

8   As he signs the credit-card slip, with its massive total price, his confidence suddenly collapses, but it is revived as wonderful grill fantasies dance in his imagination:

9   There he is atop the uppermost tier of his multilevel backyard dining and recreational area. This is the kind of deck Louis XIV would have had if Sun Gods had had decks. In his mind's eye, Patio Man can see himself coolly flipping the garlic-and-pepper T-bones on the front acreage of his new grill while carefully testing the citrus-tarragon trout filets simmering fragrantly on the rear. On the lawn below, his kids Haley and Cody frolic on the weedless community lawn that is mowed twice weekly courtesy of the people who run Monument Crowne Preserve, his townhome community.

10   Haley, the fourteen-year-old daughter, is a Travel-Team Girl who spends her weekends playing midfield against similarly ponytailed, strongly calved soccer marvels such as herself. Cody, ten, is a Buzz-Cut Boy whose naturally blond hair has been cut to lawnlike stubble, and the little that's left is highlighted an almost phosphorescent white. Cody's wardrobe is entirely derivative of fashions he has seen watching the X Games. Patio Man can see the kids playing with child-safe lawn darts alongside a gaggle of their cul-de-sac friends, a happy gathering of Haleys and Codys and Corys and Britneys. It's a brightly colored scene—Abercrombie & Fitch pink spaghetti-strap tops on the girls and ankle-length canvas shorts and laceless Nikes on the boys. Patio Man notes somewhat uncomfortably that in America today the average square yardage of boyswear grows and grows, while the square inches in the girls' outfits shrinks and shrinks. The boys carry so much fabric they look like skateboarding Bedouins, and the girls look like preppy prostitutes.

11   Nonetheless, Patio Man envisions a Saturday-evening party—his adult softball-team buddies lounging on his immaculate deck furniture, watching him with a certain moist envy as he mans the grill. They are moderately fit, sockless men in Docksiders, chinos, and Tommy Bahama muted Hawaiian shirts. Their wives, trim Jennifer Aniston lookalikes, wear capris and sleeveless tops, which look great on them owing to their countless hours on the weight machines at Spa Lady. . . .

12   They are wonderful people. Patio Man can envision his own wife, Cindy, the Realtor Mom, circulating among them serving drinks, telling parent-teacher-conference stories and generally stirring up the hospitality; he, Patio Man, masterfully wields his extra-wide fish spatula while absorbing the aroma of imported hickory chips—again, to the silent admiration of all. The sun is shining. The people are friendly. The men are no more than twenty-five pounds overweight, which is the socially acceptable male-paunch level in upwardly mobile America, and the children are well adjusted. This vision of domestic bliss is what Patio Man has been shooting for all his life.

QUESTIONS FOR DISCUSSION

1. "The Grill-Buying Guy" is satire, in this instance gentle ridicule directed at a certain segment of our population and meant to move behavior toward the author's desired norm. What would you say that norm is?

2. Americans often take pride in their individuality, but our buying habits are often not so much an expression of ourselves as they are aspirational, oriented toward the social class we would like to belong to. That is, we want to "look the part." How does this group orientation work in the case of expensive outdoor grills, as Brooks depicts it?

ASSESSING PERSUASIVE TACTICS

"The Grill-Buying Guy" might have been a *Consumer Reports*–style argument advocating that we buy the best grill for the money. Instead Brooks chose a satirical style, writing an essay that persuades indirectly, not by arguing a thesis, but by showing how funny and absurd our aspirational shopping is. Who is his intended audience? What makes this style persuasive for them? How are individuals outside his intended audience likely to respond?

False Connections

ALEX KOTLOWITZ

Alex Kotlowitz is best known as a journalist concerned with issues of race and poverty in America. His book *There Are No Children Here: The Story of Two Boys Growing Up in the Other America* won many prizes for journalism and was selected by the New York Public Library as one of the 150 most important books of the century. His more recent books are *The Other Side of the River* and a book about Chicago, *Never a City So Real*. Kotlowitz has been a writer-in-residence at Northwestern University and a visiting professor at University of Notre Dame. The selection below was originally published in Roger Rosenblatt's anthology *Consuming Desires: Consumption, Culture, and the Pursuit of Happiness*.

1 A drive down Chicago's Madison Street, moving west from the lake, is a short lesson in America's fault lines of race and class. The first mile runs through the city's downtown—or the Loop, as it's called locally—past high-rises that house banks and law firms, advertising agencies and investment funds. The second mile, once lined by flophouses and greasy diners, has hitched onto its neighbor to the east, becoming a mecca for artists and new, hip restaurants, a more affordable appendage to the Loop. And west from there, past the United Center, home to the Chicago Bulls, the boulevard descends into the abyssal lows of neighborhoods where work has disappeared. Buildings lean like punch-drunk boxers. Makers of plywood do big business here, patching those same buildings' open wounds. At dusk, the gangs claim ownership to the corners and hawk their wares, whatever is the craze of the moment, crack or smack or reefer. It's all for sale. Along one stretch, young women, their long, bare

legs shimmering under the lamplight, smile and beckon and mumble short, pithy descriptions of the pleasures they promise to deliver.

2   Such is urban decay. Such are the remains of the seemingly intractable, distinctly American version of poverty, a poverty not only "of the pocket" but also, as Mother Teresa said when she visited this section of the city, "of the spirit."

3   What is most striking about this drive down Madison, though, is that so few whites make it. Chicago's West Side, like other central-city neighborhoods, sits apart from everything and everyone else. Its inhabitants have become geographically and spiritually isolated from all that surrounds them, islands unto themselves. Even the violence—which, myth has it, threatens us all—is contained within its borders. Drug dealers shoot drug dealers. Gang members maul gang members. And the innocents, the passersby who get caught in the crossfire, are their neighbors and friends. It was that isolation which so struck me when I first began to spend time at the Henry Horner Homes, a Chicago public housing complex that sits along that Madison Street corridor. Lafeyette and Pharoah, the two boys I wrote about in my book *There Are No Children Here,* had never been to the Loop, one mile away. They'd never walked the halls of the Art Institute of Chicago or felt the spray from the Buckingham Fountain. They'd never ogled the sharks at the John G. Shedd Aquarium or stood in the shadow of the stuffed pachyderms at the Field Museum. They'd never been to the suburbs. They'd never been to the countryside. In fact, until we stayed at a hotel one summer on their first fishing trip, they'd never felt the steady steam of a shower. (Henry Horner's apartments had only bathtubs.) At one point, the boys, so certain that their way of life was the only way of life, insisted that my neighborhood, a gentrified community on the city's North Side, had to be controlled by gangs. They knew nothing different.

4   And yet children like Lafeyette and Pharoah do have a connection to the American mainstream: it is as consumers that inner-city children, otherwise so disconnected from the world around them, identify themselves not as ghetto kids or project kids but as Americans or just plain kids. And they are as much consumers as they are the consumed; that is, they mimic white America while white America mimics them. "Inner-city kids will embrace a fashion item as their own that shows they have a connection, and then you'll see the prep school kids reinvent it, trying to look hip-hop," says Sarah Young, a consultant to businesses interested in tapping the urban market. "It's a cycle."[1] A friend, a black nineteen-year-old from the city's West Side, suggests that this dynamic occurs because the inner-city poor equate classiness with suburban whites while those same suburban whites equate hipness with the inner-city poor. If he's right, it suggests that commercialism may be our most powerful link, one that in the end only accentuates and prolongs the myths we have built up about each other.

5   Along Madison Street, halfway between the Loop and the city's boundary, sits an old, worn-out shopping strip containing small, transient stores. They open and close almost seasonally—balloons mark the openings; "Close-Out Sale" banners mark the closings—as the African American and Middle Eastern immigrant owners ride the ebb and flow of unpredictable fashion tastes. GQ Sports. Dress to Impress. Best Fit. Chic Classics. Dream Team. On weekend afternoons, the makeshift mall is thronged with customers blithely unaware that store ownership and names may have changed

since their last visit. Young mothers guiding their children by the shoulders and older women seeking a specific purchase pick their way through packs of teenagers who laugh and clown, pulling and pushing one another into the stores. Their whimsical tastes are the subject of intense curiosity, longing, and marketing surveys on the part of store owners and corporate planners.

6   On a recent spring afternoon, as I made my way down Madison Street toward Tops and Bottoms, one of the area's more popular shops, I detected the unmistakable sweet odor of marijuana. Along the building's side, two teenage boys toked away at cigar-sized joints, called blunts. The store is long and narrow; its walls are lined with shoes and caps and its center is packed with shirts, jeans, and leather jackets. The owner of the store, a Palestinian immigrant, recognized me from my previous visits there with Lafeyette and Pharoah. "You're a probation officer, right?" he asked. I told him what my connection was with the boys. He completed a sale of a black Starter skullcap and then beckoned me toward the back of the store, where we could talk without distraction.

7   Behind him, an array of nearly 200 assorted shoes and sneakers lined the wall from floor to ceiling. There were the predictable brands: Nike, Fila, and Reebok, the shoes that have come to define (and nearly bankrupt) a generation. There were the heavy boots by Timberland and Lugz that have become popular among urban teens. But it was the arrangement of shoes directly in front of me that the proprietor pointed to, a collection of Hush Puppies. "See that?" he asked. "It's totally white-bread." Indeed, Hush Puppies, once of earth tones and worn by preppies, have caught on among urban black teens—and the company has responded in kind, producing the shoes in outrageous, gotta-look-at-me colors such as crayon orange and fire-engine red. I remember the first time Pharoah appeared in a pair of lime green Hush Puppies loafers—I was dumbfounded. But then I thought of his other passions: Tommy Hilfiger shirts, Coach wallets, Guess? jeans. They were the fashions of the economically well heeled, templates of those who had "made it." Pharoah, who is now off at college, ultimately found his path. But for those who are left behind, these fashions are their "in." They give them cachet. They link them to a more secure, more prosperous world, a world in which they have not been able to participate—except as consumers.

8   Sarah Young, whose clients include the company that manufactures Hush Puppies, suggests that "for a lot of these kids, what they wear is who they are because that's all they have to connect them to the rest of the larger community. It marks their status because there's not a lot else."[2]

9   It's a false status, of course. They hold on to the idea that to "make it" means to consume at will, to buy a $100 Coach wallet or an $80 Tommy Hilfiger shirt. And these brand-name companies, knowing they have a good thing going, capitalize on their popularity among the urban poor, a group that despite its economic difficulties represents a surprisingly lucrative market. The companies gear their advertising to this market segment. People such as Sarah Young nurture relationships with rap artists, who they lure into wearing certain clothing items. When the company that makes Hush Puppies was looking to increase their presence in the urban market, Young helped persuade Wyclef Jean, a singer with the Fugees, to wear powder

blue Bridgeport chukkas, which bear a sneaking resemblance to the Wallabee shoes familiar to members of my generation. In a recent issue of *Vibe,* a magazine aimed at the hip-hop market, rappers Beenie Man and Bounty Killer are pictured posing in Ralph Lauren hats and Armani sweaters, sandwiched between photographs of other rappers decked out in Calvin Klein sunglasses and Kenneth Cole shoes. The first three full-page advertisements in that same issue are for Hilfiger's athletic line, Coach handbags (with jazz singer Cassandra Wilson joyfully walking along with her Coach bag slung over her shoulder), and Perry Ellis casual wear (with a black man and three young boys lounging on the beach). This, as Pharoah told me, represents class—and, as Young suggested, the one connection that children growing up amid the ruins of the inner city have to a more prosperous, more secure world. It is as consumers that they claim citizenship. And yet that Coach handbag or that Tommy Hilfiger or Perry Ellis shirt changes nothing of the cruel realities of growing up poor and black. It reminds me of the murals painted on abandoned buildings in the South Bronx: pictures of flowers, window shades, and curtains, and the interiors of tidy rooms. As Jonathan Kozol observes in his book *Amazing Grace,* "the pictures have been done so well that when you look, the first time, you imagine that you're seeing into people's homes—pleasant-looking homes, in fact, that have a distinctly middle-class appearance."[3]

10   But the urban poor are more than just consumers. They help drive fashions as well. The Tommy Hilfiger clothing line, aimed initially at preppies, became hot in the inner city, pushed in large part by rap artists who took to the clothing maker's stylish, colorful vestments. A 1997 article in *Forbes* magazine suggests that Hilfiger's 47 percent rise in earnings over the first nine months of its fiscal year 1996–1997 had much to do with the clothing line's popularity among the kinds of kids who shop Chicago's Madison Street.[4] Suddenly, Tommy Hilfiger became cool, not only among the urban teens but also among their counterparts in the suburbs. "That gives them a sense of pride, that they're bringing a style to a new height," Sarah Young suggests.[5] Thus, those who don't have much control over other aspects of their life find comfort in having at least some control over something—style.

11   There's another facet to this as well: the romanticization of urban poverty by some white teens. In St. Joseph, Michigan, a nearly all-white town of 9,000 in the state's southwestern corner, a group of teens mimicked the mannerisms and fashions of their neighbors across the river in Benton Harbor, Michigan, a nearly all-black town that has been economically devastated by the closing of the local factories and foundries. This cadre of kids called themselves "wiggers." A few white boys identified themselves with one of the Benton Harbor gangs, and one small band was caught carrying out holdups with a BB gun. A local police detective laughingly called them "wannabes." At St. Joseph High School, the wiggers greeted one another in the hallways with a high five or a twitch of the head. "Hey, Nigger, wha's up?" they'd inquire. "Man, just chillin'."

12   But it was through fashions—as consumers—that they most clearly identified themselves with their peers across the way. They dressed in the hip-hop fashion made popular by M. C. Hammer and other rap artists, wearing blue jeans big enough for two, the crotch down at their knees. (The beltless, pants-falling-off-hips style

originated, many believe, in prison, where inmates must forgo belts.) The guys wore Starter jackets and hats, the style at the time. The girls hung braided gold necklaces around their necks and styled their hair in finger waves or braids. For these teens, the life of ghetto kids is edgy, gutsy, risky—all that adolescents crave. But do they know how edgy, how gutsy, how risky? They have never had to comfort a dying friend, bleeding from the head because he was on the wrong turf. They have never sat in a classroom where the desks are arranged so that no student will be hit by falling plaster. They have never had to say "Yes, Sir" and "No, Sir," as a police officer, dripping with sarcasm, asks, "Nigger, where'd you get the money for such a nice car?" From a safe distance—as consumers—they can believe they are hip, hip being defined as what they see in their urban counterparts. With their jeans sagging off their boxer shorts, with their baseball caps worn to the side, with their high-tops unlaced, they find some connection, though in the end it is a false bond.

13   It is as consumers that poor black children claim membership to the larger community. It is as purchasers of the talismans of success that they can believe they've transcended their otherwise miserable situation. In the late 1980s, as the drug trade began to flourish in neighborhoods such as Chicago's West Side, the vehicle of choice for these big-time entrepreneurs was the Chevrolet Blazer, an icon of suburban stability. As their communities were unraveling, in part because of their trade, they sought a connection to an otherwise stable life. And they sought it in the only way they knew how, the only way available to them: as consumers. Inner-city teens are eager to participate in society; they want to belong.

14   And for the white teens like those in St. Joseph, who, like all adolescents, want to feel that they're on the edge, what better way than to build some connection—however manufactured—to their contemporaries across the river who must negotiate that vertical drop every day? By purchasing, in complete safety, all the accoutrements associated with skirting that fall, they can believe that they've been there, that they've experienced the horrors and pains of growing up black and poor. Nothing, of course, could be further from the truth. They know nothing of the struggles their neighbors endure.

15   On the other hand, fashions in the end are just that—fashions. Sometimes kids yearn for baggy jeans or a Tommy Hilfiger shirt not because of what it represents but because it is the style of their peers. Those "wiggers," for example, may equate the sagging pants with their neighbors across the river, but kids a few years younger are mimicking them as much as their black counterparts. Fashions grow long limbs that, in the end, are only distantly connected to their roots.

16   Take that excursion down Madison Street—and the fault lines will become abundantly clear. One can't help but marvel at the spiritual distance between those shopping at Tops and Bottoms on the blighted West Side and those browsing the pricey department stores in the robust downtown. And yet many of the children have one eye trained down Madison Street, those on each side watching their counterparts and thinking they know the others' lives. Their style of dress mimics that of the others. But they're being cheated. They don't know. They have no idea. Those checking out the array of Hush Puppies at Tops and Bottoms think they have the key to making it, to becoming full members of this prosperous nation. And those trying on the jeans

wide enough for two think they know what it means to be hip, to live on the edge. And so, in lieu of building real connections—by providing opportunities or rebuilding communities—we have found some common ground as purchasers of each other's trademarks. At best, that link is tenuous; at worst, it's false. It lets us believe that we are connected when the distance, in fact, is much farther than anyone cares to admit.

NOTES

1. Sarah Young. Telephone interview with the author. Jan. 1998.
2. Ibid.
3. Jonathan Kozol, *Amazing Grace: The Lives of Children and the Conscience of a Nation,* HarperPerennial, 1996.
4. Joshua Levine, "Baad Sells," *Forbes,* vol. 159, no. 8, 21 Apr. 1997, p. 142.
5. Sarah Young. Telephone interview with the author. Jan. 1998.

QUESTIONS FOR DISCUSSION

1. What is Alex Kotlowitz's complaint about rich and poor teenage subcultures borrowing each other's styles?

2. The author refers to the "distinctively American version of poverty, a poverty not only 'of the pocket' but also . . . 'of the spirit.'" What does *spirit* mean in the context of this essay? That is, besides lacking money, what else do inner city kids lack?

3. The author concedes near the end of the essay that "fashions in the end are just that—fashions," with what's in and what's out changing faster than most of us can or want to keep up with. Yet a number of TV shows with many viewers focus on fashion. How do you account for this fascination?

FOR RESEARCH AND CONVINCING

Alex Kotlowitz's essay is about brands and social class, but his real concern is obviously poverty, which seems as stubbornly "intractable" now as it was when he wrote. Do some research on poverty in America. We think of it sometimes as an urban problem. Is it? How fluid is the economic status of the poor population in America? What causes people to fall into poverty or to remain poor all their lives? When poor people escape poverty, how do they manage to do so? Write an essay that conveys basic information about one kind of poverty you see around you, either in the community you grew up in or where you live now. What can be done to help the poor escape poverty? Take a stance and argue for whatever measures you think can eliminate or reduce the kind of poverty your essay is about.

Three Cartoons about the Consumer Society

At their best, cartoons capture the essence of our concerns, problems, and conflicts with important issues, and do so in a way we remember, in part because of the humor. Note that all three of these cartoons highlight contradictions in our attitudes toward consumerism.

Paul Fitzgerald/www.CartoonStock.com

Chris Madden/www.CartoonStock.com

© Mike Baldwin / Cornered

Mike Baldwin/www.CartoonStock.com

QUESTIONS FOR DISCUSSION

No doubt we strive for a measure of consistency, but for the most part we live in conflict and contradiction. What conflicts and contradictions do the cartoons above call attention to? How do you see your own behavior in relation to them?

Out-of-Body Image

CAROLINE HELDMAN

> Caroline Heldman, PhD, is an assistant professor of politics at Occidental College in Los Angeles. Her work centers primarily on issues of gender and race.

1   On a typical day, you might see ads featuring a naked woman's body tempting viewers to buy an electronic organizer, partially exposed women's breasts being used to sell fishing line, or a woman's rear—wearing only a thong—being used to pitch a

new running shoe. Meanwhile, on every newsstand, impossibly slim (and digitally airbrushed) cover "girls" adorn a slew of magazines. With each image, you're hit with a simple, subliminal message: Girls' and women's bodies are objects for others to visually consume.

2   If such images seem more ubiquitous than ever, it's because U.S. residents are now exposed to anywhere from 3,000 to 5,000 advertisements a day—up from 500 to 2,000 a day in the 1970s. The Internet accounts for much of this growth, and young people are particularly exposed to advertising: 70 percent of 15- to 34-year-olds use social networking technologies such as MySpace and Facebook, which allow advertisers to infiltrate previously private communication space.

3   Although mass media has always objectified women, it has become increasingly provocative. More and more, female bodies are shown as outright objects (think Rose McGowan's machine-gun leg in the recent horror movie *Grindhouse*), are literally broken into parts (the disembodied woman's torso in advertisements for TV's *The Sarah Connor Chronicles*) or are linked with sexualized violence (simulated crime scenes on *America's Next Top Model* featuring seemingly dead women).

4   A steady diet of exploitative, sexually provocative depictions of women feeds a poisonous trend in women's and girls' perceptions of their bodies, one that has recently been recognized by social scientists as self-objectification—viewing one's body as a sex object to be consumed by the male gaze. Like W. E. B. DuBois' famous description of the experience of black Americans, self-objectification is a state of "double consciousness . . . a sense of always looking at one's self through the eyes of others."

5   Women who self-objectify are desperate for outside validation of their appearance and present their bodies in ways that draw attention. A study I did of 71 randomly selected female students from a liberal arts college in Los Angeles, for example, found that 70 percent were medium or high self-objectifiers, meaning that they have internalized the male gaze and chronically monitor their physical appearance. Boys and men experience self-objectification as well, but at a much lower rate—probably because, unlike women, they rarely get the message that their bodies are the primary determination of their worth.

6   Researchers have learned a lot about self-objectification since the term was coined in 1997 by University of Michigan psychology professor Barbara Fredrickson and Colorado College psychology professor Tomi-Ann Roberts. Numerous studies since then have shown that girls and women who self-objectify are more prone to depression and low self-esteem and have less faith in their own capabilities, which can lead to diminished success in life. They are more likely to engage in "habitual body monitoring"—constantly thinking about how their bodies appear to the outside world—which puts them at higher risk for eating disorders such as anorexia and bulimia. And they are prone to embarrassment about bodily functions such as menstruation, as well as general feelings of disgust and shame about their bodies.

7   Self-objectification has also been repeatedly shown to sap cognitive functioning, because of all the attention devoted to body monitoring. For instance, a 1998 study asked two groups of women to take a math exam—one group in swimsuits, the other in sweaters. The swimsuit-wearers, distracted by body concerns, performed significantly worse than their peers in sweaters.

8   Several of my own surveys of college students indicate that this impaired concentration by self-objectifiers may hurt their academic performance. Those with low self-objectification reported an average GPA of 3.5, whereas those with high self-objectification reported a 3.1. While this gap may appear small, in graduate-school admissions it represents the difference between being competitive and being out of the running for the top schools.

9   Another worrisome effect of self-objectification is that it diminishes political efficacy—a person's belief that she can have an impact through the political process. In another survey of mine, 33 percent of high self-objectifiers felt low political efficacy, compared to 13 percent of low self-objectifiers. Since political efficacy leads to participation in politics, having less of it means that self-objectifiers may be less likely to vote or run for office.

10   The effects of self-objectification on young girls are of such growing concern that the American Psychological Association published an investigative report on it last year. The APA found that girls as young as 7 years old are exposed to clothing, toys, music, magazines and television programs that encourage them to be sexy or "hot"—teaching them to think of themselves as sex objects before their own sexual maturity. Even thong underwear is being sold in sizes for 7- to 10-year-olds. The consequence, wrote Kenyon College psychology professor Sarah Murnen in the journal

Sex Roles, is that girls "are taught to view their bodies as 'projects' that need work before they can attract others, whereas boys are likely to learn to view their bodies as tools to use to master the environment."

11   Fredrickson, along with Michigan communications professor Kristen Harrison (both work within the university's Institute for Research on Women and Gender), recently discovered that self-objectification actually impairs girls' motor skills. Their study of 202 girls, ages 10 to 17, found that self-objectification impeded girls' ability to throw a softball, even after differences in age and prior experience were factored out. Self-objectification forced girls to split their attention between how their bodies looked and what they wanted them to do, resulting in less forceful throws and worse aim.

12   One of the more stunning effects of self-objectification is its impact on sex. Nudity can cause great anxiety among self-objectifiers, who then become preoccupied with how their bodies look in sexual positions. One young woman I interviewed described sex as being an "out of body" experience during which she viewed herself through the eyes of her lover, and, sometimes, through the imaginary lens of a camera shooting a porn film. As a constant critic of her body, she couldn't focus on her own sexual pleasure.

13   Self-objectification can likely explain some other things that researchers are just starting to study. For instance, leading anti-sexist male activist and author Jackson Katz observes, "Many young women now engage in sex acts with men that prioritize the man's pleasure, with little or no expectation of reciprocity." Could this be another result of women seeing themselves as sexual objects, not agents? . . .

14   It would be encouraging if these choices reflected the sexual agency for women that feminists have fought so hard for, but they do not. The notion of objectification as empowering is illogical, since objects are acted upon, rather than taking action themselves. The real power in such arrangements lies with boys and men, who come to feel entitled to consume women as objects—first in media, then in real life.

15   At the root of this normalization of self-objectification may lie new consumer values in the U.S. Unlike the "producer citizen" of yesteryear—invoked in the 1960s by John F. Kennedy's request to "ask not what your country can do for you, ask what you can do for your country"—the more common "consumer citizen" of today asks what the country, and everyone else, can do for him or her. Consumer citizens increasingly think of relationships with others as transactions in which they receive something, making them more comfortable consuming other human beings, visually or otherwise.

16   Self-objectification isn't going anywhere anytime soon. So what can we do about it? First, we can recognize how our everyday actions feed the larger beast, and realize that we are not powerless. Mass media, the primary peddler of female bodies, can be assailed with millions of little consumer swords. We can boycott companies and engage in other forms of consumer activism, such as socially conscious investments and shareholder actions. We can also contact companies directly to voice our concerns (see *Ms.'* backpage No Comment section, for example) and refuse to patronize businesses that overtly depict women as sex objects.

17   An example of women's spending power, and the limits of our tolerance for objectification, can be found in the 12-percent dip in profits of clothing company

Victoria's Secret this year—due, according to the company's CEO, to its image becoming "too sexy." Victoria's Secret was not the target of an organized boycott: rather, its increasingly risque "bra and panty show" seems to have begun alienating women, who perhaps no longer want to simply be shown as highly sexualized window dressing.

18   Another strategy to counter one's own tendency to self-objectify is to make a point of buying products, watching programs and reading publications that promote more authentic women's empowerment. This can be difficult, of course, in a media climate in which companies are rarely wholeheartedly body-positive. For instance, Dove beauty products launched a much-lauded advertising campaign that used "real women" (i.e., not super-skinny ones) instead of models, but then Dove's parent company, Unilever, put out hypersexual ads for Axe men's body spray that showed the fragrance driving scantily clad women into orgiastic states.

19   Locating unadulterated television and film programming is also tough. Even Lifetime and Oxygen, TV networks created specifically for women, often portray us as weak victims or sex objects and present a narrow version of thin, white "beauty." Action films that promise strong female protagonists (think of the women of *X-Men,* or Lara Croft from *Tomb Raider*) usually deliver these characters in skintight clothes, serving the visual pleasure of men.

20   Feminist media criticism, at least, is plentiful. *Ms., Bitch* and others, along with publications for young girls such as *New Moon Magazine,* provide thoughtful analyses of media from various feminist perspectives. NOW's Love Your Body website (http://loveyourbody.nowfoundation.org) critiques offensive ads and praises body-positive ones. Blogs, both well-known and lesser-known, provide a platform for women and girls to vent about how the media depicts them. And there's some evidence that criticizing media helps defuse its effects: Murnen's study found that grade-school girls who had negative reactions to pictures of objectified women reported higher self-esteem.

21   A more radical, personal solution is to actively avoid media that compels us to self-objectify—which, unfortunately, is the vast majority of movies, television programs and women's magazines. My research with college-age women indicates that the less women consume media, the less they self-objectify, particularly if they avoid fashion magazines. By shutting out media, girls and women can create mental and emotional space for true self-exploration. What would our lives look like if we viewed our bodies as tools to master our environment, instead of projects to be constantly worked on? What if our sexual expressions were based on our own pleasure as opposed to a narrow, consumerist idea of male sexual pleasure? What would disappear from our lives if we stopped seeing ourselves as objects? Painful high heels? Body hatred? Constant dieting? Liposuction? Unreciprocated oral sex?

22   It's hard to know. Perhaps the most striking outcome of self-objectification is the difficulty women have in imagining identities and sexualities truly our own. In solidarity, we can start on this path, however confusing and difficult it may be.

QUESTIONS FOR DISCUSSION

1. What is "self-objectification"? To what extent is this process normal and healthy? At what point does it become excessive and therefore abnormal and unhealthy?

2. As the author points out, the use of the female body to sell things, both to men and to women, is hardly new. Do you see in the media or in the behavior of women in everyday life any signs of rebellion against the objectification of women? What forms does it take? Do you see the rebellion as genuine and meaningful?

3. The author argues that when women are viewed as objects, they lose agency because objects are acted on rather than acting. The logic may seem convincing, but do you think that women your age are in fact impaired as agents? That is, can a woman self-conscious about her appearance be using it as a tool, just in a different way than men use their bodies?

FOR RESEARCH AND CRITIQUE

Examine the advertisements in two or three fashion magazines, being sure to include depictions of men as well as of women. Choose two advertisements for analysis, one that you find appealing, and one that you find off-putting. How do you account for the difference? Is the difference a matter of an exploitative objectification of either a man or a woman or both, or do you see the difference in other terms? Write an analysis of the two ads that explains your judgment and justifies your interpretations.

X-Large Boys

ALISSA QUART

> Alissa Quart, a graduate of Columbia School of Journalism, has written two critically acclaimed books: *Branded: The Buying and Selling of Teenagers*, from which the selection below is excerpted, and *Hothouse Kids: The Dilemma of the Gifted Child*. She also writes for *The New York Times* and *The Atlantic Monthly*.

1   "Supersize your superset" proclaims one teen weightlifter, echoing female teens' urges to augment their breasts.

2   The term *superset* refers to an extraordinary number of exercises, or weightlifting sets, performed with little or no rest between them. The hope for the boys who do supersets is to grow big—bigger than their classmates, as big as male models, professional wrestlers, and bodybuilders. In a sense, teen superset obsessions result from branding efforts . . .—the selling of nutritional-supplement companies and preppy clothing manufacturers such as Abercrombie & Fitch. In just five years, these firms have created a greater sense of inadequacy among boys about their bodies than ever before. Not so coincidentally, this has produced a whole new market for underwear

and powdered drinks that teen boys now buy in an attempt to end this inadequacy. An astronomical and younger-than-ever use of steroids accompanies it all, along with a trade in dubious, over-the-counter nutritional supplements. The drive to grow big, like the drive for youthful plastic surgery, goes beyond becoming big or becoming perfect; it's the sort of self-construction that Generation Y understands. It's self-branding as an emotional palliative.

3   According to a Blue Cross-Blue Shield 2001 survey of ten-to-seventeen-year-olds, half of the 785 children interviewed said they were "aware" of sports supplements and drugs, and one in five take them. Forty-two percent did it to build muscle and 16 percent just to look better (i.e., "built"). These numbers are way up: In contrast, the 1999 BCBS survey found that no sample of kids under fourteen had taken products.

4   The push began in 1999 with the emergence of products such as Teen Advantage Creatine Serum, which made appearances on the shelves of vitamin chain stores. The marketing shows a kind of malignant genius: The formula was developed, according to the label, "especially for young aspiring athletes 8–19 years of age." (It also carries the necessary but misleadingly low-key caveat that excess dosage of creatine is not a "wise decision.") Not surprisingly, the products took off; there's nothing like a new teen-specific product that claims to alleviate a new teen-specific pathology.

5   The campaign worked so well that 52 percent of young users of performance-enhancing supplements said they had tried creatine (only 18 percent of adults surveyed used these supplements). Other supplements popular with kids—kids as young as ten—include ephedrine (which ostensibly increases endurance) and "andro," or androstenedione, an over-the-counter alternative to anabolic steroids (like steroids, androstenedione increases testosterone in the body—in fact, it also increases production of estrogen). These supplements, experts agree, range from suspect to dangerous, and even deadly, as ephedra turned out to be. In fact, some of these supplements, says Charles Yesalis, author of *The Steroids Game,* are permitted to be called supplements only because of legal loopholes and are in fact drugs that are virtually unregulated by the FDA.

6   All this supplement use does not, unfortunately, mean that kids are staying away from steroids: In the 2001 Monitoring the Future study, 2.8 percent of eighth graders, 3.5 percent of tenth graders, and 3.7 percent of twelfth graders said they had taken steroids, meaning they had "cycled" on the drugs from eight to twelve weeks at least once (only 1.7 percent of high school sophomores had taken steroids in 1992). Why? Because steroids change body fat by adding muscle and thus decrease body fat proportionally. The possible side effects of steroids include stunted bone growth, liver damage, and shrunken testicles. A cycle is also costly, ranging from a few hundred to a few thousand dollars. But, as happens with a new wardrobe or a new pair of breasts, that's not seen as much of a price for looking more attractive. Allowances are up, working hours are up; kids can afford to juice. In such an environment, the decision not to use steroids but to depend instead on supplements can seem both cautious and economical. The no-worries attitude toward supplements, and dependence on them, can be seen in Sam, a thoughtful, quiet, dedicated prep school sophomore. Sam is also a prize-winning sixteen-year-old bodybuilder who writes for teen bodybuilding sites on which he proudly posts photos of his rippling

and massive physique. Every day, Sam takes ephedrine mixed with caffeine along with 5 milligrams of creatine. He's been lifting weights since he was seven, and his punishing regimen now takes two hours of lifting daily.

7   Sam's passion for weightlifting started when he was exploring a hotel where he was staying with his family and he saw an adult lifting in the weight room. This weightlifter was his version of Edgar Allan Poe's Annabel Lee—he would never forget the image of the strong older man lifting the barbells. As soon as he got home, he bought some weights at a discount store and began working on getting big. Sam is not alone in starting so early. It's a trend that echoes the other ways in which kids are getting older younger in the market economy: Thirty-five percent of 60,000 weightlifting injuries in 1998 were for those aged from fifteen to twenty-four, and 12 percent were suffered by *children* aged from five to fourteen.

8   Today, he weighs 225 pounds, and has 6 percent body fat. He says that lifting helps him "stay healthy, look good, and feel confident," but acknowledges that for some of his peers, "exposed to weightlifting at first by popular culture," the reasons for their passions are not as hale and hearty. Some use steroids, for instance. (His own practice of taking ephedrine—an herbal supplement that can lead to heart attacks, seizures, psychoses, and death—to lose weight is arguably not such a great way of "staying healthy" either.) "There is definitely undue pressure on teen boys to look good and be big," Sam says. There is also undue pressure not to be fat given the commercial pressure to eat and the rising rates of obesity spurred on by commercials for fattening and sugary foods. In the stories of adolescents, childhood and teen obesity is a recurring theme. "The fat child is more abused than the muscled one; look at Piggy in *Lord of the Flies,*" explains Sam. "The big boy with the glasses—nobody listens to him. Teens now start lifting because they are overweight."

9   For sure, teen male body culture is a response to the now ubiquitous overweight childhoods of American boys; a fat child may put a hard body between the self that was ostracized and emasculated flesh and his new adolescent self. The teen muscle boys, like the breast augmentation girls, exchange one supersized consumerism for another: They trade family-sized packages of branded food bought in bulk at discount stores for giant, branded adult-male-looking bodies and large vats of powdered supplements.

10   Juan, a Cuban American sixteen-year-old bodybuilder who lives in New Jersey, used weightlifting to go from 225 pounds to 165 pounds in one year. He says he started weightlifting because he "got a lot of prejudice" when he was fat. "That's why I did it [weightlifting], so they wouldn't make fun of me." Now his classmates respect him, he says, and girls talk to him, although he doesn't care about girls; he's more interested in the company of other high school weightlifters. "I want to get big, really big, but natural. I wanna be feared," Juan says. Like Sam, Juan doesn't consider the supplements unnatural—he takes from 5 to 10 milligrams of creatine a day, as well as whey for protein and glutamine for joint strength.

11   The desire of adolescents to leave behind the scrawny or husky teaseable boy for the hard, well-packaged man is not a new one, of course. The virtues of the well-developed man are extolled in the writings of the Greeks and in Shakespeare's *Measure for Measure:* "O, it is excellent / To have a giant's strength; but it is tyrannous / To use

it like a giant." The wish to become big in puberty, for reasons of both dominance over one's peers and of display, can be seen in the twentieth-century in the fifty years of Charles Atlas magazine advertisements. The Atlas ads famously promised pubescents bodybuilding courses that would "make you a new man in just 15 minutes a day," that could "'RE-BUILD' skinny rundown weaklings" into creatures with "a coat of muscle straight across your stomach." In addition, bodybuilding magazines aimed at boys have a long history (and so do complementary homoerotic physique magazines). The 1977 film *Pumping Iron* also gave encouragement to boys to build themselves up.

12   However, the omnipresent gymmed-out, almost-naked male body began to make the rounds only in the late 1980s. A big force for this was a new advertising culture—the giant billboards for Calvin Klein underwear flaunting well-built models, the denuded male torsos in that same designer's perfume ads, helped to change the shape of men, literally. It is no coincidence that this was a period when the teen members of Generation Y were toddlers.

13   "When you hear girls gawking at Abercrombie & Fitch about how hot the guy is on the bag—that makes an impression," one teen bodybuilder told the *New York Times Magazine* in 1999. One of Abercrombie's countless bare-chested and buff youths had clearly been seared on that teen's mind; perhaps he still thinks of him every time he makes yet another andro shake.

14   The rise of teen male bigorexia, as media wags have called it, has also been spurred on by a new strain of magazines as well. There's the abdomen-mania of the men's magazines that these boys have grown up with, from *Men's Health* to *GQ*. In 2000, for instance, *Men's Health* even launched a magazine in celebration of the teen male abdomen called *MH-17*. According to its initial press release, *MH-17* was "aimed at the 'rapidly growing' market of male teenagers in the United States."

15   *MH-17* and its ideology of male teen "fitness" (read: male bodily self-hatred) flopped. But the tyranny of taut, ripped, and dieted teen male bodies on screen and in advertisements still rules. Teen films, for example, almost entirely lack the sloppy, scrawny, or plumpish boys of yesteryear, boys who were blissfully oblivious of the body obsession of their female counterparts. Now even those who play geeks, actors such as Jason Biggs of *American Pie 2,* are forced to have washboard stomachs or "six-packs" and to bare them constantly.

16   To achieve the required body, teen boys are willing to put in time and painful effort that many of their fathers couldn't have imagined—becoming a branded boy body takes just as much labor and pain as becoming a branded girl body. For instance, teen boy bodybuilders tend to engage in spartan, highly structured eating patterns. On the teenbodybuilder.com Web site, one boy describes the ten austere meals on his daily menu for the months when he prepares for competition. The meals are austere, obsessively observed, and protein-filled fare, one consisting of one scoop of egg white protein, one scoop of casein, half a scoop of Optimum's whey, four slices of turkey, and two pieces of whole wheat bread.

In their urge to build themselves into commercially approved hypermasculine specimens, the boys of Generation Y are in solidarity with their long-suffering female peers. Once there was a hope among feminists that girls could be taught to escape their oppressive body project. This has not occurred. Now, boys partake in it as well.

Weightlifting, enthusiasts say, is a form of self-construction. For the teen weightlifters, however—boys shooting steroids and eating egg whites for breakfast; shaving their chests and backs and legs—the line between self-betterment and a morphic pathology is a blurry one.

QUESTIONS FOR DISCUSSION

1. Quart sees the weight-lifting craze among male teens as "self-construction," that is, "self-branding as an emotional palliative." What do these terms mean? That is, how do you understand *self-construction, self-branding,* and *emotional palliative?*

2. According to the author, there are strong incentives to "supersize your superset." What are they? Can you think of other motives that might play a role in driving such obsessive behavior? How important are these motives for college-age men?

3. Heterosexuals, both male and female, have always wanted to be attractive to the opposite sex—as Quart points out, there's nothing new about this. But so far as male body building is concerned, female response is often not as positive as many men imagine. Why is that?

FOR RESEARCH, DISCUSSION, AND MEDIATION

In our experience, people that devote much of their time to physical conditioning are "true believers," strong defenders of what they do. In contrast, most medical doctors and other health professionals are just as convinced that moderate exercise is the way to go. Do some research on the benefits of exercise and its role in developing and maintaining good health and self-image. Then address these questions: What role should exercise play in the lives of people whose general health permits exercise? At what point does a good thing become too much? For those people who want to go beyond being in good physical condition, what's the safest, healthiest way to cultivate a higher level of development?

Write a paper that takes a middle ground between obsessive conditioning on the one side and moderate exercise on the other.

Does Money Buy Happiness?

DON PECK AND ROSS DOUTHAT

In the following selection, which appeared originally in *The Atlantic Monthly,* Peck and Douthat report on research into the connection between per capita income and self-reported happiness in various countries around the world. Some of the findings may surprise you.

1   Historically the province of philosophers and theologians, the relationship between wealth and happiness has recently been taken up by a cadre of social scientists seeking to quantify and compare levels of well-being worldwide.

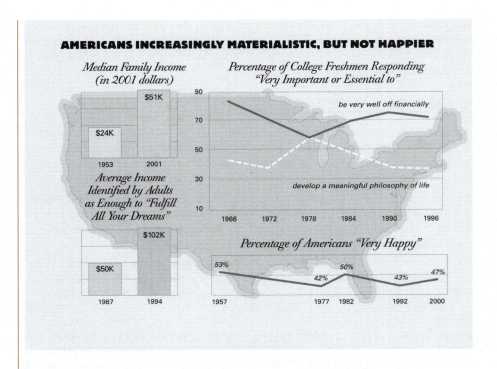

The results of their research, thus far, are clear: money does buy happiness—but only to a point. Study after study shows that the inhabitants of richer countries are, on average, significantly happier than those of poorer ones. This is true even controlling for other variables that rise with income and that may influence personal happiness: education, political freedom, women's rights, and so forth. National income appears to be one of the best single predictors of overall well-being, explaining perhaps 40 percent of the difference in contentment among nations. For individual countries, with few exceptions, self-reported happiness has increased as incomes have risen.

The chart on pages 334–335 shows survey data on happiness for fifty-four countries, compiled throughout the 1990s by the Dutch sociologist Ruut Veenhoven. These data indicate a robust, if inexact, relationship between per capita income and "life satisfaction." Veenhoven's findings provide an unexpectedly sunny view. First, they indicate that most people worldwide say they are fairly happy. It is debatable whether most people have ever viewed life as nasty, brutish, and short; but on balance, they don't now. (Even citizens of impoverished or politically star-crossed countries, such as the Philippines and Romania, or of countries with high levels of income inequality, such as Brazil and the United States, report being at least somewhat happy on average.) Moreover, though the fact that richer countries are in general happier than poorer ones may not seem terribly surprising, it does suggest that continuing economic development will generate rising happiness worldwide.

That said, there are clear limits to what money can buy. Although improvements in income produce large improvements in happiness for poor countries—gains that

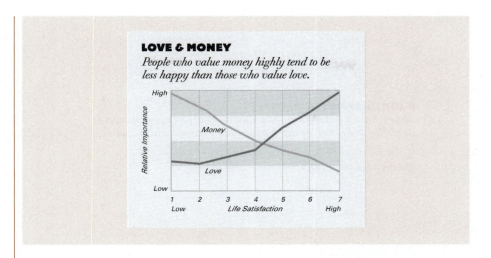

LOVE & MONEY

People who value money highly tend to be less happy than those who value love.

continue to rise with income well above the level where basic food, shelter, and sanitation needs have been met—the law of diminishing returns takes effect at higher income levels. Above about $20,000 per capita, increases in wealth yield at best minimal increases in happiness. This effect takes place at both the individual and the societal level. In poor societies those at the top of the socioeconomic ladder are significantly happier than those at the bottom; in highly developed societies there is little class difference in happiness. (In fact, oddly, in wealthy nations both those in the top 10 percent of the socioeconomic spectrum and those in the bottom 50 percent appear to be slightly happier, on average, than those in between.)

5   Robert E. Lane, a political scientist at Yale, argues that the leveling off of happiness in wealthy societies reflects more than just diminishing returns. Lane suggests that happiness is derived largely from two sources—material comfort, and social and familial intimacy—that are often incompatible. Economic development increases material comfort, but it systematically weakens social and familial ties by encouraging mobility, commercializing relationships, and attenuating the bonds of both the extended and the nuclear family. In less developed countries, where social ties are often strong and money is scarce, this tradeoff works overwhelmingly to society's advantage—the gains in material comfort more than outweigh the slight declines in social connectedness. At some point, however, the balance tips and the happiness-diminishing effects of reduced social stability begin to outweigh the happiness-increasing effects of material gain. Lane believes that the United States has passed this tipping point, and that we will actually become unhappier as incomes rise further.

6   Lane's argument is controversial. It is unclear that happiness is actually falling in the United States. Clinical depression is rising, which Lane cites as one basis for his argument, but it still afflicts only a small percentage of the population. Nonetheless, it is true that happiness in the United States has not risen over the past fifty years, despite an average increase of more than 85 percent in the real value of family income. And although the weakening of the relationship between money

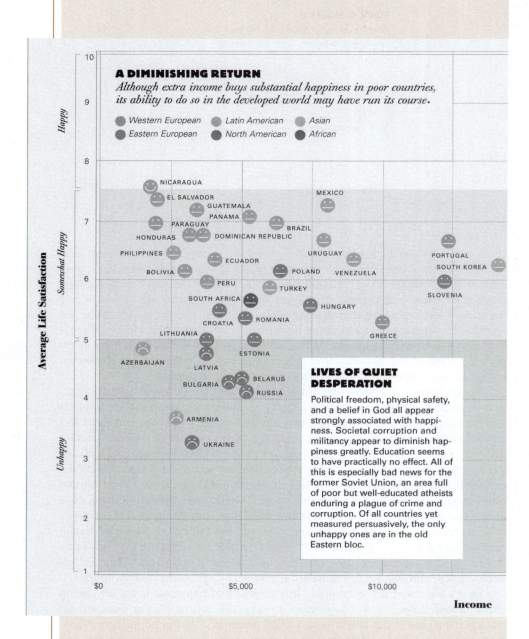

A DIMINISHING RETURN

Although extra income buys substantial happiness in poor countries, its ability to do so in the developed world may have run its course.

Western European   Latin American   Asian
Eastern European   North American   African

Average Life Satisfaction

Happy

Somewhat Happy

Unhappy

NICARAGUA
EL SALVADOR
GUATEMALA
PANAMA
MEXICO
PARAGUAY
BRAZIL
HONDURAS
DOMINICAN REPUBLIC
PHILIPPINES
ECUADOR
URUGUAY
PORTUGAL
BOLIVIA
POLAND
SOUTH KOREA
PERU
VENEZUELA
TURKEY
SLOVENIA
SOUTH AFRICA
HUNGARY
CROATIA
ROMANIA
LITHUANIA
GREECE
AZERBAIJAN
ESTONIA
LATVIA
BELARUS
BULGARIA
RUSSIA
ARMENIA
UKRAINE

LIVES OF QUIET DESPERATION

Political freedom, physical safety, and a belief in God all appear strongly associated with happiness. Societal corruption and militancy appear to diminish happiness greatly. Education seems to have practically no effect. All of this is especially bad news for the former Soviet Union, an area full of poor but well-educated atheists enduring a plague of crime and corruption. Of all countries yet measured persuasively, the only unhappy ones are in the old Eastern bloc.

$0 $5,000 $10,000

Income

SWITZERLAND

DENMARK

ICELAND   LUXEMBOURG   CANADA

IRELAND   SWEDEN

FINLAND   NETHERLANDS   NORWAY   U.S.A.
BELGIUM

U.K.   AUSTRALIA

ITALY

GERMANY

SPAIN

FRANCE   JAPAN

AUSTRIA

THE MYTH OF THE CONTENTED VILLAGER

Idyllic visions notwithstanding, there is little evidence to show that the residents of traditional villages and farming communities are particularly happy. In poor countries city-dwellers report themselves to be markedly happier than villagers. And surveys show these same villagers to be far more materialistic than urbanites, valuing money and material goods above friendship and family. Though rural residents in the United States say they are happy overall, they rate themselves as lonelier than suburbanites.

WHY ARE LATIN AMERICANS HAPPIER THAN THE JAPANESE?

Neither income nor any other quantifiable variable has fully explained cross-cultural differences in perceptions of well-being. The Japanese, for example, are far less happy than Japan's national income would suggest; life satisfaction in that country has not risen dramatically since the 1950s, despite strong income growth. Latin Americans, on the other hand, seem predisposed to happiness in spite of economic and political hardship. (The Japanese, for their part, seldom admit to being "very" anything in surveys, perhaps reflecting a cultural bias against standing out.) Thus, although social or economic changes can push happiness up or down, perceptions of well-being appear to be at least somewhat determined by a society's cultural norms.

$15,000 $20,000 $25,000 $30,000

Per Person

and contentment perhaps ought to have induced Americans to look elsewhere for sources of happiness, that hasn't happened. Indeed, as the graphs on pages 332 and 333 show, Americans have become *more* materialistic over the past three decades.

7   The Western notion of progress was shaped during a centuries-long period when rising wealth almost certainly bought rising happiness. Only recently have we left that era behind—and our society has not yet adjusted. Conditioned to value financial achievement, we may cling to materialism even as it makes the contentment we seek more elusive.

QUESTIONS FOR DISCUSSION

1. Peck and Douthat paraphrase Robert Lane's explanation of why happiness "levels off" as incomes rise (paragraph 5). Compare with John Schumaker's argument about the "happiness conspiracy" (pages 336–340). Does Schumaker's view confirm Lane's explanation?

2. Did the box labeled "The Myth of the Contented Villager" (page 335) surprise you? If so, in what way or ways exactly? If you live or have lived in a small town or a rural community, or have experience with one, would you say the global results agree with your sense of the level of happiness?

FOR RESEARCH, ANALYSIS, AND CONVINCING

Peck and Douthat deal with happiness worldwide; as a comparison, find one or two of the many existing studies of happiness in the United States. Study the data carefully, especially with regard to the sources of happiness. How much would you say that American happiness depends on our so-called consumer paradise? How much does it depend on other sources, such as "political freedom, physical safety, and a belief in God" cited in the article as important variables worldwide? (See "Lives of Quiet Desperation," page 334).

Write an essay defending your view of material wealth as a factor in happiness in the United States. Be sure to address the data indicating that happiness has not increased in the past half century despite an "85 percent [increase] in the real value of family income." Can this be explained simply by saying that we reached a "saturation point" years ago—that more money doesn't yield more happiness?

The Happiness Conspiracy: What Does It Mean to Be Happy in a Modern Consumer Society?

JOHN F. SCHUMAKER

John F. Schumaker, a clinical psychologist, was born in Wisconsin but now lives and practices in New Zealand. He has published nine books and many articles on culture and mental health. His most recent book is *In Search of Happiness: Understanding an Endangered State of Mind*. Schumaker's essay "The Happiness Conspiracy" appeared in the magazine *New Internationalist*.

1   "The trouble with normal is it always gets worse," sang the Canadian guitarist Bruce Cockburn back in 1983. Seems he was on to something. Normal doesn't seem to be working any longer. The new Holy Grail is happiness. At every turn are "how-to" happiness books, articles, TV and radio programs, videos, and websites. There are happiness institutes, camps, clubs, classes, cruises, workshops, and retreats. Universities are adding courses in Happiness Studies. Fast-growing professions include happiness counseling, happiness coaching, "life-lift" coaching, "joyology," and happiness science. Personal happiness is big business and everyone is selling it.

2   Being positive is mandatory, even with the planet in meltdown. Cynics and pessimists are running for cover while the cheerleaders are policing the game with an iron fist. Only the bravest are not being bullied into cheering up or at least shutting up.

3   But a society of "happichondriacs" isn't necessarily a healthy sign. No one is less able to sustain happiness than someone obsessed with feeling only happiness. A happy and meaningful existence depends on the ability to feel emotions other than happiness, as well as ones that compete with happiness.

4   "Happiness never appeared to me as an absolute aim," said Einstein. "I am even inclined to compare such moral aims to the ambitions of a pig. The ideals that have lighted my way are Kindness, Beauty and Truth."

5   If we've become pigs at the happiness trough, it's understandable. As higher systems of meaning have withered, life purpose has dwindled to feeling good. Innocence, the lifeblood of happiness, is obsolete. We live on cultural soil perfectly suited for depression.

6   Other happiness blockers include materialism, perpetual discontent, overcomplication, hypercompetition, stress, rage, boredom, loneliness, and existential confusion. We're removed from nature, married to work, adrift from family and friends, spiritually starved, sleep deprived, physically unfit, dumbed down, and enslaved to debt.

7   Health professionals face new epidemics of "hurry sickness," "toxic success syndrome," the "frantic family," the "over-commercialized child," and "pleonexia" or out-of-control greed.

8   Too much is no longer enough. Many are stretching themselves so far that they have difficulty feeling anything at all. At its heart the happiness boom is a metaphor for the modern struggle for meaning.

9   We laugh only a third as often as we did 50 years ago—hence the huge popularity of laughter clubs and laughter therapy. We make love less frequently and enjoy it less, even though sex is now largely deregulated and available in endless guilt-free varieties. Yet we're the least happy society in history if we measure happiness in terms of mental health, personal growth, or general sense of aliveness.

10   A society's dominant value system dictates how happiness is measured. The native Navajos in the southwest of the U.S. saw happiness as the attainment of universal beauty, or what they called Hozho. Their counterpart of "Have a nice day" was "May you walk in beauty."

11   Personal satisfaction is the most common way of measuring happiness today (via something called the Life Satisfaction Scale). This mirrors the supreme value that

consumer culture attaches to the romancing of desire and the satiation of the self. When measured this way, almost everyone seems pretty happy—even if it's primarily false needs being satisfied. A high percentage of depressed people even end up happy when "personal satisfaction" is the yardstick.

12   By the middle of the 19th century, social critics were already noticing how happiness was losing its social, spiritual, moral, and intellectual anchors and becoming a form of emotional masturbation. In his classic 1863 work, *Utilitarianism,* John Stuart Mill scorned this trend: "Better to be Socrates dissatisfied than a fool satisfied," he opined.

13   Total satisfaction can actually be a major obstacle to happiness. Artist Salvador Dali lamented: "There are days when I think I'm going to die from an overdose of satisfaction." To preserve the "rarity value" of life one must resist wrapping heaven around oneself. Keeping paradise at a distance, yet within reach, is a much better way of staying alive. People who have it all must learn the art of flirting with deprivation.

14   The highest forms of happiness have always been experienced and expressed as love. But happiness is being wooed in increasingly autistic ways that lack this vital dimension. In a recent survey only one percent of people indicated "true love" as what they wanted most in life. Our standard of living has increased but our standard of loving has plummeted.

15   The backlash against today's narcissistic happiness is rekindling interest in the ancient Greek philosophers who equated happiness with virtue. Especially celebrated by them were loyalty, friendship, moderation, honesty, compassion, and trust. Research shows that all these traits are in steep decline today—despite being happiness boosters. Like true love and true happiness, they have become uneconomic.

16   When author John Updike warned, "America is a vast conspiracy to make you happy," he was referring to the superficial mass happiness that prevails when economics successfully conspires to define our existence. I profit, therefore I am. To be happy, gulp something. Pay later.

17   Novelist J. D. Salinger was so unnerved by the happiness conspiracy that he confessed: "I'm a kind of paranoiac in reverse. I suspect people are plotting to make one happy." The wrong type of happiness is worse than no happiness at all.

18   Governments are the biggest players in the happiness conspiracy. Any political action aimed at a more people-friendly or planet-friendly happiness is certain to be met with fierce resistance. The best consumers are itchy narcissists who hop, skip, and jump from one fleeting desire to the next, never deeply satisfied, but always in the process of satisfying themselves. Our entire socioeconomic system is designed to spew out this type of "ideal citizen." Contentment is the single greatest threat to the economics of greed and consumer happiness.

19   Our ignorance of happiness is revealed by the question on everyone's lips: "Does money make us happy?" The head of a U.S. aid agency in Kenya commented recently that volunteers are predictably dumbstruck and confused by the zest and jubilance of the Africans. It's become a cliché for them to say: "The people are so poor, they have nothing—and yet they have so much joy and seem so happy."

20   I never knew how measly my own happiness was until one day in 1978 when I found myself stranded in a remote western Tanzanian village. I saw real happiness

for the first time—since then I have learned that it has vastly more to do with cultural factors than genetics or the trendy notion of personal "choice."

21   So it didn't surprise me that an African nation, Nigeria, was found recently to be the world's happiest country. The study of "happy societies" is awakening us to the importance of social connectedness, spirituality, simplicity, modesty of expectations, gratitude, patience, touch, music, movement, play, and "down time."

22   The small Himalayan nation of Ladakh is one of the best-documented examples of a "happy society." As Helena Norberg-Hodge writes in *Ancient Future,* Ladakhis were a remarkably joyous and vibrant people who lived in harmony with their harsh environment. Their culture generated mutual respect, community-mindedness, an eagerness to share, reverence for nature, thankfulness, and love of life. Their value system bred tenderness, empathy, politeness, spiritual awareness, and environmental conservation. Violence, discrimination, avarice, and abuse of power were nonexistent while depressed, burned-out people were nowhere to be found.

23   But in 1980 consumer capitalism came knocking with its usual bounty of raised hopes and social diseases. The following year, Ladakh's freshly appointed Development Commissioner announced: "If Ladakh is ever going to be developed, we have to figure out how to make these people more greedy." The developers triumphed, and a greed economy took root. The issues nowadays are declining mental health, family breakdown, crime, land degradation, unemployment, a widening gap between rich and poor, pollution, and sprawl.

24   Writer Ted Trainer says before 1980 the people of Ladakh were "notoriously happy." He sees in their tragic story a sobering lesson about our cherished goals of development, growth, and progress. For the most part these are convenient myths that are much better at producing happy economies than happy people.

25   When normality fails, as it has today, happiness becomes a form of protest. Some disillusioned folks are resorting to "culture jamming" and "subvertisements" to expose the hollow core of commercial society. Others are seeking refuge in various forms of primitivism and eco-primitivism. Spurring this on is intriguing evidence from the field of cognitive archaeology suggesting that our Paleolithic ancestors were probably happier and far more alive than people today. The shift toward "Paleo" and "Stone Age" diets also reflects the belief that they had happier bodies.

26   There is an exquisite line by the philosopher Friedrich Nietsche which touches on one of the keys to happiness: the need to appreciate "the least, the softest, lightest, a lizard's rustling, a breath, a moment." Paradoxically, happiness is closer when we kneel than when we soar. Our own nothingness can be a great source of joy.

27   We usually hitch our emotional wagons to ego, ambition, personal power, and the spectacular. But all of these are surprising flops when it comes to happiness. Today's "success" has become a blueprint for failure.

28   Visionaries tell us that the only happiness that makes sense at this perilous juncture in Earth's history is "sustainable happiness." All worthwhile happiness is life-supporting. But so much of what makes us happy in the age of consumerism is dependent upon the destruction and over-exploitation of nature. A sustainable happiness implies that we take responsibility for the wider contexts in which we live and for the well-being of future generations.

29   Sustainable happiness harks back to the classical Greek philosophies in viewing ethical living as a legitimate vehicle for human happiness. Compassion in particular plays a central role. In part it rests on the truth that we can be happy in planting the seeds of happiness, even if we might miss the harvest.

30   Some argue that as a society we are too programmed to selfishness and over-consumption for a sustainable happiness to take root. Democracy itself is a problem when the majority itches for the wrong things. But if we manage to take the first few steps, we may rediscover that happiness resonates most deeply when it has a price.

31   The greatest irony in the search for happiness is that it is never strictly personal. For happiness to be mature and heartfelt, it must be shared—whether by those around us or by tomorrow's children. If not, happiness can be downright depressing.

QUESTIONS FOR DISCUSSION

1. "Happiness never appeared to me as an absolute aim," Schumaker quotes Einstein as saying. What does this mean? If happiness is not an absolute aim, how does it relate to other aims or purposes?

2. Paragraph 6 sums up the author's critique of consumer society. Do you agree with what he says? If so, what evidence from your own experience can you cite as support? If not, do you think that he is misgauging our happiness or that genuine "happiness blockers" are other than he says they are?

3. Schumaker refers to the difference between "happy economics . . . [and] happy people" (paragraph 24). That is, we are bombarded with news about the economy when it is doing well and even more when it is doing badly. But we hear little about what makes for happy people. What makes you happy? How dependent is your happiness on money?

FOR RESEARCH AND PERSUASION

With the economy in worldwide recession recently, the case for what Schumaker calls "sustainable happiness" has been a hard sell. But the truth is that now billions of people all over the world aspire to live more like middle- or upper-middle-class Americans. Research the relationship between prosperity, the exhaustion of natural resources, and the destruction of ecosystems. The World Watch Institute is a good place to start.

Write an essay persuading Americans in your age group that sustainability is the issue that matters and that people your age should lead the way in living in a more sustainable fashion.

FOR FURTHER READING

Berger, Arthur Asa. *Shop 'Til You Drop*. Rowman & Littlefield, 2005.

Brooks, David. *On Paradise Drive: How We Live Now (And Always Have) in the Future Tense*. Simon & Schuster, 2004.

Easterbrook, Gregg. *The Progress Paradox: How Life Gets Better While People Feel Worse*. Random House, 2004.

———. "The Real Truth about Money." *Time,* 17 Jan. 2005, pp. 32–34, content.time.com/time/magazine/article/0,9171,1015883,00.html.

Glickman, Lawrence B. *Consumer Society in American History: A Reader.* Cornell UP, 1999.

Milner, Murray, Jr. *Freaks, Geeks, and Cool Kids: American Teenagers, Schools, and the Culture of Consumption.* Routledge, 2004.

Sachs, Jeffrey D. *The Price of Civilization: Reawakening American Virtue and Prosperity.* Random House, 2011.

Schor, Juliet. *Born to Buy: The Commercialized Child and the New Consumer Culture.* Scribner, 2004.

Schumaker, John F. *In Search of Happiness: Understanding an Endangered State of Mind.* Penguin New Zealand, 2006.

Speth, James Gustave. *America the Possible: Manifesto for a New Economy.* Yale UP, 2012.

Twitchell, James B. *Adcult USA: The Triumph of Advertising in American Culture.* Columbia UP, 1997.

———. *Lead Us Into Temptation: The Triumph of American Materialism.* Columbia UP, 1999.

———. *Living It Up: America's Love Affair with Luxury.* Simon & Schuster, 2003.

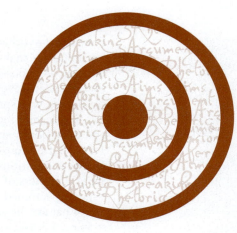

CHAPTER 13

Global Warming: What Should Be Done?

Text of the American College and University Presidents' Climate
    Commitment *344*

National Geographic, Global Warming: An Overview *347*

Scientific American, 15 Ways to Make a Wedge *352*

Bill Blakemore, Who's "Most to Blame" for Global Warming? *353*

Gregg Easterbrook, Some Convenient Truths *358*

Tim Appenzeller, The Coal Paradox *362*

Al Gore, Existing Technologies for Reducing CO$_2$ Emissions *367*

Michelle Nijhuis, Selling the Wind *368*

Union of Concerned Scientists, Ten Personal Solutions *372*

William F. Ruddiman, Consuming Earth's Gifts *375*

For Further Reading *378*

There's no issue quite like global warming. A strong consensus exists among scientists that the Earth is warming up at an alarming rate. Natural processes are involved, but most of the warming is caused by human activities, especially the burning of fossil fuels, mainly coal and oil. If something is not done and done soon—within the next decade or two—we face a long list of trouble: rising sea levels that will threaten coastal cities, droughts that will make farming difficult or impossible, increasingly destructive weather (such as the hurricane that devastated New York and New Jersey), complete loss of the already stressed coral reefs, widespread extinction of species in the ocean and on land, and so on.

Yet despite repeated warnings from scientists, often reported in the press and television news, the American public as a whole lacks a sense of urgency. The scientific consensus is not having the impact it should, and too many people think questions that have been answered with a high degree of probability are still matters of serious dispute. This chapter attempts to engage the genuine issues, as summed up in its title, What should be done?

What are the genuine issues? Some are technological. We have many "green" sources of power—wind, solar, ethanol produced from corn, biodiesel, and so on. Which should we use and in what combination? We have a 200-year supply of coal—can we use some of it while making the transition to cleaner power sources without releasing the current huge discharge of carbon dioxide (CO_2) into our atmosphere? These and many other technological issues are certainly arguable.

Other questions are economic. What approach to reducing greenhouse gases will prove least expensive to consumers and most profitable for industry and investors, many of whom are increasingly aware of both the wisdom and the money in going green? It is not obvious where economic commitments should be.

Then there are political questions. What will persuade our energy companies to think beyond fossil fuels? How can we secure the cooperation of countries like Saudi Arabia, whose wealth is too dependent on oil exports? While reducing our own greenhouse gas emissions, how can we help developing countries, like China, from becoming polluters as bad as or worse than the United States and Europe currently are? Again, the best political course of action is far from settled.

This chapter explores many facets of the global warming problem, but not all of them. It is meant to encourage you to explore both problems and solutions in greater depth. We think learning to live in harmony with our planet may be *the* most important issue we face.

Text of the American College and University Presidents' Climate Commitment

Established in 2006, the American College and University Presidents' Climate Commitment (ACUPCC) now includes a long list of signatories who have endorsed meaningful steps to make their campuses "climate neutral"—that is, the goal of emitting no more greenhouse gases than they eliminate by such measures as planting trees. The existence of this high-profile organization affirms both the seriousness of global warming and the commitment required to bring it under control.

More than ever, universities must take leadership roles to address the grand challenges of the twenty-first century, and climate change is paramount amongst these.

—Michael M. Crow, President, Arizona State University

American College and University Presidents' Climate Commitment.
www.presidentsclimatecommitment.org

1 We, the undersigned presidents and chancellors of colleges and universities, are deeply concerned about the unprecedented scale and speed of global warming and its potential for large-scale, adverse health, social, economic and ecological effects. We recognize the scientific consensus that global warming is real and is largely being caused by humans. We further recognize the need to reduce the global emission of greenhouse gases by 80% by mid-century at the latest, in order to avert the worst impacts of global warming and to reestablish the more stable climatic conditions that have made human progress over the last 10,000 years possible.

2 While we understand that there might be short-term challenges associated with this effort, we believe that there will be great short-, medium-, and long-term economic, health, social and environmental benefits, including achieving energy independence for the U.S. as quickly as possible.

3 We believe colleges and universities must exercise leadership in their communities and throughout society by modeling ways to minimize global warming emissions, and by providing the knowledge and the educated graduates to achieve climate neutrality. Campuses that address the climate challenge by reducing global warming emissions and by integrating sustainability into their curriculum will better serve their students and meet their social mandate to help create a thriving, ethical and civil society. These colleges and universities will be providing students with the knowledge and skills needed to address the critical, systemic challenges faced by the world in this new century and enable them to benefit from the economic opportunities that will arise as a result of solutions they develop.

4 We further believe that colleges and universities that exert leadership in addressing climate change will stabilize and reduce their long-term energy costs, attract

excellent students and faculty, attract new sources of funding, and increase the support of alumni and local communities. Accordingly, we commit our institutions to taking the following steps in pursuit of climate neutrality.

1. Initiate the development of a comprehensive plan to achieve climate neutrality as soon as possible.

    a. Within two months of signing this document, create institutional structures to guide the development and implementation of the plan.

    b. Within one year of signing this document, complete a comprehensive inventory of all greenhouse gas emissions (including emissions from electricity, heating, commuting, and air travel) and update the inventory every other year thereafter.

    c. Within two years of signing this document, develop an institutional action plan for becoming climate neutral, which will include:

        i.   A target date for achieving climate neutrality as soon as possible.

        ii. Interim targets for goals and actions that will lead to climate neutrality.

        iii. Actions to make climate neutrality and sustainability a part of the curriculum and other educational experience for all students.

        iv. Actions to expand research or other efforts necessary to achieve climate neutrality.

        v.   Mechanisms for tracking progress on goals and actions.

2. Initiate two or more of the following tangible actions to reduce greenhouse gases while the more comprehensive plan is being developed.

    a. Establish a policy that all new campus construction will be built to at least the U.S. Green Building Council's LEED Silver standard or equivalent.

    b. Adopt an energy-efficient appliance purchasing policy requiring purchase of ENERGY STAR certified products in all areas for which such ratings exist.

    c. Establish a policy of offsetting all greenhouse gas emissions generated by air travel paid for by our institution.

    d. Encourage use of and provide access to public transportation for all faculty, staff, students and visitors at our institution.

    e. Within one year of signing this document, begin purchasing or producing at least 15% of our institution's electricity consumption from renewable sources.

    f. Establish a policy or a committee that supports climate and sustainability shareholder proposals at companies where our institution's endowment is invested.

    g. Participate in the Waste Minimization component of the national RecycleMania competition, and adopt 3 or more associated measures to reduce waste.

3. Make the action plan, inventory, and periodic progress reports publicly available by providing them to the Association for the Advancement of Sustainability in Higher Education (AASHE) for posting and dissemination.

5 | In recognition of the need to build support for this effort among college and university administrations across America, we will encourage other presidents to join this effort and become signatories to this commitment.

Signed,

The Signatories of the American College & University Presidents, Climate Commitment

---

FOR RESEARCH AND DISCUSSION

To save space, we did not include the long list of colleges and universities that have signed the Presidents' Climate Commitment. The list is available online and worth consulting. For instance, in our own state, Texas, some of our most prominent schools are not among the signatories, probably because much of the money that supports higher education comes from fossil fuel interests.

If your school is on the list, find out why it is and what is being done to carry out the promises made in the document. In your view, is the commitment serious and sustained, or just a public relations ploy without much substance? If your school is not on the list, find out why it is not and what could be done to make your school more environmentally aware and responsible. Discuss what you discover from research, including the economic and political forces that have so much to do with a college or university's priorities and decision making.

Global Warming: An Overview

NATIONAL GEOGRAPHIC

> This recent overview of global warming was taken from *National Geographic's* website, which has much more information than we have space to include here.

1 | Glaciers are melting, sea levels are rising, cloud forests are drying, and wildlife is scrambling to keep pace. It's becoming clear that humans have caused most of the past century's warming by releasing heat-trapping gases as we power our modern lives. Called greenhouse gases, their levels are higher now than in the last 650,000 years.

2 | We call the result global warming, but it is causing a set of changes to the Earth's climate, or long-term weather patterns, that varies from place to place. As the Earth spins each day, the new heat swirls with it, picking up moisture over the oceans, rising here, settling there. It's changing the rhythms of climate that all living things have come to rely upon.

3 | What will we do to slow this warming? How will we cope with the changes we've already set into motion? While we struggle to figure it all out, the face of the Earth as we know it—coasts, forests, farms and snow-capped mountains—hangs in the balance.

WHAT IS THE GREENHOUSE EFFECT?

4   The "greenhouse effect" is the warming that happens when certain gases in Earth's atmosphere trap heat. These gases let in light but keep heat from escaping, like the glass walls of a greenhouse.

5   First, sunlight shines onto the Earth's surface, where it is absorbed and then radiates back into the atmosphere as heat. In the atmosphere, greenhouse gases trap some of this heat, and the rest escapes into space. The more greenhouse gases are in the atmosphere, the more heat gets trapped.

6   Scientists have known about the greenhouse effect since 1824, when Joseph Fourier calculated that the Earth would be much colder if it had no atmosphere. This greenhouse effect is what keeps the Earth's climate livable. Without it, the Earth's surface would be an average of about 60 degrees Fahrenheit cooler. In 1895, the Swedish chemist Svante Arrhenius discovered that humans could enhance the greenhouse effect by making carbon dioxide, a greenhouse gas. He kicked off 100 years of climate research that has given us a sophisticated understanding of global warming.

7   Levels of greenhouse gases (GHGs) have gone up and down over the Earth's history, but they have been fairly constant for the past few thousand years. Global average temperatures have stayed fairly constant over that time as well, until recently. Through the burning of fossil fuels and other GHG emissions, humans are enhancing the greenhouse effect and warming Earth.

8   Scientists often use the term "climate change" instead of global warming. This is because as the Earth's average temperature climbs, winds and ocean currents move

heat around the globe in ways that can cool some areas, warm others, and change the amount of rain and snow falling. As a result, the climate changes differently in different areas.

WHAT CAUSES GLOBAL WARMING?

9   Scientists have spent decades figuring out what is causing global warming. They've looked at the natural cycles and events that are known to influence climate. But the amount and pattern of warming that's been measured can't be explained by these factors alone. The only way to explain the pattern is to include the effect of green-house gases (GHGs) emitted by humans.

10   To bring all this information together, the United Nations formed a group of scientists called the Intergovernmental Panel on Climate Change, or IPCC. The IPCC meets every few years to review the latest scientific findings and write a report sum-marizing all that is known about global warming. Each report represents a consensus, or agreement, among hundreds of leading scientists.

11   One of the first things scientists learned is that there are several greenhouse gases responsible for warming, and humans emit them in a variety of ways. Most come from the combustion of fossil fuels in cars, factories and electricity production. The gas responsible for the most warming is carbon dioxide, also called CO_2. Other contributors include methane released from landfills and agriculture (especially from the digestive systems of grazing animals), nitrous oxide from fertilizers, gases used for refrigeration and industrial processes, and the loss of forests that would otherwise store CO_2.

12   Different greenhouse gases have very different heat-trapping abilities. Some of them can even trap more heat than CO_2. A molecule of methane produces more than 20 times the warming of a molecule of CO_2. Nitrous oxide is 300 times more power-ful than CO_2. Other gases, such as chlorofluorocarbons (which have been banned in much of the world because they also degrade the ozone layer), have heat-trapping potential thousands of times greater than CO_2. But because their concentrations are much lower than CO_2, none of these gases adds as much warmth to the atmosphere as CO_2 does.

13   In order to understand the effects of all the gases together, scientists tend to talk about all greenhouse gases in terms of the equivalent amount of CO_2. Since 1990, yearly emissions have gone up by about 6 billion metric tons of "carbon dioxide equivalent" worldwide, more than a 20 percent increase.

AREN'T TEMPERATURE CHANGES NATURAL?

14   The average global temperature and concentrations of carbon dioxide (one of the major greenhouse gases) have fluctuated on a cycle of hundreds of thousands of years as the Earth's position relative to the sun has varied. As a result, ice ages have come and gone.

15   However, for thousands of years now, emissions of GHGs to the atmosphere have been balanced out by GHGs that are naturally absorbed. As a result, GHG con-centrations and temperature have been fairly stable. This stability has allowed human civilization to develop within a consistent climate.

16   Occasionally, other factors briefly influence global temperatures. Volcanic eruptions, for example, emit particles that temporarily cool the Earth's surface. But these have no lasting effect beyond a few years. Other cycles, such as El Niño, also work on fairly short and predictable cycles.

17   Now, humans have increased the amount of carbon dioxide in the atmosphere by more than a third since the industrial revolution. Changes this large have historically taken thousands of years, but are now happening over the course of decades.

WHY IS GLOBAL WARMING A CONCERN?

18   The rapid rise in greenhouse gases is a problem because it is changing the climate faster than some living things may be able to adapt. Also, a new and more unpredictable climate poses unique challenges to all life.

19   Historically, Earth's climate has regularly shifted back and forth between temperatures like those we see today and temperatures cold enough that large sheets of ice covered much of North America and Europe. The difference between average global temperatures today and during those ice ages is only about 5 degrees Celsius (9 degrees Fahrenheit), and these swings happen slowly, over hundreds of thousands of years.

20   Now, with concentrations of greenhouse gases rising, Earth's remaining ice sheets (such as Greenland and Antarctica) are starting to melt too. The extra water could potentially raise sea levels significantly.

21   As the mercury rises, the climate can change in unexpected ways. In addition to sea levels rising, weather can become more extreme. This means more intense major storms, more rain followed by longer and drier droughts (a challenge for growing crops), changes in the ranges in which plants and animals can live, and loss of water supplies that have historically come from glaciers.

22   Scientists are already seeing some of these changes occurring more quickly than they had expected. According to the Intergovernmental Panel on Climate Change, eleven of the twelve hottest years since thermometer readings became available occurred between 1995 and 2006.

23   Some impacts from increasing temperatures are already happening.

- Ice is melting worldwide, especially at the Earth's poles. This includes mountain glaciers, ice sheets covering West Antarctica and Greenland, and Arctic sea ice.

- Researcher Bill Fraser has tracked the decline of the Adélie penguins on Antarctica, where their numbers have fallen from 32,000 breeding pairs to 11,000 in 30 years.

- Sea level rise became faster over the last century.

- Some butterflies, foxes, and alpine plants have moved farther north or to higher, cooler areas.

- Precipitation (rain and snowfall) has increased across the globe, on average.

- Spruce bark beetles have boomed in Alaska thanks to 20 years of warm summers. The insects have chewed up 4 million acres of spruce trees.

24   Other effects could happen later this century, if warming continues.

- Sea levels are expected to rise between 7 and 23 inches (18 and 59 centimeters) by the end of the century, and continued melting at the poles could add between 4 and 8 inches (10 to 20 centimeters).
- Hurricanes and other storms are likely to become stronger.
- Species that depend on one another may become out of sync. For example, plants could bloom earlier than their pollinating insects become active.
- Floods and droughts will become more common. Rainfall in Ethiopia, where droughts are already common, could decline by 10 percent over the next 50 years.
- Less fresh water will be available. If the Quelccaya ice cap in Peru continues to melt at its current rate, it will be gone by 2100, leaving thousands of people who rely on it for drinking water and electricity without a source of either.
- Some diseases will spread, such as malaria carried by mosquitoes.
- Ecosystems will change—some species will move farther north or become more successful; others won't be able to move and could become extinct. Wildlife research scientist Martyn Obbard has found that since the mid-1980s, with less ice on which to live and fish for food, polar bears have gotten considerably skinnier. Polar bear biologist Ian Stirling has found a similar pattern in Hudson Bay. He fears that if sea ice disappears, the polar bears will as well.

(*National Geographic*'s source for climate information: Intergovernmental Panel on Climate Change, *Climate Change 2007* (Fourth Assessment Report), 2007)

QUESTIONS FOR DISCUSSION

1. What are the major sources of human-caused greenhouse gas emissions?
2. The article offers examples of short-term consequences of global warming. What are they? In your view, which are the most important?
3. The article offers examples of long-term consequences of global warming. What are they? In your view, which are the most important?

FOR RESEARCH AND DISCUSSION

The article is a helpful overview, but there is much more to know about global warming or climate change. There is a wealth of information, for instance, online. Go to your search engine (for example, Google) and enter "advanced search." Browse the items that come up when you enter "global warming" and "climate change" to isolate topics worth investigating in more detail. For instance, the permafrost in the Arctic region is thawing, and as it thaws it will release huge quantities of methane gas, a much more powerful greenhouse gas than carbon dioxide.

By yourself or with two or three classmates, research one of these topics further. Do the reading and share the information you uncover. Then discuss the conclusions and implications of our current knowledge. What can we do now to reduce the impact of global warming? What should we plan to do over the next ten to twenty years?

15 Ways to Make a Wedge

SCIENTIFIC AMERICAN

This chart comes from *Scientific American*. It is helpful as a way of envisioning the many routes to reducing global warming and as a reminder that only a multifaceted approach will yield satisfactory results.

An overall carbon strategy for the next half a century produces seven wedges' worth of emissions reductions. Here are 15 technologies from which those seven

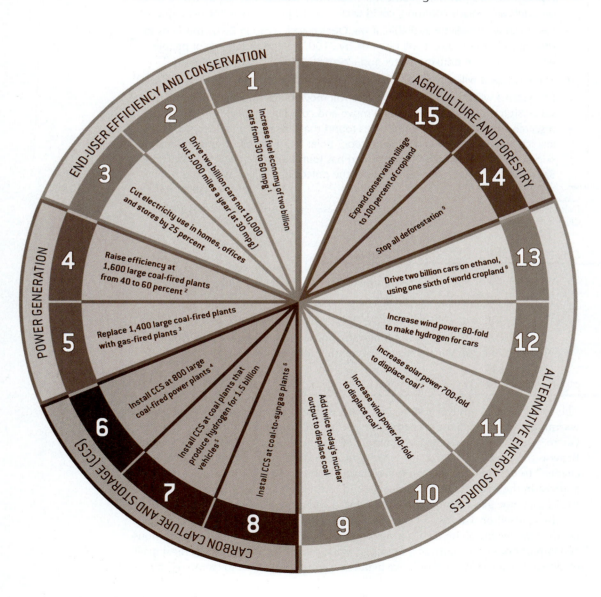

END-USER EFFICIENCY AND CONSERVATION

1 — Increase fuel economy of two billion cars from 30 to 60 mpg[1]

2 — Drive two billion cars not 10,000 but 5,000 miles a year (at 30 mpg)

3 — Cut electricity use in homes, offices and stores by 25 percent

POWER GENERATION

4 — Raise efficiency at 1,600 large coal-fired plants from 40 to 60 percent[2]

5 — Replace 1,400 large coal-fired plants with gas-fired plants[3]

CARBON CAPTURE AND STORAGE (CCS)

6 — Install CCS at 800 large coal-fired power plants[4]

7 — Install CCS at coal plants that produce hydrogen for 1.5 billion vehicles[5]

8 — Install CCS at coal-to-syngas plants[6]

9 — Add twice today's nuclear output to displace coal[7]

10 — Increase wind power 40-fold to displace coal[7]

11 — Increase solar power 700-fold to displace coal[7]

12 — Increase wind power 80-fold to make hydrogen for cars

ALTERNATIVE ENERGY SOURCES

13 — Drive two billion cars on ethanol, using one sixth of world cropland[8]

AGRICULTURE AND FORESTRY

14 — Stop all deforestation[9]

15 — Expand conservation tillage to 100 percent of cropland

can be chosen. Each of these measures, when phased in over 50 years, prevents the release of 26 billion tons of carbon. Leaving one wedge blank symbolizes that this is by no means exhaustive.

NOTES

[1] World fleet size in 2056 could well be two billon cars. Assume they average 10,000 miles a year.

[2] "Large" is one gigawatt (GW) capacity. Plants run 90 percent of the time.

[3] Here and below, assume coal plants run 90 percent of the time at 50 percent efficiency. Present coal power output is equivalent to 800 such plants.

[4] Assume 90 percent of CO_2 is captured.

[5] Assume a car (10,000 miles a year, 60 miles per gallon equivalent) requires 170 kilograms of hydrogen a year.

[6] Assume 30 million barrels of synfuels a day, about a third of today's total oil production. Assume half of carbon originally in the coal is captured.

[7] Assume wind and solar produce, on average, 30 percent of peak power. Thus replace 2,100 GW of 90-percent-time coal power with 2,100 GW (peak) wind or solar plus 1,400 GW of load-following coal power, for net displacement of 700 GW.

[8] Assume 60-mpg cars, 10,000 miles a year, biomass yield of 15 tons a hectare, and negligible fossil-fuel inputs. World cropland is 1,500 million hectares.

[9] Carbon emissions from deforestation are currently about two billion tons a year. Assume that by 2056 the rate falls by half in the business-as-usual projection and to zero in the flat path.

Illustration by Janet Chao from Robert H. Socolow and Stephen W. Pacala, "A Plan to Keep Carbon on Track," *Scientific American,* Sept. 2006. Reprinted by permission of Janet Chao.

FOR DISCUSSION AND RESEARCH

Some of the fifteen wedges are clear enough, such as increasing fuel economy in cars and trucks. The less gasoline and diesel we burn, the less carbon dioxide escapes from exhaust tailpipes into the air. Others may not be so clear, such as carbon capture and storage. In class, discuss all the wedges, listing the ones that are unfamiliar and the ones that are familiar but not understood.

Individuals or groups in the class should find out more about any of the wedges the class knows little about or does not understand. Short oral reports to the class will help bring everyone up to speed on all the existing and developing methods for reducing carbon dioxide emissions.

Another approach is to divide the class into five groups and assign them one of the categories on the outer edge of the circle. Each group should investigate its category in depth and report to the class. The advantage of this approach is that even familiar technologies, such as solar power, are in constant development and need to be grasped in considerable detail to appreciate their potential and limitations.

Who's "Most to Blame" for Global Warming?

BILL BLAKEMORE

In this 2012 article from ABC News online, Bill Blakemore answers the question posed in the title in a way that takes into account more than current levels of CO_2 pollution per year. In relation to total population, the United States is most to blame; however, the United Kingdom, in relation to its population, has polluted the most over time because the Industrial Revolution began in Britain and thus it has been polluting longer. Finally, though China pollutes now more than anyone else, because its turn to modern industry has been relatively recent, its total contribution is still far behind either the United States or Britain. Clearly we have to think about this question in more complicated ways. Just as clearly, regardless of blame, CO_2 emissions worldwide must be significantly reduced.

1   Who's most to blame for global warming? Nobody meant it to happen. But it has, and there's no debate among the world's scientists about which country is "most responsible." That is, about which nation has injected the greatest amount of the heat-trapping invisible gas CO_2 into the atmosphere, where a lot of it remains for years, piling up and only adding to the heat.

2   The answer: the United States has, with China a distant second.

3   And figured on a per person basis, the "most responsible" is the United Kingdom, with the United States a close second, Germany a close third, and China a distant seventh.

4   If you're surprised the "most to blame" isn't China, the explanation is simple: In about 2007, China did pass the United States in putting the greatest amount of CO_2 into the air *per year,* but China's economic boom only got started recently and they still have a couple of decades to go (if there are no drastic changes) before they catch up with the United States in the total cumulative amount of heat-trapping CO_2 they will have been piling up in the air.

5   (Regarding the *per person* way of thinking, the United Kingdom's population is about 62 million, America's is just over 310 million, Germany's about 82 million, and China's about 1.4 billion.)

6   The graphs below from NASA show all this responsibility in simple form. . . .

SIMPLE FACT #1:

7   A significant portion of the heat-trapping CO_2 humans put into the air stays there for years—some for 100 years, and even much longer.

8   Note that, after falling out of the atmosphere quickly during the first 50 years to about a third, the "decay" of the CO_2 emissions slows dramatically. Twenty-seven percent of it is still up there after 100 years, 17 percent after 500 years, and 14 percent after 1000 years. This "decay," say the scientists, is due to the fact that, over time, some of the excess CO_2 in the air is taken up by plants and absorbed into the soil, and some absorbed into seawater (which causes a second great problem, the growing acidification of the oceans.)

9   Scientists, including those at NASA's Goddard Institute for Space Studies, have determined that—as its widely respected longtime Director James Hansen tells ABC News—"climate change is proportional to the cumulative emissions." In other words, the build-up of global warming over the past couple of centuries has increased at rates directly proportional to the total amount of emissions that humans have been putting into the air . . . even though some of those emissions are eventually absorbed back out of the air.

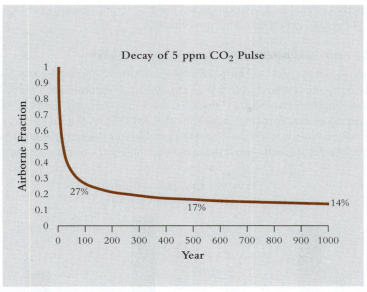

The Curvature of CO$_2$ Absorption
Note that it takes centuries for nature to deal with manmade pollution.

10   **SIMPLE FACT #2:**

The nation that has put the biggest *cumulative* portion of CO$_2$ into the air, thus helping heat the planet, is the USA.

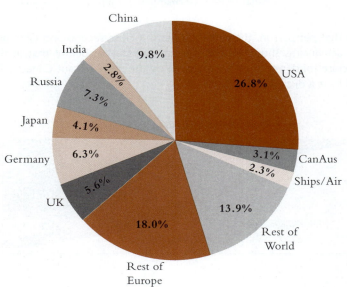

11   Note that China, India, Russia, Japan, Germany, and the UK are each a small fraction of the US . . . in total cumulative emissions.

12   **SIMPLE—AND SURPRISING—FACT #3:**

On a *per capita* basis, the biggest portion of cumulative CO_2 heating the planet was emitted not by the United States, but by the United Kingdom. That's partly because the United Kingdom created the "industrial revolution" around the year 1800, first by burning enormous amounts of coal. The UK led that revolution for so long that, on a per person basis, it is still the "most responsible" for the world's excess heat now and in the near future, with Americans a close second and Germans a close third.

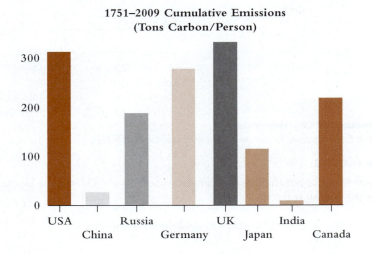

**1751–2009 Cumulative Emissions
(Tons Carbon/Person)**

13   Note that per person, the United States is a close second and Germany, whose industrial activity (as shown in this next graph) started before that in the United States, a close third, and they are followed by the more distant Canada, Russia and Japan. China is a distant seventh.

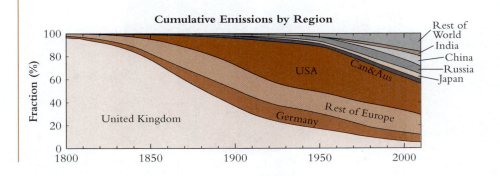

Cumulative Emissions by Region

14 | **SIMPLE FACT #4 (TO CLARIFY ANY CONFUSION ABOUT CHINA'S ROLE):**

China's economic boom only got going recently, and only started producing more CO_2 emissions *per year* than the United States in about 2007. That's why its cumulative contribution to the heat-trapping greenhouse gases is still a distant second to that of the United States. At current rates, China won't catch up to the United States for a couple of decades.

In the single year of 2010, China's total emissions (23.9 percent of the world's emissions) exceeded America's (which were 17.2 percent).

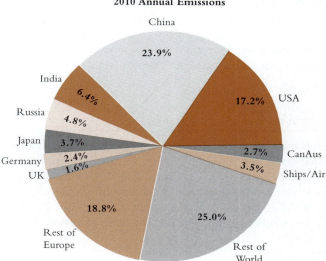

2010 Annual Emissions

15 | One more simple fact—one that bears deeply on all negotiations about how to deal with this global crisis. There are no borders in the world's constantly swirling atmosphere, nor in the ocean's many globe-girdling "conveyor belt" currents. Any heat-trapping and ocean-acidifying CO_2 gets pretty well mixed in everywhere soon after it is emitted, whatever and wherever the source.

16 | The damage so far—and for the next couple of decades (during which the heat is expected to keep rising, regardless of what nations agree to do)—will have been done more by the United States than by any other nation.

17 | But this is not, in the impression of this reporter, the main reason the countries of the world have been hoping Washington will take the lead in dealing with it. Government leaders in Europe, China, India, Russia, the Middle East, Africa and Latin America have for many years expressed hope that the United States would become the global leader in forging binding agreements to drastically cut the heat-trapping CO_2 emissions worldwide. They apparently have done so mainly because they feel that the single greatest superpower would be able to set the

tone, not only because the United States is "most to blame" in the sense of having put the single largest amount of CO_2 up there. But the fact of America having emitted the most is still a major factor in the diplomatic requests for the US to take the lead.

QUESTIONS FOR DISCUSSION

1. According to climate experts, there is enough excess CO_2 in the atmosphere already to effect significant climate change, if all polluting stopped today. What in this article helps to explain that claim?

2. As Blakemore points out, no one intended to cause global warming, and until a few decades ago the problem was not on the world's mind, as it is for the most part now. Given this circumstance, in your view, who deserves blame now for not taking reasonable action to lessen the threat of global warming?

FOR RESEARCH AND CONVINCING

It is not entirely correct to say that the United States has not taken the lead in dealing with global warming. President Clinton, for example, played a major role in the negotiations that led to the Kyoto Protocol (1997), but the U.S. Senate failed to ratify the agreement. Do research on international efforts to reduce greenhouse gas emissions since Kyoto, paying special attention to the role the United States played. Then write a paper either defending what our country has done or specifying what more it should do.

Some Convenient Truths

GREGG EASTERBROOK

Gregg Easterbrook argues that both advocates of climate control and those who oppose it are guilty of "gloom and doom" attitudes. A few enlightened government policies that encourage the entrepreneurial spirit will solve the problem, he believes.

Easterbrook is a prominent journalist who writes often about scientific subjects. He is an editor for both *The Atlantic Monthly* and *New Republic* and the author of many books, including *The Progress Paradox*. The following article was originally published in *The Atlantic Monthly*.

1   If there is now a scientific consensus that global warming must be taken seriously, there is also a related political consensus: that the issue is Gloom City. In *An Inconvenient Truth*, Al Gore warns of sea levels rising to engulf New York and San Francisco and implies that only wrenching lifestyle sacrifice can save us. The opposing view is just as glum. Even mild restrictions on greenhouse gases could "cripple our economy," Republican Senator Kit Bond of Missouri said in 2003.

Other conservatives suggest that greenhouse-gas rules for Americans would be pointless anyway, owing to increased fossil-fuel use in China and India. When commentators hash this issue out, it's often a contest to see which side can sound more pessimistic.

2   Here's a different way of thinking about the greenhouse effect: that action to prevent runaway global warming may prove cheap, practical, effective, and totally consistent with economic growth. Which makes a body wonder: Why is such environmental optimism absent from American political debate?

3   Greenhouse gases are an air-pollution problem—and all previous air-pollution problems have been reduced faster and more cheaply than predicted, without economic harm. Some of these problems once seemed scary and intractable, just as greenhouse gases seem today. About forty years ago urban smog was increasing so fast that President Lyndon Johnson warned, "Either we stop poisoning our air or we become a nation [in] gas masks groping our way through dying cities." During Ronald Reagan's presidency, emissions of chlorofluorocarbons, or CFCs, threatened to deplete the stratospheric ozone layer. As recently as George H. W. Bush's administration, acid rain was said to threaten a "new silent spring" of dead Appalachian forests.

4   But in each case, strong regulations were enacted, and what happened? Since 1970, smog-forming air pollution has declined by a third to a half. Emissions of CFCs have been nearly eliminated, and studies suggest that ozone-layer replenishment is beginning. Acid rain, meanwhile, has declined by a third since 1990, while Appalachian forest health has improved sharply.

5   Most progress against air pollution has been cheaper than expected. Smog controls on automobiles, for example, were predicted to cost thousands of dollars for each vehicle. Today's new cars emit less than 2 percent as much smog-forming pollution as the cars of 1970, and the cars are still as affordable today as they were then. Acid-rain control has cost about 10 percent of what was predicted in 1990, when Congress enacted new rules. At that time, opponents said the regulations would cause a "clean-air recession"; instead, the economy boomed.

6   Greenhouse gases, being global, are the biggest air-pollution problem ever faced. And because widespread fossil-fuel use is inevitable for some time to come, the best-case scenario for the next few decades may be a slowing of the rate of greenhouse-gas buildup, to prevent runaway climate change. Still, the basic pattern observed in all other forms of air-pollution control—rapid progress at low cost—should repeat for greenhouse-gas controls.

7   Yet a paralyzing negativism dominates global-warming politics. Environmentalists depict climate change as nearly unstoppable; skeptics speak of the problem as either imaginary (the "greatest hoax ever perpetrated," in the words of Senator James Inhofe, chairman of the Senate's environment committee) or ruinously expensive to address.

8   Even conscientious politicians may struggle for views that aren't dismal. Mandy Grunwald, a Democratic political consultant, says, "When political candidates talk

about new energy sources, they use a positive, can-do vocabulary. Voters have personal experience with energy use, so they can relate to discussion of solutions. If you say a car can use a new kind of fuel, this makes intuitive sense to people. But global warming is of such scale and magnitude, people don't have any commonsense way to grasp what the solutions would be. So political candidates tend to talk about the greenhouse effect in a depressing way."

9   One reason the global-warming problem seems so daunting is that the success of previous antipollution efforts remains something of a secret. Polls show that Americans think the air is getting dirtier, not cleaner, perhaps because media coverage of the environment rarely if ever mentions improvements. For instance, did you know that smog and acid rain have continued to diminish throughout George W. Bush's presidency?

10   One might expect Democrats to trumpet the decline of air pollution, which stands as one of government's leading postwar achievements. But just as Republicans have found they can bash Democrats by falsely accusing them of being soft on defense, Democrats have found they can bash Republicans by falsely accusing them of destroying the environment. If that's your argument, you might skip over the evidence that many environmental trends are positive. One might also expect Republicans to trumpet the reduction of air pollution, since it signifies responsible behavior by industry. But to acknowledge that air pollution has declined would require Republicans to say the words, "The regulations worked."

11   Does it matter that so many in politics seem so pessimistic about the prospect of addressing global warming? Absolutely. Making the problem appear unsolvable encourages a sort of listless fatalism, blunting the drive to take first steps toward a solution. Historically, first steps against air pollution have often led to pleasant surprises. When Congress, in 1970, mandated major reductions in smog caused by automobiles, even many supporters of the rule feared it would be hugely expensive. But the catalytic converter was not practical then; soon it was perfected, and suddenly, major reductions in smog became affordable. Even a small step by the United States against greenhouse gases could lead to a similar breakthrough.

12   And to those who worry that any greenhouse-gas reductions in the United States will be swamped by new emissions from China and India, here's a final reason to be optimistic: technology can move across borders with considerable speed. Today it's not clear that American inventors or entrepreneurs can make money by reducing greenhouse gases, so relatively few are trying. But suppose the United States regulated greenhouse gases, using its own domestic program, not the cumbersome Kyoto Protocol; then America's formidable entrepreneurial and engineering communities would fully engage the problem. Innovations pioneered here could spread throughout the world, and suddenly rapid global warming would not seem inevitable.

13   The two big technical advances against smog—the catalytic converter and the chemical engineering that removes pollutants from gasoline at the refinery stage—were invented in the United States. The big economic advance against acid rain—a

credit-trading system that gives power-plant managers a profit incentive to reduce pollution—was pioneered here as well. These advances are now spreading globally. Smog and acid rain are still increasing in some parts of the world, but the trend lines suggest that both will decline fairly soon, even in developing nations. For instance, two decades ago urban smog was rising at a dangerous rate in Mexico; today it is diminishing there, though the country's population continues to grow. A short time ago declining smog and acid rain in developing nations seemed an impossibility; today declining greenhouse gases seem an impossibility. The history of air-pollution control says otherwise.

14   Americans love challenges, and preventing artificial climate change is just the sort of technological and economic challenge at which this nation excels. It only remains for the right politician to recast the challenge in practical, optimistic tones. Gore seldom has, and Bush seems to have no interest in trying. But cheap and fast improvement is not a pipe dream; it is the pattern of previous efforts against air pollution. The only reason runaway global warming seems unstoppable is that we have not yet tried to stop it.

QUESTIONS FOR DISCUSSION

1. What reasons are offered to explain the negativism about solving the greenhouse gas problem? Do you find them convincing? Why or why not? Can you think of other reasons why the problem is not being addressed in more positive terms?

2. The author bases his optimism on previous successes with smog, CFCs, and acid rain, arguing that CO_2 emissions are just another air pollution problem, larger in scale but not fundamentally different. Do you agree? How much does the size and global extent of the problem matter?

3. Easterbrook clearly does not put much stock in international agreements, preferring instead national policies to encourage innovation, which he thinks will rapidly cross national borders. "Americans love challenges," he says. Do you find this approach appealing? Why or why not?

FOR PERSUASION

"Some Convenient Truths" is a good model for writing persuasively about environmental problems such as global warming. Using Easterbrook's essay as your inspiration, write an article of similar length for your local or college paper advocating measures ordinary citizens can take to reduce their contribution to greenhouse gases. You may want to look at later articles in this chapter or read about green movements currently under way on many college campuses. Whatever you choose to talk about, remember that taking action depends on believing that action is worthwhile. Overcoming what Easterbrook calls "listless fatalism" is essential.

The Coal Paradox

TIM APPENZELLER

Electricity is clean by the time we use it in homes, offices, and industry but not, at present, in the power plants that generate it. Many of them are coal-powered, and every ton of coal burned produces four tons of CO_2. Yet coal is abundant and relatively cheap—hence the paradox Tim Appenzeller explores in the following *National Geographic* article. We cannot seem to do without coal, but using it contributes significantly to global warming and many other problems, such as the destruction of land where the coal is mined.

Appenzeller is the news editor for *Science* and a winner of the Walter Sullivan Award for Excellence in Science Journalism.

1   On a scorching August day in southwestern Indiana, the giant Gibson generating station is running flat out. Its five 180-foot-high boilers are gulping 25 tons of coal each minute, sending thousand-degree steam blasting through turbines that churn out more than 3,000 mega-watts of electric power, 50 percent more than Hoover Dam. The plant's cooling system is struggling to keep up, and in the control room warnings chirp as the exhaust temperature rises.

2   But there's no backing off on a day like this, with air conditioners humming across the Midwest and electricity demand close to record levels. Gibson, one of the biggest power plants in the country, is a mainstay of the region's electricity supply, pumping enough power into the grid for three million people. Stepping from the sweltering plant into the air-conditioned offices, Angeline Protogere of Cinergy, the Cincinnati-based utility that owns Gibson, says gratefully, "This is why we're making all that power."

3   Next time you turn up the AC or pop in a DVD, spare a thought for places like Gibson and for the grimy fuel it devours at the rate of three 100-car trainloads a day. Coal-burning power plants like this one supply the United States with half its electricity. They also emit a stew of damaging substances, including sulfur dioxide— a major cause of acid rain—and mercury. And they gush as much climate-warming carbon dioxide as America's cars, trucks, buses, and planes combined.

4   Here and there, in small demonstration projects, engineers are exploring technologies that could turn coal into power without these environmental costs. Yet unless utilities start building such plants soon—and lots of them—the future is likely to hold many more traditional stations like Gibson.

5   Last summer's voracious electricity use was just a preview. Americans' taste for bigger houses, along with population growth in the West and air-conditioning-dependent Southeast, will help push up the U.S. appetite for power by a third over the next 20 years, according to the Department of Energy. And in the developing world, especially China, electricity needs will rise even faster as factories burgeon and hundreds of millions of people buy their first refrigerators and TVs. Much of that demand is likely to be met with coal.

6   For the past 15 years U.S. utilities needing to add power have mainly built plants that burn natural gas, a relatively clean fuel. But a near tripling of natural gas prices in the past seven years has idled many gas-fired plants and put a damper on new

construction. Neither nuclear energy nor alternative sources such as wind and solar seem likely to meet the demand for electricity.

7   Meanwhile, more than a quarter trillion tons of coal lie underfoot, from the Appalachians through the Illinois Basin to the Rocky Mountains—enough to last 250 years at today's consumption rate. You hear it again and again: The U.S. is the Saudi Arabia of coal. About 40 coal-burning power plants are now being designed or built in the U.S. China, also rich in coal, could build several hundred by 2025.

8   Mining enough coal to satisfy this growing appetite will take a toll on lands and communities. Of all fossil fuels, coal puts out the most carbon dioxide per unit of energy, so burning it poses a further threat to global climate, already warming alarmingly. With much government prodding, coal-burning utilities have cut pollutants such as sulfur dioxide and nitrogen oxides by installing equipment like the building-size scrubbers and catalytic units crowded behind the Gibson plant. But the carbon dioxide that drives global warming simply goes up the stacks—nearly two billion tons of it each year from U.S. coal plants. Within the next two decades that amount could rise by a third.

9   There's no easy way to capture all the carbon dioxide from a traditional coal-burning station. "Right now, if you took a plant and slapped a carbon-capture device on it, you'd lose 25 percent of the energy," says Julio Friedmann, who studies carbon dioxide management at Lawrence Livermore National Laboratory. But a new kind of power station could change that.

10   A hundred miles up the Wabash River from the Gibson plant is a small power station that looks nothing like Gibson's mammoth boilers and steam turbines. This one resembles an oil refinery, all tanks and silvery tubes. Instead of burning coal, the Wabash River plant chemically transforms it in a process called coal gasification.

11   The Wabash plant mixes coal or petroleum coke, a coal-like residue from oil refineries, with water and pure oxygen and pumps it into a tall tank, where a fiery reaction turns the mixture into a flammable gas. Other equipment removes sulfur and other contaminants from the syngas, as it's called, before it's burned in a gas turbine to produce electricity.

12   Cleaning the unburned syngas is cheaper and more effective than trying to sieve pollutants from power plant exhaust, as the scrubbers at a plant like Gibson do. "This has been called the cleanest coal-fired power plant in the world," says Steven Vick, general manager of the Wabash facility. "We're pretty proud of that distinction."

13   The syngas can even be processed to strip out the carbon dioxide. The Wabash plant doesn't take this step, but future plants could. Coal gasification, Vick says, "is a technology that's set up for total CO_2 removal." The carbon dioxide could be pumped deep underground into depleted oil fields, old coal seams, or fluid-filled rock, sealed away from the atmosphere. And as a bonus, taking carbon dioxide out of the syngas can leave pure hydrogen, which could fuel a new generation of nonpolluting cars as well as generate electric power.

14   The Wabash plant and a similar one near Tampa, Florida, were built or refurbished with government money in the mid-1990s to demonstrate that gasification

FACTS ABOUT COAL

WHO HAS COAL?

The world has more than a trillion tons of readily available coal. The U.S. has the largest share, but other energy-hungry countries, such as China and India, are richly endowed as well.

27%	17%	13%	10%	9%	5%	19%
U.S.	RUSSIA	CHINA	INDIA	AUSTRALIA	SOUTH AFRICA	OTHER

WHO USES COAL NOW?

Global coal consumption is roughly five billion tons a year, with China burning the most. Western Europe has cut coal use by 36 percent since 1990 by using available natural gas from the North Sea and Russia.

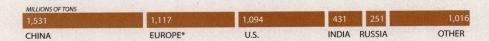

MILLIONS OF TONS

1,531	1,117	1,094	431	251	1,016
CHINA	EUROPE*	U.S.	INDIA	RUSSIA	OTHER

WHO WILL USE IT TOMORROW?

China's coal needs will more than double by 2025 to satisfy factories and consumers. The country also plans to convert coal to liquid motor fuels. Worldwide, consumption will rise by 56 percent.

MILLIONS OF TONS

3,242	1,505	853	736	288	1,602
CHINA	U.S.	EUROPE*	INDIA	RUSSIA	OTHER

*Excluding Russia

U.S. ELECTRICITY GENERATION

50%	20%	18%	9%	3%
COAL	NUCLEAR	NATURAL GAS	RENEWABLES	OIL

U.S. POWER PLANT CO$_2$ EMISSIONS

83%	13%	4%
COAL	NATURAL GAS	OIL

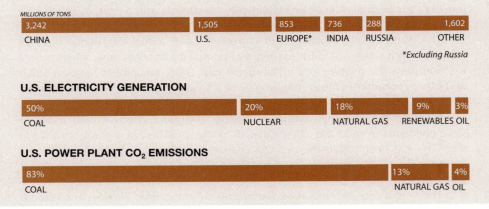

is a viable electricity source. Projects in North Dakota, Canada, the North Sea, and elsewhere have tested the other parts of the equation: capturing carbon dioxide and sequestering it underground. Researchers say they need to know more about how buried carbon dioxide behaves to be sure it won't leak back out—a potential threat to climate or even people. But Friedmann says, "For a first cut, we have enough information to say, 'It's a no-brainer. We know how to do this.'"

WHAT'S IN COAL SMOKE?

Sulfur Dioxide

The sulfur in coal forms this gas, which gives rise to acid rain when it reacts with water in clouds. Many plants control sulfur emissions by burning low-sulfur coal and passing the exhaust through scrubbers, which capture sulfur dioxide.

Nitrogen Oxides

The heat of power-plant burners turns nitrogen from the air into nitrogen oxides, which can contribute to acid rain and ground-level ozone. Pollution controls on many plants limit nitrogen oxide emissions.

Mercury

The traces of mercury in coal escape in power-plant exhaust. Falling hundreds of miles away in rain or snow, the mercury builds up in fish, making some species unsafe for children and pregnant women to eat.

Carbon Dioxide

Coal produces more CO_2 per energy unit than any other fossil fuel. CO_2 is a greenhouse gas, affecting climate by trapping heat that would otherwise escape to space. Power plants today release all their CO_2 into the atmosphere.

Particulates

Particles from coal-burning plants can harm people who have heart and breathing disorders. Soot and ash are captured before they go up the stacks, but finer particles can form later, from oxides of sulfur and nitrogen.

15   Yet that's no guarantee utilities will embrace the gasification technology. "The fact that it's proved in Indiana and Florida doesn't mean executives are going to make a billion-dollar bet on it," says William Rosenberg of Harvard's Kennedy School of Government. The two gasification power plants in the U.S. are half the size of most commercial generating stations and have proved less reliable than traditional plants. The technology also costs as much as 20 percent more. Most important, there's little incentive for a company to take on the extra risk and expense of cleaner technology: For now U.S. utilities are free to emit as much carbon dioxide as they like.

16   Cinergy CEO James Rogers, the man in charge of Gibson and eight other carbon-spewing plants, says he expects that to change. "I do believe we'll have regulation of carbon in this country," he says, and he wants his company to be ready. "The sooner we get to work, the better. I believe it's very important that we develop the ability to do carbon sequestration." Rogers says he intends to build a commercial-scale gasification power plant, able to capture its carbon dioxide, and several other companies have announced similar plans.

17 The energy bill passed last July by the U.S. Congress offers help in the form of loan guarantees and tax credits for gasification projects. "This should jump-start things," says Rosenberg, who advocated these measures in testimony to Congress. The experience of building and running the first few plants should lower costs and improve reliability. And sooner or later, says Rogers, new environmental laws that put a price on carbon dioxide emissions will make clean technology look far more attractive. "If the cost of carbon is 30 bucks a ton, it's amazing the kinds of technologies that will evolve to allow you to produce more electricity with less emissions."

18 If he's right, we may one day be able to cool our houses without turning up the thermostat on the entire planet.

QUESTIONS FOR DISCUSSION

1. According to Tim Appenzeller, why is coal the choice of so many power-generating plants? Though still producing significant amounts of CO_2, natural gas is a cleaner alternative—why don't we use natural gas exclusively?

2. What are the advantages of coal gasification? What are the disadvantages?

3. Neither conventional nor coal gasification plants currently capture and sequester the CO_2 they produce, though we are told in the article that research projects have tested this technology. In essence, in this process the gas is liquefied, pumped underground, and stored in such places as played-out oil fields. What is your reaction to such a method of pollution control?

FOR RESEARCH AND CONVINCING

Suppose that carbon sequestration will work and that economic and political forces allow it to come into widespread use. Because coal is a fossil fuel, we still have the problem that the supplies will eventually run out. Furthermore, the damage done by strip-mining will be even greater than it is now. Clearly, we need to find alternatives to coal, and natural gas has recently become more abundant because of a process of recovery called fracking.

There are basically two ways to approach the problem. The first way is to continue to build massive power-generating plants but to power them with something that is cleaner—such as natural gas or nuclear energy. The other way is to encourage what is already being done in Japan and elsewhere on a significant scale—to have each home and business generate its own power via solar or wind energy. Of course, the two ways can be combined. When the sun is shining or the wind is blowing, a home or business can go off the grid and use its own power, resorting to the centrally generated source only when necessary.

Explore these two approaches. There is much information on both. Then write a paper proposing and defending the approach or combination of approaches that you think will work best in your area.

Existing Technologies for Reducing CO₂ Emissions

AL GORE

We need to remind ourselves often that powerful technologies exist for reducing carbon dioxide emissions. The ones pictured here, most from *An Inconvenient Truth,* are only a few of many.

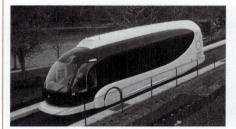

Fuel-Cell Hybrid Buses

Green Roof

Hybrid Car

Compact Fluorescent Lightbulbs

© Mark Newman/FLPA imageBROKER/Newscom
Solar Panels

Electric Car Powered by Hydrogen Fuel Cell

Geothermal Power Station

QUESTIONS FOR DISCUSSION

In the short term, we need energy conservation, ways to reduce pollution from cars and power-generating plants, and increasing use of power sources that are renewable and clean. Such measures will buy us time for more radical and permanent solutions. In the long term, we need to cease using fossil fuels as an energy source entirely, replacing them with wind, solar, tidal, hydrogen, fusion, and other potentially inexhaustible and nonpolluting sources of energy. As a class, brainstorm the possibilities both short and long term. Don't worry too much about how practical the suggestions are. After the class completes the brainstorming, examine what you have generated. Which suggestions appeal the most? Why?

Selling the Wind

MICHELLE NIJHUIS

The dream is an inexhaustible, inexpensive, and nonpolluting source of energy—a dream right now because, for instance, about 80% of the electricity generated in the United States comes from fossil fuels, but also a reality because of the many kinds of alternate energy sources already in use here and abroad. Many of these are old power sources, such as the wind, revolutionized by new technology. In the following piece from *Audubon,* the freelance writer Michelle Nijhuis discusses some of the pluses and minuses of wind power.

1   On the Emick family ranch in far southeastern Colorado, a row of antique windmills adorn the entrance road, their delicate wooden blades stilled for the moment. These windmills, some more than a century old, once helped prairie homesteaders pump water out of the ground, sustaining both families and farms. Throughout the Great Plains, such windmills are still a proud symbol of survival—of pioneer persistence in a land often too hot or too cold, too dry or too windy.

2   Today a very different sort of windmill is helping the Emick family survive on the blustery western edge of the Great Plains. In every direction, lines of cylindrical steel towers rise from the landscape, each white column topped by three sleek, swooping blades. These modern wind turbines, which measure more than 300 feet from their base to the tips of their blades, are more than 10 times taller than the frontier-era windmills at their feet.

3   The 108 turbines in this neighborhood comprise the Colorado Green project, the largest wind farm in Colorado and among the 10 largest in the nation. The project, a joint venture of Shell Wind Energy and PPM Energy (a subsidiary of Scottish-Power), produces roughly enough electricity each year to supply more than 52,000 average homes.

4   Though the Emicks and other families who lease land to wind-power companies can't divulge the details of their agreements, typical payments range from $3,000 to $6,000 per turbine per year, and generally allow farmers to continue raising crops and livestock among the towers. For agricultural families, which face the vagaries of rainfall and commodity prices, the reliable additional income is welcome. It can help

them keep their farms afloat—and keep land relatively undeveloped, in some cases preserving both wildlife habitat and open vistas.

5   Small farmers are far from the only fans of wind energy. Wind farms in the United States now have a combined capacity of more than 9,000 megawatts, generating enough electricity to power approximately 2.3 million homes. . . . While wind currently provides less than 1 percent of the country's total energy needs, many states are looking to increase their supplies of renewable energy, helping to make wind the nation's second-fastest-growing source of electricity (natural gas is tops).

6   Multinationals continue to make significant investments in wind power. GE Energy built well more than half of the new turbines in the United States last year, and Goldman Sachs, one of the world's largest investment banking firms, recently purchased a wind-power development company now called Horizon Wind Energy. Meanwhile, the U.S. Department of Energy has set a goal of helping at least 30 states increase their wind-power generating capacity to 100 megawatts each by 2010.

7   While consumers have long paid a premium for wind power, high natural gas and coal prices are enhancing wind's appeal. Last year in Colorado and in Austin, Texas, the price of wind power dipped below the price of traditional energy sources, and utility customers of all political stripes flocked to sign up for it.

8   If wind power dilutes our diet of coal and other fossil fuels, it will reduce air pollution, and even cushion the devastating, and increasingly apparent, effects of global warming. "It's critical to have a sense of urgency about dealing with global climate challenge in general, and about displacing coal in particular," says Ralph Cavanagh, an expert on renewable energy at the Natural Resources Defense Council (NRDC). "Wind is a very important part of that equation."

9   For many conservationists, however, wind power remains an uncomfortable subject. It's well known that wind turbines kill both birds and bats, though exactly how often—and why—these deaths occur remains poorly understood. Wildlife advocates hope they can push for more research, better planning, and more stringent oversight of wind farms without sabotaging the industry's hard-won momentum.

10   Much of the current controversy over wind power and wildlife stems from a place called Altamont Pass, a line of golden, oak-studded hills on the eastern outskirts of the San Francisco Bay Area. The Altamont Wind Resource Area, established in the early 1980s, was one of the first modern wind farms in the nation, and a visit to Altamont is a one-stop tour of the history of wind power.

11   On one grassy hillside stands a row of closely spaced "eggbeater" turbines, each with three busily spinning blades mounted on a latticed steel tower. Arrayed on another slope are the smooth, solid towers of newer turbines, much like those on the Emick family ranch in Colorado. Although the blades of these turbines turn more slowly than those of their smaller predecessors, each enormous turbine can generate 1.5 megawatts of power, more than twice that produced by older models. In all, more than 5,000 turbines crowd into Altamont Pass, generating enough electricity to serve some 100,000 homes.

12   But these turbines are believed to kill more birds of prey than any other wind farm in the world. Beginning in the late 1980s biologists reported that large numbers of golden eagles, hawks, and other raptors were flying into the spinning blades at

Altamont, and dying as a result. Wind-energy companies tried many measures to limit the damage, such as installing chicken wire on the latticed towers to discourage perching. But a recent five-year study by the California Energy Commission estimated that every year up to 1,300 raptors are killed at Altamont, including more than a hundred golden eagles. . . .

13   The farms and ranches of the West and Midwest are now favored homes for wind turbines, and so far they seem to be relatively safe for both raptors and song-birds. "The bird mortality we're seeing is lower than what's been seen at Altamont," says Tim Cullinan, director of science and bird conservation for Audubon Washington and a wildlife biologist. Cullinan is working with the U.S. Fish and Wildlife Service and other stakeholders such as the American Wind Energy Association and the International Association of Fish and Wildlife Agencies to strengthen siting standards for wind facilities nationwide. . . .

14   Even if biologists underestimate the number of birds killed by turbines, the damage is surely smaller, in orders of magnitude, than the numbers killed in other ways. While a 2001 study surmised that some 10,000 to 40,000 birds die in wind turbines each year, the U.S. Fish and Wildlife Service contends that these numbers are out of date and that the true mortality figures are much higher. Still, an estimated 100 million birds are killed a year by hunting housecats, and as many as 60 million die from collisions with cars and trucks.

15   Yet if the wind industry continues to boom, turbine numbers multiply, and the gaps in research persist, it is possible that collisions with turbines—and construction associated with wind farms—will become a more widespread and substantial threat, particularly for threatened and endangered species. "The fear is that with all the new wind farms rolling out, there is a new Altamont being created today," says Greg Butcher, National Audubon's director of bird conservation. "But because we don't have the data, we just don't know about it."

16   When wildlife researchers have looked closely at wind farms, disturbing numbers have emerged. One 2003 study spent seven months compiling bat fatalities at a wind-power site in the West Virginia mountains. Researchers found, to their surprise, that the 44 turbines killed as many as 4,000 migratory bats. Similarly grim findings have since been reported at wind farms in Pennsylvania and Tennessee, raising the possibility that significant bat kills are a regional or even national phenomenon.

17   The three wind farms in question stand on forested Appalachian ridges, and Ed Arnett, a conservation scientist for Bat Conservation International, speculates that tree-roosting bats hunt insects in the clearings around the turbines. But because the wind industry has only a handful of bat studies to draw on, the reasons for the kills are unclear, the number of species involved uncertain, and no one is sure how to mitigate the impacts at existing or future sites. "There's a huge dearth of research," Arnett says. "What we do know is that these are long-lived species with low reproductive rates, so a new source of mortality could drive them into serious declines very quickly."

18   Other researchers are concerned that proliferating wind turbines will take a heavy toll on night-migrating songbirds or ground-nesting birds. A 2004 study, led by Robert Robel, a biology professor at Kansas State University, found that roads and

other infrastructure disturb ground-nesting species such as the lesser-prairie chicken, a candidate for federal listing as an endangered species. Again, though, the questions far outnumber the answers.

19   In a 2005 Government Accountability Office report to Congress summarizing the research on wind farms and wildlife impacts, the authors describe "significant gaps in the literature" that "make it difficult for scientists to draw conclusions about wind power's impact on wildlife in general.". . .

20   So conservationists find themselves in a tough spot. How can they support and encourage the rapid spread of wind power—our most promising source of clean, renewable energy—while ensuring that the industry minimizes its damage to birds and other wildlife?

21   "We can't lose sight of the larger benefits of wind," says Audubon Washington's Tim Cullinan. "The direct environmental impacts of wind get a lot of attention, because there are dead bodies on the ground. But nobody ever finds the bodies of the birds killed by global warming, or by oil drilling on the North Slope of Alaska. They're out there, but we don't see them.". . .

22   The solution to this dilemma, say many conservationists, begins with early, consistent involvement in project planning. "Once those turbines go in," says biologist Pete Bloom, "they don't come down." To encourage early consideration of wildlife, environmental groups have developed guidelines and policies for wind development. Audubon Washington's guidelines, for instance, call for several seasons of bird surveys and other in-depth wildlife studies at proposed wind-power sites, and support statewide or multi-state planning efforts for wind facilities. . . .

23   By asking the right questions at the right time, conservationists can help wind power continue its growth and fulfill its promise. They can also share in the building enthusiasm for wind's wide-ranging benefits. Farmer and rancher Greg Emick, who grew up on his family's land, guesses that his ancestors—immigrants from Germany who arrived in Colorado nearly 100 years ago—would be pleased by the towering wind turbines that rise from the land they once homesteaded. "They always thought the prairie would be good for more than just raising cattle and growing a little bit of crop," says Emick, as he listens to the steady swoosh of the gigantic turbine blades above his head. "But I don't think they ever imagined we could sell the wind."

QUESTIONS FOR DISCUSSION

1. As the author emphasizes, wind energy has developed far past the old windmill on the family farm and become big business. What positive signs do you detect in the significant economic incentives for wind power?

2. When we compare 40,000 birds killed annually by wind turbines with the 100 million that cats kill or the 60 million lost to being hit by vehicles, we may be tempted to dismiss the damage done by the turbines. But other details in the article show that bird and bat mortality may be more significant than the raw numbers indicate. What details indicate this? How can we best reduce this problem?

3. Because the author is writing for conservationists whose concern is wind power's impact on wildlife and habitats, she says little about the main objection to wind turbines: many people consider them unsightly and take the NIMBY (not in my backyard) position. In view of the obvious pluses to wind power, how serious do you feel this objection is?

FOR RESEARCH AND CONVINCING

As "Selling the Wind" shows, no form of energy is without drawbacks, and some of the negatives can be quite serious, such as the radioactive waste from nuclear power plants. Nevertheless, we must give up or greatly reduce our dependence on fossil fuels. For this to happen, the general public must strongly support alternate energy sources.

Choose one of the many alternative sources—wind, water, geothermal, nuclear, hydrogen, biodiesel, ethanol, and so on—and do enough research to understand the advantages and disadvantages. Then write an editorial for your local or school newspaper urging support for the energy source. Be sure to deal with the negatives honestly, arguing either that they must be tolerated or that measures can be taken to remedy or reduce them.

FOR MEDIATION

In practical terms, no way of reducing global warming can work without negotiation among conflicting interests. Even at the personal and private level, individuals have to balance money and convenience against environmental concerns. At the public level are situations like the one Nijhuis discusses—the value of wind power versus the concerns for species loss and aesthetics. The various interests have to be fitted together somehow.

Imagine you are an advocate for wind power and that you are addressing an audience of conservationists and ordinary citizens who oppose wind turbines in their community. Compose the text of a speech that mediates—that firmly advocates increased use of wind power but does so in a way that respects and accommodates, as much as possible, the concerns of your audience. You may need to do research on wind power to find the information and lines of argument you need.

Ten Personal Solutions

UNION OF CONCERNED SCIENTISTS

We tend to think of global warming as a large-scale problem involving public issues such as the generation of electric power. But much of the solution is personal and small-scale, a matter of what you and I choose to do or not do in our daily lives. The suggestions in the following article (see www.ucsusa.org) are only a few of the many choices we can make.

1   Individual choices can have an impact on global climate change. Reducing your family's heat-trapping emissions does not mean forgoing modern conveniences; it

means making smart choices and using energy-efficient products, which may require an additional investment up front, but often pay you back in energy savings within a couple of years.

2   Since Americans' per capita emissions of heat-trapping gases is 5.6 tons—more than double the amount of western Europeans—we can all make choices that will greatly reduce our families' global warming impact.

1. **The car you drive: the most important personal climate decision.** When you buy your next car, look for the one with the best fuel economy in its class. Each gallon of gas you use releases 25 pounds of heat-trapping carbon dioxide (CO_2) into the atmosphere. Better gas mileage not only reduces global warming, but will also save you thousands of dollars at the pump over the life of the vehicle. Compare the fuel economy of the cars you're considering and look for new technologies like hybrid engines.

2. **Choose clean power.** More than half the electricity in the United States comes from polluting coal-fired power plants. And power plants are the single largest source of heat-trapping gas. None of us can live without electricity, but in some states, you can switch to electricity companies that provide 50 to 100 percent renewable energy. (For more information go to Green-e.org.)

3. **Look for Energy Star.** When it comes time to replace appliances, look for the Energy Star label on new appliances (refrigerators, freezers, furnaces, air conditioners, and water heaters use the most energy). These items may cost a bit more initially, but the energy savings will pay back the extra investment within a couple of years. Household energy savings really can make a difference: If each household in the United States replaced its existing appliances with the most efficient models available, we would save $15 billion in energy costs and eliminate 175 million tons of heat-trapping gases.

4. **Unplug a freezer.** One of the quickest ways to reduce your global warming impact is to unplug the extra refrigerator or freezer you rarely use (except when you need it for holidays and parties). This can reduce the typical family's carbon dioxide emissions by nearly 10 percent.

5. **Get a home energy audit.** Take advantage of the free home energy audits offered by many utilities. Simple measures, such as installing a programmable thermostat to replace your old dial unit or sealing and insulating heating and cooling ducts, can each reduce a typical family's carbon dioxide emissions by about 5 percent.

6. **Light bulbs matter.** If every household in the United States replaced one regular light bulb with an energy-saving model, we could reduce global warming pollution by more than 90 billion pounds over the life of the bulbs; the same as taking 6.3 million cars off the road. So, replace your incandescent bulbs with more efficient compact fluorescents, which now come in all shapes and sizes. You'll be doing your share to cut back on heat-trapping pollution and you'll save money on your electric bills and light bulbs.

7. **Think before you drive.** If you own more than one vehicle, use the less fuel-efficient one only when you can fill it with passengers. Driving a full minivan may be kinder to the environment than two midsize cars. Whenever possible, join a carpool or take mass transit.

8. **Buy good wood.** When buying wood products, check for labels that indicate the source of the timber. Supporting forests that are managed in a sustainable fashion makes sense for biodiversity, and it may make sense for the climate too. Forests that are well managed are more likely to store carbon effectively because more trees are left standing and carbon-storing soils are less disturbed.

9. **Plant a tree.** You can also make a difference in your own backyard. Get a group in your neighborhood together and contact your local arborist or urban forester about planting trees on private property and public land. In addition to storing carbon, trees planted in and around urban areas and residences can provide much-needed shade in the summer, reducing energy bills and fossil fuel use.

10. **Let policymakers know you are concerned about global warming.** Our elected officials and business leaders need to hear from concerned citizens.

QUESTIONS FOR DISCUSSION

1. The piece claims that each American produces 5.6 tons of greenhouse gas emissions each year—double the European amount. In your view, how much of this difference is a matter of circumstances, such as the size of the United States, and how much is the result of lifestyle choices that could be changed?

2. What action have you taken to reduce your personal carbon footprint? What in the list of ten suggestions appeals to you most? What has the least appeal? Do you have resistance to any of the ten items? If there are changes you do not want to make, such as the car you drive, what could you do to reduce carbon emissions in other ways?

FOR INQUIRY AND CONVINCING

Besides taking action at the personal and home or family level, each of us can urge greater concern for the environment in local institutions and workplaces. Universities and colleges, for instance, are not always models of efficient energy use. A growing student movement in the United States aims to address this problem.

As a class project, find out what your university or college is doing and plans to do to use energy more efficiently. As part of this research, walk around campus and tour the buildings. Is the level of heating and cooling appropriate? Are lights left on in rooms that are empty? Take note of anything that seems wasteful to you.

Discuss the results of your research and work together as a class to create a document to present to the central administration, urging whatever improvements the class thinks might make a difference.

Consuming Earth's Gifts

WILLIAM F. RUDDIMAN

Global warming has gotten so much attention recently that we are apt to forget that it is only one of many environmental problems. William Ruddiman, retired professor of environmental science at the University of Virginia, reminds us of another big problem—exhaustion of the Earth's resources, including water and topsoil. The following essay comes from his influential book, *Plows, Plagues, and Petroleum*, which traces human impact on climate back to the invention of agriculture, about 10,000 years ago.

1   Even though I have made the case that future climate change is likely to be large . . . , I do not rank the oncoming global warming as the greatest environmental problem of our time. Other environmental issues seem to me far more immediate and pressing, and in the future I suspect our concerns will focus heavily on the eventual depletion of key resources.

2   . . . Humankind has been steadily transforming Earth's surface for some 8,000 years, initially in Eurasia and later on all continents. Initially, we caused these transformations by clearing land for farming; later, other aspects of civilized life joined farming as important causes of this transformation. Well before the industrial era, the cumulative result over many millennia was an enormous loss of what had been "natural" on this planet.

3   During the 1800s and 1900s, human population increased from 1 billion to 6 billion, an explosion unprecedented in human history. This rise came about because new sanitary standards and medicines reduced the incidence of disease and because human ingenuity led to innovations in agriculture that fed ever-larger numbers of people. As a result, our already sizable impact on Earth's surface increased at a much faster rate. . . .

4   By most estimates, the explosive population increase still under way will end near AD 2050 as global population levels out at some 9–10 billion people, or roughly 50 percent more people than now. A major reason for the predicted stabilization will be the increase in affluence that has historically resulted in fewer children per family. . . .

5   On the other hand, as affluence and technology continue to spread, increased pressures on the environment will occur for that reason alone. If a billion or more people in China and India begin to live the way Americans and Europeans do now, their additional use of Earth's resources will be enormous. Even without population increases, humanity will continue to alter the environment in new ways.

6   The cumulative impact of so many millennia of transforming Earth's surface has inevitably come at a cost to nature. Many of the problems our actions have created have been described elsewhere by ecologists and others knowledgeable about the environment. In the process of transforming Earth's surface, we have fragmented the space that ecosystems require, transported species from the places they belong to regions where their presence is invasive to existing flora and fauna, and caused the extinction of species in numbers that no one really knows. . . .

7   Those with environmental concerns have in recent decades added a new argument to their side of this battle. Ecologists have coined the term "ecosystem services" to describe processes that nature provides for free and that have real economic value. For example, trees and other vegetation on hill slopes trap rainfall that would otherwise flow away and erode soils. As the retained water passes into subsurface layers, the soils slowly filter it and transform it into clean, drinkable water that can be retrieved from wells or springs. Some of the water flows into wetlands and is further cleansed there. Nature gives us a large supply of clean water.

8   But when the trees are cut or the wetlands are filled in, these free services are lost, and society must pick up the cost of doing nature's job. . . . The loss of nature's subsurface cleansing of water requires municipal water treatment plants and home water filters, but these remedies rarely return water of the quality nature once provided. So we buy bottled water shipped from other regions or even other continents. All in all, we pay an economic price to replace ecosystem services. Ecologists rightly argue that the costs incurred from losing ecosystem services must be included in complete "economic" analyses of land-use decisions. . . .

9   Probably as a result of my long interest in Earth's climate history, my own concerns about the future tend to focus on a related set of longer-term problems—"gifts" that nature has provided us through slow-acting processes that took place well back in Earth's past and that cannot be replaced once they are consumed.

10   My concern about these gifts is simple: When these resources run low or run out, how will we find comparably inexpensive replacements? . . . We live today in an era of remarkably cheap oil, gas, and coal. It took nature hundreds of millions of years to create the world's supply of these resources, by burying organic carbon in swamps and inland seas and shallow coastal areas, and by cooking the carbon at just the right temperature and pressure. We only began using these resources in significant amounts in the middle 1800s, and yet the first signs are already at hand that the world will reach the year of peak oil production and consumption in just one or two decades, if not sooner. World supplies of natural gas will last a bit longer, and coal for a few centuries. I wonder whether we will ever find a substitute even remotely as inexpensive as these carbon gifts. We are investigating alternative sources of energy, but as of now none of them seems likely to be as widely available and as inexpensive as the solar energy stored in carbon-based fuels.

11   At some point early in the current century, gradual depletion of this vital commodity will presumably become a major economic issue. Once world oil production begins to decline by 1 percent or so per year, it seems likely to add a measurable cost to the functioning of the global economy, in effect adding a new form of built-in "inflation" on top of the normal kind. Fuel for cars and trucks is not the only concern;

a vast array of products made from petrochemicals has become part of the basic fabric of our lives. All of them will cost more.

12   I also wonder about the long-term supply of water. With more than half of the supply of water from surface run-off already in use for irrigation and human consumption, we have for years been pumping water from aquifers deep in the ground, especially in arid and semi-arid regions into which many people are now moving. The water stored in the deep aquifers of the American West was put there tens to hundreds of thousands of years ago by melt water flowing southward from the margins of the great ice sheets, and by snow and rain water that fell during climatic conditions much wetter than today. In recent decades, the level of those aquifers has been falling as we extract water from depths where it cannot be quickly replenished by nature.

13   Pumping ever deeper will require more carbon fuel, which in turn will become more expensive. Gradually, the water from greater depths will contain ever-larger concentrations of dissolved salts that will be left on irrigated fields, making agriculture more difficult. Eventually, we will exhaust the useable water in these underground reservoirs. Little by little, agriculture will probably retreat from the arid high-plains regions of the West back toward the midcontinent regions nearer the Mississippi River, where natural rainfall supports agriculture. The same retreat will occur in other regions of extensive groundwater use across the globe.

14   I have no idea when these groundwater limits will be reached in each region, but new reports suggest the start of the problem may be close at hand in some regions. To conserve water, the municipal government of Santa Fe, New Mexico, recently began requiring home builders to retrofit six existing houses for improved water economy to offset the added water use in each new house built. In the Oklahoma-Texas panhandle region, oilman and investor T. Boone Pickens has been buying up the rights to groundwater in the glacial-age Ogallala aquifer. When municipal governments put extra burdens on local builders, and when wealthy oil tycoons invest in underground water as a scarce commodity, problems must be looming. . . .

15   I also wonder about topsoil. The most productive farms in the American Midwest can thank the ice sheets for their topsoil. Ice repeatedly gouged bedrock and scraped older soils in north-central Canada and pushed the eroded debris south, where streams of glacial melt water carried it into river valleys, and winds blew it across the western prairies. During the 1800s, farmers began breaking up the tough top layer of prairie sod, which had been held in place by extremely deep-rooted plants, and farming began at a scale the world had never seen. The midwestern American agricultural miracle has been one of the great success stories in human history.

16   But this great success came at a price. Repeated tilling exposed the rich prairie soils to decades of dry winds and floods. Estimates are that half of the original topsoil layer in the American Midwest has been lost, most of it flowing down the Mississippi River to the Gulf of Mexico. In the late 1900s, farmers began adapting new techniques that have reduced, but not stopped, the rapid removal of this precious gift. These methods and other conservation efforts will keep us from losing soil as rapidly as before, but slower rates of loss will continue to deplete soils that no longer have the natural protection provided by prairie vegetation.

17   Farmers and farm corporations now spend enormous sums of money every year on manufactured fertilizers to replenish nutrients lost to crop production and natural erosion. These fertilizers are produced from petrochemical (petroleum) products, which again brings us back to the gradual depletion (and increased expense) of carbon-based products in the coming decades. Once again, it will be a very long wait indeed until nature gets around to making more topsoil, probably 50,000 to 100,000 years until the next ice sheet bulldozes the next rich load southward. . . .

18   With no wish to be alarmist about the slow depletion of these many gifts, especially carbon-based energy sources, I still wonder: What will humankind do when they grow scarce? Will our resourcefulness as a species open up new avenues? Or will the depletion be a true loss? I have no clue what answers to these vital questions the distant future will bring.

QUESTIONS FOR DISCUSSION

1. In your own words, describe what Ruddiman means by "ecosystem services." He points to the economic costs when technology has to replace what nature once provided freely, as "gifts" to us. What other costs are involved?

2. One of the author's concerns is depletion of fossil fuels or prohibitively expensive supplies. He understands the role of such sources of energy in global warming, so why is he concerned?

3. Water is another of nature's "gifts." Why, according to the author, should we be worried about it?

4. Why is topsoil erosion a problem? Are there other ecological problems connected with it? What, for instance, happens when topsoil is washed down a river and deposited in the ocean?

FOR RESEARCH, DISCUSSION, AND PERSUASION

Environmental problems seldom have a single cause. We're losing coral reefs, for example, through a combination of forces: ocean warming, ocean acidification (caused by CO_2 from the atmosphere turning into carbonic acid), topsoil erosion (the soil smothers the reefs), pollution from many other sources, and the carelessness of boaters and divers.

Do research on coral reefs—or on rain forests, which are also in deep trouble. Investigate all the causes of their destruction or degradation, including but not limited to global warming. Then write an article aiming to raise awareness of the value of what we are losing, the complex causes, and the necessity of taking immediate action. Address your U.S. congressperson or senator.

FOR FURTHER READING

Archer, David. *Global Warming: Understanding the Forecast.* 2012.
Flannery, Tim. *The Weather Makers: How Man Is Changing the Climate and What It Means for Life on Earth.* Atlantic Monthly Press, 2005.

Gore, Al. *An Inconvenient Truth*. Rodale, 2006.

Houghton, John. *Global Warming: The Complete Briefing*. Cambridge UP, 1997.

Linden, Eugene. *The Winds of Change: Climate, Weather, and the Destruction of Civilizations*. Simon and Schuster, 2006.

McKibben, Bill. *The Global Warming Reader: A Century of Writing About Climate Change*. Penguin, 2012.

National Aeronautics and Space Administration, www.nasa.gov.

National Oceanic and Atmospheric Administration, www.noaa.gov.

Newell, Peter. *Climate for Change: Non-State Actors and the Global Politics of the Greenhouse*. Cambridge UP, 2000.

Ruddiman, William F. *Plows, Plagues, and Petroleum: How Humans Took Control of Climate*. Princeton UP, 2005.

Union of Concerned Scientists, www.ucsusa.org.

CHAPTER 14

The Millennials: Issues Facing Young Adults

Pew Research Center, Millennials: Confident. Connected. Open to Change *383*

Kit Yarrow and Jayne O'Donnell, Gen Y Is from Mercury *391*

Kim Brooks, Is It Time to Kill the Liberal Arts Degree? *395*

Stuart Rabinowitz, A Liberal Arts Education Is Still Relevant *399*

Dale Archer, College Debt: Necessary Evil or Ponzi Scheme? *402*

Richard Vedder, Forgive Student Loans? *405*

Anya Kamenetz, Waking Up and Taking Charge *408*

For Further Reading *413*

"The Millennials" refer to people born between 1980 and 2000. Also commonly called Generation Y, this group includes a high percentage of students currently enrolled in colleges and universities. It is difficult to generalize about more than 80 million people—the size of the Millennial generation—but the general opinion is that this generation is distinctive and full of promise. Our first selection offers the findings of many surveys by a leading social research group showing overall positive characteristics of the Millennial cohort. In our second selection, Kit Yarrow and Jayne O'Donnell, who have done extensive research in their capacity as retail consultants, claim that

> Having never experienced a world without computers, the Internet, cell phones, and digital cameras, Gen Yers are free of anxiety and full of playfulness when they interact with the Internet and technology of all sorts. This makes learning easier for them than it is for all but the most tech-savvy parents.

If Millennials are getting good reviews from older generations, they also face problems their parents did not. The chief problem is economic. College now costs far more than it did thirty or forty years ago, with students graduating from college on average about $26,000 in debt, not counting an additional $7,000 on credit cards. In other words, too many young people start their lives after college significantly in debt. For those who pursue graduate degrees, the debt could double or triple.

Perhaps starting in a deep hole would not be so bad if job prospects were better. Although college graduates experience less unemployment than high school graduates, according to the Bureau of Labor Statistics, in 2013, 7.7 percent of college graduates were unemployed. In addition, as Kim Brooks points out in our third reading, many graduates are underemployed, especially those with degrees in the arts and sciences traditionally known as the Liberal Arts. Therefore, an important issue for many young people is the choice of a degree and career plan. Should students search for a major that ignites their passions or opt for a secure path to a career that will merely pay the bills? In the fourth reading, the president of Hofstra University engages this debate with a strong argument in favor of the liberal arts as preparation for whatever the future holds. A third view of college as preparation for employment comes from Dale Archer, a psychiatrist and counselor, who questions the entire notion that a college education is necessary for economic security.

Finally, there is the related issue of the cost of college and the enormous debt many students carry when they graduate. In 2013, the estimated national student loan debt will be $1 trillion. The interest on student loans piles up faster than job earnings can pay them, creating a bottomless hole for young people to climb out of. One solution is for the government to forgive student loan debt, as proposed by Congressman Hansen Clarke (D-Mich.) in H.R. 4170, the Student Loan Forgiveness Act of 2012. A counterargument comes from Richard Vedder in the *National Review,* who argues that college students are already abusing taxpayers' dollars by loans that subsidize too much partying and not enough studying. But if the high cost of college and the burden of debt comprise a serious problem, what are students themselves doing to solve it? Anya Kamenetz suggests that American college students, unlike their European counterparts, have not taken advantage of their digital connectedness to unite for change.

All of the readings in this chapter offer information and viewpoints on issues involving young people today and their futures. We hope that these selections stir debate in your classes and inspire you to make your own explorations and arguments.

Millennials: Confident. Connected. Open to Change

PEW RESEARCH CENTER

> The following excerpt from an extensive report on Millennials from the highly regarded Pew Research Center offers valuable data on people approximately 18–29 years old in the United States. Visit its website at www.pewsocialtrends.org/2010/02/24/ millennials-confident-connected-open-to-change/ to read the entire report.

1   Generations, like people, have personalities, and Millennials—the American teens and twenty-somethings who are making the passage into adulthood at the start of a new millennium—have begun to forge theirs: confident, self-expressive, liberal, upbeat and open to change.

2   They are more ethnically and racially diverse than older adults. They're less religious, less likely to have served in the military, and are on track to become the most educated generation in American history.

3   Their entry into careers and first jobs has been badly set back by the Great Recession, but they are more upbeat than their elders about their own economic futures as well as about the overall state of the nation.

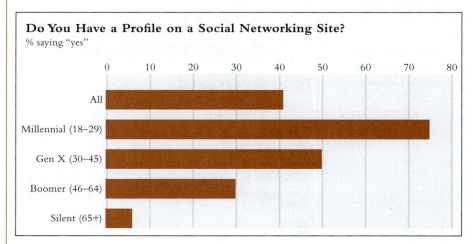

Do You Have a Profile on a Social Networking Site?
% saying "yes"

All	
Millennial (18–29)	
Gen X (30–45)	
Boomer (46–64)	
Silent (65+)	

4   They embrace multiple modes of self-expression. Three-quarters have created a profile on a social networking site. One-in-five have posted a video of themselves online. Nearly four-in-ten have a tattoo (and for most who do, one is not enough: about half of those with tattoos have two to five and 18% have six or more).

5   Nearly one-in-four have a piercing in some place other than an earlobe—about six times the share of older adults who've done this. But their look-at-me tendencies are not without limits. Most Millennials have placed privacy boundaries on their social media profiles. And 70% say their tattoos are hidden beneath clothing.

6   Despite struggling (and often failing) to find jobs in the teeth of a recession, about nine-in-ten either say that they currently have enough money or that they

will eventually meet their long-term financial goals. But at the moment, fully 37% of 18- to 29-year-olds are unemployed or out of the workforce, the highest share among this age group in more than three decades. Research shows that young people who graduate from college in a bad economy typically suffer long-term consequences—with effects on their careers and earnings that linger as long as 15 years.[1]

7   Whether as a by-product of protective parents, the age of terrorism or a media culture that focuses on dangers, they cast a wary eye on human nature. Two-thirds say "you can't be too careful" when dealing with people. Yet they are less skeptical than their elders of government. More so than other generations, they believe government should do more to solve problems.

8   They are the least overtly religious American generation in modern times. One-in-four are unaffiliated with any religion, far more than the share of older adults when they were ages 18 to 29. Yet not belonging does not necessarily mean not believing. Millennials pray about as often as their elders did in their own youth.

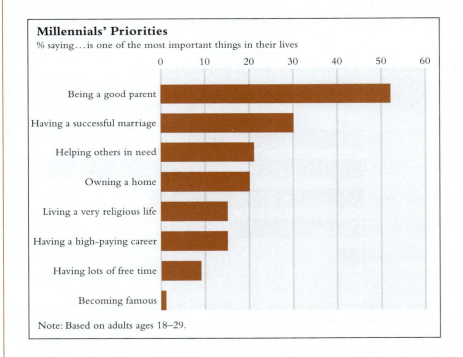

Millennials' Priorities
% saying…is one of the most important things in their lives

Note: Based on adults ages 18–29.

9   Only about six-in-ten were raised by both parents—a smaller share than was the case with older generations. In weighing their own life priorities, Millennials (like older adults) place parenthood and marriage far above career and financial success. But they aren't rushing to the altar. Just one-in-five Millennials (21%) are married now, half the share of their parents' generation at the same stage of life. About a third

(34%) are parents, according to the Pew Research survey. We estimate that, in 2006, more than a third of 18- to 29-year-old women who gave birth were unmarried. This is a far higher share than was the case in earlier generations.[2]

10   Millennials are on course to become the most educated generation in American history, a trend driven largely by the demands of a modern knowledge-based economy, but most likely accelerated in recent years by the millions of 20-somethings enrolling in graduate schools, colleges or community colleges in part because they can't find a job. Among 18- to 24-year-olds a record share—39.6%—was enrolled in college as of 2008, according to census data.

11   They get along well with their parents. Looking back at their teenage years, Millennials report having had fewer spats with mom or dad than older adults say they had with their own parents when they were growing up. And now, hard times have kept a significant share of adult Millennials and their parents under the same roof. About one-in-eight older Millennials (ages 22 and older) say they've "boomeranged" back to a parent's home because of the recession.

12   They respect their elders. A majority say that the older generation is superior to the younger generation when it comes to moral values and work ethic. Also, more than six-in-ten say that families have a responsibility to have an elderly parent come live with them if that parent wants to. By contrast, fewer than four-in-ten adults ages 60 and older agree that this is a family responsibility.

13   Despite coming of age at a time when the United States has been waging two wars, relatively few Millennials—just 2% of males—are military veterans. At a comparable stage of their life cycle, 6% of Gen Xer men, 13% of Baby Boomer men and 24% of Silent men were veterans.

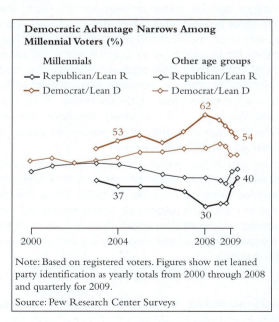

Democratic Advantage Narrows Among Millennial Voters (%)

Millennials
—◇— Republican/Lean R
—◇— Democrat/Lean D

Other age groups
—◇— Republican/Lean R
—◇— Democrat/Lean D

Note: Based on registered voters. Figures show net leaned party identification as yearly totals from 2000 through 2008 and quarterly for 2009.

Source: Pew Research Center Surveys

14   Politically, Millennials were among Barack Obama's strongest supporters in 2008, backing him for president by more than a two-to-one ratio (66% to 32%) while older adults were giving just 50% of their votes to the Democratic nominee. This was the largest disparity between younger and older voters recorded in four decades of modern election day exit polling. Moreover, after decades of low voter participation by the young, the turnout gap in 2008 between voters under and over the age of 30 was the smallest it had been since 18- to 20-year-olds were given the right to vote in 1972.

15   But the political enthusiasms of Millennials have since cooled—for Obama and his message of change, for the Democratic Party and, quite possibly, for politics itself. About half of Millennials say the president has failed to change the way Washington works, which had been the central promise of his candidacy. Of those who say this, three-in-ten blame Obama himself, while more than half blame his political opponents and special interests.

16   To be sure, Millennials remain the most likely of any generation to self-identify as liberals; they are less supportive than their elders of an assertive national security policy and more supportive of a progressive domestic social agenda. They are still more likely than any other age group to identify as Democrats. Yet by early 2010, their support for Obama and the Democrats had receded, as evidenced both by survey data and by their low level of participation in recent off-year and special elections.

OUR RESEARCH METHODS

17   This Pew Research Center report profiles the roughly 50 million Millennials who currently span the ages of 18 to 29. It's likely that when future analysts are in a position to take a fuller measure of this new generation, they will conclude that millions of additional younger teens (and perhaps even pre-teens) should be grouped together with their older brothers and sisters. But for the purposes of this report, unless we indicate otherwise, we focus on Millennials who are at least 18 years old.

18   We examine their demographics; their political and social values; their lifestyles and life priorities; their digital technology and social media habits; and their economic and educational aspirations. We also compare and contrast Millennials with the nation's three other living generations—Gen Xers (ages 30 to 45), Baby Boomers (ages 46 to 64) and Silents (ages 65 and older). Whenever the trend data permit, we compare the four generations as they all are now—and also as older generations were at the ages that adult Millennials are now.[3]

19   Most of the findings in this report are based on a new survey of a national cross-section of 2,020 adults (including an oversample of Millennials), conducted by landline and cellular telephone from Jan. 14 to 27, 2010; this survey has a margin of error of plus or minus 3.0 percentage points for the full sample and larger percentages for various subgroups. The report also draws on more than two decades of Pew Research Center surveys, supplemented by our analysis of Census Bureau data and other relevant studies. . . .

SOME CAVEATS

20   A few notes of caution are in order. Generational analysis has a long and distinguished place in social science, and we cast our lot with those scholars who believe it is not

only possible, but often highly illuminating, to search for the unique and distinctive characteristics of any given age group of Americans. But we also know this is not an exact science.

21   We acknowledge, for example, that there is an element of false precision in setting hard chronological boundaries between the generations. Can we say with certainty that a typical 30-year-old adult is a Gen Xer while a typical 29-year-old adult is a Millennial? Of course not. Nevertheless, we must draw lines in order to carry out the statistical analyses that form the core of our research methodology. And our boundaries—while admittedly too crisp—are not arbitrary. They are based on our own research findings and those of other scholars.

22   We are mindful that there are as many differences in attitudes, values, behaviors and lifestyles within a generation as there are between generations. But we believe this reality does not diminish the value of generational analysis; it merely adds to its richness and complexity. Throughout this report, we will not only explore how Millennials differ from other generations, we will also look at how they differ among themselves.

THE MILLENNIAL IDENTITY

23 Most Millennials (61%) in our January 2010 survey say their generation has a unique and distinctive identity. That doesn't make them unusual, however. Roughly two-thirds of Silents, nearly six-in-ten Boomers and about half of Xers feel the same way about their generation.

24   But Millennials have a distinctive reason for feeling distinctive. In response to an open-ended follow-up question, 24% say it's because of their use of technology. Gen Xers also cite technology as their generation's biggest source of distinctiveness, but far fewer—just 12%—say this. Boomers' feelings of distinctiveness coalesce mainly around work ethic, which 17% cite as their most prominent identity badge. For Silents, it's the shared experience of the Depression and World War II, which 14% cite as the biggest reason their generation stands apart.

What Makes Your Generation Unique?

	Millennial	Gen X	Boomer	Silent
1.	Technology use (24%)	Technology use (12%)	Work ethic (17%)	WW II, Depression (14%)
2.	Music/Pop culture (11%)	Work ethic (11%)	Respectful (14%)	Smarter (13%)
3.	Liberal/tolerant (7%)	Conservative/Trad'l (7%)	Values/Morals (8%)	Honest (12%)
4.	Smarter (6%)	Smarter (6%)	"Baby Boomers" (6%)	Work ethic (10%)
5.	Clothes (5%)	Respectful (5%)	Smarter (5%)	Values/Morals (10%)

NOTE: Based on respondents who said their generation was unique/distinct. Items represent individual, open-ended responses. Top five responses are shown for each age group. Sample sizes for sub-groups are as follows: Millennials, n = 527; Gen X, n = 173; Boomers, n = 283; Silent, n = 205.

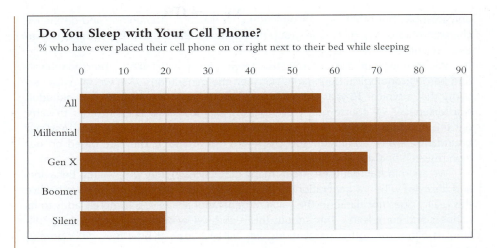

Do You Sleep with Your Cell Phone?
% who have ever placed their cell phone on or right next to their bed while sleeping

25   Millennials' technological exceptionalism is chronicled throughout the survey. It's not just their gadgets—it's the way they've fused their social lives into them. For example, three-quarters of Millennials have created a profile on a social networking site, compared with half of Xers, 30% of Boomers and 6% of Silents. There are big generation gaps, as well, in using wireless technology, playing video games and posting self-created videos online. Millennials are also more likely than older adults to say technology makes life easier and brings family and friends closer together (though the generation gaps on these questions are relatively narrow).

WORK ETHIC, MORAL VALUES, RACE RELATIONS

26   Of the four generations, Millennials are the only one that doesn't cite "work ethic" as one of their principal claims to distinctiveness. A nationwide Pew Research Center survey taken in 2009 may help explain why. This one focused on differences between young and old rather than between specific age groups. Nonetheless, its findings are instructive. Nearly six-in-ten respondents cited work ethic as one of the big sources of differences between young and old. Asked who has the better work ethic, about three-fourths of respondents said that older people do. By similar margins, survey respondents also found older adults have the upper hand when it comes to moral values and their respect for others.

27   It might be tempting to dismiss these findings as a typical older adult gripe about "kids today." But when it comes to each of these traits—work ethic, moral values, respect for others—young adults agree that older adults have the better of it. In short, Millennials may be a self-confident generation, but they display little appetite for claims of moral superiority.

28   That 2009 survey also found that the public—young and old alike—thinks the younger generation is more racially tolerant than their elders. More than two decades of Pew Research surveys confirm that assessment. In their views about interracial dating, for example, Millennials are the most open to change of any generation, followed closely by Gen Xers, then Boomers, then Silents.

Weighing Trends in Marriage and Parenthood, by Generation

% saying this is a bad thing for society				
	Millennial	**Gen X**	**Boomer**	**Silent**
More single women deciding to have children	59	54	65	72
More gay couples raising children	32	36	48	55
More mothers of young children working outside the home	23	29	39	38
More people living together w/o getting married	22	31	44	58
More people of different races marrying each other	5	10	14	26

Note: "Good thing", "Doesn't make much difference", and "Don't know" responses not shown.

29   Likewise, Millennials are more receptive to immigrants than are their elders. Nearly six-in-ten (58%) say immigrants strengthen the country, according to a 2009 Pew Research survey; just 43% of adults ages 30 and older agree.

30   The same pattern holds on a range of attitudes about nontraditional family arrangements, from mothers of young children working outside the home, to adults living together without being married, to more people of different races marrying each other. Millennials are more accepting than older generations of these more modern family arrangements, followed closely by Gen Xers. To be sure, acceptance does not in all cases translate into outright approval. But it does mean Millennials disapprove less.

A GENTLER GENERATION GAP

31   A 1969 Gallup survey, taken near the height of the social and political upheavals of that turbulent decade, found that 74% of the public believed there was a "generation gap" in American society. Surprisingly, when that same question was asked in a Pew Research Center survey last year—in an era marked by hard economic times but little if any overt age-based social tension—the share of the public saying there was a generation gap had risen slightly to 79%.

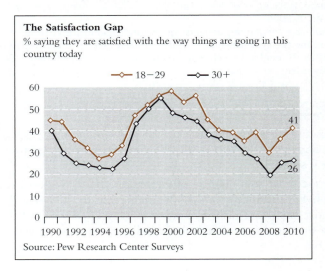

The Satisfaction Gap

% saying they are satisfied with the way things are going in this country today

18−29   30+

Source: Pew Research Center Surveys

32   But as the 2009 results also make clear, this modern generation gap is a much more benign affair than the one that cast a shadow over the 1960s. The public says this one is mostly about the different ways that old and young use technology—and relatively few people see that gap as a source of conflict. Indeed, only about a quarter of the respondents in the 2009 survey said they see big conflicts between young and old in America. Many more see conflicts between immigrants and the native born, between rich and poor, and between black and whites.

33   There is one generation gap that has widened notably in recent years. It has to do with satisfaction over the state of the nation. In recent decades the young have always tended to be a bit more upbeat than their elders on this key measure, but the gap is wider now than it has been in at least twenty years. Some 41% of Millennials say they are satisfied with the way things are going in the country, compared with just 26% of those ages 30 and older. Whatever toll a recession, a housing crisis, a financial meltdown and a pair of wars may have taken on the national psyche in the past few years, it appears to have hit the old harder than the young.

34   But this speaks to a difference in outlook and attitude; it's not a source of conflict or tension. As they make their way into adulthood, Millennials have already distinguished themselves as a generation that gets along well with others, especially their elders. For a nation whose population is rapidly going gray, that could prove to be a most welcome character trait.

NOTES

1. Lisa B. Kahn. "The Long-Term Labor Market Consequences of Graduating from College in a Bad Economy," Yale School of Management, 13 Aug. 2009 (forthcoming in *Labour Economics*).
2. This Pew Research estimate is drawn from our analysis of government data for women ages 18 to 29 who gave birth in 2006, the most recent year for which such data is available. Martin, Joyce A., et al. Births: Final Data for 2006. *National Vital Statistics Reports,* vol. 57, no. 7, 2009.
3. We do not have enough respondents ages 83 and older in our 2010 survey to permit an analysis of the Greatest Generation, which is usually defined as encompassing adults born before 1928. Throughout much of this report, we have grouped these older respondents in with the Silent generation.

QUESTIONS FOR DISCUSSION

1. Surveys often confirm what we already know or strongly suspect. Did any of the findings of this survey surprise you? Are you inclined to doubt any of them? If so, why?

2. What factor or combination of factors do you think best explains the results? For instance, many Millennials point to the Great Recession as the most important influence on their lives. How much of the results of the survey seem tied directly or indirectly to adverse economic conditions?

3. As generations age, attitudes and outlooks tend to change. For example, people tend to become more conservative and realistic. What characteristics of the Millennials do you think will change the most? What characteristics do you think will remain the same or grow more pronounced?

FOR ADDITIONAL READING, DISCUSSION, AND INQUIRY

This selection is only a summary of the results of the Pew Center's research on Millennials. Divide the class into groups and read some or all of the chapters comprising the complete report, which you can access at the address given in the headnote. Discuss the details of each chapter with the whole class. Then, taking the chapter or chapter you find most interesting, write an exploratory essay addressing some or all of the questions posed above; that is,

— Did any of the findings in this chapter surprise you? Are you inclined to doubt any of them? If so, why?

— What factor or combination of factors do you think best explains the results?

— What characteristics of the Millennials do you think will change the most? What characteristics do you think will remain the same or grow more pronounced?

Gen Y Is from Mercury

KIT YARROW AND JAYNE O'DONNELL

Kit Yarrow is a consumer psychologist, chair of the psychology department at Golden Gate University, and consultant for such companies as General Electric, Del Monte, and Nokia. Jayne O'Donnell is a prominent journalist at *USA Today,* who has done important work on product safety, especially relating to air bags and teenaged drivers. They coauthored *Gen BuY: How Tweens, Teens, and Twenty-Somethings Are Revolutionizing Retail,* from which the following excerpt comes.

1   This generation, the product of a transformed world, is to previous generations as man is to woman and Mars is to Venus. Which is to say: basically the same, but entirely different. Generation Y is unquestionably unique, and some say potentially one of the most powerful and influential generations ever.

2   Gen Y is diverse, adaptive, and confident. Fewer than two-thirds of them are white, over 25 percent are raised in single parent households, and three-quarters have working moms. Their generation's size—almost eighty-four million members—helps give them unprecedented influence; their confidence and their ability to connect with others guarantee it. . . .

THE TWO GREATEST INFLUENCES

3   Though some may point to social or political events such as the Columbine shootings, the Bill Clinton–Monica Lewinsky scandal, the fall of the Soviet Union, and even the

death of Princess Diana as the forces that have shaped Gen Y, there are two profoundly influential factors that outweigh the rest: *their adoring parents* and *the digital world.*

Adoring Parents

4   Gen Y children are considered to be the most wanted children of all time, and they've grown up in an era of exploding interest in and knowledge about child development and psychology. Unlike previous generations of parents—who certainly wanted and loved their children, but also saw them as responsibilities—or even earlier generations, who felt the same way but saw them as potential laborers—today's parents prize their children as more equal and central members of the household. Additionally, no society in history has had a greater focus on, interest in, and understanding of the child.

5   And even though nearly half of Gen Y children have divorced parents, and one-third come from single-parent households, those parents still spent more focused time with their Gen Y kids than any previous generation. The greater attention and parental involvement of fathers as central figures in parenting has also had a great effect on the sense of Gen Yers that they are important and central. Additionally, technology brings families even closer, thanks to the frequent contact between kids and parents that cell phones afford.

6   Gen Y parents have been criticized for coddling, for impairing their child's independence by hovering like helicopters, for being enmeshed in or overly dependent on their kid's approval. These characteristics are generally more true of this generation than of previous ones, and in the course of our research we certainly did see examples of just the sort of behavior that's inspired these descriptions (including moms who know who's asking whom to the prom before their kids do), and also *plenty* of parents dependent on their kids' success for their own egos. But what we also saw were "helicopters" who might also have been described as simply interested, involved parents; "coddlers" who could have been called warm, nurturing parents; and "overly dependent parents" who might have been seen as folks who value their kid's minds and opinions. . . .

7   We found it most helpful to view Gen Y parents on a normally distributed curve, with those clearly overinvolved, coddling helicopters at one end; some relatively disengaged parents at the other end; and most of the group in the middle—registering more kid-centric than the last generation of parents, but not 'coptering coddlers either.

8   Being a wanted kid in a child-centered household adds to your clout, of course. Gen Y households are the most egalitarian of all time, and Gen Y parents tend to be nonauthoritarian and to value their friendships with their kids. This is one of the primary reasons behind Gen Y's confidence and power. . . .

Their Digital World

9   The second most important factor that's shaped the uniqueness of this generation is their enmeshment with technology and their ability to harness the power of the Internet. This sophistication has increased their influence in their households, added a pedal-to-the-metal element to their cognitive and social styles, reinforced and equipped a team mentality, and empowered them.

10   ***Household Clout.*** In addition to their kid-centric clout, Gen Yers typically provide in-house tech support for their parents, which has reinforced their stature as
equals—or even superiors, at least in the IT department. It's also made them *the* great
force to be reckoned with by electronics marketers. When they have prized knowledge and expertise, it becomes pretty hard to discount the thoughts and abilities
of a kid. Previous generations had to pretend or humor their kids ("Let's frame your
Picasso!"), but in the case of this generation, their intuitive ease with technology and
their ability to adapt to technological shifts is a genuine asset to any family. Having
never experienced a world without computers, the Internet, cell phones, and digital
cameras, Gen Yers are free of anxiety and full of playfulness when they interact with
the Internet and technology of all sorts. This makes learning easier for them than it is
for all but the most tech-savvy parents. . . .

11   ***Speed, Power, and Self-Reliance.*** Put simply, they want what they want when
they want it. As the first generation raised from day one under the influence of the
Internet, the world, as they know it, means speed; multitasking; instant answers;
always available friends, parents, teachers, and experts; a connection to others that
defies geography and hierarchy; less necessity for face-to-face (or voice-to-voice)
human interaction; and free access to information for everyone.

12   Kit noticed, during a recent guest lecture at UC Berkeley, that at least half of her
students were typing. A quick cruise around the room revealed about half of those
typists were looking up her articles, an international student was checking a word
definition, and the rest were on Facebook. In other words: multitasking, available to
their friends no matter where they were, and instantly accessing free information.

13   "They are a very different generation," says Jenny Floren, founder and CEO of
Experience, which helps recruits students from nearly four thousand colleges and
universities for its business clients. Because they've been online often since they were
toddlers, they process information very differently. "That's where their friends are,
where they shop, and where they study," says Floren. "In many regards, being in
person is the same as being online."

14   The digital world that Gen Y inhabits is credited with shortening their attention spans, increasing their need for immediate gratification, and helping them to
become super speedy at processing visual data—Gen Yers live in a faster world than
anything previous generations have known.

15   Gen Yers are also proactive and empowered when it comes to information. They
seek out only the information that's relevant (or that they perceive to be relevant) to
them. Previous generations, unaided by the power of search engines, acquired information in a more passive way. For example, most boomers wouldn't have had a way
to learn more about a physical symptom or health malady—those answers were in the
hands of physicians and households lucky enough to have a set of encyclopedias. There
was no such thing as an instant answer. Not to mention that the answers available had
been edited and vetted prior to publication. So when we say "empowered" we truly
do mean power. From the information (though not the wisdom) of a physician to the
latest Van's hoodie available to a skater living 350 miles from a mall, Gen Yers have
known only one world—one in which they can get what they want when they want it.

16   Consequently, there has been an important social shift toward a mentality of self-reliance and the flattened hierarchy that accompanies democratized information. Contributing to this is a disappointment in social institutions ranging from our schools and religious institutions to our political leaders and even athletes and celebrities—all widely (and sometimes hysterically) reported through an increasingly competitive media. Businesses, in particular, have taken a big hit in confidence. Once the most likely villain in the movies was a Communist, monster, or alien—today it's a white businessman.

17   ***My Posse.*** Gen Yers, already trained in school to work as teams, have embraced technology as a way to facilitate group connections. They can and do unite with likeminded (physical) strangers from around the world to champion causes, play computer games such as World of Warcraft, stay in touch with school and business friends and colleagues indefinitely through social networking sites such as LinkedIn and Facebook, and text their moms' group about sales at Baby Gap. Whatever the interest, connections—already the social DNA of Gen Y—are enabled through technology. Gen Yers between thirteen and twenty-four tell an average of eighteen people about a website or TV show that they enjoy, whereas older adults tell an average of only ten people.

18   Although older folks sometimes struggle to learn and adapt to technological advances, they've also had the opportunity to weigh consequences and compare outcomes. Some of the anxiety we've seen in older generations regarding Gen Y is due, in part, to their fear that Gen Y won't know what they're missing or losing by relying on technology. Will all that speed and multitasking result in superficiality? Will Gen Yers have the patience to think deeply about things? Will online relating replace or diminish intimacy? Will shorthand communication, like text messaging and Twittering, and the highly portable nature of technology result in social rudeness (like loud cell phone chats in elevators) and poor formal writing and communication skills?

19   We all know the answer to the social rudeness question—and it's certainly not just the younger members of our community who are at fault. As to the other questions, some of the answer resides in the asker: it's a time-honored tradition of every senior generation to ask, "What's with these kids?" And though our Gen Yers shared some serious struggles and concerns—many of which are related to technology and even more to the high expectations they have for themselves and the world—we found overall that the kids are alright. They'll have their own set of problems to solve, just as every generation before them, but they'll also have powerful gifts and new tools to help—namely confidence, teamwork, technology, and their desire to make a positive contribution to the world. . . .

QUESTIONS FOR DISCUSSION

1. The Millennial generation is "unquestionably unique," Yarrow and O'Donnell say. What are the characteristics that make them unique?

2. "Gen Y's parents have been criticized for coddling, for impairing their child's independence by hovering like helicopters." Do you think this criticism has

merit? How important in your view is independence and how does it relate to being *inter*dependent, connected to a network of people via electronic communications?

3. One characteristic that Millennials and the parent generation may share is "a disappointment in social institutions," certainly widespread in the 1960s and 1970s. Are you disappointed in American social institutions? If so, did you acquire this attitude from your parents or from other sources?

FOR RESEARCH, DISCUSSION, AND PERSUASION

According to Yarrow and O'Donnell, older generations pose these questions about Millennials:

> Will all that speed and multitasking result in superficiality? Will Gen Yers have the patience to think deeply about things? Will online relating replace or diminish intimacy? Will short-hand communication, like text messaging and Twittering, and the highly portable nature of technology result in social rudeness . . . and poor formal writing?

All these questions have been much debated and researched, both online and in print sources. Choose one of them or a related question you would like to investigate and read what you can find on it. (Consult Chapter 6, pages 98–111 for help in doing the research.)

After discussion of research results in class, write a persuasive essay directed at the older generation urging them not to be overly concerned about your question, or directed at a Millennial audience urging them to take steps to resist or counteract the impact of electronic communication.

Is It Time to Kill the Liberal Arts Degree?

KIM BROOKS

> Whenever the economy suffers a long decline, the value of a liberal arts major comes up for debate. In this selection, a creative writer, Kim Brooks, offers an honest and balanced inquiry into the topic. Her essay appeared in the online magazine *Salon*.

1   Every year or two, my husband, an academic advisor at a prestigious Midwestern university, gets a call from a student's parent. Mr. or Mrs. So-and-so's son is a sophomore now and still insistent on majoring in film studies, anthropology, Southeast Asian comparative literature or, god forbid . . . English. These dalliances in the humanities were fine and good when little Johnny was a freshman, but isn't it time now that he wake up and start thinking seriously about what, one or two or three years down the line, he's actually going to do?

2   My husband, loyal first and foremost to his students' intellectual development, and also an unwavering believer in the inherent value of a liberal arts education, tells me about these conversations with an air of indignation. He wonders, "Aren't these parents aware of what they signed their kid up for when they decided to let him come get a liberal arts degree instead of going to welding school?" Also, he says,

"The most aimless students are often the last ones you want to force into a career path. I do sort of hate to enable this prolonged adolescence, but I also don't want to aid and abet the miseries of years lost to a misguided professional choice."

3   Now, I love my husband. Lately, however, I find myself wincing when he recounts these stories. "Well," I sometimes say, "what *are* they going to do?"

4   The answer, at least according to a recent article in the *New York Times,* is rather bleak. Employment rates for college graduates have declined steeply in the last two years, and perhaps even more disheartening, those who find jobs are more likely to be steaming lattes or walking dogs than doing anything even peripherally related to their college curriculum. While the scale and severity of this post-graduation letdown may be an unavoidable consequence of an awful recession, I do wonder if all those lofty institutions of higher learning, with their noble-sounding mission statements and soft-focused brochure photos of campus greens, may be glossing over the serious, at-times-crippling obstacles a B.A. holder must overcome to achieve professional and financial stability. I'm not asking if a college education has inherent value, if it makes students more thoughtful, more informed, more enlightened and critical-minded human beings. These are all interesting questions that don't pay the rent. What I'm asking is far more banal and far more pressing. What I'm asking is: Why do even the best colleges fail so often at preparing kids for the world?

5   When I earned my diploma from the University of Virginia in the spring of 2000, it never occurred to me before my senior year to worry too seriously about my post-graduation prospects. Indeed, most of my professors, advisors and mentors reinforced this complacency. I was smart, they told me. I'd spent four years at a rigorous institution honing my writing, research and critical-thinking skills. I'd written an impressive senior thesis, gathered recommendations from professors, completed summer internships in various journalistic endeavors. They had no doubt at all that I would land on my feet. And I did (kind of), about a decade after graduating.

6   In the interim, I floundered. I worked as a restaurant hostess and tutored English-as-a-second-language without a formal work visa. I mooched off friends and boyfriends and slept on couches. One dreary night in San Francisco, I went on an interview to tend bar at a strip club, but left demoralized when I realized I'd have to walk around in stilettos. I went back to school to complete the pre-medical requirements I'd shunned the first time through; then, a week into physics, I applied to nursing school, then withdrew from that program after a month when I realized nursing would be an environment where my habit of spacing out might actually kill someone. I landed a $12-an-hour job as a paralegal at an asbestos-related litigation firm. I got an MFA in fiction.

7   Depending on how you look at it, I either spent a long time finding myself, or wasted seven years. And while all these efforts hardly add up to a tragedy (largely because I had the luxury of supportive parents willing to supplement my income for a time), I do have to admit feeling disillusioned as I moved from one gig to another, feeling as though my undergraduate education, far from preparing me for any kind of meaningful and remunerative work, had in some ways deprepared me, nurturing my natural strengths and predilections—writing, reading, analysis—and sweeping my weaknesses in organization, pragmatic problem-solving, decision-making under the proverbial rug.

8   Of course, there are certainly plenty of B.A. holders out there who, wielding the magic combination of competency, credentials and luck, are able to land themselves a respectable, entry-level job that requires neither name tag nor apron. But for every person I know who parlayed a degree in English or anthropology into a career-track gig, I know two others who weren't so lucky, who, in that awful, post-college year or two or three or four, unemployed and uninsured and uncommitted to any particular field, racked up credit card debt or got married to the wrong person or went to law school for no particular reason or made one of a dozen other time- and money-wasting mistakes.

9   And the common thread in all these stories seems to be how surprised these graduates were by their utter unemployability, a feeling of having been misled into complacency, issued reassurances about how the pedigree or prestige of the institution they'd attended would save them. This narrative holds true whether their course of study was humanities or social sciences. My baby sitter, for example, who earned a degree in psychology from a Big Ten university, now makes $15 an hour watching my kids. "I was not the most serious student," she admits. "But I do wonder, why was I allowed to decide on a major without ever sitting down with my advisor and talking about what I might do with that major after graduating? I mean, I had to write out a plan for how I'd fit all my required courses into my schedule, but no one seemed to care if I had a plan once I left there. I graduated not knowing how to use Excel, write out a business plan, do basic accounting. With room and board and tuition, my time there cost $120,000."

10   I asked Sarah Isham, the director of career services of the College of Arts and Sciences at my alma mater about this discrepancy between curriculum and career planning, and she repeats the same reassurances I heard 10 years ago: "What we do is help students see how the patterns and themes of their interests, skills and values, might relate to particular arenas. We do offer a few self-assessment tests, as well as many other resources to help them do this."

11   When I ask how well the current services are working—that is, how many recent graduates are finding jobs, real jobs that require a degree—she can only say that "The College of Arts and Sciences does not collect statistics on post-graduation plans. I could not give you any idea of where these students are going or what they are doing. Regrettably, it's not something in place at this time."

12   I went on to ask her how the college's curriculum was adapting to meet the demands of the recession and the realities of the job market, and she directed me to a dean who asked not to be identified, and who expressed, in no uncertain terms, how tired he was of articles like mine that question the rationale, rigor or usefulness of a liberal arts education. He insisted that while he had no suggestions regarding how a 22-year-old should weather a recession, the university was achieving its goal of creating citizens of the world.

13   When I asked him how a 22-year-old with no job, no income, no health insurance and, in some cases, six figures of college debt to pay off is supposed to be a citizen of the world, he said he had no comment, that he was the wrong person to talk to, and he directed me to another dean, who was also unable to comment.

14   The chilliness of this response was a bit disheartening, but not terribly surprising. When I was an undergrad, it seemed whenever I mentioned my job-search anxieties,

my professors and advisors would get a glassy look in their eyes and mutter something about the career center. Their gazes would drift toward their bookshelves or a folder of ungraded papers. And at the time, I could hardly blame them. These were people who'd published dissertations on Freud, written definitive volumes on Virginia Woolf. The language of real-world career preparation was a language they simply didn't speak.

15   And if they did say anything at all, it was usually a reiteration of the typical liberal arts defense, that graduating with a humanities degree, I could do anything: I could go on to earn a master's or a law degree or become an editor or a teacher. I could go into journalism or nonprofit work, apply to medical school or the foreign service. I could write books or learn to illustrate or bind them. I could start my own business, work as a consultant, get a job editing pamphlets for an alumni association or raise money for public radio. The possibilities were literally limitless. It was a like being 6 years old again and trying to decide if I'd become an astronaut or a ballerina. The advantage to a humanities degree, one professor insisted, was its versatility. In retrospect, though, I wonder if perhaps this was part of the problem, as well; freedom can promote growth, but it can also cause paralysis. Faced with limitless possibilities, a certain number of people will just stand still.

16   "So let me ask you something," my husband says, my wonderfully incisive husband who will let me get away with only so much bitterness. "If your school had forced you to declare a career plan or take an accounting class or study Web programming instead of contemporary lit, how would you have felt about it at the time, without the benefit of hindsight?"

17   It's a good question, and the answer is, I probably would have transferred. There were courses I took in college, courses in Renaissance literature and the anthropology of social progress and international relations of the Middle East and, of course, writing, that will, in all likelihood, never earn me a steady paycheck or a 401K, but which I would not trade for anything; there were lectures on Shakespeare and Twain and Joyce that I still remember, that I've dreamt about and that define my sensibility as a writer and a reader and a human being. Even now, knowing the lost years that followed, I still wouldn't trade them in.

18   A new Harvard study suggests that it's not an abandonment of the college curriculum that's needed, but a re-envisioning and better preparation. The study compares the U.S. system unfavorably to its European counterparts where students begin thinking about what sort of career they'll pursue and the sort of preparation they'll need for it in middle school. Could that be the answer?

19   At the end of my interview with Sarah Isham, she asks me if I might come back to Charlottesville to participate in an alumni career panel. "We always have a lot of students interested in media and writing and the arts. It would be wonderful," she says "to have you come and talk to them." She asks me this, and I can't help but laugh. "I don't think I'd be much of a role model," I say. "I don't have what you'd call a high-powered career. I mostly do freelance work. Adjunct teaching. That sort of thing."

20   "Oh, that's fine," she insists. "Our students will love that. So many of them are terrified of sitting in a cubicle all day."

21   They should be so lucky, I think. But I would never say that—not to them and not to my own students. They'll have plenty of time later to find out just what a degree is and isn't good for. Right now, they're in those four extraordinary, exceptional years where ideas matter; and there's not a thing I'd do to change that.

This article first appeared in Salon.com, at http://www.Salon.com. An online version remains in the Salon archives. Reprinted with permission.

QUESTIONS FOR DISCUSSION

1. This selection is an example of argument as inquiry, as Brooks looks at the advantages and disadvantages of spending time in college studying arts and humanities. What evidence does she offer that challenges the choice of a liberal arts degree? What evidence supports the choice? What is her conclusion?

2. In the context of job shortages in recent years, the ending may surprise some readers, especially the comment by Sarah Isham that students are "terrified of sitting in a cubicle all day." Do you share this fear? If so, how many of your fellow students also share it? What does that say about thinking of college as career preparation? What does it say about views of entry-level jobs among young adults?

3. Brooks says that she had "the luxury of supportive parents willing to supplement [her] income" after graduation. How does this fact affect her conclusion?

FOR RESEARCH AND CONVINCING

Do Americans wait too long to decide on a career path? Is it a luxury to spend late adolescence in years of exploring one's options and interests? Compare the American college system with that of some other country or countries where students declare their career paths at an earlier age. Then write an essay that either rejects the foreign system as incompatible with American culture or that advocates American higher education as a model other nations should adopt.

A Liberal Arts Education Is Still Relevant

STUART RABINOWITZ

Stuart Rabinowitz is president of Hofstra University. Drawing on his long experience with college students and universities, he makes a strong argument for liberal arts as still a good choice for many students, and a choice that should not be evaluated on its immediate rewards but rather its long-term life and career outcomes. This essay appeared on the op-ed page of *Newsday,* February 7, 2013.

1   Our nation's ongoing economic recession, coupled with the escalating costs of higher education, has rekindled the perennial debate about the value of a liberal arts education. Just last week, North Carolina Gov. Patrick McCrory and House Majority Leader Eric Cantor (R-Va.) have publicly, and pointedly, posed the question: What good is a major in literature or philosophy when today's college graduates, already saddled with substantial debt, face so uncertain a professional future?

2   Cantor, in a speech to the American Enterprise Institute on Tuesday, called on colleges and universities to be more transparent about costs, to encourage entrepreneurship and innovation, and to provide reliable information on employment and potential earnings by academic major. Federal aid, he argued, should be used as an incentive for students to finish their studies, and get into the job market, sooner.

3   This anxiety about the economy has a significant impact on higher education. A private university without a 10-digit endowment that ignores these trends does so at its fiscal peril. Providing complete and reliable data is critical, as is investing in programs that train students to work in fields such as engineering and the health professions, where demographic trends predict abundant job opportunities. At Hofstra, we're doing both. But there's a difference between giving students resources to help them make informed decisions about where and what they study, and pushing them to pick a major based solely on perceived or projected career potential.

4   Where does this leave the liberal arts—disciplines in the humanities and more recently in the social sciences that for centuries have defined the knowledge an educated person should have? These have been criticized lately for being out of step and, even worse, irrelevant to financial and professional success.

5   Defenders rightly stress that the training a liberal arts education provides in advancing critical thinking skills and oral and written communication is essential to professional success. They contend that a liberal arts education is the foundation for an engaged citizenry, and they point out the joy and inspiration people find in experiencing literature, the arts, music and theater.

6   So what is today's college student to do? For most students, the decision about what they should major in goes beyond an analysis of employment statistics. As the following questions that students frequently ask themselves demonstrate, choosing a major in response to a changing job market is not always the most practical or rewarding way to approach one's undergraduate education.

7   **What do I want to be when I grow up?** The notion that college should provide four years of pre-professional training assumes that students begin their studies with a clear understanding of what they want to do with their lives after graduation. To be sure, there are ambitious young people whose career paths are clear from the outset. But compelling students to make decisions based on perceived job opportunities that are four years in the future deprives them of the self-discovery that is the hallmark of a liberal arts education.

8   **What if I change my mind?** Because a liberal arts education exposes students to a wide array of disciplines, students in liberal arts universities frequently discover interests they never knew they had. Partly as a consequence, a substantial percentage of undergraduates change their majors at some point during college. Students who approach their education purely in terms of occupational preparation may deprive themselves of the opportunity to find inspiration and excel in some other area of concentration.

9   **I know what I want to be but what do I major in?** For some fields, the connection between academic and career training is clear. An aspiring computer scientist should major in computer science; a future physician assistant should take a course of study in pre-PA. But most fields can be entered from a variety of undergraduate,

academic majors. Law students may major as undergraduates in disciplines ranging from English and philosophy to engineering and accounting. Medical schools are eager to expand their pool of talented applicants by recruiting students who have excelled in the humanities and social sciences, not just the more traditional majors in biology and biochemistry. Some of our alumni who have built successful business careers majored in liberal arts disciplines during their undergraduate years.

10   **But I really love art.** One of our deans told me about a student who loved graphic arts but who was concerned about its career potential. The dean advised the student to major in art—that if he loved it and could excel at it, he would find a way to make a career from it. One of the underlying assumptions of a liberal arts education is that we are all wired differently. The Bureau of Labor Statistics may forecast an abundance of jobs for software engineers, but not all of us are either interested in or suited for that. Some of us are wired with the talents to be novelists, actors, musicians or scholars. We sometimes forget that America's global leadership was attained not only through business and technological innovation, but also by the dissemination of its culture and political ideas—through art, literature, history, music and theater.

11   At Hofstra, all of our students, regardless of major, are educated about job opportunities. But we encourage them to view their college years as exploration, as well as preparation for the workplace. We want them not only to get jobs after they graduate, but to have rewarding careers and fulfilling lives.

12   **There were supposed to be jobs in these fields.** Approaching an undergraduate education based on the availability of jobs in a particular area may appear to be a low-risk/high-reward endeavor, but these trends can change with astonishing rapidity. Think of how quickly job prospects in law and finance changed from 2008 to 2009. The jobs that are seen as hot today may cool off by the time a student is ready to graduate; jobs that may be abundant in one region may be hard to come by in another. The virtue of a liberal arts education is that it provides the graduate with enduring communication and critical thinking skills that are less susceptible to the consequences of job erosion in an area where a student has devoted years of pre-professional training.

13   In today's fast-paced culture, we are often told to value the moment, but the lasting worth of one's education can only be assessed over time. Do we measure the success of the graduate's college experience by her first job or by a lifetime of professional achievement? Americans now change jobs numerous times over a lifetime and when the jobs of tomorrow may not even exist today, how significant is preparation for a student's first job? What we want—students, parents, all of us—is something of lasting worth.

14   When examined from this perspective, the liberal arts hold up very well.

From *Newsday*, February 7, 2013. © 2013 by Stuart Rabinowitz. Reprinted by permission of the author.

QUESTIONS FOR DISCUSSION

1. Make a list of the author's points in favor of the liberal arts. Which points seem strongest to you? Which seem weakest? Why?

2. "At Hofstra," the author says, "all of our students, regardless of major, are educated about job opportunities. But we encourage them to view their college years as exploration, as well as preparation for the workplace." This sounds responsible and humane, but how do you react to it? Is exploration a luxury from your point of view, given economic realities and college costs? What do you really want from college? Do the liberal arts (English, philosophy, history, political science, religious studies, and so on) connect to what you want?

3. The author refers to a well-established and indisputable fact: "Americans now change jobs numerous times over a lifetime." Sometimes these job changes are quite radically different—say, from being an investment counselor to a community college teacher, or from doing one job full time, another part time. Does it make sense, then, for any student to choose career training over getting a broad-based education?

FOR RESEARCH, DISCUSSION, AND MEDIATION

Using the arguments in this chapter and others that you locate about liberal arts vs. career-preparation views of post-secondary education, compile a list of arguments for both points of view. Discuss the arguments thoughtfully. Then ask: Is there a median position, one that would not result either in college graduates with no job prospects or college graduates who know virtually nothing outside of narrow preparation for a first job? If you see a median position, state and defend it. If you don't, argue for your version of one of the two sides, being sure to include your reasons for being a post-secondary student and your experience—and the experience of people you know—with school and work.

College Debt: Necessary Evil or Ponzi Scheme?

DALE ARCHER

College debt is a reality for many students and their families. This burden and the high cost of college causes some to question if the need for college is as real as commonly assumed. A medical doctor and psychiatrist, Dale Archer questions the value of college for all high school graduates in *Psychology Today*'s online magazine.

1   A college education ranks right along with owning your own home as the foundation of the American dream. We learned the hard way that not everyone needed to own a house after the market collapse 2008, but as for a college degree, well we all know it's necessary to be a success—right? As it turns out, in this case and so many others, the "prevailing wisdom" is often dead wrong.

2   Back in the day, a college diploma truly meant something. It represented an upward mobility and virtually guaranteed a decent job with benefits in a chosen field. Best of all it was cost effective; the return on a 4-year time/money investment was well worth it.

3   Then, once college became more common, it was no longer enough to get into college. It had to be a "good college," or a "top 25 college" or an Ivy League college. The better the school the better the job, and as with all supply and demand situations, the price for a top notch school skyrocketed. For example, when I attended Tulane University back in the 70's tuition, room and board was about $2,500 per year. Today it's over $60,000!

4   Of course, few people can afford that, but no problem. This is America! Simply take out a student loan, get in the best school you can and then make the mega bucks when you get out. But is this real?

5   The median household income between 2007–2011 was $52,762. The average tuition at a public four-year college has increased 104 percent within the past ten years. Put into hard figures, during the 2010–11 academic school year, annual tuition, room and board at public colleges was $13,600; private, nonprofit universities cashed in at $36,300. Of course, the "better" the college, the higher the price tag.

6   The national student loan debt will reach $1 trillion this year. The higher education system as a whole is broken and with the price of the diploma climbing each semester, it's quickly becoming a race to nowhere.

7   What good is the diploma if you can't repay it? We are pumping out graduates who hold a degree in their chosen field . . . yet can't find work. Many who do are able to get lower paying jobs that are not in their field, but they must work in order to repay their school loans. What happens if you have a degree with an $80,000 student loan to repay, yet are unable to find a job? Fresh out of school and immediately facing financial disaster with a debt that will never be forgiven, even with bankruptcy—now what?

8   The American dream promised our children that if they studied hard, made good grades and earned their degree they would be rewarded with success and opportunities that would otherwise not be available. In today's world that's a lie; there are no more guarantees. These students represent Generation Debt, without the benefits of previous generations with degrees. Remember, too, that this trillion dollar debt is *everybody's* debt if it's not repaid.

9   Now, let's push money aside and look at another fact. Upper education used to open doors. Not so true anymore. The degree used to be a screening tool, but that is falling by the wayside as there are a glut of college grads on the market.

10   A slew of kids enter college without a clue as to what they want to do with their life. Many graduate with the same problem. They have their degree—now what? It's not out of the ordinary for the guy with a Master's degree to be working side-by-side and earning the same wage as the guy next to him who earned his GED. The only difference is the GED guy doesn't have to pay back a six-figure student loan.

11   But there is an alternative for an education at a fraction of the cost. Trade schools (often overlooked and considered "not as good" as a college education) are making a comeback. A 2011 Harvard Graduate School of Education reports only 56 percent of students get their Bachelor's degree within six years, and actually encourage high school teachers to persuade their students to consider trade school.

12   High school graduates are encouraged to look at these trade schools, quickly and efficiently learning and training to enter the workforce to keep up with hot careers. These vocational schools intensely teach the students what they need to land a job in today's booming fields—healthcare, technology, electrical and natural resources—with relevant career-focused subject matter.

13   These grads are armed with a certificate which requires considerably less time and classes than a degree, and often pays more. Not only that, but many vocational schools will actually *find placement for you in the workforce.* Some even guarantee it.

14   Universities used to prepare young adults for the real world. I dare say the graduates today go in without a clue and graduate without a clue. It's time to acknowledge the college degree is not worth what it was in the past. Times are changing, and so is the way we prepare our youth to survive in a competitive world.

15   Unfortunately, the drumbeat that "you MUST go to college" shows no sign of abating, fostered by data that shows a lower unemployment rate for those with a degree. What this stat ignores is that those with the drive to make good grades, pass entrance exams and graduate are driven to succeed regardless of whether they have a degree or not. These people would be just as successful in the workforce without a degree, because they are hardworking achievers.

16   The college degree market today is comparable to a Ponzi scheme. Those that got in early reaped huge rewards and spread the mantra that you too can have it all if you just get your degree. But as more and more folks pursued the college dream at top flight universities, the prices kept ratcheting up to levels requiring huge loans to make the tuition. As with all pyramid schemes, those late to the party are the big losers.

Reprinted with permission from *Psychology Today* magazine. (Copyright © 2013 Sussex Publishers, LLC.)

QUESTIONS FOR DISCUSSION

1. Archer argues that while the cost of a college degree has gone up, its value has gone down. Why has it gone down, according to his argument? To what extent can students themselves determine the financial payoff of their college educations?

2. What is a Ponzi scheme? Archer makes an argument by analogy, comparing the "prevailing wisdom" about college degrees to a Ponzi scheme. Explain and evaluate the thinking behind this analogy.

3. According to the White House web page on higher education, our nation "suffer[s] from a college attainment gap, as high school graduates from the wealthiest families in our nation are almost certain to continue on to higher education, while just over half of our high school graduates in the poorest quarter of families attend college." Based on a close reading of Archer's argument, what do you infer that Archer would say about the "college attainment gap"? Would you agree or disagree with him, and why? <http://www.whitehouse.gov/issues/education/higher-education>

FOR RESEARCH AND CONVINCING

Look into the Harvard Graduate School of Education report that Archer refers to in paragraph 11. You can find it at <http://www.gse.harvard.edu/news_events /features/2011/Pathways_to_Prosperity_Feb2011.pdf>.

This report shows that 70% of high school graduates enter college with the hope of graduating with an associate or bachelor's degree. After reading the report and doing more research into employment opportunities available to graduates of vocational training schools, consider what advice high school guidance counselors should give students who cannot afford a college education without borrowing money. As you explore to find your position on this issue, you might also read arguments from other writers in this chapter, such as Stuart Rabinowitz (pages 399–401), on the value of a liberal arts education.

Forgive Student Loans?

RICHARD VEDDER

A professor at Ohio University and adjunct scholar at the American Enterprise Institute, Richard Vedder heads the Center for College Affordability and Productivity. The following article, which opposes our current student loan program for college students and argues against legislation proposed in 2012 to forgive student loans, appeared in *National Review Online.*

1   As the [Occupy] Wall Street protests grow and expand beyond New York, growing scrutiny of the nascent movement is warranted. What do these folks want? Alongside their ranting about the inequality of incomes, the alleged inordinate power of Wall Street and large corporations, the high level of unemployment, and the like, one policy goal ranks high with most protesters: the forgiveness of student-loan debt. In an informal survey of over 50 protesters in New York last Tuesday, blogger and equity research analyst David Maris found 93 percent of them advocated student-loan forgiveness. An online petition drive advocating student-loan forgiveness has gathered an impressive number of signatures (over 442,000). This is an issue that resonates with many Americans.

2   Economist Justin Wolfers recently opined that "this is the worst idea ever." I think it is actually the second-worst idea ever—the worst was the creation of federally subsidized student loans in the first place. Under current law, when the feds (who have basically taken over the student-loan industry) make a loan, the size of the U.S. budget deficit rises and the government borrows additional funds, very often from foreign investors. We are borrowing from the Chinese to finance school attendance by a predominantly middle-class group of Americans.

3   But that is the tip of the iceberg: Though the ostensible objective of the loan program is to increase the proportion of adult Americans with college degrees, over 40 percent of those pursuing a bachelor's degree fail to receive one within six years. And default is a growing problem with student loans.

4   Further, it's not clear that college imparts much of value to the average student. The typical college student spends less than 30 hours a week, 32 weeks a year, on all

academic matters—class attendance, writing papers, studying for exams, etc. They spend about half as much time on school as their parents spend working. If Richard Arum and Josipa Roksa (authors of *Academically Adrift*) are even roughly correct, today's students typically learn little in the way of critical learning or writing skills while in school.

5   Moreover, the student-loan program has proven an ineffective way to achieve one of its initial aims, a goal also of the Wall Street protesters: increasing economic opportunity for the poor. In 1970, when federal student-loan and -grant programs were in their infancy, about 12 percent of college graduates came from the bottom one-fourth of the income distribution. While people from all social classes are more likely to go to college today, the poor haven't gained nearly as much ground as the rich have: With the nation awash in nearly a trillion dollars in student-loan debt (more even than credit-card obligations), the proportion of bachelor's-degree holders coming from the bottom one-fourth of the income distribution has fallen to around 7 percent.

6   The sins of the loan program are many. Let's briefly mention just five.

7   First, artificially low interest rates are set by the federal government—they are fixed by law rather than market forces. Low-interest-rate mortgage loans resulting from loose Fed policies and the government-sponsored enterprises Fannie Mae and Freddie Mac spurred the housing bubble that caused the 2008 financial crisis. Arguably, federal student financial assistance is creating a second bubble in higher education.

8   Second, loan terms are invariant, with students with poor prospects of graduating and getting good jobs often borrowing at the same interest rates as those with excellent prospects (e.g., electrical-engineering majors at MIT).

9   Third, the availability of cheap loans has almost certainly contributed to the tuition explosion—college prices are going up even more than health-care prices.

10   Fourth, at present the loans are made by a monopoly provider, the same one that gave us such similar inefficient and costly monopolistic behemoths as the U.S. Postal Service.

11   Fifth, the student-loan and associated Pell Grant programs spawned the notorious FAFSA form that requires families to reveal all sorts of financial information—information that colleges use to engage in ruthless price discrimination via tuition discounting, charging wildly different amounts to students depending on how much their parents can afford to pay. It's a soak-the-rich scheme on steroids.

12   Still, for good or ill, we have this unfortunate program. Wouldn't loan forgiveness provide some stimulus to a moribund economy? The Wall Street protesters argue that if debt-burdened young persons were free of this albatross, they would start spending more on goods and services, stimulating employment. Yet we demonstrated with stimulus packages in 2008 and 2009 (not to mention the 1930s, Japan in the 1990s, etc.) that giving people more money to spend will not bring recovery. But even if it did, why should we give a break to this particular group of individuals, who disproportionately come from prosperous families to begin with? Why give them assistance while those who have dutifully repaid their loans get none? An arguably more equitable and efficient method of stimulus would be to drop dollars out of airplanes over low-income areas.

13   Moreover, this idea has ominous implications for the macro economy. Who would take the loss from the unanticipated non-repayment of a trillion dollars? If private financial institutions are liable for some of it, it could kill them, triggering another financial crisis. If the federal government shoulders the entire burden, we are adding a trillion or so more dollars in liabilities to a government already grievously overextended (upwards of $100 trillion in liabilities counting Medicare, Social Security, and the national debt), almost certainly leading to more debt downgrades, which could trigger investor panic. This idea is breathtaking in terms of its naïveté and stupidity.

14   The demonstrators say that selfish plutocrats are ruining our economy and creating an unjust society. Rather, a group of predominantly rather spoiled and coddled young persons, long favored and subsidized by the American taxpayer, are complaining that society has not given them enough—they want the taxpayer to foot the bill for their years of limited learning and heavy partying while in college. Hopefully, this burst of dimwittery should not pass muster even in our often dysfunctional Congress.

QUESTIONS FOR DISCUSSION

1. On average, an American college student graduates owing about $25,000. In your view, is that an acceptable level of indebtedness for an undergraduate degree and the advantages over a lifetime that college graduates enjoy over people who complete high school only?

2. Vedder is certainly correct that forgiving student loans will result in higher expenditures by the federal government, which in turn ultimately places a heavier burden on taxpayers. Is that fair? That is, can you think of any reasons why the cost of education should not be carried mainly by students and their families?

3. Vedder claims that college students are not spending enough time studying and are not learning what they should. Based on your personal experience, do you agree? If so, what do you think should be done?

FOR RESEARCH AND CONVINCING

Vedder is not the only voice claiming that federal support for higher education is a major driver of tuition costs—many argue that colleges charge so much because they can depend on the federal government to cover part of the cost through student loans and other programs. Do research on the relationship between student loans and tuition costs.

Write a paper responding to Vedder's claim that "the availability of cheap loans has almost certainly contributed to the tuition explosion." If you agree with him, provide the evidence he did not provide. If you disagree completely or in part, provide evidence showing that there is either no linkage or that student loans are not as important as other factors in driving tuition up.

Waking Up and Taking Charge

ANYA KAMENETZ

It is one thing to know we have a problem, quite another to do something to solve it, even when we understand it reasonably well. In the following excerpt from Generation Debt: Why Now Is a Terrible Time to Be Young, *Anya Kamenetz proposes action to promote needed change.*

Kamenetz, despite being a recent Yale graduate, has struggled herself with difficult economic conditions. Through writing and advocacy, she is helping to lead young adults toward becoming a potent political force.

We aren't particularly interested in "rocking the vote." . . . We're here to represent our generation because decisions are made by the people who show up.

—Virginia21, *the first student-led state political action committee, 2004*

1   If you're like me, you're a little impatient with the political sphere of action. Spend months and years supporting local candidates? Send blast faxes to your congress-people? Actually read those endless e-mail alerts?

2   Well, look, if 35 million people over fifty can band together to demand respect from Congress, so can we. Unless we're willing to continue being typecast as passive "adultescents," unless we really want to get "rolled over by greedy middle-aged and older people who have been expropriating our earnings for generations," as the economist Laurence Kotlikoff says, it's the only way. Young people urgently need a strong national generational movement—for higher education funding, fairer credit laws, a better-designed school-to-work system, justice system reform, worker protections, a living wage, health care, saving programs, support for young families and homeowners, entitlement reform, and a million other issues.

3   As college gets ever more out of reach, there are signs of a nascent movement. At my alma mater on a freezing day in February 2005, fifteen students sat in at the admissions office until removed by police. The undergraduates were demanding changes to Yale's financial aid policy to bring it in line with several other Ivies, including Harvard, Princeton, and Brown. In the past few years, these schools have all dipped into their multimillion-dollar endowments to make it easier for families to afford college without heavy loans. One week after the sit-in, Yale, too, announced that it would no longer expect any tuition contribution at all from families earning less than $45,000 a year.

4   By all accounts, the financial aid reform issue galvanized the campus. One in five Yalies signed on to the reform platform, including the president of the Yale College Republicans and other campus conservatives. "This is self-interested organizing in a positive way," Phoebe Rounds, a sophomore on financial aid who organized for six months leading up to the sit-in, told me. "The campaign has made people realize the extent to which their individual struggles are shared by a large number of students."

5   The Yale action also demonstrates, however, that without a unified voice, individual protests can make only small ripples. Tuition discounting is possible only at a tiny percentage of well-endowed private schools serving a tiny percentage of

students. At selective colleges in 2004, only 10 percent of students came from the bottom half of the income scale.

6   An effective student movement should be organized state by state, to pressure the governors who make decisions about public schools where the vast majority of students are enrolled. When it comes to the broader problems facing young people, only national political organizing will do.

7   The student loan debt explosion could potentially be more amenable to lobbying than any of the other problems facing Generation Debt. The federal government gives out most student financial aid. They say how much you can borrow in guaranteed student loans and how high an interest rate the banks can charge. Given a true reordering of our national priorities—a big given—a few amendments to the Higher Education Act could immediately bring student borrowing down to a manageable level and lower the barriers to access. Increasing the maximum Pell Grant, and making the grant an entitlement that rises automatically from year to year, are obvious first steps. In the words of the National Association of Student Financial Aid Administrators, "If we are serious about reducing student loan debt . . . making the Pell Grant Program a true entitlement, divorced from the vagaries of the appropriations process, is the only way."

8   As this book is going to press, the eighth reauthorization of the Higher Education Act is finally getting under way, a few years overdue. The Bush administration assigned the lion's share of spending cuts for the purpose of deficit reduction to the House and Senate Education committees, and they turned around and passed the pain on to student aid, with $15 billion in cuts and new fees—the biggest cuts since HEA programs were created.

9   Even if legislative reform is years in coming, a vocal activist campaign about the dangers of student loans could accomplish a lot. After all, excessive student debt is not measured by a fixed number of dollars. It's a function of each person's income, other debts, financial management skills, ability to persist in college, and expectations about the value of a diploma. Raising awareness about the long-term dangers of high debt could help all those kids who "just sign on the dotted line as an eighteen-year-old and you don't know what you're getting into," as one interviewee put it.

10   Youth activism could effectively address credit card debt, too. It would be great to reinstate usury laws nationwide and end 29 percent annual interest rates, so that twenty-somethings earning $12,000 a year are no longer profitable customers for $10,000 lines of credit. That would require a morally high-fiber Congress willing to take on one of the fastest-growing profit areas in financial services. Failing that, returning to the norms of the 1980s, when college students without incomes needed a parental cosigner for a card, would keep eighteen-year-olds from charging down that path before they realize the consequences.

11   With credit card debt, just as with student loans, a vocal activist movement could bring the problem out into the open, making kids think twice before signing up for the free Frisbees and key chains. Universities have a role to play, too, in limiting their students' exposure to credit card marketing. Just as Stella, [a] thirty-one-year-old debtor . . . , says, the next time you see the Discover Card table, RUN the other way!

12   Where is our national student antidebt crusade? Over the past four decades, college students have gained a reputation as the most engaged political activists in the country—except on issues directly affecting them. Each year, for example, *Mother Jones* magazine recognizes the top ten activist campuses in the nation. From 2001 to 2005, the list featured left-wing campaigns on free speech, the war in Iraq, AIDS, the drug war, and living wages. Missing were bipartisan student issues like mounting debt burden, aggressive credit card marketing, the lack of health insurance, and the dearth of solid entry-level jobs.

13   Standing up for world peace is utterly admirable, but the social safety net in this country was woven by people lobbying for their own lives, not fighting for causes a world away. American college students need to experience that "click" moment, as the feminists of the 1970s called it, and realize that our personal problems are also political. If we young people don't march on our own behalf, who will march for us?

14   In other countries, students get it. Many EU and Latin American countries have overwhelmingly public, centralized university systems, making organizing easier (and education cheaper). Around the world, national undergraduate student unions have lobbied forcefully for decades. They address issues like diversity and date rape, along with tuition, books, housing, health care, debt, and jobs. They win battles for their constituencies, keeping young people on the social agenda.

15   The UK's National Union of Students claims 5 million members, nearly all the country's higher education students. In October 2003, an estimated 31,000 of them rallied in London against higher school fees.

16   After huge national budget cuts in the '90s, Canadians' student loans are comparable to Americans', at an average $22,520 ($19,143 U.S.) in 2001. Educational access is worsening for lower-income Canadians, although not quite as badly as in the United States.

17   Canada's two national student lobbying organizations boast combined memberships of 750,000, nearly half the nation's college students. James Kusie, a 2002 university grad from Manitoba, served from 2003 to 2005 as the elected national director of the Canadian Alliance of Student Associations (CASA). His group, founded in 1995, represents 300,000 students at nineteen universities across Canada. Member associations fund CASA's full-time staff of five, which drafts policy in the nation's capital and builds relationships with lawmakers, both elected representatives and bureaucrats. "You can be rallying outside and shouting through the window, and that's an important piece of building public support," Kusie says. "But you also need to be at the table with them, engaging them on the issues."

18   Each year, the presidents and vice presidents of each student council in CASA come to the national capital, Ottawa, and meet in person with their elected representatives. They also hold media stunts. In November 2003, they built a 120-foot Wall of Debt out of foam blocks, bearing the signatures of 20,000 students along with the debt burdens of each.

19   Throughout the 1990s, Canadian student organizations won tuition freezes and even cuts in several provinces. Kusie glows as he describes the accomplishments of his term as CASA's chair. In 2004, the federal government adopted their proposal for a new grant to low-income students, up to $3,000, modeled on the Pell Grant.

They also changed the formulas for expected parental contributions, making up to 50,000 more students eligible for financial aid. These victories came during comparatively good economic times for Canada, but after more than a decade of deep budget cuts that shrank the size of the federal government by a third and while the country was experiencing the same increases in health care and pension costs as in the United States. CASA and the Canadian Federation of Students work to ensure that a government tending to the needs of an aging population does not forget young people.

20   "When Parliament begins a new session following an election, the government gives a 'throne speech,' setting out its priorities for the legislative session," Kusie says. "When it came to the section on education, chunks of it seemed to have come word for word from our pre-budget submission. . . . We were very happy to see that our work had paid off."

21   The United States Student Association, this nation's oldest and largest student organization, contrasts poorly with the muscle flexed abroad. Its exact membership is not available on its seldom updated website. Most students have never heard of it, and the media tend to pass it over. Its lobbying clout is dwarfed by that of the big student loan companies—it spent just $20,000 on lobbying in 2000, compared with $1.5 million spent by Sallie Mae.

22   The 80 percent of students who attend public schools are pitted against the immovable object of state budgets. In the past few years, community college and state university students from California and New York demonstrated against big tuition hikes coupled with budget cuts. Ten thousand students from California's community colleges marched to Sacramento in 2003 to protest a 120 percent rise in fees and budget cuts in the hundreds of millions. They carried paper effigies representing an estimated 200,000 students priced out of the community college system. Public college students backed by the New York Public Interest Research Group rallied strongly against tuition hikes throughout the '90s, marching 561 miles across New York State in 2003. In both cases, despite temporary responses, the budget cuts and tuition increases continued.

23   There is a model here in America of what students could be doing to focus legislators' attention on education. A state political action committee, as powerful and well organized as the student unions in other countries, has taken root in, of all places, placid suburban Virginia.

24   In 2002, students at the public College of William and Mary formed Students PAC to help pass a $900 million state bond issue for higher education. In the summer of 2003, the coalition, now called Virginia21, went statewide. It now boasts over 14,500 members at all fifteen public four-year colleges and universities in the Commonwealth.

25   VA21, the first student-led state PAC, addresses voters between eighteen and twenty-four on economic issues like tuition, book costs, and education budget cuts. They reject the popular approach of relying on mass media or celebrity to sell young voters on civic involvement. Jesse Ferguson, the twenty-four-year-old executive director, notes that voters of all ages tend to be motivated by concrete self-interest, not abstract ideals.

26   "We're trying to find a way to support mainstream, bipartisan, middle-of-the-road issues that affect all of us on a day-to-day basis," Ferguson says. He cofounded Students of Virginia PAC as a college student. Now he and a small staff work full-time in Virginia's capital to drive home their message about budget priorities. At their website, you can check the status of all the legislation they're working on, from cutting textbook prices, to increasing student financial aid, to reforming absentee voting so college students have an easier time getting to the ballot box. Their rhetoric strikes a determined but not angry note; they remind legislators that education is an investment in Virginia, and they remind students that they don't deserve to be priced out. In June 2004, Virginia21 celebrated passage of a state budget with $275 million more for higher education than the year before, the first such increase in years.

27   VA21 draws on its members for letter-writing campaigns, e-mail blasts, and rallies. They collected and trucked 200,000 pennies to the state capitol in 2004 in support of a one-cent sales tax for education. Meanwhile, Ferguson and his team haunted the halls of the capitol during their first legislative session just as all the other power players did.

28   In a bow to the realities of American politics, VA21, unlike the Canadian groups, depends on corporate contributions. Their 2003–2004 budget was $100,000. Donors included America Online, Bank of America, and Philip Morris's corporate owner. With this backing, it's hard to imagine VA21 addressing issues like unfair credit card marketing. Still, they're getting results, and lawmakers are taking them seriously.

29   Jesse Ferguson says he would seize the chance to take VA21 national if offered the funding. He calls his group a young, wired equivalent of the AARP, for its focus on issues that affect everyone of a certain age, and for its pragmatic, even insider, approach. "There's a change you can see in recent years in eighteen- to twenty-four-year-olds—they would rather have a seat at the table than a rally outside," Ferguson told me, echoing James Kusie of CASA. "It's got to be not just student activism but effective student activism."

QUESTIONS FOR DISCUSSION

1. A common charge, which Kamenetz indirectly acknowledges, is that young adults are alienated from politics, too passive in accepting whatever older adults dish out. In your experience, is there any truth in this criticism? If you pay little or no attention to politics and do not vote, how do you explain or justify your behavior?

2. Kamenetz presents VA21 in terms obviously designed to make political action attractive. Do you find the idea for a college student–young adult PAC (political action committee) appealing? Why or why not? If you had a chance to take a role in such a group, would you? Why or why not?

3. Unfortunately, there is too much in American culture that encourages young adults to think that the sky is the limit, that you can achieve anything you want to achieve—"chase your dreams" is an American credo. What is good

about such an outlook? How much do you think the credo contributes to college students and their parents taking on too much debt for college expenses? What do you think should be done to encourage young adults to assess themselves and their financial situation with greater realism and practicality?

FOR RESEARCH AND INQUIRY

The great model for an age-specific PAC is AARP (formerly known as the American Association of Retired Persons). Find out all you can about its membership, how it is organized, what it does to create a sense of group identity and purpose, and why it is effective with the political establishment.

Then write a paper exploring the possibility of creating a similar group for young adults, a group that would embrace college students and college graduates as well as the majority of young adults who do not go to or do not finish college. In what ways could such a group follow the AARP model? In what ways should it depart from it? What do you think needs to be done to make young adults a political force to be reckoned with by politicians at all levels of government?

An alternative is to research VA21 instead, the student-led PAC in Virginia that won important concessions from state government. If you take this route, ponder what VA21 accomplished and exactly why and how they managed to get things done. Would a similar PAC work in your state? Would it be better to go national—form a group that takes in all college students—or remain more local, working state by state instead?

FOR FURTHER READING

Apter, Terri. *The Myth of Maturity: What Teenagers Need from Parents to Become Adults.* Norton, 2001.

Arnett, Jeffrey Jensen. *Emerging Adulthood: The Winding Road from the Late Teens through the Twenties.* Oxford UP, 2004.

Draut, Tamara. *Strapped: Why America's 20- and 30-Somethings Can't Get Ahead.* Doubleday, 2005.

Kamenetz, Anya. *Generation Debt: Why Now Is a Terrible Time to Be Young.* Riverside Books, 2006.

Manafy, Michelle, and Heidi Gautschi. *Dancing with Digital Natives: Staying in Step with the Generation That's Transforming the Way Business Is Done.* CyberAge Books, 2011.

Snyder, Thomas. *The Community College Career Track: How to Achieve the American Dream without a Mountain of Debt.* Wiley, 2012.

Twenge, Jean M. *Generation Me: Why Today's Young Americans Are More Confident, Assertive, Entitled—and More Miserable Than Ever Before.* Free Press, 2006.

Yarrow, Kit, and Jayne O'Donnell. *Gen BuY: How Tweens, Teens, and Twenty-Somethings Are Revolutionizing Retail.* Jossey-Bass, 2009.

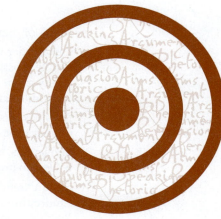

CHAPTER 15

Immigration Revisited: A New Look at a Permanent Issue

Historical Images: Our Contradictory Attitudes toward Immigration   *417*

Tamar Jacoby, The New Immigrants and the Issue of Assimilation   *418*

Samuel Huntington, One Nation, Out of Many: Why "Americanization" of Newcomers Is Still Important   *425*

Jeff Koterba, Cartoon: Playing POLITICS with the Border   *429*

Ross Douthat and Jenny Woodson, The Border   *430*

Linda Chavez, The Realities of Immigration   *434*

Chris Farrell, Obama's Next Act: Immigration Reform   *441*

Dava Castillo, Comprehensive Immigration Reform—Past, Present, and Future   *444*

Leslie Marmon Silko, The Border Patrol State   *447*

For Further Reading   *451*

About a decade ago, we had a chapter on immigration in the second edition of this book. In many important ways, little has changed:

- About 1.2 million immigrants come to the United States each year, the vast majority of whom are Hispanics and Asians.

- Many of them are undocumented aliens.

- Our border with Mexico remains leaky, with perhaps about half a million people crossing it illegally each year since 2000. Of course, the number in any given year will vary depending on how well the U.S. and Mexican economies are doing.

- All measures to control the border and significantly reduce illegal immigration have produced mixed results.

- Immigrants, both legal and illegal, contribute significantly to our economy while also imposing significant costs, especially on state and local governments.

We could extend this list, but you get the point: as the French proverb says, "The more things change, the more they stay the same."

Yet things have changed. After the 2012 election, immigration received more attention, in part because the Hispanic vote was so important. Many recent legal immigrants come from regions and countries that supplied few willing residents in the past—from Africa and India, for instance. In the past, most immigrants were confined to coastal or gateway cities and the Southwest. That is less and less the case; states such as North Carolina and Iowa now receive many new immigrants.

Furthermore, 9/11 led Americans to worry about the country's porous borders more than before. More recently, immigration has been discussed extensively in the news, on talk radio, and on thousands of Web sites, raising awareness of the issue to heights not seen since the 1920s and resulting in efforts to pass new legislation in Congress. Hardly anyone doubts that new laws will eventually pass—but what they will be no one knows for sure, and the actual impact they will have is anyone's guess.

Few issues confronting us are more poorly understood, more emotional, and more up in the air than immigration. Consequently, we need to focus on certain fundamental questions of long-term importance:

- There are now more than 300 million Americans. How long can we continue to absorb so many new people? From the standpoint of population control and ecology, *should we want to reduce the immigration rate?*

- Measures to control immigration are often both ineffective and produce unintended results, some of them clearly negative. Supposing that we want to, *can we reduce the immigration rate?* As the recent recession clearly shows, economic forces drive immigration; perhaps we should let market forces control it. If not, what measures would really work, without producing intolerably bad side effects?

- All data indicate that without immigrants many millions of jobs would go unfilled. Even assuming we would like to reduce immigration and can actually do so, *can we afford to reduce the immigration rate?*

- Finally, until recently, the pressure on new immigrants to "become Americans" was unrelenting and almost unquestioned. But now assimilation itself is an issue. *Do we really want immigrants to lose all sense of connection to their culture of origin?* If, as many people believe, the whole idea of the melting pot belongs to the past, *how much assimilation is desirable?*

The following selections address these questions directly and by implication. How we answer them will determine the nature and future of our country.

Historical Images: Our Contradictory Attitudes toward Immigration

The following posters were printed in popular publications about one hundred years ago, when immigration was highest, as measured by percentage of the total U.S. population. We think they capture in dramatic fashion the conflicting attitudes Americans have always had toward new arrivals. These and several similar drawings appeared in the magazine *Reason*.

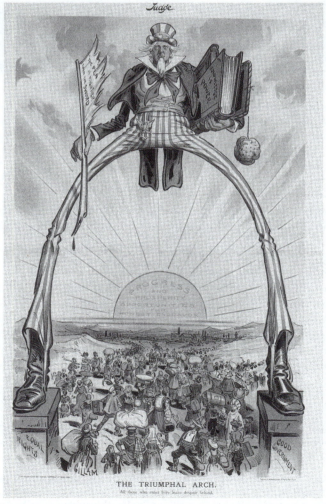

THE TRIUMPHAL ARCH.
All those who enter here leave despair behind.

The caption beneath the poster's title, "The Triumphal Arch," reads, "All those who enter here leave despair behind."

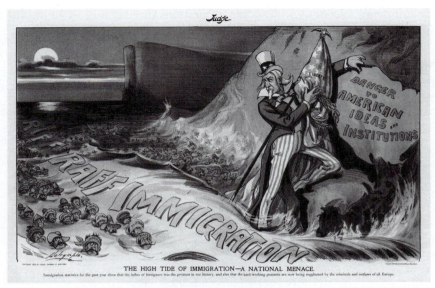

THE HIGH TIDE OF IMMIGRATION—A NATIONAL MENACE.
Immigration statistics for the past year show that the influx of foreigners was the greatest in our history, and also that the hard-working peasants are now being supplanted by the criminals and outlaws of all Europe.

The caption beneath the poster's title, "The High Tide of Immigration . . . ," reads, "Immigration statistics for the past year show that the influx of foreigners was the greatest in history, and also that the hard-working peasants are now being supplanted by the criminals and outlaws of all Europe."

QUESTIONS FOR DISCUSSION

Look carefully at the details in these two posters. What "assertions" are they making by implication? In your view, how do they reflect reality? How do they distort it?

FOR RESEARCH, ANALYSIS, AND INQUIRY

As a class project, collect recent images connected with attitudes toward immigration—photographs, cartoons, anything pictorial. Discuss each image in class, exploring both its conscious and unconscious impact, and comparing it with the posters from a century ago. How much has changed? How much remains the same?

Select two or three recent images you find particularly interesting and write an essay about the attitudes they express. Do they capture your own ideals and fears? If so, how?

The New Immigrants and the Issue of Assimilation

TAMAR JACOBY

One of the better books published on immigration is a collection of essays called *Reinventing the Melting Pot: The New Immigrant and What It Means to Be American*. The following selection is an excerpt from the first two chapters, both written by Tamar Jacoby, the editor of the volume and a senior researcher at the Manhattan Institute. She provides basic information on the current wave of immigrants and poses the issue of assimilation as we wrestle with it now.

THE BIG PICTURE

1 The immigrant influx of the last forty years is a demographic shift of historic proportions. The percentage of the population that was born abroad is slightly lower than it was when the last great wave of immigrants arrived, at the beginning of the twentieth century: 11 percent now compared to 15 percent then. But the absolute number of newcomers living in the United States today is the highest it has ever been: some 31 million. Roughly 1.2 million arrive on our shores every year. One in nine Americans is an immigrant. And half the laborers entering the American workforce in the 1990s were foreign-born. Add in their families and extended families and the picture grows more dramatic still. Together, immigrants and their children now account for one in five Americans. Hispanics, at nearly 14 percent of the population, are already the largest minority, outnumbering blacks. Asian-Americans are still a relatively small share of the nation—at only 4 percent. But despite their numbers, they, too, are going to play a major part in the country's future: already, they make up between 15 and 20 percent of the students at most Ivy League colleges.

2 Where do these new arrivals come from? Just over half the foreign-born are Hispanic and a little more than a quarter are Asian. They hail from all the corners of the globe, though more from some countries than from others. Mexicans, by far the largest category, account for roughly one in three first-generation immigrants—almost ten times more than any other nationality. The next largest groups are Filipinos and Indians, followed by Chinese, Vietnamese, Koreans, Cubans and Salvadorans—but none of these account for more than 3 or 4 percent of the total.

3 What do the newcomers do for a living? They tend to be clustered at both the top and the bottom of the job ladder. A large percentage work in dirty, demeaning, low-paid jobs that native-born Americans no longer want to do: busboys, chambermaids, farmhands, nurses' aides, sweatshop workers, on the assembly-line in meatpacking plants. But a large number also work at the top of the job pyramid: as scientists, engineers, nurses, high-tech entrepreneurs and the like. Two of the statistics that paint this picture most vividly are the percentage of U.S. farmhands who are foreign-born (an astonishing 80 percent) and the percentage of patents that are held by foreigners (an equally astonishing 26 percent). Social scientists call this a "barbell pattern," and it has some predictable corollaries. Not surprisingly, today's newcomers are either quite rich or quite poor, and they are either very well educated or hardly educated at all. Roughly a quarter have less than nine years of schooling, while an equal percentage have university degrees—a much larger share than the proportion of native-born Americans who have stayed in school that long.

4 Where in the United States do most immigrants settle? Until about ten years ago, they were concentrated in what demographers call "gateway cities": New York, Los Angeles, Miami, Houston, Chicago. But this is changing dramatically and with profound consequences for the country. States such as New York and California and

New Jersey are still home to the largest numbers. But the states with the fastest grow-ing immigrant populations are places like North Carolina, Georgia, Arkansas and Ten-nessee. Even Iowa more than doubled its share in the 1990s. The cities where the immigrant population expanded the most in the past decade are equally surprising: Greensboro, N.C., Charlotte, N.C., Raleigh, N.C., Atlanta and Las Vegas. Still more of a departure, while some of today's new arrivals still gravitate to urban areas, many head straight for the suburbs, and roughly half of all Asians and Latinos now live out-side the center city. . . .

5   Most foreigners, whether they arrive legally or illegally, come to the United States to work. Most do not come in the expectation of living on welfare: most are not entitled to most kinds of benefits for at least five years. Thanks to modern tech-nology, they generally know from other immigrants who have preceded them from their regions whether or not work is available. And in economic downturns, when there are fewer jobs to be had, fewer immigrants seem to make the trip. . . .

6   Of course, however hard they work, many poor, ill-educated immigrants who start at the bottom of the ladder remain there throughout their lives. This is not par-ticularly surprising, and it may seem to vindicate those who claim that the United States today is importing a new lower class. But that's part of the point of our immigration policy: America no longer has this kind of working class, and it turns out that we need one. And even this does not necessarily mean the newcomers will not be absorbed into the economy or do well by it. Indeed while most brand-new arrivals make considerably less than the native-born, by the time they have been in the United States for ten or fifteen years, they are usually making more. (Mexicans seem to be an exception—and a troubling one—but despite their overwhelming numbers and the way this weights any statistical measure, the overall immigrant average is still a success story.) By the time they've been in the country for fifteen to twenty years, immigrants are also less likely than the native-born to be living in poverty.

7   The trajectory of high-end immigrants—those who come with some money or an education—is even more impressive. Immigrant entrepreneurship is nothing short of astonishing—in the first and second generation and beyond. Asian and Latino business start-up rates were four times the average American rate in the 1990s. Most of these minority-owned firms were small, and most had no paid employees—but that was also true of the businesses owned by native-born Americans. . . .

8   In some cases, immigrants are not merely assimilating into a regional economy: they dominate it. In Silicon Valley in the 1990s, foreign-born scientists accounted for a third of the scientific workforce, and Chinese and Indian entrepreneurs ran a quarter of the high-tech companies. In New York, by one estimate, Korean immi-grants own 70 percent of the independent groceries, 80 percent of the nail salons and 60 percent of the dry cleaners. In Los Angeles, an increasing share of the banks are Asian-owned, and newcomers—whether from the Middle East, North Africa or Korea—control most of the $22 billion fashion industry. Whatever one calls it, there can be little question, immigrants are finding their place—and generally a productive place—in the American economy. . . .

THE TENSIONS OF ASSIMILATION

9 Like many Asian-Americans of his generation, Eddie Liu* isn't quite sure how to place or describe himself. Born in Taiwan to professional parents who moved to the United States when he was two years old, Eddie grew up in a California suburb, speaking mostly English and absorbing the manners and morals he saw on television, hardly aware of any differences between himself and his mostly Anglo school friends. Going to college changed all that: by the mid–1990s, identity politics had taken over his University of California campus, and Eddie quickly learned to see himself as an Asian-American. He took courses in Asian-American studies, joined several Chinese-American organizations, decided he could date only Asian women and grew more and more skeptical about the United States—the typical trajectory of a young, hyphenated American in the age of multiculturalism.

10 By the time I met him, he was twenty-five, and his life reflected both of these younger selves. He lived in a comfortable Los Angeles suburb, drove an expensive late-model car, dated both Asian and white women and, though he worked for an internet company that targeted Asian-Americans, knew more about American popular culture than I did. A bright and engaging young man, he grew thoughtful and a little tentative when our conversation turned to ethnic identity. Asked whether he saw himself as an excluded minority or a "person of color," he laughed good-naturedly. "Hardly," he said. And yet, when asked about the word "assimilation," he was plainly uncomfortable. "I don't know," he mused, "not if it's a one-way street. Not if you're asking me to give up who I am and fit into some 1950s 'Leave It To Beaver' America. Of course, I'm American. But I'm not sure I'm assimilated—or want to be."

11 Eddie's ambivalence is far from unique. Like most immigrants in the past, the overwhelming majority of today's brand-new arrivals know why they have come to the United States: to make a better life for themselves and their children by becoming American. These newcomers struggle against all odds to fit in—finding jobs, learning the system, picking up the rudiments of the language. And with the exception of a few community leaders who draw their status and livelihood from their separate ethnicity, first-generation immigrants have no trouble with the word "assimilation." "I don't see why people would not want to assimilate," a Chinese-American newcomer said to me recently with a certainty typical of those born in another country.

12 But the second generation, be it Asian or Latino or some other group, is often far less clear about its relationship to the new place. Like Eddie, they know what they don't want. None seek to lose themselves and their cultural heritage in a bland, homogenized America—assimilation as defined by the conformist, lily-white suburban neighborhoods of 1950s television and advertising. Multiculturalism combined with the sheer number of newcomers arriving today has laid that dream—if it ever really was anyone's dream—to rest forever. But nor do most voice the oppositional attitudes and color-coded divisiveness associated with identity politics. They are keen

---

*That isn't his real name.

to make it in America, yet reject the metaphor of the melting pot—and desperately need a way to understand just who they are and how they fit in. . . .

MAKING IT INTO THE MAINSTREAM—AS HARD IF NOT HARDER THAN EVER

13   The story of immigrant absorption is as old as America, but the new arrivals and the country they are settling in are very different today than in the past. Yesterday's newcomers were ethnically more similar to the nation they were joining: like the native born, virtually all were of European stock. In contrast, today, most immigrants hail from the developing world, more than half of them from Latin-America and a quarter from Asia. Today's newcomers include skilled, middle-class people, but many are poor and uneducated and woefully unprepared to join the knowledge economy. (Some 60 percent of those from India, for example, have completed four years of college, but only 6 percent of refugees from Cambodia have, and the average Mexican arrives with 7.6 years of schooling.) Together, immigrants and their children account for more than 60 million people, or a fifth of all U.S. residents. And by 2050, if today's projections are borne out, a third of all Americans will be either Asian or Latino.

14   The America they come to is also different: at once more prosperous and unequal economically than it was a century ago, often making it harder for newcomers to assimilate into the middle class. The gap between rich and poor is wider than ever, creating what some social scientists call an "hourglass economy." In many cities, well-paid factory jobs have been replaced by service-sector work, and for some time now, real wages at the bottom of the pay scale have been declining rather than growing. On top of this, many newcomers settle in impoverished inner cities, where crime, drugs, gangs and broken families conspire to hinder their climb up the economic ladder. Getting an education—the most critical step in assimilating into the knowledge economy—is no easy matter in the barrios of, say, south central Los Angeles. . . .

15   Some immigrant enclaves are better off: many Asian-Americans in California, for example, live in leafy, upscale suburbs. But pleasant as they are, these neighborhoods can be as insular as any ghetto: their ethnic shopping malls, ethnic restaurants and groceries, in-language newspapers, one-country Rotary Clubs, community banks, ethnic movie theaters and other amenities often make it unnecessary to have much contact with the integrated mainstream. The more newcomers arrive from the old country, the larger and more all-encompassing these enclaves—both rich and poor—grow, reducing incentives to make the difficult transition to a mixed neighborhood. Meanwhile, geographic proximity and cheap air travel allow newcomers to shuttle back and forth to their home countries and, in some cases, to maintain dual citizenship and even vote in both places.

16   Then there are the cultural factors that conspire against assimilation: everything from the internet and niche advertising to color-coded identity politics. The attacks of September 11, 2001, have sparked new patriotism and a new confidence in what brings us together as Americans. Some forty years after the Black Power movement and the ethnic revival it sparked among people of all backgrounds, the

excesses of group chauvinism seem finally to be fading a bit. But no mere swing of the cultural pendulum is going to repeal multiculturalism or erase the profound effect it has had on the way most Americans live and view the world. From the relativism that now reigns in intellectual circles to the way Congress divides up into monolithic ethnic caucuses, multiculturalism has become the civil religion of the United States. . . .

17   The drumbeat of ethnocentric messages can be constant and unavoidable. In an inner city high school, native-born minority classmates tease you for listening and doing your homework—both widely condemned by poor blacks and Latinos as "acting white" or "selling out." If this doesn't deter you, if and when you get to college, you'll be assailed by campus ethnic activists pressing you to question why you want to join the mainstream, racist and exploitative as it is seen to be. By the time you've finished your education, according to one study, you'll be far less likely to consider yourself an American, or even a hyphenated American, than you were as a young teenager. In many cases, by then, you'll see yourself simply as an aggrieved minority or as what some are now calling "ampersand Americans"—as in "Mexican & American." . . .

18   We shouldn't exaggerate the threat. Today, as before in our history when the immigrant tide was rising, nativists peddle a frightening array of grim scenarios: balkanization, civil strife, economic ruin and worse. Very few of these nightmare visions are based in fact, and all are unlikely. . . . The nation is steadily absorbing tens of millions of newcomers: people of all ages and backgrounds who are finding work, learning English, making their way through school and up into more comfortable circumstances than they knew at home or when they first arrived in America. Still, like any wholesale social shift or personal transformation of this magnitude, the integration of today's influx needs watching—and occasional tending. . . .

A NEW INTELLECTUAL CURRENT

19   What about Eddie Liu and his doubts? Is what we as a nation want to encourage really *assimilation?* The very notion is almost a dirty word today. Some who oppose it are plainly extremists: people so taken with multiculturalism that they see being absorbed into a larger America as so much cultural "genocide." Yet Eddie is no activist, and concerns like his are widely felt, particularly in his generation. To young people like him, "assimilation" implies a forced conformity. They feel that it would require them to give up what makes them special, and they dread being reduced to what they see as the lowest common denominator of what it means to be American. As for the melting pot, if anything, that seems even more threatening: who wants to be melted down, after all—for the sake of national unity or anything else?

20   Meanwhile , at the other end of the political spectrum are those who think that, desirable as it is, assimilation is no longer possible in America. Some in this camp are driven by racial concerns: they view today's immigrants as simply too different ethnically ever to fit in in the United States. Others believe that the obstacles are cultural: that America has a distinct national ethos that cannot be grasped by any but

a few newcomers—the better educated, perhaps, or those from Christian Europe. Still others feel that the problem lies less in the foreign influx than in ourselves: that in the wake of multiculturalism and the upheavals of the 1960s, we as a nation have lost the confidence to assert who we are and what we believe in. But whatever their reasoning, all three kinds of pessimists have gained a wider hearing in the wake of 9/11 as the nation has grown ever more anxious about what many imagine are the unassimilated in our midst. And together, these two groups—those who believe assimilation is impossible and those who fear it—have come to dominate most discussion of the issue, leaving little room for those in the middle who take a more positive view. . . .

21   Hemmed in on both sides, hardly heard in the din of an often emotional debate, in fact, many of the thinkers who have thought longest and hardest about immigration believe that assimilation is still possible and indeed desirable, if not inevitable, today. They don't all like or use that word—for some of the same reasons that Eddie has trouble with it. Very few imagine that it should look as it looked in the 1950s: that it requires newcomers to forget their roots or abandon their inherited loyalties. And fewer still believe that it happens automatically—that it needs no tending or attention from the nation as a whole. Still, whatever word they use, these thinkers maintain that we as a nation not only can but must continue to absorb those who arrive on our shores: absorb them economically, culturally, politically and, perhaps most important, give them a sense that they belong.

QUESTIONS FOR DISCUSSION

1. Of all the facts about immigration Jacoby provides, which ones surprised you the most? Which seem most important? Why?

2. Recent immigrants cluster at either the top or the bottom of our society—the "barbell pattern" the author refers to. In terms of actual numbers, however, most arrive poor and stay poor for some time. Given what Jacoby tells us and what you know about immigrants in general, is it accurate and fair to say we are importing a new lower class?

3. Summarize the complex view of assimilation Jacoby presents, being sure to include the opinions she characterizes as extreme and between which she seeks a middle ground. Where would you locate your own opinion in this spectrum of outlooks? How did you acquire your opinion?

FOR INQUIRY AND PERSUASION

"As for the melting pot . . . ," Jacoby asks, "who wants to be melted down . . . for the sake of national unity or anything else?" Find out as much as you can about your own background. Where did your family originate? How much of your culture of origin does your family preserve? How much is fading away or lost?

Write an essay defending the proposition that being American ought not to imply loss of our sense of origins and family cultural traditions.

One Nation, Out of Many: Why "Americanization" of Newcomers Is Still Important

SAMUEL HUNTINGTON

A professor of political science at Harvard, Samuel Huntington was a leading intellectual voice for neoconservative views for many years. In the following article he argues that "Anglo Protestant culture, values, [and] institutions" formed America and must be preserved amid a large influx of immigrants from other traditions, especially from Mexico. Without stronger efforts to "Americanize" this latest wave of immigrants, we are in danger, he believes, of becoming two nations instead of one.

The following article appeared in *The American Enterprise.* It is an excerpt from his book *Who Are We? The Challenges to America's National Identity.*

1 America's core culture has primarily been the culture of the seventeenth and eighteenth century settlers who founded our nation. The central elements of that culture are the Christian religion; Protestant values, including individualism, the work ethic, and moralism; the English language; British traditions of law, justice, and limits on government power; and a legacy of European art, literature, and philosophy. Out of this culture the early settlers formulated the American Creed, with its principles of liberty, equality, human rights, representative government, and private property. Subsequent generations of immigrants were assimilated into the culture of the founding settlers and modified it, but did not change it fundamentally. It was, after all, Anglo Protestant culture, values, institutions, and the opportunities they created that attracted more immigrants to America than to all the rest of the world. . . .

2 One has only to ask: Would America be the America it is today if in the seventeenth and eighteenth centuries it had been settled not by British Protestants but by French, Spanish, or Portuguese Catholics? The answer is no. It would not be America; it would be Quebec, Mexico, or Brazil. . . .

3 During the decades before World War I, the huge wave of immigrants flooding into America generated a major social movement devoted to Americanizing these new arrivals. It involved local, state, and national governments, private organizations, and businesses. Americanization became a key element in the Progressive phase of American politics, and was promoted by Theodore Roosevelt, Woodrow Wilson, and other leaders. . . .

4 The central institution for Americanization was the public school system. Indeed, public schools had been created in the nineteenth century and shaped in considerable part by the perceived need to Americanize and Protestantize immigrants. "People looked to education as the best way to transmit Anglo-American Protestant values and to prevent the collapse of republican institutions," summarizes historian Carl Kaestle. In 1921–22, as many as a thousand communities conducted "special public school programs to Americanize the foreign-born." Between 1915 and 1922, more than 1 million immigrants enrolled in such programs. School systems "saw public education as an instrument to create a unified society out of the multiplying diversity created by immigration," reports Reed Ueda.

5   Without these Americanizing activities starting in the early 1890s, America's dramatic 1924 reduction in immigration would in all likelihood have been imposed much earlier. Americanization made immigration acceptable to Americans. The success of the movement was manifest when the immigrants and their children rallied to the colors and marched off to fight their country's wars. In World War II in particular, racial, ethnic, and class identities were subordinated to national loyalty, and the identification of Americans with their country reached its highest point in history.

6   National identity then began to fade. In 1994, 19 scholars of American history and politics were asked to evaluate the level of American unity in 1930, 1950, 1970, and 1990. The year 1950, according to these experts, was the "zenith of American national integration." Since then "cultural and political fragmentation has increased" and "conflict emanating from intensified ethnic and religious consciousness poses the main current challenge to the American nation."

7   Fanning all of this was the new popularity among liberal elites of the doctrines of "multiculturalism" and "diversity," which elevate subnational, racial, ethnic, cultural, gender, and other identities over national identity, and encourage immigrants to maintain dual identities, loyalties, and citizenships. Multiculturalism is basically an anti-Western ideology. Multiculturalists argue that white Anglo America has suppressed other cultural alternatives, and that America in the future should not be a society with a single pervasive national culture, but instead should become a "tossed salad" of many starkly different ingredients.

8   In sharp contrast to their predecessors, American political leaders have recently promoted measures consciously designed to weaken America's cultural identity and strengthen racial, ethnic, and other identities. President Clinton called for a "great revolution" to liberate Americans from their dominant European culture. Vice President Gore interpreted the nation's motto, *E pluribus unum* (Out of many, one), to mean "out of one, many." By 1992, even some liberals like Arthur Schlesinger, Jr. were warning that the "ethnic upsurge" which had begun "as a gesture of protest against the Anglocentric culture" had become "a cult, and today it threatens to become a counterrevolution against the original theory of America as 'one people,' a common culture, a single nation."

9   These efforts by members of government to deconstruct the nation they led are, quite possibly, without precedent in human history. And important parts of academia, the media, business, and the professions joined them in the effort. A study by Paul Vitz of 22 school texts published in the 1970s and 1980s for grades three and six found that only five out of 670 stories and articles in these readers had "any patriotic theme." All five dealt with the American Revolution; none had "anything to do with American history since 1780." In four of the five stories the principal person is a girl, in three the same girl, Sybil Ludington. The 22 books lack any story "featuring Nathan Hale, Patrick Henry, Daniel Boone, or Paul Revere's ride." "Patriotism," Vitz concludes, "is close to nonexistent" in these readers.

10   The deconstructionist coalition, however, does not include most Americans. In poll after poll, majorities of Americans reject ideas and measures that would lessen national identity and promote subnational identities. Everyday Americans remain deeply patriotic, nationalistic in their outlook, and committed to their national

culture, creed, and identity. A major gap has thus developed between portions of our elite and the bulk of our populace over what America is and should be. . . .

11   The current wave of immigration to the U.S. has increased with each decade. During the 1960s, 3 million people entered the country. During the 1980s, 7 million people did. In the 1990s it was over 9 million. The foreign born percentage of the American population, which was a bit above 5 percent in 1960, more than doubled to close to 12 percent in 2002.

12   The United States thus appears to face something new in its history: persistent high levels of immigration. The two earlier waves of heavy immigration (1840s and 50s; and 1880s to 1924) subsided as a result of world events. But absent a serious war or economic collapse, over 1 million immigrants are likely to enter the United States each year for the indefinite future. This may cause assimilation to be slower and less complete than it was for past waves of immigration.

13   That seems to be happening with today's immigration from Latin America, especially from Mexico. Mexican immigration is leading toward a demographic "reconquista" of areas Americans took from Mexico by force in the 1830s and 1840s. Mexican immigration is very different from immigration from other sources, due to its sheer size, its illegality, and its other special qualities.

14   One reason Mexican immigration is special is simply because there are now so very many arrivals (legal and illegal) from that one country. Thanks to heavy Mexican inflows, for the very first time in history a majority of U.S. immigrants now speak a single non-English language, Spanish. The impact of today's large flow of Mexican immigrants is reinforced by other factors: the proximity of their country of origin; their geographical concentration within the U.S.; the improbability of their inflow ending or being significantly reduced; the decline of the assimilation movement; and the new enthusiasm of many American elites for multiculturalism, bilingualism, affirmative action, and cultural diversity instead of cultural unity. In addition, the Mexican government now actively promotes the export of its people to the United States while encouraging them to maintain their Mexican culture, identity, and nationality. President Vicente Fox regularly refers to himself as the president of 123 million Mexicans, 100 million in Mexico, 23 million in the United States. The net result is that Mexican immigrants and their progeny have not assimilated into American society as other immigrants did in the past, or as many other immigrants are doing now. . . .

15   Problems in digesting Mexican immigrants would be less urgent if Mexicans were just one group among many. But because legal and illegal Mexicans comprise such a large proportion of our current immigrant flow, any assimilation problems arising within their ranks shape our immigrant experience. The overwhelming influence of Mexicans on America's immigration flow becomes clearly visible if one poses a thought experiment. What if Mexican immigration to the U.S. somehow abruptly stopped, while other immigration continued as at present? In such a case, illegal entries in particular would diminish dramatically. Agriculture and other businesses in the southwest would be disrupted, but the wages of low-income Americans would rise. Debates over the use of Spanish, and whether English should be made the official language of state and national governments, would fade away. Bilingual education and the controversies it spawns would decline. So also would controversies

over welfare and other benefits for immigrants. The debate over whether immigrants are an economic burden on state and federal governments would be decisively resolved in the negative. The average education and skills of the immigrants coming to America would rise to levels unprecedented in American history. Our inflow of immigrants would again become highly diverse, which would increase incentives for all immigrants to learn English and absorb American culture. The possibility of a split between a predominantly Spanish-speaking America and English-speaking America would disappear, and with it a major potential threat to the cultural and possibly political integrity of the United States.

16   A glimpse of what a splintering of America into English- and Spanish-speaking camps might look like can be found in current day Miami. Since the 1960s, first Cuban and then other Latin American immigrants have converted Miami from a fairly normal American city into a heavily Hispanic city. By 2000 Spanish was not just the language spoken in most homes in Miami, it was also the principal language of commerce, business, and politics. The local media and communications are increasingly Hispanic. In 1998, a Spanish language television station became the number one station watched by Miamians—the first time a foreign-language station achieved that rating in a major American city. . . .

17   Is Miami the future for Los Angeles and the southwest generally? In the end, the results could be similar: the creation of a large, distinct, Spanish-speaking community with economic and political resources sufficient to sustain its own Hispanic identity apart from the national identity of other Americans, and also sufficient to significantly influence American politics, government, and society. The process by which this might come about, however, is different. The Hispanization of Miami has been led from the top down by successful Cuban and other Central and South American immigrants. In the southwest, the overwhelming bulk of Spanish-speaking immigrants are Mexican, and have been poor, unskilled, and poorly educated. It appears that many of their offspring are likely to be similar. The pressures toward Hispanization in the southwest thus come from below, whereas those in South Florida came from above. . . .

18   The continuation of high levels of Mexican and Hispanic immigration and low rates of assimilation of these immigrants into American society and culture could eventually change America into a country of two languages, two cultures, and two peoples. This will not only transform America. It will also have deep consequences for Hispanics—who will be in America but not of the America that has existed for centuries.

QUESTIONS FOR DISCUSSION

1. In the previous selection, Tamar Jacoby characterized one view of immigration as based on the assumption or fear that many of the new immigrants cannot be "Americanized"—that is, assimilated. Is that Huntington's view? What is the problem with "Americanization" as Huntington sees it?

2. According to Huntington, patriotic values are not being taught much in our schools. Based on your own experience as a high school student or as a parent of high school children, would you agree? If you do, should this change?

3. We all have what Huntington calls "subnational" aspects of identity, dimensions of what we are based on race, ethnicity, culture, class, and gender, among other differences. He believes that these subnational aspects have become too important, even more important than loyalty to the United States. Is he right? That is, do you recognize such attitudes in your own life? In other people you know well?

FOR RESEARCH, DISCUSSION, AND CONVINCING

As a class project, find out all you can about Hispanic immigration in general and immigration from Mexico in particular. Discuss the implications of the various points of view and the information you discover.

Then write an essay that addresses the question Huntington raises: Are we on the way to becoming two countries? Does the large influx of Hispanics pose a serious, long-term threat to U.S. national identity?

Cartoon: Playing POLITICS with the Border

JEFF KOTERBA

Like most political cartoons, this one makes a simple point forcefully: Politics may be the real barrier to handling illegal immigration intelligently.

QUESTIONS FOR DISCUSSION

Most of us get impatient with politics at least sometimes, and the accusation of "playing politics" with some serious issue is a frequent criticism. But in what way are our impatience and that accusation misdirected?

The Border

ROSS DOUTHAT AND JENNY WOODSON

This compact, fact-filled article and graphic appeared in *The Atlantic Monthly*.

1   More than 1.3 million people were caught trying to enter the United States illegally from Mexico in 2004. Nearly 200,000 were attempting to cross, often concealed in vehicles, at one of the twenty-five U.S.-Mexican Customs stations; most of the rest—those indicated on the map [on pages 432–433]—were apprehended by the U.S. Border Patrol, while making their way across the Rio Grande or the Sonora Desert or through the fences and other barriers separating Tijuana from southern California.

2   The Border Patrol has become much larger and more sophisticated in recent decades. Since the current wave of illegal Mexican immigration began, in the mid-1970s, the number of agents along the southern U.S. border has risen from 2,000 to 11,000. Roadways have been extended into remote areas to give agents better access to smuggling routes; floodlights, motion sensors, and remote video cameras have been installed; and agents have started patrolling in aircraft as well as on the ground. Last year the Border Patrol deployed a "Predator B" unmanned aerial vehicle—the first American UAV put to civilian use. It provides real-time bird's-eye views of previously inaccessible areas, transmitting images that are quickly relayed to agents on the ground.

3   But, of course, the migrants keep slipping through. The Border Patrol will not speculate about how many evade capture and enter the United States; the Pew Hispanic Center recently estimated that, on average, 485,000 Mexicans have crossed the border illegally every year since 2000, and that more illegal than legal aliens have entered the country altogether since 1995.

4   Immigration pressure from Mexico is unlikely to abate anytime soon. Nearly half of all Mexicans asked by Pew said they would come to the United States immediately if they had "the means and opportunity." Twenty-one percent said they would do so even if they had to come illegally. Indeed, many Mexicans seem to have a sense of entitlement regarding the United States: 58 percent surveyed in a 2002 Zogby poll believe that "the territory of the United States' Southwest rightfully belongs to Mexico."

5   Americans are unhappy about this state of affairs: according to recent polls, most favor beefing up the enforcement of immigration laws and using troops to police the border. A majority even voiced support for the Minuteman Project, a group of civilian vigilantes who have begun patrolling the border themselves.

6   However, political leaders in both parties (along with many business organizations, media outlets, and bipartisan interest groups) see the issue differently, believing that restricting immigration is not economically desirable. The immigration proposals currently circulating in Washington seem unlikely to reduce the influx from the south. They are aimed instead at regularizing it, by creating a temporary-visa program for migrant laborers. Although such a "guest worker" program might be paired with legislation to tighten border security and curb the hiring of illegal immigrants, as President Bush suggested in a November policy speech, there's reason to doubt that serious restrictions would actually result. The last major immigration reform, in 1986, was supposed to provide a similar tradeoff—an amnesty program for illegal aliens already in the United States was joined to commitment to crack down on employers of illegal immigrants. The amnesty was implemented; the crackdown fizzled out. And in December of 2004 Congress authorized the addition of 10,000 Border Patrol agents over a five-year period beginning in 2006—but only 210 new positions were funded for this year.

7   This gap between popular and elite opinion means that the porousness of the border is becoming a potent issue, especially for working-class voters, whose jobs may be vulnerable to guest-worker programs. Tom Tancredo, a Republican congressman from Colorado, has threatened to make an insurgent run for the 2008 GOP presidential nomination if no other candidate comes out strongly against illegal immigration, and observers speculate that Democrats might use the issue to try to outflank the GOP on the right. (Last year the governors of New Mexico and Arizona, both Democrats, declared states of emergency because of the influx of illegal immigrants, blaming the federal government for failing to secure the border.)

8   Nativist politics hasn't fared well in recent decades. And securing the border may not be feasible no matter what the public wants—at least absent a heavy military presence and the sorts of barriers used in Cold War Berlin and the Korean DMZ. (Spending on border security rose dramatically during the 1990s, but so did the number of illegal immigrants.) However, unless the gap on this issue between America's leaders and its citizenry is somehow narrowed, whether by stringent reform or by rising economic optimism on Main Street, a populist backlash could ensue—against both illegal immigrants themselves and those many see as their enablers in Washington.

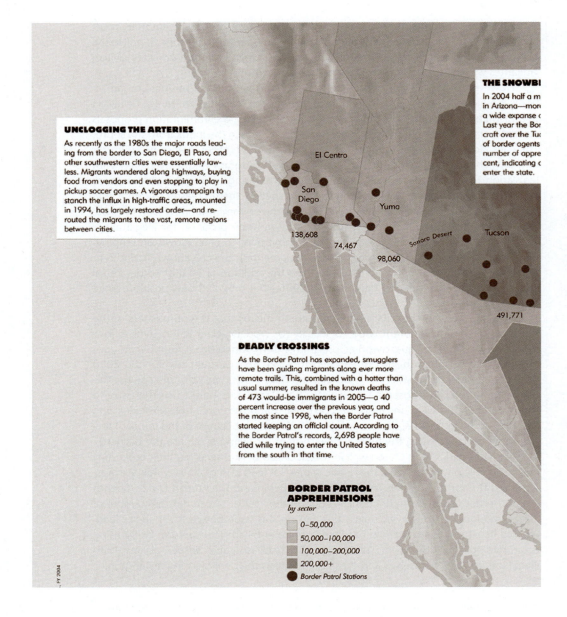

UNCLOGGING THE ARTERIES

As recently as the 1980s the major roads leading from the border to San Diego, El Paso, and other southwestern cities were essentially lawless. Migrants wandered along highways, buying food from vendors and even stopping to play in pickup soccer games. A vigorous campaign to stanch the influx in high-traffic areas, mounted in 1994, has largely restored order—and re-routed the migrants to the vast, remote regions between cities.

THE SNOWB

In 2004 half a m
in Arizona—mor
a wide expanse
Last year the Bor
craft over the Tu
of border agents
number of appre
cent, indicating
enter the state.

El Centro

San Diego

Yuma

138,608

74,467

98,060

Sonora Desert

Tucson

491,771

DEADLY CROSSINGS

As the Border Patrol has expanded, smugglers have been guiding migrants along ever more remote trails. This, combined with a hotter than usual summer, resulted in the known deaths of 473 would-be immigrants in 2005—a 40 percent increase over the previous year, and the most since 1998, when the Border Patrol started keeping an official count. According to the Border Patrol's records, 2,698 people have died while trying to enter the United States from the south in that time.

BORDER PATROL APPREHENSIONS
by sector

- 0–50,000
- 50,000–100,000
- 100,000–200,000
- 200,000+
- ● Border Patrol Stations

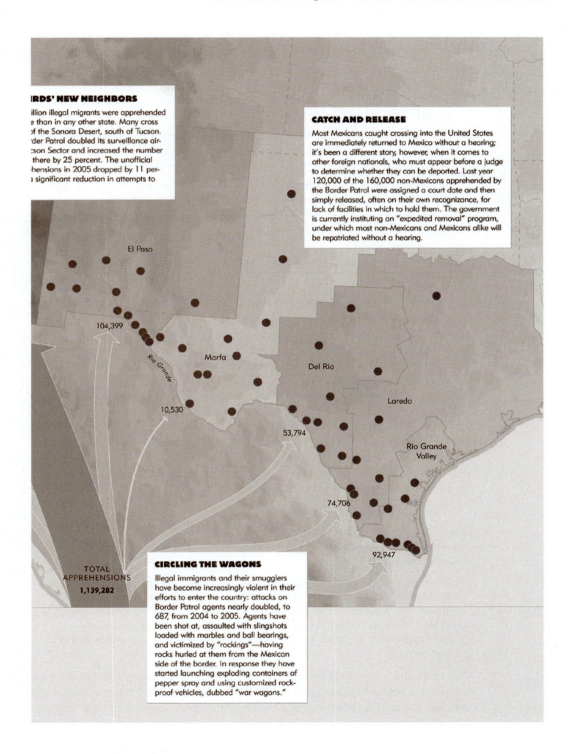

IRDS' NEW NEIGHBORS

illion illegal migrants were apprehended
e than in any other state. Many cross
of the Sonora Desert, south of Tucson.
der Patrol doubled its surveillance air-
cson Sector and increased the number
there by 25 percent. The unofficial
hensions in 2005 dropped by 11 per-
significant reduction in attempts to

CATCH AND RELEASE

Most Mexicans caught crossing into the United States
are immediately returned to Mexico without a hearing;
it's been a different story, however, when it comes to
other foreign nationals, who must appear before a judge
to determine whether they can be deported. Last year
120,000 of the 160,000 non-Mexicans apprehended by
the Border Patrol were assigned a court date and then
simply released, often on their own recognizance, for
lack of facilities in which to hold them. The government
is currently instituting an "expedited removal" program,
under which most non-Mexicans and Mexicans alike will
be repatriated without a hearing.

El Paso

104,399

Rio Grande

Marfa

10,530

Del Rio

Laredo

53,794

Rio Grande
Valley

74,706

92,947

TOTAL
APPREHENSIONS
1,139,282

CIRCLING THE WAGONS

Illegal immigrants and their smugglers
have become increasingly violent in their
efforts to enter the country: attacks on
Border Patrol agents nearly doubled, to
687, from 2004 to 2005. Agents have
been shot at, assaulted with slingshots
loaded with marbles and ball bearings,
and victimized by "rockings"—having
rocks hurled at them from the Mexican
side of the border. In response they have
started launching exploding containers of
pepper spray and using customized rock-
proof vehicles, dubbed "war wagons."

QUESTIONS FOR DISCUSSION

1. This article is an example of one kind of slightly disguised argument. It seems to be informative and, of course, is. But the information implies conclusions, arguable contentions, some spelled out, some not. What conclusions both explicit and implicit do you find?

2. What information were you unaware of? What surprised you the most? What conclusions do you draw from the information you now have? Are any of your conclusions different from the viewpoint of the authors?

3. Border control is a topic of much casual, often heated discussion. The graphic depicts the magnitude of the problem well and mentions the vast amount of manpower and money devoted to apprehending undocumented aliens. In your view, is the effort worthwhile?

FOR RESEARCH, DISCUSSION, AND MEDIATION

Many commentators point to the gap between the opinions of many ordinary Americans and those of the so-called elite concerning immigration. All the articles so far allude to it, and "The Border" highlights it. Basically, the popular view is generally anti-immigration and strongly for increased efforts to control the border with Mexico. Elite opinion—professors who study immigration, big business concerns, and many politicians—tend to be more pro-immigration and skeptical of efforts to control the border.

Do research on this rift in opinion, including current legislative proposals in Congress, which reflect the sharp contrast. Discuss the implications of what you turn up, being sure to reflect on *why* popular opinion moves one way and elite opinion another.

Then write an essay proposing an approach to border control designed to give both sides some of what they want. Defend it as a practical, middle-of-the-road way of better coping with this difficult problem.

The Realities of Immigration

LINDA CHAVEZ

Chairperson of the Center for Equal Opportunity in Washington, D.C. and author of *Out of the Barrio*, Linda Chavez is a frequent and perceptive commentator on immigration. She argues here that large-scale immigration from Mexico does not pose the threat some make it out to be, but we need a guest-worker program coupled with other measures to bring our border under greater control. Her article appeared in *Commentary*.

1   What to do about immigration—both legal and illegal—has become one of the most controversial public-policy debates in recent memory. But why it has occurred at this particular moment is something of a mystery. The rate of immigration into the U.S., although high, is still below what it was even a few years ago, the peak having been

reached in the late 1990's. President Bush first talked about comprehensive immigration reform almost immediately after assuming office, but he put the plan on hold after 9/11 and only reintroduced the idea in 2004. Why the current flap?

2   By far the biggest factor shaping the popular mood seems to have been the almost daily drumbeat on the issue from political talk-show hosts, most prominently CNN's Lou Dobbs and the Fox News Channel's Bill O'Reilly and Sean Hannity (both of whom also have popular radio shows), syndicated radio hosts Rush Limbaugh, Laura Ingraham, Michael Savage, and G. Gordon Liddy, and a plethora of local hosts reaching tens of millions of listeners each week. Stories about immigration have become a staple of cable news, with sensational footage of illegal crossings featured virtually every day.

3   Media saturation has led, in turn, to the emergence of immigration as a wedge issue in the . . . 2008 presidential campaign. Several aspiring Republican candidates—former House Speaker Newt Gingrich, Senate Majority Leader Bill Frist, and Senator George Allen—have worked to burnish their "get tough" credentials, while, on the other side of the issue, Senator John McCain has come forward as the lead sponsor of a bill to allow most illegal aliens to earn legal status. For their part, potential Democratic candidates have remained largely mum, unsure how the issue plays with their various constituencies.

4   And then there are the immigrants themselves, who have shown surprising political muscle, especially in response to legislation passed by the House that would turn the illegal aliens among them into felons. Millions of mostly Hispanic protesters have taken to the streets in our big cities in recent months, waving American flags and (more controversially) their own national flags while demanding recognition and better treatment. Though Hispanic leaders and pro-immigrant advocates point to the protests as evidence of a powerful new civil-rights movement, many other Americans see the demonstrators as proof of an alien invasion—and a looming threat to the country's prosperity and unity.

5   In short, it is hard to recall a time when there has been so much talk about immigration and immigration reform—or when so much of the talk has been misinformed, misleading, and ahistorical. Before policy-makers can decide what to do about immigration, the problem itself needs to be better defined, not just in terms of costs and benefits but in relation to America's deepest values.

6   Contrary to popular myth, immigrants have never been particularly welcome in the United States. Americans have always tended to romanticize the immigrants of their grandparents' generation while casting a skeptical eye on contemporary newcomers. In the first decades of the 20th century, descendants of Northern European immigrants resisted the arrival of Southern and Eastern Europeans, and today the descendants of those once unwanted Italians, Greeks, and Poles are deeply distrustful of current immigrants from Latin America. Congressman Tom Tancredo, a Republican from Colorado and an outspoken advocate of tighter restrictions, is fond of invoking the memory of his Italian immigrant grandfather to argue that he is not anti-immigrant, just anti-*illegal* immigration. He fails to mention that at the time his grandfather arrived, immigrants simply had to show up on American shores (or walk across the border) to gain legal entry. . . .

7   The modern immigration era commenced in 1965 with the passage of the Immigration and Nationality Act, which abolished all national-origin quotas, gave preference to close relatives of American citizens, refugees, and individuals with certain skills, and allowed for immigrants from the Western hemisphere on a first-come, first-served basis. The act's passage drew a huge wave, much of it from Latin America and Asia. From 1970 to 2000, the United States admitted more than 20 million persons as permanent residents.

8   By 2000, some 3 million of these new residents were formerly illegal aliens who had gained amnesty as part of the 1986 Immigration Reform and Control Act (IRCA). This, Congress's first serious attempt to stem the flow of illegal immigration, forced employers to determine the status of their workers and imposed heavy penalties on those hiring illegal entrants. But from the beginning, the law was fraught with problems. It created huge bureaucratic burdens, even for private individuals wanting to hire someone to cut their lawn or care for their children, and spawned a vast new document-fraud industry for immigrants eager to get hold of the necessary paperwork. The law has been a monumental failure. Today, some 11.5 million illegal aliens reside in the U.S.—quadruple the population of two decades ago, when IRCA was enacted—and the number is growing by an estimated 500,000 a year. . . .

9   The real question is not whether the U.S. has the means to stop illegal immigration—no doubt, with sufficient resources, we could mostly do so—but whether we would be better off as a nation without these workers. Restrictionists claim that large-scale immigration—legal and illegal—has depressed wages, burdened government resources, and acted as a net drain on the economy. The Federation for American Immigration Reform (FAIR), the most prominent of the pressure groups on the issue, argues that, because of this influx, hourly earnings among American males have not increased appreciably in 30 years. As the restrictionists see it, if the U.S. got serious about defending its borders, there would be plenty of Americans willing to do the jobs now performed by workers from abroad. . . .

10   Despite the presence in our workforce of millions of illegal immigrants, the U.S. is currently creating slightly more than two million jobs a year and boasts an unemployment rate of 4.7 percent, which is lower than the average in each of the past four decades. More to the point perhaps, when the National Research Council (NRC) of the National Academy of Sciences evaluated the economic impact of immigration in its landmark 1997 study *The New Americans: Economic, Demographic, and Fiscal Effects of Immigration,* it found only a small negative impact on the earnings of Americans, and even then, only for workers at lower skill and education levels.

11   Moreover , the participation of immigrants in the labor force has had obvious positive effects. The NRC estimated that roughly 5 percent of household expenditures in the U.S. went to goods and services produced by immigrant labor—labor whose relative cheapness translated into lower prices for everything from chicken to new homes. These price advantages, the study found, were "spread quite uniformly across most types of domestic consumers," with a slightly greater benefit for higher-income households.

12   Many restrictionists argue that if Americans would simply cut their own lawns, clean their own houses, and care for their own children, there would be no need for

immigrant labor. But even if this were true, the overall economy would hardly benefit from having fewer workers. If American women were unable to rely on immigrants to perform some household duties, more of them would be forced to stay home. A smaller labor force would also have devastating consequences when it comes to dealing with the national debt and government-funded entitlements like Social Security and Medicare, a point repeatedly made by former Federal Reserve Board Chairman Alan Greenspan. As he told a Senate committee in 2003, "short of a major increase in immigration, economic growth cannot be safely counted upon to eliminate deficits and the difficult choices that will be required to restore fiscal discipline." The following year, Greenspan noted that offsetting the fiscal effects of our own declining birthrate would require a level of immigration "much larger than almost all current projections assume."

13   The contributions that immigrants make to the economy must be weighed, of course, against the burdens they impose. FAIR and other restrictionist groups contend that immigrants are a huge drain on society because of the cost of providing public services to them—some $67 to $87 billion a year, according to one commonly cited study. Drawing on numbers from the NRC's 1997 report, FAIR argues that "the net fiscal drain on American taxpayers [from immigration] is between $166 and $226 a year per native household."

14   There is something to these assertions, though less than may at first appear. Much of the anxiety and resentment generated by immigrants is, indeed, a result of the very real costs they impose on state and local governments, especially in border states like California and Arizona. Providing education and health care to the children of immigrants is particularly expensive, and the federal government picks up only a fraction of the expense. But, again, there are countervailing factors. Illegal immigrants are hardly free-riders. An estimated three-quarters of them paid federal taxes in 2002, amounting to $7 billion in Social Security contributions and $1.5 billion in Medicare taxes, plus withholding for income taxes. They also pay state and local sales taxes and (as homeowners and renters) property taxes.

15   Moreover, FAIR and its ilk have a penchant for playing fast and loose with numbers. To support its assessment of immigration's overall fiscal burden, for instance, FAIR ignores the explicit cautions in a later NRC report about cross-sectional analyses that exclude the "concurrent descendants" of immigrants—that is, their adult children. These, overwhelmingly, are productive members of the workforce. As the NRC notes, when this more complete picture is taken into account, immigrants have "a positive federal impact of about $1,260 [per capita], exceeding their net cost [$680 per capita on average] at the state and local levels." Restrictionists also argue that fewer immigrants would mean more opportunities for low-skilled native workers. Of late, groups like the Minuteman Project have even taken to presenting themselves as champions of unemployed American blacks (a curious tactic, to say the least, considering the views on race and ethnicity of many in the anti-immigrant camp*).

---

*As the author and anti-immigration activist Peter Brimelow wrote in his 1995 book *Alien Nation,* "Americans have a legitimate interest in their country's racial balance . . . [and] a right to insist that their government stop shifting it." Himself an immigrant from England, Brimelow wants "more immigrants who look like me."

16   But here, too, the factual evidence is mixed. Wages for American workers who have less than a high-school education have probably been adversely affected by large-scale immigration; the economist George Borjas estimates a reduction of 8 percent in hourly wages for native-born males in that category. But price competition is not the only reason that many employers favor immigrants over poorly educated natives. Human capital includes motivation, and there could hardly be two more disparately motivated groups than U.S.-born high-school drop-outs and their foreign-born rivals in the labor market. Young American men usually leave high school because they become involved with drugs or crime, have difficulty with authority, cannot maintain regular hours, or struggle with learning. Immigrants, on the other hand, have demonstrated enormous initiative, reflecting, in the words of President Reagan, "a special kind of courage that enabled them to leave their own land, leave their friends and their countrymen, and come to this new and strange land."

17   Just as important, they possess a strong desire to work. Legal immigrants have an 86-percent rate of participation in the labor force; illegal immigrant males have a 94-percent rate. By contrast, among white males with less than a high-school education, the participation rate is 46 percent, while among blacks it is 40 percent. If all immigrants, or even only illegal aliens, disappeared from the American workforce, can anyone truly believe that poorly skilled whites and blacks would fill the gap? To the contrary, productivity would likely decline, and employers in many sectors would simply move their operations to countries like Mexico, China, and the Philippines, where many of our immigrants come from in the first place.

18   Of equal weight among foes of immigration are the cultural changes wrought by today's newcomers, especially those from Mexico. In his book *Who Are We? The Challenges to National Identity* (2004), the eminent political scientist Samuel P. Huntington warns that "Mexican immigration is leading toward the demographic *reconquista* of areas Americans took from Mexico by force in the 1830's and 1840's." . . .

19   Does it not seem likely that today's immigrants—because of their numbers, the constant flow of even more newcomers, and their proximity to their countries of origin—will be unable or unwilling to assimilate as previous ethnic groups have done?

20   There is no question that some public policies in the U.S. have actively discouraged assimilation. Bilingual education, the dominant method of instruction of Hispanic immigrant children for some 30 years, is the most obvious culprit, with its emphasis on retaining Spanish. But bilingual education is on the wane, having been challenged by statewide initiatives in California (1998), Arizona (2000), and Massachusetts (2004), and by policy shifts in several major cities and at the federal level. States that have moved to English-immersion instruction have seen test scores for Hispanic youngsters rise, in some cases substantially.

21   Evidence from the culture at large is also encouraging. On most measures of social and economic integration, Hispanic immigrants and their descendants have made steady strides up the ladder. English is the preferred language of virtually all U.S.-born Hispanics; indeed, according to a 2002 national survey by the Pew Hispanic Center and the Kaiser Family Foundation, 78 percent of third-generation Mexican-Americans cannot speak Spanish at all. In education, 86 percent of U.S.-born

Hispanics complete high school, compared with 92 percent of non-Hispanic whites, and the drop-out rate among immigrant children who enroll in high school after they come here is no higher than for the native-born. . . .

22   As for the effect of Hispanic immigrants on the country's social fabric, the NRC found that they are more likely than other Americans to live with their immediate relatives: 88.6 percent of Mexican immigrant households are made up of families, compared with 69.5 percent of non-Hispanic whites and 68.3 percent of blacks. These differences are partially attributable to the age structure of the Hispanic population, which is younger on average than the white or black population. But even after adjusting for age and immigrant generation, U.S. residents of Hispanic origin—and especially those from Mexico—are much more likely to live in family households. Despite increased out-of-wedlock births among Hispanics, about 67 percent of American children of Mexican origin live in two-parent families, as compared with 77 percent of white children but only 37 percent of black children.

23   Perhaps the strongest indicator of Hispanic integration into American life is the population's high rate of intermarriage. About a quarter of all Hispanics marry outside their ethnic group, almost exclusively to non-Hispanic white spouses, a rate that has remained virtually unchanged since 1980. And here a significant fact has been noted in a 2005 study by the Population Reference Bureau—namely, that "the majority of inter-Hispanic children are reported as Hispanic." Such intermarriages themselves, the study goes on, "may have been a factor in the phenomenal growth of the U.S. Hispanic population in recent years."

24   It has been widely predicted that, by mid-century, Hispanics will represent fully a quarter of the U.S. population. Such predictions fail to take into account that increasing numbers of these "Hispanics" will have only one grandparent or great-grandparent of Hispanic heritage. By that point, Hispanic ethnicity may well mean neither more nor less than German, Italian, or Irish ethnicity means today.

25   How, then, to proceed? Congress is under growing pressure to strengthen border control, but unless it also reaches some agreement on more comprehensive reforms, stauncher enforcement is unlikely to have much of an effect. With a growing economy and more jobs than our own population can readily absorb, the U.S. will continue to need immigrants. Illegal immigration already responds reasonably well to market forces. It has increased during boom times like the late 1990's and decreased again when jobs disappear, as in the latest recession. Trying to determine an ideal number makes no more sense than trying to predict how much steel or how many textiles we ought to import; government quotas can never match the efficiency of simple supply and demand. As President Bush has argued—and as the Senate has now agreed—a guest-worker program is the way to go.

26   Does this mean the U.S. should just open its borders to anyone who wants to come? Hardly. We still need an orderly process, one that includes background checks to insure that terrorists and criminals are not being admitted. It also makes sense to require that immigrants have at least a basic knowledge of English and to give preference to those who have advanced skills or needed talents.

27   Moreover, immigrants themselves have to take more responsibility for their status. Illegal aliens from Mexico now pay significant sums of money to "coyotes" who

sneak them across the border. If they could come legally as guest workers, that same money might be put up as a surety bond to guarantee their return at the end of their employment contract, or perhaps to pay for health insurance. Nor is it good policy to allow immigrants to become welfare recipients or to benefit from affirmative action: restrictions on both sorts of programs have to be written into law and stringently applied.

28   A market-driven guest-worker program might be arranged in any number of ways. A proposal devised by the Vernon K. Krieble Foundation, a policy group based in Colorado, suggests that government-licensed, private-sector employment agencies be put in charge of administering the effort, setting up offices in other countries to process applicants and perform background checks. Workers would be issued tamper-proof identity cards only after signing agreements that would allow for deportation if they violated the terms of their contract or committed crimes in the U.S. Although the Krieble plan would offer no path to citizenship, workers who wanted to change their status could still apply for permanent residency and, ultimately, citizenship through the normal, lengthy process.

29   Do such schemes stand a chance politically? A poll commissioned by the Krieble Foundation found that most Americans (except those with less than a high-school education) consider an "efficient system for handling guest workers" to be more important than expanded law enforcement in strengthening the country's border. Similarly, a CNN tracking poll in May found that 81 percent of respondents favored legislation permitting illegal immigrants who have been in the U.S. more than five years to stay here and apply for citizenship, provided they had jobs and paid back taxes. True, other polls have contradicted these results, suggesting public ambivalence on the issue—and an openness to persuasion.

30   Regardless of what Congress does or does not do—the odds in favor of an agreement between the Senate and House on final legislation are still no better than 50-50—immigration is likely to continue at high levels for the foreseeable future. Barring a recession or another terrorist attack, the U.S. economy is likely to need some 1.5 to 2 million immigrants a year for some time to come. It would be far better for all concerned if those who wanted to work in the U.S. and had jobs waiting for them here could do so legally, in the light of day and with the full approval of the American people.

QUESTIONS FOR DISCUSSION

1. Chavez thinks that media attention and politics are responsible for the current spotlight on immigration—implying that the issue is hyped, overblown. Based on what you have read in this section and your own knowledge, would you agree? Why or why not?

2. Chavez makes a strong case for the economic necessity of immigrant workers. Summarize her position, including her effort to refute viewpoints such as FAIR's. Do you find her case convincing? Why or why not? If you agree, what implications does your assent have for immigration policy? If you disagree, what implications does your dissent have?

Mexican migrant workers harvest organic parsley at Grant Family Farms on Oct. 11, 2011, in Wellington, Colorado.

3. Compare Chavez's view of the assimilation of Mexican immigrants with Samuel Huntington's in his selection in this chapter. Who makes the stronger case? If you think Chavez does, what points does Huntington make that must be taken into account? If Huntington does, what does Chavez say that merits attention?

FOR RESEARCH AND CONVINCING

There is a great deal of resentment toward illegal immigration at the level of local government, both state and city. It is not hard to see why—local government bears much of the cost of services required for undocumented workers. Investigate this problem and then write a paper urging the federal government to take on more of the costs of illegal immigration.

Obama's Next Act: Immigration Reform

CHRIS FARRELL

Written a month after President Obama's reelection in 2012, this article summarizes the economic case for extending citizenship to undocumented workers. Farrell writes on economics for *Bloomberg Businessweek* and appears often on public radio's business program *Marketplace*.

1 Washington won't get much of a reprieve from verbal pyrotechnics once the drama of the fiscal cliff is over. Up next: major immigration reform. President

Obama has made it clear that a comprehensive overhaul of the nation's badly frayed immigration system is a second-term priority. Many Republican lawmakers are convinced the big takeaway from the 2012 election results is that conservatives need to rethink their hard-line stance on immigration—including illegal immigrants.

2   Here's what Washington should do before tackling the tough job of rewriting the immigration laws: Create a quicksilver path to citizenship for the 11 million to 12 million undocumented workers in the U.S. (excluding the small number convicted of violent crimes or multiple felonies). The shift in status acknowledges that these foreign-born newcomers, like previous generations of immigrants, overcame significant obstacles to come to the U.S. to make a better life for their families. Illegal immigrants are neighbors heading off to work, sending their kids to school, and attending church. Their everyday lives would vastly improve by moving from the shadows of society into the mainstream.

3   More important from a public-policy perspective, the change would give a boost to the economy's underlying dynamism. "What you're doing in the short run is making it easier for workers to move between jobs, a relatively small effect," says Gordon Hanson, a professor of economics at the University of California at San Diego. "The larger effect from eliminating uncertainty for these immigrants is creating incentives for them to make long-term investments in careers, entrepreneurship, education, homes, and community."

4   Let's state the obvious: A rapid transformation of illegal immigrants into legal immigrants isn't in the cards. Amnesty—let alone citizenship—is an anathema to large parts of the electorate. Too bad, since the scholarly evidence is compelling that immigrants—documented or not, legal or illegal—are a boon to the net economy. "Competition fosters economic growth," says Michael Clemens, senior fellow at the Center for Global Development in Washington.

5   The economic return from attracting skilled immigrants to the U.S. is well known. Foreign-born newcomers account for some 13 percent of the population, yet they are responsible for one-third of U.S. patented innovations. The nation's high-tech regions such as Silicon Valley, the Silicon Hills of Austin, Tex., and Boston's Route 128 rely on immigrant scientists, engineers, entrepreneurs, and employees. Better yet, economist Enrico Moretti at the University of California at Berkeley calculates that a 1 percent increase in the share of college-educated immigrants in a city hikes productivity and wages for others in the city.

6   Less appreciated is how much the economy gains from the efforts of less-skilled immigrants, including illegal workers. Throughout the country, foreign-born newcomers have revived beaten-down neighborhoods as immigrant entrepreneurs have opened small businesses and immigrant families have put down stakes. Immigrant workers have played a vital role keeping a number of industries competitive, such as agriculture and meatpacking. Cities with lots of immigrants have seen their per capita tax base go up, according to David Card, an economist at UC Berkeley. Despite the popular impression that a rising tide of immigrants is associated with higher crime rates, research by Robert Sampson of Harvard University and others offer a compelling case that it's no coincidence that the growing ranks of immigrants tracks the reduction in crime in the U.S.

7   But don't newcomers—legal and illegal—drive down wages and job opportunities for American workers? Not really. A cottage industry of economic studies doesn't find any negative effect on native-born wages and employment on the local level. On the national level the research shows the impact on native-born Americans doesn't drift far from zero, either positively or negatively. "In both cases, immigrants are more likely to complement the job prospects of U.S.-born citizens than they are to compete for the same jobs as U.S.-born citizens," Giovanni Peri, an economist at the University of California at Davis, writes in *Rationalizing U.S. Immigration Policy: Reforms for Simplicity, Fairness, and Economic Growth.*

8   The counterintuitive results reflect a numbers of factors. Immigrants expand the size of the economic pie by creating new businesses, new jobs, and new consumers. Middle-class families find it easier to focus on careers with affordable immigrant labor offering gardening, child care, and other services. Many illegal immigrants aren't fluent in English, so they don't compete for the same jobs as native-born workers. Another factor behind the lack of direct competition is the higher educational level of native-born Americans. In 1960 about half of U.S.-born working-age adults hadn't completed high school, while the comparable figure today is about 8 percent.

9   The real downside concern is on the fiscal side of the immigrant ledger. Yes, more taxes would go into Social Security, Medicare, and the like with legalization, but more people would qualify for Medicaid, welfare, and other benefits. At the local level, many school districts are strained financially from educating immigrant children, legal and illegal. That said, the prospect of fiscal costs would diminish as newly legalized immigrant workers move freely around the country seeking jobs, entrepreneurs are comfortable expanding their payrolls, and immigrant parents push their children to live the American Dream. "Over time, as entrepreneurs emerge and families are better able to get their kids through high school and college, you're reducing the long-run fiscal claim of the group," says Hanson.

10   There is no economic evidence that making roughly 6 percent of the workforce illegal will benefit the economy. Plenty of research supports the opposite case. A fast track to legality offers Washington a rare twofer: a just move that's economically efficient.

QUESTIONS FOR DISCUSSION

1. Compare this 2012 article to the previous essay by Linda Chavez, written about six years earlier. Pay special attention to what both writers say about the economics of immigration. On what points do they agree? On what points do they disagree?

2. Besides being good for the economy, Farrell contends that a fast track to citizenship for undocumented workers is also just. Is it? Is it just for undocumented workers to receive the same treatment as people who immigrate legally? Why or why not?

3. There is no doubt that the main driver of immigration, legal and illegal, is economics, as it has been throughout the history of the United States. However, there are other motives, such as the desire of immigrants to escape political persecution in their countries of origin. What other motivations do you know about?

FOR RESEARCH, DISCUSSION, AND MEDIATION

As a class research project, compile information about the ongoing effort at immigration reform. What are the battle lines in Congress and how do they relate to what President Obama wants to do? Discuss the implications of the information you have and then write a paper indicating what you think needs to be done and what compromises will have to be made so that meaningful reform can happen.

Comprehensive Immigration Reform—Past, Present, and Future

DAVA CASTILLO

Published a month after President Obama's reelection in 2012, this online article advocates the DREAM Act, which failed to become law in 2010. Castillo, who is a writer for Allvoices, an online source of news and news commentary, argues for doing the right thing as she sees it, taking action especially to stop the recent large-scale deportation of undocumented workers.

1   In Charles Dickens' classic novel "A Christmas Carol," Ebenezer Scrooge, who has been a notorious penny-pinching miser most of his life, is visited in a dream by the ghosts of Christmas Past, Present and Future. The Spirit of Christmas Past visited Scrooge first:

> Scrooge reverently disclaimed all intention to offend or any knowledge of having willfully bonneted the Spirit at any period of his life. He then made bold to inquire what business brought him there.
> "Your welfare!" said the Ghost.
> Scrooge expressed himself much obliged, but could not help thinking that a night of unbroken rest would have been more conducive to that end. The Spirit must have heard him thinking, for it said immediately:
> "Your reclamation, then. Take heed!"
> It put out its strong hand as it spoke, and clasped him gently by the arm.
> "Rise! and walk with me!"

2   Will the ghost of comprehensive immigration reform visit President Obama this holiday season and offer a chance to reclaim past political campaign promises? Obama was elected in 2008 and re-elected in 2012 with the support of the voting Latino population under the mandate that comprehensive immigration reform would be a priority by his administration, and it is still waiting to be addressed. Since Obama's election in 2008, deportations have continued, and the program Secure Communities has wreaked havoc in Hispanic communities by wrongly netting Latino American citizens in an effort to deport criminals. The president used executive order to slow the deportation of young Hispanics who came here with their parents as children, but the DREAM Act, which would ensure by law that these children can remain in the United States, still remains controversial and politicized. It has not been passed by Congress, where it has languished since 2001.

DEPORTATIONS SINCE OBAMA TOOK OFFICE

3   For the first three years of Obama's administration, the Republicans praised the number of immigrant deportations like it was a badge of honor to separate families. Immigration reform advocates, however, view the deportation of 1.2 million undocumented individuals in the first three years of Obama's administration in direct contrast to his 2008 campaign promise for comprehensive immigration reform.

4   A 2011 report by the Transactional Records Access Clearinghouse (TRAC), a data-gathering, research and distribution organization at Syracuse University, reported that the number of deportation legal proceedings initiated between October and December 2011 fell by 33 percent from the previous quarter, causing outrage by Congressional Republicans, according to a *Huffington Post* report. Still, the deportations numbers remained high.

5   The Congress has budgeted for 400,000 deportations a year to ensure deportation rates remain high. According to Immigrations and Customs Enforcement (ICE), the annual number of deportations was stable in the last few years: 370,000 in Fiscal Year 2008, 390,000 in FY 2009, 393,000 in FY 2010, and 397,000 in FY 2011, the October and December 2011 decline in deportations notwithstanding. Despite the relatively high numbers of average yearly deportations, the call by Republicans echoed for ICE to fill the quotas.

SECURE COMMUNITIES

6   The Secure Communities Program, which is an arm of Homeland Security and ICE, was piloted in 2008 by the then-president George Bush in a Texas jurisdiction, but the program did not go into full operation until Obama took office. Nationwide implementation came in 2011, when it was expanded to 1,210 jurisdictions with a projection by ICE to have 3,141 state, county and local jails and prisons signing on to the program by 2013.

7   It is not coincidental that the expansion coincides with the 2011 TRAC report and the Republican complaint that the quota for deportations was not being met. The president appeased the Republicans with expansion of a defective program that captures innocent Latino American citizens and prevents the undocumented from reporting crimes for fear of reprisal.

8   The quota system for deportation has inherent flaws. It is bad public policy to have a system that incentivizes law enforcement, in this case ICE, for the accomplishment of arrest quotas, then grades the policy success based on the fulfillment of a quota set by Congress. Maintaining high deportation numbers is counterintuitive to non-punitive, successful immigration policy which would automatically realize a decrease in deportations.

RELIEF FOR DREAMERS

9   Relief for DREAMers began as a student movement to stop deporting immigrant youth and separating their families. The Congress' failure to pass the DREAM Act spirited students to launch the "End Our Pain" campaign in 2011, which

proved a success in an election year. In response the Obama administration issued an executive order in June 2012, which many believe was to reel in Hispanic voters in November, and it worked. The order stopped deportation of Latino youth brought here by their parents, and instead issued work permits to law abiding youth. The administration's decision could affect as many as 800,000 immigrant youth.

10   In Charles Dickens' novel, Scrooge is transformed after the ghostly visitations. The ghost of "Christmas Yet to Come," which is the future, gives Scrooge some choices. Crying out, Scrooge realizes his transgressions: "Men's courses will foreshadow certain ends, to which, if persevered in, they must lead," said Scrooge. "But if the courses be departed from, the ends will change." In other words, change is possible if the past is recognized and replaced by new strategies which reflect an enlightened course of action.

11   Immigration policy aimed at punishing and criminalizing the undocumented is not written in stone, nor should future public policy become rooted in political party ideology or be designed to appease a political party. The guide is protecting human rights, civil liberties, and encouraging American diversity, which has always been the bedrock of our society.

12   Make the DREAM Act federal law and not just an abstraction left to languish in the halls of Congress. The past need not be prologue, and 2013 needs to be the year that the Congress acts with a conscience and President Obama stands firm on his campaign promises to expedite intelligent, comprehensive immigration reform to our Hispanic brothers and sisters who have supported him since 2008 and our nation for so many years.

RESOURCES

www.huffingtonpost.com/2012/03/01/deportation-numbers-obama_n_1314916.html
www.nycpba.org/publications/mag-05-spring/murray.html
www.swer.org/blog/2012/06/15/relief-for-dreamers/
en.wikipedia.org/wiki/Ghost_of_Christmas_Yet_to_Come
www.literature.org/authors/dickens-charles/christmas-carol/chapter-02.html

QUESTIONS FOR DISCUSSION

1. Around Christmas time every year, Dickens' "A Christmas Carol" is retold in one medium or another. Writing in December 2012, Castillo attempts to use the story to persuade her readers. Do you think this tactic worked well? If so, why? If not, why not?

2. Did you know about the number of deportations of the undocumented that went on during Obama's first term? Did the numbers surprise you? What view do you take of that policy?

3. Castillo says that "it is bad public policy to have a system that incentivizes law enforcement," that gives the police or other law enforcement officials special reason to enforce the law. Yet, it is commonly done in the United States, for example, to encourage traffic citations. What is your response to the notion of incentives?

FOR RESEARCH AND CONVINCING

Some people justify current immigration policy in part by appealing to the need to control criminal activity and to prevent terrorism. Do research on the behavior of the current undocumented population and on the rationale for and actual consequences of the Secure Communities program. Is there any connection between criminal activity in general or terrorism in particular and current immigration policy? How strong is the connection? Has the Secure Communities program played a constructive role? What negative impact has it had?

Write a paper defending or attacking the Secure Communities program. You may concentrate on either its rationale or its actual practices or on both.

The Border Patrol State

LESLIE MARMON SILKO

> Whenever illegal immigration is discussed, someone asserts that we have lost control of our borders. The contention is typically accepted as a fact rather than thought about seriously. This classic article examines the notion seriously, while calling attention to violations of the civil rights of American citizens by Border Patrol agents.
>
> Leslie Marmon Silko is a celebrated Native American writer. Her article appeared originally in *The Nation*.

1   I used to travel the highways of New Mexico and Arizona with a wonderful sensation of absolute freedom as I cruised down the open road and across the vast desert plateaus. On the Laguna Pueblo reservation where I was raised, the people were patriotic despite the way the U.S. government had treated Native Americans. As proud citizens, we grew up believing the freedom to travel was our inalienable right, a right that some Native Americans had been denied in the early twentieth century. Our cousin, old Bill Pratt, used to ride his horse 300 miles overland from Laguna, New Mexico, to Prescott, Arizona, every summer to work as a fire lookout.

2   In school in the 1950s, we were taught that our right to travel from state to state without special papers or threat of detainment was a right that citizens under communist and totalitarian governments did not possess. That wide open highway told us we were U.S. citizens; we were free. . . .

3   Not so long ago, my companion Gus and I were driving south from Albuquerque, returning to Tucson after a book promotion for the paperback edition of my novel *Almanac of the Dead.* I had settled back and gone to sleep while Gus drove; but I was awakened when I felt the car slowing to a stop. It was nearly midnight on New Mexico State Road 26, a dark, lonely stretch of two-lane highway between Hatch and Deming. When I sat up, I saw the headlights and emergency flashers of six vehicles—Border Patrol cars and a van were blocking both lanes of the highway. Gus stopped the car and rolled down the window to ask what was wrong. But the closest Border Patrolman and his companion did not reply; instead, the first agent ordered us to "step out of the car." Gus asked why, but his question seemed to set them off. Two more Border Patrol agents immediately approached our car, and one of them snapped, "Are you looking for trouble?" as if he would relish it.

4   I will never forget that night beside the highway. There was an awful feeling of menace and violence straining to break loose. It was clear that the uniformed men would be only too happy to drag us out of the car if we did not speedily comply with their request (asking a question is tantamount to resistance, it seems). So we stepped out of the car and they motioned for us to stand on the shoulder of the road. The night was very dark, and no other traffic had come down the road since we had been stopped. All I could think about was a book I had read—*Nunca Mas*—the official report of a human rights commission that investigated and certified more than 12,000 "disappearances" during Argentina's "dirty war" in the late 1970s.

5   The weird anger of these Border Patrolmen made me think about descriptions in the report of Argentine police and military officers who became addicted to interrogation, torture and the murder that followed. When the military and police ran out of political suspects to torture and kill, they resorted to the random abduction of citizens off the streets. I thought how easy it would be for the Border Patrol to shoot us and leave our bodies and car beside the highway, like so many bodies found in these parts and ascribed to "drug runners."

6   Two other Border Patrolmen stood by the white van. The one who had asked if we were looking for trouble ordered his partner to "get the dog," and from the back of the van another patrolman brought a small female German shepherd on a leash. The dog apparently did not heel well enough to suit him, and the handler jerked the leash. They opened the doors of our car and pulled the dog's head into it, but I saw immediately from the expression in her eyes that the dog hated them, and that she would not serve them. When she showed no interest in the inside of the car, they brought her around back to the trunk, near where we were standing. They half-dragged her up into the trunk, but still she did not indicate any stowed-away human beings or illegal drugs.

7   The mood got uglier; the officers seemed outraged that the dog could not find any contraband, and they dragged her over to us and commanded her to sniff our legs and feet. To my relief, the strange violence the Border Patrol agents had focused on us now seemed shifted to the dog. I no longer felt so strongly that we would be murdered. We exchanged looks—the dog and I. She was afraid of what they might do, just as I was. The dog's handler jerked the leash sharply as she sniffed us, as if to make her perform better, but the dog refused to accuse us: She had an innate dignity that did not permit her to serve the murderous impulses of those men. I can't forget the expression in the dog's eyes; it was as if she were embarrassed to be associated with them. I had a small amount of medicinal marijuana in my purse that night, but she refused to expose me. I am not partial to dogs, but I will always remember the small German shepherd that night.

8   Unfortunately , what happened to me is an everyday occurrence here now. . . .

9   I was [also] detained once at Truth or Consequences, despite my and my companion's Arizona driver's licenses. Two men, both Chicanos, were detained at the same time, despite the fact that they too presented ID and spoke English without the thick Texas accents of the Border Patrol agents. While we were stopped, we watched as other vehicles—whose occupants were white—were waved through the checkpoint. White people traveling with brown people, however, can expect to be stopped

on suspicion they work with the sanctuary movement, which shelters refugees. White people who appear to be clergy, those who wear ethnic clothing or jewelry and women with very long hair or very short hair (they could be nuns) are also frequently detained; white men with beards or men with long hair are likely to be detained, too, because Border Patrol agents have "profiles" of "those sorts" of white people who may help political refugees. (Most of the political refugees from Guatemala and El Salvador are Native American or mestizo because the indigenous people of the Americas have continued to resist efforts by invaders to displace them from their ancestral lands.) Alleged increases in illegal immigration by people of Asian ancestry means that the Border Patrol now routinely detains anyone who appears to be Asian or part Asian, as well.

10   Once your car is diverted from the Interstate Highway into the checkpoint area, you are under the control of the Border Patrol, which in practical terms exercises a power that no highway patrol or city patrolman possesses: They are willing to detain anyone, for no apparent reason. Other law-enforcement officers need a shred of probable cause in order to detain someone. On the books, so does the Border Patrol; but on the road, it's another matter. They'll order you to stop your car and step out; then they'll ask you to open the trunk. If you ask why or request a search warrant, you'll be told that they'll have to have a dog sniff the car before they can request a search warrant, and the dog might not get there for two or three hours. The search warrant might require an hour or two past that. They make it clear that if you force them to obtain a search warrant for the car, they will make you submit to a strip search as well. . . .

11   This is the police state that has developed in the southwestern United States since the 1980s. No person, no citizen, is free to travel without the scrutiny of the Border Patrol. In the city of South Tucson, where 80 percent of the respondents were Chicano or Mexicano, a joint research project by the University of Wisconsin and the University of Arizona recently concluded that one out of every five people there had been detained, mistreated verbally or nonverbally, or questioned by I.N.S. [Immigration and Naturalization Service] agents in the past two years.

12   Manifest Destiny may lack its old grandeur of theft and blood—"lock the door" is what it means now, with racism a trump card to be played again and again, shamelessly, by both major political parties. "Immigration," like "street crime" and "welfare fraud," is a political euphemism that refers to people of color. Politicians and media people talk about "illegal aliens" to dehumanize and demonize undocumented immigrants, who are for the most part people of color. Even in the days of Spanish and Mexican rule, no attempts were made to interfere with the flow of people and goods from south to north and north to south. It is the U.S. government that has continually attempted to sever contact between the tribal people north of the border and those to the south.[1]

---

[1] The Treaty of Guadalupe Hidalgo, signed in 1848, recognizes the right of the Tohano O'Odom (Papago) people to move freely across the U.S.–Mexico border without documents. A treaty with Canada guarantees similar rights to those of the Iroquois nation in traversing the U.S.–Canada border. [Author's note]

13   Now that the "Iron Curtain" is gone, it is ironic that the U.S. government and its Border Patrol are constructing a steel wall ten feet high to span sections of the border with Mexico. . . . Like the pathetic multimillion-dollar "antidrug" border surveillance balloons that were continually deflated by high winds and made only a couple of meager interceptions before they blew away, the fence along the border is a theatrical prop, a bit of pork for contractors. Border entrepreneurs have already used blowtorches to cut passageways through the fence to collect "tolls," and are doing a brisk business. . . .

14   It is no use; borders haven't worked, and they won't work, not now, as the indigenous people of the Americas reassert their kinship and solidarity with one another. A mass migration is already under way; its roots are not simply economic. The Uto-Aztecan languages are spoken as far north as Taos Pueblo near the Colorado border, all the way south to Mexico City. Before the arrival of the Europeans, the indigenous communities throughout this region not only conducted commerce, the people shared cosmologies, and oral narratives about the Maize Mothers, the Twin Brothers and their Grandmother, Spider Woman, as well as Quetzalcoatl the benevolent snake. The great human migration within the Americas cannot be stopped; human beings are natural forces of the Earth, just as rivers and winds are natural forces. . . .

15   One evening at sundown, we were stopped in traffic at a railroad crossing in downtown Tucson while a freight train passed us, slowly gaining speed as it headed north to Phoenix. In the twilight I saw the most amazing sight: Dozens of human beings, mostly young men, were riding the train; everywhere, on flat cars, inside open boxcars, perched on top of boxcars, hanging off ladders on tank cars and between boxcars. I couldn't count fast enough, but I saw fifty or sixty people headed north. They were dark young men, Indian and mestizo; they were smiling and a few of them waved at us in our cars. I was reminded of the ancient story of Aztlán, told by the Aztecs but known in other Uto-Aztecan communities as well. Aztlán is the beautiful land to the north, the origin place of the Aztec people. I don't remember how or why the people left Aztlán to journey farther south, but the old story says that one day, they will return.

QUESTIONS FOR DISCUSSION

1. Silko refers to the "weird anger" (paragraph 5) of the Border Patrol officers. Why does she call it "weird"? What might explain their anger?

2. "Immigration," like "street crime" and "welfare fraud," Silko claims, "is a political euphemism that refers to people of color." Is she right? What do these terms make you think of? How do such associations distort clear thinking about immigration, legal or illegal?

3. Originally "The Border Patrol State" appeared under the caption "America's Iron Curtain," an allusion to the Berlin Wall, one of the great symbols of tyranny for Americans of Silko's generation. Thus, the editors of *The Nation* compare our border walls to the Berlin Wall, torn down only a few years before Silko's article appeared. How apt is the analogy?

FOR RESEARCH, DISCUSSION, AND MEDIATION

Silko reminds us of how short-sighted views of immigration can be—they tend to focus on the current situation without much awareness of the history, for example, of peoples moving back and forth along the U.S. border with Mexico. Find out all you can about the movement of peoples along our southern border, being sure to go all the way back to when there was no border and the region was populated by Native Americans only. Answer these questions: What does the history tell us about cultural ties among the people who live on both sides of the current border? How much should what we know from history influence our thinking now about border control and immigration?

Write an essay proposing an approach to border control based on your new knowledge of history. Use your knowledge to propose a solution in between the current extremes: shutting off illegal immigration entirely and creating completely open borders.

FOR FURTHER READING

Bray, Ilona. *U.S. Immigration Made Easy*. 15th ed. Nolo, 2011.

Huntington, Samuel P. *Who Are We? The Challenges to America's Identity*. Simon and Schuster, 2004.

Gerber, David A. *Immigration: A Very Short Introduction*. Oxford UP, 2011.

Jacoby, Tamar, ed., *Reinventing the Melting Pot: The New Immigrants and What It Means to Be American*. Basic Books, 2004.

Reason, Aug.–Sept. 2006. A series of provocative articles in a special section of the issue. See especially Carolyn Lockheed, "The Unexpected Consequences of Immigration Reform."

Schrag, Peter. *Not Fit for Our Society: Immigration and Nativism in America*. U of California P, 2011.

Wilson Quarterly, Summer 2006. Some interesting pieces on recent immigration trends, including legal immigration from Africa.

Zollberg, Aristide R. *A Nation by Design: Immigration Policy in the Fashioning of America*. Harvard UP, 2004.

A common example of incivility is bullying. While bullying is not new, the instances of reported bullying in schools increased by almost 25% during the period from 2003 to 2007, according to the National Center for Education Statistics.

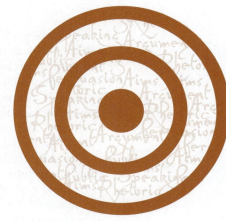

CHAPTER 16

Declining Civility:
Is Rudeness on the Rise?

P. M. Forni, What Is Civility?   455

Sara Rimer, Play with Your Food, Just Don't Text   459

Elizabeth Bernstein, Why We Are So Rude Online   462

Leonard Pitts, Jr., Going beyond Edgy—and Falling off the Cliff   465

Tufts Now, Left Is Mean But Right Is Meaner, Says New Study of
  Political Discourse   467

Brian McGee, Can Political Rhetoric Be Too Civil?   470

Frank D. Adams and Gloria J. Lawrence, Bullying Victims: The Effects
  Last into College   472

Emily Bazelon, Don't Be a Bystander   479

For Further Reading   *482*

Examples of rude behavior are not hard to find these days. On the roads, aggressive drivers seem more common than courteous ones. In the news, we see a tennis player verbally assault a line judge and a rap singer barge onstage to interrupt another singer's awards acceptance speech. At meals, people are texting while ignoring others sitting with them around the table. And in college classes, students and professors report that they regularly observe rude behavior such as text messaging, talking, sleeping, allowing cell phones to ring, and packing up books before the end of class.

Behavior that goes beyond rudeness is all too common. Nearly every day we hear of instances of verbal and physical bullying in schools and the subsequent effects on the victims. Obscene and vulgar language proliferates on television and the Internet, filtering from the screen into people's everyday lives, where it is overheard and repeated.

On the political landscape, language has become more heated and divisive along party lines, with both major parties taking off the gloves and hurling insults and personal attacks. When Congressman Joe Wilson of South Carolina shouted "You lie!" during President Obama's speech on health care reform in September of 2009, even members of his own Republican Party criticized him as having gone too far. Politicians, news commentators, and radio talk show hosts have found that incivility gets them more attention than politeness.

Incivility, however, does not persuade. For Aristotle, good character—or ethos—was an essential element of persuasion. It is also an important element of democracy, which depends on cooperation. Civility makes all communication more effective. A course in college writing is therefore a good place to examine civility and its role in our personal and public lives.

The readings in this chapter begin with a definition of civility from a professor of literature, P. M. Forni, whose book *Choosing Civility* has become a best-seller since its publication in 2002. Civility "is imagination on a moral track." He advocates teaching civility in college to help students reach their full human potential. "To be fully human," he writes, "we must be able to imagine others' hurt and to relate it to the hurt we would experience if we were in their place." Other readings show examples of people's failure to act in civil ways: in private life, such as texting at the dinner table, and in the public world, in politics, journalism, social media, and the halls and classrooms of America's schools. We include a report about two Tufts University professors' findings about the increasing use of "outrage talk" in a wide variety of political discourse genres.

What are the consequences of incivility? If civility is, as Forni claims, moral behavior, then choosing incivility is choosing to be immoral. Other readings explore the causes, consequences, and possible solutions to the kinds of incivility all people are exposed to in daily life. Elizabeth Bernstein explores the effects of anonymity on social media, while *Miami Herald* writer Leonard Pitts asks us to consider the line between edgy humor and hateful speech intended as humor. And no discussion of incivility can ignore the age-old problem of bullying and what to do about it. The scholarly article by Frank Adams and Gloria Lawrence shows that the consequences of school bullying can last far beyond the childhood years, affecting victims' self-esteem and other personality traits. The chapter closes with a reading by Emily Bazelon on how young people might begin to take responsibility for changing the culture of bullying.

The readings in this chapter should stimulate interest in the role of civility in the public realm and in our daily personal interactions. You might consider how individuals could begin to change the larger culture of incivility by speaking up when they witness rudeness and cruelty in any of its forms.

What Is Civility?

P. M. FORNI

The first reading comes from a best-selling book, *Choosing Civility: The Twenty-five Rules of Considerate Conduct.* The author is a professor of Italian literature and civility at Johns Hopkins University, where he directs the Johns Hopkins Civility Initiative. Before giving readers his "rules" for showing consideration towards others, Forni lays the groundwork with his careful definition of civility.

Maybe I was coming down with change-of-season influenza. If so, I should really consider buying a little white half mask for my subway ride home.

—Sujata Massey

1   For many years literature was my life. I spent most of my time reading, teaching, and writing on Italian fiction and poetry. One day, while lecturing on *The Divine Comedy,* I looked at my students and realized that I wanted them to be kind human beings more than I wanted them to know about Dante. I told them that if they knew everything about Dante and then they went out and treated an elderly lady on the bus unkindly, I'd feel that I had failed as a teacher. I have given dozens of lectures and workshops on civility in the last few years, and I have derived much satisfaction from addressing audiences I could not have reached speaking on literature. I know, however, that reading literature can develop the kind of imagination without which civility is impossible. To be fully human we must be able to imagine others' hurt and to relate it to the hurt we would experience if we were in their place. Consideration is imagination on a moral track.

2   Sometimes the participants in my workshops write on a sheet of paper what civility means to them. In no particular order, here are a number of key civility-related notions I have collected over the years from those sheets:

Respect for others	Decency
Care	Self-control
Consideration	Concern
Courtesy	Justice
Golden rule	Tolerance
Respect of others' feelings	Selflessness
Niceness	Etiquette
Politeness	Community service
Respect of others' opinions	Tact

Maturity	Equality
Kindness	Sincerity
Manners	Morality
Being accommodating	Honesty
Fairness	Awareness
Trustworthiness	Going out of one's way
Friendship	Friendliness
Table manners	Lending a hand
Moderation	Propriety
Listening	Abiding by rules
Compassion	Good citizenship
Being agreeable	Peace

This list tells us that

- Civility is complex.
- Civility is good.
- Whatever civility might be, it has to do with courtesy, politeness, and good manners.
- Civility belongs in the realm of ethics.

3   These four points have guided me in writing this book. Like my workshop participants, I am inclusive rather than exclusive in defining civility. Courtesy, politeness, manners, and civility are all, in essence, forms of awareness. Being civil means being constantly aware of others and weaving restraint, respect, and consideration into the very fabric of this awareness. Civility is a form of goodness; it is gracious goodness. But it is not just an attitude of benevolent and thoughtful relating to other individuals; it also entails an active interest in the well-being of our communities and even a concern for the health of the planet on which we live.

4   Saying "please" and "thank you"; lowering our voice whenever it may threaten or interfere with others' tranquillity; raising funds for a neighborhood renovation program; acknowledging a newcomer to the conversation; welcoming a new neighbor; listening to understand and help; respecting those different from us; responding with restraint to a challenge; properly disposing of a piece of trash left by someone else; properly disposing of dangerous industrial pollutants; acknowledging our mistakes; refusing to participate in malicious gossip; making a new pot of coffee for the office machine after drinking the last cup; signaling our turns when driving; yielding our seat on a bus whenever it seems appropriate; alerting the person sitting behind us on a plane when we are about to lower the back of our seat; standing close to the right-side handrail on an escalator; stopping to give directions to someone who is lost; stopping at red lights; disagreeing with poise; yielding with grace when losing an argument, these diverse behaviors are all imbued with the spirit of civility.

5   *Civility, courtesy, politeness,* and *manners* are not perfect synonyms, as etymology clearly shows.

> In life courtesy and self-possession, and in the arts style, are the sensible impressions of the free mind, for both arise out of a deliberate shaping of all things, and from never being swept away, whatever the emotion, into confusion or dullness.
>
> —William Butler Yeats

Courtesy is connected to *court* and evoked in the past the superior qualities of character and bearing expected in those close to royalty. Etymologically, when we are courteous we are courtierlike. Although today we seldom make this connection, courtesy still suggests excellence and elegance in bestowing respect and attention. It can also suggest deference and formality.

> The very essence of politeness seems to be to take care that by our words and actions we make other people pleased with us as well as with themselves.
>
> —Jean de La Bruyere

6   To understand *politeness,* we must think of *polish.* The polite are those who have polished their behavior. They have put some effort into bettering themselves, but they are sometimes looked upon with suspicion. Expressions such as "polite reply," "polite lie," and "polite applause" connect politeness to hypocrisy. It is true that the polite are inclined to veil their own feelings to spare someone else's. Self-serving lying, however, is always beyond the pale of politeness. If politeness is a quality of character (alongside courtesy, good manners, and civility), it cannot become a flaw. A suave manipulator may appear to be polite but is not.

> There is always a best way of doing everything, if it be to boil an egg. Manners are the happy way of doing things; each once a stroke of genius or of love, now repeated and hardened into usage.
>
> —Ralph Waldo Emerson

7   When we think of good *manners* we often think of children being taught to say "please" and "thank you" and chew with their mouths closed. This may prevent us from looking at manners with the attention they deserve. *Manner* comes from *manus,* the Latin word for "hand." *Manner* and *manners* have to do with the use of our hands. A manner is the way something is done, a mode of handling. Thus *manners* came to refer to behavior in social interaction—the way we handle the encounter between Self and Other. We have good manners when we use our hands well—when we handle others with care. When we rediscover the connection of *manner* with *hand,* the hand that, depending on our will and sensitivity, can strike or lift, hurt or soothe, destroy or heal, we understand the importance—for children and adults alike—of having good manners.

> Being civil to one another is much more active and positive a good than mere politeness or courtesy, but like many other important goods, such as generosity, gratitude, or solidarity, it is not the sort of thing that can be "demanded" as a matter of duty, like a moral entitlement.
>
> —Robert B. Pippin

8 | *Civility's* defining characteristic is its ties to *city* and *society.* The word derives from the Latin *civitas,* which means "city," especially in the sense of civic community. *Civitas* is the same word from which *civilization* comes. The age-old assumption behind civility is that life in the city has a civilizing effect. The city is where we enlighten our intellect and refine our social skills. And as we are shaped by the city, we learn to give of ourselves for the sake of the city. Although we can describe the civil as courteous, polite, and well mannered, etymology reminds us that they are also supposed to be good citizens and good neighbors.

QUESTIONS FOR DISCUSSION

1. Forni begins by arguing that learning to be kind to others is as important to a college education as learning literature—or presumably any other area of academic study. Do you think a university ought to play some role in developing students' character as well as their knowledge? If so, what are some of the ways this could happen?

2. Have you previously thought about reading literature as a way to develop empathy for other people? If so, what books, poems, and stories would you recommend?

3. In paragraph 3, Forni says awareness of others is the basis of civility. How do some of the examples in paragraph 4 show an awareness of others? What are some habits and conditions of daily life that hinder such awareness, causing our attentions to be self-directed?

4. Forni believes the etymology, or origins, of words can open up our understanding of meanings. How does the discussion of the origins of the words *courtesy, politeness,* and *manners* add to your understanding of what it takes to be a civil person?

FOR RESEARCH AND INQUIRY

Do research into the problem of incivility on college campuses (including observations on your own campus) and how schools are dealing with it. Many schools have instituted codes of conduct, which are often posted on the Internet. Then do research into opinions about the usefulness of such codes. How effective are they? What other solutions have been proposed? Conclude by endorsing a plan for dealing with the problem.

FOR RESEARCH AND CONVINCING OR MEDIATION

Many groups feel that hazing has a good purpose in forming bonds among members of an organization. It was common for first-year college students to be hazed, a tradition going back hundreds of years but now mostly eliminated by student codes of conduct. However, other campus institutions continue the practice to some degree. Look into arguments for and against hazing. Does it build character or teach incivility? Write an argument against the practice as uncivil, using some of the ideas of P. M. Forni about why colleges should teach civility. Or write an essay to mediate that arrives at a position that would satisfy people on both sides.

Play with Your Food, Just Don't Text

SARA RIMER

This article, which originally appeared in *The New York Times*, offers a range of opinions about the common habit of texting at the table. Before reading, consider your own attitude toward texting while dining with others. Have you done it? How do you feel when others do it?

Danah Boyd and Gilad Lotan, a married couple, regularly bring their iPhones to the dinner table.

1   Anytime Anne Fishel and her family talk about behaviors that are out of bounds during family meals, they come back to the Yom Kippur Incident.

2   Two years ago, 14 people had gathered at her dining room table in Newton, Mass., to break the fast on the most solemn of Jewish holidays. As Dr. Fishel looked around, it seemed that everyone—her husband, their two college-age sons, Gabe and Joe, their friends—was enjoying her cooking and sharing the sense of an important family dinner.

3   Except, she noticed, for Gabe's friend from college. Wait a second, what was he doing? With a furtive downward glance, he was surreptitiously texting—and not just once or twice, but almost continuously, from the apple-squash soup to the roast turkey.

4   Dr. Fishel, who directs the family and couples therapy program at Massachusetts General Hospital, wasn't about to embarrass the young man. But another of Gabe's friends, seated next to the stealth texter, spoke up. "You really shouldn't be doing that here," she admonished him, and not in a whisper.

5   "Why not?" the texter said. "It's not like this is a formal dinner or something."

6   Texting anarchy, Emily Post's great-granddaughter, Cindy Post Senning, calls it. "People are texting everywhere," she said.

7   Husbands, wives, children and dinner guests who would never be so rude as to talk on a phone at the family table seem to think it's perfectly fine to text (or e-mail, or Twitter) while eating.

8   Dr. Post Senning is here to tell you that it is not perfectly fine. Not at all. So new is the problem that her latest book, *Emily Post's Table Manners for Kids* (HarperCollins, 2009), written with Peggy Post, covered it only generally, in a blanket ruling: "Do NOT use your cell phone or any other electronic devices at the table."

9   She now finds it necessary to weigh in on the texting issue specifically: No texting at the dinner table, particularly at home. "The family meal is a social event," she said in a phone interview, "not a food ingestion event."

10   "Be aware that others can see your thumbs working even when they are in your lap," she wrote in a follow-up e-mail message, laying down the official rule of etiquette. "If you are in a situation where your attention should be focused on others, you should not be texting." And she means no e-mailing, either.

11   That means you, George d'Arbeloff. Or so his wife, P. A. d'Arbeloff, told him after she caught him peeking at the iPhone in his lap during Thanksgiving dinner at their home in the Jamaica Plain neighborhood of Boston. "I tried to catch his eye," said Ms. d'Arbeloff, director of the Cambridge Science Festival in Cambridge, Mass., "but he was looking down."

12   He may have been scrolling through work-related e-mail messages or, possibly, checking sports scores, conceded Mr. d'Arbeloff, who is the chairman of a Los Angeles–based dental laser company. Because the company is on the West Coast, e-mail messages tend to flood in just as he is sitting down to eat.

13   "I have never texted at the dinner table," he said in a telephone interview. "I will admit: I do read e-mails." He paused, listening to his wife, who was in the room with him. "P. A. says I send."

14   A few months ago, a family meeting was convened. The d'Arbeloffs' 7-year-old twin daughters made their feelings known. Their father agreed to cease using his iPhone during dinner. "I'm 95 percent reformed," he said.

15   "Maybe people think they can time-share: both texting and talking at once," said Harry Lewis, a Harvard computer science professor and one of the authors of *Blown to Bits: Your Life, Liberty and Happiness After the Digital Explosion* (Addison-Wesley, 2008). Beware, he says: You're not fooling anybody. "No one thinks someone on the cellphone can really be paying attention to another person."

16   Texting while eating has become a major issue among couples in counseling, says Evan Imber-Black, a prominent family therapist. And, yes, she says, it seems the men are the ones who can't sit down for dinner for a half-hour without tapping away at their phones. (The reverse is true among teenagers, where the girls are the nonstop texters.)

17   "I think it has to do with the erosion of a boundary between work and family, particularly for men in any kind of business where they're just afraid to stop working practically 24-7," said Dr. Imber-Black, one of the authors of the book *Rituals in Families and Family Therapy.*

18   Evvajean Mintz's husband, Richard, a partner in a Boston law firm, arrives at the table with his BlackBerry clipped to his belt. "If there's one second of spare time, and if you look away from him and lose eye contact, he immediately whips it out and starts looking at it," she said. "I suggested I'd throw it out the window."

19   Like a lot of couples, the Mintzes have conflicting views of the rate of tableside BlackBerry use. Mr. Mintz, who is working part time at 87, thought he was doing it only when his wife was preoccupied—when, for example, she ducks into another room to catch a few minutes of television.

20   "I try not to do it in a way that upsets her," Mr. Mintz said. "I guess I'm not doing it as well as I should."

21   Another family therapist, Peter Fraenkel, director of the Center for Work and Family at the Ackerman Institute for the Family in Manhattan, said he recently counseled a real estate broker and his wife, who works as a headhunter. The couple has two children, ages 6 and 4. She wanted two BlackBerry-free hours each night, including dinner.

22   Dr. Fraenkel said that he had the husband log his incoming e-mail messages, texts and calls for two weeks. Which ones had to be handled immediately, or else the deal would be lost?

23   After the husband concluded that none of the calls were urgent, Dr. Fraenkel said, he was able to create the two-hour BlackBerry-free family zone.

24   As for teenagers and texting, says Danah Boyd, a researcher at Microsoft who studies the ways young people use technology, they're just doing what they've always done: hanging out with their friends.

25   The cellphone makes it possible to bring your social circle to the dinner table. "You don't really have to disconnect," she said.

26   Brigid Wright, 17, from Needham, Mass., said that like many teenagers, she has honed the skill of eating with one hand and texting with the other. But, she said (and her family confirms), she does not text at the table at home.

27   "No teenager wants to look up from a glowing cellphone screen to see a disappointed parent frowning across the table," she wrote in an e-mail message.

28   Ms. Boyd is 31. Sometimes she looks up from her glowing iPhone screen to see her husband, Gilad Lotan, a Microsoft designer, frowning at her across the table.

29   "If I'm sitting there privately responding to messages, Gilad might say, 'Hey, I thought we were at dinner,' " she said. "I'll be, like, 'Hmm, sorry, just doing this quickly.'"

30   They both bring their iPhones to the table, she said, using them as conversational tools. If they're debating a question, for instance, they might use their phones to look up the answer.

31   They try to avoid texting, she said, "if it's a dinner where we're trying to be engaged." (As opposed to a dinner "where we both need food in our systems so we can both get back to work.")

32   There is no texting or e-mailing at the dinner table in Lydia Shire's home, in Weston, Mass. "My son would never dream of texting at the table," said Ms. Shire, a chef and restaurant owner in Boston. "And he wouldn't do it at anyone else's table, either."

33   True, said her 19-year-old son, Alex Pineda. To take out his BlackBerry Dream would be to distract from his mother's amazing cooking, and the conversation with her and his father.

34   But he did have to explain it to a friend who came to dinner not long ago. Just as they were sitting down at the table, Alex said, "he started texting."

35   Fortunately, his mother was still occupied with serving the food. "She didn't notice," Alex said. "I told him to put it away."

QUESTIONS FOR DISCUSSION

1. The "Yom Kippur Incident" seems like an egregious breach of manners. Why do you think the texting college student was not aware that others would find his actions very rude?

2. Cell phones and laptops have made it possible to combine work and personal life. What does this habit reveal about the values and priorities of those who do not establish a boundary between work and family life? Why might they be afraid to be unconnected to their work?

3. What is Danah Boyd's attitude toward teens texting at the table? Is there anything wrong with teens preferring to socialize with their friends rather than with their family at the table?

FOR PERSUASION

Do research into the benefits of the family dinner hour, where children and parents sit down to a technology-free social exchange rather than a "food ingestion event," to use the words of the etiquette writer Cindy Post Senning. Make a persuasive argument to parents about the value of reestablishing a technology-free family dinner hour.

Why We Are So Rude Online

ELIZABETH BERNSTEIN

Elizabeth Bernstein is a columnist for *The Wall Street Journal Online.* Her article pulls together accounts about online hostility with recent expert commentary and analysis that help to explain lack of civility online.

1   Jennifer Bristol recently lost one of her oldest friends—thanks to a Facebook fight about pit bulls. The trouble started when she posted a newspaper article asserting that pit bulls were the most dangerous type of dog in New York City last year. "Please share thoughts . . . 833 incidents with pitties," wrote Ms. Bristol, a 40-year-old publicist and animal-welfare advocate in Manhattan.

2   Her friends, many of whom also work in the animal-welfare world, quickly weighed in. One noted that "pit bull" isn't a single official breed; another said "irresponsible ownership" is often involved when dogs turn violent. Black Labs may actually bite more, someone else offered. Then a childhood pal of Ms. Bristol piped up with this: "Take it from an ER doctor . . . In 15 years of doing this I have yet to see a golden retriever bite that had to go to the operating room or killed its target."

3   That unleashed a torrent. One person demanded to see the doctor's "scientific research." Another accused him of not bothering to confirm whether his patients were actually bitten by pit bulls. Someone else suggested he should "venture out of the ER" to see what was really going on.

4   "It was ridiculous," says Ms. Bristol, who stayed out of the fight. Her old buddy, the ER doctor, unfriended her the next morning. That was eight months ago. She hasn't heard from him since.

5   Why are we so nasty to each other online? Whether on Facebook, Twitter, message boards or websites, we say things to each other that we would never say face to face. Shouldn't we know better by now?

6   Anonymity is a powerful force. Hiding behind a fake screen name makes us feel invincible, as well as invisible. Never mind that, on many websites, we're not as anonymous as we think—and we're not anonymous at all on Facebook. Even when we reveal our real identities, we still misbehave. According to soon-to-be-published research from professors at Columbia University and the University of Pittsburgh, browsing Facebook lowers our self-control. The effect is most pronounced with people whose Facebook networks were made up of close friends, the researchers say.

7   Most of us present an enhanced image of ourselves on Facebook. This positive image—and the encouragement we get, in the form of "likes"—boosts our self-esteem. And when we have an inflated sense of self, we tend to exhibit poor self-control. "Think of it as a licensing effect: You feel good about yourself so you feel a sense of entitlement," says Keith Wilcox, assistant professor of marketing at Columbia Business School and co-author of the study. "And you want to protect that enhanced view, which might be why people are lashing out so strongly at others who don't share their opinions." These types of behavior—poor self control, inflated sense of self—"are often displayed by people impaired by alcohol," he adds.

8   The researchers conducted a series of five studies. In one, they asked 541 Facebook users how much time they spent on the site and how many close friends they had in their Facebook networks. They also asked about their offline lives, including questions about their debt and credit-card usage, their weight and eating habits and how much time they spent socializing in person each week.

9   People who spent more time online and who had a high percentage of close ties in their network were more likely to engage in binge eating and to have a greater body mass index, as well as to have more credit-card debt and a lower credit score, the research found. Another study found that people who browsed Facebook for five minutes and had strong network ties were more likely to choose a chocolate-chip cookie than a granola bar as a snack.

10   In a third study, the professors gave participants a set of anagrams that were impossible to solve, as well as timed IQ tests, then measured how long it took them

to give up trying to solve the problems. They found people who spent more time on Facebook were more likely to give up on difficult tasks more quickly. A Facebook spokesman declined to comment.

11   Why are we often so aggressive online? Consider this recent post to this column's Facebook page, from someone I don't know: "Why should I even bother writing you? You won't respond."

12   We're less inhibited online because we don't have to see the reaction of the person we're addressing, says Sherry Turkle, psychologist and Massachusetts Institute of Technology professor of the social studies of science and technology. Because it's harder to see and focus on what we have in common, we tend to dehumanize each other, she says.

13   Astoundingly, Dr. Turkle says, many people still forget that they're speaking out loud when they communicate online. Especially when posting from a smartphone, "you are publishing but you don't feel like you are," she says. "So what if you say 'I hate you' on this tiny little thing? It's like a toy. It doesn't feel consequential."

14   And for Facebook, its very name is part of the problem. "It promises us a face and a place where we are going to have friends," says Dr. Turkle, author of the book *Alone Together: Why We Expect More from Technology and Less from Each Other.* "If you get something hurtful there, you're not prepared. You feel doubly affronted, so you strike back."

15   It's high season for online bickering about politics, as Chip Bolcik well knows. Mr. Bolcik, 54, a TV announcer and registered Independent from Thousand Oaks, Calif., likes to pose political questions on his Facebook page. "I am very interested in how people think who have different views than mine," he says. "And sometimes I will write a provocative question for the entertainment purpose of watching people yell at each other."

16   Over the past few months, Mr. Bolcik lost two real-life friends because of online political spats. The first friend got mad at him after he posted a status update asking people to debate whether Mormons are Christians. ("You are so off base you don't know what you are talking about," she wrote on his page, followed later by: "You're an idiot.") Mr. Bolcik blocked her from his page. "I will allow free discussion until you irritate me," he says. Sometimes, he erases entire conversation threads.

17   The second friendship ended even more abruptly, after one of Mr. Bolcik's old friends offended several of his Facebook friends, as well as Mr. Bolcik himself, by repeatedly posting his views. "He was spouting about politics, rather than discussing," Mr. Bolcik says. Mr. Bolcik wrote his friend and told him he was going to block him from the page if he didn't pipe down. In response, his friend told him off using vulgar language and unfriended him. "I was pretty upset," Mr. Bolcik says.

18   Still, he sometimes can't restrain himself from fanning the flames. When a political discussion thread becomes heated and he doesn't like the way it is going—"right or left," he says—he privately messages one of his "attack dog" friends and suggests he or she join the discussion. "I will say, 'Gee, this discussion doesn't seem right to me, what do you think?'" he says. "Then they will go on there and berate the person who is upsetting me, and I will look like the good guy."

QUESTIONS FOR DISCUSSION

1. List the various explanations offered for online incivility. Which seem strongest to you? Which weakest? Why?

2. When we choose to become part of any discussion of a controversial topic—whether on or offline—we take on a degree of risk not usually present in merely chatting with other people. Part of this risk is hostile remarks from people who feel strongly about the rightness of their point of view. To what extent, then, do you see the unfriending in the accounts above as simply the result of not entering into the spirit of controversy or of having too-thin skin?

3. We all say things among close friends and relatives that we would not say in a more public context—for example, in a class discussion. To what extent do you think that Facebook and similar media blur the difference between private/informal and public/formal? How much of the misbehavior in the accounts above might be explained at least in part by such blurring?

FOR CLASS DISCUSSION AND INQUIRY

Share your negative experiences on the Net, especially times you have said or someone else has said something hurtful or offensive. Are the accounts similar to the ones discussed in Bernstein's article? If not, how are they different? Why are they different?

When the discussion is over, write a blog entry or short essay about the negative experiences that you thought were especially revealing. Offer an explanation of why things went wrong and what needs to be done to prevent destructive communication in the future. Be sure to consider the explanations for online incivility in the Bernstein article, even if you think your own explanations offer more insight.

Going beyond Edgy—and Falling off the Cliff

LEONARD PITTS, JR.

> This op-ed piece from the *Miami Herald* argues against the no-holds-barred tastelessness of too much popular culture, especially in the too-fast-for-thought online world. Leonard Pitts, Jr., is a syndicated columnist and novelist.

1   The tweet went as follows: "Everyone else seems afraid to say it, but that Quvenzhane Wallis is kind of a [expletive], right?"

2   The missing word is a bit of verbal sewage sometimes used to disparage women. Begins with "c," rhymes with "hunt." Its target here, however, was not a woman. Quvenzhane Wallis is the actress who was nominated for an Academy Award for her performance as Hushpuppy in the celebrated film, *Beasts of the Southern Wild.* She was all of six when the movie was filmed. She is nine now.

3   The tweet, penned by a so-far anonymous writer and posted by the *Onion*, the satirical newspaper and website, was intended as a joke, a meta-commentary on

the sniping and backbiting of Hollywood. Yes, the *Onion* snatched the tweet back an hour later. Yes, it promptly apologized. And yes, funny covers a multitude of sins. The problem though, is that this was not remotely funny. It was, however, profoundly illustrative.

4   There are some things you just do not say. Not because there is a law against them, not because you don't have the right. No, you don't say them because you don't. You know better. Or at least, you did. These days, there is a good chance you don't. These days, we worship at the altar of edgy.

5   You know edgy, of course. It is the *sine qua non* of pop culture, represents rejection of the straightjacket of propriety and political correctness, celebrates the freedom found in bare-knuckle, impolitic truth. As such, it has become a value unto itself, a synonym for good. Once upon a time, a comedian worked to be funny. Now, it seems they work to be edgy.

6   There is nothing wrong with edgy. Some of us can tell you how Lenny Bruce invented it, Richard Pryor perfected it and Norman Lear gave it a TV show. Some of us applauded as the new ethos made hamburger out of sacred cows, gave grandma the vapors and drove bluenose prudes to arias of apoplexy. Some of us knew that "edgy" allowed the saying of necessary things. But what was said about Wallis, not to put too fine a point on it, was even less necessary than funny.

7   This is not a prayer for the resurrection of Bob Hope and Milton Berle or a plaint for the return of the day when Lucille Ball could not say "pregnant" on television. It is not a screed against potty-mouthed language nor even a rant against the *Onion* which, most days, hits the mark squarely with satire sharp enough for surgery.

8   No, this is simply an observation that something is lost when going too far becomes both the end and the means thereto. And that, in making "edge" its defining value, American popular culture increasingly winds up embodying what it purports to lampoon. This is what happened with the Wallis "joke" which, it bears repeating, was meant to satirize the nastiness of Hollywood gossip. Instead, it becomes an example thereof.

9   Something similar happened when Oscar host Seth MacFarlane performed a song about women who have played nude scenes on film. *We Saw Your Boobs* was no spoof of misogyny. It was misogyny.

10   In making "edge" the prime directive of American culture, we lose the ability—and willingness—to tell the difference. In embracing tastelessness for its own sake, we coarsen our own selves and embrace a self-perpetuating mindset under which to even take offense is to render yourself irrelevant, a pious naif who doesn't get the whole concept of self-aware humor for a self-aware age.

11   But it is possible to get that concept, indeed, to have been laughing along as it was invented—and yet feel there is something broken about a culture and time where it is possible to call a nine-year-old girl a hateful thing and expect laughter. It suggests a culture that has, indeed, gone to the edge—and fallen off.

QUESTIONS FOR DISCUSSION

1. Suppose that the actress Pitts identifies in paragraph 2 was a woman—29, let us say, rather than 9. Would the comment then be acceptable? That is, is age the issue here? If not, what is?

2. "There are some things you just do not say," Pitts claims. He is talking about social or cultural norms of behavior. In your view, do such norms still exist among the people you associate with regularly? What difference does it make—if any—that the attempt to be funny, because it was a tweet, was public rather private?

3. Do you agree with Pitts that "there is nothing wrong with edgy"? What motivates edgy? That is, why does popular culture pursue it so relentlessly?

FOR RESEARCH, DISCUSSION, AND PERSUASION

Pitts values "the freedom found in bare-knuckle, impolitic truth." That is, he thinks that speaking the truth, even when it is harsh and politically incorrect, has value. Humor makes impolitic truth more palatable. What he objects to is when edginess becomes an end in itself.

For two or three evenings watch some popular television shows. Based on what you see and hear, is Pitts' distinction clear to you or not? Put another way, are you witnessing edginess with a point, in good taste, or only coarseness? Discuss your evaluations in class, comparing your judgments with those of your classmates.

Then write an op-ed of your own about the difference between good edginess and bad edginess. Be sure to use concrete examples to distinguish the two, as Pitts does.

Left Is Mean But Right Is Meaner, Says New Study of Political Discourse

TUFTS NOW

The reading below is a news release about two Tufts professors' analysis of recent political discourse on television, blogs, radio, and other media. After reading, you may want to access the study cited in the article and in our "For Further Reading" list at the end of this chapter.

1   **Medford/Somerville, Mass.**—While the tragic shooting in Arizona has spotlighted the vitriol that seems to pervade political commentary, objective research examining the scope of this disturbing phenomenon has been lacking. In the first published study of its kind, social scientists at Tufts University's School of Arts and Sciences have found that outrage talk is endemic among commentators of all political stripes, but measurably worse on the political right, and is more prevalent than it was even during the turmoil of the war in Viet Nam and the Watergate scandal.

2   In their study, Tufts Assistant Professor of Sociology Sarah Sobieraj and Professor of Political Science Jeffrey Berry systematically scrutinized what they call "outrage

talk" in leading talk radio, cable news analysis, political blogs and newspaper columns. Their findings, "From Incivility to Outrage: Political Discourse in Blogs, Talk Radio, and Cable News," appear in the February 2011 issue of the journal *Political Communication.*

3   The term "outrage talk" refers to a form of political discourse involving efforts to provoke visceral responses, such as anger, righteousness, fear or moral indignation, through the use of overgeneralizations, sensationalism, misleading or patently inaccurate information, ad hominem attacks and partial truths about opponents.

4   The Tufts scientists' analysis of both ideologically conservative and liberal content revealed that outrage talk, often infused with hateful terminology and imagery, is pervasive, not just an occasional emotional eruption.

5   During a 10-week period in the spring of 2009, four researchers reviewed evening cable TV, national radio talk shows, ideological political blogs and mainstream newspaper columns for 13 variables, such as insulting language, name calling and misrepresentative exaggeration. Researchers also judged overall tone of each sample and proportion of outrage language.

6   Almost 9 out of 10 cases sampled, or 89.6 percent, contained at least one outrage incident. One hundred percent of TV episodes and 98.8 percent of talk radio programs contained outrage incidents, while 82.8 percent of blog posts incorporated outrage writing. In some cases, outrage speech or behavior occurred at a rate of more than one instance per minute.

MORE OUTRAGEOUS: LIBERALS OR CONSERVATIVES?

7   When it comes to inflammatory language, is one side really worse than the other? Yes, found the Tufts researchers: "Our data indicate that the right uses decidedly more outrage speech than the left. Taken as a whole, liberal content is quite nasty in character, following the outrage model of emotional, dramatic and judgment-laden speech. Conservatives, however, are even nastier."

8   The data showed the political right engaging in an average of 15.57 outrage acts per case, while the left engaged in 10.32 acts per case.

9   However, as Sobieraj and Berry noted, although the left and right do not use outrage equally, they use it in ways that are remarkably similar.

10   "Whether it's MSNBC's Keith Olbermann* spitting out his coffee because of some conservative transgression or radio host Michael Savage venomously impugning the character of immigrants, cable television, talk radio and blogs overflow with outrage rhetoric, and even mainstream newspaper columns are not above the fray," they said.

NEW: OUTRAGE IN NEWSPAPERS

11   Unexpectedly the Tufts researchers found that outrage language is now common among the nation's leading newspaper columnists. To determine whether this outrage is new, or simply more of the same, Sobieraj and Berry studied 10 widely syndicated columnists during 10-week periods in both 1955 and 1975. They chose

---

*Keith Olbermann no longer works for the cable news network MSNBC.

these dates to see if the tumultuous period of the civil rights movement, the Vietnam War protests and the Watergate scandal led to greater outrage in newspapers at that time. They found the answer was no.

12   "Outrage is virtually absent from both the 1955 *and* the 1975 columns, in contrast to the columns of 2009 which contain, on average, nearly six instances of outrage per column," said the Tufts scholars. "The titans of American journalism in 1955 and 1975 remained restrained in their language despite the impassioned politics of protest."

13   In contrast, according to the researchers, today's model of outrage-oriented political commentary succeeds because of an increasingly polarized populace and content providers facing an incredibly competitive environment who are desperate to attract audience members and in turn advertisers.

14   Whether outrage is ultimately corrosive, constructive or both to the health of democracy is still an unanswered question, said the authors.

QUESTIONS FOR DISCUSSION

1. A definition of "outrage talk" appears in paragraph 3. Using the leads about where such speech appears, find an example to listen to or read, and be ready to discuss it rhetorically: What is the topic or issue being discussed? What is the author or speaker's main point? What does the tone of the writing reveal about the character of the speaker? Who is the intended audience? What effect might this example of "outrage talk" have on its audience? Do you think your example is "corrosive" or "constructive" to healthy democratic debate on this topic?

2. What factors do the authors of the study see as contributing to the rise of outrage talk in politics? Would you agree that these are plausible reasons? Can you think of any other explanations?

3. Were you aware of the extent of outrage talk in political discourse today? Were you surprised that the study found that conservatives were more "outraged" than liberals? What effects do you think such pervasive negative speech might have on the electorate?

FOR INQUIRY AND CONVINCING

The next reading, by Brian McGee, argues that a certain amount of incivility is necessary for political change to occur. Read his argument and compare his main points with points made in this summary of the study by Sarah Sobieraj and Jeffrey Berry. Look at some primary sources on political topics from 1955 to 1975. What do you notice about the tone and level of civility in these speeches or writings? Were the authors "restrained in their language despite the impassioned politics of protest" as the Tufts scholars report? After inquiry, make a case for what you think is acceptable incivility in political discourse.

Can Political Rhetoric Be Too Civil?

BRIAN MCGEE

This guest editorial in the Charleston, South Carolina newspaper, *The Post and Courier,* was written by Brian McGee, chairman of the Department of Communication at the College of Charleston. Consider whether ranting might qualify as an example of the impolite kinds of discourse he says are sometimes necessary.

1   Every few years, in response to one or more widely publicized episodes of rowdiness or rudeness, someone bemoans the decline of civility in U.S. politics.

2   Such complaints sometimes suggest the good old days were more polite than they are today, as when the *New York Times* noted in 1997 an "epidemic of incivility" in public meetings.

3   In other instances Americans are described as worrisomely inconsiderate. Turning once again to the *New York Times,* we find the editors opining in 1876 that the U.S. was the "rudest of nations," with a problem of "national incivility."

4   This time-honored anxiety about civility is with us today. Harry Pastides, president of the University of South Carolina, is worried about the "decline in the civil tenor of our national discourse." Pastides has committed the eight campuses of his university to teaching civility because "the people of this nation deserve better."

5   I do not doubt that Pastides's goals are admirable and the product of deeply held convictions. However, I don't think his efforts will be successful.

6   Initially, any commitment to teaching civility to university students implies they do not fully understand the merits of politeness or the political and societal advantages of civility.

7   I have no first-hand experience with Pastides's students, but my institution's students are the politest people I've ever met in a teaching career that covers 20 years and six states. Individually, some of my students are rude on some days, but they long ago learned they shouldn't be. They understand the basic rules of civility, even if they choose to ignore those rules.

8   Moreover, Pastides isn't talking about student-teacher interactions. He wants more civil discourse about politics, which I certainly appreciate. The problem is that 22-year-olds and graduate students are not the primary sources of shouting in contemporary political forums, as far as I can tell. Retirees and middle-aged workers have been responsible for more than their fair share of incivility in town hall meetings. A revised university code of conduct isn't going to influence the over-40 crowd.

9   So, my sense is that familiarity with politeness norms is most productively and most commonly cultivated in grade school and in family life. There is no student knowledge vacuum in the area of decorum and civil discourse that universities must rush to fill.

10   Our students have the basic idea. Politeness generally is good. Rudeness generally is not.

11   What can universities do about incivility? In part, they can study why ordinarily civil people choose to be uncivil. As one example, I want to suggest why incivility has a role to play in American politics and in any democratic society.

12   Those who hold political power always would prefer to have a polite debate, hold a vote in which their side will prevail, and consider the democratic niceties fulfilled.

13   Politeness, as the politically powerful know, is boring. Incivility attracts attention. Those in the minority are particularly likely to be uncivil because incivility encourages uncommitted voters and media organizations to pay attention, to consider and promote minority views and, possibly, to change hearts and minds.

14   The list of impolite people and groups in politics is long and distinguished. There is good reason to believe that incivility was important in the successes of the movements to end slavery; secure civil rights for African Americans, women, and gay men; and reduce property taxes in California and other states, among many other causes.

15   Like most people, I prefer friendly and civil conversations about all topics, including politics. Debate about important issues in most cases can and should be both spirited and cordial.

16   In saying so, however, I would not uncritically make civil discourse into another tool of congressional or legislative majorities, whether Democratic or Republican. If political ideas, whether conservative or liberal, cannot withstand the passionate and disorderly speech of the minority, those political ideas usually will not endure in the long run.

17   So, at all our universities, let's explain why talk should be preferred to violence, and why all points of view must be heard if we want democracy to work. But let's celebrate the merits of civility with some qualification. In particular, let's not maintain that incivility is OK for our side, but terrible when it comes from the other side.

18   Politics in a democratic society can be a messy, unpleasant business. We always will be happiest when politics and politeness coexist in a productive way. Sometimes, however, the people of this nation both want and need a little incivility.

QUESTIONS FOR DISCUSSION

1. Several of the readings in this chapter refer to concern over rising incivility. McGee was motivated to write this column in response to the decision of the University of South Carolina president, Harry Pastides, to teach civility on all campuses in the state system. Why does McGee oppose the idea? Do you agree that college students already have the needed knowledge about civility?

2. Would you agree that impolite discourse is often initiated by those who do not hold the power in any political situation? What examples can you give to show that minorities have had to be impolite or not civil in order to get the attention that will dislodge the status quo? Consider the examples of progress McGee mentions in paragraph 14: What are some examples of political discourse that helped lead to these examples of progress?

3. What is the difference between the kind of speech that greases the wheels of democracy and the kind that throws sand in the wheels? What is the difference between "messy and unpleasant" but necessary versus divisive and counterproductive to a democratic government?

FOR INQUIRY AND CONVINCING

Examine a famous speech that helped to bring about some progressive legislation such as the end of segregation in the South. (A powerful example is Susan B. Anthony's 1873 speech for woman's right to vote, just a little over five hundred words and readily available on the Internet.) Does your analysis of this particular speech—or another of your choice—support McGee's point that people wishing to challenge the status quo must use uncivil language?

Bullying Victims: The Effects Last into College

FRANK D. ADAMS AND GLORIA J. LAWRENCE

The following study shows that bullying does not end with high school and can have significant impact on college students. It appeared in *American Secondary Education*. The survey questions are listed after the reading under the heading "For Research and Discussion." Professors Adams and Lawrence teach at Wayne State College.

ABSTRACT

This study examined whether those bullied in schools continued to show the effects of being bullied after they enrolled in an institution of higher education. There were 269 undergraduate students participating in the study. Previous studies (2006; 2008) conducted by the authors suggested the effects of bullying upon both the victim and bully are long lasting; victims of bullying at the college level indicated histories of being bullied throughout their school years. The results of this study suggest bullying in junior high and/or high school continues into college.

1   The act of bullying, or being bullied, has been viewed as a "rite of passage" (Brown, 2006, para.1); until a violent act occurs to focus attention on bullying, it has generally received little attention from educators. Research suggests that, as a result of their experience of being bullied, some victims became bullies themselves. Others performed poorly in their academic work and eventually dropped out of school, and still others chose a more dramatic response to having been bullied, such as committing suicide (Lawrence & Adams, 2006; Olweus, 1978; & Smith, 2011).

2   Various types and degrees of bullying have been described by Monks and Smith (2010). Monks and Smith reviewed various definitions and rationale for bullying behaviors. They also examined bullying at various age levels and concluded it exists at all age levels in varying degrees.

3   Cyberbullying (Rubin, 2008; Strom & Strom, 2005) and workplace bullying (Fritzgerald, 2010) are now being more closely examined owing to the widespread and potentially negative effects on the victims. Bullying in the workplace has been examined from the perspective of an "ongoing behavior" developed from an educational setting (Smith, Singer, Hoel, & Cooper, 2003). Newman, Holden, and Delville indicated that a history of victimization was associated with increased levels of stress and avoidant coping strategies during the college years. As Oliver and Candappa (2003) suggested, bullies are everywhere; so, too, are the victims.

PROBLEM STATEMENT

4 | Do students who have experienced episodes of being bullied in school continue to exhibit characteristics or effects of being bullied after having been enrolled in an institution of higher education?

REVIEW OF CURRENT LITERATURE

5 | Investigations of the effects of bullying received wide recognition in the 1970s with the work of Olweus (1978) whose studies were triggered by the suicides of several young victims of bullying. Olweus pointed out that the power differences between bully and victim are a crucial component of the interactions. Parker & Asher (1987) discussed the negative consequences for children bullied in elementary school, including middle school adjustment difficulties and the greater likelihood of quitting school. Adams, Lawrence, and Schenck (2008) and Lawrence and Adams (2006) suggested that greater notice has been taken of the presence of bullying between the elementary school and the secondary school years. They stressed the "continuous effect" of bullying experienced during the lower grades on the middle school grades and continuing into the secondary school years.

6 | Pellegrini, Bartini, and Brooks (1999) examined the occurrence of bullying, victimization, and aggressive victimization during early adolescence (5th grade); they reported that bullies were more emotional and physical than their elementary school peers. Bullies sought peer friendships with other aggressive individuals; the friendships existed primarily as a "cover." Nansel et al. (2001) reported that bullying occurred with greater frequency among middle school-aged youth than among high school-aged youth; mobility of the secondary student was one factor for the reduced number of bullies at that level.

7 | Espelage and Swearer (2003) indicated that bullying at all levels—early elementary, middle, or secondary school—included an ongoing and escalating physical and/or verbal aggression by one or more individuals who seek to attain dominance, status, or property at the various levels. They cited a wide range of bully-victim behaviors or roles: a bully, a victim, a bully-victim, and/or a bystander. The researchers noted the growing presence of female bullies affecting both genders with their aggressive behavior. Tritt and Duncan (1997) indicated that bullied adults, young adults and their victims reported significantly more loneliness than those not involved in bullying situations. They also reported that there were similar levels of lower self-esteem in young adults who were childhood bullies or victims than those not involved in bullying experiences.

8 | The present study was conducted to determine whether those bullied in schools continued to show the effects of being bullied after they entered college. Adams, Lawrence, and Schenck (2008) suggested that the effects of bullying on the victims were long-lasting; the current study investigated whether victims of bullying at the college level have histories of being bullied throughout the school years.

9 | The process of bullying is complex, involving many factors. There is no single causal factor for a bully to select one or many victims, but the individuals who are already struggling socially to "fit in" and who appear awkward in various social

settings are much more vulnerable to the bully. There is also no single factor for an individual to become a victim.

PARTICIPANTS

10   A total of 269 undergraduate students (56 freshmen, 65 sophomores, 67 juniors, and 81 seniors) at a midwestern state college (total enrollment 3,500) volunteered to participate. Participants were 176 females and 93 males, closely approximating the 2:1 female-to-male distribution of the college student body. Participants' ages were 19–23 years (240), 24–29 years (20), and 30+ years (9).

DEVELOPMENT OF THE INSTRUMENT

11   The questions used for this study were developed from a review of current and relevant journal articles, and reports, as well as information gained from individual discussions held with a variety of ages of individuals (ranging from 12 to 47) who identified themselves as having been bullied either during middle school, secondary school, or college years. None of the individuals involved in these discussions were included in the study.

PROCEDURE

12   Participants for the study were recruited from randomly selected classes at a rural college; informed consents and questionnaires were distributed by a student assistant to reduce bias and/or implied pressure to participate in the study. A debriefing statement was read after all questionnaires were completed and returned to the assistant. Any questions relating to the survey instrument were addressed by the student assistants administering the survey.

13   Participants first signed an informed consent stating a description of the study concerning bullying behaviors at the college level. The informed consent was followed by a self-report questionnaire; the questionnaire provided demographics (age, gender, and year in school, etc.), twenty statements on which participants responded using the 5-point Likert scale (5 = strongly agree to 1 = strongly disagree), as well as a section for any additional comments that could be made anonymously.

FINDINGS

14   Scores 5 to 1 were assigned to the responses (5 = strongly agree to 1 = strongly disagree). The only relationships that failed to reach significance were the relationships between feeling "safe" (Statement 1), feeling "alone and isolated" (Statement 4), "threatened with physical harm" (Statement 7), and "individuals laugh at me" (Statement 17).

15   A total of 100 (37.2%) participants reported they had been bullied in high school or junior high school by answering "strongly agree" or "agree" to that statement. They were assigned to the Bullied group. The Non-Bullied group consisted of 160 (59.5%) participants who answered "strongly disagree" or "disagree." Data from nine participants (3.3%) were eliminated from analyses, because they failed to respond to the statement or they answered "no opinion." . . .

DISCUSSION

16   These data do not support previous data suggesting that bullying decreases as grade level increases to approximately 5% in the 9th grade (Olweus, 1999). In the present study, 37% of participants had been bullied in high school and/or junior high school. The data also suggest that bullying occurs in schools in rural areas; participants of this study were members of a college population in which 65% came from high schools whose senior classes had less than 100 students.

17   The data suggest that students who are bullied in high school and/or junior high school continue to be victimized (called names, excluded from class activities, physically abused, etc.) in college. Whether a consequence of being bullied in high school, in junior high school, or in college, the victims feel alone and isolated. They find it hard to make friends, and they feel that no one will listen to them while in college. Victims also reported that they do not know how to fight back when individuals say hurtful things to them (Statement 9); they report this to a much greater degree than those not bullied.

18   The only relationships that failed to reach significance were between feeling safe in their dorm room and feeling alone and isolated, threatened with physical harm, and being laughed at. No significant difference was found between groups on feeling safe only in their dorm room; both groups scored relatively high.

19   Data from previous studies (Lawrence & Adams, 2006; Adams, Lawrence, & Schenck, 2008) indicated that bullying continued from early elementary grades through secondary school years. The data from the current study indicate that the effects of bullying continue from the secondary school environments into institutions of higher education. The negative effects of bullying are associated with the characteristics of being victimized. The data for this study reflect much of previous research conducted on bullying behavior and characteristics of both bully and victim. The current study builds upon information presented in the various research reports (Lawrence & Adams, 2006; Adams, Lawrence, & Schenck, 2008); there was no attempt to continue or replicate previous research.

20   The research of Nansel et al. (2001) and Espelage and Swearer (2003) provided a background for the current researchers to identify and describe seven terms reflecting the data from this study. Guided by the work of Nansel et al. and Espelage and Swearer, we use the following terms to describe the characteristics and lasting effects of bullying.

1. Safety. Being unsure of a secure location within which one may be able to relax, or feel comfortable; the individual's security has been compromised. Victims only feel safe in their dorm rooms, or a confined space which has a restricted access. They are afraid someone will say something hurtful, afraid to tell anyone about electronic messages, afraid to go to certain classes, and find few places they feel safe.

2. Exclusion. Being "left out" of conversations, groupings, or lack a sense of belonging to a group. Victims feel they are often excluded from class or group activities.

3. Isolation. Feeling a lack of inclusion, or being a member. Victims feel alone and isolated much of the day and feel that no one will listen to them.

4. Abuse. Receiving negative comments or treated in a disrespectful manner after having expressed behavior and/or conversation deemed inappropriate by an individual or a group. Victims report having been abused for expressing their opinions, having received insulting/degrading text messages, and being laughed at when responding to questions in class.

5. Alienation. Feeling or sensing an inability to connect, or communicate in a positive manner with other individuals or groups. Victims report it is hard for them to make friends.

6. Lonely. Feeling that there is no one willing to communicate, feeling a sense of having no friend or acquaintance for conversations. Victims feel alone and isolated, feel that no one will believe them, and only wish to sleep. . . .

21 | **CONCLUSIONS**

The current study supports conclusions reported by Barker et al. (2008): Youths victimized by their peers were at an increased risk, in turn, of victimizing others as they move from one environment to another. The Center for Disease Control (2011) reported bullying continues to occur at all levels within the educational environment. This study provides supporting data indicating bullying initiated in middle/senior high school years continues in other educational settings. The State of Massachusetts reported in the Journal of the American Medical Association (2011) that bullying continues today at various levels within the school years. This study supports that bullying continues beyond the school years—into either institutions of higher education or into the workplace.

22 | Exclusion, abuse, alienation, and loneliness reported in this study are poignantly reflected in current legal action taken against a school district that refused to take a positive stand against harassment and bullying (Smith, 2011). The district elected to use a policy of "neutrality." Smith indicated the message present in an environment of this type is clear—who you are is "not OK"; bullying is permissible throughout the educational environment until "you change."

23 | With more focus being directed to and from a variety of venues, such as the media (Miller, 2010), academic settings (Rigby 2010), and the workplace (Oade, 2009), more information and resources are available on bullying; however, there is a need for more information examining the long-term effects of the bullying behavior on both the victim and the bully.

REFERENCES

Adams, F. D., Lawrence, G. J., & Schenck, S. (2008, Spring). A survey on bullying: Some reflections on the findings. *NASCD News & Notes, 8,* 1–7.

Barker, E. D., Arseneault, L., Brendgen, M., Fontaine, N., & Maughan, B. (2008, September). Joint development of bullying and victimization in adolescence: Relations to delinquency and self-harm. *Journal of the American Academy of Child & Adolescent Psychiatry, 47*(9), 1030–1038.

Brown, N. L. (2006, December 23). Harassment and bullying: Not a rite of passage. Retrieved from http://www.healthline.com/blogs/teen_health/2006/12/harassment-and-bullying-not-rite-of.html

Centers for Disease Control and Prevention. (2011). *Morbidity and Mortality Weekly Report. Bullying among middle school and high school students—Massachusetts, 2009. The Journal of the American Medical Association, 22*(305), 2283–2286.

Cohen, J. M. (1977). Sources of peer group homogeneity. *Sociology of Education, 50,* 227–241.

Espelage, D. L., & Swearer, S. M. (2003). Research on school bullying and victimization: What have we learned and where do we go from here? *School Psychology Review, 32*(3), 365–383.

Fritzgerald, B. (2010, August 13). Did UVA administration respond to claims of "workplace bullying"? C-VILLE Charlottesville News & Arts. Retrieved from http://www.c-ville.com/index

Lawrence, G. J., & Adams, F. D. (2006, Fall). For every bully there is a victim. *American Secondary Education, 35*(1), 66–71.

Miller, T. W. (Ed.). (2010). *Handbook of stressful conditions across the lifespan.* New York, NY: Springer.

Monks, C. P., & Smith, P. K. (2010, December). Definitions of bullying: Age differences in understanding of the term and the role of experience. *British Journal of Developmental Psychology, 24*(A), 801–821.

Nansel, T. R., Overpeck, M., Pilla, R. S., Ruan, W. J., Simons-Morton, B., & Scheidt, P. (2001, April 25). Bullying behaviors among US youth: Prevalence and association with psychosocial adjustment. *The Journal of the American Medical Association, 285*(16), 2094–2100.

Newman, M. L., Holden, G. W., & Delville, Y. (2011, March). Coping with the stress of being bullied: Consequences of coping strategies among college students. *Social Psychological and Personality Science, 2*(2), 205–211.

Oade, A. (2009). *Managing workplace bullying: How to identify, respond to and manage bullying behavior in the workplace.* New York, NY: Palgrave & MacMillan.

Oliver, C., & Candappa, M. (2003). *Tackling bullying: Listening to the views of children and young people. Special Report.* London, UK: Thomas Coram Research Unit, Institute of Education, Department for Education and Skills.

Olweus, D. O. (1978). *Aggression in the schools: Bullies and whipping boys.* Washington, DC: Hemisphere Press (Wiley).

Olweus, D. O. (1993). *Bullying at school: What we know and what we can do.* Oxford, UK: Blackwell.

Olweus, D. O. (1999). The nature of school bullying (pp. 28–48). In P. K. Smith, Y. Morita, J. Junger-Tas, D. Olweus, R. Cantalano, & P. Slee (Eds.). (1999). *The nature of school bullying: A cross-national perspective.* Florence, KY: Taylor & Frances/Routledge.

Parker, J. C., & Asher, S. R. (1987). Peer relations and later personal adjustment: Are low-accepted children at risk? *Psychological Bulletin, 103,* 357–389.

Pellegrini, A. S., Bartini, M., & Brooks, F. (1999). School bullies, victims, and aggressive victims. Factors relating to group affiliation and victimization in early adolescence. *Journal of Educational Psychology, 7*(2), 216–224.

Rigby, K. (2010). *Bullying interventions in schools: Six basic approaches.* Victoria, AU: Australian Council for Educational Research Press.

Rubin, R. (2008). "Electronic aggression": Another form of bullying. *USA Today.com,* para. 1.

Smith, K. (2011, July 22). Anoka-Hennepin sued over bullying. *Minneapolis Star Tribune.* Retrieved from http://www.startribune.com/local/north/125958688.html

Smith, P. K., Singer, M., Hoel, H., & Cooper, C. L. (2003, May). Victimization in the school and the workplace: Are there any links? *The British Journal of Psychology, 94*(2), 175–188.

Strom, P. S., & Strom, R. D. (2005). Cyberbullying by adolescents: A preliminary assessment. *The Educational Forum, 70,* 21–36.

Tritt, C., & Duncan, R. D. (1997, September). The relationship between childhood bullying and young adult self-esteem and loneliness. *Journal of Humanistic Education and Development, 36*(1), 35–44. ERIC Document EJ568410

QUESTIONS FOR DISCUSSION

1. What do you think motivates bullying? How deep in human nature do the motivations go?

2. Regardless of age and place, people have ways of punishing those who depart too much from a group's norms. At what point or in what ways can enforcing conformity become bullying?

3. In your experience, what strategy copes with bullying best? For instance, is it best to resist, perhaps even to the point of blows? Or is it best to endure, not answering bad behavior with more bad behavior? How about telling persons in authority? Does it help or make matters worse?

FOR RESEARCH AND DISCUSSION

Adams and Lawrence used the following questionnaire in their study:

1. I feel safe only in my dorm room.

2. Students in my class call me names, say something hurtful to me, or say something loud enough for me to hear.

3. I am often excluded from class activities.

4. For much of the day I feel alone and isolated.

5. I have been physically abused by someone in my classes, more than once, for expressing my opinion.

6. As I walk to and from class, I am afraid someone will say something hurtful to me.

7. I have been threatened with physical harm this week.

8. I have received more than one email which had insulting comments about me.

9. I don't know how to fight back when individuals say hurtful things to me, or about me.

10. I have received more than one text message that was insulting and degrading to me.

11. I am afraid to tell anyone about being hurt or harmed from emails, text messages, or instant messages.

12. No one believes me about being hurt, insulted, or harmed from emails or instant messages.

13. I am afraid to go to certain classes because of individuals present in those classes.

14. I experienced acts of bullying during my years in high school and/or junior high school.

15. During the day, or in my classes, I only wish to sleep.

16. I find that I have great difficulty concentrating in class because of certain individuals in that class.

17. When I respond to an instructor's question, there is always laughter from individuals in the class.

18. It is hard for me to make friends.

19. No one will listen to me; I feel so alone and isolated.

20. There are few places in the school where I feel safe.

Discuss these questions as a class. Are there any questions you would take out? Are there questions you would add?

Have your class take the questionnaire you decide on and compile the results. Are your findings similar to those in the study? If not, why do think they differ? What conclusions do you draw from your data?

Don't Be a Bystander

EMILY BAZELON

A senior fellow at Yale Law School and an editor for the online magazine *Slate,* Emily Bazelon is the author of *Sticks and Stones: Defeating the Culture of Bullying and Rediscovering the Power of Character and Empathy* (Random House). In the following article, she offers a partial solution to the problem of bullying.

Experts are working with kids to teach them that speaking up and coming to the defense of bullying victims can bring an end to the cruelty.

1   One of the most frustrating facts about bullying is this: In the vast majority of cases, it takes place in front of an audience of other kids—88 percent of the time, according to one study. And yet kids who are bystanders intervene only 20 percent of the time. When they *do* step forward, however, they stop half the bullying they try to head off.

2   Bystanders, then, represent a major opportunity: Convert more of them into defenders or allies of the target of bullying, and you could take the sting out of one of childhood's enduring harms. Except that it's not so easy. Adults constantly exhort kids to stand up for kids who are the victims of taunting and cruelty. It's what many of us want to see from our own children—I know I expect my own sons to stand up for the kid getting picked on. But stepping into the middle of a conflict to confront an aggressor is usually asking a lot. "As bullies are often perceived as popular and powerful, it takes a lot to thwart their behavior," as the Finnish psychologist Christina Salmivalli, a leader in the field, puts it in a 2010 paper. In a new study from Harvard, based on in-depth interviews with 23 middle-schoolers, every single one said they supported the idea of being an "upstander" rather than a passive bystander, but "half of them acknowledged that in practice they often laugh when they see others victimizing a peer in school," as the authors put it.

3   Kids want to help, and know they should, but they don't always do it. It's an example of the classic bystander problem that also affects adults: In a famous study in the late 1960s, researchers showed that people who watch a dangerous situation unfold take longer to help if there are many fellow onlookers. The presence of multiple bystanders diffuses responsibility and also makes people unsure of social cues—they hesitate to be the first one to make a move if no one else has.

4   These findings help explain how Kitty Genovese was brutally and infamously murdered by a knife-wielding attacker in New York in 1964, even though she cried out for help to neighbors in a nearby apartment building. The facts of the story aren't quite as awful as the original telling: Someone did initially scare off the killer by opening a window to yell, "Let that girl alone!" And it may be that none of the neighbors realized that he actually came back. Still, it did take a half-hour for someone to finally call the police—for Genovese, too late.

5   One of the experts I've come to respect in writing my book on bullying is a former guidance counselor and researcher, Stan Davis, who points out that kids can also help the targets of bullying in quieter, after-the-fact ways, by asking them if they're OK or sending a sympathetic text. Having even one single defender reduces the negative effects for the victim—it makes the bullying less upsetting.

6   What do we know about kids who come to the aid of the targets of bullies—and how could we expand their number? Salmivalli points out that not surprisingly, kids are more likely to stick up for kids they're friends with. Kids are also more likely to be upstanders if they're in a social circle of friends in which other kids don't bully. The few kids in the Harvard study who stood up for victims of bullying outside their friend group had an objective sense of moral responsibility, "a common commitment to address issues of unfairness," as the researchers put it. They were also "very powerful members of the peer group"—kids with status.

7   But we can't only rely on the kids who happen to be both moral and high in status. The key is to figure out how the environment of a classroom—or a whole school—can add to their ranks. There is plenty of evidence that aggression and meanness among students can pay off in terms of popularity—it's often a route to moving up the social ladder. So how can a school, or a community, turn that around to reward a kid's willingness to put themselves on the line to stop cruelty instead? It's a question at the heart of every good bullying prevention effort, and one that explains why the programs with success encompass the whole school.

8   Salmivalli focuses on one with particular promise: a program in Finland, called KiVa, that has generated a lot of international interest based on its record of reducing bullying and increasing peer support for victims. She emphasizes the importance of showing kids that bullying isn't the norm—that most people don't do it. When very few kids step up to challenge bullying, on the other hand, "children may infer that *the others think bullying is OK.*"

9   In the United States, bullying prevention programs like Olweus and Steps to Respect try to encourage more upstanding. But no one here has completely solved the riddle. One person who is trying is Nancy Willard, a longtime advocate in the field who directs Embrace Civility in the Digital Age. Willard has designed a new program with a couple of features I haven't seen before that seem promising, like encouraging teachers and other staff to watch for students who act as allies, not to make them an object of public praise, since that could make them uncool and backfire, but so that the principal can send a letter of thanks home. It's a small idea, but that's somehow how larger cultural shifts start.

QUESTIONS FOR DISCUSSION

1. If we want to understand bullying, surely one point the author makes merits special consideration: "There is plenty of evidence that aggression and meanness among students can pay off in terms of popularity." Based on your own experience, would you say the claim is true? If so, why does aggression and meanness pay off?

2. Perhaps another important insight comes from the author's discussion of the bystander problem (paragraphs 3 and 4). What is her point? Do you see it as having any value in explaining why victims of bullying sometimes aren't aided by people who witness but do not participate in the bullying itself? Why or why not?

3. The author describes the characteristics of people who do intervene in an effort to stop bullying. What are these characteristics? In your experience, which characteristic or characteristics are most important? Why? Do you see in these characteristics any implications for reducing bullying?

FOR RESEARCH, DISCUSSION, AND CONVINCING

Probably the greatest barrier to dealing with bullying more effectively is the widespread belief that nothing can be done about it. As a class, do research on bullying, beginning with Bazelon's book mentioned in the headnote and the sources she refers to in the article. Discuss your findings in class.

Write an essay meant to convince your peer group that both the incidence and severity of bullying can be reduced. Based on the research, defend what you think the most promising approach or approaches are.

FOR FURTHER READING

Bazelon, Emily. *Sticks and Stones: Defeating the Culture of Bullying and Rediscovering the Power of Character and Empathy.* Random House, 2013.

Calandra, Lion. "Public Grooming: Duck! It's a Wayward Toenail Clipping." *New York Times,* 8 Nov. 2009, query.nytimes.com/gst/fullpage.html?res=9900E0DE113DF93BA35752C1A96F9C8B63.

Carter, Stephen L. *Civility: Manners, Morals, and the Etiquette of Democracy.* Basic Books, 1998.

Forni, P. M. *Choosing Civility: The Twenty-five Rules of Considerate Conduct.* St. Martin's, 2002.

——. *The Civility Solution: What to Do When People Are Rude.* St. Martin's, 2009.

Gilroy, Marilyn. "Colleges Grappling with Incivility." *Education Digest,* vol. 74, no. 4, Dec. 2008, pp. 36–40. *EBSCOHost,* connection.ebscohost.com/c/articles/35617812/colleges-grappling-incivility.

Herbst, Susan. *Rude Democracy: Civility and Incivility in American Politics.* Temple UP, 2010.

"Minding Manners: Civility Project Compiles Rules Using Washington's Models." *The University of Virginia Magazine,* Winter 2009, uvamagazine.org/articles/minding_manners.

Parker, Kathleen. "'New' Media Have Fueled Our Incivility." *Arizona Daily Star,* 17 Nov. 2009, tucson.com/news/opinion/new-media-have-fueled-our-incivility/article_9978427d-addb-5414-ace0-21d2e537ea43.html.

Siegel, Lee. *Against the Machine: Being Human in the Age of the Electronic Mob.* Random House, 2008.

Sobieraj, Sarah, and Jeffrey M. Berry. "From Incivility to Outrage: Political Discourse in Blogs, Talk Radio, and Cable News." *Political Communication,* vol. 28, no. 1, 2011, pp. 19–41.

Twenge, Jean. "Incivility—or Narcissism?" *Psychology Today,* 18 Sept. 2009, www.psychologytoday.com/blog/the-narcissism-epidemic/200909/incivility-or-narcissism.

Cycling champion Lance Armstrong bared all to Oprah Winfrey.

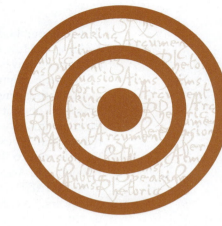

CHAPTER 17

Enhancing Humans: How Far Is Too Far?

Carl Elliott, The Tyranny of Happiness   *487*

Benedict Carey, Brain Enhancement Is Wrong, Right?   *492*

Barbara Sahakian and Nora Volkow, Professor's Little Helper?   *495*

Gregory Stock, Choosing Our Genes   *501*

John Naish, Genetically Modified Athletes   *506*

Arthur L. Caplan, A Shot in the Rear: Why Are We Really against Steroids?   *509*

Ed Smith, Lance Armstrong and the Cult of Positive Thinking   *514*

Larry Gonick and Mark Wheelis, Cartoon: Gene-Splicing as Big Business   *517*

C. Ben Mitchell, On Human Bioenhancements   *519*

For Further Reading   *521*

Human beings have always found ways to enhance their lives by improving on what nature provides. That is what technology is all about, from the first stone tools to today's computers and cell phones. Now technology has the potential to alter not only the tools we use but also our genetic makeup, the "software" that tells our bodily "hardware" what shapes to take and what to do. The question is: How far is too far? Where should our nearly compulsive efforts to enhance ourselves stop?

Genetic engineering receives much attention in the news, but at present manipulating genes is not a significant share of enhancement. Rather, as Carl Elliott points out in the first selection, using drugs intended to treat disease for their capacity to enhance our energy level, increase our capacity to focus, reduce anxiety, and in other ways make us more productive dominate the scene. We refer not to illegal drugs but prescription drugs such as Adderall, Ritalin, Provigil, and Aricept, developed to treat clinical problems like attention-deficit disorder (ADD) and Alzheimer's, but now used by healthy people as "brain enhancers." As the second and third selections in this chapter indicate, the use of such drugs is widespread on and off college campuses, and not just by students wanting a boost during final exams, but by professors, workaholic executives, and the like.

Outside of breaking the law by using prescription medications intended for somebody else in off-label ways, what is the problem? After all, we have "real" drug problems, such as crystal meth, heroin, and the abuse of steroids, against which someone getting a dose or two of Ritalin from an ADD patient for occasional use may seem trivial. But in fact the abuse of prescription drugs is a major concern, a bigger problem in some ways than the traffic in illegal drugs. They pose health risks and raise ethical questions such as how fair it is for a student to seek an advantage on a test that comes from anything else than studying hard. Will other students feel pressure to take drugs such as Ritalin to maintain their competitive edge? Are we headed toward a society not just addicted to Starbucks but where doping is as routine as coffee and energy drinks?

In general, our drive to enhance ourselves in all ways requires careful thought, each choice a balancing of such considerations as benefit, risk, effort expended, and cost. Where to draw the line is never easy: Even dieting and exercise can go too far.

More specifically, we will face increasing temptations to use knowledge of genetics not just to prevent and treat disease—surely a legitimate use of the technology—but to increase the chances to have children that are smarter, more attractive, more talented, and so on than the roll of the dice in ordinary human mating permits. Gregory Stock and C. Ben Mitchell address these temptations with different attitudes and ways of thinking, but both alert us to how serious such choices are. Again, the question is, How far is too far? Should we stop with restoring normal function, using stem cells, for instance, to help a paralyzed person walk again? Or should we aim at fashioning better human beings, better in the sense of having higher IQs? Is it possible to be too smart? Or to have too much athletic or musical talent? These are hard questions that must be pondered as a powerful technology unfolds before our eyes.

The Tyranny of Happiness

CARL ELLIOTT

Carl Elliott teaches philosophy and bioethics at the University of Minnesota. The following selection comes from the last chapter of his book *Better Than Well: American Medicine Meets the American Dream.*

Elliott is concerned with the American passion for—some would say "compulsion toward"—enhancement of all kinds. He analyzes its motives and traces it to self-fulfillment as the goal of happiness. The problem is that such a notion of the good lacks social connection and eludes definition and assessment. How can we know what fulfills us? How can we know when we are fulfilled?

In America I have seen the freest and best educated of men in circumstances the happiest to be found in the world, yet it seemed to me that a cloud habitually hung on their brow, and they seemed serious and almost sad even in their pleasures.

—Alexis de Tocqueville

1   Thirty-five years ago, at the beginning of a twelve-year Senate inquiry into the drug industry, Senator Gaylord Nelson opened the session on psychotropic drugs by comparing them to the drugs in *Brave New World.* "When Aldous Huxley wrote his fantasy concept of the world of the future in the now classic *Brave New World,* he created an uncomfortable, emotionless culture of escapism dependent on tiny tablets of tranquility called soma."[1] Thirty-five years later, *Brave New World* is still invoked, time and again, as a warning against the dangers that await us if we embark on new enhancement technologies. News stories about psychotropic drugs, stem cells, reproductive technologies, or genetic engineering inevitably appear with headlines reading Brave New Medicine, Brave New Babies, Brave New Minds, or Brave New People. It is as if we have no other metaphors for these technologies, no competing visions of possible futures. Whatever the new technology of the moment happens to be, we hear the same cautionary tale: it will lead us to a totalitarian society where generic workers are slotted into castes and anesthetized into bliss. The people in these totalitarian societies are not so much unhappy as they are ignorant of what true happiness is, because they have been drugged and engineered to want nothing more than that which their station allows them.

2   We keep returning to this story, I suspect, partly because we like stories of individuals battling the forces of authority, and partly because it allows both teller and listener to collude in the shared sense that we, unlike our neighbors and coworkers and maybe even our family members, have figured out what is really bad about a technology that looks so good. This story says, "Our neighbors may have been sold a bill of goods, they may think that they have found happiness in a Prozac tablet and a Botox injection, but you and I know it's a crock. You and I are too smart to believe the cosmetic surgery Web sites, the drug companies peddling Sarafem and Paxil, and the psychiatrists who tell us we have adult ADHD." Yet as much as we like the *Brave New World* story, as many times as we read it and repeat it and write high school essays about it, somehow it never seems to apply to us. For men, the story of enhancement technologies is about the vanity of women; for women, it is about the sexual gaze

of men; for Europeans and Canadians, it is about shallowness of American values; for Americans, it is about "other" Americans—the ones who are either too crooked or deluded to acknowledge what is really going on. If we blame anyone for the ill effects of enhancement technologies, it is either someone in power (the FDA, the media, Big Pharma, "the culture") or the poor suckers who have allowed themselves to be duped (Miss America contestants, neurotic New Yorkers, Michael Jackson). We imagine second-rate TV stars lining up for liposuction and anxious middle managers asking their family doctors for Paxil, and we just shake our heads and laugh. "Why can't they learn to accept themselves as they are?" we ask. Then we are asked to sing a solo in the church choir and can't sleep for a week, or our daughter starts getting teased at school for her buck teeth, and the joke doesn't seem so funny anymore.

3   We all like to moralize about enhancement technologies, except for the ones we use ourselves. Those technologies never seem quite so bad, because our view of them comes not from television or magazines but from personal experience, or the shared confidences of our troubled friends. There is often striking contrast between private conversation about enhancement technologies and the broader public discussion. In public, for example, everyone seems to be officially anti-Prozac. Feminists ask me why doctors prescribe Prozac more often for women than for men. Undergraduates worry that Prozac might give their classmates a competitive edge. Philosophy professors argue that Prozac would make people shallow and uncreative. Germans object that Prozac is not a natural substance. Americans say that Prozac is a crutch. Most people seem to feel that Prozac is creating some version of what historian David Rothman called, in a *New Republic* cover story, "shiny, happy people."

4   In private, though, people have started to seek me out and tell me their Prozac stories. They have tried Prozac and hated it; they have tried Prozac and it changed their life; they have tried Prozac and can't see what the big deal is. It has begun to seem as if everyone I know is on Prozac, has been on Prozac, or is considering taking Prozac, and all of them want to get my opinion. Most of all, they want me to try Prozac myself. "How can you write about it if you've never even tried it?" I can see their point. Still, it strikes me as a strange way to talk about a prescription drug. These people are oddly insistent. It was as if we were back in high school, and they were trying to get me to smoke a joint.

5   People who look at America from abroad often marvel at the enthusiasm with which Americans use enhancement technologies. I can see why. It is a jolt to discover the rates at which Americans use Ritalin or Prozac or Botox. But "enthusiasm" is probably the wrong word to describe the way Americans feel about enhancement technologies. If this is enthusiasm, it is the enthusiasm of a diver on the high platform, who has to talk himself into taking the plunge. . . . I don't think Americans expect happiness in a handful of tablets. We take the tablets, but we brood about it. We try to hide the tablets from our friends. We worry that taking them is a sign of weakness. We try to convince our friends to take them too. We fret that if we don't take them, others will outshine us. We take the tablets, but they leave a bitter taste in our mouths.

6   Why? Perhaps because in those tablets is a mix of all the American wishes, lusts, and fears: the drive to self-improvement, the search for fulfillment, the desire to

show that there are second acts in American lives; yet a mix diluted by nagging anxieties about social conformity, about getting too much too easily, about phoniness and self-deception and shallow pleasure. This is not a story from *Brave New World*. It is not even a story of enhancement. . . . It is less a story about trying to get ahead than about the terror of being left behind, and the humiliation of crossing the finish line dead last, while the crowd points at you and laughs. You can still refuse to use enhancement technologies, of course—you might be the last woman in America who does not dye her gray hair, the last man who refuses to work out at the gym—but even that publicly announces something to other Americans about who you are and what you value. This is all part of the logic of consumer culture. You cannot simply opt out of the system and expect nobody to notice how much you weigh.

7   Why here, why now? On one level, the answer seems obvious: because the technology has arrived. If you are anxious and lonely and a drug can fix it, why stay anxious and lonely? If you are unhappy with your body and surgery can fix it, why stay unhappy? The market moves to fill a demand for happiness as efficiently as it moves to fill a demand for spark plugs or home computers. It is on a deeper level that the question of enhancement technologies becomes more puzzling. What has made the ground for these technologies so fertile? The sheer variety of technologies on display is remarkable. . . . Black folks rub themselves with cream to make their skin lighter, while white folks broil in tanning parlors to make their skin darker. Bashful men get ETS surgery to reduce blood flow above the neck, while elderly men take Viagra to increase blood flow below the belt. Each technology has its own rationale, its own cultural niche, a distinct population of users, and an appeal that often waxes or wanes with changes in fashion or the state of scientific knowledge. But do they have anything in common? Is there anything about the way we live now that helps explain their popularity?

8   The "self that struggles to realize itself," as philosopher Michael Walzer puts it, has become a familiar notion to most people living in the West today.[2] We tend to see ourselves as the managers of life projects that we map out, organize, make choices about, perhaps compare with other possible projects, and ultimately live out to completion. From late adolescence onward, we are expected to make important decisions about what to do for a living, where to live, whether to marry and have children, all with the sense that these decisions will contribute to the success or failure of our projects. Yet as Walzer points out, there is nothing natural or inevitable about this way of conceptualizing a life. Not everyone in the West today will think of their lives as planned projects, and most people at most times in history have probably thought of their lives differently. Marriages are arranged; educational choices are fixed; gods are tyrannical or absent. A life might be spontaneous, rather than planned; its shape might be given to us, rather than created. The shapes of lives can be determined not by the demands of personal values or self-fulfillment, but by those of God, family, social station, caste, or one's ancestors.

9   This notion of life as a project suggests both individual responsibility and moral uncertainty. If I am the planner and manager of my life, then I am at least partly responsible for its success or failure. Thus the lure of enhancement technologies: as tools to

produce a better, more successful project. Yet if my life is a project, what exactly is the purpose of the project? How do I tell a successful project from a failure? Aristotle (for example) could write confidently about the good life for human beings because he was confident about what the purpose of being a human being was. Just as a knife has a purpose, so human beings have a purpose; just as the qualities that make for a good knife are those that help the knife slice, whittle, and chop, the qualities that make a human being better are those that help us better fulfill our purpose as human beings.

10   Our problem, of course, is that most of us don't have Aristotle's confidence about the purpose of human life. Good knives cut, that much we can see, but what does a good human being do, and how will we know when we are doing it? Is there even such a thing as a single, universal human purpose? Not if we believe what we are told by the culture that surrounds us. From philosophy courses and therapy sessions to magazines and movies, we are told that questions of purpose vary from one person to the next; that, in fact, a large part of our life project is to discover our own individual purpose and develop it to its fullest. This leaves us with unanswered questions not just about what kinds of lives are better or worse, but also about the criteria by which such judgments are made. Is it better to be a successful bail bondsman or a second-rate novelist? On what yardstick do we compare the lives of Reform Jews, high-church Episcopalians, and California Wiccans? Where exactly should the choices we make about our lives be anchored?

11   Many people today believe that the success or failure of a life has something to do with the idea of self-fulfillment. We may not know exactly what a successful life is, but we have a pretty good suspicion that it has something to do with being fulfilled— or at the very least, that an unfulfilled life runs the risk of failure. In the name of fulfillment people quit their jobs in human resources and real estate to become poets and potters, leave their dermatology practices to do medical mission work in Bangladesh, even divorce their husbands or wives (the marriage was adequate, but it was not fulfilling). Women leave their children in day care because they believe that they will be more fulfilled with a career; they leave their jobs because they believe that it will be more fulfilling to stay home with the kids. Fulfillment has a strong moral strand to it—many people feel that they *ought* to pursue a career, that they *ought* to leave a loveless marriage—but its parameters are vague and indeterminate. How exactly do I know if I am fulfilled? Fulfillment looks a little like being in love, a little like a successful spiritual quest; it is a state centered largely on individual psychic well-being. If I am alienated, depressed, or anxious, I can't be completely fulfilled.

12   If I am not fulfilled, I am missing out on what life can offer. Life is a short, sweet ride, and I am spending it all in the station. The problem is that there is no great, overarching metric for self-fulfillment, no master schedule that we can look up at and say, "Yes, I've missed the train." So we look desperately to experts for instructions— counselors, psychiatrists, advice columnists, self-help writers, life coaches, even professional ethicists. We read the ads on the wall for cosmetic dentistry, and we look nervously at the people standing next to us in line. Does she know something that I don't? Is she more fulfilled? How does my psychic well-being compare to hers? . . .

13   In other times and places, success or failure in a life might have been determined by fixed and agreed-upon standards. You displeased the ancestors; you

shamed your family; you did not accept Jesus Christ as your personal savior. You arrived late to the station, and the train left without you. But our situation today is different—not for everyone, of course, but for many of us. We have gotten on the train, but we don't know who is driving it, or where, some point off in the far distance, the tracks are leading. The other passengers are smiling, they look happy, yet underneath this facade of good cheer and philosophical certainty, a demon keeps whispering in our ears: "What if I have gotten it all wrong? What if I have boarded the wrong train?"

14   Tocqueville hinted at this worry over 150 years ago when he wrote about American "restlessness in the midst of abundance." Behind all the admirable energy of American life, Tocqueville saw a kind of grim relentlessness. We build houses to pass our old age, Tocqueville wrote, then sell them before the roof is on; we clear fields, then leave it to others to gather the harvest; we take up a profession, then leave it to take up another one or go into politics. Americans frantically pursue prosperity, and when we finally get it, we are tormented by the worry that we might have gotten it quicker. An American on vacation, Tocqueville marveled, "will travel five hundred miles in a few days as a distraction from his happiness."[3]

15   Tocqueville may well have been right about American restlessness, but it took another Frenchman, surrealist painter Philippe Soupault, to put his finger on the form that it has taken today. According to Soupault, Americans see the pursuit of happiness not just as a right, as the Declaration of Independence states, but as a strange sort of duty. In the United States, he wrote, "one is always in danger of entrapment by what appears on the surface to be a happy civilization. There is a sort of obligation to be happy." Humans are born to be happy, and if they are not, something has gone wrong. As Soupault puts it, "Whoever is unhappy is suspect."[4] Substitute self-fulfillment for happiness and you get something of the ethic that motivates the desire for enhancement technologies. Once self-fulfillment is hitched to the success of a human life, it comes perilously close to an obligation—not an obligation to God, country, or family, but an obligation to the self. We are compelled to pursue fulfillment through enhancement technologies not in order to get ahead of others, but to make sure that we have lived our lives to the fullest. The train has left the station and we don't know where it is going. The least we can do is be sure it is making good time.

NOTES

1. Mickey Smith, *A Social History of the Minor Tranquilizers: The Quest for Small Comfort in an Age of Anxiety.* Praeger, 1989, p. 178.
2. Michael Walzer, *Thick and Thin: Moral Argument at Home and Abroad.* Notre Dame UP, 1994, pp. 23–24.
3. Alexis de Tocqueville, *Democracy in America.* Translated by George Lawrence, edited by J. P. Mayer. Harper and Row, 1988, p. 536.
4. Philippe Soupault, "Introduction to Mademoiselle Coeur Brise (Miss Lonely-hearts)," *Nathanael West: A Collection of Critical Essays,* edited by Jay Martin. Prentice-Hall, 1971, pp. 112–13.

QUESTIONS FOR DISCUSSION

1. According to Elliott, why do people appeal so often to Huxley's novel, *Brave New World,* when enhancement technologies, especially new ones, are discussed? Why does he consider the connection essentially misleading?

2. Elliott claims that American culture and values emphasize "life as a project"—hence, "the lure of enhancement technologies: as tools to produce a better, more successful project." Do you see this as the drive behind such popular TV shows as *What Not to Wear* and *Extreme Makeover?*

3. "If I am alienated, depressed, or anxious, I can't be completely fulfilled," Elliott says, and the solution becomes a pill, plastic surgery, occupational change, divorce—something that will "fix" the problem. But are there circumstances when people ought to feel alienated, depressed, or anxious? Can such feelings be positive and productive rather than negative and counterproductive?

4. Elliott cites the French surrealist painter Philippe Soupault, who claims that in the United States "there is a sort of obligation to be happy. . . . Whoever is unhappy is suspect." Thus, according to Elliott, the pursuit of happiness is not a right but rather "a strange sort of duty . . . an obligation to the self." Do you find this diagnosis persuasive? What, according to Elliott, makes such an understanding of the pursuit of happiness unsatisfying and ultimately self-defeating?

FOR PERSUASION

"Our problem," Elliott claims, "is that most of us don't have Aristotle's confidence about the purpose of human life. . . . [W]hat does a good human being do, and how will we know when we are doing it?"

Are we Americans so much in doubt about what we ought to be doing as Elliott claims? Write an essay arguing against his assertion of complete relativity where our notion of the good is concerned. Support it by referring to popular culture—to movies and TV dramas, for instance—which often reflect our values and sometimes expose them for reflection.

Brain Enhancement Is Wrong, Right?

BENEDICT CAREY

Benedict Carey is a writer on science and medical topics for *The New York Times,* where the following article originally appeared.

1   So far no one is demanding that asterisks be attached to Nobels, Pulitzers or Lasker awards. Government agents have not been raiding anthropology departments, riffling book bags, testing professors' urine. And if there are illicit trainers on campuses, shady tutors with wraparound sunglasses and ties to basement labs in Italy, no one has exposed them.

2   Yet an era of doping may be looming in academia, and it has ignited a debate about policy and ethics that in some ways echoes the national controversy over performance enhancement accusations against elite athletes like Barry Bonds and Roger Clemens.

3   In a recent commentary in the journal *Nature,* two Cambridge University researchers reported that about a dozen of their colleagues had admitted to regular use of prescription drugs like Adderall, a stimulant, and Provigil, which promotes wakefulness, to improve their academic performance. The former is approved to treat attention deficit disorder, the latter narcolepsy, and both are considered more effective, and more widely available, than the drugs circulating in dorms a generation ago.

4   Letters flooded the journal, and an online debate immediately bubbled up. The journal has been conducting its own, more rigorous survey, and so far at least 20 respondents have said that they used the drugs for nonmedical purposes, according to Philip Campbell, the journal's editor in chief. The debate has also caught fire on the Web site of the *Chronicle of Higher Education,* where academics and students are sniping at one another.

5   But is prescription tweaking to perform on exams, or prepare presentations and grants, really the same as injecting hormones to chase down a home run record, or win the Tour de France?

6   Some argue that such use could be worse, given the potentially deep impact on society. And the behavior of academics in particular, as intellectual leaders, could serve as an example to others.

7   In his book *Our Posthuman Future: Consequences of the Biotechnology Revolution,* Francis Fukuyama raises the broader issue of performance enhancement: "The original purpose of medicine is to heal the sick, not turn healthy people into gods." He and others point out that increased use of such drugs could raise the standard of what is considered "normal" performance and widen the gap between those who have access to the medications and those who don't—and even erode the relationship between struggle and the building of character.

8   "Even though stimulants and other cognitive enhancers are intended for legitimate clinical use, history predicts that greater availability will lead to an increase in diversion, misuse and abuse," wrote Dr. Nora Volkow, director of the National Institute on Drug Abuse, and James Swanson of the University of California at Irvine, in a letter to *Nature.* "Among high school students, abuse of prescription medications is second only to cannabis use."

9   But others insist that the ethics are not so clear, and that academic performance is different in important ways from baseball, or cycling.

10 "I think the analogy with sports doping is really misleading, because in sports it's all about competition, only about who's the best runner or home run hitter," said Martha Farah, director of the Center for Cognitive Neuroscience at the University of Pennsylvania. "In academics, whether you're a student or a researcher, there is an element of competition, but it's secondary. The main purpose is to try to learn things, to get experience, to write papers, to do experiments. So in that case if you can do it better because you've got some drug on board, that would on the face of things seem like a plus."

11   She and other midcareer scientists interviewed said that, as far as they knew, very few of their colleagues used brain-boosting drugs regularly. Many have used Provigil for jet lag, or even to stay vertical for late events. But most agreed that the next generation of scientists, now in graduate school and college, were more likely to use the drugs as study aids and bring along those habits as they moved up the ladder.

12   Surveys of college students have found that from 4 percent to 16 percent say they have used stimulants or other prescription drugs to improve their academic performance—usually getting the pills from other students.

13   "Suppose you're preparing for the SAT, or going for a job interview—in those situations where you have to perform on that day, these drugs will be very attractive," said Dr. Barbara Sahakian of Cambridge, a co-author with Sharon Morein-Zamir of the recent essay in *Nature*. "The desire for cognitive enhancement is very strong, maybe stronger than for beauty, or athletic ability."

14   Jeffrey White, a graduate student in cell biology who has attended several institutions, said that those numbers sounded about right. "You can usually tell who's using them because they can be angry, testy, hyperfocused, they don't want to be bothered," he said.

15   Mr. White said he did not use the drugs himself, considering them an artificial shortcut that could set people up for problems later on. "What happens if you're in a fast-paced surgical situation and they're not available?" he asked. "Will you be able to function at the same level?"

16   Yet such objections—and philosophical concerns—can vaporize when students and junior faculty members face other questions: What happens if I don't make the cut? What if I'm derailed by a bad test score, or a mangled chemistry course?

17   One person who posted anonymously on the *Chronicle of Higher Education* Web site said that a daily regimen of three 20-milligram doses of Adderall transformed his career: "I'm not talking about being able to work longer hours without sleep (although that helps)," the posting said. "I'm talking about being able to take on twice the responsibility, work twice as fast, write more effectively, manage better, be more attentive, devise better and more creative strategies."

18   Dr. Anjan Chatterjee, an associate professor of neurology at the University of Pennsylvania who foresaw this debate in a 2004 paper, argues that the history of cosmetic surgery—scorned initially as vain and unnatural but now mainstream as a form of self-improvement—is a guide to predicting the trajectory of cosmetic neurology, as he calls it.

19   "We worship at the altar of progress, and to the demigod of choice," Dr. Chatterjee said. "Both are very strong undercurrents in the culture and the way this is likely to be framed is: 'Look, we want smart people to be as productive as possible to make everybody's lives better. We want people performing at the max, and if that means using these medicines, then great, then we should be free to choose what we want as long as we're not harming someone.' I'm not taking that position, but we have this winner-take-all culture and that is the way it is likely to go."

20   People already use legal performance enhancers, he said, from high-octane cafe Americanos to the beta-blockers taken by musicians to ease stage fright, to antidepressants to improve mood. "So the question with all of these things is, Is this enhancement, or a matter of removing the cloud over our better selves?" he said.

21   The public backlash against brain-enhancement, if it comes, may hit home only after the practice becomes mainstream, Dr. Chatterjee suggested. "You can imagine a scenario in the future, when you're applying for a job, and the employer says, 'Sure, you've got the talent for this, but we require you to take Adderall.' Now, maybe you do start to care about the ethical implications."

QUESTIONS FOR DISCUSSION

1. "The desire for cognitive enhancement is very strong, maybe stronger than for beauty, or athletic ability," Carey cites Barbara Sahakian as saying. Does this statement seem true to you? If so, what are its implications?

2. Reread paragraph 17 carefully, noting the claims of the person who posted to *The Chronicle of Higher Education*'s Web site. He believes that Adderall has "transformed his career," which makes the scenario discussed in the last paragraph not as unrealistic as it may seem. What are the ethical implications of being *required* to take performance-enhancing drugs, say, to be an air traffic controller?

FOR DISCUSSION AND MEDIATION

The strength of Carey's article is that he reports the opposing positions on performance-enhancing drugs so well. Reread the article, paying special attention to the views of Francis Fukuyama, Nora Volkow, Martha Farah, and Anjan Chatterjee. Then consider the proposition that, good or bad, greater use of such drugs will almost certainly happen.

Given that people will use them, what would be the best position for us to take regarding *responsible and ethical use?* That is, take and defend a position designed to draw the assent of the widest possible audience, one that will take into account both the viewpoints of those who oppose the use of performance-enhancers and those who see no objection to them.

Professor's Little Helper?

BARBARA SAHAKIAN AND NORA VOLKOW

Perhaps no one knows more about cognitive-enhancing drugs than Barbara Sahakian, a neourologist at Cambridge University, and Nora Volkow, head of the National Institute of Drug Abuse in the United States. They were interviewed by Lynn Neary on "Talk of the Nation," a National Public Radio program. We offer an abridged version of the transcript here.

1   I'm Lynn Neary in Washington.

2   If you could take a drug that might help you think better or perform more effectively and efficiently in school or at work, would you do it? And if so, do you think

that's the same as taking a drug that helps you hit more home runs? That's one of the questions being raised in the debate over brain-enhancement drugs. Once prescribed mainly for people with disabilities, brain-enhancement drugs are now being used more frequently by students who are about to take a tough test or by academics and other professionals who may be getting ready for a big presentation. Is it cheating or not?

3   Joining us now from the BBC studios in Cambridge, England, is Barbara Sahakian. She is professor of clinical neuropsychology at Cambridge University. Her commentary on brain-enhancement drugs, titled "Professor's Little Helper," appeared in the journal *Nature.*

4   **Neary:** What drugs are we talking about?

5   **Prof. Sahakian:** [Among others, she mentions Ritalin, for treating attention deficit hyperactivity disorder (ADHD) and Aricept, for treating Alzheimer's.]

6   **Neary:** So if you do not have any kind of disability or condition that requires the use of these drugs, how does it affect you?

7   **Prof. Sahakian:** We've done studies with Ritalin using Cambridge undergraduates who are already functioning very well. But even Cambridge undergraduates show improvements when they take Ritalin on the different tests that we've used, such as test of what we call working memory [recall of information for a short time]. We showed very good enhancement.

8   Another drug we used was modafinil, known as Provigil, for the treatment of excessive daytime sleepiness or narcolepsy. We've shown that normal, healthy volunteers do very well on that and increased their memory, planning ability and so forth.

9   **Neary:** So people now are using these drugs for what purpose? Give me an example of why somebody might take one of these drugs?

10   **Prof. Sahakian:** We gave a questionnaire to some colleagues I knew who were taking these drugs. They say they take them for jetlag. If they have to give a big lecture and feel that they've got jetlag, they take the drug. And they say it improves their ability to attend, their working memory, and word finding, which you can imagine for a lecturer is very important.

11   I have colleagues also who they say they took it because they want to just increase their mental energy and improve their thinking when they're trying to have a particularly productive day.

12   **Neary:** When we talk about performance-enhancing drugs in sports or in physical activity, we say that it makes you stronger. Can you say that these drugs make you smarter?

13   **Prof. Sahakian:** It depends what you mean by smarter. We're not talking I.Q., but it helps to keep your attention focused and to remember what you're trying to do in order to complete the task.

14   **Neary:** So this is where some of the ethical questions might come up. In this country, for instance, there's the SAT, the college entrance exams. If some

students are starting to take these drugs to help them perform better and others are not, then those who are taking them might have an unfair advantage.

15   **Prof. Sahakian:** Well, exactly, that's one of the ethical questions because it could result in coercing other people to take the drug because they fear they will be at a disadvantage if they don't. . . .

16   I don't know if you're aware but at some college campuses where they've done surveys about 16 to 20 percent of college students have used Ritalin for studying purposes and to enhance cognition for exams. So it's fairly widespread in the USA on college campuses.

17   **Neary:** We are talking about brain-enhancement drugs and debate over some of the ethical issues involved. If you'd like join our discussion, our number is 800-989-8255. We're going to take a call now from Conway, Arkansas.

18   **Caller:** I'm a student here in Conway, a senior, graduating this year. And I've taken these brain-enhancing drugs and it's difficult because it seems students that are really excelling are taking them and it's hard to compete in a busy academic environment without the drugs. There's so many people overloading themselves and using them to improve their performance.

19   **Neary:** So you started doing it because you felt other kids were doing it to keep up?

20   **Caller:** I did it the first time because I was behind and I had too much work to do and it was an easy way out. You just see how many people do it, especially during finals and keeping them awake to write papers.

21   **Neary:** Can you explain what the effect is, exactly?

22   **Caller:** It makes it easier to stay up for long amounts of time and focus on a single task without getting distracted, which is really easy to do when you're surrounded by thousands of people.

23   **Neary:** I'm assuming that there's an underground, a way of buying them on campus?

24   **Caller:** It's not really underground; it's pretty open. There's a lot of people that are prescribed Ritalin and Adderall, and it's not hard to find some of it.

25   **Neary:** Do you have any concerns about what you are able to accomplish with these drugs as compared to a friend who does not take them?

26   **Caller:** I don't necessarily feel that it gives me an advantage, just that I am able to do more work when I am stressed out. . . . I've stopped using the drugs. They give me the jitters, make me feel bad afterwards.

27   **Neary:** Thank you so much for calling in. Barbara Sahakian, can you comment?

28   **Prof. Sahakian:** I think what he said is very typical, so it was helpful that he was forthright about it. We had letters responding to my "Professor's Little Helper" commentary, and one of the letters came from Nora Volkow, head of the National Institute of Drug Abuse in America. Her point was that there is a large amount of these prescriptions that are being passed on or sold, a concern for the NIDA.

29   **Neary:** We have to take a break here and when we come back, Dr. Volkow is going to join us. . . .

30   It's so good to have you with us. Welcome to the program. Dr. Volkow, can you tell us how addictive these drugs are?

31   **Dr. Nora Volkow:** Stimulant medications have an effect that is similar to that of drugs of abuse. So yes, indeed, both amphetamine as well as Ritalin has the potential for producing dependency.

32   **Neary:** We heard from a caller already who was describing the effect. He said, sometimes you get jittery from these drugs. I wonder if you can expand on this.

33   **Dr. Volkow:** Well, responses to stimulant medication vary enormously and the effects of Ritalin are somewhat different from those of amphetamine. Amphetamine is more potent and its effects longer lasting. And because it's stimulating dopamine [a brain chemical] at much higher levels than normal, these can be perceived by individuals as making them restless or jittery, and these can be very, very uncomfortable.

34   Also, he mentioned that he didn't like how he felt after the drug's effects are over. It is described by some individuals as feeling like a crash. They lack energy and cannot concentrate.

35   When you use these medications outside the prescribed purposes, you produce adaptation changes in your brain that can be deleterious to performance.

36   Furthermore, not everybody improves when they take a stimulant medication. There are numerous stories that for some individuals and certain tasks, performance can actually deteriorate.

37   **Neary:** How would they deteriorate?

38   **Dr. Volkow:** For example, you can concentrate much better but that concentration can go to the extreme, make you perseverate on that particular task when you need to shift to another. . . .

39   **Neary:** Oh, I see, so you're focusing so intensely on one thing that you're not able to go back and forth and . . .

40   **Dr. Volkow:** Exactly.

41   **Neary:** You don't have the breadth that you need for true knowledge, really?

42   **Dr. Volkow:** Exactly.

43   **Neary:** Okay. Let's take a call. We're going to go to Joe. He is calling from Salt Lake City, Utah.

44   Joe, go ahead.

45   **Joe:** Thank you for letting me participate. I'm a physician and I've prescribed stimulants as well as Provigil. And I was with a group of other physicians discussing the ethical aspects of it, and two things came to us. One was whether or not the drugs were addictive; the other was whether or not there was competition, in the same way sports players take steroids to enhance their performance.

46   We thought it was ethically dubious for a student who otherwise doesn't have a diagnosis to be taking a stimulant to improve test scores. It made it unfair for them to be in the same arena as students who aren't taking stimulants. However, we thought it may not be as ethically dubious for individuals who are not directly competing, such as, say, the physician who is a resident, who has been on call late nights and he takes modafinil to be more alert the next day—or the long-haul truck driver who may be taking it to be more alert.

47   **Neary:** So you're saying that, as a doctor, you would prescribe this drug to someone who doesn't have a physical or mental condition where they need it but for their job?

48   **Joe:** Yes—well, yes and no. Modafinil is indicated for shift workers, and residents and truck drivers do shift work. I wouldn't necessarily prescribe it to someone whose livelihood or safety doesn't depend on it, but I actually haven't had anyone ask me to prescribe it to them.

49   **Neary:** Oh, I see. Okay. . . .

50   Barbara Sahakian, let me ask you to reply, to respond first.

51   **Prof. Sahakian:** I thought Joe's point was very interesting because it has been suggested that there may be conditions in which we want to encourage people to take cognitive-enhancing drugs—for instance, air-traffic controllers.

52   And he also pointed out that, thus far anyway, modafinil doesn't seem to have the same abuse potential, true also of some other drugs.

53   **Neary:** Dr. Volkow was turning thumbs down on a certain point when you were talking, so I just want to hear what she was responding to.

54   **Dr. Volkow:** I think that giving stimulant medication for people on night shifts is accepted medical practice. At the same time, there has been concern that some judgments have been inadequate when people have been sleep deprived—many misjudgments have been directly linked with the effects of amphetamine. Amphetamine can not only increase paranoid thinking but also cause sleep deprivation. So, again, not everybody responds well to stimulant medications.

55   I was smiling at modafinil because new studies done on humans show that, just like stimulants, it increases dopamine in the brain.

56   **Neary:** I was going to ask you, what's the difference between this and, say, what used to be called speed, which kids used to use before exams.

57   **Dr. Volkow:** Well, Dexedrine or speed is an amphetamine-like compound and with Adderall, you have Dexedrine plus amphetamine. That's a very effective medication for attention deficit disorder.

58   **Neary:** All right. We're going to take a call now. Carolyn. She's calling from San Jose, California.

59   **Carolyn:** Hi. Thank you for taking my call. Good program. I just am concerned at the widespread use of drugs for everything and nothing in our culture. And

you know, Dr. Joe a little while ago was talking about prescribing these drugs for the resident who didn't get a good night's sleep. Frankly, I'd rather be treated by a resident who did have a good night's sleep and not by one who's on drugs. And what's next? Are we going to drug test students?

60   **Neary:** All right, thanks so much for calling, Carolyn.

61   Barbara Sahakian or Dr. Volkow?

62   **Prof. Sahakian:** Well, I'd like to respond. First, to the very important point she made: our drug use is a reflection of our society and we should really be looking at the broader context of why healthy people would choose to use a drug in the first place. There are other options for coping with everyday stresses. We could improve the work–life balance or learn relaxation techniques. And the best way to enhance cognition is through education and other means. So we have other ways of tackling these problems.

63   Yes, we may have to drug-test, I suppose, if people are against using the drugs in competitive situations.

64   **Neary:** Dr. Volkow.

65   **Dr. Volkow:** There's another aspect that is important to consider which we haven't discussed. It has been shown that ADHD kids on stimulant medications perform better, but when tested off the stimulant, they actually perform worse than they did before initiation of the stimulant. They recover, but there's a period where the performance is actually worse than it was before. And this is likely to happen when people are taking stimulants outside the context of ADHD.

66   Furthermore, if a stimulant medication helps you pass an exam, what will be the outcome two or three months later? Will you be able to remember as well the information as you might have done with proper sleep and putting in the hours that it takes to learn without sleep deprivation? If you're doing it just to pass an exam—well, that's one issue—but if you're doing it to build up a knowledge base that will allow you to succeed—well, we do not have any information about these medications on that score.

QUESTIONS FOR DISCUSSION

1. Is there any difference between taking a cognitive-enhancing drug to do better on the SAT and taking steroids to hit more home runs? Do both amount to cheating?

2. The college student identified as Caller, who called in from Conway, Arkansas, mentions that his peers are "overloading themselves." Would you say that you or some of your friends are doing too much, either as a matter of choice or necessity? Is that the underlying reason why drugs like Ritalin and Provigil appeal so much?

3. Nora Volkow supplies a number of reasons not to use the drugs. What are they? Which do you find most persuasive?

FOR DISCUSSION AND INQUIRY

"Our drug use is a reflection of our society," Barbara Sahakian correctly says, "and we should be looking at the broader context of why healthy people would choose to use a drug in the first place." Explore this statement in class, drawing on all the selections in this chapter so far.

Then write an exploratory essay offering your own tentative explanation for why healthy people resort so often to over-the-counter and prescription drugs. What needs to change for this kind of drug abuse to diminish? Draw on your own experience or that of people you know.

Choosing Our Genes

GREGORY STOCK

> Gregory Stock is director of the Program on Medicine, Technology, and Society at UCLA and author of the best-seller *Redesigning Humans*. In his book and the following article from *The Futurist,* he offers a detailed discussion of what is likely to happen soon in applying genetics to enhance human beings.

1 Technologies giving us control over our genetic destiny will be developed, whether they are banned or not. But clumsy regulatory efforts could greatly impede our progress toward improving the future health and well-being of our descendants.

2 What is causing all the fuss are technologies that will give parents the ability to make conscious choices about the genetics and traits of their children. For the foreseeable future, genetically altering adults is not in the cards, other than for treating a handful of specific diseases like cystic fibrosis. Changing the genes of an adult is far too daunting, and there are simpler, safer, and more effective ways of intervening to restore or enhance adult function.

3 Germinal choice technology refers to a whole realm of technologies by which parents influence the genetic constitutions of their children at the time of their conception. The simplest such intervention would be to correct genes. It is not a particularly radical departure, since it would have exactly the same effect as could be accomplished by screening multiple embryos and picking one with the desired genes. In fact, such embryo screening is being done now in preimplantation genetic diagnosis. Such technology has been in use for more than a decade, but what can be tested for is going to become increasingly sophisticated in the next 5 to 10 years. And as these technologies mature, the kinds of decisions that parents can make will become much more complex.

4 Farther into the future will be germline interventions—alterations to the egg, sperm, or more likely the first cell of an embryo. These procedures are being done already in animal systems, but using approaches that don't have the safety or reliability that would be required in human beings. . . .

GOALS OF GERMINAL CHOICE

5 The prevention of disease will likely be the initial goal of germinal choice. And the possibilities may soon move well beyond the correction of aberrant genes. Recent

studies suggest, for example, that children who have Down syndrome have close to a 90% reduction in the incidence of many cancers. It is possible that trisomy 21—i.e., having a third copy of chromosome 21, with increased gene expression levels that lead to the retardation and other symptoms of Down syndrome—may be protective against cancer. What if we could identify which of the genes on that chromosome are responsible for this protection from cancer? Geneticists might take a set of those genes and place them on an artificial chromosome, then add it to an embryo to reduce the incidence of cancer to the levels seen with Down syndrome, but without all the problems brought by the duplication of the other genes on chromosome 21. Many other similar possibilities will no doubt emerge, and some will almost certainly prove beneficial.

6   The use of artificial chromosomes might work quite well, particularly because the chromosomes themselves could be tested within the laboratory environment before any human use. They could be tested on animals, validated, and used in humans in essentially the same state they were tested in. Today, each gene therapy is done anew, so it is impossible to gain that kind of reliability. . . .

7   All sorts of ideas will occur to future gene therapists, who will then test them out to see if they are possible. If they are, then we will not forgo them. Reducing the incidence of cancer and heart disease, for example, or retarding aging are health enhancements that will be seen as very, very desirable.

GENETICALLY EXTENDING LIFESPANS

8   Antiaging will be an especially significant area of research because such interventions seem so plausible and are so strongly desired by large numbers of people. If it turns out that there are interventions that could—through our unraveling of the underlying process of aging—allow us to develop pharmaceutical and other interventions that are effective in adults, then that is what everybody would want. . . .

9   But embryo engineering will likely be easier and more effective than gene therapy in an adult. This is because genes placed in an embryo are copied into every single cell in the body and could be given tissue-specific control elements. So there may well be interventions to an embryo that are infeasible in an adult. And in this case, parents will likely look at conception as their one chance to give their child significant health advantages—a chance that will never again be available.

10   A "cure for aging" might be greatly accelerated by an infusion of funds into research on the biology of aging. Right now, the area is rather underfunded. Much more money is being spent to find treatments for diseases of aging than to understand the underlying process that may be responsible for a wide variety of age-related diseases, such as cancer, heart disease, Alzheimer's, arthritis, and diabetes. . . .

11   Antiaging—offering one's children longer lifespans—will probably be a key goal of germline interventions, but not the only one. To do what is best for our children is a very human response. In fact, international polls have shown that in every country polled there is at least a significant minority who are interested in enhancing the physical or mental well-being of their children. They are thinking not of simple therapy to avoid particular diseases, but interventions aimed at actually improving (at least in their eyes) a child's beauty, intelligence, strength, altruism, and other qualities.

AN UNWELCOME CHOICE?

12 Society may not welcome some parents' choices. Sex selection is legal in the United States, but illegal in Britain and a number of other countries. And quite a few people think the procedure should be illegal in the United States as well, despite the fact that in the West, where no serious gender imbalances arise, it is hard to see who is injured by such choices. Another immediate decision will be whether parents screen for broad numbers of genetic diseases, some of which may not be terribly serious. And soon, parents will likely be able to make choices about the height or IQ of their children, or other aspects of temperament and personality—predispositions and vulnerabilities that may soon be rather obvious in each of our genetic readouts.

13 The first wave of possibilities from germinal choice technology will be in genetic testing and screening, choosing one embryo instead of another. Initially, it will be very difficult for a lot of people to accept this, but it will be almost impossible to regulate, since any such embryo could have arrived completely naturally. These choices may prove agonizing, but they won't be dangerous, and I suspect they will bring us more benefits than problems.

14 Some people worry about a loss of diversity, but I think a more wrenching issue may be parents who decide to specifically select an embryo that would result in a child with a serious health condition. Should parents be allowed to make such choices?

15 In the deaf community, for instance, there is a whole movement that is very opposed to the use of cochlear implants, because it hurts deaf culture and treats deafness like a disability. This is exactly the way most hearing people view it. And there are deaf parents who say that they would use germinal choice technology to ensure that their children were deaf. That is not to say they would take an embryo and damage it, but they would select an embryo that would develop into a deaf child.

16 That becomes a real issue for society when, for example, such health problems have medical costs that society must bear. If we feel that parents do have the right to make such choices and that there is no reason to value the birth of a healthy individual any more than someone with serious health challenges, then we won't regulate such choices. But if we decide there is a problem, and really want to come to grips with it, we may find it very challenging.

FRIGHTENING OURSELVES TO DEATH

17 Shortly after reports were heard of the first pregnancy resulting from a human cloning program (reports that most scientists believe are a total fabrication), U.S. President George W. Bush voiced his support for a Senate bill that would outlaw all forms of human cloning, including biomedical research aimed at creating embryonic stem cells that would not be rejected when transplanted, so-called therapeutic cloning.

18 I believe such a ban is premature, futile, extremely misguided, and just plain wrong. It would not significantly delay the arrival of reproductive cloning, which in my view is almost certain to occur within this decade somewhere in the world. It would inject politics, religion, and philosophy into the workings of basic research and inquiry, which would be a dangerous precedent. It would legislate greater concern for a microscopic dot of cells than for real people with real diseases and real suffering. And it would threaten embryo researchers with criminal penalties so extreme (10 years in

prison) that they are almost unbelievable in the United States, a country where women during their first trimester have the right to an abortion for any reason whatsoever.

19   U.S. restraints on embryo research have already had an impact on the development of biomedical technologies directed toward regenerative medicine. Those restraints have slowed progress in this realm in the United States, which has the most powerful biomedical research effort in the world. Such research has now moved to Britain and other countries, such as Singapore, which is funding a huge program to explore embryonic stem cells. But such delays are very unfortunate because of the might-have-beens that still are not. For most people, a delay of a decade or two is not a big problem, but this is not so for people like actor Michael J. Fox and others who are undergoing progressive decline from serious diseases like Parkinson's or Alzheimer's. . . .

20   No matter how much it disturbs us, human germinal choice is inevitable. Embryo selection is already here, cloning is on the way, and even direct germline engineering in humans will arrive. Such technology is inevitable because many people see it as beneficial, because it will be feasible in thousands of labs all over the world, and, most importantly, because it will be a mere spin-off of mainstream biomedical research to decipher our biology. . . .

A DEMOCRATIZING TECHNOLOGY?

21   The effort to block these new reproductive technologies renders them extremely divisive socially, because it will guarantee that they are only available to the wealthy who are able to circumvent any kinds of restrictions rather easily, either by traveling to other locations or by simply paying money to get black-market services.

22   At their core, germinal choice technologies—if handled properly—could be very democratizing, because the kinds of interventions that will be available initially are going to compensate for deficits. It will be much easier to lift someone with an IQ of 70 up to 100 (the population average) than to raise someone's IQ from 150 (the top fraction of a percent of the population) up to 160. And the same will be true in selecting the predispositions of future children. . . .

23   The genetic lottery can be very, very cruel. Ask anybody who is very slow or has a genetic disease of one sort or another. They don't believe in some abstract principle of how wonderful the genetic lottery is. They would like to be healthier or have more talent in one way or another. The broad availability of these technologies would thus level the playing field in many ways, because it would give opportunities to those who otherwise would be genetically disadvantaged.

24   Another point is that these technologies, as do any technologies, evolve rather rapidly. The differences will not so much be between the wealthy and the poor in one generation (although obviously there will be more things available to those who have more resources), but between one generation and the next. Today, even a Bill Gates could not obtain the genetic enhancements or services for his child that will seem primitive compared with what any middle-class person is going to have access to in 25 years. . . .

LOSING OUR HUMANITY—OR CONTROLLING IT?

25   Another misplaced fear is that, by tampering with our biology, we risk losing our humanity. But does "humanity" have to do with very narrow aspects of our biology, or

does it have to do with the whole process of engaging the world and with our interactions with one another? For instance, if our lifespan were to double, would that make us "not human" in some sense? It would certainly change the trajectory of our lives, the way we interact with one another, our institutions, our sense of family, and our attitudes about education. But we would still be human, and I daresay we would soon adjust to these changes and wonder how we could ever have lived without them. . . .

26   Humans now are just in the very early stages of their evolution—early adolescence at most. A thousand years from now, when future humans look back at this era, they're going to see it as a primitive, difficult, and challenging time. They will also see it as an extraordinary, rather glorious moment when we laid down the foundations of their lives. It is hard to imagine what human life will be like even a hundred years from now, but I suspect that the reworking of our own biology will figure heavily in our future.

QUESTIONS FOR DISCUSSION

1. According to Stock, why is genetic alteration of adults "not in the cards" for the most part?

2. "Correcting genes" in embryos would not be, Stock claims, "a particularly radical departure" from current practices used in in vitro fertilization. Why does he say this? How does it differ from what he calls "preimplantation genetic diagnosis"?

3. Stock points to an interesting "side effect" of Down syndrome—that children afflicted by it also "have close to a 90% reduction in the incidence of many cancers" (paragraph 5). How does he propose that such knowledge could be used to reduce cancer in the general population?

4. "Society may not welcome some parents' choices," Stock admits. He points out that some deaf parents will want deaf children as an example. What other choices might society find troubling?

5. Stock argues that genetic manipulation of human embryos could be a democratizing technology. What does he offer to support his view?

6. How does Stock view the question of what makes human beings human? Do you agree that gene manipulation will not fundamentally change what it means to be human?

FOR RESEARCH AND DISCUSSION

"The genetic lottery can be very, very cruel," Stock observes, and to verify that all you need to do is visit the cancer ward at a children's hospital or encounter an example or two of other congenital diseases. It is difficult to extol natural processes when about 2% of all live births result in genetically impaired children.

Compile a list of diseases linked to genetic defects. Individually or in groups, select a disease, then find out about symptoms and current, nongenetic treatment, including what it costs. Give a short, informative presentation about each disease.

Then discuss this question in class: Can there be any reasonable objection to genetic research designed to prevent such diseases either through screening embryos or through altering germ cells that produce or can produce genetic illnesses?

FOR CONVINCING

Stock points to the area of greatest controversy where applications of genetic knowledge are concerned—enhancing human traits a culture considers desirable. It is one thing to cure disease, the common argument goes, quite another to extend lifetimes or raise IQs or design children to be more attractive or less susceptible to depression.

Suppose that we have the knowledge and the means to select the traits our children will have. Suppose also that it is affordable and that conception would be the result of sexual intercourse only—no petri dishes and artificial means of insemination. In a short essay, make a case for using or not using that technology.

Genetically Modified Athletes

JOHN NAISH

The following news story, published in the London *Daily Mail* on July 31, 2012, calls our attention to a fundamental issue about the integrity of sport competitions. Is there any way to prevent cheating, especially as methods for doing so become more and more sophisticated?

The controversy over Chinese swimmer Ye Shiwen's astonishing gold medal performance is no longer confined to just the suspicions of drug abuse, which she emphatically denies. It has raised concerns about another worrying—and infinitely more sinister—threat to the world of honest competition: the genetic enhancement of athletes.

1 John Leonard, the highly respected American director of the World Swimming Coaches Association, described the 16-year-old's world-record-breaking performance as "suspicious," "disturbing" and "unbelievable. . . . Any time someone has looked like superwoman in the history of our sport they have later been found guilty of doping," he added. He went on to say that the authorities who tested Ye Shewin for drug abuse should also check to see "if there is something unusual going on in terms of genetic manipulation."

2 A Chinese anti-doping official, Jiang Zhixue, described Leonard's claims as completely unreasonable. The astonishing suggestion seems to be that London 2012 may be the first Olympics in which competitors are attempting to cheat by altering their genes to build muscle and sinew, and boost their blood's oxygen-carrying powers.

3 Laboratory experiments have already shown that the science can work. In 2005, Ronald Evans, a hormone expert working at the Salk Institute of Biological Studies in La Jolla, California, showed how genetic modification can increase the athletic power of mice. Evans produced a group of genetically modified mice with an increased amount of slow-twitch muscle fiber. This type of fiber is associated with strong cardiovascular muscles and boosts an athlete's endurance. Evans's mice could run for an hour longer than normal mice, were resistant to weight gain no matter what they were fed on, and remained at peak fitness even when they took no exercise. A form of genetic modification is already being tested in medicine, in the form of gene therapy for diseases such as cystic fibrosis.

4 Most gene modification techniques involve placing genetically modified DNA inside a virus and injecting it into the human body. The virus then enters human cells, and its modified DNA attaches itself to the human DNA inside those cells.

5 Gene therapy is at a very early stage in development and has become possible as a result of our discovery in 2003 of how to map the human genome. This meant we could identify specific genes that cause disease—cystic fibrosis is caused by one faulty gene, for example, and the idea is that gene therapy can replace the faulty gene with one that works. In the same way, it may well be possible for athletes to use a virus to introduce a gene that spurs the production of oxygen-carrying red blood cells or muscle-building hormones. And the heightened blood-cell counts or hormone levels might simply appear to the doping agencies to be the product of an extraordinary athlete's body.

6 Tests are being developed to detect this kind of manipulation, but at the moment, the World Anti-Doping Agency does not have one. Anna Baoutina, a senior research scientist at the National Measurement Institute in Sydney, told the Tackling Doping in Sport conference in London earlier this year that no gene test was in place for the 2012 Olympics. "The major advantage of gene doping is that it is very difficult to detect compared to drug doping. The doping gene is very similar to natural cells found in the body," she told journalists. "We are developing methods to fight it."

7 Olympics leaders say, however, that they are confident they will soon be able to detect the first generations of genetically super-powered cheats. For example, Patrick Schamasch, medical director of the International Olympic Committee (IOC), has said that the viruses used to smuggle genes into the body leave behind traces which can

be detected. But this will probably not be the case for long, he warned: "I'm certain viruses will be invented that won't leave traces."

8   Olympics officials are banking on the success of their newly introduced "biological passport." This keeps track of the athlete's overall physiological profile, and triggers alarm if anything about it changes in a suspicious manner—for example if everyday hormone levels take an unusual leap.

9   Many scientists, though, question the authorities' confidence in their ability to catch dopers and point out that cheats are already using biological methods to avoid detection. In particular they are concerned about the lack of a test for an increasingly popular form of cheating—a blood transfusion where athletes store pints of their own blood and re-inject them later, before a race, for example. This boosts the number of oxygen-carrying red cells in the blood, improving power and stamina. But it is hard to detect such transfusions, because they involve the athlete's own blood, so don't contain traces of any foreign body. The WADA has funded research into developing a test for the transfusions, but it is still not ready.

10   Professor Dominic Wells, a gene therapy researcher who has studied the possibility of modifying athletes, believes we are still some way off being able to use genes to significantly change athletes' performance. "There is a real possibility, however, that this will work for athletes in the future because we have some of the best brains in medicine working on it," he says.

11   If genetic manipulation does become common, the Olympic doping authorities at least have time on their side. New cheating methods will always remain undetected until the authorities develop scientific methods of spotting them. Olympic chiefs have therefore decided to keep medal-winners' blood samples for eight years, so they can subject them to new tests when they are developed.

12   Last week, for example, Arne Ljungqvist, the anti-doping chief of the International Olympic Committee, disclosed that about 100 samples from the Athens Games in 2004 had been retested—and six athletes who competed have been identified as possible drug cheats. "The longer you wait the better, if you want to catch someone," he said. There is, however, a real penalty to pay for this. Whenever we cheer a new champion on the podium, we must always wonder whether their shiny medal will be taken back in ignominy years down the line. The idea of retrospective testing tarnishes Olympic achievement. But if that is the price we have to pay to keep the specter of genetically-modified, unbeatable Franken-athletes at bay, then sadly, it does seem to be worth paying.

QUESTIONS FOR DISCUSSION

1. What is the difference between so-called doping—injecting steroids, for example—and the genetic modification discussed in this article? Is there any reason to object to the second more than the first, or vice versa?

2. The basic problem with cheating in sports is that the stakes can be so high: national prestige, the competitor's desire for fame, and the fortune that often comes with it. Given the high stakes, is it realistic to think any measures will significantly reduce cheating?

3. Just as we breed farm animals to develop certain desired traits, so we can breed humans to increase the likelihood of high athletic prowess. To some extent this occurs "naturally," when successful athletes marry and have children. Can you see any reason to object to artificial ways of doing this, such as the use of test-tube fertilization and surrogate mothers?

FOR DISCUSSION AND PERSUASION

It is not hard to imagine why athletes are tempted to cheat. The stakes are high, such as the multi-million dollar contracts so common in professional sports, the competition is stiff, and the likelihood of getting caught is, in some cases, slim, with relatively minimal negative consequences as compared to the immediate rewards. Besides that, athletes may cheat because they suspect others are and they don't want to be at a disadvantage—perhaps some cheaters genuinely believe that they are only keeping the playing field level. What, then, is the root of the cheating problem, in your view? Given how you see it, can anything be done to solve the problem?

Write an essay stating your point of view in response to these two key questions and defending any action or actions you think ought to be taken.

A Shot in the Rear: Why Are We Really against Steroids?

ARTHUR L. CAPLAN

Professor Caplan, a member of the Science Progress advisory board, holds a distinguished chair in Bioethics at the University of Pennsylvania. The following article reviews and analyzes arguments about performance-enhancing drugs in a way that helps us think more clearly and deeply about their use in sports and elsewhere in contemporary society.

1   Professional and amateur sports are awash in steroids and have been for many years. It seems self-evident that this is a problem. The amount of media and political attention paid to steroids and other pharmacologic forms of enhancement in sports might even suggest that it is one of the greatest moral problems the world faces.

2   Admittedly, putting the challenge of dealing with steroids on the same moral plane as battling poverty is a bit of a stretch. Still, a lot of people all over the world are clamoring for those in charge to get steroids out of sports. That is what makes the recent publication of a number of articles and books challenging the idea that performance enhancement is morally wrong so interesting. While it may seem obvious that athletes using steroids to build strength or gain endurance is wrong, could those intuitions be mistaken?

3   In one sense they cannot. Steroids are dangerous and there is a real need to protect children who admire athletes from taking serious risks with their health in imitating what their idols do. But put the safety issue aside. Someday we may get drugs that do what steroids do without any real risk of harm to the user. Would we still want them banned? John Harris, a British bioethicist, is a useful example

of someone who is not at all sure that a bit of the "juice" is such a bad thing in athletic competition. In his *Enhancing Evolution* (2007), he argues that performance enhancement is not only ethically acceptable, but that sometimes it may be morally obligatory.

4   Harris sees a legitimate role for the use of drugs and genetic engineering to improve performance in sport. But sports are not his main target. He sees a future in which parents happily and willingly use genetic and reproductive technologies to design their children with more capacities and abilities than they otherwise would have had. His main argument in the book is that there are no convincing arguments against performance enhancement and plenty that support it.

5   Can Harris's positive view of enhancement be used to as an antidote to the wave of anti-steroid mania tearing through the sports and editorial pages? In Harris's sports world, the genetically engineered, chemically enhanced, and optimally trained ought to serve as our heroes. They will give us performances to remember. And that is the point of sport. Or is it?

6   Harris's eloquent defense of performance enhancement as entirely ethical stands in stark contrast to the efforts of sports authorities and prosecutors all over the world to vigorously chase down and defrock of honors athletes who have used steroids and other performance enhancing substances. Are the prosecutions really persecutions? Should performance enhancement simply be accepted as a part of sport? Are those who want seconds shaved off of the time it takes to run a mile or who want to see baseball sluggers smash seventy or more home runs in a single season really all that interested in whether these records are achieved by those who use no drugs in achieving these record performances? The international brouhaha over drug use to improve performance gives some evidence that the road to better living through biochemical engineering may be laced with more ethical potholes than are dreamt of in Harris's philosophy.

7   Consider first just a tiny bit of the mess that efforts at drug-based performance enhancement have produced in contemporary sports. The world of cycling is just about kaput as a result of drug allegations and revelations. Marion Jones, the dazzling Olympic sprinter who won three gold medals and two bronzes at the games in Sydney, Australia, has confessed in a U.S. Federal courtroom to using steroids and jail awaits. Her tearful admission came after years of angry denials that she had ever gone near performance enhancing drugs.

8   Baseball's all-time home run hitter, Barry Bonds, faces federal charges for lying about steroid use as part of a larger investigation of an illegal steroids lab, the BALCO company of Burlingame, California. The BALCO probe has turned up the names of many high-profile professional athletes from around the world, as BALCO steroids customers include baseball players, track and field stars, football players, cyclists, and boxers. . . . Bonds realizes that baseball fans would dismiss his achievements as the product of a chemically enhanced body were he to admit what is obvious from changes in his body over the years—that he used steroids and other performance enhancing drugs.

9   Roger Clemens, perhaps the preeminent pitcher in the history of baseball, a seven-time Cy Young Award winner—a prize given each year to the best pitcher in

baseball—spent a dreary four hours in front of the House Oversight Committee jousting with its chair, Henry Waxman. While there he failed to persuade anyone except a few star-struck, fawning conservative representatives that he had not gotten steroid injections from his personal trainer when he played for the New York Yankees.

10   After all didn't Jones, Bonds, Clemens, and others give us remarkable and memorable performances?

11   Clemens's best friends on the team, Andy Pettitte and Chuck Knoblauch, have admitted using. So did Clemens's wife! She said she had the trainer shoot her up in preparing for a swimsuit photo-shoot. These admissions make it a feat of epistemological legerdemain to believe that Roger knew what those closest to him were doing but that he did not know he was getting steroids injected into his rump when his trainer inserted a needle there.

12   An additional problem for crediting Clemens's denials that he ever used steroids is that his own career performance statistics contradict him. He was at his most productive late in his career at a time in his life when nearly every other pitcher has begun to lose their speed and stamina. Admitting a flow of steroids through his body would make not only a mockery of his denials but also of the virtuous character he seeks to claim for himself in explaining how he could improve his abilities at a time when nearly every other pitcher in the history of baseball was seeing theirs wane.

13   The list of steroid scandals goes on and on. But, as these examples make clear, using steroids and other drugs to improve athletic performance grates on the perceptions of fans, the media, sports management and many politicians. But why exactly is that so?

14   One of the most interesting critics of pharmacologic enhancement in sport is Harvard political scientist Michael Sandel. Sandel has argued in a series of articles and a book, *The Case against Perfection* (2007), that the causal role of human agency plays a key role in substantiating our admiration of athletic performance. In commenting on drug use in baseball he observes that "as the role of (drug) enhancement increases, our admiration for the new achievement fades—or, rather, our admiration for the achievement shifts from the player to his pharmacist." Something like this explanation is at the heart of sports's current struggle with steroids. Sandel is clearly on to something when he argues that chemically produced performance enhancement undermines our willingness to esteem the performance of the winners of the Tour de France, Roger Clemens, Barry Bonds, or Marion Jones.

15   This is where Harris weighs in. He does not see much merit in Sandel's caution that chemistry corrodes admiration for athletic effort. He argues that great efforts are not always required to achieve great performance. Moreover, in sport an athlete still has to train in order to perform well even when using steroids. Using performance enhancing drugs is not a substitute for effort. Rather, Harris argues, the drugs enhance the results of the effort.

16   Well, Harris is right that you don't need to make a great effort to accomplish great things. Every once in a while someone wins the lottery or finds an old heirloom

worth a lot of money in the attic and no one seems to mind that they have advanced themselves through luck, not exertion. But that is not true in sport. A lucky bounce or a gust of wind can determine the outcome, but athletes get praise for performance linked to effort, not luck. The whole point of sport is to try and reward effort even if luck plays a crucial role in the outcome. Harris's point that small efforts can produce big rewards does not moot the point that big efforts that produce big rewards get the praise, not just the notice. Outcomes don't define sport—the process leading to outcomes does.

17   And it is true, as Harris says, that no one gets to be a great athlete simply by taking steroids or growth hormone. You get an edge or an advantage over others who are just as naturally gifted and train just as hard as you do. What Harris misses though, is that some performances are explicitly associated, by the nature of the rules governing the activity, with great effort—admittedly as a matter of history or culture—but nonetheless, it is the effort that is valued. If someone takes a pill and lifts a lot of weight it may be amazing. But it is only a weightlifter's willingness both to train and to show extraordinary effort that makes weightlifting an athletic achievement as opposed to an exhibition.

18   Sport is only sport if it is measuring human abilities, as varied as those may be. Sport also links the results achieved to training, will, and effort. Outcomes don't define sport—the process leading to outcomes does. That is why short circuiting your way to success by pills or hormones as Jones, Bonds, and Clemens did undercuts their performance since both process and outcome are required in assessing performance.

19   "Professional" wrestling has many fans in North America, Mexico, Asia, and Europe. Its athletes can do impressive feats involving agility and strength. They are very strong certainly due to steroids. But no one seriously thinks that pro wrestling is a sport—despite having all the external accoutrements. It is a steroid-infused exhibition. Harris might say "redefine the sport—there is nothing intrinsically sacrosanct about effort leading to performance." Except that there is. The definition of sport is human effort based on talent and training leading to performance. This is an activity that need not be preserved but if it is to be preserved—and most baseball, track and cycling fans have an exquisite sensitivity to history—then drugs, huge shifts in equipment, and competing in venues that distort the value of effort, e.g., very high altitudes, won't work.

20   So at least in sports, if not on Wall Street or in the classroom, it is how the performance is achieved and not just the performance that is valued. That link between human effort and agency and output may be contingent. But it is surely definitive of what sport is.

21   Sandel has one more volley to offer in defense of steroid-free sports. He argues that it is the very "giftedness" of talent that make drugs unwelcome. We appreciate that some are borne inclined to be great sprinters and others great pitchers, and drugs—not to mention genetic engineering—ruin all that.

22   I am not sure about this and neither is Harris. The idea that we value a performance because we admire the random luck of the lottery of life that gives some of us genes for singing, others for strength and still others for superb vision seems

implausible. Why is randomness to be admired? Looking for value in the natural distribution of talents and skills is like looking for the source of free will and autonomy in the random nature of evolution or the Heisenberg uncertainty principle. Estimable value does not lurk in random luck. We can accept that luck can bring us fortune and enjoy it, but it is hard to see what role the luck of the draw in genetics has in esteeming sports performances.

23   The battle over performance enhancement is often fought out as if one size fits all—what makes performance enhancement acceptable in one domain, sports, will make it acceptable in all aspects of life. What the fight between Harris and Sandel reveals is that this is not so. There are reasons to believe that steroids don't belong in sports, even putting safety concerns aside. But this does not mean that performance-enhancing drugs have no appropriate role in any areas of life and achievement. The decision about what role pharmacology and genetics ought to play depends on whether you are trying to travel to another planet, solve a difficult math problem, learn a new language, or hit a home run.

This article was first published by *Science Progress* (online), www.scienceprogress.org

QUESTIONS FOR DISCUSSION

1. According to Caplan, the bioethicist John Harris argues that "remarkable and memorable" achievements are all that really matter in sports. Do you think this is true for most sports fans? Would they prefer that the battle over doping be stopped, so that they can just enjoy watching their favorite sports heroes perform?

2. "Why is randomness to be admired?" Caplan asks. That is, he believes that good luck in the genes you happen to have has nothing to do with admiring athletic achievement, yet we admire Einstein's achievements in physics so much that we have preserved his brain and studied it carefully. *Do* we in fact admire randomness in athletic achievement? Do we admire it in achievement in other human endeavors?

3. Caplan attempts to distinguish pro wrestling from what he considers genuine sports (paragraph 19). Yet the players call major league baseball "the show," and if the Super Bowl is not an exhibition, what is it? Is there a *significant* distinction between pro wrestling and pro baseball or football? If so, how would you distinguish between them?

FOR RESEARCH, DISCUSSION, AND CONVINCING

Caplan concludes his argument as follows:

There are reasons to believe that steroids don't belong in sports, even putting safety concerns aside. But this does not mean that performance-enhancing drugs have no appropriate role in any areas of life and achievement. The decision about what role pharmacology and genetics ought to play depends on whether you are trying to travel to another planet, solve a difficult math problem, learn a new language, or hit a home run.

Read or reread the articles by Carey, Sahakian and Volkow, and Stock in this chapter. Think about the relevance of what they say to Caplan's belief that performance-enhancing drugs (PEDs) may be acceptable in some contexts but not in others.

Write an essay defending or attacking Caplan's position that we should not approach PEDs with a one-size-fits-all attitude.

Lance Armstrong and the Cult of Positive Thinking

ED SMITH

Enhancement is not always a matter of taking something or submitting to gene therapy. For the most part, in fact, self-improvement hinges more on changing one's attitudes than on changing one's body chemistry. The following article from *New Statesman* (September 10, 2012) brings this home in the context of a fallen hero, Lance Armstrong, who pushed the cult of positive thinking so common in American culture.

1   He might be disgraced as a sportsman but his advocacy of relentless willpower has brought hope to millions of cancer sufferers. That is the conventional view of Lance Armstrong. Sadly, the doping case against Armstrong is the least of it. Applied to sport, Armstrong's deification of the power of positive thinking is mere fantasy. When it is applied to the question of life and death it moves into far more dangerous territory.

2   Armstrong built a brand in answer to the question, "What made the difference, Lance?" He nourished a narrative that apparently began as a lie and hardened into full-scale fantasy. Not talent (though he possessed plenty of that). Not drugs (though his teammates now say he was a "pioneer of doping"). No, the difference in Armstrong's view was his mental ability to eliminate human frailty. Armstrong recovered from testicular cancer; he then won seven yellow jerseys in the Tour de France. Those two processes became blurred in his mind—so much so that when people accused him of doping in cycling he would imply they were belittling those who had recovered from cancer.

FANATICAL HATRED

3   Does Armstrong still believe he is a genuine champion, unfairly wronged? Many people accused of doping allow themselves some wriggle room, even before they are caught. Armstrong responded to his accusers with fanatical hatred. They were cynics trying to cheat the world of genuine miracles that he, Armstrong, had made real.

4   Is lying the appropriate word for such a fantasist? Or do fantasists lose possession of those facts that don't fit the version of events on which their self-image relies? Armstrong's racing was informed by a simple mantra: I believe, therefore I will win.

Armstrong's doping denials were similarly straightforward: I believe, therefore it is true. Both sport and life had been reduced to a narrative in which willpower could defy any odds.

5   Armstrong told us to "believe in miracles." But if you follow his own logic, believing in miracles doesn't quite capture it. After all, he believed he had the power to make miracles, not just to benefit from them. He was the agent, not just the recipient. There is a term for those who can will miraculous events: gods. That is how Armstrong viewed himself. The rules that govern normal human beings no longer applied to him. There are echoes of Tiger Woods, who has long regarded his own humanity as something that needs to be overcome rather than embraced. Feelings, emotions, vulnerabilities: they are problems that need to be ironed out, like flaws in a faulty backswing.

6   But compare Armstrong's alleged deceit with the relatively trifling deception of Woods. Woods pretended to be a family man to make a few extra million dollars in easy sponsorship deals. He was exposed but his achievements on the golf course remain valid. With Armstrong, the deceit seems far deeper and sadder.

7   Armstrong found many willing allies in the promotion of his myth. The public lapped up the Lance legend with hysterical enthusiasm. He was the perfect hero for our times: an icon of willpower. In sport—and in life—self-belief is now routinely invoked as the explanation for almost everything. Commentators blithely assure us that it is "all about who wants it the most," as though sporting podiums are arranged exactly according to the amount of willpower that went into the struggle. Bronze: considerable self-belief; silver: still stronger self-belief; gold: self-belief on an epic scale.

8   This is pure nonsense. Inferring an exact and causal relationship between determination and success is a delusional fantasy of a society obsessed by just deserts. The true differentiating factors in elite sport are far more complex. What goes in to the making a champion? It is the subtle interplay of genes, talent, opportunity, hard work, willpower, pure luck and, in some cases, drugs. Willpower is just one factor.

9   Armstrong's oversimplification of success becomes even more problematic when it is applied to the question of life and death. The misleading phrase "the battle against cancer" has a lot to answer for. A friend of mine recently died of breast cancer. It would be hard to imagine a braver, stronger-willed woman. But the cancer "won," as cancers often do. That her death could be interpreted as a failure of willpower or positive thinking is a gross insult.

MODERN GODS

10   It is an insult that has been implied by the Armstrong message. The truth about "positive thinking" is much more nuanced. It is often a very good thing. It may even be necessary. But it is never sufficient. The Armstrong philosophy veers dangerously close to the self-help mantra of books such as *The Secret.* Its author, Rhonda Byrne, mused after the Java tsunami of 2006 that such events only ever afflicted people who were "on the same frequency as the event." *Smile or Die,* Barbara

11 Ehrenreich's exposé of the positive-thinking industry, includes a chilling story from a psychiatrist at a New York cancer clinic: "Patients come in with stories of being told by well-meaning friends, 'I've read all about this—if you got cancer, you must have wanted it.'"

12 Every age has its deities. The medieval mindset placed its blind faith in God. The Enlightenment anointed reason and science. Our own age has indulged a pseudoscientific cult of willpower: the deification of determination. At its best, it is a questionable creed. At its worst, it suggests that all losers must also be weaklings.

With luck, Armstrong's career—and the legend that surrounded it—will one day be seen as the high-water mark of the voodoo cult of willpower. Paradoxically, Armstrong's downfall may do more long-term good than his ascent. We now know that pure willpower was only one strand of Armstrong's career. That corrective applies to all success and, by extension, to all failure. Armstrong spent his career trying to prove that willpower is the whole story. Instead, he has demonstrated that life is always far more complicated than that.

QUESTIONS FOR DISCUSSION

1. We all get caught up in media obsession with news surrounding celebrities of all kinds, Lance Armstrong being only an especially famous example. This article offers a diagnosis of why Armstrong fell into disgrace. What is the diagnosis? Do you find it persuasive? Why or why not?

2. Smith concedes that the power of positive thinking "is often a very good thing. It may even be necessary. But it is never sufficient." Why, according to Smith, is it never sufficient? Why is it unfair and even sometimes cruel to attribute success or failure to it?

3. Perhaps most human beings who achieve tell themselves and others stories about why they achieved that amount to self-deceit—at least, in part, as oversimplification. Is this human tendency necessarily bad, something we should strive to avoid? Or is it mostly harmless? At what point does self-deceit become self-destructive and dangerous to other people?

FOR RESEARCH AND CRITIQUE

As the most common form of "enhancement" in our culture, the self-help industry is a multibillion dollar money maker every year. Go to any bookstore and you will find a large section devoted to self-help books. Find one that sounds interesting to you and select a chapter or part of a chapter for careful study and analysis.

Using Ed Smith's article as a model, write a critique of the selection you have chosen.

Cartoon: Gene-Splicing as Big Business

LARRY GONICK AND MARK WHEELIS

If you want to learn about genetics and have fun at the same time, read *The Cartoon Guide to Genetics* (HarperCollins), from which the following satire comes.

QUESTIONS FOR DISCUSSION

There has been a great deal of concern about the alliance between business and American colleges in recent years. So the questions raised by the appalled academics in the cartoon are serious questions, even if the economic incentives for turning discoveries into profits are so great that they tend to overwhelm them. What do you think about the issues raised, especially as they bear on business applications of genetic engineering?

On Human Bioenhancements

C. BEN MITCHELL

C. Ben Mitchell is Graves Professor of Moral Philosophy at Union University and editor of *Ethics and Medicine,* the journal in which the following editorial first appeared.

1 Human beings are obsessive innovators. *Homo sapiens* (knower) is by nature *Homo faber* (fabricator). Life without what philosopher Michael Novak has called "the fire of invention" doubtless would be nasty, bloody, and brutish. Since biomedicine and biotechnology are two spheres where innovation is especially rewarded, it is no surprise that we stand on the threshold of the development of human biological enhancements.

2 We have attempted enhancement in many different ways, especially for our children: diet, exercise, music lessons, tutoring, athletics, and even cosmetic surgery. But for many people, there is something deeply troubling about bioenhancement technologies, whether they are reproductive, genetic, neurological, or prosthetic technologies. By 'bioenhancement' I mean that these technologies magnify human biological function *beyond species typical norms.*

THERAPY VERSUS ENHANCEMENT

3 Ethical reflection about these technologies requires that we make some distinction between therapy and enhancement. Therapies would include medical interventions that restore human functioning to species typical norms. So, kidney dialysis, lasik surgery, and angioplasty are therapies; but adding twenty IQ points to someone who already has a normal IQ would be an enhancement.

4 Both proponents and critics of bioenhancements have argued, however, that the line between therapy and enhancement is vanishingly thin. But it may not be as faint as some imagine. I was once in a conversation with a prominent fertility specialist who used preimplantation genetic diagnosis (PGD) to help couples have children without genetically-linked diseases. He told of a couple who came to him requesting that he assist them to have a child who would have perfect musical pitch. Since they were both orchestral musicians and because there may be a gene associated with aural acuity, they wanted a child to follow in their footsteps. He steadfastly refused. He said he could not say exactly why, but his intuition was that it was unethical. Just because we cannot always make finely tuned distinctions does not mean distinctions are impossible. Just because a bright line may not be drawn does not mean no line can be drawn.

5   We should resist human bioenhancement technologies at least for a number of reasons, including their inconsistency with the goals of medicine, their violation of the principle of justice, and their complicity with cultural stereotypes.

THE GOALS OF MEDICINE

6   Human bioenhancements should be resisted, first, because they are inconsistent with the goals of medicine. The first goal of medicine is healing for the "patient's good." The principle of medical beneficence assumes either that a patient is enjoying homeostasis, and the role of the physician is to assist him or her to maintain or optimize normal functioning, or that a patient is suffering diminished capacity due to illness or disease, and medicine's role is to help restore as much normal function as possible. This aim of medicine is as old as the Hippocratic Oath. Whether we call it healing, wellness, or shalom, the goals of medicine are restorative and preventive.

7   Only recently have we begun to imagine medicine as a way to move beyond therapy. Medicine is seen less today as a profession and more as a commercial service. Physicians are not seen as professionals, they are merely body plumbers (no offense to plumbers). Consumerism thrives on giving the customer what he or she desires. While human bioenhancements are not consistent with the traditional aims of medicine, they are very consistent with desire-satisfaction where, as ethicist Carl Elliott so elegantly puts it, "American medicine meets the American dream." So now consumers employ doctors to make them "better than well."

THE PRINCIPLE OF JUSTICE

8   Another reason to reject bioenhancements is the principle of justice. Having recently witnessed the Olympic games in Beijing, and heard the hoopla over doping in the Tour de France, we should be sensitive to the ways even the hint of enhancements threaten the fairness of competition. By analogy, technologically enhanced IQ, speed, dexterity, hearing, musical ability, etc., would create injustices, at least in cultures where those qualities are valued. The enhanced individual potentially would have unfair advantage over others in employment or life, just as blood-doping and steroids created advantages over other athletes. Furthermore, enhancing already wealthy Westerners while so many individuals lack access to basic therapeutic medicine, seems patently unjust. In fact, most of the world's people do not want enhancements, they want basic healthcare.

THE PROBLEM OF CULTURAL COMPLICITY

9   Georgetown philosopher Margaret Little has argued that enhancements contribute to cultural differences that lead to personal dissatisfaction and even stigmatization. For instance, Western culture's valorization of the Barbie-doll figure leads to body dysmorphic disorder among American teenage girls. Some Asian girls are having cosmetic surgery to make their eyes rounder and less almond-shaped in order to fit the Western ideal. For a culture to legitimize enhancement is to be complicit in these

pathologies. And this would seem especially heinous after spending untold social capital, tax-dollars, and educational resources trying to convince our culture that persons with disabilities should be respected equally as those without them.

10   Human bioenhancements seem to be a very dubious investment of time and other scarce resources. Only those already well-off can afford the luxury of enhancements. The sick need a physician.

QUESTIONS FOR DISCUSSION

1. In paragraph 4, Mitchell describes a case where a doctor refused to help a couple engineer a child with perfect pitch, obviously an asset for musicians. The doctor said "his intuition was that it [the request] was unethical." Do you agree? If so, can you give reasons for turning the couple down?

2. One of Mitchell's reasons for resisting bioenhancements is that money and resources are expended "to magnify human biological function" when so many people in the world lack even basic medical care, including millions in the United States. Should individual choice be limited by such considerations? How do you feel about wealthy people having access to biological enhancements when the vast majority of people in the United States and other countries do not?

FOR RESEARCH AND CONVINCING

"Medicine is seen less today," Mitchell claims, "as a profession and more as a commercial service." Do research on how medicine is practiced today to discover how much truth there is in Mitchell's assertion. If you see the commercialization of medicine as a problem, propose a solution that would move the practice of medicine more toward professional responsibility. If you see the commercialization of medicine as free enterprise at work, defend current practice against Mitchell's criticism.

FOR FURTHER READING

Chapman, Audrey R., and Mark S. Frankel, editors. *Designing Our Descendants: The Promises and Perils of Genetic Engineering.* Farrar, 2002.

Elliott, Carl. *Better Than Well: American Medicine Meets the American Dream.* Norton, 2003.

Fukuyama, Francis. *Our Posthuman Future: Consequences of the Biotechnology Revolution.* Farrar, 2002.

Gonick, Larry, and Mark Wheelis. *The Cartoon Guide to Genetics.* Harper, 2005.

Mottram, David, ed. *Drugs in Sport.* 5th ed., Routledge, 2011.

Naam, Ramez. *More Than Human: Embracing the Promise of Biological Enhancement.* 2nd ed., Broadway Books, 2010.

Savulescu, Julian, and Nick Bostrom, editors. *Human Enhancement.* Oxford UP, 2011.

Stock, Gregory. *Redesigning Humans: Our Inevitable Genetic Future.* Houghton Mifflin, 2002.

A Brief Guide to Editing and Proofreading

Editing and proofreading are the final steps in creating a finished piece of writing. Too often, however, these steps are rushed as writers race to meet a deadline. Ideally, you should distinguish between the acts of revising, editing, and proofreading. Because each step requires that you pay attention to something different, you cannot reasonably expect to do them well if you try to do them all at once.

Our suggestions for revising appear in each of Chapters 8–11 on the aims of argument. *Revising* means shaping and developing the whole argument with an eye to audience and purpose; when you revise, you are ensuring that you have accomplished your aim. *Editing,* on the other hand, means making smaller changes within paragraphs and sentences. When you edit, you are thinking about whether your prose will be a pleasure to read. Editing improves the sound and rhythm of your voice. It makes complicated ideas more accessible to readers and usually makes your writing more concise. Finally, *proofreading* means eliminating errors. When you proofread, you correct everything you find that will annoy readers, such as misspellings, punctuation mistakes, and faulty grammar.

In this appendix, we offer some basic advice on what to look for when editing and proofreading. For more detailed help, consult a handbook on grammar and punctuation and a good book on style, such as Joseph Williams's *Ten Lessons in Clarity and Grace* or Richard Lanham's *Revising Prose.* Both of these texts guided our thinking in the advice that follows.

EDITING

Most ideas can be phrased in a number of ways, each of which gives the idea a slightly distinctive twist. Consider the following examples:

In New York City, about 74,000 people die each year.

In New York City, death comes to one in a hundred people each year.

Death comes to one in a hundred New Yorkers each year.

To begin an article on what becomes of the unknown and unclaimed dead in New York, Edward Conlon wrote the final of these three sentences. We can only speculate about the possible variations he considered, but because openings are so crucial, he almost certainly cast these words quite deliberately.

For most writers, such deliberation over matters of style occurs during editing. In this late stage of the writing process, writers examine choices made earlier, perhaps unconsciously, while drafting and revising. They listen to how sentences sound, to patterns of rhythm both within and among sentences. Editing is like an art or craft; it can provide you the satisfaction of knowing you've said something gracefully and effectively. To focus on language this closely, you will need to set aside enough time following the revision step.

In this section, we discuss some things to look for when editing your own writing. Don't forget, though, that editing does not always mean looking for weaknesses. You should also recognize passages that work well just as you wrote them, that you can leave alone or play up more by editing passages that surround them.

Editing for Clarity and Conciseness

Even drafts revised several times may have wordy and awkward passages; these are often places where a writer struggled with uncertainty or felt less than confident about the point being made. Introductions often contain such passages. In editing, you have one more opportunity to clarify and sharpen your ideas.

Express Main Ideas Forcefully

Emphasize the main idea of a sentence by stating it as directly as possible, using the two key sentence parts (*subject* and *verb*) to convey the two key parts of the idea (*agent* and *act*).

As you edit, first look for sentences that state ideas indirectly rather than directly; such sentences may include (1) overuse of the verb *to be* in its various forms (*is, was, will have been,* and so forth), (2) the opening words "There is . . ." or "It is . . . ," (3) strings of prepositional phrases, or (4) many vague nouns. Then ask, "What is my true subject here, and what is that subject's action?" Here is an example of a weak, indirect sentence:

> It is a fact that the effects of pollution are more evident in lower-class neighborhoods than in middle-class ones.

The writer's subject is pollution. What is the pollution's action? Limply, the sentence tells us its "effects" are "evident." The following edited version makes pollution the agent that performs the action of a livelier verb, "fouls." The edited sentence is more specific—without being longer.

> *Pollution* more frequently *fouls* the air, soil, and water of lower-class neighborhoods than of middle-class ones.

Editing Practice   The following passage about a plan for creating low-income housing contains two weak sentences. In this case, the weakness results from wordiness. (Note the overuse of vague nouns and prepositional phrases.) Decide what the true subject is for each sentence, and make that word the subject of the verb. Your edited version should be much shorter.

> As in every program, there will be the presence of a few who abuse the system. However, as in other social programs, the numbers would not be sufficient to justify the rejection of the program on the basis that one person in a thousand will try to cheat.

Choose Carefully between Active and Passive Voice

Active voice and passive voice indicate different relationships between subjects and verbs. As we have noted, ideas are usually clearest when the writer's true subject is also the subject of the verb in the sentence—that is, when it is the agent of the action. In the passive voice, however, the agent of the action appears in the predicate or not at all. Rather than acting as agent, the subject of the sentence *receives* the action of the verb.

The following sentence is in the passive voice:

> The air of poor neighborhoods is often fouled by pollution.

There is nothing incorrect about the use of the passive voice in this sentence, and in the context of a whole paragraph, passive voice can be the most emphatic way to make a point. (Here, for example, it allows the word *pollution* to fall at the end of the sentence, a strong position.) But, often, use of the passive voice is not a deliberate choice at all; rather, it's a vague and unspecific way of stating a point.

Consider the following sentences, in which the main verbs have no agents:

> It *is believed* that dumping garbage at sea is not as harmful to the environment as *was* once *thought*.

> Ronald Reagan *was considered* the "Great Communicator."

Who thinks such dumping is not so harmful? environmental scientists? industrial producers? Who considered former president Reagan a great communicator? speech professors? news commentators? Such sentences are clearer when they are written in the active voice:

> Some environmentalists believe that dumping garbage at sea is not as harmful to the environment as they used to think.

> Media commentators considered Ronald Reagan the "Great Communicator."

In editing for the passive voice, look over your verbs. Passive voice is easily recognized because it always contains (1) some form of *to be* as a helping verb and (2) the main verb in its past participle form (which ends in *-ed, -d, -t, -en,* or *-n,* or in some cases may be irregular: *drunk, sung, lain,* and so on).

When you find a sentence phrased in the passive voice, decide who or what is performing the action; the agent may appear after the verb or not at all. Then decide if changing the sentence to the active voice will improve the sentence as well as the surrounding passage.

Editing Practice

1. The following paragraph from a student's argument needs to be edited for emphasis. It is choking with excess nouns and forms of the verb *to be,* some as part of passive constructions. You need not eliminate all passive voice, but do look for wording that is vague and ineffective. Your edited version should be not only stronger but shorter as well.

   Although emergency shelters are needed in some cases (for example, a mother fleeing domestic violence), they are an inefficient means of dealing with the massive numbers of people they are bombarded with each day. The members of a homeless family are in need of a home, not a temporary shelter into which they and others like them are herded, only to be shuffled out when their thirty-day stay is over to make room for the next incoming herd. Emergency shelters would be sufficient if we did not have a low-income housing shortage, but what is needed most at present is an increase in availability of affordable housing for the poor.

2. Select a paragraph of your own writing to edit; focus on using strong verbs and subjects to carry the main idea of your sentences.

Editing for Emphasis

When you edit for emphasis, you make sure that your main ideas stand out so that your reader will take notice. Following are some suggestions to help.

Emphasize Main Ideas by Subordinating Less Important Ones

Subordination refers to distinctions in rank or order of importance. Think of the chain of command at an office: the boss is at the top of the ladder, the middle management is on a lower (subordinate) rung, the support staff is at an even lower rung, and so on.

In writing, subordination means placing less important ideas in less important positions in sentences in order to emphasize the main ideas that should stand out. Writing that lacks subordination treats all ideas equally; each idea may consist of a sentence of its own or may be joined to another idea by a coordinator (*and, but,* and *or*). Such a passage follows with its sentences numbered for reference purposes.

(1) It has been over a century since slavery was abolished and a few decades since lawful, systematic segregation came to an unwilling halt. (2) Truly, blacks have come a long way from the darker days that lasted for more than three centuries. (3) Many blacks have

entered the mainstream, and there is a proportionately large contingent of middle-class blacks. (4) Yet an even greater percentage of blacks are immersed in truly pathetic conditions. (5) The inner-city black poor are enmeshed in devastating socioeconomic problems. (6) Unemployment among inner-city black youths has become much worse than it was even five years ago.

Three main ideas are important here—that blacks have been free for some time, that some have made economic progress, and that others are trapped in poverty—and of these three, the last is probably intended to be the most important. Yet, as we read the passage, these key ideas do not stand out. In fact, each point receives equal emphasis and sounds about the same, with the repeated subject-verb-object syntax. The result seems monotonous, even apathetic, though the writer is probably truly disturbed about the subject. The following edited version, which subordinates some of the points, is more emphatic. We have italicized the main points.

> *Blacks have come a long way* in the century since slavery was abolished and in the decades since lawful, systematic segregation came to an unwilling halt. Yet, although many blacks have entered the mainstream and the middle class, *an even greater percentage is immersed in truly pathetic conditions.* To give just one example of these devastating socioeconomic problems, *unemployment among inner-city black youths is much worse now than it was even five years ago.*

Although different editing choices are possible, this version plays down sentences 1, 3, and 5 in the original so that sentences 2, 4, and 6 stand out.

As you edit, look for passages that sound wordy and flat because all the ideas are expressed with equal weight in the same subject-verb-object pattern. Then single out your most important points, and try out some options for subordinating the less important ones. The key is to put main ideas in main clauses and modifying ideas in modifying clauses or phrases.

Modifying Clauses Like simple sentences, modifying clauses contain a subject and verb. They are formed in two ways: (1) with relative pronouns and (2) with subordinating conjunctions.

Relative pronouns introduce clauses that modify nouns, with the relative pronoun relating the clause to the noun it modifies. There are five relative pronouns: *that, which, who, whose,* and *whom.* The following sentence contains a relative clause:

> Alcohol advertisers are trying to sell a product *that is by its very nature harmful to users.*

> —Jason Rath (student)

Relative pronouns may also be implied:

> I have returned the library book [that] *you loaned me.*

Relative pronouns may also be preceded by prepositions, such as *on, in, to,* or *during:*

> Drug hysteria has created an atmosphere *in which civil rights are disregarded.*

Subordinating conjunctions show relationships among ideas. It is impossible to provide a complete list of subordinating conjunctions in this short space, but here are the most common and the kinds of modifying roles they perform:

> To show time: *after, as, before, since, until, when, while*
>
> To show place: *where, wherever*
>
> To show contrast: *although, though, whereas, while*
>
> To show cause and effect: *because, since, so that*
>
> To show condition: *if, unless, whether, provided that*
>
> To show manner: *how, as though*

By introducing it with a subordinating conjunction, you can convert one sentence into a dependent clause that can modify another sentence. Consider the following two versions of the same idea:

> Pain is a state of consciousness, a "mental event." It can never be directly observed.
>
> *Since pain is a state of consciousness, a "mental event,"* it can never be directly observed.
>
> —Peter Singer, *"Animal Liberation"*

Modifying Phrases   Unlike clauses, phrases do not have a subject and a verb. Prepositional phrases and infinitive phrases are most likely already in your repertoire of modifiers. (Consult a handbook if you need to review these.) Here, we remind you of two other useful types of phrases: (1) participial phrases and (2) appositives.

Participial phrases modify nouns. Participles are created from verbs, so it is not surprising that the two varieties represent two verb tenses. The first is present participles ending in *-ing:*

> *Hoping to eliminate harassment on campus,* many universities have tried to institute codes for speech and behavior.
>
> The desperate Haitians fled here in boats, *risking all.*
>
> —Carmen Hazan-Cohen (student)

The second is past participles ending in *-ed, -en, -d, -t,* or *-n:*

> Women themselves became a resource, *acquired by men much as the land was acquired by men.*
>
> —Gerda Lerner

> *Linked more to the Third World and Asia than to the Europe of America's racial and cultural roots,* Los Angeles and Southern California will enter the 21st century as a multi-racial and multicultural society.
>
> —Ryszard Kapuscinski

Notice that modifying phrases should immediately precede the nouns they modify.

An *appositive* is a noun or noun phrase that restates another noun, usually in a more specific way. Appositives can be highly emphatic, but more often they are tucked into the middle of a sentence or added to the end, allowing a subordinate idea to be slipped in. When used like this, appositives are usually set off with commas:

> Rick Halperin, *a professor at Southern Methodist University,* noted that Ted Bundy's execution cost Florida taxpayers over six million dollars.
>
> —Diane Miller (student)

Editing Practice

1. Edit the following passage as needed for emphasis, clarity, and conciseness, using subordinate clauses, relative clauses, participial phrases, appositives, and any other options that occur to you. If some parts are effective as they are, leave them alone.

   The monetary implications of drug legalization are not the only reason it is worth consideration. There is reason to believe that the United States would be a safer place to live if drugs were legalized. A large amount of what the media has named "drug-related" violence is really prohibition-related violence. Included in this are random shootings and murders associated with black-market transactions. Estimates indicate that at least 40 percent of all property crime in the United States is committed by drug users so they can maintain their habits. That amounts to a total of 4 million crimes per year and $7.5 billion in stolen property. Legalizing drugs would be a step toward reducing this wave of crime.

2. Edit a paragraph of your own writing with an eye to subordinating less important ideas through the use of modifying phrases and clauses.

Vary Sentence Length and Pattern

Even when read silently, your writing has a sound. If your sentences are all about the same length (typically fifteen to twenty words) and all structured according to a subject-verb-object pattern, they will roll along with the monotonous rhythm of an assembly line. Obviously, one solution to this problem is to open some of your sentences with modifying phrases and clauses, as we discuss in the previous section. Here we offer some other strategies, all of which add emphasis by introducing something unexpected.

1. Use a short sentence after several long ones.

    [A] population's general mortality is affected by a great many factors over which doctors and hospitals have little influence. For those diseases and injuries for which modern medicine can affect the outcome, however, which country the patient lives in really matters. Life expectancy is not the same among developed countries for premature babies, for children born with spina bifida, or for people who have cancer, a brain tumor, heart disease, or chronic renal failure. *Their chances of survival are best in the United States.*

    —John Goodman

2. Interrupt a sentence.

    The position of women in that hippie counterculture was, *as a young black male leader preached succinctly,* "prone."

    —Betty Friedan

    Symbols and myths—*when emerging uncorrupted from human experience*—are precious. Then it is the poetic voice and vision that informs and infuses—*the poet-warrior's, the prophet-seer's, the dreamer's*—reassuring us that truth is as real as falsehood. And ultimately stronger.

    —Ossie Davis

3. Use an intentional sentence fragment. The concluding fragment in the previous passage by Ossie Davis is a good example.
4. Invert the order of subject-verb-object.

    Further complicating negotiations is the difficulty of obtaining relevant financial statements.

    —Regina Herzlinger

    This creature, with scarcely two thirds of man's cranial capacity, was a fire user. Of what it meant to him beyond warmth and shelter, we know nothing; with what rites, ghastly or benighted, it was struck or maintained, no word remains.

    —Loren Eiseley

Use Special Effects for Emphasis

Especially in persuasive argumentation, you will want to make some of your points in deliberately dramatic ways. Remember that just as the crescendos stand out in music because the surrounding passages are less intense, so the special effects work best in rhetoric when you use them sparingly.

Repetition Deliberately repeating words, phrases, or sentence patterns has the effect of building up to a climactic point. Here is an example from the conclusion of an argument linking women's rights with environmental reforms:

> Environmental justice goes much further than environmental protection, a passive and paternalistic phrase. *Justice requires that* industrial nations pay back the environmental debt incurred in building their wealth by using less of nature's resources. *Justice prescribes that* governments stop siting hazardous waste facilities in cash-poor rural and urban neighborhoods and now in the developing world. *Justice insists that* the subordination of women and nature by men is not only a hazard; it is a crime. *Justice reminds us that* the Earth does not belong to us; even when we "own" a piece of it, we belong to the Earth.
>
> —H. Patricia Hynes

Paired Coordinators Coordinators are conjunctions that pair words, word groups, and sentences in a way that gives them equal emphasis and that also shows a relationship between them, such as contrast, consequence, or addition. In grade school, you may have learned the coordinators through the mnemonic *FANBOYS,* standing for *for, and, nor, but, or, yet, so.*

Paired coordinators emphasize the relationship between coordinated elements; the first coordinator signals that a corresponding coordinator will follow. Some paired coordinators are:

both _____ and _____

not _____ but _____

not only _____ but also _____

either _____ or _____

neither _____ nor _____

The key to effective paired coordination is to keep the words that follow the marker words as grammatically similar as possible. Pair nouns with nouns, verbs with verbs, prepositional phrases with prepositional phrases, and whole sentences with whole sentences. (Think of paired coordination as a variation on repetition.) Here are some examples:

> Feminist anger, or any form of social outrage, is dismissed breezily—*not* because it lacks substance *but* because it lacks "style."
>
> —Susan Faludi

> Alcohol ads that emphasize "success" in the business and social worlds are useful examples *not only* of how advertisers appeal to people's envy *but also* of how ads perpetuate gender stereotypes.
>
> —Jason Rath (student)

Emphatic Appositives While an appositive (a noun or noun phrase that restates another noun) can subordinate an idea, it can also emphasize an idea if it is placed at the beginning or the end of a sentence, where it will command attention. Here are some examples:

> *The poorest nation in the Western hemisphere,* Haiti is populated by six million people, many of whom cannot obtain adequate food, water, or shelter.
>
> —Sneed B. Collard III

> [Feminists] made a simple, though serious, ideological error when they applied the same political rhetoric to their own situation as women versus men: *too literal an analogy with class warfare, racial oppression.*
>
> —Betty Friedan

Note that at the end of a sentence, an appositive may be set off with a colon or a dash.

Emphatic Word Order   The opening and closing positions of a sentence are high-profile spots, not to be wasted on weak words. The following sentence, for example, begins weakly with the filler phrase "there are":

> *There are* several distinctions, all of them false, that are commonly made between rape and date rape.

A better version would read:

> My opponents make several distinctions between rape and date rape; all of these are false.

Even more important are the final words of every paragraph and the opening and closing of the entire argument.

Editing Practice

1. Select one or two paragraphs from a piece of published writing you have recently read and admired. Be ready to share it with the class, explaining how the writer has crafted the passage to make it work.

2. Take a paragraph or two from one of your previous essays, perhaps even an essay from another course, and edit it to improve clarity, conciseness, and emphasis.

Editing for Coherence

Coherence refers to what some people call the "flow" of writing; writing flows when the ideas connect smoothly, one to the next. In contrast, when writing is incoherent, the reader must work to see how ideas connect and must infer points that the writer, for whatever reason, has left unstated.

Incoherence is a particular problem with writing that contains an abundance of direct or indirect quotations. In using sources, be careful always to lead into the quotation with some words of your own, showing clearly how this new idea connects with what has come before.

Because finding incoherent passages in your own writing can be difficult, ask a friend to read your draft to look for gaps in the presentation of ideas. Here are some additional suggestions for improving coherence.

Move from Old Information to New Information

Coherent writing is easy to follow because the connections between old information and new information are clear. Sentences refer to previously introduced information and set up reader expectations for new information to come. Notice how every sentence fulfills your expectations in the following excerpts from an argument on animal rights by Steven Zak.

> The credibility of the animal-rights viewpoint . . . need not stand or fall with the "marginal human beings" argument.

Next, you would expect to hear why animals do not have to be classed as "marginal human beings"—and you do:

> Lives don't have to be qualitatively the same to be worthy of equal respect.

At this point you might ask upon what else we should base our respect. Zak answers this question in the next sentence:

> One's perception that another life has value comes as much from an appreciation of its uniqueness as from the recognition that it has characteristics that are shared by one's own life.

Not only do these sentences fulfill reader expectations, but each also makes a clear connection by referring specifically to the key idea in the sentence before it, forming an unbroken chain of thought. We have italicized the words that accomplish this linkage and connected them with arrows.

> The credibility of the animal-rights viewpoint . . . need not stand or fall with the *"marginal human beings"* argument.
>
> Lives don't have to be *qualitatively the same* to be worthy of *equal respect*.
>
> One's perception that *another life has value* comes as much from an *appreciation of its uniqueness* as from the recognition that it has characteristics that are shared by one's own life.
>
> One can imagine that the lives of various kinds of animals *differ radically.* . . .

In the following paragraph, reader expectations are not so well fulfilled:

> We are presently witness to the greatest number of homeless families since the Great Depression of the 1930s. The cause of this phenomenon is a shortage of low-income housing. Mothers with children as young as two weeks are forced to live on the street because there is no room for them in homeless shelters.

Although these sentences are all on the subject of homelessness, the second leads us to expect that the third will take up the topic of shortages of low-income housing. Instead, it takes us back to the subject of the first sentence and offers a different cause—no room in the shelters.

Looking for ways to link old information with new information will help you find problems of coherence in your own writing.

Editing Practice

1. In the following paragraph, underline the words or phrases that make the connections back to the previous sentence and forward to the next, as we did earlier with the passage from Zak.

   The affluent, educated, liberated women of the First World, who can enjoy freedoms unavailable to any women ever before, do not feel as free as they want to. And they can no longer restrict to the subconscious their sense that this lack of freedom has something to do with—with apparently frivolous issues, things that really should not matter. Many are ashamed to admit that such trivial concerns—to do with physical appearance, bodies, faces, hair, clothes—matter so much. But in spite of shame, guilt, and denial, more and more women are wondering if it isn't that they are entirely neurotic alone but rather that something important is indeed at stake that has to do with the relationship between female liberation and female beauty.

   —Naomi Wolf

2. The following student paragraph lacks coherence. Read through it, and put a slash (/) between sentences expressing unconnected ideas. You may try to rewrite the paragraph, rearranging sentences and adding ideas to make the connections tighter.

   Students may know what AIDS is and how it is transmitted, but most are not concerned about AIDS and do not perceive themselves to be at risk. But college-age heterosexuals are the number-one high-risk group for this disease (Gray and Sacarino 258). "Students already know about AIDS. Condom distribution, public or not, is not going to help. It just butts into my personal life," said one student surveyed. College is a time for exploration and that includes the discovery of sexual freedom. Students, away from home and free to make their own decisions for maybe the first time in their lives, have a "bigger than life" attitude. The thought of dying is the farthest from their minds. Yet at this point in their lives, they are most in need of this information.

Use Transitions to Show Relationships between Ideas

Coherence has to be built into a piece of writing; as we discussed earlier, the ideas between sentences must first cohere. However, sometimes readers need help in making the transition from one idea to the next, so you must provide signposts to help them see the connections more readily. For example, a transitional word like *however* can prepare readers for an idea in contrast to the one before it, as in the second sentence in this paragraph. Transitional words can also highlight the structure of an argument ("These data will show three things: first . . . , second . . . , and third . . ."), almost forming a verbal path for the reader to follow. Following are examples of transitional words and phrases and their purposes:

To show order: *first, second, next, then, last, finally*

To show contrast: *however, yet, but, nevertheless*

To show cause and effect: *therefore, consequently, as a result, then*

To show importance: *moreover, significantly*

To show an added point: *as well, also, too*

To show an example: *for example, for instance*

To show concession: *admittedly*

To show conclusion: *in sum, in conclusion*

The key to using transitional words is similar to the key to using special effects for emphasis: Don't overdo it. To avoid choking your writing with these words, anticipate where your reader will genuinely need them, and limit their use to these instances.

Editing Practice   Underline the transitional words and phrases in the following passage of published writing:

When people believe that their problems can be solved, they tend to get busy solving them.

On the other hand, when people believe that their problems are beyond solution, they tend to position themselves so as to avoid blame. Take the woeful inadequacy of education in the predominantly black central cities. Does the black leadership see the ascendancy of black teachers, school administrators, and politicians as an asset to be used in improving those dreadful schools? Rarely. You are more likely to hear charges of white abandonment, white resistance to integration, conspiracies to isolate black children, even when the schools are officially desegregated. In short, white people are accused of being responsible for the problem. But if the youngsters manage to survive those awful school systems and achieve success, leaders want to claim credit. They don't hesitate to attribute that success to the glorious Civil Rights movement.

—William Raspberry

PROOFREADING

Proofreading is truly the final step in writing a paper. After proofreading, you ought to be able to print your paper out one more time; but if you do not have time, most instructors will be perfectly happy to see the necessary corrections done neatly in ink on the final draft.

Following are some suggestions for proofreading.

Spelling Errors

If you have used a word processor, you may have a program that will check your spelling. If not, you will have to check your spelling by reading through again carefully with a dictionary at hand. Consult the dictionary whenever you feel uncertain. Note also that spell checkers can be unreliable; a word that is spelled correctly but is the wrong word won't be caught. You might consider devoting a special part of your writer's notebook to your habitual spelling errors: some students always misspell *athlete,* for example, whereas others leave the second *n* out of *environment.*

Omissions and Jumbled Passages

Read your paper out loud. Physically shaping your lips around the words can help locate missing words, typos (*saw* instead of *was*), or the remnants of some earlier version of a sentence that did not get fully deleted. Place a caret (^) in the sentence and write the correction or addition above the line, or draw a line through unnecessary text.

Punctuation Problems

Apostrophes and commas give writers the most trouble. If you have habitual problems with these, you should record your errors in your writer's notebook.

Apostrophes

Apostrophe problems usually occur in forming possessives, not contractions, so here we discuss only the former. If you have problems with possessives, you may also want to consult a good handbook or seek a private tutorial with your instructor or your school's writing center.

Here are the basic principles to remember.

1. Possessive pronouns—*his, hers, yours, theirs, its*—never take an apostrophe.

2. Singular nouns become possessive by adding -*'s.*

   A single parent's life is hard.

   A society's values change.

   Do you like Mr. Voss's new car?

3. Plural nouns ending in -*s* become possessive by simply adding an apostrophe.

   Her parents' marriage is faltering.

   Many cities' air is badly polluted.

   The Joneses' house is up for sale.

4. Plural nouns that do not end in -*s* become possessive by adding -*'s.*

   Show me the women's (men's) room.

   The people's voice was heard.

If you err by using apostrophes where they do not belong in nonpossessive words ending in -*s*, remember that a possessive will always have a noun after it, not some other part of speech such as a verb or a preposition. You may even need to read each line of print with a ruler under it to help you focus more intently on each word.

Commas

Because commas indicate a pause, reading your paper aloud is a good way to decide where to add or delete them. A good handbook will elaborate on the following basic principles. The example sentences have been adapted from an argument by Mary Meehan, who opposes abortion.

1. Use a comma when you join two or more main clauses with a coordinating conjunction.

    Main clause, conjunction (and, but, or, nor, so, yet) *main clause.*

    Feminists want to have men participate more in the care of children, but abortion allows a man to shift total responsibility to the woman.

2. Use a comma after an introductory phrase or dependent clause.

    Introductory phrase or clause, main clause.

    To save the smallest children, the Left should speak out against abortion.

3. Use commas around modifiers such as relative clauses and appositives unless they are essential to the noun's meaning. Be sure to put the comma at both ends of the modifier.

    _____, *appositive,*_____

    _____, *relative clause,*_____

    One member of the 1972 Presidential commission on population growth was Graciela Olivarez, a Chicana who was active in civil rights and anti-poverty work. Olivarez, who later was named to head the Federal Government's Community Services Administration, had known poverty in her youth in the Southwest.

4. Use commas with a series.

    __x__, __y__, and __z__

    The traditional mark of the Left has been its protection of the underdog, the weak, and the poor.

Semicolons

Think of a semicolon as a strong comma. It has two main uses.

1. Use a semicolon to join two main clauses when you choose not to use a conjunction. This works well when the two main clauses are closely related or parallel in structure.

    Main clause; main clause.

Pro-life activists did not want abortion to be a class issue; they wanted to end abortion everywhere, for all classes.

As a variation, you may wish to add a transitional adverb to the second main clause. The adverb indicates the relationship between the main clauses, but it is not a conjunction, so a comma preceding it would not be correct.

Main clause; transitional adverb (however, therefore, thus, moreover, consequently), *main clause.*

When speaking with counselors at the abortion clinic, many women change their minds and decide against abortion; however, a woman who is accompanied by a husband or boyfriend often does not feel free to talk with the counselor.

2. Use semicolons between items in a series if any of the items themselves contain commas.

___,___ ; ___,___ ; ___,___

A few liberals who have spoken out against abortion are Jesse Jackson, a civil rights leader; Richard Neuhaus, a theologian; the comedian Dick Gregory; and politicians Mark Hatfield and Mary Rose Oakar.

Colons

The colon has two common uses.

1. Use a colon to introduce a quotation when both your own lead-in and the words quoted are complete sentences that can stand alone. (See the section in Chapter 6 entitled "Incorporating and Documenting Source Material" for more on introducing quotations.)

Main clause in your words: "Quoted sentence(s)."

Mary Meehan criticizes liberals who have been silent on abortion: "If much of the leadership of the pro-life movement is right-wing, that is due largely to the default of the Left."

2. Use a colon before an appositive that comes dramatically at the end of a sentence, especially if the appositive contains more than one item.

Main clause: appositive, appositive, and appositive.

Meehan argues that many pro-choice advocates see abortion as a way to hold down the population of certain minorities: blacks, Puerto Ricans, and other Latins.

Grammatical Errors

Grammatical mistakes can be hard to find, but once again we suggest reading aloud as one method of proofing for them; grammatical errors tend not to "sound right" even if they look like good prose. Another suggestion is to recognize your habitual errors and then look for particular grammatical structures that lead you into error.

Introductory Participial Phrases

Constructions such as these often lead writers to create dangling modifiers. To avoid this pitfall, see the discussion of participial phrases earlier in this appendix. Remember that an introductory phrase dangles if it is not immediately followed by the noun it modifies.

> *Incorrect:* Using her conscience as a guide, our society has granted each woman the right to decide if a fetus is truly a "person" with rights equal to her own.

(Notice that the implied subject of the participial phrase is "each woman," when in fact the subject of the main clause is "our society"; thus, the participial phrase does not modify the subject.)

> *Corrected:* Using her conscience as a guide, each woman in our society has the right to decide if a fetus is truly a "person" with rights equal to her own.

Paired Coordinators

If the words that follow each of the coordinators are not of the same grammatical structure, then an error known as nonparallelism has occurred. To correct this error, line up the paired items one over the other. You will see that the correction often involves simply adding a word or two to, or deleting some words from, one side of the paired coordinators.

> not only _____ but also _____

> *Incorrect:* Legal abortion not only protects women's lives, but also their health.

> *Corrected:* Legal abortion protects not only women's lives but also their health.

Split Subjects and Verbs

If the subject of a sentence contains long modifying phrases or clauses, by the time you get to the verb you may make an error in agreement (using a plural verb, for example, when the subject is singular) or even in logic (for example, having a subject that is not capable of being the agent that performs the action of the verb). Following are some typical errors:

> The *goal* of the courses grouped under the rubric of "Encountering Non-Western Cultures" *are* . . .

Here the writer forgot that *goal,* the subject, is singular.

> During 1992, *the Refugee Act of 1980,* with the help of President Bush and Congress, *accepted* 114,000 immigrants into our nation.

The writer here should have realized that the agent doing the accepting would have to be the Bush administration, not the Refugee Act. A better version would read:

> During 1992, the Bush administration accepted 114,000 immigrants into our nation under the terms of the Refugee Act of 1980.

Proofreading Practice   Proofread the following passage for errors of grammar and punctuation.

> The citizens of Zurich, Switzerland tired of problems associated with drug abuse, experimented with legalization. The plan was to open a central park, Platzspitz, where drugs and drug use would be permitted. Many European experts felt, that it was the illegal drug business rather than the actual use of drugs that had caused many of the cities problems. While the citizens had hoped to isolate the drug problem, foster rehabilitation, and curb the AIDS epidemic, the actual outcome of the Platzspitz experiment did not create the desired results. Instead, violence increased. Drug-related deaths doubled. And drug users were drawn from not only all over Switzerland, but from all over Europe as well. With thousands of discarded syringe packets lying around, one can only speculate as to whether the spread of AIDS was curbed. The park itself was ruined and finally on February 10, 1992, it was barred up and closed. After studying the Swiss peoples' experience with Platzspitz, it is hard to believe that some advocates of drug legalization in the United States are urging us to participate in the same kind of experiment.

APPENDIX B

Fallacies—and Critical Thinking

Arguments, like [people], are often pretenders.

—Plato

Throughout this book we have stressed how to argue well, accentuating the positive rather than dwelling on the negative, poor reasoning and bad arguments. We would rather say "do this" than "do not do that." We would rather offer good arguments to emulate than bad arguments to avoid. In stressing the positive, however, we have not paid enough attention to an undeniable fact. Too often unsound arguments convince too many people who should reject them. This appendix addresses a daily problem—arguments that succeed when they ought to fail.

Traditionally, logicians and philosophers have tried to solve this problem by exposing "fallacies," errors in reasoning. About 2,400 years ago, the great ancient Greek philosopher Aristotle was the first to do so in *Sophistical Refutations*. "Sophistry" means reasoning that *appears* to be sound. Aristotle showed that such reasoning only seems sound and therefore should not pass critical scrutiny. He identified thirteen common errors in reasoning. Others have since isolated dozens more, over a hundred in some recent treatments.

We respect this ancient tradition and urge you to learn more about it. Irving M. Copi's classic textbook, *Introduction to Logic*, offers an excellent discussion. It is often used in beginning college philosophy courses. However, our concern is not philosophy but arguments about public issues, where a different notion of fallacy is more useful. Let's start, then, with how we define it.

WHAT IS A FALLACY?

Our concern is arguing well, both skillfully and ethically, and arguments have force through *appeals to an audience*. Therefore, we define *fallacy* as "the misuse of an otherwise common and legitimate form of appeal."

A good example is the appeal to authority, common in advancing evidence to defend reasons in an argument. If I am writing about flu epidemics, for instance, I may cite a scientist studying them at the national Centers for Disease Control to support something I have said. As long as I report what he or she said accurately, fully, and without distortion, I have used the appeal to authority correctly. After all, I am not a flu expert and this person is—it only makes sense to appeal to his or her authority.

But suppose that my authority's view does not represent what most experts believe—in fact most leading authorities reject it. Perhaps I just do not know enough to realize that my authority is not in the mainstream. Or perhaps I do know, but for reasons of my own I want my audience to think a minority view is the majority view. It does not matter whether I intend to deceive or not—if I present my authority in a misleading way, I have misused the appeal to authority. I have committed a fallacy in the meaning we are giving it here.

Here is the point of our definition of fallacy: There is nothing wrong with the appeal to authority itself. Everything depends on how it is used in a particular case. That is why fallacies must be linked with critical thinking. Studying fallacies can lead to mindless "fallacy hunts" and to labeling all instances of a kind of appeal as fallacious. Fallacies are common, but finding them requires *thinking through any appeal that strikes us as suspect for some reason*. We have to decide in each case whether to accept or reject the appeal—or more often, how much we should let it influence our thinking.

WHY ARE FALLACIES SO COMMON?

Fallacies are common because they are deeply rooted in human nature. We must not imagine that we can eliminate them. But we can understand some of their causes and motivations and, with that understanding, increase our critical alertness.

We have distinguished unintended fallacies from intentional ones. We think most fallacies are not meant to deceive, so let's deal with this bigger category first. Unintentional fallacies can result from not knowing enough about the subject, which we may not realize for a number of reasons:

- *Inaccurate reporting or insufficient knowledge.* Arguments always appeal to the facts connected with a controversial question. Again, as with the appeal to authority, there is nothing wrong with appealing to what is known about something. It is hard to imagine how we would argue without doing so. But we have to get the facts right and present them in a context of other relevant information.

  So, for example, experts think that about 300,000 undocumented, foreign-born people immigrate to the United States each year. Not 3,000 or 30,000, but 300,000, and not per month or decade, but annually. The first way we can misuse the appeal to facts is not to report the information accurately. Mistakes of this kind occur often. Magazines and newspapers frequently acknowledge errors in their stories from previous issues.

If we cite the correct figure, 300,000 per year, to support a contention that the Border Patrol is not doing its job, we would be guilty of a fallacy if we did not know that about half of these immigrants come legally, on visas, and simply stay. They are not the Border Patrol's problem. So, even if we cite information accurately, we can still misrepresent what it means or misinterpret it. Accuracy is important but not enough by itself to avoid fallacies. We have to double-check our facts and understand what the facts mean.

- *Holding beliefs that are not true.* If what we do not know can hurt us, what we think we know that is false does more damage. We pick up such beliefs from misinformation that gets repeated over and over in conversation and the media. For example, many Americans equate Islam with Arabs. But most Muslims are not Arabs, and many Arabs are not Muslims. The linkage is no more than a popular association. Furthermore, many terrorists are neither Arabs nor Muslims—we just do not hear about them much. Unfortunately, even when informed people point out the facts just mentioned, they tend not to register or be forgotten quickly. Such is the hold of incorrect beliefs on the minds of many people.

- *Stubbornly adhering to a belief despite massive counterevidence.* At one time most climate scientists resisted the notion that human activities could influence the weather, much less cause global warming. But as more and more evidence accumulated, the overwhelming majority eventually came to agree that carbon dioxide emissions, especially from vehicles and power-generating plants, are the major cause of global warming. But dissenters still exist, and not all of them are being paid by oil companies. Some may sincerely feel that natural variation in the Earth's climate is the real cause of global warming. Some may enjoy the role of outsider or maverick. Some may say that often the majority opinion turns out to be wrong, which is true enough, and somebody needs to play the skeptic. Whatever the motivation may be, the dissenters are brushing aside an enormous amount of evidence. Their fallacious arguments have helped to convince too many Americans that we do not have a problem when we do. We cite this example to show that fallacies are not restricted to popular arguments. Scientists can be as stubborn as anyone. It is human nature, against which no degree of expertise can protect us.

- *Dodging issues we do not understand or that disturb or embarrass us.* The issues that immigration, both legal and illegal, raise, for example, are more often avoided or obscured than confronted. People talk about immigrants becoming "good Americans" and worry about whether the latest wave can or will "assimilate." But what is a "good American"?

The question is rarely posed. Exactly what does "assimilate" involve? Again, few ask the question. Thus, arguments about this subject often dodge the important questions connected with it. In many cases those making these arguments do so while thinking they are confronting it.

If you recognize yourself and people you know in some or all of these causes and motivations that drive fallacious arguments, welcome to the club. We are all guilty. Without meaning to, we all get the facts wrong; we all pick up notions we take to be true that are not; and we all are at times stubborn and evasive.

Fortunately, unintended fallacies usually have telltale signs we can learn to detect, such as these:

- the reported fact that seems unlikely or implausible
- the interpretation that reduces a complex problem to something too simple to trust
- the belief that does not fit what we know of the world and our own experience
- the argument that strains too hard to downplay or explain away data that would call it into question
- the argument that dances around issues rather than confronting them

The good news is that unintended fallacies are seldom skillful enough to fool us often or for long. They tend to give themselves away once we know what to look for and care enough to exercise our natural critical capacity.

The bad news is that arguments coldly calculated to deceive, although less common than arguments that mislead unintentionally, are often much harder to detect. What makes the problem especially tough is that deceit comes too often from people we want and even need to trust. Why? Why do people sometimes set out to deceive others? We think the philosopher and brilliant fallacy hunter Jeremy Bentham had the best answer. He called the motivation "interest-begotten prejudice." What did he mean?

He meant that all human beings have interests they consider vital—status, money, and power they either have and seek to protect or strive to acquire. As a direct result of these interests, their outlook, thinking, and of course their arguments are shot through with prejudices, unexamined judgments about what is good, desirable, worthwhile, and so on. For example, through much of American history, Native Americans had something the American government wanted—land. When it did not take it by force, it took it by treaty, by persuading Native Americans to make bad bargains that often the government never intended to keep anyway. The whole process rode on prejudices: Native Americans were savages or children in need of protection by the Great Father in Washington; besides that, they did not "do anything" with the land they had. Because the deceit paid off handsomely for its perpetrators, it went on until there was little land remaining to take.

We would like to tell you that deliberate deceit in argument does not work—that deceivers are exposed and discredited at least, if not punished for what they do. We would like to endorse Abraham Lincoln's famous statement: "You can fool all of the people some of the time, and some of the people all the time, but you can't fool all of the people all of the time." Maybe so— many Native Americans and some independent-thinking white people were not fooled by the false promises of the treaties. But the humorist James Thurber's less famous observation is probably closer to the truth: "You can fool too many of the people too much of the time." This is so because the interest-begotten prejudices of the powerful coincide with or cooperate with the prejudices of a large segment of the audience addressed. That is why Hitler and his propaganda machine was able to create the disastrous Third Reich and why Joseph Stalin, who murdered more Russians than Hitler did, remains a national hero for many Russians even now, after his brutal regime's actions have long been exposed.

So, what can be done about the fallacious arguments of deliberate deceivers, backed as they often are by the power of the state or other potent interests? The most important thing is to examine our own interest-begotten prejudices, because that is what the deceivers use to manipulate us. They will not be able to push our buttons so easily if we know what they are and realize we are being manipulated. Beyond that, we need to recognize the interests of others, who may be in the minority and largely powerless to resist when too many people are fooled too much of the time. We can call attention to the fallacies of deliberate deceivers, exposing their game for others to see. We can make counterarguments, defending enlightened stances with all our skill. There is no guarantee that what should prevail will, but at least we need not lend support to exploiters nor fall into silence when we ought to resist.

SOME COMMON FALLACIES

For reasons that should be clearer now, people often misuse legitimate forms of appeal. We have mentioned two examples already—the misuse of the appeal to authority and the misuse of the appeal to facts. All legitimate appeals can be misused, and because there are too many to discuss them all, we will confine our attention to those most commonly turned into fallacies.

In Chapter 10, "Motivating Action: Arguing to Persuade," we described and illustrated all the forms of appeal (pages 236–237). In sum, we are persuaded by

- *ethos:* the character of the writer as we perceive him or her
- *pathos:* our emotions and attitudes as the argument arouses them
- *style:* how well something is said
- *logos:* our capacity for logic, by the force of reasons and evidence advanced for a thesis

You will encounter people, including many professors, who hold that only logos, rational appeal, *should* persuade. Anything else from their point of view is irrelevant and probably fallacious. We say in response that, regardless of what should be the case, people *are* persuaded by all four kinds of appeal—that we always have been and always will be. It therefore does not help to call appeals to ethos, pathos, and style fallacious. It *can* help to understand how these legitimate forms of appeal can be misused or abused.

The Appeal to Ethos

We do not know many people well whose arguments we encounter in print or in cyberspace. Typically, we do not know them at all. Consequently, we ordinarily rely on their qualifications and reputation as well as our impression of their character from reading what they have written. If ethos is not important or should not matter, we would not find statements about an author's identity and background attached to articles and books they have written. Speakers would not be introduced by someone providing similar information. But ethos does matter; as Aristotle said long ago, it is probably the most potent form of appeal. If we do not trust the person we are hearing or reading, it is highly unlikely we will be persuaded by anything said or written. If we do, we are inclined to assent to all of it. Consequently, appeals to ethos are often misused. Here are some of the common ways.

Personal Attack

There are people we ought never to trust—confidence men who bilk people out of their life savings, pathological liars, and so on. There is nothing wrong with exposing such people, destroying the ethos they often pretend very persuasively to have, thereby rendering their arguments unpersuasive.

But too often good arguments by good people are undermined with unjustified personal attacks. The most common is name-calling. Someone offers an argument opponents cannot see how to refute, so instead of addressing the argument, they call him or her "a liberal," a "neocon," or some other name the audience equates with "bad."

This fallacy is so common in politics that we now refer to it as "negative ads" or "negative campaigning." We ought not to dismiss it because experience and studies show that it often works. It works because once a label is attached to someone it is hard to shake.

Common Opinion

It is hard to find any argument that does not appeal to commonly accepted beliefs, many of which are accurate and reliable. Even scientific argument, which extols the value of skepticism, assumes that some knowledge is established beyond question and that some ways of doing things, like experimental design, are the right ways. When we indicate that we share the common opinions of our readers, thinking and behaving as they do, we establish or increase our ethos.

Used fallaciously, a writer passes off as commonly accepted either a belief that is not held by many informed people or one that is held commonly but is false or highly doubtful. "Of course," the writer says, and then affirms something questionable as if it was beyond question. For example, "Everybody knows that AIDS is spread by promiscuous sexual behavior." Sometimes it is, but one sexual act with one person can transmit the virus, and infection need not be transmitted sexually at all—babies are born with it because their mothers have AIDS, and addicts sharing needles is another common way AIDS is spread. Furthermore, health care workers are at higher risk because they often are exposed to bodily fluids from infected people. The common opinion in this and many other instances is no more than a half-truth at best.

Tradition

Few can see the opening of the musical *Fiddler on the Roof* and not be at least temporarily warmed by the thought of tradition. Tradition preserves our sense of continuity, helps us maintain stability and identity amid the often overwhelming demands of rapid change. No wonder, then, that writers appeal to it frequently to enhance their ethos and often in ways that are not fallacious at all. It was hardly a fallacy after 9/11, for instance, to remind Americans that part of the price we pay for liberty, our supreme traditional value, is greater relative vulnerability to terrorism. A closed, totalitarian society like North Korea can deal with terrorism much more "efficiently" than we can, but at the price of having no liberty.

Many of the abuses of tradition as a source of ethical appeal are so obvious as to need no discussion: politicians wrapping themselves in the flag (or at least red, white, and blue balloons), television preachers oozing piety to get donations. You can easily provide your own examples. Much more difficult to discern is invoking tradition not to dupe the naïve but to justify resisting constructive change. Tradition helped to delay women's right to vote in the United States, for example, and plays a major role in the high illiteracy rate for women in India and many other countries now.

Like all fallacious uses of legitimate appeals, ethical fallacies can be revealed by asking the right questions:

For *personal attack,* ask, "Are we dealing with a person whose views we should reject out of hand?" "Is the personal attack simply a means to dismiss an argument we ought to listen to?"

For *common opinion,* ask, "Is this belief really held by well-informed people?" If it is, ask, "Does the common belief hold only in some instances or in every case?"

For *tradition,* ask, "Have we always really done it that way?" If so, ask, "Have conditions changed enough so that the old way may need to be modified or replaced?"

The Appeal to Pathos

After people understand the indispensable role ethos plays in persuasion, few continue to view it only negatively, as merely a source of fallacies. Pathos is another matter. In Western culture, the heart is opposed to the head, feeling and emotion contrasted with logic and clear thinking. Furthermore, our typical attitudes toward pathos affect ethos as well: Emotional people cannot be trusted. Their arguments betray a disorganized and unbalanced mind.

With cause, we are wary of the power of emotional appeal, especially when passionate orators unleash it in crowds. The result often enough has been public hysteria and sometimes riots, lynchings, and verbal or physical abuse of innocent people. We know its power. Should it, then, be avoided? Are emotional appeals always suspect?

Let's take a brief look at a few of them.

Fear

"The only thing we have to fear is fear itself," Franklin Roosevelt declared, at a time when matters looked fearful indeed. The Great Depression was at its height; fascism was gaining ground in Europe. The new president sought to reduce the fear and despair that gripped the United States and much of the world at the time.

About a year later, in 1933, Hitler came to power, but the authorities in Britain, France, and other countries failed to realize the threat he represented soon enough, despite warnings from Winston Churchill and many others. As a result, the Allied powers in Europe fell to the Nazis, and Britain came to the brink of defeat. Fear can paralyze, as Roosevelt knew, but lack of it can result in complacency when genuine threats loom.

How can we tell the difference? With appeals to fear, as with all appeals to any emotion, this hard-to-answer question is the key: *Does reality justify the emotion a speaker or writer seeks to arouse or allay?* Recently, for instance, it has been easy to play on our fear of terrorists. But the odds of you or me dying in a terrorist plot are very low. The risk of death is greater just driving a car. Far more Americans will die prematurely from sedentary ways than Osama bin Laden's associates are ever likely to kill. 9/11 has taught us yet again that "eternal vigilance is the price of liberty," but the sometimes nearly hysterical fear of terrorism is not justified.

Pity

Fear has its roots in the body, in the fight-or-flight rush of adrenaline that helps us to survive. Pity, the ability to feel sorry for people suffering unjustly, has social roots. Both are fundamental emotions, part of being human.

Like the appeal to fear, the appeal to pity can be used fallaciously, to mislead us into, for example, contributing to a seemingly worthy cause which is really just a front for con artists. But if pity can be used to manipulate us, we can also fail to respond when pity is warranted. Or we can substitute the emotion for action. The suffering in Darfur in recent years has been acute, but the response of the rest of the world has usually been too little, too late. Like fear, then, we can fail to respond to appeals for pity when they are warranted.

Which is worse? To be conned sometimes or to be indifferent in the face of unjust suffering? Surely the latter. Because fear can lead to hysteria and violence, we should meet appeals to it skeptically. Because unjust suffering is so common, we should meet appeals to pity in a more receptive frame of mind. But with both emotions we require critical thinking. "I just feel what I feel" is not good enough. We have to get past that to distinguish legitimate emotional appeals from fallacious ones.

Ridicule

We mention ridicule because student writers are often advised to avoid it. "Do not ridicule your opponents in an argument" is the standard advice, advice you will find elsewhere in this book. So, is ridicule always fallacious, always a cheap shot, always a way to win points without earning them?

Well, not always. With most positions on most issues, we are dealing with points of view we may not agree with but must respect. But what if a position makes no sense, has little or no evidence to support its contentions, and yet people persist in holding it? What then? Is ridicule justified, at least sometimes?

If it is not, then satire is not justified, for satire holds up for scorn human behavior the satirist considers irrational and destructive. We all enjoy political cartoons, which thrive on ridicule of the absurd and the foolish. How many stand-up comedians would have far less material if ridicule was never justified?

Like pity, ridicule is a social emotion. It tries to bring individuals who have drifted too far away from social norms back into the fold. It allows us to discharge our frustration with stupid or dishonest positions through largely harmless laughter—far better than "let's beat some sense into old So-and-So." Ridicule, then, has its place and its functions.

But it also has its fallacies. Most commonly an intelligent, well-reasoned, and strongly supported position suffers ridicule simply because it is unpopular, because most people have difficulty getting their minds around it. Clearly, the fact that an argument has been dismissed as ridiculous or absurd does not mean that it is, and we must be especially careful when we unthinkingly join in the ridicule.

Like the fallacies related to ethos, pathetic fallacies can be revealed with the right questions:

1. Is the emotion appropriate to the situation, in proportion to what we know about what is going on in the world?

2. What are the consequences of buying into a particular emotional appeal? Where will it take us?

3. Does the emotional appeal *substitute* for reason, for a good argument, or does it reinforce it in justified ways?

4. What is the relation of the appeal to unexamined and possibly unjustified prejudice or bias? Are we being manipulated or led for good reasons to feel something?

The Appeal to Style

Most experienced and educated people are aware of the seductions of ethos and pathos. They know how easy it is to be misled by people they trust or manipulated by emotion into doing something they ordinarily would not and should not do. They have been fooled enough to be wary and therefore critical. However, even experienced and educated people often are not alert to the power of style, to the great impact that something can have *just because it is stated well*. One of the great students of persuasion, the American critic Kenneth Burke, explained the impact of style. He said that when we like the *form* of something said or written, it is a small step to accepting the *content* of it as well. We move very easily from "Well said" to "I agree," or even "It must be true." It is almost as if we cannot distrust at a deep level language that appeals to our sense of rhythm and sound.

Yet fallacies of style are a major industry. It is called advertising. People are paid handsomely to create slogans the public will remember and repeat. From some time ago, for instance, comes this one: "When guns are outlawed, only outlaws will have guns." Has a nice swing to it, doesn't it? The play on words is pleasing, hard to forget, and captures in a powerful formula the fears of the pro-gun lobby. Of course, in reality there has never been a serious movement to outlaw guns in the United States. No one is going to take away your guns, so the slogan is nothing more than scaremongering at best.

Now compare this slogan with another memorable phrase: "Justice too long delayed is justice denied." Martin Luther King used it to characterize the situation of black Americans in 1963 in his classic "Letter from Birmingham Jail." He got the phrase from a Supreme Court justice, but its appeal has less to do with the source of the statement than with its formula-like feeling of truth. It stuck in King's mind so he used it in his situation, and once you read it, you will not forget it either. In other words, it works in much the same way that the fallacious slogan works. But King's use of it is not at all fallacious. As a matter of undisputed fact, black Americans were denied their civil rights legally and illegally for more than a century after the Emancipation Proclamation.

The point, of course, is that the form of a statement says nothing about its truth value or whether it is being used to deceive. If form pushes us toward unthinking assent, then we must exert enough resistance to permit critical thought. Even "justice too long delayed is justice denied" may require some careful thought if it is applied to some other situation. Many people who favor the death penalty, for example, are outraged by the many years it usually takes to move a murderer from conviction to execution. They could well apply the phrase to this state of affairs. How much truth should it contain for someone who has no legal, moral, or religious objections to capital punishment? It is true that often the relatives of a victim must wait a decade or more for justice. It is true that sometimes, for one reason or another, the execution never happens. Is that justice denied? But it is also true that convicted felons on death row have been found innocent and released. Some innocent ones have been executed. Has justice been too long delayed or not? Would it be wise to shorten the process? These are serious questions critical thought must address.

The appeal of style goes well beyond slogans and formulas. We have not offered a list of common stylistic devices and how they may be misused because there are far too many of them. All can be used to express the truth; all can be used to package falsehood in appealing rhythm and sound. Separating ourselves from appeals of language long enough to think about what is being said is the only solution.

The Appeal to Logos

Before we present a short list of common errors in reasoning, the traditional focus of fallacy research, let's review a fundamental point about logic: An argument can be free of errors in reasoning, be logically compelling, and yet be false. Logic can tell us whether an argument makes sense but not whether it is true. For example, consider the following statements:

> Australia began as a penal colony, a place where criminals in England were sent.

> Modern Australians, therefore, are descendents of criminals.

There is nothing wrong with the logical relation of these two statements. But its truth value depends on the *historical accuracy* of the first statement. It depends also on the *actual origins* of all modern Australians. As a matter of fact, Australia was used by the English as a convenient place to send certain people the authorities considered undesirable, but they were not all criminals. Furthermore, native Australians populated the country long before any European knew it existed. And most modern Australians immigrated long after the days of the penal colony. So the truth value of these perfectly logical statements is low. It is true enough for Australians to joke about sometimes, but it is not really true.

Here is a good rule of thumb: *The reality of things reasoned about is far more varied and complex than the best reasoning typically captures.* Sometimes errors in reasoning lead us to false conclusions. But false conclusions result much more often from statements not being adequate to what is known about reality.

With that in mind, let's look at a few fallacies of logical appeal.

False Cause

We have defined *fallacy* as the misuse of a legitimate form of appeal. There is nothing more common or reasonable than identifying the cause of something. We are not likely to repair a car without knowing what is causing that wobble in the steering, or treat a disease effectively, or come up with the right solution to almost any problem without knowing the cause.

The difficulty is that just because "a" follows "b," "b" did not necessarily cause "a." Yet we tend to think so, especially if "a" always follows "b." Hence, the possibility of "false cause," reasoning that misleads by confusing sequence with cause. If we flip a light switch and the light does not go on, we immediately think, "The bulb is burned out." But if we replace the bulb, and it still does not work, we think the problem must be the switch. We may tinker with that for a while before we realize that none of the lights are working: "Oh, the breaker is cut off." By a process of trial and error, we eliminate the false causes to find the real one.

But if we are reasoning about more complex problems, trial and error usually is not an option. For example, a recent newspaper article attributed the decline in the wages of Americans despite increased productivity to the influx of illegal aliens, especially from Mexico. Because they are paid less than most American citizens are, attributing the cause of lower wages to them may seem plausible. But actually some groups of Americans have endured a steady decline for some time, as high-paying industrial jobs were lost and lower-paying service work took their place. Globalization has allowed companies to force wages down and reduce the power of labor unions by taking advantage of people in other countries who will work for much less. It is highly unlikely that depressed wages are caused by illegal aliens alone. But if we do not like them, it is especially tempting to blame them for a more complex problem with which they are only associated. That is called *scapegoating,* and false cause is how the reasoning works that justifies it.

As a rule of thumb, let's assume that complex problems have multiple causes, and let's be especially suspicious when common prejudices may motivate single-cause thinking.

Straw Man

Nothing is more common in argument than stating an opponent's position and then showing what is wrong with it. As long as we state our opponent's position fully and accurately and attack it intelligently, with good reasons and evidence, there is nothing fallacious about such an attack.

The temptation, however, is to seek advantage by attributing to our opponents a weak or indefensible position they do not hold but which resembles their position in some respects. We can then knock it down easily and make our opponents look dumb or silly in the process. That is called "creating a straw man," and it is a common ploy in politics especially. It works because most people are not familiar enough with the position being distorted to realize that it has been misrepresented, and so they accept the straw man as if it was the real argument. Often people whose views have been caricatured fight an uphill battle, first to reestablish their genuine position and then to get it listened to after an audience has accepted the distorted one as genuine. Thus, many fallacies succeed because of ignorance and ill will on the part of both the fallacious reasoner and the audience.

Slippery Slope

Human experience offers many examples of "one thing leading to another." We decide to have a baby, for instance, and one thing follows another from the first diaper change all the way to college graduation, with so much in between and beyond that a parent's life is altered forever and fundamentally. Furthermore, it is always prudent to ask about any decision we face, "If I do *x,* what consequent *y* am I likely to face? And if *y* happens, where will that lead me?"

The slippery-slope fallacy takes advantage of our commonsense notion that actions have consequences, that one thing leads to another. The difference between the truth and the fallacy is that the drastic consequences the arguer envisions could not or are not likely to happen. Those who opposed making the so-called morning-after pill available without a prescription sometimes warned of a wholesale decline in sexual morality, especially among young adults. That has not happened, and in any case, technology is one thing, morality another. What makes sex right or wrong has little to do with the method of contraception.

The slippery-slope fallacy plays on fear, indicating one of the many ways that one kind of appeal—in this case, to logic, or reasoning about consequences—connects with other kinds of appeal—in this case, to emotion. Working in tandem, such appeals can be powerfully persuasive. All the more reason, then, to stand back and analyze any slope an argument depicts critically. Is the predicted slide inevitable or even probable? In many cases, the answer will be no, and we can see through the appeal to what it often is: a scare tactic to head off doing something that makes good sense.

Hasty Generalization

We cannot think and therefore cannot argue without generalizing. Almost any generalization is vulnerable to the charge of being hasty. All that is required for what some logicians label as "hasty generalization" is to find a single exception to an otherwise true assertion. So "SUVs waste gas." But the new hybrid SUVs are relatively gas efficient. "Since 9/11 American Muslims have felt that their loyalty to the United States has been in doubt." Surely we can find individual Muslims who have not felt insecure at all.

The problem with hasty generalization is not exceptions to statements that are by and large true. The problem, rather, is generalization based on what is called a biased (and hence unrepresentative) sample, which results in a generalization that is false. If you visit an institution for the criminally insane, you will probably encounter some schizophrenics. You may conclude, as many people have, that schizophrenics are dangerous. Most of them, however, are not, and the relatively few who are do not pose a threat when they stay on their meds. The common fear of "schizo street people" results from a hasty generalization that can do real harm.

Begging the Question

We end with this because it is especially tricky. Every argument makes assumptions that have not been and in some cases cannot be proven. We simply could not argue at all if we had to prove everything our position assumes. Hence, virtually all arguments can be said to "beg the question," to assume as true that which has not been shown definitively as true. Furthermore, we can never tell when an assumption that almost no one doubts can turn out to be very doubtful as new information emerges. Assumptions we used to make routinely can become hot issues of controversy.

Consequently, we should confine "begging the question" to *taking as settled the very question that is currently at issue.* Someone is charged with a crime, and the press gives it much ink and air time. Inevitably, some people jump to the conclusion that the accused is guilty. This can be such a big problem that it is hard to impanel a jury that has not been hopelessly biased by all the coverage.

We beg the question whenever we assume something that can not be assumed because it is the very thing we must prove. Fallacies of this kind are usually no harder to spot than the juror who thinks the defendant is guilty simply because he or she has been charged with a crime. Pro-lifers, for example, argue in ways that depend on the fetus having the legal status of a person. Of course, if the fetus is a person, there is no controversy. Abortion would be what pro-lifers say it is, murder, and thus prohibited by law. The personhood of the fetus is *the* issue; assuming the fetus is a person is begging the question.

The following exercise does not include what many such exercises offer—fallacies so obvious they would fool no one over the age of ten. You will have to think them through, discuss them at length. In some cases, rather than flatly rejecting or accepting the arguments, you may want to give them "partial credit," a degree of acceptance. That is fine, part of learning to live with shades of gray.

EXERCISE

The following examples come from instances of persuasion that appeared in earlier editions of this book. Some may not be fallacious in any way. Assess them carefully and be prepared to defend the judgment you make.

1. From an ad depicting the VW Beetle: "Hug it? Drive it? Hug it? Drive it?"

2. From a cartoon depicting a man holding a pro-life sign, above which appear two specimen jars, one containing "a dead abortion doctor,"

the other "a dead fetus." The man is pointing at the jar with the dead fetus. The caption reads "We object to this one."

3. From an essay called "The End of Life," James Rachels offers the following interpretation of the Biblical prohibition against taking human life: "The sixth commandment does not say, literally, 'Thou shalt not *kill*'— that is a bad translation. A better translation is, Thou shalt not commit *murder,* which is different, and which does not obviously prohibit mercy killing. Murder is by definition *wrongful killing;* so, if you do not think that a given kind of killing is wrong, you will not call it murder" [author's emphasis].

4. From a panel discussion in *Newsweek* about violence in the media: The moderator asks a representative of the movie industry why the rating NC-17 is not applied to "gratuitously violent movies." The response is "because the definition of 'gratuitous' is shrouded in subjectivity. . . . Creative people can shoot a violent scene a hundred different ways. Sex and language are different, because there are only a few ways [you can depict them on screen]. . . . Violence is far more difficult to pin down."

5. From an essay critical of multiculturalism comes the following quotation from the political scientist Samuel B. Huntington, whose view the essay's author endorses: "Does it take an Osama bin Laden . . . to make us realize that we are Americans? If we do not experience recurrent destructive attacks, will we return to the fragmentation and eroded Americanism before September 11?"

6. From an essay advocating multiculturalism: "The attack on affirmative action isn't really about affirmative action. Essentially it is another tactic in today's war on the gains of the 1960's, a tactic rooted in Anglo resentment and fear. A major source of that fear: the fact that California will almost surely have a majority of people of color in 20 to 30 years at most, with the nation as a whole not far behind."

7. From an essay urging us to move beyond the multiculturalism debate, written by a naturalized American citizen who was born in India: "I take my American citizenship very seriously. I am a voluntary immigrant, and not a seeker of political asylum. I am an American by choice, and not by the simple accident of birth. I have made emotional, social, and political commitments to this country. I have earned the right to think of myself as an American."

8. From an article arguing that militant Islam and Islamic terrorism is like Nazism: "Once again, the world is faced with a transcendent conflict between those who love life and those who love death both for themselves and their enemies. Which is why we tremble."

9. From an article arguing that American foreign policy provokes terrorism and that the root of it all is "our rampant militarism": "Two of the most

influential federal institutions are not in Washington but on the south side of the Potomac River: the Defense Department and the Central Intelligence Agency. Given their influence today, one must conclude that what the government outlined in the Constitution of 1787 no longer bears much relationship to the government that actually rules from Washington. Until that is corrected, we should probably stop talking about 'democracy' and 'human rights.'"

10. From an article that attempts to explain human mating in evolutionary terms: "Feelings and acts of love are not recent products of particular Western views. Love is universal. Thoughts, emotions, and actions of love are experienced by people in all cultures worldwide—from the Zulu in the southern tip of Africa to the Eskimos in the north of Alaska."

For additional examples of fallacies for analysis, see "Stalking the Wild Fallacy" <http://www.fallacyfiles.org/examples.html>.

active voice A statement that has the doer of the action as the subject of the sentence, followed by the verb and the person or thing that receives the action. "The President (subject) criticized (verb) the Congress (receiver of the action) for delaying passage of the legislation." See also **passive voice.** Favor active voice sentences because they are easier to understand and make a stronger impression on readers.

allusion A reference to a person, event, or text the author thinks readers will recognize without explanation. Usually a quick Google search will clarify allusions you do not recognize.

analogy The comparison of one subject to another, implying that they are similar. Analogies are often used in arguments to reason that what the opposition accepts as valid for one subject should also be accepted as valid for the other.

annotation Typically a handwritten note in the margins of something we are reading that, for instance, helps us to relocate a major point in a text or raises a question about something the author has said. Form the habit of writing in the margins of print texts and typing in comments for electronic ones, necessary for both critical reading and research.

argument An opinion backed by a reason—for instance, "We should cap tuition (opinion) because too many college students cannot afford the increasing costs" (reason). Arguments are developed into cases by adding more reasons and evidence that supports each reason.

assumptions Principles or values an argument takes for granted and so does not state or defend. "We should cap tuition because too many college students cannot afford the increasing costs" assumes what most Americans take for granted: that extending higher education to as many people as possible is a good thing. When we make arguments, we should examine our assumptions to make sure that they do not need defending. When we assess the arguments of other people, we should expose the assumptions to make sure they should go unchallenged.

audience Also called "readership," designates the particular group of people we hope to reach with an argument. There is no point in trying to convince an audience that already agrees with us, nor an audience unalterably opposed to our opinion. Choose an audience weakly inclined your way, inclined against you but open to reason, or with no position at all. In this middle range of groups, pick the audience you know best and then consciously develop your argument to appeal to their values and interests.

bibliography A list of sources on a particular topic, arranged in alphabetical order according to the last name of the author or, in the case of sources with no author, the first major word in the title. Called "Works Cited" in the Modern Language Association (MLA) handbook used in most English courses.

blog Short for "web log," designates online sites maintained by people who wish to register their opinions on many issues. A vast, democratic expansion of access for popular opinion as compared to print. Increasingly important for the discussion of controversial subjects worldwide.

case structure An outline of a case, including the claim or thesis you are defending, the reasons that justify or explain your thesis, and the evidence you will offer to develop and support each reason. Useful as a plan for writing a paper. Typically does not include your ideas for beginning and ending the paper and perhaps other details, such as showing why a possible objection to your case does not hold.

claim Also called "thesis," the central statement an argument defends, the belief or action you want your audience to accept. A claim is a carefully stated and more specific version of your opinion about something. For example, you may be opposed to the war in Afghanistan (opinion) but your claim might be, "We should withdraw all American troops from Afghanistan within the next year."

climate of opinion The range of existing common viewpoints on any controversial question. As an arguer you need to be acquainted with what people are thinking and what motivates the varying points of view, which usually amounts to the perceived interests of the contending parties.

common knowledge A convention that governs the need for citation of sources. If the information is widely known—say, the kind of information available in a general use encyclopedia or what people who keep up with the news would know—there is no need to provide parenthetical notation or an entry in your Works Cited page. Our advice is to cite anyway if you are in doubt about whether an item qualifies as common knowledge.

connotation What a word or statement implies. For instance, both "famous" and "notorious" mean that someone is well known, but "notorious" implies well known for bad reasons. Because the connotations of words register unconsciously most of the time, and therefore are not usually criticized, choosing words carefully for their connotations has a powerful impact on readers. See also **denotation.**

context A word with many meanings, used most commonly in two ways: context of text, which means the place from which a quotation is taken, and context of situation, which means the circumstances in which a writer writes or an interpreter of a text interprets. So, Abraham Lincoln's famous words, "With malice toward none, with charity for all," come near the end of his Second Inaugural, where he is discussing the attitude he would take in victory when the Civil War is over (context of text), a position he argued against those that would punish the South for starting the war (context of situation). See also **rhetorical context.**

conviction An earned opinion achieved through thought, research, and discussion. We often have casual opinions that need to be examined thoroughly to see what they are worth. Many

Americans believe, for instance, that Japanese- and German-made vehicles are always better than domestics—are they? What does the best current data show? We should argue (make claims about) only opinions that we have earned.

convincing One of the four aims of argument; to seek assent to a claim not directly tied to taking action. Convincing, or case-making, is especially valued in the academic world, where we are often debating issues or topics about which no action can be taken. "What caused the Great Depression?" for example, is an important question in an American history course, crucial to understanding the past.

critical distance The kind of thinking that comes from stepping back far enough to inquire into opinions dispassionately and methodically.

critical reading Also called "close reading," a thoughtful examination of a text with the intent of analyzing and evaluating it. Instead of reading a text just to know what it says, we slow down enough to think through what it says and whether or not we should accept what it says as accurate and true.

critical thinking The process of evaluating the reasoning in an argument regardless of whether you agree with it.

critique A written evaluation of some kind of performance.

denotation The dictionary meaning of a word, apart from what it implies. The term "white," for example, in the United States designates anyone whose skin color and facial features allows him or her to pass as white whatever the racial mix in ancestry might be. See also **connotation.**

dialogue Also known as "dialectic," a serious conversation where opinions are both offered and examined critically, often through a process of questioning. If someone says, "We must secure our borders," a legitimate question for exploring the assertion would be, "What do you mean by 'secure'?" What sort of people do you want to prevent entering or leaving our country without documents?

editing As contrasted with revision, or significant rewriting of a paper to improve content, designates attention to such matters as awkward sentences, paragraph coherence, and errors; as such, editing comes after revision and before proofreading. Editing is indispensable to writing well. See also **revision** and **proofreading.**

ethos A word that means "character" in Greek, used to designate how a writer appeals through self-presentation, conforming to what readers admire: being intelligent, well informed, fair, aware of reader fears and desires, and so on. Perhaps the most potent form of appeal because people we do not trust cannot convince or persuade us.

evidence Reasoning, data, and expert opinion advanced to justify or confirm a reason. The amount of evidence needed to support a reason depends on the degree of resistance you estimate your audience will have.

fallacies The misuse of a legitimate form of appeal, sometimes with the intent to deceive. For example, on matters requiring specialized knowledge, we cite expert opinion, as in the case of the law with regard to a particular practice. There is nothing wrong with citing expert opinion, but we must cite a genuine expert and represent his or her opinion accurately to avoid committing a fallacy.

field research Generating your own information through observation, experiment, surveys, and the like rather than using sources. A valuable way to test your opinions and to provide evidence about issues that existing data do not address. If you want to know what students at your college think about living together before marriage, for instance, conducting a survey may be the only way to secure such information.

graphics Visual supplements to a text, including tables, charts, pie graphs, drawings, and the like. Widely used in publications but not exploited nearly enough in academic writing by students.

identification Linking the reader's interest and values with what a writer has said, achieved most commonly and powerfully through shared experiences, such as participation in the same war, the same activity or place, and so on. The writer who advocates preservation of nature by describing a trip as a

child to a national park is seeking the identification of readers with the cause.

implied questions All statements we write or read answer (mostly unstated) questions, so that the statement, "The first one hundred days of a new President are not as important as many people think," answers the question, "How well does the first one hundred days predict the success of an administration?" Learning to ask what questions a statement implies can help you with argument in two ways: With your own arguments, you can see better the sequence of questions your sentences are answering, and possibly detect other questions you need to answer and a better sequence for the ones you have answered. With the arguments of others, you can more easily detect different possible answers to the questions the writer's sentences imply.

inquiry One of the four aims of argument, inquiry uses reasoning to analyze and critique existing arguments, as part of the process of arriving at the truth as you see it. Asking and pursuing questions is the key to effective inquiry. See also **conviction.**

issue A controversial question connected to a subject matter or topic. If we are discussing health care, for example, an issue would be, "Should access to health care be considered a right for all U.S. citizens?" See also **stasis.**

logos A Greek word that means "reasoning," used to designate the logical appeal of an argument. Readers respond to well-reasoned cases by saying "This makes sense to me" or "Your logic is compelling," the kind of response logical appeal seeks.

mediation One of the four aims of argument, used to find common ground and agreement on a course of action when parties to a dispute are in sharp and seemingly irreconcilable conflict. You will encounter mediating positions on all controversial topics, from which you can learn the valuable skill of bringing people together who, in many cases, have stopped talking to one another.

opinion Most arguments begin with opinions, with something as simple as "I didn't like that movie." When we take an opinion like this and think it through, developing it into a thesis or claim we could defend in a movie review, including good reasons and evidence, we have moved to what we need for arguing well. The same as **position;** contrast with **conviction.**

paraphrase   Your own wording for what someone else has said or written. Paraphrase is an alternative to quotation, and should be used more often than quotations, which should be reserved for statements where the exact wording matters—for instance, when you want to comment on the wording.

passive voice   A sentence where the doer or subject of the verb's action is either left out or moved to a position after the verb. "Congress was criticized by the President for delaying passage of the legislation." Passive voice is harder for readers to understand, and so active voice is preferred. However, passive voice is useful when you do not know who did something or when you do not want to emphasize responsibility for an action. Prefer active voice, but use passive voice when you have a good reason to do so. See also **active voice.**

pathos   A Greek word that means "feeling" or "emotion," used to refer to moving readers to act by, for example, showing photographs of people suffering from a natural disaster that has left them destitute. When appropriate emotional appeals are used to supplement sound reasoning, pathos is a legitimate way to persuade others.

persuasion   One of the four aims of argument, persuasion moves people to act by combining logical argument with emotional appeals. Advertising is the most common form of persuasion in our culture, but you will find it whenever action is at stake, such as an election, a vaccination campaign, contributions for disaster relief, and so on.

plagiarism   The act of presenting someone else's words or ideas as your own, without acknowledging the source. The most common forms of plagiarism result from not supplying parenthetical documentation for information you have paraphrased or paraphrasing in language too close to your source even with documentation. Be careful to supply all documentation and put your source aside when you paraphrase to avoid using the language of your source. See also **paraphrase.**

prewriting   The same as preparing to write, designates everything done prior to the first draft. Good writing results from effort in prewriting and revision, or rewriting. You cannot put too much effort into preparing to write and into revision of first drafts.

proofreading   The last phase of writing, coming after revision and editing, the purpose of which is to detect small remaining errors, such as typos and misspellings. A good technique is to read your paper slowly, sentence-by-sentence, beginning with the last paragraph and working back toward the first. This will help you detect errors by breaking up the flow of the prose. See also **revision** and **editing.**

qualifier   Acknowledging the strength of one's claim: "Counterinsurgency usually fails when the government of a country lacks popular support." The word "usually" is a qualifier, allowing for exceptions to the claim.

reason   A sentence saying why a claim should be accepted as true.

rebuttal   Anticipating objections to your argument a reader is likely to have and showing why they do not hold. Normally appears after you make your case, but if the objections to your case are strongly adhered to by your audience, sometimes the refutation should come first.

responsible reasoning   In contrast to unexamined arguments, responsible reasoning depends on careful and disciplined thought. A person who reasons responsibly has inquired into a range of opinions on an issue and is both well-informed and open to constructive criticism. Responsible arguments seek to win assent from readers rather than provoke resistance. Responsible reasoning is the goal of this book.

revision   Literally, "to see again," refers to big changes to improve the quality of a first draft, such as adding content, rearranging the order of presentation, and rewriting to make points clearer and more forceful. See also **editing** and **proofreading.**

rhetoric   The art of argument, techniques that convince or persuade. See also **responsible reasoning.**

rhetorical context The knowledge of circumstances required to understand a text and therefore to respond to it well: information about the time and place in which it was written, about the author, who published it, and the ongoing debate to which it contributed. Online searches can turn up helpful information quickly and with little effort.

sampling A fast and not necessarily sequential reading of a text, such as reading the first sentence in each paragraph, to get a feeling for the territory it covers and as preparation for a more careful reading.

stasis Means "stop" or "stay," and refers to ordering the issues connected with a controversial topic to discover what you should argue. For instance, the proposed sending of astronauts to Mars begins with the question, "Is such a mission worthwhile?" If you say "no," then you stop with this issue and make your case. If you say "yes," then the next issue is technical feasibility. "Can we actually send a human mission to Mars?" If you say "yes," you make your case that it should and can be done. And so on, through other issues connected with the Mars mission. Stasis is a valuable approach to understanding how issues connected with a topic relate to one another. See also **issue**.

summary A shortened version of a passage or text, reduced to its essential ideas stated in your own words. Summaries are usually one-third or less the length of the original passage. In arguments, writers often summarize an opposing view in order to examine or refute it.

thesis See **claim**.

topic A subject matter, such as "American policy in the Middle East." Typically arguments are restricted to some part of a topic, and often to a single issue related to it. Narrowing topics to something that can be handled within the length allowed for an assignment is an important part of prewriting or preparing to write. See also **issue**.

visual rhetoric The use of images, sometimes with sound or other appeals to the senses, to persuade one's audience to act as the image-maker would have them act. Advertising and political cartoons are examples of visual rhetoric.

voice Your voice in writing should be a slightly more formal version of how you speak when you are talking to people you do not know well and whose opinion of you matters. The result is "conversational prose," in general the norm of good writing now. Voice also needs to be adapted to your subject matter, audience, and purpose, so that, for instance, writing about the quality of medical care available to wounded veterans has a high seriousness that, say, a parking problem does not.

warrant In an argument, an underlying belief or assumption that one would have to accept in order to see the reasons and evidence as valid support for the claim. For example, the argument that to improve the quality of education, schools should hire more teachers depends on the warrant, or assumption, that students learn more in small classes than in large ones.

CREDITS

Text Credits

Chapter 1

p. 10: **Kelby S. Carlson,** "Fighting Words: Why Our Public Discourse Must Change," *The Vanderbilt Torch,* March 17, 2012. © 2012 The Vanderbilt Torch. Reprinted with permission.

Chapter 2

p. 21: **Sally Jenkins,** "A Major Gain for College Sports?" *Washington Post,* October 6, 2011. Reproduced with permission of Washington Post Co. via Copyright Clearance Center.

p. 33: **Mariah Burton Nelson,** Response to Sally Jenkins, "A Major Gain for College Sports?" *Washington Post,* October 6, 2011. Reprinted by permission of the author.

p. 35: **Keith A. Williams,** "A Technological Cloud Hangs Over Higher Education," *The Chronicle of Higher Education,* June 3, 2012. Reprinted by permission of the author.

Chapter 4

p. 54: **Tom Stafford,** "Why Sherry Turkle Is So Wrong," Posted April 27, 2011 on idiolect blog. Reprinted by permission of the author.

p. 59: **David Fryman,** "Open Your Ears to Biased Professors," *The Justice,* September 1, 2004, p. 10. © 2004 David Fryman and The Justice at Brandeis University.

p. 70: **D. D. Solomon,** "How Professors Should Deal with Their Biases." Reprinted with permission.

Chapter 5

Color Insert, Figure C-8: Analysis by Twenge, Campbell, and Gentile based on the American Freshman Survey, in William Kremer, "Does Confidence Really Breed Success?" *BBC News Magazine,* January 3, 2013, http://www.bbc.co.uk/news/magazine-20756247. Reprinted by permission of Dr. Jean Twenge.

p. 86: **Ryan Herrscher,** "The Image of Happiness: An Analysis of Coca-Cola's 'Open Happiness' Campaign." Reprinted with permission.

Chapter 6

p. 117: **Richard Moe,** "Battling Teardowns, Saving Neighborhoods." Speech given to the Commonwealth Club, San Francisco, California, June 28, 2006. © 2006 National Trust for Historic Preservation. Reprinted with permission.

p. 152: **Julie Ross,** "Why Residential Construction Needs to Get a Conscience." Reprinted with permission.

Chapter 7

p. 166: **Pat Joseph,** "Start by Arming Yourself with Knowledge: Al Gore Breaks Through with His Global-Warming Message," *Sierra,* September/October 2006. Reprinted with permission from *Sierra,* the magazine of The Sierra Club.

Chapter 8

pp. 180, 181: From *Oxford English Dictionary Online* definitions of "narcissism" and "Narcissus." By permission of Oxford University Press.

p. 181: **John F. Schumaker,** "The Paradox of Narcissism" from *In Search of Happiness: Understanding an Endangered State of Mind,* pp. 167–173. Copyright © 2006 by John F. Schumaker. Reprinted by permission of Penguin Group (NZ).

p. 187: **Duncan Greenberg,** © 2007 Duncan Greenberg, "Generation Y and the New Myth of Narcissism." From the *Yale Herald.* Reprinted by permission.

p. 197: **Ian Fagerstrom,** "Comparison of Perspectives on Narcissism." Reprinted with permission from Ian Fagerstrom.

Chapter 9

p. 209: **Wilbert Rideau,** "Why Prisons Don't Work" from *Time* (March 21, 1994). Copyright © 1994 by Wilbert Rideau. Reprinted with the permission of the author, c/o The Permissions Company, Inc., www.permissionscompany.com

p. 212: **T. Boone Pickens,** "The Pickens Plan to Free the United States from Dependency on Oil," http://www.pickensplan.com. Reprinted with permission.

p. 231: **Noelle Alberto,** "Multitasking: A Poor Study Habit." Reprinted with permission from Noelle Alberto.

Chapter 10

p. 239: **Tom Beaudoin,** "Consuming Faith: Integrating Who We Are With What We Buy," *Tikkun,* Volume 19, no. 4, pp. 13–14. Copyright, 2004, Tikkun Magazine. All rights reserved. Republished by permission of the copyright holder, and the present publisher, Duke University Press. www.dukeupress.edu

p. 260: **Natsumi Hazama,** "Is Too Much Pressure Healthy?" Reprinted with permission from Natsumi Hazama.

Chapter 11

p. 268: **Roger Kimball,** Editor, *The New Criterion.* From "Institutionalizing Our Demise: America vs. Multiculturalism" from *Lengthened Shadows: America and Its Institutions in the Twenty-First Century,* edited by Roger Kimball and Hilton Kramer. San Francisco: Encounter Books, 2004. First published by Encounter Books. Reprinted by permission of the author.

p. 275: **Elizabeth Martínez,** "Reinventing 'America': Call for a New National Identity" from *De Colores Means All of Us: Latina Views for a Multi-Colored Century* by Elizabeth Martínez. Copyright © 1998 by Elizabeth Martínez. Reprinted by permission of South End Press.

p. 287: **Bharati Mukherjee,** "Beyond Multiculturalism: Surviving the Nineties" by Bharati Mukherjee. Copyright © 1996 by Bharati Mukherjee. Originally published in *Journal of Modern Literature.* Reprinted by permission of the author.

p. 297: **Angi Grellhesl,** "Mediating the Speech Code Controversy." Reprinted with permission of Angi Grellhesl.

Chapter 12

p. 306: Excerpt from pp. 4–9 from *The Substance of Style* by Virginia Postrel. Copyright © 2003 by Virginia Postrel. Reprinted by permission of HarperCollins Publishers.

p. 310: **Erik Kain,** "In Defense of Consumerism," November 30, 2009, http://trueslant.com/erikkain/2009/11/30/in-defense-of-consumerism. © 2009 Erik Kain. Reprinted by permission of the author.

p. 315: **Alex Kotlowitz,** "False Connections." From *Consuming Desires: Consumption, Culture, and the Pursuit of Happiness,* edited by Roger Rosenblatt. Copyright © 1999 by Island Press. Reproduced by permission of Island Press, Washington, DC.

p. 322: **Caroline Heldman,** "Out-of-Body Image," *Ms.* magazine, Spring 2008, pp. 52–55. Reprinted by permission of *Ms.* magazine. © 2008.

p. 327: From *Branded: The Buying and Selling of Teenagers* by Alissa Quart. Copyright © 2003 Alissa Quart. Reprinted by permission of Basic Books, a member of the Perseus Books Group.

p. 336: **John F. Schumaker,** "The Happiness Conspiracy: What Does It Mean to Be Happy in a Modern Consumer Society?" *New Internationalist,* July 2006. Reprinted by kind permission of the New Internationalist. Copyright New Internationalist. www.newint.org.

Chapter 13

p. 347: **National Geographic,** "Global Warming: An Overview," three articles from http://environment.nationalgeographic.com/environment/global-warming. © National Geographic Society. Reprinted with permission.

p. 353: Excerpts from **Bill Blakemore,** "Who's 'Most to Blame' for Global Warming?" ABC News online, July 22, 2012. http://abcnews.go.com/blogs/technology/2012/07/whos-most-to-blame-for-global-warming. Copyright © 2012 ABC News Internet Ventures. Reprinted with permission.

p. 358: **Gregg Easterbrook,** "Some Convenient Truths," *The Atlantic Monthly,* September 2006, pp. 29–30. © 2006 by Gregg Easterbrook. Reprinted by permission of the author.

p. 362: **Tim Appenzeller,** "The Coal Paradox," *National Geographic,* March 2006. Reprinted by permission of National Geographic Society.

p. 368: **Michelle Nijhuis,** from "Selling the Wind" by Michelle Nijhuis. First published in *Audubon* magazine, September–October 2006. © 2006 by the National Audubon Society. Reprinted by permission of Audubon magazine.

p. 372: **Union of Concerned Scientists,** "Ten Personal Solutions." © 2006 Union of Concerned Scientists. Reprinted with permission. (www.ucsusa.org)

p. 375: **William F. Ruddiman,** "Consuming Earth's Gifts" from *Plows, Plagues, and Petroleum: How Humans Took Control of Climate* by William F. Ruddiman. Copyright © 2005 by Princeton University Press. Reprinted by permission of Princeton University Press.

Chapter 14

p. 383: **Pew Research Center,** *Millennials: Confident. Connected. Open to Change.* Executive Summary. Pew Research Social & Demographic Trends, February 24, 2010. Copyright © 2010 Pew Research Center. Reprinted with permission.

p. 391: **Kit Yarrow and Jayne O'Donnell,** from "Gen Y is from Mercury" from *Gen BuY: How Tweens, Teens, and Twenty-Somethings Are Revolutionizing Retail,* pp. 1–2, 5–11. Copyright © 2009 by Kit Yarrow and Jayne O'Donnell. Reproduced with permission of John Wiley & Sons Inc.

p. 405: **Richard Vedder,** "Forgive Student Loans? It's the Second-Worst Idea Ever," *National Review Online,* October 11, 2011. © 2011 by National Review, Inc. Reprinted by permission.

p. 408: **Anya Kamenetz,** "Waking Up and Taking Charge," from *Generation Debt* by Anya Kamenetz, copyright © 2006 by Anya Kamenetz. Used by permission of Riverhead Books, an imprint of Penguin Group (USA) Inc.

Chapter 15

p. 418: **Tamar Jacoby,** from *Reinventing the Melting Pot: The New Immigrants and What It Means to Be American,* edited by Tamar Jacoby. Copyright © 2004 Tamar Jacoby. Reprinted by permission of Basic Books, a member of the Perseus Books Group.

p. 434: **Linda Chavez,** "The Realities of Immigration," *Commentary,* July–August 2006, pp. 34–39. Reprinted by permission of Commentary Magazine.

p. 441: **Chris Farrell,** "Obama's Next Act: Immigration Reform," *Business Week,* December 13, 2012. © 2012 Bloomberg L.P. All Rights Reserved. Reprinted with permission.

p. 444: **Dava Castillo,** "Comprehensive Immigration Reform—Past, Present, Future," Allvoices.com, December 24, 2012, http://www.allvoices.com/contributed-news/13675429-comprehensive-immigration-reformpresent-past-and-future. Copyright © 2012 by Allvoices.com. Reprinted with permission.

p. 447: "Border Patrol State" by Leslie Marmon Silko, originally published in The Nation. Copyright © 1996 by Leslie Marmon Silko, used by permission of The Wylie Agency LLC.

Chapter 16

p. 455: **P. M. Forni,** "What Is Civility?" from *Choosing Civility: The Twenty-five Rules of Considerate Conduct* © 2003 by P. M. Forni. Reprinted by permission of St. Martin's Press. All Rights Reserved.

p. 467: "Left Is Mean But Right Is Meaner, Says New Study of Political Discourse," *Tufts Now,* February 10, 2011. Reprinted with permission.

p. 470: **Dr. Brian McGee,** "Can Political Rhetoric Be Too Civil?" Originally published with the title "Too Much Civility Can Serve Agenda of the Powers That Be" in *Post & Courier,* November 21, 2009. Reprinted by permission of the author.

p. 472: **Frank D. Adams and Gloria J. Lawrence,** "Bullying Victims: The Effects Last into College," *American Secondary Education,* vol. 40, no. 1 (Fall 2011). Reprinted by permission of the publisher.

Chapter 17

p. 495: **Barbara Sahakian and Nora Volkow.** © 2008 National Public Radio, Inc. NPR® news report titled "Professor's Little Helper" was originally broadcast on NPR's *Talk of the Nation®* on March 17, 2008, and is used with the permission of NPR. Any unauthorized duplication is strictly prohibited.

p. 501: **Gregory Stock**, "Choosing Our Genes." Originally published in *The Futurist*, vol. 36, no. 4 (July–August 2002), pp. 17–23. Used with permission from The World Future Society (www.wfs.org).

p. 506: **John Naish**, "Genetically Modified Athletes," *Daily Mail* (London), July 31, 2012. Reprinted by permission of Solo Syndication, agents for the *Daily Mail*.

p. 514: **Ed Smith**, "Lance Armstrong and the Cult of Positive Thinking." Originally published with the title "The Voodoo Cult of Positive Thinking: Lessons from Lance Armstrong's Disgrace" in *New Statesman*, vol. 141, issue 5122 (September 7, 2012), p. 62. Reprinted by permission of New Statesman.

p. 519: **C. Ben Mitchell**, "On Human Bioenhancements," *Ethics & Medicine*, 25:3 (Fall 2009), pp. 133–134. Reprinted by permission of The Bioethics Press Limited.

Photo Credits

About the Authors

Page xiii(top, bottom): © Dave Tyler Photography.

Chapter 1

Figure 1.1: The J. Paul Getty Museum, Villa Collection, Malibu, California. Interior attributed to Meidias Painter, Attic Red-Figure Kylix, 410 B.C. Terracotta 12.4x13 82.AE.38. detail. © J. Paul Getty Museum.

Chapter 5

Color Insert 1: © Image courtesy of The Advertising Archives; C-2: © U.S. Postal Service/AP Photo; C-3: © Holzman & Kaplan Worldwide, Bret Wills, photographer; C-4: © f4foto/ Alamy C-5: © adidas. adidas, the 3-Bars logo and the 3-Striples mark are registered trademarks of the adidas Group; C-6: © Seth Wenig/AP Photo; C-7: © Frances Fife/ AFP/Getty Images; 5.4: © Digital Vision/Getty Images RF; 5.5: © Orhan Cam/Shutterstock; 5.6: © Russ Widstrand/ Getty Images; 5.7: © Astrid Riecken/The Washington Post/ Getty Images; 5.8a: © Julio Cortez/AP Photo; 5.8b: © Spencer Platt/Getty Images.

Chapter 6

Figure 6.1: © Drexel University, All Rights Reserved; 6.2–6.3: Screenshot Courtesy of the Library of Congress, www.loc. gov; 6.4–6.5: Screenshot Courtesy of the University of Massachusetts, Amherst, Libraries; 6.6–6.7: © Southern Methodist University. Reprinted with permission; 6.8: © 2007 EBSCO Industries, Inc. All rights reserved. Reprinted with permission; 6.9: Google and Google logo are registered trademarks of Google Inc., used with permission; 6.11–6.12: © 2007 National Trust for Historic Preservation. Reprinted with

permission; pp. 140–141: © Pew Research Hispanic Center, www.pewhispanic.org; pp. 154–159: © Carolyn Channell.

Chapter 7

Page 169: © John Engstead/Hulton Archive/Getty Images.

Chapter 8

Figure 8.1: © John William Waterhouse/The Bridgeman Art Library/Getty Images.

Chapter 9

Page 214: © 2010 3TIER, Inc.; p. 215: Civic NGV image provided courtesy of American Honda Motor Co., Inc. © 2009 American Honda Motor Co., Inc.; p. 216(left): © Glen Allison/Getty Images RF; p. 216(right): © moodboard/Super-Stock RF.

Chapter 10

Page 238: Screenshot Courtesy of Subaru of America, Inc.

Chapter 12

Opener: © Peter Macdiarmid/Getty Images; p. 324: © Banana-Stock/PunchStock RF.

Chapter 13

Opener: NASA; p. 345: © Second Nature, Inc.; p. 348: © Peter Essick/Aurora Photos; p. 367(fuel cell bus): © Koichi Kamoshida/Getty Images; p. 367(green roof): Courtesy of City of Chicago; p. 367(hybrid car): © David Paul Morris/ Getty Images; p. 367(lightbulbs): © William Thomas Cain/ Getty Images; p. 367(solar panels): © Mark Newman/FLPA imageBROKER/Newscom; p. 367(fuel cell): © Joe Raedle/ Getty Images; p. 367(power station): © Photodisc/Getty Images RF.

Chapter 14

Opener: © ZUMA Wire Service/Alamy.

Chapter 15

Opener: © The McGraw-Hill Companies, Inc./John Flournoy, photographer; p. 417: © Picture History/Newscom; p. 418: Image courtesy www.printsofpropaganda.com; p. 441: © John Moore/Getty Images.

Chapter 16

Opener: © SW Productions/Photodisc/Getty Images RF; p. 459: © Mark Ostow/*The New York Times*/Redux Pictures; p. 479: © Weston Colton/Getty Images RF.

Chapter 17

Opener: © Timothy A. Clary, Torsten Blackwood/AFP/Getty Images; p. 506: © Fabrice Coffrini/AFP/Getty Images.

action appeal, 242–243, 245, 246, 257

active and passive voice, 525–526

Adams, Frank D., 472–477, 478

advertisements
as arguments, 34
consumer society and body image, 322–331
discussion questions on, 75–76
in persuasive argument, 238–239
as visual arguments, 75–76
in works cited or reference lists, 139, 150

"The Aesthetic Imperative" (Postrel), 306–309

aesthetics, 306–309

Alberto, Noelle, 227–228, 230–233

alternative form argument
discussion questions on, 37
reading and reading preparation, 33–38
responding to, 38

American College and University Presidents' Climate Commitment, 344–347

American Psychological Association (APA)
direct quotations using style of, 129–130, 132–133
documentation style, 128, 129–130, 132–133, 143–151
reference lists in style of, 133, 143–151
student sample research paper in style of, 177–180

analogies, 62–63

analysis. See specific topics

annotation
bibliographic, 126–127
collaborative discussion of, 23–24
in critical reading, 19–20, 35
informal writing employing source, 121

anthologies, 98–99, 135–136

Apenzeller, Tim, 362–366

apostrophes, 536–537

appeal, four forms of, 237. See also emotion and emotional appeals (pathos); good character (ethos);

persuasive argument; reason and reasoning (logos); style
action, 242–243, 245, 246, 257
emotional, 254, 545, 548–550
in persuasive argument, 237, 242–243, 245, 246, 254, 545–554
style in, 545, 550–551

appositive, 529

Archer, Dale, 402–404

argument. See also alternative form argument; convincing argument; critique, argument; inquiry argument; mediatory argument; persuasive argument; visual argument; writing, research-based argument
advertisement and story as, 34
aims of, 13–15, 266
critical reading of, 17–18
definition and nature of, 3–4
example of, 3–4, 6–7, 40
listening as part of, 7
paraphrasing, 26
proposal example, 21–23
reading, 17–38
responding to, 25–26, 29–33, 38
as responsible reasoning, 5–6, 7–10
rhetorical context of, 19
schematic layout of, 24–25
Toulmin method for analyzing, 39
vivid description, voice, and style for, 34

Aristotle, 4, 541

Armstrong, Lance, 514–516

art reproduction, 139

assertion, levels, 202

assignment, writing
for editorial cartoon analysis, 85–89
inquiry argument, 189–190
visual argument of college promotion, 89
visual argument through posters and flyers, 88–89
visual argument using graphics, 89

assimilation, immigrant, 418–428

assumptions, argument critique, 62–63

audience
in argument critique, 58
arguments needing, 4
best practices in reasons for, 253
case-making for, 205, 218–219
concept close-up analysis of, 249
in convincing argument, 201–202, 208
inquiry argument, 189, 201
persuasive argument, 247, 248, 249
responsible reasoning considering, 8, 9–10

audiovisual materials, 100

author. See books; reference lists; works cited; writer; specific topics

"Battling Teardowns, Saving Neighborhoods" (Moe), 117–121, 123–125

Bazelon, Emily, 479–481, 482

Beaudoin, Tom, 239–243

begging the question reasoning, 554

beliefs, untrue, 543

best practices
action appeal revision checklist, 257
for annotation in critical reading, 20
for argument critique, 62
for argument response questions, 31
for argument rhetorical context, 19
for audience-based reasons, 253
for case and case outline draft, 228, 229
critique revision checklist, 69
difference understanding questions, 283
for direct quotation leading, 132
for graphics' use, 90
internet source evaluation, 114
paraphrase guidelines as, 27
perspective comparison revision checklist, 196
for perspective comparison strategy, 190
for question organization, 195
source writing guidelines, 126
summarizing guidelines, 125
team research, 221
Toulmin method analysis, 49
writing preparation, 251

"Beyond Multiculturalism: A Two-Way Transformation" (Mukherjee), 287–293
bias, 112, 115
bibliographies and bibliographic information
  annotated, 126–127
  case, 223
  source evaluation and recording, 111–112
Blakemore, Bill, 353–358
blogs, listservs, usenet groups, and message boards
  as internet sources, 101, 111
  in works cited or reference lists, 142, 151
body image, 322–331
books
  in library online catalogue, 104, 105–106
  monographs, anthologies, and reference, 98–100
  in reference lists, 146–148
  as sources, 98–99
  in works cited, 134–138
boolean searching, 102
"The Border" (Douthat and Woodson), 430–433
"The Border Patrol State" (Silko), 447–450
"Brain Enhancement Is Wrong, Right?" (Carey), 492–495
Brando, Marlon, 168, 169
Brooks, David, 312–315
Brooks, Kim, 395–399
Brummett, Barry, 6
bullying
  college impact from, 472–477
  as incivility form, 452, 454, 472–482
"Bullying Victims: The Effects Last Into College" (Adams and Lawrence), 472–477
Burton Nelson, Martha, 33

"Can Political Rhetoric Be Too Civil?" (McGee), 470–472
Caplan, Arthur L., 509–514
capsule summaries, 126–127
Carden, Art, 42–44
Carey, Benedict, 492–495
Carlson, Kelby, 10–12
cartoon
  consumer society, 320–322
  editorial, 76–77, 85–89

gene-splicing, 517–518
immigration, 429
case and case-making
  assertion levels of, 202
  for audience, 205, 218–219
  best practices for draft and draft outline of, 228, 229
  collaborative activity on topic of, 220
  considered opinion in, 222
  in convincing argument, 202–205
  critical reading detection and outlining of, 23–24
  defensible opinion required in, 223–224
  example, 203–204
  informal writing, 218, 222, 226
  issue, 220–221
  method for making, 203–205
  problem-solution/cause-and-effect reasoning, 211–212
  reasons, 202–203, 226–229
  research, 222–224
  strategies, 207–208, 211–212, 216–217
  structure, 25, 203, 204, 207–208, 211, 217
  thesis, reasons, and evidence of, 203, 207–208
  topic, 218, 219–224
  voice and style of, 219
  writing preparation, 224–226
Castillo, Dava, 444–446
"Changes in Narcissism" (Twenge), 185–187
Chavez, Linda, 434–441
"Choosing Our Genes" (Stock), 501–505
chunking, 28, 38
civility. *See also* incivility
  courtesy, politeness, and manners compared to, 457
  definition and nature of, 454, 455–458
  discussion questions on, 458
  in politics, 469–472
claim, 24, 25, 28, 31
  in critique of argument, 62–63
  defined, 3–4
  example argument involving, 40
  qualifier limiting or clarifying, 41–42
  Toulmin method analyzing, 44–45, 49
clarity and conciseness
  active and passive voice for, 525–526

editing for, 524–526
  main idea forceful expression for, 524–525
"The Coal Paradox" (Appenzeller), 362–366
cognitive-enhancing drugs, 495–500
coherence
  defined, 532
  editing for, 532–535
  old to new information for, 533–534
  transitions for idea relationships in, 534–535
collaborative activity
  alternative form argument and chunking strategy, 38
  annotation discussion, 23–24
  case structure, 211, 217
  case topic, 220
  inquiry argument topic subdivisions as, 191
  narcissism examples found in, 181
  paraphrase comparison, 27
  persuasive argument, 246, 250, 252
  rephrasing in own words as, 192
  warrants found in, 41–44, 47
college, bullying, 472–477
"College Debt: Necessary Evil or Ponzi Scheme?" (Archer), 402–404
colons, 538
commas, 537
commentary, 192–193
commercial internet domains, 109
common ground, mediatory argument, 285–286
common opinion, 546–547
comparative grid, 193
comparing perspective. *See* perspective comparison
component parts, 28–29, 38
"Comprehensive Immigration Reform- Past, Present, and Future" (Castillo), 444–446
concept close-up
  annotated bibliography sample entry, 127
  argument aims compared in, 15
  audience analysis, 249
  case-making and structure in, 25, 203, 204
  context and critique, 52
  of convincing compared to inquiry argument, 202
  critical reading defined in, 18

four appeal forms, 237
of mediation characteristics, 266
persuasive argument, 236, 237, 249
of plagiarism, 165, 166
responsible reasoning, definition
and criteria of, 6, 8
rhetoric defined in, 5
synthesis defined in, 176
Toulmin model diagram, 48
conciseness. *See* clarity and
conciseness
connections, 193–194
constructive criticism, 8, 9
consumer society
advertising and body image in,
322–331
aesthetics and, 306–309
cartoons, 320–322
discussion questions concerning,
306, 310, 312, 315, 320, 322,
327, 331, 336, 340
happiness in, 331–340
nature of, 303–304
quotations on, 305–306
shopping, spending, and fashion,
310–320
writing concerning, 310–340
"Consuming Earth's Gifts" (Ruddiman), 375–378
"Consuming Faith" (Beaudoin),
239–242
context
argument rhetorical, 19
critical reading and skimming for,
18–19
critique and, 52
responsible reasoning understanding, 8, 10
visual argument and rhetorical, 74
controversial, 218
convincing argument. *See also* case
and case-making
as argument aim, 13–14, 15
audience for, 201–202, 208
case in, 202–205
discussion questions concerning,
207, 211, 216
enhancement of human lives, 506,
513–514, 521
on incivility, 458–459, 469, 472,
482
inquiry argument compared to,
201–202
paper draft and revision of,
229–233

readings for, 205–208
revision of, 230
sample, 205–207, 209–210, 212–216
voice in, 208–209
courtesy, 457
critical distance, 53, 61
critical reading
annotation in, 19–20, 35
of arguments, 17–18
case detection and outline in, 23–24
context skimming and content reading in, 18–19
defined, 18
discussion questions on, 23
paraphrasing in, 26
of sources, 111–114
strategies and application, 18–23,
26, 27–28, 29–30
summarizing in, 27–28
writer and bias identification in,
112
critical thinking, 52–53
critique, argument
analogies, assumptions, implications, and key terms in, 62–63
analysis, 61–64
assessment example, 70
audience in, 58
claim, reasons, and evidence in,
62–63
context and, 52
critical distance in, 53, 61
definition and nature of, 51
discussion questions concerning, 57
enhancement of human lives, 516
example, 54–57, 59–61
first impression and response in, 61
items not worth challenging in, 61
locating and choosing, 58–59
paper draft elements and steps for,
66–72
reaction compared to, 52–58
reader, purpose, and tone in, 66
reality test for, 64–65
research for, 64–65
revision and revision checklist in,
69–72
stance formulated, determined, and
refined for, 66
strategies, 53–54
summarizing, 65
topic and focus, 58
critique paper, drafting
in argument critique, 66–72
development in, 67–68

discovery sample excerpts, 68–69
editing as part of, 72
organization, 67
revision, 68–70

description and descriptive outline,
28–29, 34
development
in paper drafting, 195, 229, 255–256
paper drafting involving, 67–68
dialogue
inquiry argument through, 13
source, 127
differences
mediatory argument and factual, 282
mediatory argument and interest, value, and interpretational,
282–285
discussion questions
on advertisements, 75–76
alternative form argument, 37
argument response, 33
on civility and incivility, 458, 462,
465, 467, 469, 471, 478, 481
consumer society, 306, 310, 312,
315, 320, 322, 327, 331, 336,
340
convincing argument, 207, 211, 216
critical reading, 23
on critique of argument, 57
editorial cartoon, 76–77
enhancement of human lives, 492,
495, 500, 505, 508–509, 513,
516, 521
global warming, 351, 358, 361,
368, 371–372, 374, 378
immigration, 418, 424, 428–429,
430, 434, 440–441, 443, 446, 450
inquiry argument, 180, 187, 189
involving Toulmin method, 44
mediatory argument, 295
on millennials, 390–391, 394–395,
399, 401–402, 404, 407,
412–413
on narcissism, 187, 189
on news photographs, 82
persuasive argument, 242
public sculpture, 81
responsible reasoning, 7, 12–13
documentation and incorporation. *See
also* government agency or document; reference lists; works cited
APA style, 128, 129–130, 132–133,
143–151
direct quotations in, 129–131, 132

documentation and
  incorporation—*Cont.*
  indirect quotations in, 131–133
  MLA style, 128, 129, 131–132,
    133–143
  of sources, 128–151
"Does Money Buy Happiness?"
  (Douthat and Peck), 331–336
domains, internet and website, 108–
  109, 114–115
"Don't Be a Bystander" (Bazelon),
  479–481
double-entry notebook
  argument response through, 30,
    32–33
  making, 32–33
  text observations and responses in,
    30, 32
Douthat, Ross, 331–336, 430–433
drafting. *See* paper, drafting and
  revising
drugs. *See* enhancement of human
  lives

Easterbrook, Gregg, 358–361
editing. *See also* clarity and conciseness; coherence; emphasis; paper,
  drafting and revising; proofreading; revision
  appositive in, 529
  for clarity and conciseness,
    524–526
  for coherence, 532–535
  definition and nature of, 523
  for emphasis, 526–532
  in paper drafting, 72
  participial phrases in, 528–529
  practice, 529, 534
  relative pronouns in, 527–528
  style and, 523–524
  subordination and subordinating
    conjunctions in, 526–527, 528
editorial cartoons
  discussion questions concerning,
    76–77
  persuasive power activity on, 77
  as visual argument, 76–77
  writing assignment analyzing,
    85–89
education and college debt, millennial,
  395–407, 408–412
educational institution internet
  domains, 109
Elliott, Carl, 487–492

ellipses, 130–131
emotion and emotional appeals (pathos)
  fallacies involving, 545, 548–550
  fear in, 548
  in mediatory essay, 293–294
  in persuasive argument, 254, 545,
    548–550
  pity in, 548–549
  ridicule in, 549–550
  visual argument and, 74
emphasis
  editing for, 526–532
  main idea, 526–529
  modifying clauses and, 527–528
  modifying phrases and, 528–529
  sentence length and pattern vari-
    ance for, 529–530
  special effects for, 530–532
encyclopedia. *See* reference books or
  work
enhancement of human lives
  bio-, 487–491, 519–521
  brain, 492–495
  cognitive drugs for, 495–500
  convincing argument on, 506,
    513–514, 521
  critique argument, 516
  definition, nature, and examples for,
    485–486
  discussion questions on, 492, 495,
    500, 505, 508–509, 513, 516, 521
  gene-splicing in, 517–518
  genetic athletic, 506–508
  germinal technology, 501–505
  happiness in, 487–491
  inquiry argument on, 501
  mediatory argument, 495
  persuasive argument on, 492, 509
  positive thinking in, 514–516
  steroid, 509–513
ethical writing. *See also* plagiarism
  good character or ethos and, 163
  good study habits and, 172
  source use violation and, 164–170
  unethical help given and received
    impacting, 170–172
ethics
  for millennials, 388–389
  plagiarism as violation of, 166
  visual argument and appeal of, 74
ethos. *See* good character (ethos)
evaluation. *See also* sources
  source, 111–117
  website, 114–117

Everything Good Is Bad for You
  (Johnson), 3–4, 6–7
evidence, 18, 24–25, 28, 31, 33–34
  in case structure, 203
  in critique of argument, 62–63
  example argument involving, 40
  in persuasive argument, 237, 252,
    253
  reason and arranging, 227–229
  Toulmin method for analyzing,
    45–46, 49
"Existing Technologies for Reducing
  CO2 Emissions" (Gore), 367

"The Factories of Lost Children"
  (Weber), 243–245
fallacies. *See also* emotion and emotional appeals (pathos); good
  character (ethos); reason and
  reasoning (logos)
  Aristotle on, 541
  common, examples, 545–550
  common, reasons for, 542–545
  definition and nature of, 541–542,
    552
  emotion or pathos involved in, 545,
    548–550
  exercise involving persuasive,
    554–556
  good character or ethos involved in,
    545, 546–547
  intentional, 544–545
  persuasive argument, 541–556
  of reasoning or logos,
    545, 551–554
  of style, 545, 550–551
  unintentional, 542–544
false cause reasoning, 552
"False Connections" (Kotlowitz),
  315–320
Farrell, Chris, 441–443
fear, 548
field research
  interviews in, 97–98
  observations as, 96
  questionnaires and surveys in,
    96–97
  in research-based writing, 96–98
"Fighting Words: Why Our Public
  Discourse Must Change" (Carlson), 10–12
first impression, 61
focus. *See* inquiry argument, topic and
  focus of; topic

"Forgive Student Loans?" (Vedder), 405–407
Forni, P. M., 454, 455–458
freewriting or notebook entry, 45, 47, 121–122
Fryman, David, 59–64, 68–69, 70–71

"Gen Y Is from Mercury" (O'Donnell and Yarrow), 391–394
"Generation Y and the New Myth of Narcissus" (Greenberg), 187–189
"Gene-Splicing as Big Business" (Gonick and Wheelis), 517–518
gene-splicing cartoon, 517–518
genetic athletic enhancement, 506–508
"Genetically Modified Athletes" (Naish), 506–508
germinal technology enhancement, 501–505
global warming
    American College and University Presidents' Climate Commitment and, 344–347
    coal in, 362–366
    countries responsible for, 353–358
    discussion questions, 351, 358, 361, 368, 371–372, 374, 378
    earth resource exhaustion and, 375–378
    existing technologies for reducing, 367
    issue through student example concerning, 94–95
    mediatory argument for, 372
    National Geographic overview of, 347–351
    nature of, 343–344
    pessimism concerning, 358–361
    Scientific American on reducing, 352–353
    ten personal solutions to, 372–374
    wind power in reducing, 368–371
    writing concerning, 344–351, 352–361, 362–366, 367, 368–371, 372–374, 375–378
"Going beyond Edgy- and Falling off the Cliff" (Pitts), 465–467
Gonick, Larry, 517–518
good character (ethos), 58
    ancient Greece and, 4, 541
    common opinion, 546–547
    ethical writing and, 163
    fallacies involving, 545, 546–547

in mediatory essay, 293
personal attack, 546, 547
in persuasive argument, 237, 247, 254, 545, 546–547
tradition and, 547
Google Scholar and specialized searches, 110
Gore, Al, 166–167, 367
government agency or document
    internet domains, 109
    reference list treatment of, 147
    works cited for, 142
grammatical errors
    introductory participial phrase, 539
    paired coordinator, 539
    proofreading for, 538–540
    split subject and verb, 539–540
graphics
    best practices for use of, 90
    nature and types of, 83–84
    photographs as, 84–85
    visual argument writing assignment using, 89
    as visual arguments, 83–85
Greece, ancient, 4–5, 541
Greenberg, Duncan, 187–189
"The Grill-Buying Guy" (Brooks, D.), 312–314

happiness, 86–88
    in consumer society, 331–340
    in enhancement of human lives, 487–491
"The Happiness Conspiracy: What Does It Mean to Be Happy in a Modern Consumer Society?" (Schumaker), 336–340
hasty generalization reasoning, 553–554
Heldman, Caroline, 322–327
Herrscher, Ryan, 86–88
Hollander, Anne, 168
"How Professors Should Deal with Their Biases" (Solomon), 70–71
human bioenhancement, 487–491, 519–521
Huntington, Samuel, 425–429

identity, millennial, 387–388
"The Image of Happiness" (Herrscher), 86–88
images
    historical immigration, 417–418
    visual argument and "reading," 74

immigration
    assimilation and, 418–428
    border control and, 430–440, 447–451
    cartoon, 429
    discussion questions on, 418, 424, 428–429, 430, 434, 440–441, 443, 446, 450
    historical images of, 417–418
    media and political influence on, 435
    mediatory argument concerning, 268–286
    reform, 441–446
    state and statistics, 415–417, 436, 437
    U.S. acceptance of, 435–436
implications, argument critique, 62–63
"In Defense of Consumerism" (Kain), 310–311
inaccurate reporting, 542–543
incivility
    bullying as form of, 452, 454, 472–482
    definition, nature, and examples of, 453–455
    discussion questions on, 458, 462, 465, 467, 469, 471, 478, 481
    online, 462–467
    persuasive argument on, 462
    in politics, 467–472
    popular culture, 465–467
    research, 158–159, 482
    research, convincing, and mediatory argument on, 458–459, 469, 472, 482
    texting at table, 459–462
incorporation. See documentation and incorporation
"The Indispensable Opposition" (Lippmann), 7
information
    bibliographic, 111–112, 126–127, 223
    coherence in old to new, 533–534
    research and interpretation versus, 222–223
inquiry argument. See also paper, drafting and revising; perspective comparison
    abstract in, 178
    as argument aim, 13, 15
    assignment, 189–190

inquiry argument—*Cont.*
  audience, voice, and style in, 189,
    201
  convincing argument compared to,
    201–202
  defined, 175
  discussion questions, 180, 187, 189
  on enhancement of human lives,
    501
  introduction, 178–179
  on narcissism, 181–189
  paper drafted and revised for,
    194–197
  perspective comparison in, 175
  research and sources for, 190
  sample, 177–180
  student draft revision example,
    197–200
  writer in, 177
  writing assignment suggestions,
    189–190
inquiry argument, topic and focus of,
    189
  choosing, 190
  collaborative activity finding subdi-
    visions in, 191
  exploration of, 190–194
  exploratory stance maintained in
    finding, 194
  main points, 191–192
  paraphrasing and summarizing
    main points in, 191, 192–193
"Institutionalizing Our Demise:
    America *vs.* Multiculturalism"
    (Kimball), 268–275
internet
  advanced web-searching on,
    109–110
  best practices for source evaluation
    from, 114
  blogs, listservs, message boards, and
    chat groups, 101, 111
  commercial, nonprofit, educational,
    and government sources on, 109
  domains, 108–109, 114–115
  issue found through, 93
  library resources and catalogue on,
    104–108
  plagiarism rising from, 163–164,
    165–166
  reference list on sources from,
    150–151
  research, 108–111
  research-based writing employing, 98

search term precision in research-
    ing, 101–103
  sources, 100–101, 108–111, 114,
    139–143, 150–151, 163–165
  subject directories, 110
  website evaluation, 114–117
  works cited for sources from,
    139–143
interpretation, 222–223
interviews. *See also* personal
    communication
  in field research, 97–98
  works cited or reference lists for
    broadcast or published, 143, 151
in-text citations and references
  to electronic sources, 133
  lacking author or editor, 145
  for multiple authors, 144–145
  paraphrased, 143–144
  personal communication, 146
  for quotations, 144, 145
  in reference lists, 143–146
introduction, inquiry argument,
    178–179
"Is It Time to Kill the Liberal Arts
    Degree?" (Brooks, K.), 395–399
issue
  in case-making, 220–221
  global warming student example,
    94–95
  internet for finding, 93
  lectures, panel/class discussions, and
    conversations for, 94
  library databases and resources for
    finding, 93
  magazines and newspapers for find-
    ing, 93
  in news, 93–94
  personal observations for identify-
    ing, 94
  research-based writing and finding,
    92–95
  topic compared to, 92

Jacoby, Tamar, 418–424, 428
Jenkins, Sally, 20, 21–33
Johnson, Steven, 3–4, 6–7
Judson, Olivia, 205–208, 216–217

Kain, E. D., 310–312
Kamenetz, Anya, 408–412
keyword searching, 102
Kimball, Roger, 268–275
knowledge, insufficient, 542–543

Kohn, Alfie, 40
Kotlowitz, Alex, 315–320

"Lance Armstrong and the Cult of
    Positive Thinking" (Smith),
    514–516
Lawrence, Gloria J., 472–477, 478
lectures, panel/class discussions, and
    conversations, 94
"Let's Be Blunt: It's Time to End the
    Drug War" (Carden), 42–44
"A Liberal Arts Education Is Still Rel-
    evant" (Rabinowitz), 399–401
library, databases and resources
  books and periodicals in online
    catalogue of, 104–106
  issue found through, 93
  keyword search, 105
  online and online catalogue, 104–108
  research, 103–108
  research-based writing employing, 98
  search term precision in searching,
    101–103
  searching, 103–108
  sources, 98–100
  subject search, 105
  title search, 104
  works cited for, 142
Light, Richard J., 169–170
Lippmann, Walter, 7
listening, in argument, 7
logical analysis, 48
logos. *See* reason and reasoning
    (logos)

magazines
  issue found through, 93
  as periodical sources, 100
  in reference lists, 149, 150
  in works cited, 138, 142
main idea
  clarity and conciseness in forceful
    expression of, 524–525
  emphasis, 526–529
"A Major Gain for College Sports"
    (Jenkins), 21–23
manners, 457
Martínez, Elizabeth, 275–280
McGee, Brian, 469, 470–472
media, immigration influence of,
    434–440
mediatory argument, 402, 434
  as argument aim, 14–15, 266
  common ground found in, 285–286

definition and nature of, 265–266
discussion questions on, 295
enhancement of human lives, 495
factual differences in, 282
for global warming, 372
immigration conflict for, 268–286
on incivility, 458–459
interests, values, and interpretational differences in, 282–285
mediatory essay in, 287–295
Rogerian form of, 267–268
writers' positions analyzed, 280–281
mediatory essay
emotional appeal in, 293–294
good character in, 293
in mediatory argument, 287–295
reasons in, 294–295
student example of, 297–299
writing, drafting, and revising, 295–299
millennials
definition, nature, and issues facing, 381–382, 383–386
discussion questions concerning, 390–391, 394–395, 399, 401–402, 404, 407, 412–413
education and college debt for, 395–407, 408–412
greatest influences on, 391–394
identity of, 387–388
as open, connected, and confident, 383–390
work ethic, moral values, and race relations for, 388–389
writing concerning, 383–390, 391–394, 395–401, 402–404, 405–407, 408–412
Mitchell, C. Ben, 519–521
MLA. *See* Modern Language Association
Modern Language Association (MLA)
documentation, 128, 129, 131–132, 133–143
quotations using style of, 129, 131–132
student sample of research paper in style of, 152–161
works cited using, 133–143
modifying
clauses, 527–528
phrases, 528–529
Moe, Richard, 117–121, 123–125, 129–130

monographs, 99
moves, summarizing, 29
Mukherjee, Bharati, 287–295
"Multitasking: A Poor Study Habit" (Alberto), 231–233

Naish, John, 506–508
narcissism, 191
collaborative activity for finding examples of, 181
definition and nature of, 180–181
discussion questions concerning, 187, 189
inquiry arguments concerning, 181–189
readings on, 180–181
National Geographic global warming overview, 347–351
need, persuasive argument, 248–250
"The New Immigrants and the Issue of Assimilation" (Jacoby), 418–424
news issues, 93–94
news photographs
discussion questions concerning, 82
persuasiveness analysis activity on, 82
as visual argument, 81–83
newspapers
issue found through, 93
as periodical sources, 100
in reference lists, 148–150
in works cited, 138–139, 142
Nijhuis, Michelle, 368–371
nonprofit internet domains, 109
notebook entry. *See* freewriting or notebook entry

"Obama's Next Act: Immigration Reform" (Farrell), 441–443
observations, personal
in field research, 96
issue identified through, 94
O'Donnell, Jayne, 391–394
OED. *See Oxford English Dictionary*
omissions and jumbled passages, 536
"On Human Bioenhancements" (Mitchell), 519–521
"One Nation, Out of Many: Why 'Americanization' of Newcomers Is Still Important" (Huntington), 425–428
online incivility, 462–467

online resources and catalogue, library, 104–108
"Open Your Ears to Biased Professors" (Fryman), 59–61
opinion, defensible
case-making requiring, 223–224
research results for assessing, 224
as thesis, 224–225
"Optimism in Evolution" (Judson), 205–207, 216–217
organization
best practices involving question, 195
in paper drafting, 67, 195, 229
source, 114
origin, source, 113–114
"Out-of-Body Image" (Heldman), 322–327
Oxford English Dictionary (OED), 180–181

paired coordinators, 539
paper, drafting and revising, 68–70. *See also* critique paper, drafting
convincing argument, 229–233
development and organization in, 67, 195, 229, 255–256
for inquiry argument, 194–197
mediatory essay, 295–299
persuasive argument, 255–263
planning for, 194
student example, 197–200, 230–233, 257–263
paper, purchasing, 164–165
"The Paradox of Narcissism" (Schumaker), 181–184, 191
paraphrasing
argument, 26
collaborative comparison of, 27
commentary on, 192–193
in critical reading, 26
defined, 26
guidelines, 27
inquiry argument topic through, 191, 192–193
in-text citation, 143–144
plagiarism in unnamed source, 168–170
plagiarism through inadequate, 167–168
practicing, 26–27
source use through, 122–124
voice in, 26

participial phrases
  in editing, 528–529
  grammatical errors in introductory,
    539
passive voice. *See* active and passive
  voice
pathos. *See* emotion and emotional
  appeals (pathos)
Peck, Don, 331–336
periodicals
  in library online catalogues, 105
  in reference lists, 148–150
  scholarly journals, magazines, and
    newspapers as, 99–100
  as sources, 99–100
  in works cited, 138–139, 142
personal attack, 546, 547
personal communication
  in-text citations, 146
  in reference lists, 151
perspective comparison
  application of and questions to ask
    in, 177
  best practice strategies for, 190
  comparative grid activity for, 193
  connections tracked in, 193–194
  inquiry argument involving, 175
  nature and genre examples of, 176
  revision checklist best practices, 196
  writing for, 176
persuasive argument. *See also* fallacies
  advertisement, 238–239
  as argument aim, 14, 15
  assignment, 247
  audience, 247, 248, 249
  collaborative activity, 246, 250, 252
  concept close-up concerning, 236,
    237, 249
  definition and nature of, 235–238
  discussion questions concerning, 242
  enhancement of human lives, 492,
    509
  fallacies of, 541–556
  four appeal forms in, 237, 242–243,
    245, 246, 254, 545–554
  on incivility, 462
  need in, 248–250
  paper drafting and revising of,
    255–263
  readings for, 239–246
  reasons, evidence, and good char-
    acter in, 237–238, 247, 251–252,
    253, 254, 545, 546–547,
    551–554

student example, 252–253,
    257–263
  style in, 545, 550–551
  topic for, 247, 248–250
  voice in, 247
  writing, 236, 239, 247–263, 361
persuasiveness, 82
photographs
  as graphics, 84–85
  news, 81–83
phrase searching, 102
Pickens, T. Boone, 212–216, 217
Pitts, Leonard, Jr., 465–467
pity, 548–549
plagiarism
  defined, 164, 165
  ethical violation of, 166
  help given and received as, 170–172
  inadequate paraphrasing as,
    167–168
  internet giving rise to, 163–164,
    165–166
  paper found online as, 165
  paper purchase as, 164–165
  paraphrasing without source named
    as, 168–170
  priority in, 170
  research-based writing and, 92
  student, 163–164
  uncited source passage as, 165–167
"A Plan for Reducing American
    Dependence on Foreign Oil"
    (Pickens), 212–216
"Play with Your Food, Just Don't
    Text" (Rimer), 459–462
politeness, 457
politics
  immigration influenced by, 434–440
  incivility in, 467–472
popular culture, incivility in, 465–467
positive thinking, 514–516
Postrel, Virginia, 306–310
priority, plagiarism, 170
"Professor's Little Helper?" (Sahakian
    and Volkow), 495–500
proofreading
  definition and nature of, 523, 535
  grammatical errors, 538–540
  for omissions and jumbled
    passages, 536
  practice, 540
  for punctuation problems,
    536–538
  spelling errors, 536

public sculpture
  discussion questions concerning, 81
  as visual argument, 77, 79–81
punctuation problems
  apostrophes within, 536–537
  colons in, 538
  commas in, 537
  proofreading for, 536–538
  semicolons in, 537–538
purpose, argument critique, 66

qualifier
  claim limited or clarified by, 41–42
  Toulmin method revealing, 41–42,
    49
Quart, Alissa, 327–331
question, organization, 195
questionnaires and surveys, field
    research, 96–97
questions. *See* discussion questions
quotations
  APA style, 129–130, 132–133
  best practices for leading into
    direct, 132
  block, 131
  documentation of direct, 129–131,
    132
  documentation of indirect, 131–133
  ellipses and square bracket altera-
    tion of direct, 130–131
  in-text citations for, 144, 145
  MLA style, 129, 131–132

Rabinowitz, Stuart, 399–401
reaction
  critical distance and, 53
  critique compared to, 52–58
reader, argument critique, 66
reading. *See also* critical reading;
    proofreading; *specific topics*
  alternative form arguments, 33–38
  arguments, 17–38
  for convincing argument, 205–208
  images in visual argument, 74
  narcissism, 180–181
  persuasive argument, 239–246
  responsible reasoning, 10–12
"The Realities of Immigration"
    (Chavez), 434–440
reality test, argument critique, 64–65
reason and reasoning (logos), 24–25,
    29, 31, 33–34. *See also* respon-
    sible reasoning
  in ancient Greece, 4, 541

argument as responsible, 5–6, 7–10
begging the question, 554
best practices for audience-based,
    253
in case structure, 203, 207–208
case-making, 202–203, 226–229
in critique of argument, 62–63
defined, 3–4
evidence arranged with, 227–229
example argument involving, 40
fallacies of, 545, 551–554
false cause, 552
four criteria of responsible, 8–10
hasty generalization, 553–554
mediatory essay incorporating,
    294–295
persuasive argument through, 237–
    238, 251–252, 545, 551–554
rule of thumb for, 551
slippery slope, 553
straw man, 552–553
Toulmin method for analyzing,
    45–46, 49
rebuttal, Toulmin method, 42, 47, 49
reference books or work
    as book sources, 99
    in reference lists, 148, 151
    in works cited, 137, 142
reference lists
    APA style, 133, 143–151
    books in, 146–148
    examples of, 146
    in-text citations in, 143–146
    periodicals in, 148–150
"Reinventing 'America': Call for a
    New National Identity" (Mar-
    tínez), 275–280
relative pronouns, 527–528
reliability, source, 112–113
religious text, 137–138
rephrasing, 192
research. See also evaluation; internet;
    library, databases and resources;
    sources; writing, research-based
    argument; specific topics
for argument critique, 64–65
best practices for team, 221
case, 222–224
field, 96–98
for incivility, 158–159, 482
information versus interpretation
    in, 222–223
inquiry argument, 190
library and internet, 98–111

opinion assessed from results of,
    224
research-based argument writing. See
    writing, research-based argument
response, argument, 25–26, 29
    alternative form, 38
    in critique of argument, 61
    discussion questions
        concerning, 33
    double-entry notebook in, 30,
        32–33
    example, 33
    questions for, 31
"Response to 'A Major Gain for
    College Sports'" (Burton
    Nelson), 33
responsible reasoning
    audience considered in, 8, 9–10
    context understood in, 8, 10
    discussion questions on, 7, 12–13
    as open to constructive criticism,
        8, 9
    reading concerning decline of,
        10–12
    as well informed, 8, 9
revision. See also paper, drafting and
    revising
    in argument critique, 69–72
    checklist, 69, 230, 257
    of convincing argument, 230
    definition and nature of, 523
    paper drafting involving, 68–70
    perspective comparison checklist
        for, 196
    strategy, 70
    student example of, 197–200
rhetoric
    in ancient Greece, 4–5
    argument and context of, 19
    definition and nature of, 4–6
    visual, 74, 86–88
    in visual argument, 73–74, 76
The Rhetoric of Popular Culture
    (Brummett), 6
Rideau, Wilbert, 209–210, 211–212
ridicule, 549–550
Rimer, Sarah, 459–462
Rogerian argument, 267–268
Rogers, Carl, 267
Ross, Julie, 94–95, 100, 102, 115,
    152–161
Rudd, Andy, 177–180
Ruddiman, William F., 375–378
rudeness. See incivility

Sachs, Jeffrey D., 304
Sahakian, Barbara, 495–501
scholarly journals
    as periodical sources, 99
    reference list treatment of, 149,
        150, 151
    works cited for online, 142
Schumaker, John F., 181–184, 191,
    192, 336–340
Scientific American, 352–353
search. See specific topics
search term precision
    keyword, phrase, and boolean, 102
    in library and internet research,
        101–103
    subject words used in, 102–103
"Selling the Wind" (Nijhuis), 368–371
semicolons, 537–538
sentence, length and pattern variance,
    529–530
"A Shot in the Rear: Why Are
    We Really against Steroids?"
    (Caplan), 509–513
Silko, Leslie Marmon, 447–451
slippery slope reasoning, 553
Smith, Ed, 514–516
Solomon, D. D., 68–72
"Some Convenient Truths" (Easter-
    brook), 358–361
sophistry, 541
sources. See also plagiarism; reference
    lists; works cited
    annotation of, 121
    audiovisual, 100
    best practices for evaluating inter-
        net, 114
    best practices writing guidelines
        for, 126
    bibliographic information recorded
        for, 111–112
    blogs, listservs, usenet groups, and
        message board, 101, 111
    books as, 98–99
    critical reading of, 111–114
    dialogue about, 127
    documentation and incorporation
        of, 128–151
    eliminating inappropriate, 111
    ethical violation in use of, 164–170
    evaluation of, 111–117
    example use of, 117–121
    informal writing for mastery of,
        121–127
    inquiry argument, 190

sources—*Cont.*
internet, 100–101, 108–111, 114, 139–143, 150–151, 163–165
in-text references to electronic, 133
library, 98–100
notebook for use of, 121–122
origin, organization, and aims of, 113–114
paraphrasing, adequate and inadequate examples, 123–124
paraphrasing important ideas from, 122–124
periodicals as, 99–100
reliability of, 112–113
research-based writing and finding, 95–96
research-based writing and misusing, 92
research-based writing and types of, 98–101
summarizing, 124–127
use of, 117–128
website, 100
special effects, 530–532
spelling errors, 536
split subjects and verbs, 539–540
square brackets, 130
Stafford, Tom, 54–57
steroids, 509–513
Stock, Gregory, 501–505
story, 34
strategy
argument critique, 53–54
case and case-making, 207–208, 211–212, 216–217
chunking, 38
critical reading, 18–23, 26, 27–28, 29–30
revision, 70
straw man reasoning, 552–553
student
inquiry argument draft revision example, 197–200
mediatory essay example, 297–299
persuasive argument example, 252–253, 257–263
plagiarism, 163–164
student sample analysis
of APA style research paper, 177–180
of MLA style research paper, 152–161
of visual rhetoric, 86–88
works cited, 160–161

study habits, 172
style. *See also specific topics*
argument through, 34
case voice and, 219
editing and, 523–524
fallacies of, 545, 550–551
inquiry argument voice and, 189
in persuasive argument, 545, 550–551
subject directories, 110
subject words, 102–103
subordination and subordinating conjunctions, 526–527, 528
summarizing
argument critique, 65
best practice guidelines for, 125
capsule, 126–127
chunking in, 28, 38
component parts and moves, 28, 38
as critical reading strategy, 27–28
defined, 27
descriptive outline in, 29
example of, 30
inquiry argument focus through, 191
source, 124–127
synthesis, 176

"A Technological Cloud Hangs over Higher Education" (Williams), 35–37
texting, table, 459–462
thesis
of case structure, 203, 207
as defensible opinion, 224–225
unpacking, 226
tone, argument critique, 66
topic. *See also* inquiry argument, topic and focus of
case, 218, 219–224
inquiry argument focus and, 189
issue compared to, 92
persuasive argument, 247, 248–250
Toulmin, Stephen, 39–40
Toulmin method
analysis summary, 47, 49
argument analyzed through, 39
claim analyzed in, 44–45, 49
demonstration of, 44–47
discussion questions involving, 44
evidence and reasons analyzed in, 45–46, 49
example argument, 42–44

freewriting or notebook entry for applying, 45, 47
model diagram, 48
overview of, 39–41
qualifier revealed in, 41–42, 49
rebuttal in, 42, 47, 49
warrant, or unspoken assumption, in, 40–41, 46–47, 49
tradition, 547
transitions, idea relationship, 534–535
Twenge, Jean M., 185–187
Twenty Ads That Shook the World (Twitchell), 75
Twitchell, James B., 75
"The Tyranny of Happiness" (Elliott), 487–491

United States (U.S.), immigration, 435–436
The Uses of Argument (Toulmin), 39

Vedder, Richard, 405–407
visual argument. *See also* visual rhetoric
advertisements as, 75–76
context, emotional, and ethical appeal in, 74
five common types of, 75–85
graphics as, 83–85
images "read" in, 74
news photographs as, 81–83
public sculpture as, 77, 79–81
as rhetorical, 73–74
rhetorical appeal activity for, 76
writing assignment for college promotion, 89
writing assignment using graphics, 89
writing assignment using posters/flyers, 88–89
visual rhetoric
definition and nature of, 74
rhetorical analysis of, 74
student sample analysis of, 86–88
voice, 58
in appeal to action, 246
argument through, 34
case style and, 219
in convincing argument, 208–209
defined, 208
inquiry argument style and, 189
in paraphrasing, 26
persuasive argument, 247
Volkow, Nora, 495–501

"Waking Up and Taking Charge"
    (Kamenetz), 408–412
warrant
    collaborative activity for finding,
        41–44, 47
    Toulmin method involving, 40–41,
        46–47, 49
Weber, Katharine, 243–246
websites
    bias and mission of, 115
    domain of, 108–109, 114–115
    evaluation of, 114–117
    as sources, 100
    works cited for, 140–141
well informed, responsible reasoning,
    8, 9
"What Is Civility?" (Forni), 455–458
Wheelis, Mark, 517–518
"Which Character Should Sports
    Develop" (Rudd), 177–180
"Who's 'Most to Blame' for Global
    Warming?" (Blakemore),
    353–358
"Why Prisons Don't Work" (Rideau),
    209–210
"Why Sherry Turkle Is So Wrong"
    (Stafford), 54–57
"Why We Are So Rude Online" (Bern-
    stein), 462–464

Williams, Keith A., 34–38
Woodson, Jenny, 430–433
works cited
    advertisements and art reproduc-
        tion in, 139
    books in, 134–138
    for internet sources, 139–143
    MLA styles for, 133–143
    periodicals in, 138–139, 142
    student sample research paper,
        160–161
writer
    critical reading in identification of,
        112
    as inquirer, 177
    mediatory argument and positions
        of, 280–281
    source aim of, 114
writing. See also critique paper,
    drafting; ethical writing; paper,
    drafting and revising
    on aesthetics, 306–309
    best practices in preparation for, 251
    case-making and preparation for,
        224–226
    on consumer society, 310–340
    on global warming, 344–351,
        352–361, 362–366, 367,
        368–371, 372–374, 375–378

mediatory essay, 295–299
    on millennials, 388–390, 391–394,
        395–401, 402–404, 405–407,
        408–412
    for perspective comparison, 176
    persuasive argument, 236, 239,
        247–263, 361
writing, research-based argument. See
    also documentation and incor-
    poration; field research; internet;
    issue; library, databases and
    resources; sources
    field research in, 96–98
    finding sources for, 95–96
    issue found in, 92–95
    library and internet research for,
        98–111
    nature and purpose of, 91–92
    plagiarism and, 92
    source misuse in, 92
    source types in, 98–101
"writing in the middle," 117

"X-Large Boys" (Quart), 327–331

Yarrow, Kit, 391–394